TEMAS (Tell-Me-A-Story) Assessment in Multicultural Societies

TEMAS (Tell-Me-A-Story) Assessment in Multicultural Societies

Giuseppe Costantino
Lutheran Medical Center
Lutheran Family Health Centers
Brooklyn, New York

Richard H. Dana
Portland State University
Regional Research Institute

Robert G. Malgady
New York University

LAWRENCE ERLBAUM ASSOCIATES, PUBLISHERS
2007   Mahwah, New Jersey   London

Lawrence Erlbaum Associates, Inc., Publishers
10 Industrial Avenue
Mahwah, NJ 07430

Cover design by Tomai Maridou

Library of Congress Cataloging-in-Publication Data

Costantino, Giuseppe.
TEMAS (Tell-Me-A-Story) Assessment in
multicultural societies / Giuseppe Costantino,
Richard H. Dana, Robert G. Malgady.
    p. ; cm.
    Includes bibliographical references and index.
ISBN 0–8058–4451–1 (cloth : alk. paper)
WS 105.5.E8 C758t 2007]
RJ503.7.B42C66 2007
618.92′89—dc22

                        2006016215

Books published by Lawrence Erlbaum Associates are printed on
acid-free paper, and their bindings are chosen
for strength and durability.

Printed in the United States of America
10 9 8 7 6 5 4 3 2 1

For My spouse, Maryse, and my daughter, Erminia, whose love, empathy, and fair-mindedness, exhibited by their multicultural personae, are the meaning of this book.

And In Memoria. For my mother, Erminia who taught me the Art of Storytelling and instilled in me motivation to achieve, and for my father, Gaetano, who, as an immigrant shoemaker in several foreign countries, taught me appreciation of culturally diverse societies.

—*Giuseppe Costantino*

For William Behn, Richard Dana, and Rose Dana, my grandchildren in blood and emotional presence, this volume expresses my hope that your future world can nourish understanding of persons as individuals in cultural contexts sufficient for quality living in a healthier society.

—*Richard Dana*

For my mother, Marie Calabrese Malgady, from Valva, Italy.

—*Robert G. Malgady*

Contents

Foreword   ix
Preface   xv
Acknowledgments   xxi

PART I INTRODUCTORY CONSIDERATIONS   1

1 Child/Adolescent Mental Health Needs
 and Services   5
2 Promoting Cultural Competency in Mental
 Health Service Delivery   61
3 Picture-Story Performance Instruments for
 Children and Adolescents   101
4 TEMAS: Description and Development   129

PART II ESSENTIALS OF TEMAS ASSESSMENT   163

5 Administration and Scoring   165
6 Psychometric Properties   201
7 Cross-Cultural Findings   229

PART III CLINICAL UTILITY OF TEMAS: CASE STUDIES   289

8 European American Case Study   295
9 Hispanic/Latino Case Study   321
10 Asian American Case Studies   345
11 Diverse Cross-Cultural Studies   373
12 Forensic Case Study   429

Author Index   461
Subject Index   473

Foreword

The mental health needs of children and adolescents are not met in the United States. The majority of children with special social, emotional, educational, and behavioral needs or psychiatric problems do not receive services. Ethnic minority and multicultural children and adolescents are the most poorly served. The problem is not merely a matter of providing services, although that clearly is pivotal. The entire infrastructure and continuity of professional development underlies the problem. Thus, there is an enormous need for researchers, training programs, service providers, culturally informed and sensitive interventions, and novel models of service delivery to address the problem. Pointing out the growing population of ethnic minorities in the United States is one way of conveying the need, but something even more obvious is rarely stated. Our science and services are intended to understand and help *people*—not people in one country or of one ethnicity or even a few ethnicities. Millions of underserved children and adolescents are in need throughout the world. International mental health is a goal of our profession. Consequently, cultural and ethnic diversities are the beginning point of departure for our science and service, not an after thought, and not treated as special interests or special interest groups.

This book represents an important advance in relation to this broader point of departure. The book features an important assessment device and strategy, TEMAS (Tell Me A Story), applicable to ethnically and culturally diverse children and adolescents ages 5–18. Positive characteristics of individual functioning are included as well as aspects of maladjustment to permit use of the measure as a basis for assessment, diagnosis, and evaluation of preventive and treatment interventions. TEMAS is an interesting combination of qualitative and quantitative traditions. The richness of the stories, following the format of projective tests, allows one to capture diverse facets of affect, cognition, personality, and clinical information. Yet, there is rigorous psychometric information in relation to normative data, reliability, and validity. Extensive background information and data are presented on the measure, its scoring, and use with diverse populations.

Measures for children are usually developed with one target population, usually a majority sample. Use with other samples is then based on translation and back translation, procedures that are well accepted. A difficulty is that core features of the measures (e.g., any stimulus material) and the ways in which items are initially selected and framed are critical from a multicultural perspective. Translating and back translating do not help if the original scale itself omitted features pertinent to groups of a particular ethnicity or culture. The stimulus material in TEMAS and culturally informed delivery and administration of the measure (e.g., meeting cultural expectations, emphasizing assessor-assessee match) are exemplary. Thus, the significance of this book stems not only from developing a much needed measure, but also for providing a model of measurement development.

Three facets of the book can be distinguished. First, there is the scholarly presentation of needs of ethnic minority children, the woeful services provided for them, and the barriers to assessment and treatment. Second, the current status of available assessments for youths, criteria for their evaluation, and their relative strengths are covered. Third, research on TEMAS development, scoring, and use is detailed. The research conveys the accomplishments, current use, and great potential for further use. Each of the three features is exemplary. That they are woven together in such a seamless and scholarly fashion is remarkable. TEMAS is superb in the model it conveys for developing measures in theoretically, clinically, and culturally informed ways. It is difficult to find other examples. Hopefully, this book will spawn similar efforts in the future.

Alan E. Kazdin
Yale University School of Medicine

TEMAS (Tell-Me-A-Story) Assessment of Children in Multicultural Societies is the culmination of more than two decades of research on a culturally-appropriate assessment instrument for children of color. My first exposure to the instrument was through the 1984 article in the *Journal of Clinical and Consulting Psychology* by Dr. Costantino and his colleagues. I incorporated several TEMAS research articles into my class, Psychological Interventions with Minority Populations, which I taught from 1987 to 1990. I also ordered TEMAS and used it as a practicing psychologist in community mental health settings in urban neighborhoods of New York City. The TEMAS test served me well as both a tool for training doctoral students in culturally-sensitive approaches to psychological assessment, and as a practical instrument to inform my clinical decisions. This book comes at an opportune time due to growing interest in the intersection between cultural competence and evidence-based practices in the mental health field. The authors provide significant evidence of the psychometric soundness of the TEMAS test, as well as providing case studies to illustrate its use in culturally competent mental health care for minority and nonminority children. It is my belief that this book will contribute significantly to the literature on psychological assessment and will serve as a model of how to integrate research and practice, especially in relation to approaches to culturally competent assessment and treatment grounded in strong empirical evidence.

Arthur L. Whaley
*Hogg Foundation for Mental Health
and University of Texas at Austin*

In an era of globalization and the integration of ideas, beliefs, cultures and languages, it is clear that recognizing the need to provide mental health services, in the most genuine and relevant of ways, is imperative to our overall conceptions of mental well being, particularly within the United States. To this end, it is timely and important that so-called "culturally-sensitive" approaches and instruments be devised with both a theoretical and practical application that has been well thought out, well tested, and proven to provide a valid measure of psychological functioning. This book acutely demonstrates how this can be done from start to finish in the most comprehensive manner and with the interest of the health and well being of the general public in mind. Works such as, *Strategies for Building Multicultural Competence in Mental Health and Educational Settings*, by Constantine and Sue (2005), for example, and that of others, begin to set out guidelines for scholars, researchers, and practitioners in providing comprehensive treatment programs and interventions that maximize positive outcomes in mental health settings. The work of Altarriba and others, for example, (Altarriba & Santiago-Rivera, 1994; Santiago-Rivera & Altarriba, 2002) examines the role of beliefs, customs, and particularly language in developing therapeutic avenues and applications that are relevant to populations of individuals who are bicultural/bilingual and/or share ethnic worldviews that may be different from the majority population. In this vein, TEMAS serves to emphasize the importance of cultural competency and cultural relevance in mental health assessment and treatment, as this instrument provides the opportunity for culturally and linguistically diverse children to tell personal stories in their own dominant language and within the context of their own culture. Indeed, one of the most important contributions of the use of TEMAS is the fact that, from its inception, it has been developed to be a culturally and linguistically sensitive approach to mental health assessment. Interest in research and scholarly endeavor in the area of multicultural psychological assessment and treatment is rapidly growing. However, models for the development of precise instruments are far too few. The present piece, however, provides a serious entry into the development of such tools as the work is grounded in theoretical work on topics such as acculturation, cultural identity, personality theory, psychopathology, and the like, and in particular, to their development within childhood and adolescence. The development of TEMAS is to be seen as an important milestone in developing sound, valid, and reliable measures, as applied to cultural and multicultural contexts. Not only does the present text provide an instrument that has been shown to be flexible enough to cover a variety of ethnic backgrounds, it is to be seen as a model for doing so, for other researchers interested in the development of assessment tools and their validation. The current book then takes the reader through the various steps of instrument development from the outlining of the importance of the variables included in its development, to the characteristics and design of the TEMAS instrument itself, to measures of its validity and applicability to various populations. Actual measures are included that validate its use, as well as a number of case studies and examples that serve as a road map for the application of this instrument. In agreement with the authors of this book, it is clear that it can be an important reference manual from which to guide a classroom of students or a group of practitioners through not only the use of this tool but to the underpinnings of its development, as well. This kind of comprehensive treatment of an assessment tool is critical to having the field of multicultural counseling and assessment raised to an exceptional standard within the field of mental health. It should serve as an example for years to come, and this text will surely become a standard in the field entering into the mainstream of mental health in the larger psychological field.

Jeanette Altarriba
University at Albany, State University of New York

REFERENCES

Altarriba, J., & Santiago-Rivera, A. L. (1994). Current perspectives on using linguistic and cultural factors in counseling the bilingual Spanish-speaking client. *Professional Psychology: Research and Practice, 25,* 388–397.

Constantine, M., & Sue, D. W. (2005). *Strategies for building multicultural competence in mental health and educational settings.* New York: John Wiley and Sons.

Santiago-Rivera, A. L., & Altarriba, J. (2002). The role of language in therapy with the Spanish-English bilingual client. *Professional Psychology: Research and Practice, 33,* 30–38.

Preface

This book was prepared for prospective readers with interests in child and adolescent psychological health and dysfunction. Ethnic minority children, in contrast with nonminorities, have not enjoyed equal access or benefit from the contemporary mental health system. These students now comprise over 40% of the entire school population and 75% of students in the 100 largest cities. This book examines the health/mental health care system in which professional service providers, including psychologists, labor to provide quality care for youth in the United States. Quality care for this population necessitates comprehensive assessment for all children and adolescents. However, only the availability and presence of culturally competent assessment instruments and assessors can provide equitable entrée into mental health systems of care.

Our approach to responsible professional assessment in this book is from the perspective of TEMAS, an assessment instrument explicitly designed for all children/adolescents employing minority and non-minority versions. TEMAS proficiency requires both cultural competency and instrument competency as a consequence of dedicated courses, supervised practice experience, and awareness of relevant research. This TEMAS textbook amplifies the earlier test manual, expands the contents of a number of positive reviews, reviews the history of instrument-specific research, and presents a variety of case examples representing multicultural populations in the United States and internationally.

Following a brief summary of book contents, this preface describes the prospective audience for this book and reaffirms the importance of TEMAS for professional psychology with the advocacy, enthusiasm, and excitement the authors feel for this first and exemplary multicultural assessment instrument.

CONTENTS

TEMAS offers a relatively brief, multifaceted, clinically descriptive, and diagnostically-useful test for describing the emotional and adjustment problems of cultural/racial minority children and adolescents. Scoring variables and a theoretical rationale were developed from mainstream professional psychology resources. TEMAS has been used in schools, community mental health facilities, and the private sector.

TEMAS is the first test designed, constructed, and validated for multicultural populations. Tests constructed and normed primarily for mainstream populations serve ethnic minority children and adolescents inequitably due to lack of demonstrated cultural equivalence and an absence of independent acculturation and racial identity status evaluation. These deficits diminish the likelihood of applying existing standard interventions with maximum benefit due to instrument bias, insufficient client information, and/or misdiagnosis. Furthermore, the potential relevance and suitability of adapting standard interventions for multicultural populations, or interventions designed for culture-specific problems-in-living, cannot be ascertained using standard instruments.

The first three introductory chapters in Part I of this book present a rationale and context for employing TEMAS as a major multicultural assessment instrument and re-examines the rationale for comprehensive assessment to facilitate understanding all youth. These chapters describe the mental health status of the population-at-risk as well as systems of care for youth in which assessment and intervention are necessary components. A failure to incorporate comprehensive assessment instruments for their historically documented purposes within contemporary mental health care has had adverse effects on quality care for all youth. Despite a recent history of declining use, these instruments continue to have a distinct, vital, and salutary role in alleviating problems inherent in mental health services for all children and adolescents.

One salient outcome of minimizing comprehensive assessment is the precarious fit between presenting problems and the full range of potentially effective interventions. Moreover, blurring the distinction between diagnosis-based and problem-based interventions contributes to an uneven treatment/intervention evaluation literature with predominantly mediocre outcomes. These initial chapters suggest how more comprehensive assessment, including routine use of TEMAS, can foster the development of more coherent, responsible, and coordinated child and adolescent interventions in the United States.

TEMAS description and development is contained in chapter 4. In Part II, chapter 5 is devoted to administration and scoring; Chapter 6 examine psychometric properties. Chapter 7, Cross-Cultural Findings, summarizes cross-cultural TEMAS validation and provides examples of Latin American,

Caribbean, Italian, and Taiwanese studies. In Part III, chapters 8–12 present TEMAS case examples of European American, Hispanic/Latino, Asian American, Diverse Cross-Cultural, and Forensic Studies.

READERSHIP

This book was written for professional providers in health/mental health professions and particularly for (a) instructors who teach standard assessment courses; (b) clinicians, counselors, school psychologists and other mental health practitioners; (c) assessment specialists and other mental health researchers; and (d) administrators concerned with mental health services designed for children and adolescents.

Instructors of comprehensive assessment courses now need to decide whether standard assessment instruments are adequate for employment with ethnic minority populations in the absence of satisfactory cross-cultural equivalence demonstrations. Although it is generally acknowledged that standard assessment training should include multicultural assessment, there is controversy concerning whether standard and multicultural assessment training can be provided in the same courses. TEMAS is a complex instrument similar to the MMPI–2 or Rorschach. Dedicated courses are mandatory to present the TEMAS rationale, acquire skill in reliable usage of the scoring system, facilitate report preparation, and provide interpretation experiences within a milieu of expanding assessor multicultural knowledge.

We believe that TEMAS should be offered as an independent multicultural assessment course, regardless of whether or not standard and multicultural assessment are combined in other courses. Learning TEMAS and practicing multicultural assessment with TEMAS is a giant step toward cultural competency. Not only was TEMAS constructed for multicultural assessment practice, but TEMAS administration and interpretation necessitates a depth of cultural knowledge. This knowledge includes ethnic/racial identity development, health/illness beliefs, and culture-bound syndromes for preparation of cultural formulations, as well as cultural and identity conceptualizations described in this book.

TEMAS

TEMAS enjoys a unique role in contemporary psychological assessment as a comprehensive projective-narrative method for individually focused personality-psychopathology evaluation. TEMAS is the premier instrument currently available for multicultural assessment practice, training, and research. Furthermore, TEMAS can partially restore awareness of the historically recognized benefits of comprehensive standard assessment employing traditional psychometric instruments. Objective and standardized assessment instruments yield quantified normative information. Such information identifies personality resources and emotional/behavioral problems, facilitates responsible clinical diagnoses, and contributes to treatment planning, monitoring, and evaluation.

TEMAS meets the following criteria for culturally relevant assessment methods to a much greater extent than other comparable narrative instruments: (a) development by members of informed ethnic minority and cultural communities; (b) comprehensive theoretical rationale; (c) administration using credible social etiquette; (d) culturally familiar figures and backgrounds in stimulus pictures; (e) objective scores derived from theory and/or empirical research; (f) normative data for U.S., ethnic minority populations and nationals in other countries; and (g) research-driven expanding context of cultural knowledge useful for interpretation. Ethnic minority assessment practitioners developed TEMAS in mental health settings serving cultural/racial populations. The theoretical rationale uses a dynamic-cognitive model employing social-cognitive learning theory and combining aspects of cognitive, interpersonal, and narrative psychology. Components of this model are currently in the process of careful empirical scrutiny for applications with ethnic minority populations. For each ethnic minority child/adolescent, credible social etiquette and the client's first language are used during TEMAS administration.

TEMAS pictorial stimuli were developed with figures and backgrounds appropriate for the ethnic minority populations in the United States and national populations in other countries. The figures and backgrounds in the nonminority TEMAS cards are appropriate for mainstream Caucasian populations in the United States. These stimulus characteristics have been associated with productivity and contribute to "card pull" demonstrated by earlier TAT research with TEMAS scoring variables.

The TEMAS scoring system was developed from a theoretical rationale containing variables of documented importance for diagnosis of psychopathology and delineation of problems-in-living. Culture-specific, or emic normative TEMAS data is available, but these scores have origins in a U.S. dynamic-cognitive model. As a consequence, TEMAS scoring variables must eventually meet cultural equivalence standards on the basis of multicultural and cross-cultural research demonstrations. Moreover,

TEMAS requires research on cultural identity/racial identity status to facilitate interpretation using the available culture-specific normative data. Demonstrations for fine-tuning TEMAS scores to avoid confounds with psychopathology have MMPI/MMPI-2 antecedents; an available research model is discussed in this book.

Normative data is available for populations of interest in the United States and internationally. These normative data resources can be augmented by corrections for traditional cultural identity for Hispanics and Asian Americans and/or for emerging racial identity among African Americans. Because TEMAS interpretation relies on theoretical and practical understanding of personality-psychopathology information within identified cultural contexts, multicultural assessor competency is required.

TEMAS is an assessment centerpiece with hitherto unappreciated prospects for implementation of multicultural assessment competency as well as for cross-cultural international applications using standard instruments to facilitate more effective liaison between assessment and intervention for all children and adolescents.

—*Richard H. Dana*

Acknowledgments

These acknowledgments appear in two sections. The first section corresponds to chapters 1–3, by Richard Dana, which contain a mental health context for TEMAS. The second section corresponds to chapters 4–12, by Giuseppe Costantino, which present a complete TEMAS manual including history, construction, and research as well as national and international case studies. Chapters 1, 2, and 3 in this book, as well as all of Richard Dana's professional activities since 1989, resulted from the good will and continuous facilitation provided by Portland State University through the Regional Research Institute for Human Services (RRI) and the Graduate School of Social Work. The RRI has been a safe haven for my "retirement" years because of Director, Nancy Koroloff, her Assistants, Ron Talarico and Jennifer Williams, and computer technical support from Terell Avery and Ivan Hernandez. This comfortable, consistently affable, and nurturing climate resulted in four major books as well as a plethora of book chapters and research publications. Since May, 2004, Art Emlen has graciously shared his office with me and has increased my enjoyment with his occasional presence, good nature, and his willingness to share his profound understanding of an adjacent and hospitable professional world.

Denise Schmit constructed the author index for this book with the same meticulousness and accuracy demonstrated in my earlier Erlbaum publications. Sara Schwartz and Lita Rafia worked with me assiduously on the subject index. Michael Conner graciously permitted me to describe in detail his groundbreaking Step One Screening Program (www.InCrisis.org) prior to the publication of his book, *Crisis Intervention with Adolescents: A Parent Guide* (Conner, 2005). I am indebted to my wife, Dr. Joan Dayger Behn for careful and helpful reading of materials in this book, including the preface, and for her patience, support, and understanding during a long process of manuscript preparation and throughout longer process of book production.

Chapters 1, 2, and 3 require specific acknowledgments. Chapter 1 draws on available RRI resources and the research conducted during the last 20 years. This chapter benefited directly from a careful and informed reading by an RRI colleague, Michael D. Pullmann, now a predoctoral research fellow at Vanderbilt University. Michaele P. Dunlap, President,

Mentor Research Institute, also examined chapter 1 with a critical and helpful editorial eye.

Chapter 1 describes the present status and continuing applications of the Multicultural Assessment-Intervention Process (MAIP) model developed originally for multicultural assessment practice described in two Erlbaum books, *Multicultural Assessment Principles, Applications, and Examples* (Dana, 2005) and *Handbook of Cross-Cultural and Multicultural Personality Assessment* (Dana, 2000). Glenn Gamst, Professor of Psychology and Department Chair, University of La Verne (ULV), and Aghop Der-Karabetian, Associate ULV Dean, shared the MAIP model transition from assessment origins to the public sector mental health service delivery system in California. The published and unpublished MAIP research literature and related materials cited in this chapter were developed with many others. The opportunity to conduct MAIP model research in the Tri-City Mental Health Center, Pomona, CA, under the administrative auspices of Terry Kramer and LuAnn Martensen, is acknowledged with gratitude. Rachel Guerrero, Chief, Office of Multicultural Services, California Department of Mental Health, facilitated the development and adoption of MAIP training materials for statewide cultural competency training in California. Barbara Friesen, Professor Emeritus, Portland State University, and formerly Director, Research and Training Center on Family Support and Children's Mental Health, RRI, facilitated my presentation of a MAIP Seminar to social work doctoral students in January of 2005.

Chapter 2 presents the cultural competency perspectives of each mental health profession and describes a model for pan-professional cultural competency training. These diverse multidisciplinary perspectives are represented in the RRI as a consequence of Nancy Koroloff's leadership and Barbara Friesen's participation in the landmark research, Transforming Mental Health Care for Children and Their Families, published in the *American Psychologist* in 2005.

Chapter 3 recognizes the role of a human-centered science of psychology, consistent with a positive psychology within a recovery vision, to serve the needs of the entire child and adolescent population. An expanded psychological science includes comprehensive assessment and interventions consistent with broadly defined research-informed, evidence-based practice advocated by an American Psychological Association Presidential Task Force and reported in the *American Psychologist* in 2006. This chapter owes much to the participants in the 2005 Hogg Foundation for Mental Health Expert Panel on Cultural Adaptations of Evidence-Based Practices facilitated by King Davis and

Arthur Whaley. Furthermore, my thinking in this chapter concerning the relevance of a humanized psychological science to assessment and intervention research has been consistently scrutinized, critiqued, and nourished by Jim Allen, University of Alaska Fairbanks. Without his wisdom and support, my post-retirement professional writing would have been of lesser quality and clarity. Finally, the Society for Personality Assessment enabled preparation of my professional autobiography, subsequently published by the *Journal of Personality Assessment* and Springer. This "psychological report on myself" was replete with examples of students including Jeff Brookings (Wittenburg University), Shirley Leech (Memphis, TN), and Rodger Hornby (Sinte Gleska University) whose professional lives embodied the credibility of a human science by transforming the lives of students and patients while contributing to their own integrity. I thus acknowledge with gratitude the immediate and long-term contributions of many others whose professional substance and personal realities were shared sufficiently with me to be recognizable retrospectively in the substance, contents, and organization of these three chapters.

—Richard H. Dana

Were it not for the formal presentation of this book, I would entitle this section *Thanksgiving,* because the highest intellectual capacity and moral responsibility of a person does not reside in discursive understanding but in an understanding heart.

The research reported in this book represents a thirty-year endeavor to develop a multiculturally competent assessment instrument. Because of its magnitude, duration, and complexity, this project would never have been completed without the commitment and dedication of numerous persons and the cooperation of various institutions. Attempts will be made to thank all individuals who directly contributed to this book and those persons and institutions that advance and support the development of TEMAS. If anyone is omitted, it will be the failure of the mind, but not of the heart. This section is subdivided into three parts: **Contributors** whose work on TEMAS is reported in this book; **Promoters** whose direct interest has promoted the advancement of the instrument; and **Individuals within the institutions** who offered their support to continue the TEMAS research program.

Contributors from the USA and Puerto Rico. Erminia Costantino, BS, Director of the American Multicultural Institute (AMI) contributed her creative input throughout the writing, and her excellent editorial and computer skills during the production of the book. Without her dedication, the production of this book would have been greatly delayed. Maryse Costantino, MS, provided her expert artwork suggestion for the cover as well as the artwork of the Record Booklets of the case studies. She also worked with dedication f or two years in the normative data collection. Peter Aiello, BA, contributed his computer expertise on several chapters. Elsa Cardalda, Ph.D., Clinical Director of the Doctoral Program at Carlos Albizu University (UCA) in San Juan, Puerto Rico, has made a decade-long research contribution for the validation of TEMAS both in New York City and in Puerto Rico. She has also been instrumental in the teaching of the TEMAS at UCA. Dr. Cardalda was assisted by her diligent and dedicated TEMAS team members José V. Martínez, Ph.D., Sean Sayers, Ph.D., Mariela León-Velázquez, MA, Victoria Jiménez-Suárez, MA, Nyrma Ortiz-Vargas, MA, and Lili M. Sardinas, MA; and her work represents the most comprehensive body of psychometric research conducted on TEMAS. Isabel Bernal, Ph.D., conducted an important study to show that TEMAS was a valid test with Mexican-American children in the Los Angeles area and that it was more culturally competent in comparison with the RATC. Thanks to Teri Elliot, Ph.D., whose strong interest in narrative and projective assessment motivated her to conduct a study on the differential validity of TEMAS with the Rorschach Comprehensive System as criterion. At the Sunset Park Mental Health Center of Lutheran Medical Center, I would like to express my deep-felt thanks to Melanie Perez, Ph.D., clinical psychologist and research associate, for her dedicated clinical and research interest in TEMAS and her important work in using the instrument in the school settings. Ianna Kalogiros, Ph.D., psychology trainee conducted an insightful clinical case study. Sherry Gaines Cutler, Psy. D., former psychology intern, conducted a clinically useful case study. Elen Tsui, Ph.D., clinical psychologist, whose interest in TEMAS spans for almost two decades, and who conducted two culturally competent case studies; and Tracy Poon, Ph.D., staff psychologist, who also carried out a culturally insightful case study. Charlene Beckford, Ph.D., former psychology intern, contributed a forensically valid and clinically useful case. Mark Rand, Ph.D., Chief Psychologist, whose interest in the test spans for more than 15 years, contributed a clinically valid forensic case. Dr. Rand has been instrumental in introducing TEMAS training as part of the curriculum and has continually motivated students to use the test. William Bracero, Ph.D. senior psychologist, an expert in culturally competent assessment and treatment, contributed an insightful discussion on cross-cultural clinical test validity, has been training students in the clinical use TEMAS and conducted pilot studies using TEMAS pictures as therapeutic technique with psychiatric patients in acute care unit. Pietro Lofu, Ph.D., former psychology intern, contributed three clinically useful cross-cultural studies. Also, Miriam Rivera diligently assisted in the several TEMAS studies.

My gratitude is offered to highly respected psychologists, Rosemary Flanagan, Ph.D., Director of the School Psychology Program, Adelphi University, Derner Institute, for her decade-long interest, teaching and conducting research with the TEMAS, and for writing an endorsement for this book. Alan E. Kazdin, Ph.D., Director of the Study Center and John M. Musser Professor of Psychology at Yale University, originally recognized the importance of our innovative, culturally competent research program and kindly wrote one part of the Foreword in this book. Arthur Whaley, Ph.D., formerly Associate Director for Mental Health Services Research and Professor of Psychology at the University of Texas at Austin, Hogg Foundation for Mental Health, whose interest on the multicultural utility of the TEMAS goes back several years, wrote the second part of the Foreword. And Jeanette Altarriba, Ph.D., Associate Dean and Professor, University at Albany, State University of New York, who has shown much interest on this test, wrote the third part of the Foreword. Lisa A. Suzuki, Ph.D., Professor, New York University, with her long-standing interest in TEMAS, included several TEMAS chapters in her Multicultural Assessment books, and wrote an endorsement for this book. Sincere thanks to Barry Ritzler, Ph.D., Professor, Long Island University, for his continuous interest in TEMAS, early positive review of the test, his writing about the multicultural validity of the instrument, his sponsoring of a dissertation, and his present endorsement. And special thanks to, Anthony J. Marsella, Ph.D., Emeritus Professor, University of Hawaii, for his endorsement of this book.

Contributors from Argentina, Italy, and Taiwán. Daniel Gomez Dupertuis, Ph.D., Professor at Universidad de Buenos Aires and at Universidad Nacional de La Plata, Argentina, made a scholarly contribution to the adaptation and validation of TEMAS. Assisted by his capable colleagues, Ernesto Pais, Psy.D.; Veronica Silva Arancibia, Psy.D.; Cynthia Fernandez, Psy.D.; Virginia Rodino, MA; and Maria de los Angeles Ropaldo, Psy.D., Dr. Gomez Dupertuis continues to make important contributions for the standardization and validation of TEMAS in Argentina in particular and in Latin America in general. Thanks are also extended to Prof. Maria Martina Casullo at Universidad de Buenos Aires for the mid–1980s research validating TEMAS with Argentinean children.

Dr. GianMarco Sardi, Dr. Barbara Summo, Dr. Carla Cornabuci and Dr. Cinzia Sulfaro conducted the first four significant studies on the validity of TEMAS with Italian children as part of their dissertations at L'Universita di Roma "La Sapienza", Italy. Special thanks are extended to Dr. Sardi, who continued his training in TEMAS and cross-cultural psychology for three years with this author, and upon his return to Italy became an expert psychologist in Traffic Psychology. He is Director of Human Resources and Training of the SIPSiVi and of various European Projects on road safety. Italy and other EU countries are experiencing a need to develop culturally competent assessment and treatment techniques to deal with large numbers of ethnic minorities. Dr. Francesca Fantini and her mentor, Professor Patrizia Bevilacqua at L'Universita Cattolica di Milano, with great diligence have carried out the first most important study on the cross-cultural clinical utility of TEMAS with Hispanic children living in Milan. Motivated by the strong commitment of Prof. Bevilacqua to promote TEMAS in Italy, several psychology students at the Catholic University are pursuing research on emic and etic validity of the test. Hence *mille grazie* to Prof. Bevilacqua and to Dr. Fantini who, assisted by her colleagues, Dr. Filippo Aschieri and Cristina Augello, is working on the standardization of TEMAS as her Ph.D. dissertation. In addition, thanks are also offered to Professor Vittorio Cigoli, Director of Graduate Psychology Studies at the Catholic University for his strong interest in culturally competent assessment and TEMAS. Special thanks are offered to Chien-Ming Yang, Ph.D., professor at the National Chemgghi University, Department of Psychology, Research Center for Mind, Brain, & Learning, Taipei, Taiwan, who obtained his Ph.D. from CCNY and learned TEMAS in the USA as a psychology intern under the supervision of this author and conducted pioneer research with the Asian-American version of the test in Taiwan, assisted by his graduate student, Liang-Hsan Kuo, MA. Meei-Ju Lin, Ph.D., graduate of Purdue University, is presently a Professor of Psychology at the National Hualien University of Education, Hualien, Taiwan. Dr. Lin, with an interest in TEMAS for several years, conducted the first study comparing the validity of TEMAS and CAT with Tatwanese children, and completed her second study on the validity of TEMAS with Taiwanese children.

My heartfelt thanks are offered to my physicians, who indirectly contributed to the completion of this book by providing me with quality medical care before, during, and after the quadruple bypass operation in March, 2006. Mario Costantino, MD, my immediate "family" doctor; Mauro Gasperini, MD, internist; John Ruisi, MD, outpatient cardiologist;

Michael Gambino, MD, angioplasty surgeon; and above all, Scott Shoeback, MD, Chief of Thoracic Cardiovascular Surgery Department, both of Winthrop University Hospital.

My gratitude is also expressed to the following individuals, who indirectly contributed to this book by giving me the opportunity to emigrate to *America* in the early 1960s from Nocera Terinese, Italy. Professor Mario Pontieri urged his writer to take an examination to study English and Psychology at New York University while sitting in a *Cafe*. Professor Francesco Costanzo, a childhood friend highly proficient in English, helped this writer to complete his successful NYU application. And Doctor Leopoldo Rossi, President of the Cassa di Risparmio di Calabria, gave this writer a loan "come to study in America" with his book of poetry, *Dove la Valle e Verde—Where the Valley is Green*, his as a collateral. Nicholas Tomaino, the American uncle, gave this writer guidance and support to study and achieve in the new country.

Promoters in the USA and Europe. My warmest thanks are extended to all those individuals who have conducted studies and dissertations, used the TEMAS as a non-biased clinical tool, and/or have motivated others to learn the test and have facilitated its clinical use and research studies. The majority of these people previously worked or are now working at the Sunset Park Mental Health Center (SPMHC), recently renamed, Sunset Terrace Outpatient Behavioral Health Center, of the Lutheran Medical Center, where the test was further developed. Prominent among those are Jean Bailey, Ph.D., Director of Child and Adolescent Services, who conducted one of the early TEMAS doctoral dissertations on the effects of racial similarities responses among Latino, Black, and White children. She also helped in the development of the scoring TEMAS system and continues to supervise several waves of doctoral psychology interns. Carmen Rivera, Ph.D., Director of the Psychology Internship Program, included the TEMAS in the training curriculum, wrote about its culturally competent validity in the training booklet, strongly promotes its use, and continues to motivate new psychology interns to use the test to assess culturally diverse children. Adela Castillo, Psy.D., former psychologist in training, and Thomas Faiola, Ph.D., former psychology intern, conducted a cross-cultural TEMAS study comparing Argentinean and Peruvian children. Maria Sesin, Ph.D., staff psychologist in training, has shown a long-lasting interest in TEMAS as an assessment tool and as a narrative therapy modality. She diligently used the two modalities clinically and conducted several studies. As result of her training, Dr. Sesin, in collaboration with Dr. William Bracero, developed a new projective tool, the Freda Kahlo Assessment Technique. Tanya

Hernandez, LCSW, clinician, worked with great interest on various TEMAS projects, including the Child/Adolescents Treatment and Service (CATS) project. Jacquelyn Guajardo, Ph.D., former staff psychologist, and Trauma Unit Coordinator, diligently trained several psychology students in the use of TEMAS as an assessment instrument and expertly coordinated the CATS project wherein the TEMAS Narrative Therapy and CBT were used as treatment modalities. Marie Borges, FMG (Foreign Medical Graduate), MPH, Research Coordinator, diligently contributed to several TEMAS studies and successfully coordinated the data collection of the CATS project. Fernando Peña collected data on the use of TEMAS with the elderly and worked with diligence and enthusiasm on the collection of CATS outcome data. My deeply felt thanks are also extended to Dr. Carolina Meucci of L'Universita di Roma "La Sapienza" and CCNY John Jay College of Criminal Justice in New York City, who dedicated several years to the training of TEMAS, assisted in conducting research such as the CATS project, and was the second author in translation and adaptation of the Italian TEMAS Manual. Elizabeth Messina, Ph. D., co-Director of the Assembly of Italian-American Psychologists, has promoted the advancement of the test. Special thanks are offered to Phil Jacobs, who dedicated his artistic talent in drawing TEMAS pictures from its inception in 1977 to its 1987 publication and thereafter. Phil is continuing to collaborate with this author in other projects. His artistic skills have contributed immensely to the national and international recognition of the TEMAS pictures.

The following psychologists with strong interest in culturally competent assessment conducted their doctoral dissertations using TEMAS. Carmen Vazquez, Ph.D., former Director of the Psychology Internship Program, Bellevue Hospital in NYC, conducted the first important dissertation using TEMAS, wherein she demonstrated that TEMAS was a culturally competent test with Latino children. Fred Millan-Arzuaga, Ph.D., Associate Professor and Chair, Psychology Department, CUNY College of Old Westbury, NY, used this test in his dissertation study to assess the worldview of Latino adolescents and their parents; Melanie Challender, Ph.D., formerly of City University of New York, assessed racial self-concept and global self-concept and anxiety among Black girls using TEMAS; Rene Krinsky, Ph.D., utilized TEMAS to assess delayed gratification, achievement motivation and aggression in children of alcoholics. Gloria Torres, Ph.D. conducted her dissertation on school achievement, self-concept, and trait anxiety in bilingual Latino children. Gerardita Colon-Malgady, MS, conducted her Master thesis using TEMAS to assess attention deficit disorders in culturally diverse children. This author would also like to thank all other psychologists who conducted their dissertation studies on TEMAS, and whose work is not presently known to him. Sincere thanks to Vera S. Paster, Ph.D., former Director of Bureau of Child Guidance, and former Psychology Professor at City College of New York, for granting the original authorization to conduct TEMAS research in New York Public Schools and for sponsoring TEMAS dissertations at CCNY. Anderson Franklyn, Ph.D., Director of the Clinical Psychology Program at CCNY for promoting the test among the minority students at the college. Gilbert Trackman, Ph.D., former Director of the School Psychology Program at NYU for promoting the test among his students and sponsoring a dissertation. And the late Kenneth Clark, Ph. D., former professor emeritus at CCNY for giving the first positive oral evaluation of the culturally competent validity of the TEMAS pictures.

Special thanks are extended to Joan Riley Walton, Ed. D., Ronald Nuttall, Ph.D., both of Boston College, and Ena Vazquez Nuttall, Ph.D., of Northeastern University, for using TEMAS in their significant cross-cultural study of post-war adjustment of Salvadoran children.

My sincere thanks are expressed to King Davis, Ph.D., LMSW-ACP, Executive Director; Chair in Mental Health and Social Policy School of Social Work, at the Hogg Foundation for Mental Health, University of Texas at Austin, for his strong interest in TEMAS as a culturally competent, evidence-based assessment instrument. Very special thanks are offered to Irving B. Weiner, Ph.D., President of the Board of Trustees, Society For Personality Assessment, and former Chief Editor of LEA for his 30-year guidance in the development of TEMAS. The late John E. Exner, Ph.D., former president of Rorschach Workshops, and Professor Emeritus, Long Island University, for his "paternal" suggestions in the early development of the test. To Steve Rutter, Editorial Director, Nicole Buchmann, Editorial Assistant, and Claudia Dukeshire, Production Editor, LEA, for their instrumental help in publishing this book.

Dr. PierAngelo Sardi, former president of the AUPI, Associazione Unitaria di Psicologi Italiani and Italian Charter of Psychologists, and presently member of the Executive Council of the EFPA, the European Federation of Psychologists' Association, and Vice President of CEPLIS, the European Council of Liberal Professions, published TEMAS in the AUPI Journal in 1997, and strongly promoted this test among psychologists in Italy and the European Union. Dr. Vito Tummino, president of the Federazione Italiana Societa Scientifiche di Psicologia (FISSP), Chief Psychologist at Como Medical Center, and Editor of *LINK*, an Italian psychology journal, was instrumental in introducing the TEMAS in Italy, and has been working with strong interest to train Italian psychologists in the clinical use of TEMAS. Dr. Giovanni Cavadi conducted TEMAS assessment of adult Italian patients with sexual dysfunctions, obtaining significant clinical results.

Institutional and Organizational Support. My gratitude is extended to several institutions and organizations and the key individuals within them who provided their support for the development of TEMAS. Professor Raymond Di Giuseppe, presently Chairperson of the Psychology Department, instituted the teaching of TEMAS in the graduate school program at St. John's University in the mid–1990s. Professor Louis Primavera, Chairperson of the Psychology Department at that time, and presently professor and former dean at Adelphi University, Derner Institute, supported the TEMAS course at St John's University, and subsequently helped to institute a TEMAS course in the School Psychology Program at Adelphi under the directorship of Prof. Rosemary Flanagan. Rafael Javier, Professor at St. John's University, continues to show his long-standing interest in TEMAS. Thanks to Neil Maron, Ph.D., President of Supreme Evaluations, Inc, Brooklyn, NY, for his continuous interest. Salvador Santiago-Negron, Ph.D., former President of Carlos Albizu University (UCA), displayed strong interest and was instrumental in introducing the teaching of the TEMAS at the university. Jose Cabiya, Ph.D., Professor and Director of the Research Institute at UCA, has maintained continued interest in the test and promoted it among his graduate students. Guillermo Bernal, Ph.D. Director of Psychological Research Center, University of Puerto Rico, promotes the cultural competence and evidence-based validity of the test. And Victor Alvarez, Ph.D., President of *Innovaciones Psicoeducativas*, has supported the teaching of TEMAS at UCA and the clinical use of TEMAS in Puerto Rico. Special thanks are extended to Western Psychological Services, publisher of the TEMAS test, and its original president, the late Ira Manson; its current president, Sarah Manson; and her administrative assistant, Susan Weinberg, as well as Research Director in the mid–1980's; David Lachar, Ph.D., was instrumental in the publication of test. Robert Zachary, Ph.D. and William Reynolds, Ph.D., former directors of clinical research, and Christian Gruber, Ph.D, current Director of clinical research at WPS, assisted in the standardization and/or promotion of TEMAS.

In addition, this author would like to express his warmest thanks to the following people for their interest in establishing a Masters in Multicultural Psychological Assessment at the University of Salerno. Dr. Franco Vaccaro, a dear childhood friend and former Coordinator of Commerce and Agriculture Development of the Campania Region, Italy, and currently Professor of Sociology at L'Universita di Salerno; and

Professor Raimondo Pasquino, Rettore (Rector) dell'Universita' degli Studi di Salerno. Thanks are also expressed to Giuseppe Macchione, a childhood friend, formerly a teacher and currently a recognized painter and graphic artist in Italy, for his interest in the pictorial aspect of the test. My gratitude is offered to two great institutions and its key individuals for their long lasting continuous support of the TEMAS development. a) The Hispanic Research Center, Fordham University, and its director Lloyd Rogler, Ph.D., provided support and contributed early research and writing on the test. b) The Lutheran Medical Center, the Sunset Park Mental Health Centers, and the Sunset Park Family Health Centers, including the executive staff from the original President and CEO, George Adams, to the current president and CEO, Wendy Goldstein, and Claudia Caine, Executive VP and Chief Operating Officer, have given institutional support, that is continuing after 30 years. Jim Stiles, MPH, former Executive VP, has given long-lasting support, that has been continued and augmented by Larry McReynolds, MPH, the present Executive VP and Executive Director of Lutheran Family Health Centers, whose uncondi- tional support was instrumental in the publication of this book and an inspiration to continue culturally competent research at the center. In addi- tion, Angel La Porte, Senior VP; Merle Cunningham, MD, Medical Director; Bradford Goff, MD, Chairperson of the Department of Psychiatry; Violeta Maya, President of Sunset Park Health Council, Inc.; John Fitzpatrick, Ph.D., Associate Director; and Michael Lardiere, LCSW, Administrative Director of the Sunset Terrace Outpatient Behavior Health Center, continue to support and promote TEMAS and collaborate in cul- turally competent research. Sincere thanks are also offered to the Lutheran Health Care System IRB Unit, especially to Vincent Vigorita, MD, former Medical Director and IRB Chairperson; to Claudia Lyons, MD, current IRB Chairperson; Kell Julliard, MS, Director of Research, for their continued interest and support.

    And lastly, but not the least, my deepest thanks are expressed to my teachers, the late Doctor Michele Macchione, my elementary school teacher; Dr. Vittorio Mendicino, my Middle School instructor; Dr. GianBattista Odoardi, MD, Chief of Internal Medicine at Consenza Hospital, monitored my school progress; and Dr. Gaetano Cirmeni, Director of *Avviemento Professionale*-Agriculture Institute, gave me my first position as an art and music teacher; all in Nocera Terinese, Italy. Also, Angelo Dispenzieri, Ph.D., former professor of the City of New York, Baruch College; Victor Sanua, Ph.D., and the late Irving Singer, Ph.D., both former professors at CCNY Graduate School of Education. And the late Isador Chein, Ph.D., the late

Stanley Lehman, Ph.D., and Walter Neff, Ph.D., former professors at New York University's Clinical and Community Psychology Program. Howard Eisman, Ph. D., Chief Psychologist, Coney Island Hospital, NYC. All shared their knowledge and creativity to forge and foster my professional growth as psychologist and taught this writer the fluency of the human heart so that, in turn, I could pass knowledge and skills into other students.

—*Giuseppe Costantino, Ph.D.*

I

INTRODUCTION

Part I consists of four chapters designed to provide a context for TEMAS.

Chapter 1 describes the contemporary mental health system for children and adolescents in the United States. For at least 50 years, the seriousness and range of child/adolescent mental health problems has gradually increased and now merits national concern. Definitive, consistent, and consensual definitions of psychological distress have been lacking for this population and contribute to confusion and inefficiency in accessing relevant and helpful services. Responsive, adequate, quality care is infrequent, particularly for services of documented utility using research-driven, improved technologies that satisfy consumers. As difficult as these circumstances have been for mainstream, middle-class, Caucasian children/adolescents, ethnic minority children and those from poverty-ridden families have suffered more and received even less relevant and satisfactory services. Mental health resource allocation commensurate with the numbers of these children and families has not occurred. Managed care has been generally less responsible in the public sector due to health care policy subordinating mental health, medical model service priorities, minimization of individual and cultural differences, and restrictive cost-effective standards for care.

In providing this context for TEMAS, chapter 1 examines the existing child/adolescent systems of care and offers a research-driven, outcome-oriented, cost-effective model of public sector care—the Multicultural Assessment-Intervention Process model (MAIP). The MAIP model for quality care responds to the burgeoning multicultural child/adolescent population by embedding culturally competent assessment and intervention services at the client–consumer, agency, and community levels. This model is consistent with the California statewide public sector cultural competency initiative and a recovery-oriented vision for quality mental health care. This recovery vision emphasizes strengths and a positive psychology of human functioning within a developmental science framework. TEMAS figures conspicuously in the MAIP model as a comprehensive assessment instrument applicable for entire child/adolescent populations and necessary for a responsible intake process within managed-care time constraints. TEMAS meets some of the most salient youth assessment needs by providing medical model diagnostic input-but also develops comprehensive, culturally relevant information concerning personality resources consistent with a recoveryorientation.

Chapter 2 examines the cultural competency concept within the health/mental health professions. Beginning with the Child and Adolescent Service System Program (CASSP) minority cultural initiatives in the late 1980s, minority cultural initiatives have been present with varying degrees of advocacy, acceptance, and centrality in all of these professions. These initiatives are all relevant and necessary for the development of an interdisciplinary cultural competency model described in this chapter. This model is identified by attributes, construct dimensions, training modalities, and outcome characteristics of professional mental health service providers. This competency model can reaffirm, extend, and improve the quality of assessment training, practice, and research. TEMAS provides continuity for picture-story performance methods by attending to historical TAT deficiencies as a test and has reestablished and legitimized the TAT legacy for comprehensive narrative assessment of children/adolescents. TEMAS has a unique and essential role in the development of multicultural assessment competency in the United States and internationally.

Chapter 3 describes a gradual change from a method-centered, positivist-empiricist science toward a human-centered science of psychological assessment. This enlarged perspective permits an overview of current assessment training limitations partially responsible for the diminishing role of comprehensive assessment with performance measures. The availability of TEMAS to provide consistent, reliable, and useful personality-psychopathology information lies at the heart of a reconstituted assessment process for all children and adolescents. TEMAS, as a major storytelling test, contributes to a renaissance of comprehensive assessment signaled by the development of psychometrically respectable performance measures. TEMAS is also consistent with therapeutic assessment within a judgment-based practice of care.

Chapter 3 reviews similar and dissimilar picture-story instruments. Except for TEMAS, picture-story instruments have been unsystematically and partially adapted for multicultural children/adolescents rather than by deliberate construction for these populations. Adaptations have included the nature of stimuli, administration directions, service delivery social etiquette, and moderator variables, as well as special norms and interpretation guidelines. Although these instrument adaptations serve to reduce bias, there has been controversy concerning their legitimacy. This controversy was due to the false assumption that these instruments were universal in nature and required only translation for multicultural/cross-cultural use. A rationale for application of adapted storytelling instruments for multicultural populations included specific comparative criteria, or desiderata. Comparing the adequacy of adapted storytelling instruments on these criteria for multicultural applications strongly favors TEMAS.

Chapter 4 presents a history of TEMAS origins and development that is descriptive, detailed, and comprehensive. This chapter chronicles TAT origins with improvements including research-derived card adaptations, an objective scoring system, low and high inference interpretation, and culture-specific as well as international child/adolescent normative data.

In contrast to the TAT, TEMAS uses card stimuli representing age, gender, and specific minority and nonminority versions delineating physical appearance in culturally relevant and familiar backgrounds. These card sets have been employed with several multicultural populations in the United States (i.e., Hispanics, African Americans, and Asian Americans) and an increasing number of different foreign countries. Designed to depict conflict situations amenable to problem solving in urban settings, cards of medium ambiguity and definite structure were printed in color to stimulate affect. These adaptations were designed to maximize card pull. Long and short parallel forms of 9 and 23 cards, respectively, present identical themes. Separate cards in each form were developed to depict a single gender and both genders as well as age-specific settings. Multicultural characters are presented in both the minority and nonminority versions.

A scoring system rationale incorporated social, cognitive, and narrative theoretical models. TEMAS stories are reliably scored for18 cognitive functions, 9 personality functions, and 7 affective dimensions. These scores provide information concerning personality strengths and deficits, and adaptive and maladaptive personality development, and they facilitate measurement and interpretation of psychopathology and personality within sociocultural systems.

1

Child/Adolescent Mental Health Needs and Services

A series of nationally disseminated reports from 1969 to 2003 indicated consensus concerning the magnitude of child adolescent mental health problems and the insufficiency of available mental health resources. However, these reports embodied goals of contemporary quality mental health care for eliminating barriers to access, endorsing increased consumer-family responsibilities, screening, comprehensive assessment, and prevention within research-driven services and improved technologies for service delivery and evaluation. A recovery-oriented vision within a developmental science framework affirms that recovery from severe mental illnesses can and does occur. Implementation of this vision now requires reintegration of comprehensive assessment within a multicultural competency model for delivery of quality care for children and adolescents.

Comprehensive assessment using standard tests and methods has largely been omitted in managed care in favor of simpler, routine diagnoses of mental health disorders as preferred avenues for decisions relevant to subsequent services. This omission exacerbates the currently incomplete relationship between problem specification and problem alleviation, particularly for ethnic minorities. Standard tests and methods as well as new instruments are now required for assessment of these populations. Multicultural assessment is now essential for evaluating the adequacy of mental health care as well as for implementing a positive mental health psychology.

The continuing necessity for comprehensive assessment during a transformation of the mental health system must also affirm that assessment/diagnosis and intervention/treatment components are coequal, interdependent, and necessary components of quality care. There is a crucial role for multicultural assessment, particularly for the Tell-Me-A-Story Test (TEMAS), in concert with the Multicultural Assessment-Intervention Process model (MAIP) to foster effective services and service delivery embracing the full range of child adolescent consumers. TEMAS and the MAIP model are complementary avenues for implementing a positive, strength-based recovery vision.

This chapter examines the mental health needs and services context for TEMAS and describes agency-driven MAIP model components of access/ intake (including screening and comprehensive assessment), multicultural competency training, formulations and conceptualizations for diagnosis and treatment planning, treatments/interventions, and outcome evaluations within a research aegis.

MENTAL HEALTH STATUS: A POPULATION AT-RISK

Adults face increasingly high stress from multiple stressors in managing the social and economic aspects of their lives, and family discord is rampant. Caring for children is often compromised and diluted by fewer two-parent homes and absence of support from intact, extended families. The child adolescent population is increasingly distressed by multiple and complex conflicting demands, expectations, and contradictions. Parents are frustrated and often discouraged by their ongoing and frequently unrewarding efforts to seek help for their children.

The contemporary mental health care milieu for children and adolescents described in this chapter begins with the mental health status of this at-risk population and their burgeoning needs for adequate and effective mental health services. A report by the Joint Commission on the Mental Health of Children (1969) and a subsequent description of the prevalence of children with untreated serious emotional disturbances (Knitzer, 1982) led to awareness that the mental health system was inadequately funded and unprepared to provide adequate services. During the early 1980s, the National Institutes of Mental Health (NIMH) initiated the Child and Adolescent Service System Program (CASSP). Core values and guiding principles for a system of care philosophy (SOC; Stroul & Friedman, 1986) presaged the 1999 and 2001 reports by the Surgeon General and the 2003 New Freedom Initiative.

Unfortunately, there is no consensually accepted or consistent definition of child adolescent psychological distress (Friedman, Kutash, & Duchnowski, 1996). In addition to psychiatric diagnosis, *Psychosocial Impairment* refers to conditions not meeting DSM criteria. Various other labels have been used descriptively to underscore the presence of a diagnosable DSM disorder resulting in functional impairment of family, school, or emotional activities in a compilation of federal definitions by the Bazelon Center for Mental Health Law (1993) including *Developmental Disability, Seriously Emotionally Disturbed,* and *Serious Emotional Disturbance* (SED). All of these definitions are confusing in terminology, lack clarity or consistency, and have contributed to difficulties in epidemiological studies.

Functional impairment was defined in the Mental Health Administration Reorganization Act (Public Law 102–321) as difficulties substantially interfering or limiting functioning in one or more basic life activities, instrumental living skills, and functioning in social, family, or educational/vocational contexts (Friedman et al., 1996). Among 9- to 17-year-old students, extreme functional impairment occurs in 5%, who are unable to function in major areas of their lives, while 11% have significant functional impairment leading to problems and 21% have minimum impairment (U. S. Public Health Service, 2000).

SED, included in the Bazelon report and employed by the Center for Mental Health Services (CMHS), is not a diagnostic category but a definition of targeted youth that includes diagnosis and other characteristics providing eligibility criteria for mental health services. Research to determine SED prevalence has employed a number of instruments to assess functional impairment including the Children's Global Assessment Scale (CGAS; Shaffer et al., 1996), and the Diagnostic Interview Schedule for Children (DISC; Shaffer, Fisher, & Lucas, 2004). These global measures report different percentages of impairment affected by geographical location, cultural bias, and use of a single score or several key areas (Friedman et al., 1996). Forness and Knitzer (1992) recommended replacing of SED with *Emotional or Behavioral Disorders* and additionally requiring adverse effects on educational performance and presence of disability in schools and at least one other setting.

Our knowledge of the extent and gravity of child adolescent psychiatric disorders in the United States remains incomplete in the absence of representative population sampling, although this has been accomplished in Great Britain and Australia (Costello, Mustillo, Keeler, & Angold, 2004). These authors describe worldwide prevalence rates for these disorders as piecemeal, cobbled together from relatively small-scale studies, diverse methodologies, and time frames. Twenty-one studies used the Diagnostic and Statistical Manual of the American Psychiatric Association (DSM) or the International Classification of Diseases (ICD; World Health Organization, 2005) with child and/or parent informants in the United States, six European countries, Canada, Australia, and New Zealand. Versions of the DISC (Costello, Edelbrock, Kalas, Kessler, & Klaric, 1984), the most frequently used instrument, were employed in eight of these 21 studies, as was a variety of other instruments and clinical interviews. An estimated range from 8.2% to 42% and a median international estimate between 25% and 26% for "any psychiatric disorder" were reported.

The U. S. population-at-risk now contains more than 63 million children and adolescents. At least 1.5 million are abused or neglected each year, 300,000 require foster care, 7 million live with alcoholic parents, and one third of these youth can anticipate mental illness during their lifetime (Mrazek & Haggerty, 1994). A recent census figure indicates 21% of the child adolescent population with diagnosable mental disorders (U.S. Census Bureau, 2001). In addition, critical mental health related problems in male and female adolescents, respectively, include disabling sadness/ unhappiness/depression (33%/34%), suicide attempts requiring medical attention (2%/3%), drinking and driving (17%/10%), alcohol consumption prior to age 13 (34%/24%), physical fights (43%/33%), carrying weapon at school (19%/3%), and chlamydia trachomatis (16%/12%, Elster & Marcell, 2003). About 12% of this population experiences serious behavioral or emotional problems (Institute of Medicine [IOM], 1989; Saxe, Cross, & Silverman, 1988), and 2.5 million receive treatment (Office of Technology Assessment, 1986). However, no mental health services whatsoever are received by 80% of youth with diagnosable disorders (Ringel & Sturm, 2001), although these untreated disorders are frequently debilitating (Kataoka, Zhang, & Wells, 2002). Following treatment for behavioral and psychosomatic complaints, children and adolescents have fewer emergency room visits and make less use of medical services (Finney, Riley, & Cataldo, 1991).

Among youth who are undiagnosed and undiagnosable using DSM-III-R, various measures of caseness yielded a 9.4% rate of psychosocial symptomatic impairment (Angold, Costello, Farmer, Burns, & Erkanli, 1999). Estimates of need for mental health services among primary medical care child/adolescent patients are as high as 70% and although 40% are referred, only 10% actually receive any services (Cummings, 2002). For example, primary care physicians, as first responders, devote approximately 13 minutes per visit to treat an average of six mental health problems (Williams, Ross, & Dietrich, 1999). Furthermore, physicians and mental health service providers differ remarkably in the manner of providing services, including communication style, level of interaction, and amount of time with patients (Levin, Hanson, & Hennessy, 2004). As a consequence, only 6.0% to 7.5% of those 6 to 17 years of age in need of mental health evaluation actually receive services. In many areas of the country, especially rural areas, the primary mode of mental health treatment is juvenile justice.

These data on prevalence, persistence, and interrelatedness of problems, as well as more recent estimates of problem frequencies, document a national emergency for youth in urgent need of mental health services, especially for ethnic minority children in urban schools or in rural areas where children are placed in the Juvenile Justice system instead of mental health care. These needs are long-term in nature, frequently co-occurring (one mental disorder plus alcohol/drug use), demand early screening/ intervention, and impair functioning across family, education, social network, and work domains. Furthermore, the magnitude of psychosocial disorders, particularly antisocial behavior (e.g., crime, alcohol/drugs) as well as depression, eating disorders, and suicide/suicidal behaviors) has appreciably worsened during the last 50 years, probably due in part to greater diagnostic sensitivity (Fonagy, Target, Cottrell, Phillips, & Kurtz, 2002) in the absence of consensus concerning causal mechanisms. Smith and Rutter (1995) suggested strengthening the research infrastructure to permit cross-national comparisons of shifts in moral concepts that result in conflict between individualistic values and rising expectations as a potential avenue to increase understanding.

These rates of unmet needs are even greater and underutilization of available mental health services is more likely to occur among the uninsured and all ethnic minority youth (Kataoka et al., 2002; Snowden, 2003). Furthermore, the population now contains 30.6% non-Whites (U.S. Census Bureau, 2004) with disproportionately higher numbers of children and adolescents among ethnic minorities due to their higher birth rates (U.S. Census Bureau, 2001). Urban school children in districts within the 100 largest cities now are 75% non-White (Ponterotto, Mendelsohn, & Belzaire, 2003), whereas the composition of the total school-age population contains 40% ethnic minorities (Rogers, 2005).

An evaluation of cultural differences in access to care examined practice implications of these earlier reports in recent research for transforming the mental health system to provide culturally responsible interventions for children and adolescents (Snowden & Yamada, 2005). These authors concluded that disparities continue to exist and adequate explanations remain elusive. As a consequence, they believe it is imperative for researchers to "design and conduct more studies of treatment-seeking pathways that favor nonspecialty sources of assistance, improve trust and treatment receptiveness, eliminate stigma, and accommodate culturally distinctive beliefs about mental illness and mental health and styles of expressing mental health-related suffering" (p. 161).

SYSTEMS OF CARE

CAASP Philosophy

In 1984, the CASSP philosophy became the SOC cornerstone for the child and adolescent population (Stroul & Friedman, 1986). This philosophy advocated community-based systems employing a full array of individualized, clinically appropriate assessment and intervention services, responsive to the needs of children and families. Envisioned were early problem identification and ensuing services provided in the least restrictive, most normative environment, incorporating families as full participants, with linkages between various agencies. Protection of children's rights and provision of equitable, non-discriminatory services recognizing special cultural needs with easy transitions to the adult care system were objectives (Stroul, 1993).

This CASSP philosophy, under NIMH auspices, now impacts all 50 states and a number of territories. In more than 100 projects, these systems aspire to demonstrate the effects of early identification and comprehensive, individualized services coordinated by collaboration among partners reflecting administration/policy, agencies, and providers within system, program, and practice levels (Stroul, 2002).

U.S. Surgeon General Reports

Reports on mental health provided an agenda for children's mental health, recognizing the need for transformation in organization, financing, and operations of behavioral health services within integrated SOC services (U.S. Department of Health and Human Services, 1999, 2001a; U.S. Public Health Services, 2000). Children's rights were protected and advocacy was recommended, with families fully participating in planning and delivery of services. Equitable access to culturally competent services responsive to the disproportionate burden of unmet mental health needs among ethnic minority youth was strongly endorsed. These reports also called for increased recognition of children's mental health needs by improved assessment procedures and development of a sound scientific basis in research for prevention and treatment to improve quality of care.

New Freedom Initiative

Access to mental health facilities and quality care were examined, including barriers imposed by stigma, private insurance carriers, and fragmentation of the mental health system (New Freedom Commission on Mental Health, 2003). Other goals were also articulated: (a) mental health is essential to overall health; (b) mental health care is consumer and family driven; (c) elimination of disparities in mental health services; (d) early mental health screening, assessment, and referral to services; (e) mandated excellent mental health care and research; and (f) use of technology to access mental health care and information.

OVERVIEW OF SYSTEMS

SOC were authorized, developed, and funded nationally and within states as a response to the CAASP 1989 philosophy to partially resolve the crisis of too many distressed and at-risk youth for an overburdened mental health system. These systems contained core values, and guiding principles, as well as a variety of mental health services and a number of related services designed to provide comprehensive quality care for children and families commensurate with fiscal accountability while recognizing consumer needs and rights to access and treatment. The mental health services were nonresidential (i.e., prevention, early identification and intervention, assessment, outpatient treatment, home-based services, day treatment, and emergency services) and residential (i.e., therapeutic foster and group care, therapeutic camp services, independent living, residential treatment and crisis residential services, and inpatient hospitalization). These services were coordinated with social, educational, health, substance abuse, vocational, and recreational services as well as operational facilitation by case management, support and self-help groups, and a variety of ancillary services. SOC were designed to provide services responsive to cultural/racial differences that were individualized, child-centered, family-focused, and community-oriented.

However, a focus on cost containment emphasizes short-term alleviation of immediate distress rather than prevention and long-term care. As a result, access and services were provided for only a small percentage of distressed children and adolescents and specific interventions have only mediocre empirical outcomes. Psychiatric interventions, social service models, and SOC, authorized and funded as partial solutions for the emotional and behavioral dilemmas of youth, have received critical international and national evaluations.

EVALUATION OF SYSTEMS

Internationally, the U.S. health care system ranked #37 among 191 countries (World Health Organization, 2000), a commentary on the magnitude of need for continued scrutiny and improvement. This evaluation contained five indicators: (a) overall level of population health; (b) health disparities; (c) system responsiveness to individuals (i.e., patient satisfaction plus quality of system action); (d) system responsiveness to socio economic status; (e) financial burden within population. In the United States, private health expenses represented 56% of total costs while the total cost, a GDP percentage of 13.7 as well as per capita cost, exceeded any other country.

This international appraisal reaffirms Kiesler's (1992) judgment that the shift from a social welfare to health policy aegis for mental health has trivialized and subordinated the role of these services. In Kiesler's words, "Left underemphasized in U.S. health policy are preventive services needed by at least 40% of the population; the needed behavioral changes in the population that could lead to healthier practices; and various chronic health problems, especially those experienced by the elderly, children and youth" (p. 1078).

Following consolidation of health and mental health services in managed care, these policy issues severely impacted the numbers of ethnic-specific agencies and truncated similar services and programs available in the mainstream agencies. Although ethnic-specific programs operated by community-based organizations have the capacity to retain clients for continuous services and report client improvement (e.g., Chow & Wyatt, in press; Kouyoumdjian, Zamboanga, & Hensen, 2003; Leong & Lau, 2001), Snowden and Yamada (2005) suggest that organizational norms and operational procedures rather than clinical factors may account for these positive findings.

Lyons (2004) believes the sheer size, scope, organization, and management of systems has been responsible for inefficiency and something less than optimal service outcomes or satisfactory funding. These structures constitute systems *in name only* because they lack cohesive functioning of service components within simplified, consumer-friendly organizations. Reduction of mental illness stigma, a goal of recent reports, requires careful educational effort using expanded information resources.

SYSTEM BARRIERS

Four overarching and interrelated SOC barriers to receiving equitable mental health services by consumers include: (a) access limitations; (b) narrow assessment objectives; (c) medical specification of problems within a for-profit model; and (d) restrictions limiting the kinds, range, and effectiveness of available interventions (Lyons, 2004). These barriers undoubtedly contribute to system malfunction but may be amenable to partial resolution due to collective awareness and an understanding of salient limitations in available services.

In a democratic society, however, there are other more fundamental issues concerning how medical and mental health services are funded and dispensed and what constitutes a legitimate locus of power for control, regulation, and utilization of these services. For example, can medicalized mental health services be effective using a business model as opposed to a medical model or intervention-driven model integrating several sources of authority and responsibility? This question deserves careful consideration within the new information-driven and goal-oriented context of reports by the Surgeon General and the New Freedom Commission. The presence of an informed and shared perspective with laudable societal goals for alleviating suffering among children and adolescents is not sufficient in the absence of the political will to implement these goals in a socially responsible manner. Political power in this society potentially can trump scientific acumen and professional consensus.

Consumer Access

Access to care has not substantially increased nor have mental health services for children/adolescents improved in the number and variety of available interventions or the adequacy of outcome evaluation. Nonetheless, access can be facilitated by broadening the definition of consumer eligibility, feasible in combined insurance-provider systems by careful management of the cost–benefit ratio. Within these systems, local control and management of services, as contrasted with central control, provides more flexibility in addressing multiple needs using different assessment and intervention strategies. Central control of services requires complex bureaucratic policies and procedures that interfere with services to consumers.

Access of ethnic minority persons can be facilitated to increase utilization by routinely employing culturally credible service delivery social etiquette, evaluating acculturation/racial identity status, considering the necessity and usefulness of ethnic/linguistic matching of consumers with providers, and recognizing that cultural formulations or conceptualizations can increase the reliability of clinical diagnoses and contribute to effectiveness of subsequent interventions. As an example, the Multicultural Assessment-Intervention Process (MAIP) model, described in this chapter, provides a feasible modus operandi for facilitating access and responding to culture-specific necessities for ethnic minority consumers.

Narrow Assessment Objectives

An expanded assessment role is required to encompass more comprehensive definitions of behavioral functioning in health, disorder, and disease. There is urgent need for the cost-effective screening procedures to provide comprehensive, organized, and treatment-relevant information resources. This information can be used immediately and directly for diagnostic formulations and personality conceptualizations or as a prelude to further assessment using standard, comprehensive instruments of documented psychometric status or instruments/methods designed exclusively for clinical diagnosis or symptom description.

Medical Problem Specification/Business Model

Medicalization of the entire range of human problems reduces prevention options and curtails multimodal interdisciplinary approaches. There is also a need to recognize that medical identification and definition of problems as well as insufficient regard for the medical offset literature, even with recently suggested limitations (Olfson, Sing, & Schlesinger, 1999), has reduced awareness of the potential effectiveness of nonmedical, psychological, and psychosocial interventions. Restrictions on the range and kind of available interventions often conflict with research findings suggesting more beneficial intervention options than those currently employed. Moreover, an overly narrow focus on available intervention and treatment modalities limits the scope of outcome evaluations, including quality of life measures. This issue, however, remains contextualized with a business model incentive for health and mental health care.

A business model incentive legitimizes overuse/misuse of pharmacological interventions as psychiatric interventions of choice consistent with a medical aegis and cost-effectiveness. The demonstrated positive pharmacological benefits of symptom suppression are diluted by adverse side effects, resulting in problems of medication management, consumer compliance, and viable, ongoing communication with providers. The documented differences among ethnic minority populations in medication effects require physicians and psychiatrists not only to have special knowledge but multicultural competency as well. A locus of curative power and responsibility exclusively in physicians serves policy goals and political objectives inherent in incorporating an earlier relatively separate mental health system within the health care system. Exclusive medical prerogatives may contribute to the emergence of new accountability problems in meeting needs for quality mental health care.

A business model for authorizing financing and/or reimbursing services in managed care systems originally provided a risk-pooling strategy in the form of a nontaxable benefit to employees. Health care insurance pays only for diagnosable medical conditions and for symptom-alleviating medical interventions, ultimately supervised by physicians. This definition of services and eligible consumers also covers mental health disorders and symptoms. Within a business model, an inevitable focus on profit led to an emphasis on cost containment achieved by cost-effective services. However, profit margins can vary from a nominal percentage to cover overhead and reasonable compensation (e.g., Medicare, Kaiser Permanente) to exorbitant margins in some managed care corporations. Medical decisions regarding the definition, composition, and implementation of quality services led to potential conflict concerning the balance of product cost and desired corporate profitability. Accountability requires outcome management strategies and performance-based contracting with reimbursement only for interventions with empirically supported outcomes in addition to research evaluation of the specific utilities of intervention modalities.

Such an accountability format omits a more comprehensive and adequate definition of quality services and requires identification of provider skill deficits as well as examination of the contents, efficacy, relevance, and credibility of an array of specific interventions for particular consumers. Because the mental health problems of consumers-at-risk are more complex than specific psychiatric diagnoses or symptomatology per se, nonmedical or extramedical conceptualizations, interventions, and broader outcome criteria for quality care are frequently necessary. A biopsychosocial perspective articulating quality-of-life outcome criteria is thus more inclusive than the prevailing medical model perspective.

The conflict between business model cost-efficiency objectives and medical model quality care standards results in an uneasy, unwieldy, and frequently unequal balance of power between parents and professionals for decision-making with regard to care of individual children and adolescents. This conflict restrains ethical medical practice. Whenever the exercise of power is exclusively in the hand of insurance carriers who do not have responsibility for delivery of services, a business model can also interfere with quality care. However, when the insurer is also responsible for providing services, the balance of power favors physician-defined quality criteria including consensual medical standards for definitions, ingredients, interventions, and outcomes. Nonetheless, simultaneous employment of insurance/business and clinical models creates a potential for imbalance between quality services and accountability. The diverse and often conflicting goals of administrators, providers, and consumers remain sources of chronic tensions.

An obvious solution to this inherent dilemma lies in recognizing that mental health care must be family- and consumer-driven, as recommended consistently in federal reports, with ultimate power invested by law in parents who are provided with sufficient screening information to effectively implement responsible decisions with regard to an array of available interventions of demonstrated goodness-of-fit with presenting complaints, problems, and diagnoses. It should be noted that the Surgeon General emphasized that only a balanced partnership can provide coordination and integration of care: "Not only is family involvement therapeutic for the patient, but it is the key to sustaining continuity of care and providing high-quality care" (U.S. Department of Health and Human Services, 2001b, p. 2).

A RECOVERY VISION

Anthony (1993) called the 1990s a decade of recovery and argued that service delivery systems predicated on this vision require new initiatives and standards (Anthony, 2000). A recovery vision emphasizes optimism, hope, and the possibility of augmented self-determination and independent living. This vision has been recently addressed sensitively and comprehensively (Green-Hennessy & Hennessey, 2004) within "a positive culture of healing" (Jacobson & Greenley, 2001, p. 484).

An overarching issue for children and adolescents pertains to the locus of authority and responsibility for implementing this vision with individual youth. In the current discussion of power sharing, a fine line exists between beneficence and paternalism. Beneficence requires practice in the best interest of clients, whereas paternalism invokes assumed knowledge of what constitutes best interest (McCubbin & Cohen, 1996; Pellegrino, 1994). Parents have a history of personal nurturing experiences, emotional ties, and established relationship, as well as an intimate knowledge of a child's development and behaviors across multiple settings and over time. Informed decisions concerning the welfare of a child provide the basis for competent parenting. As a societal responsibility, parents who do not possess sufficient or adequate parenting skills merit training in decision making for and with their children. A discussion of the extent, limits, and conditions governing parental responsibility for children in health, illness, and distress is now mandatory to increase public awareness of the necessity for a responsive and responsible system of child/adolescent mental health care.

This issue has been a source of perennial conflict between parents and providers who often impose their own values and usurp parental decisions by virtue of their training, professional experience, and status. Medical providers, for example, have severe time constraints as well as a legacy, at least in the United States, of an impersonal service delivery style and authoritarian stance that can render physicians only minimally able to discuss collaborative issues with parents. As a potential remedy, a New York State dialogue process between psychiatrists and ex-patient mental health professionals examined the meaning of recovery in a search for common ground (Blanch, Fisher, Tucker, Walsh, & Chassman, 1993). This dialogue yielded a manifold, active, individualized, ongoing recovery process distinct from treatment. In addition to experiencing symptoms, recovery is related to how one deals with abuse, discrimination, and stigma as secondary assaults to personal equilibrium. Recovery is fueled by hope that invokes a sense of control that includes self-directed coping and constructing meaning through a self-conscious tracking of progress and connectedness to valued activities and human relationships. Recovery is thus complex and ultimately driven by the individual response to professional care.

A recovery-oriented vision necessary for quality care requires a metatheoretical framework from the emerging discipline of developmental science that cannot be implemented by single-factor interventions (e.g., cognitive-behavioral; pharmacological) for the multiple and interrelated risks of childhood and adolescence (Farmer & Farmer, 2001). This new holistic science of child/adolescent care incorporates an interface of developmental psychology, developmental biology, molecular biology, physiology, neuropsychology, social psychology, sociology, anthropology, and other disciplines (Cairns, 2000; Magnusson, 2000). A tripartite approach can unite developmental science with prevention models as well as interventions. Developmental science can unify services by delivering interventions that rely on prevention models to relate risk factors to subsequent child and adolescent difficulties (Farmer & Farmer, 2001).

A positive psychology of human functioning consistent with this new interdisciplinary coalescence eschews a pathology-based science in favor of "a science of positive subjective experience, positive individual traits, and positive institutions...to improve quality of life...and allow individuals, communities, and societies to flourish" (Seligman & Csikszentmihalyi, 2000, p. 5). Positive psychology emphasizes psychological assessment (Lopez & Snyder, 2003) and can focus on youth development (Larson, 2000) by recognizing that emotional states promote good health and well-being (Salovey, Detweiler, Steward, & Rothman, 2000).

Quality care within a recovery-oriented system can now be defined by evidence-based practices requiring documentation by complementary quantitative and qualitative research (Anthony, Rogers, & Farkas, 2003). These authors believe that a recovery vision can only be implemented by focusing on recovery criteria deemed critical by consumers, emphasizing the credibility of subjective outcomes, and examining the role of helper–consumer relationships as well as underlying humanistic values. Acculturation status and ethnicity affect problem identification, pinpoint appropriate interventions, and identify competent providers for ethnic minority populations. These issues can affect relevance and generalizability of evidence-based practices in diverse geographical settings (e.g., Cauce et al., 2002; Drake, Goldman, Leff, 2001; Manson, 2000; Prieto, McNeill, Walls, & Gomez, 2001; Wang, Berglund, & Kessler, 2000).

Evidence-based practice in medicine originated in 1981 among Canadian epidemiologists concerned with teaching physicians to examine and classify empirical research evidence hierarchically for evidentially supported applications to patient care (Singh & Oswald, 2004). These practices are now incorporated in many mental health service settings due to demonstrated improvement in client outcomes (Drake et al., 2001), although questions remain concerning how "evidence" is defined and the relevance of research conditions and methodologies to the complexity and diversity of clinic and community settings. Moreover, the small number of adequately researched interventions and the necessity for family and consumer choice and decision-making prerogatives invoke caution consistent with the development of specific strategies for using evidence-based interventions in practice, expressed by the Task Force on Evidence-Based Interventions in School Psychology (Kratochwill & Shernoff, 2004).

The implementation of evidence-based practices has been difficult, complex, and beset with a variety of intervention-specific research limitations regarding populations, outcomes, and contents. For example, these practices have primarily led to research that was neither conceived nor undertaken to implement a recovery-oriented vision, but rather to demonstrate that efficacy-based designs carefully control experimental conditions and maximize treatment outcomes. Moreover, treatment outcome research with children has been largely restricted to behavioral and cognitive interventions rather than examining the psychodynamic, family, and eclectic interventions more typical in clinical child practice (Lonigan, Elbert, & Johnson, 1998).

Efficacy designs testing maximal treatment impact under laboratory conditions are necessary but not sufficient for evaluation of psychosocial interventions. Clinical approaches cannot be adequately examined without employing *effectiveness designs* to "assess intervention effects under ordinary clinical conditions, with treatment delivered to average or representative patients or clients, by average or representative practitioners, working under conditions that reflect typical practice realities (e.g., full caseloads and clinic productivity pressures)" (Weisz & Kazdin, 2003, p. 447).

Nonequivalence of outcomes in clinical trials/research therapy and less controlled conventional clinic therapy in over 200 studies provides a cautionary note because generalizing the positive laboratory findings in controlled outcomes studies is hazardous; different procedures or conditions suggest that the transcontextual validity issue has not been resolved (Weisz, Weiss, & Donenberg, 1992). For these reasons, Kazdin and Kendall (1998) suggested targeting disorder-specific processes and testing variations in intensity, focus, and duration of interventions. An examination of possible moderators of intervention efficacy using meta-analysis found only severity and treatment type independently associated with large effects (Weisz, Donenberg, Han & Weiss, 1995).

The question of whether or not efficacious treatments generalize to ethnic minority populations has been reviewed, documented, and supported by Miranda, Bemal, Lay, Kohn, Hwang, et al. (2005). Outcomes of depression are improved for Latinos and African Americans, but there is less data for Asian populations and Native Americans Alaska Natives. These authors conclude that "in the absence of efficacy studies, the combined used of protocols or guidelines that consider culture and context with evidence-based care is likely to facilitate engagement in treatment and probably to enhance outcomes" (p. 134). Research methodologies for tailoring these interventions for specific ethnic minority populations were recommended.

Quality care is dependent on a developmental science framework with a focus on positive subjective experience to provide a rationale for implementing a simplified process model of care, restoring assessment, and increasing the likelihood of congruence between the array of presenting problems and the dimensions and contents of available interventions. Description of behaviors relevant to internal and external factors necessary for holistic understanding of development and functioning over time thus becomes mandatory. Internal factors include cognitive, emotional, endocrine, morphological, neurobiological, perceptual, and physiological subsystems. External factors include family, peer group, neighborhood, and culture subsystems. An understanding of multiple factors on multiple levels coordinated by timing issues is vital for understanding preventive and treatment interventions. In addition to more complete and comprehensive early description of problems by screening, subsequent assessment can facilitate long-term monitoring and evaluation of the contribution of specific interventions to health-relevant behaviors and ultimately to quality of life. An interdisciplinary, recovery-oriented science is now an overarching necessity to provide individualized, accessible, culturally competent, quality care predicated on informed primary parental responsibility.

TOWARD A TRANSFORMED MENTAL HEALTH SYSTEM

Popular endorsement of a transformed health-mental health system is now necessary to forestall any political misapprehension of the means to reach mental health goals in the United States. Such a system requires clear, coherent, feasible, and ultimately consensual steps toward implementation and can be initiated by a recovery-oriented vision within a developmental science framework for multidisciplinary preventive and intervention options. These options should be provided within a clearly delineated and simplified process model for delivering mental health services. This model necessitates the inclusion of a number of components within local community networks. A locus of responsible power within the family to focus these cooperative efforts, advocated by the Surgeon General (U.S. Department of Health and Human Services, 2001b), is a controversial but necessary feature.

This section describes the present status of these mental health care system components (i.e., screening, prevention, assessment, intervention, evaluation, training, and research) and how interrelations among these components can be facilitated and monitored by employing the flexible, research-driven MAIP model permitting monitoring, modifying, and evaluating individual child and adolescent consumers and their providers.

Screening

Comprehensive mental health screening for mental and addictive disorders and subsequent referral for all children under 18 and the 52 million students in 114,000 public schools was envisioned in the New Freedom Initiative (see New Freedom Commission on Mental Health, 2003; Garrett Lee Smith Memorial Act, S.2634). Mandatory screening has been accepted on a state-by-state basis. Illinois adopted an enhanced screening, assessment, and support services system for children and adolescents in crisis as part of their 2003 Children's Mental Health Act (Public Act 93-0495).

Screening can be accomplished by either a qualified professional, or a qualified assistant, or computer-assisted for interviewing, information gathering, and information processing (Conner, 2004). A qualified professional, using information from parents, the child, teachers, paper-and-pencil questionnaires, or computer information systems, requires 1 to 5 hours. A similar process by an assistant can be supplemented by a re-interview, further examination, and report by the professional supervisor. Screening can also be accomplished via the Internet to permit better screening. Computer-assisted patient interviews can encourage larger and more representative numbers of respondents, and are less costly and more reliable than face-to-face interviews (Paperny, 1997; Paperny & Hedberg, 1999).

The TeenScreen Columbia Program has screened more than 20,000 in 27 states and 69 sites from 1999 through 2003, and cost approximately $14 million to develop and $92 per student initially, although the objectives are to decrease per student costs to $32 or less, screen 40,000 plus, and refer 10,000 for treatment annually (Hogan & Flynn, 2003). The TeenScreen Instrument, a 10-minute, self-completion questionnaire with English and Spanish versions, identifies depressive feelings and/or suicidal thoughts/attempts as well as alcohol/substance abuse and general areas of physical health in 14- to 18-year-old youth. Because a positive screen may identify brief depressive, non-clinically significant episodes, more comprehensive follow-up assessment with the DISC or evaluation by a mental health professional is recommended.

A number of other screening instruments have been employed for diagnostic purposes (e.g., Dierker et al., 2001; Grisso, Barnum, Fletcher, Cauffman & Peuslchold, 2001), perhaps as a substitute for more comprehensive assessment. Dierker et al. (2001) compared three major anxiety and depression instruments using a structured DSM-IV interview for those students above and below an 80th percentile cut-off score. These instruments yielded important internalizing and externalizing gender differences and were adequate for identifying specific symptoms but required relatively large expenditures of time and clinical skill. Grisso et al. (2001) employed a brief screen, the Massachusetts Youth Screening Instrument (MAYSI-2), administered within the juvenile justice system. The MAYSI-2 permitted an economical, self-report, first level screen and provided ethnic difference data for alcohol/drug use, anger-irritability, depression-anxiety, somatic complaints, suicide ideation, thought disturbance, and traumatic experiences.

With the development and availability of low cost on-line screening in the private sector, comparative research on comprehensive screening instruments is now imperative. Connor (2004) employed 21 criteria for comparisons of six recognized screening systems and instruments with his online StepOne Adolescent Clinical Screening Questionnaire (ASCQ) developed for Internet-based use by parents. These instruments/systems included the Devereux Scale of Mental Disorders (DSMD; Naglieri, LeBuffe, & Pfeiffer, 1994), Adolescent Symptoms Inventory (ASI-4; Gadnow & Spratkin, 1997), Behavior Assessment System Children (BASC; Reynolds & Kamphaus, 1992), Child Behavior Checklist (CBCL; Achenbach, 1992), Computerized Diagnostic Interview Schedule for Children (C-DISC; Shaffer, Fisher, & Lucas, 2004, p. 267), and the TeenScreen (Hogan & Flynn, 2003).

In terms of comparative options, StepOne is similar to other instruments employing a parent informant for risk assessment monitoring behavior and treatment, but differs by not employing children or teachers as informants, and by not providing a parent intervention report. Uniquely, StepOne is Internet-based, with parental control of privacy and immediate availability of flexible, customized screening or advanced child-focused specific and individualized reports providing parent education information and feasible treatment outcomes using community-specific norms and results. StepOne can be immediately updated and is available free or at nominal cost, contrasting with the $15 to $75 fee for other instruments. Selection of a screening system is dictated by implementation methodology as well as unique system characteristics. These comparisons are necessary because the screening method chosen can have financial, legal, ethical, social, and political implications. Consistent with limitations of other systems, StepOne is available only in English and has not been adapted for applications with ethnic minority populations in the United States or foreign nationals from diverse cultures, although such adaptation is necessary and would expand the number of potential consumers. Screening can also be employed as an intervention, although there is disagreement on whether the purpose of screening is diagnosis or intervention. Under ideal circumstances, screening or assessment solely for diagnostic purposes may be laudable. However, screening and assessment can be therapeutic and cost-effective when both of these objectives are served simultaneously, and many system-of-care sites use their program evaluation in this manner.

Prevention

Addressing problems before they are manifest, inculcating strengths and coping skills at an early age, or minimizing trauma due to abuse or environmental conditions exerts a salutary impact on future development. An early typology of primary, secondary, and tertiary prevention classified most interventions as preventive (Commission on Chronic Illness, 1957). Leaf (1999), however, preferred distinctions between preventive interventions, defined by Mrazek and Haggerty (1994) as *universal* or desirable for everyone, *selective* or directed toward at risk subgroups, and *indicated preventive interventions* applicable with persons experiencing demonstrable but subclinical problems. These preventive interventions focus on differing segments of the risk continuum.

Low-cost, preventive mental health programs for parenting and skills building have been available in existing primary health care, schools, and work settings, largely independent of mental health services. Programs serving as universal interventions for millions of low-income families include Head Start/Early Head Start, State Child Health Insurance Program (SCHIP), Medicaid, and Aid to Families with Dependent Children (AFDC), as well as child care for working mothers. Head Start, a preschool program, has included detection of emotional and behavior problems since 1965, although the benefits of associated mental health services have not been systematically evaluated, linked to developmental processes among ethnic minority children, or received adequate political support or research funding (Piotrkowski, Collins, Knitzer, & Robinson, 1994; Takanishi & DeLeon, 1994). Nonetheless, the psychosocial educational objectives of mental health education partnerships in preschool programs represent a continuing opportunity for family outreach and monitoring the status of children in the community (Edlefsen & Baird, 1994).

Indicated preventive interventions have not been clearly distinguishable from treatments for DSM disorders. Leaf (1999) suggested eliminating the fuzzy distinction between preventive interventions and clinical treatment by integrating preventive and remedial services, although this cost-effective remediation has occurred only infrequently in communities.

Despite these technical issues, the success of prevention strategies has been empirically established by a meta-analysis conducted by Durlak and Wells (1997) to demonstrate the effectiveness of 177 preventive intervention programs for child adolescent emotional and behavioral problems. This achievement stimulated commentaries by Trickett (1997) and Manson (1997) focusing attention on omissions in these programs relevant to the direction and nature of future research on preventive interventions.

Trickett (1997) examined the importance of assumptions inherent in an ecological perspective concerning the embeddedness of behavior in social and cultural contexts, interventionist-setting relationships, and community development goals. These sociocultural contexts affect how participants construe the relevance, appropriateness, and meaning of setting-specific interventions as well as the validity of constructs pertinent for durable change over time. Trickett (1997) employed the term "coupling with the host environment" (p. 198) to describe an interventionist-setting relationship affecting empowerment of participants resulting from an intervention. Empowerment is conditional on relevant sources of input, effects on composition of the intervention, and accountability of researchers to the community. Finally, the design, implementation, and evaluation of preventive interventions

> is intended to integrate the spirit of understanding the setting, crafting a collaborative and empowering relationship, and implementing discrete interventions in such a way as to create resources in the setting for future problem-solving. Doing so involves an explicit self-consciousness about how to integrate the process of relationship development with the demands of local ecology to serve the goal of community development (Trickett, 1997, p. 199).

A second commentary on Durlak and Wells (1997) noted the omission of ethnic or racial characteristics in 48% of these studies and that participants in a majority of studies were either non-White, or evenly divided between White and non-White (Manson, 1997). Citing recognition of the link between success/failure of preventive intervention research, programming, and cultural competence proposed by Mrazek and Haggerty (1994), Manson (1997) provided research examples of community–researcher relationships, identification of culturally mediated issues and theoretical frameworks, and preparation of culturally relevant content, format, and delivery within appropriate narrative structures. Studies incorporating natural helpers and existing support networks can ensure the inclusion of culture-specific decision-making processes and intervention points. Manson (1997) sought answers to the following specific questions concerning the omission of cultural variation relevant to issues raised by Trickett's (1997) ecological perspective.

> Given this potentially important source of variation, one cannot help but wonder: How do significantly non-white samples distribute across program types and is this similar to their white counterparts? Do program effects differ in terms of the ethnic and racial background of intervention participants? That is, what are the effect sizes for the samples (25.4%) comprising essentially white populations as compared to those (26.5%) noted above? Do mean effect sizes vary in any systematic way by ethnicity/race? (Manson, 1997, p. 217).

These questions can be more adequately addressed employing existing psychological research guidelines in designing future preventive intervention programs (Council of National Psychological Associations for the Advancement of Ethnic Minority Interests, 2000) coupled with an understanding of research predicated on selective use and misuse of scientific method (e.g., Malgady, 1996; Rogler, 1989; Sue & Sue, 2003).

Assessment

The goodness-of-fit between presenting distress signals and effective intervention modalities remains incompletely understood. There is continued recognition that reliable sources of comprehensive individualized information necessarily precedes accurate descriptions of problems, including formulations and conceptualizations for clinical diagnoses leading to treatment as well as other interventions for problem remediation.

Contemporary assessment instruments available for children/ adolescents have a variety of theoretical origins and measurement perspectives and thus provide distinctive diagnostic and descriptive assessment contributions. The reputations, credibility, and usage of particular projective instruments, although supported by substantive research demonstrations (e.g., Meyer, Finn, Eyde, Kays Moreland, et al., 2001), have been challenged and defended within the assessment establishment (e.g., Lilienfeld, Lynn, & Lohr, 2003; Society for Personality Assessment, 2005).

Routine assessment in child mental health settings requires easily acquired, narrowly defined, cost-effective diagnostic skills as well as single and multisource, multidimensional measures (Lachar, 2004). Although standard tests administered in battery format remain prominent, there is increasing use of parent and teacher ratings scales. Single-source measures include the Minnesota Multiphasic Personality Inventory-Adolescent (MMPI-A; Archer, 1992), the Adolescent Psychopathology Scale (APS; Reynolds, 1998), the Beck Youth Inventories of Emotional and Social Development (BYI; Beck, Beck, & Jolly, 2001), the Comprehensive Behavior Rating Scale for Children (CBRSC; Neeper, Lahey, & Frick, 1990), and the Millon Adolescent Clinical Inventory (MACI; Millon, 1993). Comprehensive, multidimensional measures include the Personality Inventory for Children, Second Edition (PIC-2; Kamphaus & Frick, 1996), the Personality Inventory for Youth (PIY), the Student Behavior Survey (SBS), the Behavior Assessment System for Children (BASC; Reynolds & Kamphaus, 1992), the Connors' Rating Scales-Revised (CRS-R; Connors, 1997), and the Child Behavior Checklist (CBC; Achenbach & McConaughy, 1997). School settings use various assessment technologies (i.e., interview/ records, observational systems, checklists/self-reports, projective methods, standardized tests of cognitive abilities/academic achievement, and response-to-intervention approaches) for eligibility decisions for special services. In the private sector, assessment remains a luxury incorporating a wide range of tests and methods often restricted to an initial session, a referral option, or as therapeutic assessment, a treatment option.

Assessment benefits from traditional instruments have been minimized and eroded by managed care in the public sector. There is an increasing preference for brief, symptom-focused instruments (Piotrowski, 1999) that can be administered, scored, and interpreted in less than two hours (Camara, Nathan, & Puente, 2000). Recognizing a narrowing focus on DSM diagnosis, Fox (1994) predicted "the continued growth and development of professional psychology may ultimately stand or fall on the integrity of the educational system that prepares future generations of practitioners" (p. 200). A recent review of managed care practices affecting professional psychology acknowledges preoccupation with diagnosis and suggests that symptom checklists may ultimately replace standard tests and test batteries (Sanchez & Turner, 2003).

Despite this contemporary assessment climate, assessment information contributes to understanding the applicability of intervention options. The lack of correspondence between categorical approaches to diagnosis in the Diagnostic and Statistical Manual of Mental Disorders (DSM-IV; American Psychiatric Association, 1994) and "real-world manifestations of emotional and behavioral disorders" (Liao, 2001, p. 14) contributes to a poor fit between assessment/diagnosis and intervention/treatment and complicates an adequate understanding of childhood distress. DSM disorders often involve functional impairment with multiple diagnoses. As a consequence, functional impairment and severity of symptoms require simultaneous evaluation (Roberts, Attkisson, & Rosenblatt, 1998) in order to plan for services with improved effectiveness in community settings. Different kinds of assessment information, including the subjective DSM-IV classification system and empirically derived objective systems, increase understanding and suggest specific resources for coping with problems-in-living and potential psychopathologies.

Intervention

There is reasonable consensus concerning the intervention areas for emotionally disturbed children and adolescents originally described by Stroul and Friedman (1986). These five general areas are psychiatric hospitalization, partial hospitalization/day treatment, outpatient services, residential treatment, and special education. Lyons (2004) has summarized the current status of these intervention areas. Psychiatric hospital admissions for children have remained constant despite the presence of fewer state hospitals and numbers of beds for children coupled with reductions in length of hospital stays. Partial hospital/day treatment provides educational activities, treatment, and rehabilitation for children/adolescents with behavioral difficulties in regular classrooms as an alternative to full hospitalization. Although there are few well-controlled studies, approximately 75% of children return to public schools and this intervention has some cost-effectiveness. Nonetheless, there is need for consistent eligibility guidelines, treatment models, outcome criteria, and expectations for length of stay.

Outpatient services provide individual and group psychotherapy and counseling for children/adolescents and families, typically on a weekly basis.

Presenting problems include attention deficit/hyperactivity, depression, disruptive behavior, and trauma including posttraumatic stress disorder. There has been some dispute concerning the effectiveness of supportive and psychodynamic psychotherapies with this population. In New York State, therapy is typically terminated on a no-show basis for various reasons with only 10% successful outcomes and another 10% requiring more intensive interventions (Lyons, 2004).

Residential treatment includes a range of facilities including institutions with campus settings, homes for small groups, treatment foster care, and outdoor/wilderness programs. A living environment is provided to support varied and eclectic active treatment by a multidisciplinary team. Short stays and behavioral approaches are frequently employed to increase accountability and clarify outcomes. Residential treatment is a major component of the public mental health care system, with funded support from the child welfare and juvenile justice systems. In 2000 there were over 28,000 residents primarily under 18 years of age, with two thirds between 13 and 17.

Special education services are available for about 1% of students, although the need has been estimated at 20% of the school population. These children have an unexplained inability to learn or build/maintain interpersonal relationships, coupled with inappropriate behaviors, pervasive depressed mood, and physical symptoms. A majority of these emotionally disturbed students are in self-contained classrooms for at least half the school day, with frequent use of behavioral strategies to control aversive behaviors without equal focus on positive behaviors.

These summaries provide helpful introductory material but do not adequately describe particular interventions with credible application histories and supportive research or illustrate how these interventions may be employed with multiple problems. Interventions designed for specific public or private sector applications are available and can be employed separately (e.g., intensive case management, cognitive-behavior therapy, multisystemic therapy, etc.) or contained in individualized regimens (e.g.,wraparound) implemented and supervised by family members, community volunteers, or mental health professionals and agencies.

Unfortunately, interventions are employed selectively by physicians and professional child-care workers, frequently on the basis of availability or cost-effectiveness. Unbiased effectiveness evaluations across a number of competing interventions for a particular child/adolescent are infrequent. There are also insufficient information resources for parents in a context of inadequate consideration or respect for their opinions as responsible adults. In other words, there has been scant public attention to how, by whom, and on what basis decisions concerning interventions for particular children/adolescents are made. Responsibility for authorization, conduct, monitoring, supervision, and evaluation of interventions currently varies from a preferred exclusive professional aegis to partial parental authority, control, and autonomy. Parental empowerment enables parents to more assertively select and control quality care for their child/adolescent. Responsibility should begin with parental authorization for individualized screening prior to any other assessment by mental health professionals. Parental consent for particular interventions is predicated on information-rich descriptions of contemporary intervention options for their children/adolescents, the availability of particular interventions within the family residential locale, and recourse to responsible feedback on the desirability and relevance of each potential intervention for their own child/adolescent. Some of this information is already available on the InCrisis website for parents, including a ranking of potentially efficacious interventions predicated by StepOne screening, and in a recent book for parents (Conner, 2005). A nontechnical, research-based evaluation of each intervention for strengths and limitations should be included, as well as the rankings of potential interventions. The InCrisis website serves to inform parental decision making and results in more responsible oversight by collaborating parents.

It is now known that the utilization of mental health care as well as the feasibility–acceptability of particular interventions or the likelihood of successful application with a particular child/adolescent depends on cultural attitudes and health–illness beliefs. Similarly, consumer comfort in treatment settings is facilitated by décor respecting cultural values. Consistent use of credible social etiquette by all staff members during the service delivery process is a complementary and necessary human contribution to quality care of multicultural consumers.

Complicating the diagnostic process are cultural differences in acceptable and maladaptive child/adolescent behaviors, affects, cognitions, and interpersonal relationships, as well as culturally determined constraints affecting the contents of parental reports, especially of family relevant events, experiences, and trauma. The extent to which specific interventions can be helpful is also dramatically affected by the role of the family as a sanctioned (and sometimes unique) pathway to any externally imposed interventions. Moreover, there are strong cultural preferences for gender and age of potential service providers, the increased comfort afforded by group or individual treatment, and the location, privacy, or nonprivacy of intervention sites.

Each intervention has diagnostic and/or problem-specific information prerequisites, varying in kind and scope, that facilitate compliance with assessment and evaluation objectives. Moreover, contemporary mental health services often occur too late in time and fail to provide immediate succor or support as well as long-term remediation or enhanced quality of life. In as much as information and immediacy of responsiveness are critical attributes of mental health care, screening with StepOne provides information needed by parents to make informed decisions. Local settings require a wider range of available interventions with demonstrated positive and beneficial effects. These interventions should be predicated on more effective usage of screening as an intervention per se as a responsible professional objective and/or as a precursor of comprehensive assessment. In the absence or unavailability of adequate screening information, comprehensive independent assessment remains a necessity.

Evaluation/Training/Research (ETR)

ETR is used here to describe a combination of necessary and associated assets readily and continuously accessible within a child/adolescent mental health care facility. A constant, consistent, and continuing evaluation of consumers, providers, diagnostic reliabilities, intervention/treatment outcomes, and cost–benefits can be readily accomplished within any treatment setting. Local settings must have available computerized facilities for tracking identified intake and outcome profiles of all consumers as well as monitoring their providers and evaluating effectiveness of designated interventions, particularly when matched according to local research findings and/or preferences. The ability to evaluate provider multicultural competencies and limitations, permitting monitoring clinical service skills during service delivery and services, is of equivalent importance and relevance.

A research aegis provides an ongoing, flexible, data-driven, computerized format for monitoring individual consumers across system components (i.e., intake/screening, diagnostic formulations/conceptualizations, interventions/treatments, and outcome evaluation as well as multicultural skills training for providers) and for rapid acquisition of archival data for research purposes and system refinement. Such informed tracking can be accomplished readily and cost-effectively within a continuously modifiable assessment-intervention model as increased understanding and greater numbers of clients contribute to efficacy demonstrations. Preparation for ETR includes careful knowledge of ethnic minority population demographics in the agency catchment area, community empowerment to facilitate design/evaluation/review of all services, and to establish and maintain viable interconnections with community schools, agencies, and indigenous healers.

A major issue historically has been that effective mental health interventions in one locale/setting do not readily generalize to other facilities or catchment areas with different population demographics. For this reason, successful interventions/programs may require alterations within a context of local community empowerment, input, and knowledge as necessary conditions for transportability.

MAIP ASSESSMENT SERVICE DELIVERY MODEL

The MAIP model emerged from a variety of sources including a social justice ideology, multicultural competence training in counseling psychology, multicultural assessment, and culturally sensitive research (e.g., Dana, 1993, 1997, 1998b; 2000a, 2002a, 2005a, 2005b). Originally developed to provide a context for culturally sensitive assessment of psychopathology and personality, this model examines the assessment- intervention process at five points employing a series of questions to clarify cultural orientation (acculturation/racial identity status), instrument usage, need for cultural formulations or conceptualizations, and interventions (standard or modified). These questions refer to particular times during the assessment-intervention process when cultural issues embedded in the mental health service delivery process can signal the potential usefulness of additional information resources (Figure 1–1):

1. Availability of a universal instrument for all clients?
2. Cultural Orientation status?
3. Diagnosis necessary?
4. Culture-specific instruments?
5. Anglo-American norms?
6. Cross-cultural interaction stress?
7. Diagnosis necessary?

With regard to Question 1, although ostensibly universal instruments are available, they must be used with extreme caution at present because they

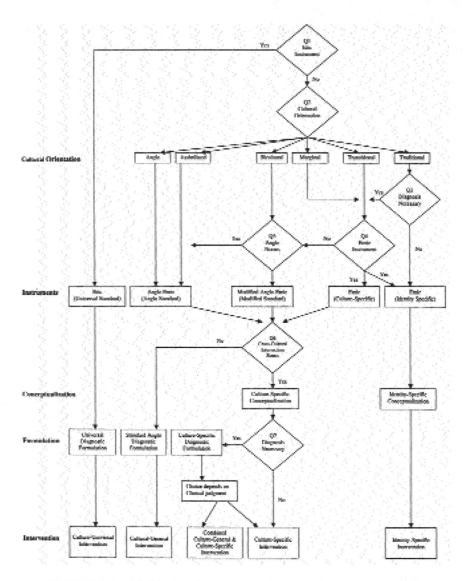

FIGURE 1–1.   Multicultural assessment–intervention process model.

Note. From *Handbook of Cross-Cultural and Multicultural Personality Assessment* (p. 7), by R. H. Dana, 2000c, Mahwah, NJ: Lawrence Erlbaum Associates, Inc. Copyright 2000 by Lawrence Erlbaum Associates, Inc. Adapted with permission.

do not adequately represent culture-specific traits and employ international samples similar to Western samples (Triandis & Suh, 2002). The existence of global or universal traits remains controversial in the absence of convincing demonstrations of cross-cultural construct equivalence (Dana, 2000b, 2005a). There is also compelling evidence that depression as well as other personality characteristics and their identified symptom constellations have few or many culture-specific descriptors and are clustered and identified differently across countries (e.g., Brandt & Boucher, 1986).

The etic instruments in Question 1 are more accurately described as imposed etics rather than genuine etics (Lonner, 1985). These imposed etic instruments have been used in the United States with ethnic minority populations and exported internationally as if they were genuine etics with identical meanings in nonoriginating cultures. However, before describing these instruments as genuine etics, it is mandatory to establish their cultural equivalence (see Allen & Dana, 2004). MAIP explicitly acknowledges the necessity for proper labeling of etic instruments as imposed etic instruments with the present limitations on cultural equivalence interpretations.

Cultural equivalence is demonstrated by cross-cultural translation (also referred to as item or linguistic equivalence) as well as construct/concept, metric/scalar (Brislin, 1993), and functional equivalence (Berry, 1980). Translation is a necessary first step toward establishing cultural equivalence, but it is never sufficient to report only translation equivalence without commensurate research attention to the full range of necessary equivalencies (Dana, 2000b). In the absence of construct and metric equivalence demonstrations for standard instruments, caution in multicultural/cross-cultural interpretation is mandatory (Dana, 2005a).

Question 2 requires identification and understanding of cultural orientation categories describing the relationship between an original cultural identification and assimilation to a host culture for major cultural groups. Four of these modes of acculturation—Assimilation, Separation, Marginalization, and Integration—were originally developed by Berry (1989) and correspond with MAIP cultural orientations of Anglo/Assimilated, Traditional, Marginal, and Bicultural. The Anglo and Assimilated orientations, characteristic of many mainstream individuals in the United States, are consistent with ignoring and disengaging from cultures of origin. Traditional clients maintain original cultural identities and value systems while rejecting the cultural norms of the dominant culture. Marginal clients selectively reject aspects of both mainstream culture and their culture of origin. A Transitional cultural orientation status describes bilingual Native Americans/Alaska Natives who question traditional values and religion (LaFromboise,

Trimble, & Mohatt, 1990). Cultural orientation status may be determined by interview questions or established moderators for the four major cultural/racial groups in the United States (e.g., Dana, 1993, 2005a; Lin & Kelsey, 2000; Van de Vijver & Phalet, 2004)).

Cultural orientation and racial identity status (CRI) describe an individual balance between original and acquired cultural/racial identities. Cultural orientation status measures are available for all groups, including African Americans (Dana, 1993, 2005a). These measures should be distinguished from African American racial identity developmental measures (Burlew, Bellow, & Lovett, 2000). CRI statuses markedly affect score elevations on standard objective assessment instruments. For example, measured acculturation may be confounded with psychopathology on the MMPI/MMPI–2 as well as other instruments not explicitly constructed for ethnic minority populations (Dana, 1993, 2005a). Racial identity developmental status may also be confounded with psychopathology for African Americans on the MMPI (Whatley, Allen, & Dana, 2003).

CRI information is often necessary for differentiating between diagnosis of psychopathology and description of personality on standard assessment instruments when these instruments are used for subsequent treatment planning decisions and specific interventions. For example, traditional individuals, as well as some marginal individuals, have historically underutilized or failed to benefit from standard ethnic-general mental health interventions. These interventions may lack credibility because majority culture professional service delivery etiquette was not employed or can be simply inappropriate for culturally relevant problems requiring culture-specific interventions, contain culturally relevant elements, or necessitate culturally informed clinicians for responsible service delivery.

Question 3 calls attention to a potential psychopathology-culture or psychopathology-racial identity confound whenever standard tests/ methods are used as imposed emics with traditional, transitional, or marginal individuals, and the effects of these instruments with bicultural individuals are not known. When the MAIP was developed, there were very few emic instruments, although the handbook of African American instruments now provides numerous examples of emic measures for this population (Jones, 1996). These emics provide useful information to document the necessity for subsequent conceptualizations suggesting the usefulness of culture-specific or identity-specific interventions whenever a DSM diagnosis may not be relevant or appropriate.

Question 4 helps the clinician decide whether or not to rely on standard Anglo emics/imposed etic instruments. These standard instruments may require adaptations for applications with specific cultural populations or use of emic instruments developed for these cultural populations. Emic instruments provide useful information not only concerning the relevance, accuracy, and usefulness of DSM diagnosis but are necessary for developing culture-specific or identity-specific conceptualizations as well as for understanding the cultural self (Dana, 1998c).

Question 5 raises issues concerning the adequacy of using the normative data available for mainstream tests/methods with ethnic minority populations. Standard assessment erroneously assumes that these available norms are sufficient regardless of the numbers, representativeness, or matching criteria for ethnic minority and mainstream participants. One solution to the dilemma of inappropriate norms is to employ acculturation/racial identity status norms to correct standard objective tests such as the MMPI/MMPI–2 (Dana, 2000b). Acculturation/racial identity status delineation identifies the need for relevant diagnostic formulations/conceptualizations as well as for the availability of culturally sensitive treatment alternatives. The continuing presence of these unresolved issues suggests that MAIP model applications in the public sector may benefit from a nonnormative comparative approach to consumer ethnicity.

Question 6 provides an opportunity to evaluate relevant life history information from individuals who are at risk for misdiagnosis because they experience stress in their cross-cultural interactions. Whenever standard interventions are employed with ethnic minority clients, their personality characteristics are vulnerable to distortion and/or misunderstanding. Reactivity to racist events may also lead to realistic paranoia and erroneous pathology diagnoses for these individuals. Because racist events may orchestrate potentially dysfunctional behaviors, or predispose individuals to situation-specific behaviors misconstrued as psychopathology, differentiating these stress-related interactions from psychopathology per se is aided by formulations and conceptualizations. These formulations and conceptualizations are required preparation for interventions dealing with interpersonal interactions involving discrimination and racism. As a consequence, either treatment or alternative culturally sensitive psychological interventions may be necessary.

Question 7 reiterates the necessity for diagnosis by changing the context from an imposed etic or emic assessment instrument recommendation to a recommendation for culture-general, cultural-specific, or combined intervention options. This strategy forces attention to the potential availability and usefulness of non-medical-psychiatric interventions for problems-in-living conducted by culturally competent clinicians in both private and public sector settings. The MAIP classifies these treatments/interventions as ethnic-general or culture-general (i.e., suitable for majority culture, assimilated, and acculturated individuals, as well as for self-selected bicultural, marginal, and transitional individuals) or culturally sensitive interventions including various combined culture-general/culture-specific as well as culture-specific interventions (for review by ethnic/racial group, see Dana, 1998a).

MAIP RESEARCH

Research with this model provides studies on the effects of matching or not matching certain factors believed to be important in the therapeutic relationship. These factors include clinician–client ethnicity, language preference, and gender. A number of studies report conflicting effects of matching on clinical outcomes (e.g., Gamst, Dana, Der-Karabetian, & Kramer, 2000, 2001, 2004; Gamst, Dana, Der-Karabetian, Aragon, Arellano, & Kramer, 2002; Jerrell, 1995, 1998; Maramba & Hall, 2002; Russell, Fujino, Sue, Cheung, & Snowden, 1996; Shin et al., 2005).

Despite the lack of clear-cut, consistent, consensual findings of these studies, some limited conclusions require emphasis:

1. Beneficial match findings were clearer for Latinos and Asians Americans than for African Americans and White Americans (Gamst et al., 2000, 2004b).
2. Match was much more important for ethnic minority consumers (Maramba & Nagayama Hall, 2002), although match per se may be of less predictive significance than provider cultural competency (Martin, 1995).
3. Match should not be considered independently of ethnic-specific services (e.g., service delivery style, combined culture-general + culture-specific, or culture-specific interventions) for Asian Americans (Lau & Zane, 2001).
4. Part of the variability found among studies reporting statistically significant matching effects may be attributed to undocumented language matching rather than specifically due to ethnic or racial matching per se (Shin et al., 2005).
5. Variability in the published literature on ethnic matching may be due to lack of clarity concerning the service providers' professional identities as well as inconsistency and insufficient descriptive detail in reporting this information.

Gamst et al. (2002) observed the practical and research relevance of the fact that mental health clients are typically seen by a variety of providers (e.g., psychiatrist, psychologist, marriage and family therapist, case manager, etc.). The mental health service provider who had the most frequent contact with a particular client during a specific time frame as determined by billing records was subsequently operationalized by the concept of *modal provider/modal therapist.*

PUBLIC SECTOR MAIP MODEL

Managed care service delivery systems have insufficiently acknowledged individual, cultural, and social class differences among their consumers (Dana, 1998d; Dana, Conner, & Allen, 1996). Policy decisions for cost-containment prioritized health care and emphasized human similarities rather than differences. These decisions minimized the range of available assessment and treatment options and eschewed responsibility for inclusion of medical-offset approaches, adequate opportunities for preventive services, and sufficient long-term care. A multicultural research and practice agenda requires careful planning, coordination, training of staff, elicitation of feedback from consumers, and meticulous tracking of all assessments and dispositional decisions by supervisory staff under the aegis of the concerned and participant multicultural communities and agency clients. In managed care agencies, this agenda provides a tradeoff between implementation costs of staff time and resources and anticipated benefits of higher consumer satisfaction with services, clinical outcomes, and lower dropout rates that drive up mental health care costs. A managed-care focus on language and interpreter services to satisfy cultural competency may be tempered by the necessity to serve all populations, which overlooks embedding issues throughout services.

MAIP MODEL ESSENTIALS

History

The MAIP model was introduced and applied over a period of years in the Tri-City Community Mental Health Center (Dana, Aragon, & Kramer, 2002). This application began with employment of the Agency Cultural Competence Checklist (ACCC; Dana, Behn, & Gonwa, 1992), continued with development of a research management process for tracking and managing data (Gamst & Dana, 2005) that facilitated the completion of the empirical studies described in an earlier section of this chapter, and was terminated with the demise of the agency in 2005.

Foundations for Public Sector Application

This section describes the status of five essential MAIP components providing the foundations for public sector applications: (a) performance measurement design; (b) disposition coordination; (c) dedicated computerized tracking system; (d) statistical model for simultaneous assessment of practice parameters; and (e) in-service provider cultural competency training. The materials in this section and MAIP summary section were developed from a series of published and unpublished papers documenting MAIP history and application (Dana, 2002c, 2005b; Dana, Aragon, & Kramer, 2002; Gamst & Dana, 2005).

Performance Measurement Design

The necessity of embedding cultural competency in mental health services and the MAIP components for achieving this objective are congruent with public sector performance measurement design currently under consideration by the California Department of Mental Health (2005). In the public domain, performance is measured at client, program, and community levels-of-analysis. The MAIP model provides an effective way to operationalize objective cultural competency indicators at the client and program levels and is consistent with the necessity for mental health services to function with community-level oversight.

At the individual-level collection of client outcome data, 15 indicators are recommended (i.e., housing, crime, employment, education, hospitalization, income, family preservation, symptoms, suicide, functioning, substance use, quality of life, illness self-management, individual goals, and physical health). MAIP employment would also include client-level data assessing ethnic identity as well as acculturation and racial identity status.

The second level provides the "mental health system accountability" data necessary for monitoring programs and systems, quality assurance, and multistakeholder coordination. In this level the focus is on client satisfaction scales with adult clients and completed by parents/caregivers for their children. In addition, the MAIP model tracks and assesses cultural factors affecting clinical outcomes (e.g., client–provider match preferences). Staff cultural competence is also examined at this level to facilitate assignment of clients to providers and to determine future training needs.

At the community level, performance measurement emphasizes community outreach, education, prevention, and public relations and thus provides a forum for community aegis on services for community members. For example, what are the most successful ways of conducting mental health outreach in each cultural community? What special strategies need to be employed to overcome mental health service stigma for each racial/ethnic group? How can mental health practitioners tap strengths, resiliencies, and capacity for positive growth within various ethnic communities? A tripartite levels-of-analysis measurement and evaluation system (i.e., client, agency, community) serving the interests of all consumers can be realized using the MAIP model.

Disposition Coordination

The MAIP model systematically mobilizes, allocates, and channels agency resources to meet each client's needs. Following the initial intake interview and clinical/cultural assessment, clients are connected to appropriate modal providers and culturally generic or specific programs on a case-by-case basis. This "disposition" process occurs on a weekly or more frequent basis with a midlevel clinical staff team. The MAIP disposition process encourages an agency to consistently attempt to accommodate client-requested preferences for a specific gender, language, or ethnic match. Whenever feasible, the disposition team funnels unacculturated clients to culturally competent staff or programs best equipped to meet client needs. Acculturated clients with no specific matching preferences can be routed to less culturally competent or sophisticated staff and/or ethnic-general treatment programs.

Computerized Tracking System

The MAIP model was predicated on the simultaneous coordination of multiple factors. Such a complex mix of strategic variables required a dedicated tracking system, typically available at community health agencies to assist in billing and other business-side activities. A prototype tracking form, the Consumer Outcome Profile (COP), was routinely generated for each client after the initial intake processing and completed during discharge/termination or annual review. The COP example provides pertinent demographic and descriptive information about the client, together with any outcome data and a description of the modal therapist characteristics.

The COP example, presented in Figure 1–2, indicates the client was a Latina, English-speaking mental health consumer with a mood disorder diagnosis. She was referred from a nonpsychiatric private hospital and indicated no particular cultural or language preferences. The client had a tenth-grade education and was living alone in a house or apartment. Her intake GAF score was 50 and increased to 75 at termination. Her modal therapist was also a Latina; hence both gender and ethnic match occurred without a specific request by the client. The client's Time 2 Brief Psychiatric Rating Scale (BPRS; Overall & Gorham, 1988) total score (and subscale scores) are well within the "not severe" range. Client service satisfaction was also consistently high for the various Consumer Survey scales associated with a Mental Health Report Card prepared for the Mental Health Statistics Improvement Program (Teague et al., 1997). At the end of treatment, a "disconnect" between the client's objective and subjective quality of life self-appraisals was observed. Objective quality of life (e.g., number of friends, family contacts, financial resources) was perceived to be low while subjective quality of life (e.g., happiness with current life situation) was relatively high.

Simultaneous Assessment of MAIP Model Parameters

In multicultural mental health research, key variables are seldom examined in their relationship to each other. A statistical model is necessary to assess the simultaneous effects of key MAIP variables of ethnic match, client acculturation status, client ethnic identity, provider cultural competence, client therapeutic intervention (ethnic-general, ethnic-specific), and their relationship to prediction of client outcome measures. A structural equation modeling (SEM) application for the MAIP model, described in Meyers, Gamst, and Guarino (2005), was subsequently used to obtain evidence of the invariance of the MAIP model for successful therapeutic outcomes among four ethnic minority mental health consumers. Four latent variable pathways predicted by theory or supported by previous research—Client Racial Identity, Acculturation Status, Client Matching, Therapist Cultural Competence—were hypothesized to have a direct effect on Successful Therapeutic Outcomes. In addition, Racial Identity, Acculturation Status, and Client Matching have an indirect effect on Successful Therapeutic Outcomes mediated by Therapist Cultural Competency. Employment

Tri-City Mental Health Center Consumer Outcome Profile
    Consumer Information 5/14/03

Gender: F   Diagnosis Type: MOOD D/O Culture Preference: Doesn't matter
Ethnicity: Latino   Trauma Code: Gender Preference: Doesn't matter
Language: English Program: 160   Language preference: English only
Education: 10ᵗʰ grade NONPAYCH PRIV HOSP GAF T1: 50
                    GAF T2: 75
Living: Lives alone Home/Apt

Modal Staff Information: Last Activity Date 4/10/03
3 -   Gender: F   Ethnicity: LATINO Degree: N/A Language: ENG

Outcome Measures:

BPRS
Anxious/Depression   5 (00–21) Not Severe
Hostile/Suspiciousness 3 (00–21) Not Severe
Thinking Disturbance 4 (00 21) Not Severe
Withdrawal/Retardation 0 (00–14) Not Severe
        Total Score   18

MHSIP
Access   4.67 (00 05) High
Appropriateness   5.00 (00–05) High
Outcomes   5.00 (00 05) High
Satisfaction   4.67 (00 05) High
        Total Score   4.88

QL-SF OBJECTIVE 0.92 (00–05) Low
QL-SF-SUBJECTIVE 5.22 (00 05) High

FIGURE 1–2.   Tri-City Mental Health Center Consumer Outcome Profile

of SEM provided substantive empirical MAIP evidence for successful therapeutic outcomes among African American, Latino, Asian, and Caucasian mental health consumers in the public sector (Dana, Gamst, Meyers, & Guarino, 2005; Gamst et al., in preparation).

In-Service Cultural Competency Training

While the MAIP empirical studies described earlier were in process, Rachel Guerrero, Chief, Office of Multicultural Services, California Department of Mental Health, provided support and an interface between this research program and the cultural competency training objectives of her department. This interest was shared, facilitated, and sponsored jointly with the California Institute for Mental Health, the University of La Verne, and the Eli Lilly Company.

In-service cultural competency training was initiated by the availability of the California Brief Multicultural Competence Scale (CBMCS), a composite of earlier competency instruments identified as a major component of the MAIP model (Gamst et al., 2004a). The CBMCS was developed from the item contents of these earlier instruments, with 1,244 California public mental health workers using a principal components analysis, expert panel item content evaluations, and confirmatory factor analysis (Gamst et al., 2004a). CBMCS factors include awareness of culture, sensitivity to consumers, multicultural knowledge, and sociocultural diversities. The CBMCS provided a standard, open-ended, psychometrically adequate instrument for measurement of cultural knowledge and abilities organized by these four relevant training areas. The CBMCS provided for assessment of training needs within a context of continuous monitoring and evaluation of the effects of training on outcomes of mental health services for clients in community settings.

These CBMCS objectives were implemented by a structured, organized training curriculum, the California Multicultural Competency Training Program (Dana, Gamst, & Der-Karabetian, 2006). Evaluation of a CBMCS training program pilot was completed by 38 experienced, sophisticated, and ethnically diverse community mental health practitioners representing 15 California counties during 6 days of training in 2004 (Gamst & Der-Karabetian, 2004).

PowerPoint presentations, small-group activities, and handouts were employed during this training. Program participants completed the CBMCS before and after the training and responded to open-ended and Likert scale questions for each module and on a separate readiness questionnaire at the conclusion of training. This questionnaire, together with ongoing written and oral commentary on the modules and feedback from focus groups, tapped their readiness to train others using this program. Participants significantly improved their pre–post total CBMCS scores and sociocultural diversity scale scores. The four modules were considered effective by 75% of participants, slightly over 50% expressed confidence in training others, and nearly 60% wanted to be considered as a pilot training-site cadre helping to improve the program.

SUMMARY: APPLICATION STEPS, COMPONENTS, AND OBJECTIVES

MAIP application steps (i.e., Intake, Training, Diagnosis/No Diagnosis, Intervention, Outcome) are dovetailed with their component processes and activities for salient objectives within public sector mental health facilities (Table 1–1). These steps all embed cultural issues in mental health services, but Intake, structured by Initial Contact and Initial Interview, is of overarching importance for Access and subsequent utilization of services. These early steps afford opportunities for clients to decide the potential usefulness of these services for themselves and/or their children and whether or not the agency and/or service providers are capable of assistance in a credible and acceptable manner. Thus, there is much to be accomplished in the process, particularly for ethnic minorities, by communicating to them that safe, comfortable, respectful, and culturally competent access is indeed feasible.

Intake

Table 1–1 separates Access into a number of components. Initial Contact, Intake Interview, Psychosocial Assessment, Pretest Outcome Measures, and Parent/Child assessments for child consumers.

A variety of means are used to schedule an intake interview. The quality, content, and the social etiquette employed during the initial contact often determines whether or not a client will return for services. During initial contact, basic demographic and other descriptive information is obtained. In the interval between contact and intake, critical questions still require empirical work. For example, what percent of clients fail to show for this appointment? How long is the average delay interval between initial contact and intake? Are appropriate language services available? Is the agency conducting effective and appropriate outreach for members of all groups in the community? These questions can be explored within an agency by using the ACCC for self-study.

The intake interview provides an opportunity for the provider to obtain presenting problem and case history information on client functioning and culture and to provide a Global Assessment of Functioning (GAF) rating, a DSM-IV diagnosis, and clinical formulations, as well as

TABLE 1–1   Steps, Components, and Objectives in Public Sector
MAIP Model Applications

Step	Component	Objective
Intake	*Initial Contact:*	First opportunity for credible social etiquette to facilitate establishing professional relationship
	Intake Interview:	Establish/consolidate relationship
	Presenting problem	Screening information
	Case history, GAF (pre)	Describe community functioning
	DSM-IV	Clinical diagnosis, Cultural Formulation, Cultural/Identity Conceptualizations
	Agency information/ Consumer goals	Information processing dialogue with consumer
	Psychosocial Assessment: Ethnic identity/gender Acculturation/racial dentity status for adults and/children and parent/ child assessments	Comprehensive intake questionnaire to establish provider–consumer match preferences/ requirements or employ various measuring instruments
	Pretest Outcome Measures: Clinical outcome measures Multicultural assessment (e.g., ARSMA, MEIM, SMAS)	Cost-effective performance assessment to capture consumer functioning + cultural information for resource allocation Multicultural clinical intake snapshot as benchmark for client functioning and guide for selecting treatment strategies
Training	*Cultural competence (modal provider)*	CBMCS description is basis for in-service cultural competence training (32 hours or determined by CMBCS factor scores)
Diagnosis/ No Diagnosis	*Cultural formulation Non-DSM conceptualization*	Confirm DSM-IV diagnosis Prepare Cultural Conceptualization Prepare Identity Conceptualization

TABLE 1–1   *(Continued)*

Step	Component	Objective
Intervention	*Ethnic-general* *Ethnic-specific*	Distinction recognizes current research limitations for describing ethnic-specific interventions
Outcome	*Disposition coordination* *Discharge/Annual* *Review Outcome* *Evaluation*	COP summary, post GAF, clinical outcome and consumer satisfaction measures

cultural and identity formulations as needed for diagnosis and treatment. In addition, the intake interview is a second opportunity to practice credible service delivery social etiquette to continue the process of developing a therapeutic relationship while serving to guide selection of agency treatment strategies and allocation of human resources.

Psychosocial assessment permits use of a questionnaire or instruments to establish preferences for provider–consumer gender, ethnic, racial identity, or acculturation status matches for children and adults. In the California mental health center conducting the MAIP research, match assignments were requested by approximately 20% of consumers. Multicultural assessment measures examined for use with the MAIP model include (a) the Acculturation Rating Scale for Mexican Americans (ARSMA—II; Cuellar, Arnold, & Maldonado, 1995); (b) the Multigroup Ethnic Identity Measure (MEIM), Phinney, 1992); the Stephenson Multigroup Acculturation Scale (SMAS; Stephenson, 2000); the Twenty Statements Test (Dana, 2005a), and the Self-Categorization Test and Ethnic Identification Scale (Van de Vijver & Phalet, 2004).

Acceptable cost-effective client-level pretest outcome measures in managed care organizations must be seamless in design and nonintrusive for providers and consumers. Moreover, these measures must be linked to empirically identified evaluation outcomes of services and employed with flexible tracking of service delivery and services. The California-mandated measures enumerated earlier, clinical outcome measures (American Psychiatric Association, 2000), and MAIP-relevant multicultural assessment measures and devices (Dana, 1993, 1998a, 2000c), are employed as needed.

A multicultural clinical intake snapshot is prepared to summarize the available information. Preparation requires knowledge provider skills, training levels, and cultural competency for consumer–provider matching for ethnicity, gender, or language on the basis of preference or prior local research findings. This initial information is part of a tracking form, the Consumer Outcome Profile (COP; Gamst & Dana, 2005). Figure 1-1 contains a COP example. Table 1-1 indicates the use of COP in a MAIP model public sector application.

Training

All providers need in-service cultural competency assessment and subsequent training predicated on CBMCS-measured cultural competency. Cultural competency in the initial contact, the intake interview, and all subsequent services can only be assured by adequate in-service training for all providers. The effectiveness of this training must be demonstrated by routine agency monitoring of client outcomes, with feedback to providers using a computerized tracking system. The modal provider concept recognizes that services often require several different providers for research and evaluation purposes, although the tracking system provides individual provider accountability as a basis for cultural competency assessment and evaluation of in-service training requirements.

Diagnosis/No Diagnosis

The MAIP recognizes that a universal diagnostic formulation is not available at present (see Figure 1–1). A standard Anglo diagnostic formulation prevails except when a cultural formulation is employed. Cultural formulations for ethnic minority individuals who are immigrants, or first generation, as well as for some second-generation individuals, are frequently necessary. Many of these individuals present culture-bound disorders, and epidemiological studies suggest these diagnoses occur with much greater frequency in traditional individuals than hitherto anticipated by psychiatrists (e.g., Dana, 2002b). Presenting problems-in-living rather than psychopathologies may suggest non-DSM cultural and identity conceptualizations as more descriptive of reactions to prejudice/discrimination or personal identity issues. Table 1–1 simplifies Figure 1–1 by recognizing only Diagnosis and No Diagnosis categories. This is done because a cultural formulation may lead to a diagnosis of a culture-bound disorder as well as a DSM-IV disorder. The No Diagnosis category recognizes that cultural and identity conceptualizations lead to interventions for problems-in-living.

Interventions

The original MAIP specified five categories of interventions (Figure 1–1): culture-universal, culture-general, combined culture-general/culture-specific, culture-specific, and identity-specific. As culture-universal interventions are not yet available, consumers with identified psychopathology also require interventions that are either standard ethnic-general or culturally sensitive and ethnic-specific (Table 1–1). Culturally sensitive interventions were defined in the original MAIP (Figure 1–1) as interventions containing components representing both culture-general and culture-specific interventions or exclusively culture-specific components (Dana, 1998a). However, the efficacy studies providing the evidence base for treatments do not adequately include ethnic minorities, although evidence-based treatment for depression does improve outcome for Latinos and African Americans, and established psychosocial care may be beneficial for Asians (Miranda et al., 2005). Thus, although there are cogent and compelling examples of successful adaptation of interventions for ethnic minorities, it is premature to rely on the original MAIP categorizations. Table 1–1 thus recognizes the necessity for both ethnic-general and ethnic-specific interventions that are susceptible to evaluation within the model.

Outcome

Outcomes are described in Table 1–1 by the COP summaries amplified by post-GAF, consumer satisfaction, and a variety of outcome measures. These summaries, including disposition coordination, discharge or annual review, posttest outcome assessment, computerized tracking system, and the simultaneous of MAIP model parameters. Although there is no consensus on outcome measures (Hoagwood, Jensen, Petti, & Burns, 1996; Jensen, Hoagwood, & Petti, 1996), the GAF Axis 5 rating of the Diagnostic and Statistical Manual IV (DSM-IV; American Psychological Association, 1994) is widely used in practice and research.

Clients terminating therapy on their own volition, discharged by the agency after successful treatment, or reaching 6-month or annual review for chronic disorders are all given the same set of outcome measures they received at intake except for cultural assessment instruments. Adult outcome/satisfaction measures used with the MAIP include the Brief Psychiatric Rating Scale (BRPS; Overall & Gorham, 1988), the Mental Health Statistics Improvement Program (MHSIP; Teague et al., 1997), and the Quality of Life Scale (QL-SF; Lehman, 1988). For children and adolescent clients, the Ohio Scales (Ogles, Melendez, Davis, & Lunnen, 2001) and the Columbia Impairment Scale (CIS; Bird, Schwab-Stone, Andrews, Goodman, & Duncan, 1996) were used. Service satisfaction has been assessed using the Youth Services Survey (YSS; Brunk, 2001) and the Youth Services Survey for Families (YSS-F; Brunk, 2001) with children and parents/caregivers, respectively. Multicultural assessment consonant with the MAIP model include the MEIM (Phinney, 1992), ARSMA-II (Cuellar et al., 1995), and the Stephenson Multigroup Acculturation Scale (Stephenson, 2000).

At the mental health systems accountability level, the focus is on monitoring systems and programs, quality assurance, and multistakeholder coordination. Client service satisfaction inventories are completed by parents/caregivers and children, and MAIP cultural factors affect clinical outcomes at the program/system accountability level. For example, client–therapist match preferences could be assessed at this level and tracked (e.g., ethnic/racial match, gender match, language match). Staff cultural competence assessment would determine future training needs and the assignment of clients to mental health providers.

TEMAS-MAIP Adaptations

Extending the adult-oriented MAIP model to children/adolescents requires adaptation in each step or component. Intake becomes more complicated by inclusion of family members. CRI differences between parents and children affect intergenerational relationships. Conflicts with parents often result from increasing child biculturality and dual language skills. These conflicts exacerbate differences between parental and peer cultures in values pertinent to family cohesion, discipline, and child behaviors.

The assessment necessary to determine goodness-of-fit between an ethnic minority child/adolescent and a particular intervention thus may differ substantially in content, breadth, and depth from adult measures. This aspect of the assessment–intervention relationship has not been carefully considered in the public sector due to the increased time required for comprehensive assessment of children and adolescents. Nonetheless, the short-form TEMAS can be completed during intake within a two-hour assessment time allocation (Camara et al., 2000). TEMAS is particularly useful in agency settings because diagnostic information is available within the context of a broader range of information relevant for development of consensual eligibility criteria for any recommended interventions for all children/adolescents. As subsequent chapters with TEMAS examples indicate, the substantial increase in relevant test information also provides increased knowledge for parents and adult nonprofessional caregivers and contributes to informed decision making. TEMAS findings can also be useful to positively affect communication and contribute to joint decision-making responsibility by parents and professional providers. A role for TEMAS in cultural formulations or cultural and identity conceptualizations is feasible, but research is necessary for this suggested usage.

The MAIP model is also congruent with common characteristics of 23 successful programs (Roberts, 1994). These programs focus on the ecology of the child in family, peer, school, and community, require strong leadership to reduce barriers to access, provide collaborative efforts across agencies, and employ clearly defined, comprehensive, and versatile services. These services should be accountable and have demonstrated effectiveness that can be replicated and adapted.

REFERENCES

Achenbach, R. M. (1992). *Manual for Child Development Checklist/2-3 & 1992 Profile.* Burlington, VT: University Vermont Department of Psychiatry.

Achenbach, R. M., & McConaughy, S. H. (1997). *Empirically based assessment of child and adolescent psychopathology: Practical implications* (2nd ed). Thousand Oaks, CA: Sage.

Allen, J., & Dana, R. H. (2004). Methodological issues in cross-cultural and multi-cultural Rorschach research. *Journal of Personality Assessment, 82,* 189–206.

American Psychiatric Association (1994). *Diagnostic and statistical manual of mental disorders* (4th ed). Washington, DC: Author.

American Psychiatric Association (2000). *Handbook of psychiatric measures.* Washington, DC: Author.

Angold, A., Costello, E. J., Farmer, E. M. Z., Burns, B. J., & Erkanli, A. (1999). Impaired but undiagnosed. *Journal of the American Academy of Child and Adolescent Psychiatry, 38,* 129–137.

Anthony, W. A. (1993). Recovery from mental illness: The guiding vision of the mental health service systems in the 1990s. *Psychiatric Rehabilitation Journal, 16(4),* 11–23.

Anthony, W. A. (2000). A recovery-oriented system: Setting some system level standards. *Psychiatric Rehabilitation Journal, 24(2),* 159–168.

Anthony, W. A., Rogers, E. S., & Farkas, M. (2003). Research on evidence-based practices: Future directions in an era of recovery. *Community Mental Health Journal, 39,* 101–114.

Archer, R. P. (1992). *MMPI-A: Assessing adolescent psychopathology.* Hillsdale, NJ: Lawrence Erlbaum Associates.

Bazelon Center for Mental Health Law (1993). *Federal definitions of children with serious emotional disturbance.* Washington, CD: Author.

Beck, J. S., Beck, A. T., & Jolly, J. B. (2001). *Beck Youth Inventories of emotional and social impairment manual.* San Antonio, TX: The Psychological Corporation.

Berry, J. W. (1980). Introduction to methodology. In H. C. Triandis & J. W. Berry (Eds.), *Handbook of cross-cultural psychology* (Vol. 2, pp. 1–28). Boston: Allyn & Bacon.

Berry, J. W. (1989). Psychology of acculturation. *Nebraska Symposium on Motivation, 21,* 257–277.

Berry, J. W. (1999). Emics and etics: A symbolic conception. *Culture & Psychology, 5,* 165–171.

Bird, H., Schwab-Stone, M., Andrews, H., Goodman, S., Dulcan, M. et al., (1996). Global measures of impairment for epidemiologic and clinical use with children and adolescents. *Journal of Methods in Psychiatric Research, 6,* 295–308.

Blanch, A., Fisher, D., Tucker, W., Walsh, D., & Chassman, J. (1993). Consumer-practioners and psychiatrists share insights about recovery and coping. *Disability Studies Quarterly, 13(2),* 17–20.

Brandt, M. E., & Boucher, J. D. (1986). Concepts of depression in emotion lexicons of eight cultures. *International Journal of Intercultural Relations, 10,* 321–346.

Brislin, R. W. (1993). *Understanding culture's influence on behavior.* New York: Harcourt Brace.

Brunk, M. (2001, October). *Youth Services Surveys.* Paper presented at the meeting of the Mental Health Data Infrastructure Grant Annual Meeting, Washington, DC.

Burlew, A. K., Bellow, S., & Lovett, M. (2000). Racial identity measures: A review and classification system. In R. H. Dana (Ed.), *Handbook of cross-cultural and multicultural personality assessment* (pp. 173–196). Mahwah, NJ: Lawrence Erlbaum Associates.

Cairns, R. B. (2000). Development science: Three audacious implications. In L. R. Bergman, R. B. Cairns, L. G. Nielson, & L. Nystedt (Eds.), *Developmental science and the holistic approach* (pp. 49–62). Mahwah, NJ: Lawrence Erlbaum Associates.

California Department of Mental Health (2005). *Preliminary discussion of the performance measurement design for the California Mental Health Services Act.* Department of Mental Health, Sacramento, CA.

Camara, W. J., Nathan, J. S., & Puente, A. E. (2000). Psychological test usage: Implications in professional psychology. *Professional Psychology: Research and Practice, 31,* 141–154.

Cauce, A. M., Domenech-Rodriguez, M., Paradise, M., Cochran, B. N., Shea, J. M., Srebnik, D., et al. (2002). Cultural and contextual influence in mental health help seeking: A focus on ethnic minority youth. *Journal of Consulting and Clinical Psychology, 70,* 44–55.

Chow, J., & Wyatt, P. (in press). Ethnicity, language capacity, and perception of ethnic-specific service agencies in Asian American and Pacific Islander communities. *Journal of Immigration and Refugee Services.*

Commission on Chronic Illness (1957). *Chronic illness in the United States* (Vol. 1). Cambridge, MA: Harvard University Press.

Conner, M. (2004). A comparison of mental health screening methods and systems. Retrieved November, 21, 2004, from http://www.incrisis.org/Articles/System ReviewComparisons.htm.

Conner, M. (2005). *Crisis intervention with adolescents: A parent guide.* Wilmington, IN: Author House.

Conners, C. K. (1997). *Conners' Rating Scales—Revised technical manual.* North Tonowanda, NY: Multi-Health Systems.

Costello, A., Edelbrock, C., Kalas, R., Kessler, M., & Klaric, S. (1984). *NIMH diagnostic interview schedule for children (DISC-C).* Rockville, MD: National Institutes of Mental Health.

Costello, E. J., Mustillo, S., Keeler, G., & Angold, A. (2004). Prevalence of psychiatric disorders in childhood and adolescence. In B. L. Levin, Petrilla J. & K. D. Hennessy, (Eds.), *Mental health services: A public health perspective* (2nd ed). New York: Oxford University Press.

Council of National Psychological Association for the Advancement of Ethnic Minority Interests. (2000). *Guidelines for research in ethnic minority communities.* Washington, DC: American Psychological Association.

Cuellar, I., Arnold, B., & Maldonado, R. (1995). An Acculturation Rating Scale for Mexican Americans-II (ARSMA-II): A revision of the original ARSMA scale. *Hispanic Journal of Behavioral Sciences, 17,* 275–304.

Cummings, N. (2002, December). *Integrated practice in the 21st century.* Paper presented at the Brief Therapy Conference, Orlando, FL.

Dana, R. H. (1993). *Multicultural assessment perspectives for professional psychology.* Boston: Allyn & Bacon.

Dana, R. H. (1997). Multicultural assessment and cultural identity: An assessment-intervention model. *World Psychology, 3(1–2),* 121–141.

Dana, R. H. (1998a). *Understanding cultural identity in intervention and assessment.* Thousand Oaks, CA: Sage.

Dana, R. H. (1998b). Multicultural assessment in the United States: Still art, not yet science, and controversial. *European Journal of Personality Assessment, 14,* 62–70.

Dana, R. H. (1998c). Personality assessment and the cultural self: Emic and etic contexts as learning resources. In L. Handler & M. Hilsenroth (Eds.), *Teaching and learning personality assessment* (pp. 325–345). Hillsdale, NJ: Lawrence Erlbaum Associates.

Dana, R. H. (1998d). Problems with managed mental health care for multicultural populations. *Psychological Reports, 83*, 283–294.

Dana, R. H. (2000a). Multicultural assessment of child and adolescent personality and psychopathology. In A. L. Comunian & U. Gielen (Eds.), *International perspectives on human development.* Lengerich, Germany: Pabst Science Publishers.

Dana, R. H. (2000b). Culture and methodology in personality assessment. In I. Cuellar & F. Paniagua (Eds.), *Handbook of multicultural mental health: Assessment and treatment of diverse groups* (pp. 97–120). San Diego, CA: Academic Press.

Dana, R. H. (Ed.) (2000c). *Handbook of cross-cultural and multicultural personality assessment.* Mahwah, NJ: Lawrence Erlbaum Associates.

Dana, R. H. (2002a). Mental health services for African Americans: A cultural/racial perspective. *Cultural Diversity and Ethnic Minority Psychology, 8*, 3–18.

Dana, R. H. (2002b). Examining the usefulness of DSM-IV. In K. Kurasaki, S. Okazaki, & S. Sue (Eds.), *Asian American mental health: Assessment, theories, and methods* (pp. 29–46). New York: Kluwer Academic/Plenum Publishers.

Dana, R. H. (2002c). The development of cultural competence in California public sector mental health services. In S. Lurie (Chair), *International innovations in community mental health health I.* Symposium conducted at the XXVIIth International Congress of Law and Mental Health, Amsterdam, The Netherlands.

Dana, R. H. (2005a). *Multicultural assessment principles, applications, and examples.* Mahwah, NJ: Lawrence Erlbaum Associates.

Dana, R. H. (2005b). *The Multicultural Assessment-Intervention Process Model (MAIP).* Unpublished paper.

Dana, R. H., Aragon, M., & Kramer, T. (2002). Public sector mental health services for multicultural populations: Bridging the gap from research to clinical practice. In M. N. Smyth (Ed.), *Health Care in Transition* (Vol. 1, pp. 1–13). Hauppauge, NY: Nova Science Publishers.

Dana, R. H., Behn, J. D., & Gonwa, T. (1992). A checklist for examination of cultural competence in social service agencies. *Research in Social Work Practice, 2*, 220–233.

Dana, R. H., Conner, M. G., & Allen, J. (1996). Cost containment and quality in managed mental health care: Policy, education, research, advocacy. *Psychological Reports, 79*, 1395-1422.

Dana, R. H., Gamst, G., & Der-Kerabetian, A. (2006). *The California Brief Multicultural Competence Scale-Based Training Program: A manual for trainers.* La Verne, CA: University of La Verne

Dana, R. H., Gamst, G., Meyers,, L., & Guarino, A. J. (2005). *Assessing the invariance of the Multicultural Assessment-Intervention Process model (MAIP) among African-American, Latino, Asian, and Caucasian mental health consumers.* Unpublished paper.

Der-Karabetian, A., Gamst, G., Dana, R. H., Aragon, M., Arellano, L., Morrow, G., et al. (2002). *California Brief Multicultural Competence Scale (CBMCS): User guide.* La Verne, CA: University of La Verne.

Dierker, L. C., Albano, A. M., Clarke, G. N., Heimberg, R. G., Kendall, P. C., Merikangas, K. R., et al. (2001). Screening for anxiety and depression in early adolescence. *Journal of the American Academy of Child and Adolescent Psychiatry, 40,* 929–936.

Drake, R. E., Goldman, H. H., Leff, S., Lehman, A. F., Dixon, L., Mueser, K. T., & Torrey, W. C. (2001). Implementing evidence-based practices in routine mental health service settings. *Psychiatric Services, 52(1),* 179–182.

Durlak, J. A., & Wells, A. M. (1997). Primary prevention mental health programs for children and adolescents: A meta-analytic review. *American Journal of Community Psychology, 25,* 115–152.

Edlefsen, M., & Baird, M. (1994). Making it work: Preventive mental health care for disadvantaged preschoolers. *Social Work, 39,* 566–573.

Elster, A. B., & Marcell, A. V. (2003). Health care of adolescent males: Overview, rationale, and recommendations. *Adolescent Medicine: State of the Art Reviews, 14(3),* 525–540.

Farmer, T. W., & Farmer, E. M. Z. (2001). Developmental science, systems of care, and prevention of emotional and behavioral problems of youth. *American Journal of Orthopsychiatry, 71,* 171–181.

Finney, F. I., Riley, A, W., & Cataldo, M. F. (1991). Psychology in primary health care: Effects of brief therapy on children's mental health care utilization. *Journal of Pediatric Psychology, 16,* 447–461.

Fonagy, P., Target, M., Cottrell, D., Phillips, J., & Kurtz, Z. (2002). *What works for whom? A critical review of treatments for children and adolescents.* New York: Guilford.

Forness, S. R., & Knitzer, J. (1992). A new proposed definition and terminology to replace "serious emotional disturbance" in the Individuals with Disabilities Education Act (IDEA). *School Psychology Review, 21,* 12–20.

Fox, R. E. (1994). Training professional psychologists for the twenty-first century. *American Psychologist, 49,* 200–206.

Friedman, R. M., Kutash, K., & Duchowski, A. J. (1996). The population of concern: Defining the issues. In B.A. Stroul (Ed.), *Children's mental health: Creating systems of care in a changing society.* Baltimore: Paul H. Brookes.

Gadnow, K., & Spratkin, J. (1997). *Adolescent Symptom Inventory 4.* Stony Brook, NY: Checkmate Plus.

Gamst, G., & Dana, R. H. (2005). *Testing the MAIP model: A proposed method for assessing culturally sensitive mental health service delivery for adults and children.* Unpublished paper.

Gamst, G., Dana, R. H., Der-Karabetian, A., Aragon, M., Arellano, L., & Kramer, T. (2002). Effects of Latino acculturation and ethnic identity on mental health outcomes. *Hispanic Journal of Behavioral Sciences, 24,* 479–505.

Gamst, G., Dana, R. H., Der-Karabetian, A., Aragon, M., Arellano, L., Morrow, G. et al. (2004a). Cultural competency revised: The California Brief Multicultural

Competence Scale. *Measurement and Evaluation in Counseling and Development, 37,* 163–183.

Gamst, G., Dana, R. H., Der-Karabetian, A., & Kramer, T. (2000). Ethnic match and client ethnicity effects on global assessment and visitation. *Journal of Community Psychology, 28,* 547–564.

Gamst, G., Dana, R. H., Der-Karabetian, A., & Kramer, T. (2001). Asian American mental health clients: Cultural responsiveness and global assessment. *Journal of Mental Health Counseling, 23,* 57–71.

Gamst, G., Dana, R. H., Der-Karabetian, A., & Kramer, T. (2004b). Ethnic match and treatment outcomes for child and adolescent mental health center clients. *Journal of Counseling and Development, 82,* 457–465.

Gamst, G., Dana, R. H., Der-Kerabetian, A., Meyers, L., & Guarino, A. J. (2006). *Assessing the validity of the Multicultural Assessment Intervention Process (MAIP) model for mental health consumers.* Manuscript submitted for publication.

Gamst, G., & Der-Karabetian, A. (2004). *Preliminary evaluation of the California Brief Multicultural Competency Training Program.* La Verne, CA: University of La Verne.

Green-Hennessy, S., & Hennessy, K. D. (2004). The recovery movement: Consumers, families, and the mental health system. In B. L. Levin, J. Petrila, & K. D. Hennessy (Eds.), *Mental health services: A public health perspective* (2nd ed). New York: Oxford University Press.

Grisso, T., Barnum, R., Fletcher, K. E., Cauffman, E., & Peuslchold, D. (2001). Massachusetts Youth Screening Instrument for mental health needs of juvenile justice youths. *Journal of the American Academy of Child and Adolescent Psychiatry, 40,* 541–548.

Hoagwood, K., Jensen, P. S., Petti, T., & Burns, B. J. (1996). Outcomes of mental health care for children and adolescents: I. A comprehensive conceptual model. *Journal of the American Academy of Child and Adolescent Psychiatry, 35,* 1055–1063.

Hogan, M., & Flynn, L. (2003, September). *Catch them before they fall. How to implement mental health screening programs for youth as recommended by the President's New Freedom Commission on Mental Health.* New York: Carmel Hill Center for Early Diagnosis and Treatment.

Institute of Medicine (1989). *Research on children and adolescents with mental, behavioral, and developmental disorders.* Washington, DC: National Academy Press.

Jacobson, N., & Greenley, D. (2001). What is recovery? A conceptual model of recovery. *Psychiatric Services, 52,* 482–485.

Jensen, P. S., Hoagwood, K., & Petti, T. (1996). Outcomes of mental health care for children and adolescents: II. Literature review and application of a comprehensive model. *Journal of the American Academy of Child and Adolescent Psychiatry, 35,* 1064–1077.

Jerrell, J. M. (1995). The effects of client-counselor match on service use and costs. *Administration and Policy in Mental Health, 23,* 119–126.

Jerrell, J. M. (1998). Effect of ethnic matching of young children and mental health staff. *Cultural Diversity and Mental Health, 4,* 297–302.

Joint Commission on the Mental Health of Children. (1969). *Action for mental health for children.* New York: Basic Books.

Jones, R. (Ed.). (1996). *Handbook of tests and measurements for Black populations* (Vols. 1 & 2). Hampton, VA: Cobb & Henry.

Kamphaus, R. W., & Frick, P. J. (1996). *Clinical assessment of child and adolescent personality and behavior.* Boston: Allyn & Bacon.

Kataoka, S. H., Zhang, L., & Wells, K. B. (2002). Unmet need for mental health care among U.S. children: Variation by ethnicity and insurance status. *American Journal of Psychiatry, 159,* 1548–1555.

Kazdin, A. E., & Kendall, P. C. (1998). Current progress and future plans for developing effective treatments: Comments and perspectives. *Journal of Clinical Child Psychology, 27,* 217–226.

Kiesler, C. A. (1992). U.S. mental health policy: Doomed to fail. *American Psychologist, 47,* 1077–1082.

Knitzer, J. (1982). *Unclaimed children: The failure of public responsibility to children and adolescents in needs of mental health services.* Washington, DC: Child Defense League.

Kouyoumdjian, H., Zamboanga, B. L., & Hensen, D. J. (2003). Barriers to community mental health services for Latinos: Treatment considerations. *Clinical Psychology, 10,* 394–422.

Kratchowill, T. R., & Shernoff, E. S. (2004). Evidence-based practice: Promoting evidence-based practice in school psychology. *School Psychology Review, 33,* 34–48.

Lachar, D. (2004). Psychological assessment in child mental health settings. In J. R. Graham & J. A. Naglieri (Eds.)., *Handbook of psychology (Vol. 10): Assessment psychology.* New York: Wiley.

LaFromboise, T. D., Trimble, J. E., & Mohatt, G. V. (1990). Counseling intervention and American Indian tradition: An integrative approach. *The Counseling Psychologist, 18,* 628–654.

Larson, R. W. (2000). Toward a psychology of positive youth development. *American Psychologist, 55,* 170–183.

Lau, A., & Zane, N. (2001). Examining the effects of ethnic-specific services: An analysis of cost-utilization and treatment outcome for Asian American clients. *Journal of Community Psychology, 28,* 63–67.

Leaf, P. J. (1999). A system of care perspective on prevention. *Clinical Psychology Review, 19,* 403–413.

Lehman, A. F. (1988). A Quality of Life Interview for the chronically mentally ill. *Evaluation and Program Planning, 11,* 51–62.

Leong, F. T. L., & Lau, A. S. L. (2001). Barriers to providing effective mental health services to Asian Americans. *Mental Health Services Research, 3,* 201–214.

Levin, B. L., Hanson, A., & Hennessy, K. D. (2004). Overview of prevention, integration, and parity. In B. L. Levin, J. Petrilla, & K. D. Hennessy (Eds.), *Mental health services. A public health perspective* (2nd ed). New York: Oxford University Press.

Liao, Q. (2001). Describing the population of adolescents served in systems of care. *Journal of Emotional & Behavioral Disorders, 9,* 13–30.

Lilienfeld, S. O., Lynn, S. J., & Lohr, J. M. (2003). *Science and pseudoscience in psychology.* New York: Guilford.

Lin, S. S., & Kelsey, J. L. (2000). Use of race and ethnicity in epidemiological research. *Epidemiologic Reviews, 22,* 187–202.

Lonigan, C. J., Elbert, J. C., & Johnson, S. B. (1998). Empirically supported psychosocial interventions for children: An overview. *Journal of Clinical Child Psychology, 27,* 138–145.

Lonner, W. J. (1985). Issues in testing and assessment in cross-cultural counseling. *The Counseling Psychologist, 13,* 599–614.

Lopez, S. J., & Snyder, C. P. (Eds.). (2003). *Positive psychological assessment. Handbook of models and measures.* Washington, DC: American Psychological Association.

Lyons, J. S. (2004). *Redressing the emperor: Improving our children's public mental health system.* Westport, CT: Praeger.

Magnusson, D. (2000). The individual as the organizing principle in psychological inquiry: A holistic approach. In L. R. Bergman, R. B. Cairns, L. G. Nilsson, & L. Nystedt (Eds.), *Developmental science and the holistic approach* (pp. 33–47). Mahwah, NJ: Lawrence Erlbaum Associates.

Malgady, R. G. (1996). The question of cultural bias in assessment and diagnosis of ethnic minority clients: Let's reject the null hypothesis. *Professional Psychology, 27,* 73–77.

Manson, S, M. (1997). One small step for science, one giant step for prevention. *American Journal of Community Psychology, 25,* 215–219.

Manson, S. M. (2000). Mental health services for American Indians and Alaska Natives: Need, use, and barriers to effective care. *Canadian Journal of Psychiatry, 45,* 617–626.

Maramba, G. G., & Hall, G. C. (2002). Meta-analyses of ethnic match as a predictor of dropout, utilization, and level of functioning. *Cultural Diversity and Ethnic Minority Psychology, 8,* 290–297.

Martin, T. W. (1995). Community mental health services for ethnic minority adolescents: A test of the cultural responsiveness hypothesis. *Dissertation Abstracts International, 55(7-B),* 3018 (Abstract only).

McCubbin, M., & Cohen, D. (1996). Extremely unbalanced interest divergence: Interest divergence and power disparities between clients and psychiatry. *International Journal of Law and Psychiatry, 19,* 1–25.

Meyer, G. J., Finn, S. E., Eyde, L. D., Kay, G. G., Moreland, K. L., Dies, R. R., et al. (2001). Psychological testing and psychological assessment: A review of evidence and issues. *American Psychologist, 56,* 128–165.

Meyers, L., Gamst, G., & Guarino, A. J. (2005). *Applied multivariate research: Design and interpretation.* Thousand Oaks, CA: Sage.

Millon, T. (1993). *Millon Adolescent Clinical Inventory (MACI) manual.* Minneapolis: National Computer Systems.

Miranda, J., Bernal, G., Lay, A., Kohn, L., Hwang, W-C, & LaFromboise, T. (2005). State of the science on psychosocial interventions for ethnic minorities. *Annual Review of Clinical Psychology, 1,* 113–142.

Mrazek, P. J., & Haggerty, R. J. (Eds.). (1994). *Reducing risks for mental disorders: Frontiers for preventive intervention research.* Washington, DC: National Academy Press.

Naglieri, J., LeBuffe, P. A., & Pfeiffer, S. (1994). *Devereux Scale of Mental Disorders Manual.* San Antonio, TX: Psychological Corporation.

Neeper, R., Lahey, B. B., & Frick, P. J. (1990). *Comprehensive behavior rating scale for children.* San Antonio, TX: Psychological Corporation.

New Freedom Commission on Mental Health (2003). *Achieving the promise: Transforming mental health care in America.* (SMA 02–3832). Rockville, MD: Substance Abuse and Mental Health Services Administration.

Office of Technology Assessment (1986). *Children's mental health: Problems and services: A background paper.* (Publication No. OTA-BP-_H–33). Washington, DC: U.S. Government Printing Office.

Ogles, B. M., Melendez, G., Davis, D. C., & Lunnen, K. M. (2001). The Ohio Scales: Practical outcome assessment. *Journal of Child and Family Studies, 10,* 199–212.

Olfson, M., Sing, M., & Schlesinger, H. J. (1999). Mental health/health care cost offsets: Opportunities for managed care. *Health Affairs, 18(2),* 79–90.

Overall, J. E., & Gorham, D. R. (1988). The Brief Psychiatric Rating Scale (BRPS): Recent developments in ascertainment and scaling. *Psychopharmacological Bulletin, 24,* 97–99.

Paperny, D. M. (1997). Computerized health assessment and education for adolescent HIV and STD prevention in health care settings and schools. *Health Education and Behavior, 24,* 54–70.

Paperny, D. M., & Hedburg, V. (1999). Computer-assisted health counselor visits: A low cost model for comprehensive adolescent preventive services. *Archives of Pediatric Adolescent Medicine, 153,* 63–66.

Pellegrino, E. D. (1994). Patient and physician autonomy: Conflicting rights and obligations in the physician–patient relationship. *Journal of Contemporary Health and Law Policy, 10,* 47–68.

Phinney, J. S. (1992). The Multigroup Ethnic Identity Measure: A new scale for use with diverse groups. *Journal of Adolescent Research, 7,* 156–176.

Piotrkowski, C. S., Collins, R. C., Knitzer, J., & Robinson, R. (1994). Strengthening mental health services in Head Start. *American Psychologist, 49,* 133–139.

Piotrowski, C. (1999). Assessment practices in the era of managed care: Current status and future directions. *Psychological Assessment, 7,* 787–796.

Ponterotto, J. G., Mendelsohn, J., & Belizaire, L. (2003). Assessing teacher multicultural competence: Self-report instruments, observer report evaluations, and a portfolio assessment. In D. B. Pope-Davis, H. L. K. Coleman, W. M. Liu, & R. C. Toporek (Eds.), *Handbook of multicultural competencies in counseling and psychology* (pp. 191–210). Thousand Oaks, CA: Sage.

Prieto, L. R., McNeill, B. W., Walls, R. G., & Gomez, S. P. (2001). Chicanas/os and mental health services: An overview of utilization, counselor preference, and assessment issues. *Counseling Psychologist, 29,* 18–54.

Reynolds, C. R., & Kamphaus, R. W. (1992). *Behavior Assessment System for Children.* Circle Pines, MN: American Guidance.

Reynolds, W. M. (1998). *Adolescent Psychopathology Scale(APS): Administration and interpretation manual. Psychometric and interpretation manual.* Odessa, FL: Psychological Assessment Resources.

Ringel, J. S., & Sturm, R. (2001). National estimates of mental health utilization and expenditures for children in 1998. *Journal of Behavioral Health Services and Research, 28,* 319–332.

Roberts, M. C. (1994). Models for service delivery in children's mental health: Common characteristics. *Journal of Clinical Child psychology, 23,* 212–219.

Roberts, R. E., Attkisson, C. C., & Rosenblatt, A. (1998). Prevalence of psychopathology among children and adolescents. *American Journal of Psychiatry, 155(6),* 715–725.

Rogers, M. R. (2005). Multicultural training in school psychology. In C. Frisby & C. R. Reynolds (Eds.), *Comprehensive handbook of multicultural school psychology* (pp. 993–1022). San Francisco: Jossey-Bass.

Rogler, L. H. (1989). The meaning of culturally sensitive research in mental health. *American Journal of Psychiatry, 146,* 296–303.

Russell, G. L., Fujino, D. C., Sue, S., Cheung, M-K., & Snowden, L. R. (1996). The effects of counselor-client ethnic match on assessment of mental health functioning. *Journal of Cross-Cultural Psychology, 27,* 598–615.

Salovey, P., Detweiler, J. B., Steward, W. T., & Rothman, A. (2000). Emotional states and physical health. *American Psychologist, 55,* 110–121.

Sanchez, L. M., & Turner, S. M. (2003). Practicing psychology in the era of managed care: Implications for practice and training. *American Psychologist, 58,* 116–129.

Saxe, L., Cross, T., & Silverman, N. (1988). Children's mental health: The gap between what we know and what we do. *American Psychologist, 43,* 800–807.

Shaffer, D., Fisher, P., Dulcan, M. K., Davies, M., Piacentini, J., Schwab-Stone, M. E., et al. (1996). The NIMH Diagnostic Interview Schedule for Children Version 2.3 (DISC-2.3): Description, acceptability, prevalence rates, and performance in the MECA study. Methods for the Epidemiology of Child and Adolescent Mental Disorders study. *Journal of the American Academy of Child and Adolescent Psychiatry, 35,* 865–877.

Seligman, M. E. P., & Csikszentmihalyi, M. (2000). Positive psychology: An introduction. *American Psychologist, 55,* 5–14.

Shaffer, D., Fisher, P., & Lucas, C. (2004). The Diagnostic Interview Schedule for Children (DISC). In M.J. Hilsenroth & D.L. Segal (Eds.), *Comprehensive handbook of psychological assessment (Vol. 2): Personality Assessment* (pp. 256–279). New York: Wiley.

Shaffer, D., Gould, M., Brasic, J., Ambrosini, P., Fischer, P., Bird, H., et al. (1983). A children's global assessment scale (CGAS). *Archives of General Psychiatry, 40,* 1228–1231.

Shin, S. M., Chow, D., Camacho-Gonsalves, T., Levy, R. J., Allen, I. I., & Leff, H. S. (2005). A meta-analytic review of racial/ethnic matching for African American and Caucasian American clients and clinicians. *Journal of Counseling Psychology, 52,* 45–56.

Singh, N. N., & Oswald, D. P. (2004). Evidence-based practice. Part I: General methodology. *Journal of Child & Family Studies, 13,* 129–143.

Smith, D. J., & Rutter, M. (1995). Time trends in psychosocial disorders of youth. In M. Rutter & D. J. Smith (Eds.), *Psychosocial disorders in young people: Time trends and their causes.* New York: Wiley.

Snowden, L. R. (2003). Bias in mental health assessment and intervention: Theory and evidence. *American Journal of Public Health, 93,* 239–242.

Snowden, L. R., & Yamada, A-M. (2005). Cultural differences in access to care. *Annual Review of Clinical Psychology, 1,* 143–166.

Society for Personality Assessment (2005). *The status of the Rorschach in clinical and forensic practice: An official statement by the Board of Trustees of the Society for Personality Assessment.* Falls Church, VA: Author.

Stephenson, M. (2000). Development and validation of the Stephenson Multigroup Acculturation Scale (SMAS). *Psychological Assessment, 12,* 77–88.

Stroul, B. A. (1993). *Systems of care for children and adolescents with severe emotional disturbances: What are the results?* Washington, DC: Georgetown University.

Stroul, B. A. (2002). *Issue brief-System of care: A framework for system reform in children's mental health.* Washington DC: Georgetown University.

Stroul, B. A., & Friedman, R. M. (1986). *A system of care for children and youth with severe emotional disturbances* (Rev. ed). Washington, DC: Georgetown University.

Sue, S., & Sue, L. (2003). Ethnic research is good science. In G. Bernal, J. E. Trimble, A. K. Burlew, & F. T. L. Leung (Eds.), *Handbook of racial and ethnic minority psychology* (pp. 198–207). Thousand Oaks, CA: Sage.

Takanishi, R., & DeLeon, P. H. (1994). A Head Start for the 21st century. *American Psychologist, 49,* 120–122.

Teague, G. B., Hornik, J., Ganju, V., Johnson, J. R., & McKinney, J. (1997). The MHSIP Mental Health Report Card: A consumer-oriented approach to monitoring the quality of health plans. *Evaluation Review, 21(3),* 330–341.

Triandis, H. C., & Suh, E. M. (2002). Cultural influences on personality. *Annual Review of Psychology, 53,* 133–160.

Trickett. E. J. (1997). Ecology and primary prevention: Reflections on a meta-analysis. *American Journal of Community Psychology, 25,* 197–205.

U.S. Census Bureau (2001). *Profile of general demographic characteristics 2000: 2000 census of population of children placed solely to obtain mental health services.* Report GAO-03-397.Gao(2003).

U.S. Census Bureau (2004). *U. S. Interim Projections by Age, Sex, Race, and Hispanic Origin.* Retrieved December 8, 2005 from http://www.census.gov/ipc/www/usinterimproj/

U.S. Department of Health and Human Services (1999). *Mental health: A report of the Surgeon General.* Rockville, MD: U.S. Department of Health and Human Services. Washingon, DC: Department of Health and Human Services.

U.S. Department of Health and Human Services (2001a). *Mental health: Culture, race, and ethnicity–A supplement to Mental health: A report of the Surgeon General.* Rockville, MD: U.S. Department of Health and Human Services.

U.S. Department of Health and Human Services (2001b). *Report of Surgeon General's working meeting on the integration of mental health services and primary health care.* Rockville, MD: Office of the Surgeon General.

U.S. Public Health Service (2000). *Report of the Surgeon General's Conference on Children's Mental Health: A national action agenda.* Washington, DC: Department of Health and Human Services.

Van de Vijver, F. J. R., & Phalet, K. (2004). Assessment of multicultural groups: The role of acculturation. *Applied Psychology: An International Review, 53,* 215–236.

Wang, P. S., Berglund, P., & Kessler, R. C. (2000). Prevalence and conformance with evidence-based recommendations. *Journal of General Internal Medicine, 15,* 284–292.

Weisz, J. R., Donenberg, G. R., Han, S. S., & Weiss, B. (1995). Bridging the gap between laboratory and clinic in child and adolescent psychotherapy. *Journal of Consulting and Clinical Psychology, 63,* 688–701.

Weisz, J. R., & Kazdin, A. E. (2003). Concluding thoughts. Present and future evidence-based psychotherapies for children and adolescents. In A. E. Kazdin & J. R. Weisz (Eds.), *Evidence-based psychotherapies for children and adolescents.* (pp. 439–451). New York: Guilford.

Weisz, J. R., Weiss, B., & Donenberg, G. R. (1992). The lab versus the clinic: Effects of child and adolescent psychotherapy. *American Psychologist, 47,* 1578–1585.

Whatley, R., Allen, J., & Dana, R. H. (2003). Racial identity and the MMPI in African American male college students. *Cultural Diversity and Ethnic Minority Psychology, 9,* 344–352.

Williams, J. W., Ross, K., & Dietrich, A. J. (1999). Primary care physicians' approach to depressive disorders: Effects of physician specialty and practice structure. *Archives of Family Medicine, 8,* 58–67.

World Health Organization. (2005). *International classification of diseases and related health problems.* Geneva: Author.

World Health Organization. (2000). *World health report-2000: Health systems: Improving performance.* Geneva: Author.

2

Promoting Cultural Competency in Mental Health Service Delivery

Chapter 1 described the mental health status of children and adolescents at the provider level, as well as more complex evaluation efforts at program and system levels. A recovery vision and a positive psychology of human functioning, accompanied by a new holistic science of child/adolescent development, was designed to increase access to quality mental health services for all consumers. Access to quality mental health care within the available service delivery systems, however, remains inadequate, particularly for ethnic minorities. Cultural competency of service providers and mental health agencies and systems of care was invoked to remedy underutilization and dissatisfaction by these populations with available mental health resources. Cultural competency in professional psychology is also known as multicultural competency (Pope-Davis, Coleman, Liu, & Toporek, 2003), racial–cultural competence (Carter, 2005), and intercultural competence (Lonner & Hayes, 2004). These cultural competency terms contribute to a recovery vision by fostering an enlarged, redesigned, and more inclusive perspective for understanding the role of cultural issues in reshaping mental health care.

Profound changes in the mental health care of ethnic minority children and adolescents were advocated by three independent cultural competency progenitors. These historic antecedents include the social welfare philosophy contained in the Child and Adolescent Service System Program (CASSP) minority cultural initiatives, multicultural competency conceptualizations in counseling psychology, and development of a research context in several international psychology associations and in the United States. Cultural sensitivity in systems of care and in each of the health/mental health professions contributes to access and participation in culturally competent services. These diverse cultural sensitivity/proficiency activities are relevant to the development of a cultural competency model. This model delineates a complex panorama of culture-relevant attributes within disparate professional training perspectives designed for general and specialty practice with profession-specific service populations in designated health/mental health settings. Each profession interfaces with patients/clients differing in race/ethnicity/culture as well as special nonethnic diversity populations (e.g., age, gender, sexual orientation, disability/handicap, and socioeconomic status. This model facilitates reexamining cultural competency in counseling/psychotherapy and assessment applications. As a comprehensive narrative instrument for children and adolescents, TEMAS has a special status and a major role in multicultural assessment nationally and internationally.

HISTORICAL RESOURCES

CASSP

The CASSP initiative examined essential elements for culturally competent systems, agencies, and programs serving ethnic minority children and adolescents. This philosophy led to developing agency evaluation instruments and stimulated training of service providers. CASSP ingredients in these projects contributed to advocacy for implementation of cultural competency in child/adolescent assessment. An ensuing climate of demonstration projects increased national awareness of cultural issues. However, despite the impetus provided by the Surgeon General's Reports and the New Freedom Initiative, the primary CAASP objective of embedding cultural competency into mental health systems was not achieved in managed care settings due to inadequate linkages of cultural competence to access, cost, and quality of care for ethnic minority populations.

Counseling Psychology

Counseling Psychology advocated multicultural competency as a primary professional training objective. The development of a multicultural competency model containing constructs representing knowledge, attitudes/beliefs, and skills stimulated widespread awareness of the need for culturally competent mental health services (Sue, Bernier, Duran, Feinberg, Pedersen et al., 1982). These constructs were operationalized by a number of self-report measures (Ponterotto, Fuertes, & Chen, 2000), and multicultural competency became "the central core of the counseling profession's identity" (Ponterotto, Gretchen, Utsey, Rieger, & Austin, 2002, p. 153). Counseling psychology training, research, practice, and evaluation subsequently incorporated measures of these three constructs within a literature affirming the necessity of understanding the role of culture in all human services. More recently, a fourth construct—Sociocultural Diversities—emerged from the items in these earlier measures (Gamst Dana, Der-Karabetian, Aragon, Arellano et al., 2004). This new, additional construct broadened the definition of diversity and provided an empirically derived rationale for cultural competency training that extends construct facets to other disadvantaged client groups.

Research Context

Three international psychology research disciplines—Cross-Cultural, Cultural, and Indigenous Psychology—developed disparate conceptual and methodological approaches to psychological research on culture–behavior relationships (Greenfield, 2000). Cross-Cultural Psychology operationalized culture as antecedent or independent indexical variables. Cultural processes were examined in individuals comparatively as dependent variables using psychometric procedures. Cultural Psychology focused the discourse inside the individual, and problems and procedures were derived from analyzing the nature of culture as process rather than index. Indigenous Psychology transformed folk theories of psychological functioning into psychological theories and legitimized ethnopsychological sources of formal psychological models by empirical investigation.

Berry (2000) believed these three approaches were necessary and complementary resources for understanding culture–behavior relationships within the health/mental health professions. Understanding behavior by transporting current psychological knowledge to other cultural contexts provides opportunities to examine the validity and cultural equivalence of this knowledge and ultimately integrates disparate knowledge sources. Berry (1999) recognized that culture-specific and culture-general perspectives, designated by *emic* and *etic*, were not dichotomous but overlapping and complementary viewpoints of equivalent value representing symbiotic approaches.

An international research context increased the sophistication and fueled the efforts of research scientists in the United States to develop more adequate research knowledge of ethnic minority populations, including the importance of cultural/racial identity and the within-group magnitude of individual variability. The entire research process has been reexamined to develop and disseminate adequate cultural knowledge resources for culturally competent mental health services (e.g., Council of

National Psychological Associations for the Advancement of Ethnic Minority Interests, 2000; Sue & Sue, 2003).

CULTURAL SENSITIVITY APPLICATIONS IN MENTAL HEALTH SYSTEMS

Mental health care has become an inseparable and minor subsidiary of health policy, and service delivery now occurs within a managed care business-insurance model. As a consequence, it is necessary to establish linkages between structural factors, process variables, and outcomes in order to focus responsibly on access, cost, and quality of mental health care for ethnic minority populations, described by Abe-Kim and Takeuchi (1996). Research on these linkages has not occurred in a sufficiently timely manner to influence managed care policy, medical and psychiatric service delivery, or their business and insurance industry partners and managers.

Quality has been conceptualized to include *structural factors* (e.g., necessary resources, services, staff), *process variables* (e.g., diagnostic procedures, referral sources, interventions, compliance), direct *outcome variables* (e.g., patient satisfaction, quality of life, clinical status, symptomatology), and indirect *outcome variables* (e.g., utilization rates, premature termination, length of treatment, and GAF; Donabedian, 1978). Indirect outcome variables are of limited utility although they have been examined more frequently than the direct outcome variables.

Quality care evaluation requires measurement of treatment effects on quality assurance criteria and other activities within the institutional framework, including relevant patient outcomes and expanding the conceptual framework to include the broader context of community and client attributes relevant for access (McGlynn, Norquist, Wells, Sullivan, & Liberman, 1988).

As a result, implementation of cultural sensitivity as a critical ingredient in quality care of ethnic minority populations still remains to be accomplished. Abe-Kim and Takeuchi (1996) suggested that the question of cultural sensitivity can only be addressed and properly examined in managed care by "incorporating cultural competence as a central feature of quality" (p. 289). Implementation by self-assessment and audit tools can now occur for all system levels within a community health psychology model that specifies access, appropriate utilization, and delivery of services within a climate of continuous quality improvement (De La Cancela, Chin, & Jenkins, 1998). To date, however, cultural responsivenss/competence has been defined primarily by language and interpreter services rather than by evaluation of stakeholder perspectives (Chin, 2002). In Chin's (2000) words;

Cultural competence has a very different meaning for organizations dedicated to serving culturally specific populations than for those dedicated to serving all populations. While cultural competence is core to the missions and programs of culture-specific organizations, their goal is not to be diverse but to fulfill unmet needs and advocate for the larger system to be more responsive to all segments of the population. (pp. 26–27)

The time is already past due for embedding cultural issues in mental health care. Embedding recognizes the pervasive and continuing importance of adequate identification of consumers requiring or requesting language, cultural, or racial match with providers, provision of culturally credible service delivery social etiquette, culturally sensitive provider training, interventions containing relevant cultural contents, and consistent evaluation of outcomes of services. CAASP and others (e.g., Wells & Brook, 1989) identified these critical components as important decision points in service delivery. As described in Chapter 1, the MAIP model embeds culture in mental health care at critical points where decisions for ethnic minority clients are required for quality care.

The MAIP provides a practical means of utilizing health/mental health resources at every level (i.e., federal, state, local), in each area (i.e., health and mental health care, education, business and industry, criminal justice, social welfare), and within each contributing profession (e.g., psychiatry, psychology, social work, medicine, nursing, etc). However, it is now evident that contemporary systems of care have not made cultural issues conspicuous in the structure, process, and outcomes of child/adolescent mental health services. Moreover, the mental health status of ethnic minority populations remains marginal because inadequate research knowledge of ethnic minority populations contributes to the continuing chasm between empirical knowledge and clinical practice. Nonetheless, there is now awareness of avenues to improve these knowledge resources in mental health disciplines (e.g., psychiatry, psychology, social work) and associated areas (e.g., anthropology, sociology). This awareness, however, has remained largely peripheral for a majority of primary care health providers and other medical specialists.

CULTURAL COMPETENCY IN HEALTH/MENTAL HEALTH PROFESSIONS

There is widespread but not unanimous recognition across these professions of the importance of cultural competency described in terms of knowledge, attitude, skill, and nonethnic factors. Cultural competency now provides the modus operandi for transformation of the health/ mental health system despite continuing barriers to access including bias, cultural insensitivity of providers, systems, and interventions, higher percentages of uninsured families, and the gap between culturally competent research knowledge and clinical practice.

These barriers can be reduced by culturally relevant information available from a variety of sources (e.g., Dana, 1998a), but most effectively from empirical research and evidence-based practices implementing a recovery-oriented vision (Farmer & Farmer, 2001). Such knowledge is necessary but insufficient without commensurate personal exposure of all service providers to training that increases awareness of their own assumptions, biases, and values within a context of culturally sensitive relationship, assessment, and intervention skills for competent multicultural practice within each of these professions.

Counseling psychology, clinical psychology, social work, psychiatry, nursing, and medicine have dealt with cultural sensitivity/proficiency to the extent permitted by their special interests, disparate objectives, and needs of their members. Cultural sensitivity has been evidenced in professional activities relevant for training, assessment, intervention, and research. However, these professions have not shared knowledge and cooperative endeavor due to an academic status hierarchy and histories of relative isolation, values of autonomy, and self-sufficiency. Thus, profession-specific cultural competency domains are coupled with distinctive perspectives and some skepticism concerning the quality, scientific status, meaning, and social relevance of each other's activities. It is helpful to understand the extent, style, and impact of cultural competency within these health/mental health professions. The profession-specific exemplars in this discussion provide an external appreciation of the breadth and extent of cultural competency. These exemplars introduce pan-professional multicultural counseling psychotherapy and assessment competencies for which adequate training is required.

Counseling Psychology

Counseling psychology envisioned an integrative training model for multicultural counseling/psychotherapy competency in all programs and assumed leadership in advocating culturally competent professional training. Attempts to implement this objective in counseling psychology rely on single courses as well as areas of concentration within programs and interdisciplinary or integrative models introduced by Copeland (1982) and elaborated over time (e.g., LaFromboise & Foster, 1992; D. Sue, 1997; Vazquez & Garcia-Vazquez, 2003). Single courses do not require total faculty or program commitment. Areas of concentration and interdisciplinary approaches may not reach all students. Integration approaches require faculty commitment and time as well as total program evaluation. There has been preference for integrating relevant cross-cultural content into all courses as a program responsibility.

Counseling psychology training objectives have not been uniformly achieved despite ethnic minority student and faculty membership at critical mass for significant influence, APA accreditation guidelines require only a single course for compliance and not all programs have emphasized the necessity for intensive examination of student and faculty cultural/racial identity development as a constructive deterrent to inadvertent racism. Although counseling psychology emphasized multicultural competency in counseling/psychotherapy, relatively little attention has been devoted to multicultural assessment training as an essential professional contribution to assessment per se (e.g., Ponterotto, Gretchen, & Chauhan, 2000), and particularly to an assessment-intervention service delivery system (Dana, 1998b).

There has often been a poor fit between Eurocentric counseling/psychotherapy training and the emergent, changing needs of ethnic minority individuals who differ in acculturation status, racial identity development, and personal preferences for particular therapists and/or specific interventions. As one solution for training bias, culture-centered microskills training can be employed to develop identified, replicable, and transportable skills (Pedersen & Ivey, 1993) as an alternative to training that provides information and attitudinal resources for subsequent development of practice skills with particular culture/racial groups.

Counseling psychologists have provided a variety of multicultural competency models (for review/evaluation, see Mollen, Ridley, & Hill, 2003). The major model (D. W. Sue, 2001a) has been criticized for construct oversimplification, and eight less elaborate models suffer from lack of validation studies. For example, Toporek and Reza's model (2001) provides additional competencies of context, modes of changes, and process for assessment and planning. Lopez (1997) identified process domains elaborating engagement with clients, assessment of client functioning, client conceptualization/explanation of therapy, and methods facilitating therapeutic change. Finally, Mollen et al. (2003) examined the effects of implicit assumptions contained in therapist—client matching, modified and unmodified conventional counseling, and culture-specific counseling.

These assumptions are explicit in the MAIP formulation of culturally competent mental health services and amenable to examination as potential mediators of client outcomes.

A variety of creative teaching methods developed by counseling psychologists (e.g., Pope-Davis et al., 2003) are illustrated by the following selected examples. Carter (2003) developed a required laboratory course predicated on an earlier training model (Carter, 1995) including lectures, small group, skill-building dyads, and feedback from self-exploration, genograms, structured questions concerning reference groups, and a weekly journal. Narrative approaches provide opportunities for increasing self-identity using self-introductions, an identity paper, and other personal stories from readings and presentations by guest speakers (Kerl, 2002). Facilitating student awareness of personal bias, defensiveness, and privilege by employing Cultural Self-Awareness Assessment portfolios documents progress structured by learning goals, objectives, and evaluation (Sodowsky, 2004). A year-long "transformative" training seminar (Sevig & Etzkom, 2001) for counseling and social work interns provides a supplement for piecemeal academic training approaches.

Unfortunately, implementing cultural competency using single courses and training procedures has been the most frequent means of satisfying APA accreditation requirements. Single courses provide scant evidence for the presence and usefulness of holistic integrative approaches deemed desirable and necessary for multicultural competency (Abreu, Chung, & Atkinson, 2000). Moreover, client perspectives on the practice outcomes of multicultural competency training have not been examined sufficiently to provide evidence for preferences and expectations (Pope-Davis, Liu, Toporek, & Brittan-Powell, 2001).

Surveys report modest increases in multicultural training opportunities in counseling psychology programs over time (e.g., Hills & Strozier, 1992; Murphy, Wright, & Bellamy, 1995) but program graduates have consistently questioned the adequacy, completeness, and relevance of their multicultural competency training (e.g., Allison, Crawford, Echemendia, Robinson & Knepp, 1994). These early internship surveys reported training deficiencies still apparent in the most recent survey conclusion that "training with ethnic minority patients occurred with low rates in most settings" (Stedman, Hatch, Schoenfeld, & Keilin, 2005, p. 5). Stedman et al. (2005) reported major internship rotations with ethnic minority patients in 49% of programs, while only 16% offered multicultural therapy rotations. Assessment was the most frequent specialty available in these programs (64%), especially prevalent in child facilities (92%) providing access to the largest ethnic minority populations. The quality of multicultural competency academic training could not be examined in this study due to an online source of program information. As a consequence, there is little evidence that counseling psychology programs have succeeded in their objective to make multicultural competency central to professional training, although counselor-training leaders aver that knowledge, self-awareness, and skill all contribute to multicultural competency on the basis of research.

Rogers (2005) reviewed training in counseling, clinical, and school psychology programs with exemplary multicultural training "reflecting a sophisticated system of academic supports" (p. 1009). Program excellence resulted from a commitment to multicultural initiatives by programs, faculty, and students. These programs used an integration multicultural training model, originally identified by Copeland (1982), with at least one required course, exposed their students to diverse clients in supervised settings, emphasized research on ethnic minority populations, and examined students on cross-cultural knowledge. These programs employed personal contacts by faculty to recruit ethnic minority students, involved these students in subsequent recruiting activities, and solicited students from other university programs. The programs retained students by supportive institutional climates, faculty mentoring to stimulate relevant research, and by providing support groups. Such program commitment fosters a learning environment that places multicultural competency issues at the heart of program activities and is consistent with a desired holistic integrated training model emphasized as a major structural device "for acquainting students with multicultural service issues and thereby enhancing intercultural sensitivity (with the) ultimate purpose of training for cultural competence ... to develop ethnorelative thinking" (Dana, 1993, pp. 6–7).

In Rogers' (2005) exemplary counseling programs, ethnic minority faculty and student numbers approached a critical mass of 30%, greatly exceeding their numbers in other APA-approved programs. These programs were examined using a design consistent with an earlier national study of internship directors' nomination of interns receiving competent academic preparation for internship (Dana, Gilliam, & Dana, 1976) and followed by intensive studies of competency training in specific clinical programs (Dana, 1978). Nonetheless, there is little evidence that available multicultural competency training resources in counseling psychology are sufficient to implement multicultural competency in the absence of a program environment dedicated to this objective and followed by internship supplementation, subsequent in-service training, and continuing lifelong professional education.

Counseling psychology continues to advocate a social obligation defined by the multicultural competency objective for professional education, training, research, and practice. A humanized professional construction of the counseling/psychotherapy reality for professional practice invites intraprofessional self-scrutiny and social accountability, although APA accreditation policies and procedures have not sufficiently encouraged these programs to fully address their multicultural ideals and advocacy by training.

Clinical Psychology

Clinical and counseling psychology programs were originally distinguished and separated by professional training loci in hospitals or counseling centers as well as by designating psychopathological or student populations of primary interest (Dana & May, 1987). These two psychology domain areas have become increasingly homogenized over time and now share similar training and professional activities, largely as a consequence of professional oversight by the American Psychological Association. Nonetheless, residual differences between these programs are apparent in the breadth and catholicity of scientific attitudes and the relative importance of cultural competency in professional training. These program characteristics are responsible for differences in student demographics as well as in preferences for relevant training and research activities.

In clinical psychology literature, multicultural sensitivity has slowly become more salient over time (e.g., Beutler, Brown, Crothers, Booker, & Seabrook, 1996; Case & Smith, 2000; DeLeon & VandenBos, 2000; Munley, Anderson, Baines, Borgman, Briggs et al., 2002; Nilsson, Berkel, Flores, Love, Wendler et al., 2003), although the more prestigious journals have neglected ethnic minority populations (Hall & Maramba, 2001). Insufficient attention to culturally sophisticated research methodology for investigation of intervention strategies/techniques has resulted in failure to establish whether or not psychotherapy modifications are essential for multicultural therapeutic competence, and ethnic differences in spirituality, discrimination, and interdependence remain inadequately explored (Hall, 2001).

The extent to which other professional areas accept the counseling/psychotherapy reality in counseling psychology is a function of their consensual scientific values, histories of admission criteria, and conservative or liberal attitudes, as well as openness to change, tolerance of professional ambiguity, and resiliency of professional identity perspectives. All of these ingredients are influential, but only when the ethnic/racial membership exceeds critical mass can multicultural competency become embedded in program philosophy and all training activities. Training that fosters student self-awareness and examination of cultural/racial identity is especially difficult with preponderantly White students (Jackson, 1999) because of the necessity for exploration of the role of White privilege and sense of entitlement that supports bias, categorical thinking, and stereotyping others (Pack-Brown, 1999).

Debate between counseling and clinical psychology concerns the self-report nature of cultural competency measurement, employment of qualitative methodologies, and an opinion forum provided by counseling psychology journals. Clinical psychologists have a more parsimonious construction of scientific reality as a consequence of self-identification as behavioral scientists, greater acceptance of medical model attitudes that depersonalize, objectify, and strip patients of their cultural identities, and fewer publication outlets and editorial gatekeepers espousing a multicultural perspective. An even more pervasive consequence has been noted in academic clinical psychology training that continues to fail the comfort test with conversations about race and ethnicity (Cardemil & Battle, 2003). White-dominated thinking, punctuated by defensive reactivity to challenges to power and privilege, still characterize an uneasy status quo in professional psychology. A quote epitomizing D. W. Sue's (2003) reaction to racism originally appeared in Ponterotto's (2004) book review and is pertinent here:

> You do not have to be actively racist to contribute to the racism problem. Inaction, itself, is tacit agreement that racism is acceptable; and because White Americans enjoy the benefits, privileges, and opportunities of the oppressive system, they inevitably are racist by both commission and omission. As a result, it is my contention that White racism is truly a White problem and that is it the responsibility of the White brothers and sisters to be centrally involved in combating and ending racial oppression. (p. 99)

This quote exposes the deficit of not explicitly confronting White power and privilege attitudes in professional training affecting research and ingrained in practice, particularly in clinical psychology.

APA extols professional ideals of social equality and justice, although commensurate professional responsibility has not been communicated by accreditation guidelines, ethical percepts, or research standards. APA conservatism may be simply a function of lacking a 30% ethnic minority critical mass, although increased efforts to counteract implicit institutionalized racism within the profession could positively affect recruitment of ethnic minority psychologists in specializations other than counseling psychology.

Social Work

Social work practitioners are committed by core values to "a sense of concern for the vulnerable, the oppressed, and the poor ... and there is evidence that social workers accommodate their practice styles more than other professionals" (Snowden, 2000, p. 439). While consistently espousing a mandate for services to disadvantaged and disenfranchised populations, including European immigrants and ethnic/racial groups, early attempts at infusing teaching and training with relevant contents were largely ignored (e.g., Chau, 1990; Eldridge, 1982; Del Valle, Merdinger, Wrenn, & Miller, 1991). However, over time, social work training has become more responsive to issues of values, social responsibility, and social change relevant for policy and practice (e.g., Bent-Goodley, 2003; Council on Social Work Education, 2003). In this context, special attention has been directed toward facilitating empowerment by recognizing client needs and individual strengths within social environments (Lohmann & Lohmann, 2002; Simon, 1994). More recently, Direct Practice Social Work (Allen-Meares & Garvin, 2000) incorporates multicultural perspectives and assessment/measurement issues to provide a cultural competence context including consultation, training staff, services in languages other than English, and monitoring caseloads for proportional representation of ethnic minorities (Snowden, 2000). Available guidelines include a number of components within each of several dimensions (i.e., cultural awareness, knowledge acquisition, skill development, and inductive learning) within a hierarchal ordering across levels (Lum, 1999).

Social work has a history of textbooks sensitive to a cultural construction of care as part and parcel of everyday personal and communal experience predicated on local and historical knowledge (e.g., Green, 1999; Iglehart & Becerra, 1995; Weaver, 2005). These texts describe culturally sensitive therapeutic interventions for families, adults, children, and immigrants in specific community ethnic minority groups and social class contexts. Green (1999), for example, describes a model of cross-cultural help-seeking service relationships specifying common, shared understandings of disability symptoms as personal crises with distinctive meanings adapted from Kleinman (1977, 1978). Within a context of client and professional cultures, this model proceeds from client problem recognition, labeling, and diagnosis to utilization of indigenous and professional help providers for problem resolution. Problem resolution entails a knowledge plan that recognizes the cultural salience of presenting problems, individualizes the client, identifies the roles of cultural competence and power, and emphasizes thinking and working comparatively. Green employed a stepwise approach to cultural competency beginning with a personal assessment of functioning in cross-cultural situations (McPhatter, 1997), followed by awareness of the need for a help-seeking behavior map (McMiller & Weisz, 1996) to expedite acquiring local knowledge (Thyer, 1997), preparing cultural formulations (Rogler, 1996), developing culturally responsive interventions (Lee, 1996), and appreciating practice complexities (Rounds, Weil, & Bishop, 1994).

Weaver (2005) begins by carefully examining the vocabulary of *culture* and associated terms in search of conceptual clarity and unambiguous definition as one aspect of identity. Although cultural identity develops for intrinsically human reasons, cultural/racial socialization serves to provide resiliency for survival in racist societies. An understanding of culture and cultural identity are primary ingredients for social work practice. Lists of cultural traits obscure recognition of diversity and foster stereotypy by categorical thinking, whereas transactional thinking recognizes that norms imposed by a power elite limit appreciation of individuality and obstruct participation in a democratic society. Because this particular issue is generally misunderstood or ignored by professionals, Weaver's more precise words follow:

> The result of categorical thinking is to shape the person being categorized rather than adjust the categories. ... In other words, difference exist between people rather than someone in the minority or with less power simply being different from someone with the power to set the norm. (p. 33)

Weaver understands that culture is flexible, whereas identity is multiply layered, and more than six million persons have multiracial ancestry (Kahn & Denmon, 1997). Culture is conceived as constantly changing and affects specific values and behaviors (e.g., independence–interdependence, defining success/setting priorities, raising children, gender roles/sexuality, perception of physical/mental differences, and equality/inequality as well as help-seeking behaviors). These dimensions define major arenas for culturally competent social work practice.

Weaver knows that an examination of cultural diversity within each profession is critical for overcoming bias, demonstrating respect in practice, and learning cultural competency attitudes and behaviors. Shifts in values are necessary and require the courage for self-examination and participation in cultural encounters and immersion experiences during training and thereafter as nonacademic continuing education in understanding cultural relativism. Cultural competence is a continuous, ongoing process rather than an outcome. Evidences of this process include identification of meaningful aspects of cultural identity using strength-based holistic assessment tools, a client's cultural norms, and awareness of the dynamics of power and oppression. Practical applications of multicultural competency for eight groups illustrate fusing knowledge with values/attitudes, and skills for engaging, assessing, and intervening. Culture-specific case examples, social policies, social agencies, and community interventions illustrate multicultural competency. Microlevel cultural competence embraces interventions with clients and influencing colleagues. Macrolevel cultural competency influences social policies, social agencies, professional education, communities, and the social work profession.

Weaver (2005) has tracked cultural competency from a culture-specific Native American perspective. Social work history is synthesized within a conceptualization of culture and cultural identity that facilitates group cultural/racial practice exemplars pertinent to micro and macro avenues for advocating profound changes in contemporary professional mental health activities. She has distilled the meaning and relevance of a complex multidisciplinary literature on the basis of her own personal and professional identities.

Although a comprehensive understanding of cultural competency requires distinctive profession-specific perspectives, these interpretations remain incomplete without the availability of culture-specific/profession-specific constructions providing sharp contrast with the pervasive White Euro-American male modes of selective perception and integration of the cultural competence domain. Social work has historic and contemporary advantages of providing services for individuals in sociocultural contexts but has not been able to incorporate cultural competency routinely or uniformly in training programs. Textbooks for single multicultural courses have historically presented multicultural issues, but only very recent publications include a culture-specific perspective (Weaver, 2005), or elucidation of multicultural ethical issues (Pack-Brown & Williams, 2003).

Sophisticated assessment skills have been recently legitimized for social work research and practice (Jordan & Franklin, 2003). Assessment is an ongoing process of understanding individual clients' characteristics such as their personality, problems, and strengths and related information about the social and interpersonal environments that are impacting clients. Multiple methods are often used to collect and evaluate ongoing information from clients. These methods are diverse and include face-to-face interviews with people, behavioral observations, reviews of written documents, and the use of measurement instruments. Assessment includes psychosocial, problem-solving, cognitive-behavioral, multimodal, life model, ecobehavioral, family systems, task-centered, strengths, and solution-focused models. These integrative models discourage long history taking by task-centered planning and goal orientations. Shared, brief, time-limited, and collaborative information processing have common features including preference for viewing clients in family, group, and community contexts as well as strength and resiliencies in addition to problems and psychopathologies. The sheer size and complexity of the social work profession necessitated many competing subdisciplines (e.g., administration, policy, research, etc.) that have been center stage rather than cultural competency.

Psychiatry

Historically, psychiatrists invested their cultural sensitivity in developing and integrating knowledge derived from a number of antecedent areas including cultural anthropology, medical sociology, and cross-cultural psychology. A number of descriptive labels have been employed including cross-cultural psychiatry (Herrera, Lawson, & Sramek, 1999) and particularly transcultural psychiatry (Wittkower & Prince, 1974). However, cultural psychiatry, a more inclusive term and a subfield of general psychiatry, describes a clinical science interested in theory and research focused on clinical applications of culturally relevant patient care (e.g., Gaw, 2001; Tseng, 2001, 2003). Cultural psychiatrists have also examined ethnic-specific reactions to pharmacological interventions (Ruiz, 2000).

Criticisms of earlier DSM diagnostic inadequacies for women and ethnic minorities led to intensive efforts by cultural psychiatrists to render the DSM-IV more applicable for ethnic minority populations by routinely including cultural formulations (e.g., Lu, Lin, & Mezzich, 1995; Mezzich,

Kleinman, Fabrega, & Parron, 1996; Rogler, 1993). The journal *Culture, Medicine, and Psychiatry* has devoted conspicuous space to training examples of multicultural case formulations (see, Lewis-Fernandez, 1996). Multicultural training to increase the reliability of clinical diagnoses by using cultural formulations has also been emphasized by social scientists (e.g., Castillo, 1997; Dana, 1998c, 2002a; Paniagua, 2000, 2005).

In addition to acquiring cultural knowledge, Tseng (2001; 2004) describes the shift from cultural sensitivity to cultural competency. This shift requires sharpening cultural sensitivity, enhancing cultural empathy, learning credible relationships with ethnic minorities, and selecting and applying culturally relevant treatments. Tseng suggests topics to be covered in several stages of training, using a teaching format with a formal didactic seminar, bedside clinical teaching, cultural psychiatry rounds, supervision, and consultation, as well as other teaching strategies. He also recommends advanced training opportunities including mentoring, culture-related academic courses, workshops, cross-cultural research, participation in international conferences, and professional activities in foreign countries. In addition to training in general residency programs, there are a small number of special programs in the absence of any consensus on a model curriculum for all medical students, psychiatric residents, and cultural psychiatry fellows (Foulks, Westermeyer, & Ta, 1998), although a residency training curriculum has been proposed including religion and spirituality (Larson, Lu, & Swyers, 1997).

Nursing

In the nursing profession, Leininger (1970) pioneered ethnonursing research, leading to the global discipline of Transcultural Nursing. Transcultural Nursing was defined "as a formal area of study and practice focused on comparative human-care (caring) differences and similarities of the beliefs, values, and patterned lifeways of cultures to provide culturally congruent, meaningful, and beneficial health care to people" (Leininger & McFarland, 2002, pp. 5–6). This discipline is identified by specialized doctoral programs, three editions of a seminal 1978 textbook, a journal, a professional society, and an international association. Within Transcultural Nursing, a cultural frame of reference is central to the experience of human beings, and culture-specific care is vital. An acknowledged primacy of culture-specific care, or culturally based ways of helping and healing, requires nurses to incorporate self-knowledge with systematic study of diverse caring activities in order to develop and practice cultural care competencies. More than 50 years of advocacy for transcultural training in the United States has resulted in transcultural nursing options in only 1% of doctoral programs and 18% of master's degree programs (Leininger & McFarland, 2002).

Leininger (1991) also developed the Sunrise Model to depict the underlying theory of cultural care diversity and universality and designed to help nurse administrators and consultants employ emic and etic research-based findings. This model mobilizes worldview dimensions of cultural and social, structure including interrelated cultural beliefs, values/lifeways, kinship/social and political/legal factors forming a language and ethnohistory environmental context. Religious/philosophical, economic, technological, and educational factors also influence expressions of care and practices of holistic health, illness, and death. These factors and the outcomes of their influences embrace individuals, families, groups, communities, and institutions by providing health contents of folk care, nursing care, and professional care–cure practices. These diverse practices are responsible for transcultural care decisions and actions that comprise culturally congruent care.

In a second major context, Lipson (1996) described cultural sensitivity in nursing. Awareness of culture, socioeconomic status, gender, race, sexual orientation, and disability within a complex combination of knowledge, attitudes, and skills are necessary to provide culturally competent nursing care. Cultural assessment entails identifying the patient's ethnicity by birthplace, time in the United States, and strength of affiliation. Support persons, community ties, language ability, nonverbal communication style, religion, food preferences/prohibitions, economic status, health/illness beliefs, practices, and customs around birth, illness, and death transitions are also described (Lipson & Meleis, 1985).

A pocket information guide for cultural assessment (Lipson, Dibble, & Minarik, 1996) contains suggestions for dealing with language differences including work with interpreters and culturally derived communication variations. A consistent format, used by ethnic minority nurses, represented each of the 24 U.S. populations exceeding 100,000. This format yields chapters containing consistent information on cultural/ethnic identity, communication, daily living activities, food practices, symptom management, birth rituals and new mother/baby care, death rituals, family relationships, spiritual/religious orientation, illness beliefs, and health practices. Appendices include population tables and maps, diversity of spiritual/religious beliefs, and world maps from selected regions.

Medicine

The medical profession has made few conspicuous or effective attempts to infuse cultural competency into medical training and health care in a manner similar to nursing. For example, during the 1980s, recommended curriculum guidelines were developed by a task force to facilitate formal instruction concerning health and culture in family practice residency programs (Like, Steiner, & Rubel, 1996). In introducing a ten-year repetition of a special journal issue on cross-cultural medicine, Barker (1992) noted the history of medical anthropology to develop relevant programs in medical schools for improved services to immigrants and indigenous groups.

Historically, there has also been significant interest in developing cultural assessment as part of health promotion and disease prevention guidelines. For example, the Cultural Assessment Framework (Huff & Kline, 1999) has relevant questions at five distinct levels. These levels include culture-specific demographics, epidemiological–environmental influences, cultural characteristics (e.g., cultural/ethnic identity, cosmology, time orientation, self and community perceptions, social norms, customs, and values, and communication patterns), health care beliefs/practices, and Western health care areas amenable to cultural sensitivity and competence.

This apparent indifference in medicine may be due to conservatism in scientific and empirical attitudes as well as professional dependence on managed care service delivery systems that are largely unresponsive to cultural issues. These careful elaborations of cultural issues have been largely unexamined in primary care medical practice. Advocacy for cultural competency has simply not existed historically in medicine despite a long interest in psychiatry. National health policy now restricts mental health care to patients with DSM diagnoses and limited psychiatric care with supplemental preventive and educational experiences, primarily as group services by ancillary providers. This policy has also limited psychiatric advocacy primarily to cultural formulations for clinical diagnosis.

Recent public policy initiatives, however, fueled by burgeoning multicultural populations, are responsible for new legislation that will provide some limited cultural competency training in medical schools accompanied by continuing medical education (CME) requirements. For example, a 2005 law in New Jersey (Senate Bill 144) now mandates their 30,000 licensed physicians to raise cultural awareness and sensitivity by specialized training as determined by the State Board of Medical Examiners (www.njleg.state.nj.us). Arizona Senate Bill 1468 requires students to complete a cultural competency course, and physicians need a course for licensing/license renewal (www.azleg.state.az.us/DocumentForBill. asp?Bill_Number=1468). In Illinois, Senate Bill 522 would create the Cultural and Linguistic Competency of Physicians Program. This program would provide voluntary foreign language classes as well as courses in understanding the roles that culture and race play in doctor–patient relationships, diagnosis, and treatment (www.ilga.gov/legislation). In New York, Assembly Bill 3751 requires medical students to complete one or more competency courses before graduation, and physicians would complete at least 16 hours of training for relicensing (www.assembly. state.ny.us).

As reported by American Medical News (www.amednews.com) (Adams, June 28, 2004), cultural competency training for physicians and other medical professionals will soon be available for continuing medical education (CME) credit on the Internet, and similar training has already been completed by 95% of Aetna physicians and nurses on clinical staff. The Cultural and Linguistic Competency of Physicians Act, sponsored by the California Hispanic Health Care Association and the California Medical Association, requires CME credits (www.leginfo.ca.gov/bilinfo. html). In California, the primary language of over 12.4 million people, or 40% of the state population, is not English; many physicians thus require not only language skills or translator assistance but knowledge of the culture beliefs and service delivery styles affecting medical practice.

CLINICAL COMPETENCY AND/OR CULTURAL COMPETENCY?

General therapeutic or clinical competency as an area of expertise has been described in rich detail (e.g., Skovholt & Jennings, 2004). Cultural competency, however, was omitted historically as a major contributor to therapeutic competency, despite similarities between master therapists and culturally competent therapists (Goh, 2005). General and cultural competency domains are arguably related (Fuertes, Bartolomeo, & Nichols, 2001), highly correlated (Fuertes & Brobst, 2002), perhaps inseparable (Coleman, 1998) and considered a higher order or superordinate competency (Sue & Sue, 2003).

Coleman (1998) posed the question of whether these competencies were different as "apples" and "oranges." Some consensus now exists that these competencies may be simply apples and better apples. Nonetheless, cultural competency is a complex, multifaceted, value-laden term with diffuse definitions. Operationalization remains difficult despite consensus among counseling psychologists concerning the necessity to make desirable competency characteristics amenable to training (Pope-Davis et al., 2003). Over time and with shifts in population demographics in the United States, contemporary distinctions between clinical competency and cultural competency will disappear as the mental health workforce more closely mirrors the general population.

A new composite self-report measure, the California Brief Multicultural Competence Scale (CBMCS), provides a quantitative basis for in-service cultural competency training, as described in chapter 1. Constructed by compiling available research and practice contents relevant for each item, a training program was developed for statewide application in California. The CBMCS was developed to examine the effects of key variables on ethnic minority mental health services encompassed by the MAIP model.

As the earlier discussion noted, all interested health/mental health professions now differ in the extent to which cultural competency is perceived and implemented as a desirable objective. The following sections summarize similarities and differences among professions that highlight the relevance of their unique contributions to training, practice, and research with particular emphasis on assessment and counseling/psychotherapy as an introduction to a training model for cultural competency.

PROFESSION-SPECIFIC CULTURAL COMPETENCY

Major and minor contributions to cultural competency in the health/ mental health professions are summarized and referenced in Table 2–1. This table describes the profession-specific cultural competency areas and includes salient references. In this table, "major" or central and "minor" or peripheral importance refers to the manner and extent to which each profession has incorporated cultural competency ingredients into its training programs.

Some clinical psychology programs have a single cultural competency course, or specialty areas, but the primary contribution of these programs has been developing student cultural research competencies as a result of mentoring by individual faculty mentors. The small number of cultural assessment and intervention texts in clinical psychology are of relatively recent origins. Specialized courses in these areas are not routinely available. A few professional psychology programs have a continuing interest in cultural competency in assessment training (e.g., Alliant University, Carlos

TABLE 2–1. Culturally Relevant Domains of Major/Minor
Importance in Professions

Profession	Major	Minor
Counseling Psychology	Multicultural Competency (Pope-Davis et al., 2003) Research (Brown/Lent, 2000) Counseling/Psychotherapy (Ancis, 2004) Racism (D.W. Sue, 2001b) Racial-Cultural Psychology (Carter, 2005)	Assessment (Suzuki et al., 2001) (Vernon/Clements, 2005;
Clinical Psychology	Research (S. Sue/L. Sue, 2003) (CNPAAEMI, 2000)	Intervention (Dana, 1998c; Hays, 2001) Assessment (Dana, 1993, 2000, 2005) (Gopaul-McNichol et al, 2002)
Social Work	Focus on individuals in sociocultural contexts (Council on SW Ed, 2003) (Bent-Goodley, 2003) Social Administration (Lohmann/ Lohmann, 2002) Direct Practice SW (Allen-Meares/Garvin, 2000)	Multicultural Competency (Weaver, 2005) Assessment (Jordan/Franklin, 2003). Multicultural ethics (Pack-Brown/ Williams, 2003)
Psychiatry	Cultural Formulation (Mezzich et al., 1996) Cultural Context (Kleinman, 1988) Cultural psychiatry (Tseng, 2004)	Clinical diagnosis (Castillo, 1997) Psychopharmacology (Ruiz, 2000)
Nursing		Transcultural Nursing (Leininger, 1991) Cultural assessment (Lipson et al., 1996)
Medicine		Cultural Assessment (Huff & Kline, 1999) Family Practice Residency (Like et al., 1996) Cross-culture medicine (Barker, 1997)

Albizu University-San Juan, Fielding Institute-Santa Barbara), although other professional school programs provide only minimal training in conventional assessment.

Despite the history of social work practice in sociocultural contexts and recent direct practice initiatives, cultural competency training is still not generally available across programs. Responsible textbooks for cultural competency, assessment, and ethics are very recent additions to their training literature. It should be noted, however, that these recent textbooks provide models and training exemplars relevant for professional psychology as well as for social work.

Cultural psychiatry has a prehistory in cultural anthropology, medical sociology, and cross-cultural psychology. Cultural psychiatry has recently emerged as a distinct specialty area in response to cultural formulation to increase the reliability of DSM-IV clinical diagnoses with ethnic minority patients. Culturally relevant interventions with increasing research credibility are slowly becoming available, although opportunities to employ them occur primarily during residency or thereafter.

The nursing profession has a long history of culture care with a transcultural nursing model for practice that includes cultural assessment. This practice model has been represented by a training option in a small percentage of master's and doctoral programs and has not appreciably influenced training of medical students.

Medicine was slow to provide interviewing training for their students despite available early textbooks developed from hands-on, supervised experience with mental hospital patients (e.g., Bernstein & Dana, 1970; Bernstein, Bernstein, & Dana, 1974). Similarly, cultural competency training for medical students has not occurred, although some residency programs have recognized the need for such training. Recent state legislation now requires remedial attention to cultural competency in medical school education. State medical licensing boards are beginning to consider cultural competency educational requirements for licensure.

Summary

Cultural competency in counseling/psychotherapy has been a primary counseling psychology objective of long duration. Social work enjoys a recent direct practice focus and new texts augur well for the immediate future of cultural competency training. Clinical psychology has been conservative in implementing cultural competency in training and practice, although individual clinical psychologists have assumed leadership in developing culturally appropriate research methodologies and advocacy for an empirical knowledge basis for professional practice. Cultural psychiatry has contributed sustained interest in cultural formulations to increase reliability of clinical diagnosis. Nursing provided a cultural care model that unfortunately has not influenced medical education, although several states are in the process of the mandating multicultural competency training requirements for medical licensure.

CULTURAL COMPETENCY: A MODEL AND PRACTICE APPLICATIONS

Competency optimizes individual adaptation for survival by employing specific local cultural resources, priorities, values, and consensually accepted behavioral rules and styles. Different conceptions of competence exist within and between cultures. For ethnic minority individuals in the United States, competencies inhering from cultural/racial socialization interact with acculturation status and majority culture prerogatives to provide sufficient conformity for adaptive functioning within the larger society.

Students bring with them a set of demographic, social class, and ethnic/cultural attributes. Professional programs attempt to provide students with the diverse contents of one or more constructs representing cultural knowledge, attitudes/values, assessment/intervention skills, and nonethnic abilities. Table 2–2 summarizes these attributes, construct dimensions, and training modalities relevant for ethnocultural thinking/relativism as a cultural competency outcome.

Two considerations in this table are noteworthy. First, attitudes/values are the primary professional training concern and are difficult to examine and modify as a result of conventional professional training modalities. Employment of experiential training modalities and *in situ* living experiences can run counter to established conventional pedagogy. Second, the addition of a fourth empirically identified CBMCS construct dimension expands the cultural competency domain to include sociocultural diversities or other sociocultural groups suffering from discrimination and oppression (for examples of these groups, see Pedersen, Draguns, Lonner, & Trimble, 2002).

Moreover, the following discussion recognizes that a professional practice lifetime for acquisition of multicultural skills is necessary to develop and maintain competency. Lifetime learning from clients, colleagues, mentors, students, and friends occurs in formal professional settings and

Table 2–2.   Cultural Competency Model: Attributes, Constructs,
Training, and Desired Outcome

Attributes	Construct Dimensions	Training Modalities	Outcome
Ethnicity/Race	Multicultural	Courses, Workshops	Ethnocultural
Social Class	knowledge		Relativism/
Urban/Rural	Attitudes/Values	Personal growth,	Ethnorelativistic
Age	(awareness of cultural	extended experiences	Thinking
Gender	barriers; sensitivity	in cross-cultural living	
Acculturation	to consumers)	Practicum, Internship	
	Multicultural skills	Continuing Education	
Personal	(Interviewing)		
Qualities:	(Assessment)		
Curiosity,	(Interventions)		
Flexibility,	(Research)		
Openness,	Sociocultural	Profession-specific	
Ambiguity	Diversities	service populations/	
Tolerance		practice specialties	
Nonjudgmental		(e.g., age, gender,	
		sexual orientation,	
		disability,	
		socioeconomicstatus)	

informally in daily life. This proposed model provides secondary attention to the necessity for lifelong learning as a necessary and recognized
component (see Pope-Davis et al., 2003).

Individual Attributes

Individual personal components encourage, stimulate, and facilitate new
learning about other persons and precede professional socialization.
Included in these attributes are curiosity, flexibility, openness to experience, toleration of ambiguity, and non-judgmental respect for differences.
A report presaging Boulder model clinical psychology training (American
Psychological Association, 1947) began by recognizing personal qualities
relevant for a scientist-professional program. Research documenting personality characteristics associated with clinical competency or cultural
competency has not been a major training objective, although counseling

psychology admission criteria have consistently appreciated and understood the goodness-of-fit between student personality and program values.

Personal attributes develop by socialization experiences associated with ethnicity/race, social class, age, gender, and acculturation status in different cultures. There are extreme individual differences in the development of these personal attributes by students and professionals. Personal attitudes, an unexamined heart of cultural competency training, provide some parameters for professional socialization and instructional modalities relevant for ethnorelativisitic thinking, a hallmark of cultural competency. These attributes interface with early socialization and affect the impact of significant positive or negative life experiences. First-person accounts of identity development contribute life stories that exemplify ethnocultural relativism or cultural competency (see autobiographies in Ponterotto, Casas, Suzuki, & Alexander, 2001). Cultural/racial identity models of identity development for Whites and non-Whites have been described (e.g., Dana, 1998c, ch. 4; Kohatsu & Richardson, 1996), used for training (Ponterotto, 1998), and as personal examples of lifelong progression toward an understanding of cultural identity and ethnocultural relativism (Dana, 2004, 2005, pp. 77–79).

Construct Dimensions

Training in some professions endorses personal soundness and addresses personal distress or potential psychopathology by facilitating counseling or psychotherapy for students or contributes to personal growth using a variety of modalities. Professional socialization complements preexisting individual CRI development of a worldview with gender roles, values germane to individualism or collectivism, and a personal style for guiding behavior and imposing structure on professional activities. Cultural identity is thus coextensive with professional identity and provides the core of a cultural competency model.

Professional socialization, however, may coincide or radically depart from a pre-existing CRI. The extent to which preexisting CRIs can affect professional socialization and professional identity depends on whether or not critical mass for representation of ethnic minority individuals within the specific professional arena has been achieved, the status of these individuals within the organization and their mentoring activities, and the distribution of political power within the program.

Existing cultural competency agendas serve practical needs within each profession for establishing relationships with clients/patients, fostering particular intervention activities, and contributing to consensually desirable outcomes. The definitions, descriptions, measurement, and evaluation of cultural competency to date have followed profession-specific guidelines and program-specific implementations for particular research and practice objectives. Measurement may or may not be considered absolutely necessary to describe personal or professional competency, identify specific skills, or develop training procedures, but measurement certainly contributes to credibility and consensus of program activities to achieve training objectives.

Despite the contents of cultural competency models and descriptive examples of program applications, professional training does not necessarily focus on socialization artifacts providing the basis for ethnocentrism or ethnorelativism. The United States is not yet a postracist society. Ethnocentrism persists among many White students who have experienced privilege and entitlement, as well as among some students of color who have experienced oppression. Examining scientific attitudes that emphasize similarities and minimize differences and understanding the function of categorical thinking can lead to awareness of bias, caricature, stereotyping, and pathologizing. Categorical thinking is a deeply ingrained and seldom recognized habit of thought. Categorical thinking is an imposed etic that distorts the cultural reality of ethnic minority individuals by ascribing majority culture personality traits and psychopathologies to them without their consent and often in situations where they are unaware of what is happening and thus are powerless to dissent.

Attitudes and values thus constitute the most important part of new cultural competency learning, particularly for White students who ordinarily have to learn second-hand about oppression because they have not experienced explicit or implicit daily affronts to their human integrity. However, attitude change as a result of educational practices is an extraordinarily difficult emotional experience because personal growth is demanded in the presence of anger, anxiety, and internalized distress and turmoil. Although these emotional reactions can inhibit or disrupt many conventional learning modalities, training has to be directed toward development of transactional thinking that encourages ethnocultural relativism and embodies cultural competency. Transactional thinking recognizes the presence of unacknowledged mainstream elitist norms limiting an appreciation of culturally different individuality and fostering disparities in health/mental health services. It is thus not surprising that change is slow, particularly within professional associations responsive primarily to internal pressure from ethnic minority members that may run counter to larger societal pressures for maintaining the status quo.

The practice of human science remains inherently conservative, modeled on physical science, and shaped by political pressures that mute advocacy to prevent or minimize conflict. Nonetheless, issues of inequality and oppression in a democratic society have to remain in the forefront of professional consciousness. These issues must be routinely and consistently addressed in cultural competency training, research, and practice. Only in this manner can the health/mental health professions engage in reducing existing disparities in access and utilization of health/mental health services for ethnic minority populations.

MULTICULTURAL ASSESSMENT APPLICATIONS

Unfortunately, psychological assessment training has decreased in quality, scope, and adequacy during recent years. First, very limited numbers of tests of intelligence, psychopathology, and personality have been consistently employed (Camara, Nathan, & Puente, 1998: Piotrowski & Belter, 1999). Second, there is been insufficient investigation of how assessment training is conducted (Childs & Eyde, 2002). Third, the median number of required reports using standard instruments in training programs has been too few to demonstrate competence (Stedman, Hatch, & Schoenfeld, 2001). Fourth, most internship programs attempt to remedy perceived deficiencies in assessment skills with standard instruments (Clemence & Handler, 2001). Fifth, graduate training in projective methods for assessment practice during the next century was deemphasized by Division 12 (APA, 1999). This pronouncement has stimulated and supported recent controversy concerning the scientific credibility of projective methods (e.g., Lilienfeld, Wood, & Garb, 2000). Finally, there is insufficient training in measurement and research methodology to minimize bias and develop more credible and substantive knowledge of ethnic minority populations despite the availability of abundant and well-publicized resources within clinical psychology.

As suggested earlier in this chapter, clinical competency and cultural competency have been examined for counseling/psychotherapy, although multicultural assessment competency has not received similar scrutiny. Within counseling psychology, multicultural assessment has been examined in descriptive rather than comparative terms (e.g., Suzuki, Ponterotto, & Meller, 2001). In comparative terms, Dana (2005) described multicultural assessment as coextensive with and predicated upon standard assessment using conventional instruments not explicitly designed for ethnic minority populations in the United States and international populations. Multicultural assessment practice is predicated on multicultural assessment training in courses integrating standard and multicultural assessment (Dana, 2002b) as well as skills training and routine supervision with ethnic minority assessees (Allen, 2006). Professional consensus probably prefers limited training in special courses, workshops, or continuing education.

TEMAS

A projective narrative measure with empirical origins in the research history of the TAT, TEMAS occupies a unique and essential role in the development of assessment competency with multicultural populations. Despite an early history of objective scores and validation for personality and psychopathology description, the TAT has never enjoyed a consensual scoring system in the United States or possessed adequate and contemporary normative data resources. As a result, professional respect for this method eroded over time. Only superficial interpretation training remains in professional doctoral programs (Rossini & Moretti, 1997), although the TAT has retained some residual popularity among clinical and school psychologists and those assessing adolescents (Piotrowski, 1999). By recognizing the merits of projective narratives as assessment resources and attending to historical deficiencies as a test, TEMAS reaffirms, revitalizes, and literally has reinvented the TAT as a major contemporary assessment instrument.

TEMAS is the only comprehensive assessment instrument constructed for ethnic minority and nonminority children/adolescents. TEMAS uniquely considers multicultural assessment test criteria including cultural aegis, theory, stimuli, service delivery social etiquette, scores, norms, and interpretation (Dana, 1993, 1999, in press) described in Table 2–3.

Cultural aegis refers to informed participation in all construction and validation phases. TEMAS developers were expert service providers in the original Puerto Rican/African American cultural communities, and this condition was met for subsequent applications in Taiwan, Argentina, and Italy.

TEMAS has theoretical foundations representing a cross-section of dynamic-cognitive models in psychology. The power of this comprehensive eclecticism is evident in the goodness-of-fit with the new developmental science of positive, strength-based, recovery-oriented human functioning. These test stimuli are congruent with three major ethnic minorities in the United States. Only Native Americans are omitted, and another TAT-derivative card set has been available for use with these populations (Dana, 1982). TEMAS clinicians employ explicit, credible, appropriate

TABLE 2–3. TEMAS Addresses Criteria for a Culturally Sensitive
Assessment Method

Criteria	Description
Cultural Aegis	Developers were either cultural representatives or bicultural/bilingual service providers within each cultural community.
Theory	Dynamic-cognitive assessment model (cognitive psychology, ego psychology, interpersonal psychology, social-cognitive learning theory).
Stimuli	Three sets of pictures in color (Black/Hispanic, Asian, White) represent children/adolescents in everyday conflict-laden situations.
Service Delivery	Routine employment of the client's first language with credible, appropriate, comfortable social etiquette by clinicians who were culturally competent and typically shared cultural identity with clients.
Scores	Quantitative and qualitative objective scores are available for cognitive, emotional, and personality constructs. However, cultural equivalency demonstrations, in addition to translation equivalence, are ultimately necessary.
Norms	Long and short form normalized t scores and percentiles for three age groups and four racial/ethnic groups for urban United States and other countries. To date, normative data has not been stratified by acculturation status moderators.
Interpretation	Normative and idiographic. Social problem-solving/coping skills within culture-specific contexts differentiates specific disorders (e.g., ADHD) and between normal and clinical groups.

service delivery social etiquette for test administration because of a shared common cultural milieu and languages with clients.

The objective TEMAS scores for cognitive, personality, and affective functions are clearly associated with earlier TAT interpretation. The cognitive scores represent formal or structural story features, personality scores address stimulus card pull, and affective scores are derived from portrayal of story characters. In addition to linguistic equivalence of translations, demonstrations of metric and construct equivalencies are ultimately necessary.

Long and short form norms in t-score format and percentiles are available for three age groups and for primarily urban racial/ethnic groups in the United States and other countries. However, this normative data has not been stratified using acculturation status modifiers in the United States for Puerto Ricans and Asian Americans.

TEMAS incorporates both normative and idiographic interpretation. Low inference interpretation from these scores provides information on problem-solving/coping skills within culture-specific contexts. High inference interpretation is used to describe clinical status or specific DSM psychopathology.

TEMAS provides strength-based assessment of positive and negative child/adolescent personality/psychopathology characteristics with direct relevance to diagnosis, prognosis, and development of individualized interventions. TEMAS is also a major contributor to treatment planning and subsequent outcome evaluations. When used as a MAIP model component, TEMAS can be employed cost-effectively in mental health settings that embed multicultural issues in service delivery and services.

REFERENCES

Abe-Kim, J. S., & Takeuchi, D. T. (1996). Cultural competence and quality of care: Issues for mental health service delivery in managed care. *Clinical Psychology: Knowledge and Practice, 3,* 273–295.

Abreu, J. M., Chung, R. H. G., & Atkinson, D. R. (2000). Multicultural counselor training: Past, present, and future directions. *The Counseling Psychologist, 28,* 641–656.

Allen, J. (2006, March). Multicultural assessment supervision: Process, interpretation, and report writing. In R. H. Dana (Chair), *Assessment training and supervision: Tests/methods and reports.* Symposium conducted at the midwinter meeting of the Society for Personality Assessment, San Diego, CA.

Allen-Meares, P., & Garvin, C. (2000). *The handbook of direct practice social work.* Thousand Oaks, CA: Sage.

Allison, K., Crawford, I., Echemendia, R., Robinson, L., & Knepp, D. (1994). Human diversity and professional competence: Training in clinical and counseling psychology revisited. *American Psychologist, 49,* 792–796.

American Psychological Association. (1947). Recommended graduate program in clinical psychology. *American Psychologist, 2,* 539–558.

American Psychological Association. (1999). Assessment for the 21st century: A model curriculum. *Clinical Psychologist, 52,* 10–15.

Ancis, J. R. (2004). *Culturally responsive interventions: Innovative approaches to working with diverse populations.* New York: Brunner-Routledge.

Barker, J. C. (1992). Cross-culture medicine: A decade later. Cultural diversity-Changing the context of medical practice. *Western Journal of Medicine, 157,* 248–254.

Bent-Goodley, T. B. (Ed). (2003). *African-American social workers and social policy.* New York: Haworth Social Work Practice Press.

Bernstein, L., & Dana, R. H. (1970). *Interviewing and the health professions.* New York: Appleton-Century-Crofts.

Bernstein, L., Bernstein, R., & Dana, R. H. (1974). *Interviewing: A guide for health professionals* (2nd ed). New York: Appleton-Century-Crofts.

Berry, J. W. (1999). Emics and etics: A symbiotic conception. *Culture & Psychology, 5(2),* 165–171.

Berry, J. W. (2000). Cross-cultural psychology: A symbiosis of cultural and comparative approaches. *Asian Journal of Social Psychology, 3,* 197–205.

Beutler, L. E., Brown, M. T., Crothers, L., Booker, K., & Seabrook, M. K. (1996). The dilemma of factitious demographic distinctions in psychological research. *Journal of Consulting and Clinical Psychology, 64,* 892–902.

Brown, S. D., & Lent, R. W. (2000). *Handbook of counseling psychology* (3rd ed.). New York: Wiley.

Camara, W. J., Nathan, J. S., & Puente, A. E. (1998). *Psychological test usage in professional psychology: Report to the APA Practice and Science Directorates.* Washington, DC: American Psychological Association.

Cardemil, E. V., & Battle, C. L. (2003). Guess who's coming to therapy? Getting comfortable with conversations about race and ethnicity in psychotherapy. *Professional Psychology: Research and Practice, 34,* 278–286.

Carter, R. T. (1995). *The influence of race and racial identity in psychotherapy: Toward a racially inclusive model.* New York: Wiley.

Carter, R. T. (2003). Becoming racially and culturally competent: The racial–cultural counseling laboratory. *Journal of Multicultural Counseling and Development, 31,* 20–30.

Carter, R. T. (Ed.). (2005). *Handbook of racial-cultural psychology and counseling: Training and practice* (Vol. 2). Hoboken, NJ: Wiley.

Case, L., & Smith, T. B. (2000). Ethnic representation in a sample of the literature of applied psychology journals. *Journal of Consulting and Clinical Psychology, 68,* 1107–111.

Castillo, R. (1997). *Culture and mental illness: A client-centered approach.* Pacific Grove, CA: Brooks/Cole.

Chau, K. L. (1990). A model for teaching cross-cultural practice in social work. *Journal of Social Work Education, 26,* 124–133.

Childs, R. A., & Eyde, L. D. (2002). Assessment training in clinical psychology doctoral programs: What should we teach? What do we teach? *Journal of Personality Assessment, 78,* 130–144.

Chin, J. L. (2002). Assessment of cultural competence in mental health systems of care for Asian Americans. In K. S. Kurasaki, S. Okazaki, & S. Sue (Eds.), Asian American mental health: Assessment, theories, and methods. New York: Kluwer Academic/Plenum Publishers.

Chin, J. L. (2000). Culturally competent health care. *Public Health Reports, 115*, 25–33.

Clemence, A. J., & Handler, L. (2001). Psychological assessment on internship: A survey of training directors and their expectations for students. *Journal of Personality Assessment, 76*, 18–47.

Coleman, H. L. K. (1998). General and multicultural counseling competency: Apples and oranges? *Journal of Multicultural Counseling and Development, 26*, 147–156.

Copeland, E. J. (1982). Minority populations and traditional training programs. *Counselor Education and Supervision, 21*, 187–193.

Council of National Psychological Associations for the Advancement of Ethnic Minority Interests (CNPAAEMI), (2000). *Guidelines for research in ethnic minority communities.* Washington, DC: American Psychological Association.

Council on Social Work Education (2003). *Challenge and change in social work education: Toward a world view. Selected papers by Harman B. Stein.* Alexandria, VA: Author.

Dana, R. H. (1978). Comparisons of competence training in two successful clinical programs. *Psychological Reports, 42*, 919–926.

Dana, R. H. (1982). *Picture-story cards for Sioux/Plains Indians.* Fayetteville, AR: University of Arkansas.

Dana, R. H. (1993). *Multicultural assessment perspectives for professional psychology.* Boston: Allyn & Bacon.

Dana, R. H. (1998a). Personality assessment and the cultural self: Etic and emic contexts as learning resources. In L. Handler & M. Hilsenroth (Eds.)., *Teaching and learning personality assessment* (pp. 325–345). Hillsdale, NJ: Lawrence Erlbaum Associates.

Dana, R. H. (1998b). Multicultural assessment in the United States: Still art, not yet science, and controversial. *European Journal of Personality Assessment, 14*, 62–70.

Dana, R. H. (1998c). *Understanding cultural identity in intervention and assessment.* Thousand Oaks, CA: Sage.

Dana, R. H. (1999). Cross-cultural-multicultural use of the Thematic Apperception Test. In L. Geiser & M. I. Stein (Eds.), *Evocative images: The Thematic Apperception Test and the art of projection* (pp. 177–190). Washington, DC: American Psychological Association.

Dana, R. H. (2000). Culture and methodology in personality assessment. In I. Cuellar & F. Paniagua (Eds.), *Handbook of multicultural mental health: Assessment and treatment of diverse groups* (pp. 97–120). San Diego, CA: Academic Press.

Dana, R. H. (2002a). Examining the usefulness of DSM-IV. In K. Kurasaki, S. Okazaki, & S. Sue (Eds.), *Asian American mental health: Assessment, theories, and methods* (pp. 29–46). New York: Kluwer Academic/Plenum Publishers.

Dana, R. H. (2002b). Introduction to symposium-Multicultural assessment: Teaching methods and competence evaluation. *Journal of Personality Assessment, 79*, 195–199.

Dana, R. H. (2004). A report on myself: The science and/or art of assessment. *Journal of Personality Assessment, 82,* 245–256.

Dana, R. H. (2005). *Multicultural assessment principles, applications, and examples.* Mahwah, NJ: Lawrence Erlbaum Associates.

Dana, R. H. (in press). Culturally competent school assessment: Performance measures of personality. *Psychology in the Schools.*

Dana, R. H., Gilliam, M., & Dana, J. (1976). Adequacy of academic–clinical preparation for internship. *Professional Psychology, 7,* 112–116.

Dana, R. H., & May, W. T. (1987). Overview. In R. H. Dana & W. T. May (Eds.). *Internship training in professional psychology* (pp. 3–74). New York: Hemisphere.

De La Cancela, V., Chin, J. L., & Jenkins, Y. M. (1998). *Community health psychology: Empowerment for diverse communities.* New York: Routledge.

DeLeon, P. H., & VandenBos, G. R. (2000). Reflecting and leading, progress in professional practice of clinical psychology. *Professional Psychology: Research and Practice, 31,* 595–597.

Del Valle, A. G., Merdinger, J. M., Wrenn, R. M., & Miller, D. (1991). The field practicum and transcultural practice. *Journal of Multicultural Social Work, 1,* 45–55.

Donabedian, A. (1978). The quality of medical care: Methods for assessing and monitoring the quality of research for research and for quality assurance programs. *Science, 200,* 856–864.

Eldridge, W. D. (1982). Our preset methods of teaching ethnic and minority content—Why they can't work. *Education, 102,* 335–338.

Farmer, T. W., & Farmer, T. M. Z. (2001). Developmental science, systems of care, and prevention of emotional and behavioral problems of youth. *American Journal of Orthopsychiatry, 71,* 171–181.

Foulks, E., Westermeyer, J., & Ta, K. (1998). Developing curricula for transcultural mental health for trainees and trainers. In S. O. Okpaku (Ed.), *Clinical methods in transcultural psychiatry* (pp. 339–362). Washington, DC: American Psychiatric Press.

Fuertes, J. N., Bartolomeo, M., & Nichols, C. M. (2001). Future research directions in the study of counselor multicultural competency. *Journal of Multicultural Counseling and Development, 29,* 3–12.

Fuertes, J. N., & Brobst, K. (2001). Clients' ratings of counselor multicultural competency. *Cultural Diversity and Ethnic Minority Psychology, 8(3),* 214–233.

Fuertes, J. N., & Brobst, K. (2002). Clients' ratings of counselor multicultural competency. *Cultural Diversity and Ethnic Minority Psychology, 8,* 214–223.

Gamst, G., Dana, R. H., Der-Karabetian, A., Aragon, M., Arellano, L. Morrow, G. et al. (2004). Cultural competency revised: The California Brief Multicultural Competency Scale. *Measurement and Evaluation in Counseling and Development, 82,* 163–183.

Gaw, A. (2001). *The concise guide to cross-cultural psychiatry.* Washington, DC: American Psychiatric Publishing, Inc.

Goh, M. (2005). Cultural competence and master therapists: An inextricable relationship. *Journal of Mental Health Counseling, 27(1)*, 71–81.

Green, J. W. (1999). *Cultural awareness in the human services: A multiethnic approach* (3rd ed.). Boston: Allyn & Bacon.

Greenfield, P. M. (2000). Three approaches to the psychology of culture: Where do they come from? Where can they go? *Asian Journal of Social Psychology, 3*, 223–240.

Hall, G. C. N. (2001). Psychotherapy research with ethnic minorities: Empirical, ethical, and conceptual issues. *Journal of Consulting and Clinical Psychology, 69*, 502—510.

Hall, G. C. N., & Maramba, G. G. (2001). In search of cultural diversity: Recent literature in cross-cultural and ethnic minority psychology. *Cultural Diversity and Ethnic Minority Psychology, 7*, 12–26.

Hays, P. A. (2001). *Addressing cultural complexities in practice: A framework for clinicians and counselors.* Washington, DC: American Psychological Association.

Herrera, J., Lawson, W., & Sramek, J. (Eds.). (1999). *Cross-cultural psychiatry.* New York: Wiley.

Hills, H. I., & Strozier, A. L. (1992). Multicultural training in APA-approved counseling psychology programs: A survey. *Professional Psychology: Research and Practice, 23*, 43–51.

Huff, R. M., & Kline, M. V. (1999). The cultural assessment framework. In R. M. Huff & M. V. Kline (Eds.), *Promoting health in multicultural populations: A handbook for practitioners* (pp. 481–489). Thousand Oaks, CA: Sage.

Iglehart, A., & Becerra, R. M. (1995). *Social services and the ethnic community.* Boston: Allyn & Bacon.

Jackson, L. C. (1999). Ethnocultural resistance to multicultural training: Students and faculty. *Cultural Diversity and Ethnic Minority Psychology, 5*, 27–36.

Jordan, C., & Franklin, C. (2003). *Clinical assessment for social workers: Qualitative and quantitative methods* (2nd ed.). Chicago: Lyceum Books.

Kahn, J. S., & Denmon, J. (1997). An examination of social science literature pertaining to multiracial identity: A historical perspective. *Journal of Multicultural Social Work, 6(1/2)*, 117–137.

Kerl, S. B. (2002). Using narrative approaches to teach multicultural competency. *Journal of Multicultural Counseling and Development, 30*, 135–143.

Kleinman, A. (1977). Lessons from a clinical approach to medical anthropology research. *Medical Anthropology Newsletter, 8*, 11–16

Kleinman, A. (1978). Concepts and a model for the comparison of medical systems as cultural systems. *Social Science & Medicine, 12*, 85–93.

Kleinman, A. (1988). *Rethinking psychiatry: From cultural category to personal experience.* New York: Free Press.

Kohatsu, E. L. & Richardson, T. Q. (1996). Racial and ethnic identity assessment. In L. A. Suzuki, P. J. Miller, & J. G. Ponterroto (Eds.), *Handbook of multicultural assessment: Clinical, psychological, and educational applications* (pp. 611–650). San Francisco, CA: Jossey-Bass.

LaFromboise, T. D., & Foster, S. L. (1992). Cross-cultural training: Scientist-practitioner model and methods. *The Counseling Psychologist, 20,* 472–489.

Larson, D. B., Lu, F. G., & Swyers, J. P. (Eds.), (1997) *Model curriculum for psychiatry residency training programs: Religion and spirituality in clinical practice* (Rev. ed). Rockville, MD: National Institute for Healthcare Research.

Lee, M.-Y. (1996). A constructivist approach to the help-seeking process of clients: A response to cultural diversity. *Journal of Clinical Social Work, 24,* 187–202.

Leininger, M. (1970). *Nursing and anthropology: Two worlds to blend.* New York: Wiley.

Leininger, M. (1991). *Culture care diversity and universality: A theory of nursing.* New York: National League for Nursing Press.

Leininger, M., & McFarland, M. R. (2002). *Transcultural nursing concepts, theories, research, and practice* (3rd ed). New York: McGraw-Hill.

Lewis-Fernandez, R. (1966). Cultural formulations of psychiatry diagnosis. *Culture, Medicine, and Psychiatry, 20,* 133–144.

Like, R. C., Steiner, R. P., & Rubel, A. J. (1996). Recommended core curriculum guidelines on culturally sensitive and competent health care. *Family Medicine, 27,* 291–297.

Lilienfeld, S. O., Wood, J. M., & Garb, H. N. (2000). The scientific status of projective techniques. *Psychological Science in the Public Interest, 1(2),* 27–66.

Lipson, J. G. (1996). Culturally competent nursing care. In J. G. Lipson, S. L. Dibble, & P. A. Minarik (Eds), *Culture and nursing care: A pocket guide* (pp. 1–6). San Francisco: UCSF Nursing Press.

Lipson, J. G., Dibble, S. L., & Minarik, P. A. (Eds.). (1996). *Culture and nursing care: A pocket guide.* San Francisco: UCSF Nursing Press.

Lipson, J. G., & Meleis, A. I. (1985). Culturally appropriate care: The case of immigrants. *Topics in Clinical Nursing, 7(3),* 48–56.

Lohmann, R. A., & Lohmann, N. (2002). *Social administration.* New York: Columbia University Press.

Lonner, W. J., & Hayes, S. A. (2004). Understanding the cognitive and social aspects of intercultural competence. In R. J. Sternberg & E. L. Grigorenko (Eds.), *Culture and competence: Contexts of life success* (pp. 89–110). Washington, DC: American Psychological Association.

Lopez, S. R. (1997). Cultural competence in psychotherapy: A guide for clinicians and their supervisors. In C. E. Watkins (Ed.), *Handbook of psychotherapy supervision* (pp. 570–588). New York: Wiley.

Lu, F. G., Lin, R. F., & Mezzich, J. E. (1995). Issues in the assessment and diagnosis of culturally diverse individuals. In J. M. Oldham & M. B. Riba (Eds.), *Review of psychiatry* (Vol. 14, pp. 477–510). Washington, DC: American Psychiatric Press.

Lum, D. (1999). *Culturally competent practice.* Pacific Grove, CA: Brooks/Cole.

McGlynn, E. A., Norquist, G. S., Wells, K. B., Sullivan, G., & Liberman, R. P. (1988). Quality of care research in mental health: Responding to the challenge. *Inquiry, 25,* 157–170.

McMiller, W. P., & Weisz, J. R. (1996). Help-seeking preceding mental health clinic intake among African-American, Latino, and Caucasian youths. *Journal of the American Academy of Child and Adolescent Psychiatry, 35,* 1086–1094.

McPhatter, A. R. (1997). Cultural competence in child welfare: What is it? How do we achieve it? What happens without it? *Child Welfare, 50,* 255–278.

Mezzich, J. E., Kleinman, A., Fabrega, H. Jr., & Parron, D. L. (1996). *Culture and psychiatric diagnosis: A DSM-IV perspective.* Washington, DC: American Psychiatric Press.

Mollen, D., Ridley, C. R., & Hill, C. L. (2003). Models of multicultural counseling competence. In D. B. Pope-Davis, H. L. K. Coleman, W. M. Liu, & R. L. Toporek (Eds.), *Handbook of multicultural competencies in counseling and psychology* (pp. 21–37. Thousand Oaks, CA: Sage.

Munley, P. H., Anderson, M. Z., Baines, T. C., Borgman, A. L., Briggs, D., Dolan, J. P. Jr. et al. (2002). Personal dimensions of identity and empirical research in APA journals. *Cultural Diversity and Ethnic Minority Psychology, 8,* 357–365.

Murphy, M. C., Wright, B. V., & Bellamy, D. E. (1995). Multicultural training in university counseling center predoctoral psychology internship programs: A survey. *Journal of Multicultural Counseling and Development, 23,* 170–180.

Nilsson, J. E., Berkel, L. A., Flores, L. Y., Love, K. M., Wendler, A. M., & Mecklenberg, E. C. (2003). An 11-year review of professional psychology: Research and practice: Content and sample analysis with an emphasis on diversity. *Professional Psychology: Research and Practice, 34,* 611–616.

Pack-Brown, S. P. (1999). Racism and White counselor training: Influence of White racial identity theory and research. *Journal of Counseling and Development, 77,* 87–92.

Pack-Brown, S. P., & Williams, C. B. (2003). *Ethics in a multicultural context.* Thousand Oaks, CA: Sage.

Paniagua, F. (2000). Culture-bound syndromes, cultural variations, and psychopathology. In I. Cuellar & F. Paniagua (Eds), *Handbook of multicultural mental health: Assessment and treatment of diverse populations* (pp. 139–169). San Diego: Academic Press.

Paniagua, F. (2005). *Assessing and treating culturally diverse individuals* (3rd ed.). Thousand Oaks, CA: Sage.

Pedersen, P. B., Draguns, J. G., Lonner, W. J., & Trimble, J. E. (Eds.). (2002). *Counseling across cultures* (5th ed.). Thousand Oaks, CA: Sage.

Pedersen, P. B., & Ivey, A. (1993). *Culture-centered counseling skills.* Westport, CT: Greenwood Press.

Piotrowski, C. (1999). Assessment practices in the era of managed care: current status and future directions. *Journal of Clinical Psychology, 55,* 787–796.

Piotrowski, C., & Belter, R. W. (1999). Internship training in psychological assessment: Has managed care had an impact? *Assessment, 6,* 381–389.

Ponterotto, J. G. (1998). Charting a course for research in multicultural counseling training. *The Counseling Psychologist, 26,* 43-68.

Ponterotto, J. G. (2004). Racism: The White problem. *Counseling Psychology APA Review of Books, 49,* 663–666.

Ponterotto, J. G., Casas, J. M., Suzuki, L. A., & Alexander, C. M. (Eds.). (2001). *Handbook of multicultural counseling* (2nd ed.). Thousand Oaks, CA: Sage.

Ponterotto, J. G., Fuertes, J. N., & Chen, E. C. (2000). Models of multicultural counseling. In J. S. Brown & R. W. Lent (Eds.), *Handbook of counseling psychology* (3rd ed; pp. 639–669). New York: Wiley.

Ponterotto, J. G., Gretchen, D., & Chauhan, R. V. (2000). Cultural identity and multicultural assessment: Quantitative and qualitative tools for the clinician. In L. A. Suzuki, J. G. Ponterotto, & A. P. Meller (Eds.), *Handbook of multicultural assessment: Clinical, psychological, and educational applications* (2nd ed; pp. 67–99). San Francisco: Jossey-Bass.

Ponterotto, J. G., Gretchen, D., Utsey, S. O., Rieger, B. P., & Austin, R. (2002). A revision of the Multicultural Counseling Awareness Scale. *Journal of Multicultural Counseling and Development, 30,* 153–180.

Pope-Davis, D. B., Coleman, H. L. K., Liu, W. M. & Toporek, R. L. (2003). *Handbook of multicultural competencies in counseling and psychotherapy.* Thousand Oaks, CA: Sage.

Pope-Davis, D. B., Liu, W. M., Toporek, R. L., & Brittan-Powell, C. S. (2001). What's missing from multicultural competency research: Review, introspection, and recommendations. *Cultural Diversity and Ethnic Minority Psychology, 7,* 121–138.

Rogers, M. R. (2005). Multicultural training in school psychology. In C. L. Frisby & C. R. Reynolds (Eds.), *Comprehensive handbook of multicultural school psychology* (pp. 993–1022). Hoboken, NJ: Wiley.

Rogler, L. H. (1993). Culturally sensitizing psychiatric diagnosis. *The Journal of Nervous and Mental Disease, 181,* 401–408.

Rogler, L. H. (1996). Framing research on culture in psychiatric diagnosis: The case of DSM-IV. *Psychiatry, 59,* 145–155.

Rossini, E. D., & Moretti, R. J. (1997). Thematic Apperception Test (TAT) interpretation: Practice recommendations from a survey of clinical psychology doctoral programs accredited by the American Psychological Association. *Professional Psychology: Research and Practice, 28,* 393–398.

Rounds, K. A., Weil, M., & Bishop, K. K. (1994). Practice with culturally diverse families of young children with disabilities. *Families in Society, 75,* 3–15.

Roysircar, G. (2004). Cultural self-awareness: Practice examples from psychology training. *Professional Psychology: Research and Practice, 35,* 658–666.

Ruiz, P. (Ed). (2000). *Ethnicity and psychopharmacology.* Washington, DC: APPI Press.

Sevig, T., & Etzkom, J. (2001). Transformative training: A year-long seminar for graduate students. *Journal of Multicultural Counseling and Development, 29,* 57–73.

Simon, B. L. (1994). *The empowerment tradition in American social work: A history.* New York: Columbia University Press.

Skovholt, T. M., & Jennings, L. (2004). *Master therapists: Exploring expertise in therapy and counseling.* Boston: Allyn & Bacon.

Snowden, L. R. (2000). The new world of practice in physical and mental health: Comorbidity, cultural competence, and managed care. In P. Allen-Meares & C. Garvin (Eds), *The Handbook of Social Work Practice* (pp. 437–450). Thousand Oaks, CA: Sage.

Stedman, J. M., Hatch, J. P., & Schoenfeld, L. S. (2001). The current status of psychological assessment training in graduate and professional schools. *Journal of Personality Assessment, 77,* 398–407.

Stedman, J. M., Hatch, J. P., Schoenfeld, L. S., & Keilin, W. G. (2005). The structure of internship training: Current patterns and implications for the future of clinical and counseling psychologists. *Professional Psychology: Research and Practice, 36,* 3–8.

Sue, D. (1997). Multicultural training. *International Journal of Intercultural Relations, 21,* 175–193.

Sue, D. W. (2001a). Multidimensional facets of cultural competence. *The Counseling Psychologist, 29,* 790–821.

Sue, D. W. (2001b). The superordinate nature of cultural competence. *The Counseling Psychologist, 29,* 850–857.

Sue, D. W. (2003). *Overcoming our racism: The journey to liberation.* San Francisco: Jossey-Bass.

Sue, D. W., Arredondo, P., & McDavis, R. J. (1992). Multicultural counseling competencies and standards: A call to the profession. *Journal of Counseling and Development, 70,* 477–486.

Sue, D. W., Bernier, J. E., Duran, A., Feinberg, L., Pedersen, P., Smith, E. J. et al. (1982). Position paper: Cross-cultural counseling competencies. *The Counseling Psychologist, 10,* 45–52.

Sue, D. W., & Sue, D. (2003). *Counseling the culturally diverse: Theory and practice* (4th ed). New York: John Wiley & Sons.

Sue, S., & Sue, L. (2003). Ethnic science is good science. In G. Bernal, J. E. Trimble, A. K. Burlew, & F. T. Leong, (Eds.), *Handbook of racial and ethnic minority psychology* (pp. 198–207). Thousand Oaks, CA: Sage.

Suzuki, L. A., Ponterotto, J. G., & Meller, P. J. (2001). *Handbook of multicultural assessment: Clinical, psychological, and educational applications* (2nd ed). San Francisco: Jossey-Bass.

Thyer, B. A. (1997). *Controversial issues in social work education.* Boston: Allyn & Bacon.

Toporek, R. L., & Reza, J. V. (2001). Context as a critical dimension of multicultural counseling: Articulating personal, professional, and institutional competence. *Journal of Multicultural Counseling and Development, 29,* 13–31.

Tseng, W-S. (2001). *Handbook of cultural psychiatry.* San Diego: Academic Press.

Tseng, W-S. (2003). *Clinician's guide to cultural psychiatry.* New York: Elsevier.

Tseng, W-S, & Streltzer, J. (Eds.). (2004). *Cultural competence in clinical psychiatry.* Washington, DC: American Psychiatric Press.

Vazquez, L. A., & Garcia-Vazquez, E. (2003). Teaching multicultural competence in the counseling curriculum. In D. B. Pope-Davis, H. L. K. Coleman, W. M. Liu, &

R. L. Toporek (Eds.), *Handbook of multicultural competencies in counseling and psychology* (pp. 547–561). Thousand Oaks, CA: Sage.

Vernon, A., & Clemente, R. (2005). *Assessment and intervention with children and adolescents: Developmental and multicultural approaches* (2nd ed). Alexandria, VA: American Counseling Association.

Weaver, H. N. (2005). *Explorations in cultural competence: Journeys to the four directions.* Belmont, CA: Thomson Brooks/Cole.

Wells, K. B., & Brook, R. H. (1989). The quality of mental health services: Past, present, and future. In C. Taube, D. Mechanic, and A. Hohmann (Eds.), *The future of mental health services* (DHHS Publication No. ADM 89-1600, pp. 203–224). Washington, DC: U.S. Government Printing Office.

Wittkower, E. D., & Prince, R. (1974). A review of transcultural psychiatry. In G. Caplan (Ed.), *American handbook of psychiatry* (2nd ed.; Vol. 2, pp. 535–550). New York: Basic Books.

3

Picture-Story Performance Instruments for Children and Adolescents

This chapter initially addresses the changing role of psychological science in shaping the contemporary development of storytelling instruments. These instruments contribute to a renaissance of comprehensive personality-psychopathology assessment for all child/adolescent populations. Availability of adequate, consistent, and reliable personality and psychopathology information lies at the heart of a reconstituted multicultural assessment-intervention process. This process provides a vehicle for the new recovery-oriented, positive science of human development for all children and adolescents, nationally and internationally.

In the United States, picture-story instruments began with the TAT during an era when psychologists were deciding their future scientific destiny. Author and TAT progenitor Henry Murray was a scholar, trained in medicine, psychoanalysis, and physiological chemistry. His conception of personality included biology and behavior flavored by assumptions of unconscious motivation, determinism, levels of personality, and the pervasive influence of the environment. He believed human beings constituted an open system with possibilities for growth and change; he explicitly denied premature closure to his theory by describing it as a "scaffolding" because "life is a continuous procession of explorations, surmises, hunches, guesses, and experiments, failures and successes, of relearnings-agings, consisting of a sequence of gradual and occasionally abrupt indurations (rigidifications, solidifications, fixations, hardenings) both of forms and functions" (Murray, 1959, pp. 18–19).

Murray's "precocious and omnivorous awareness of all manifestations of science provided a catholicism that rendered him a human science model practitioner before there was a proper label for this orientation" (Dana, 1982a, p. 22). History, however, provided an ironic fate for Murray by neglecting his *presses* and pursuing a rigorous approach to measuring a small number of *needs* by coding systems within a context of psychological science that forestalled any immediate development of a comprehensive, consensual TAT scoring system (Dana, 1968). As a result, the subsequent history of personality assessment in the United States was not appreciably influenced by Murray's scientific eclecticism. TAT low inference scores for needs survived for research purposes independently of the high inference primarily psychodynamic interpretation typically employed in practice (Rossini & Moretti, 1997).

Psychological science, as a proper model for understanding human beings, was not guided by Murray's catholicism but instead was subsequently shaped by Boring's (1929) eloquence, scholarship, and persuasiveness. Arguing for an experimental science derived from biology and Newtonian classical physics, nature was defined as independent of human beings and, thus, objectively observable and ultimately amenable to human control. A legitimate science for Boring was conducted in the laboratory with procedures to control a process dictating where the investigation looked and what was to be observed. A 19th-Century science, congruent with Euro-American population homogeneity, relatively slow change, and perdurable values, was less viable in the presences of political, economic, and social stressors attending the transformation from an agrarian to an industrial society punctuated by two world wars.

Boring's science was an ideology, an organized set of measurable ideas, passionately advocated, controversial, and lacking unequivocal substantiation (Tomkins, 1963). The experimental psychologists implementing Boulder model training preferred students who shared their scientific ideology advocating compliance to a norm, standard, or ideal essence as contrasted with a humanistic ideology identifying the person as the locus of value (Nesbitt, 1959). These contrasting interpretations of reality yield somewhat different perspectives for understanding human beings.

A method-centered science served strong needs for reassurance and certainty during societal change, although many psychologists perceived this science as incomplete for describing human beings. For example, "The stipulation that psychology be adequate to science outweighed the commitment that it be adequate to man" (Koch, 1969, p. 64). Koch (1981) also described method-generated knowledge as *ameaningful thought* and identified *epistemopathies* as pathologies of knowledge constraining an understanding of human beings. Sampson subsequently (1985) described the use of scientific method and derivative psychometrics in the United States as a centralized, coherent, equilibrium-preserving structure within a society driven by a person system of money, power, and *egocentric control* in the relative absence of *sociocentric coherence,* a person system fostering blurred self–other distinctions with cross-cutting ties and many-sided relationships.

The implications of this controversy permit description of several inter-related contemporary assessment outcomes: (a) student selection and assessment training; (b) preoccupation with low inference interpretation; (c) failure to develop comprehensive scoring systems for storytelling instruments; (d) and delayed consensus on the codetermining, coextensive, and inseparable nature of assessment and intervention. These assessment outcomes provide a context for evaluating the major storytelling instruments.

STUDENT SELECTION AND ASSESSMENT TRAINING

Shakow (1976) advocated a blend of scientific and humanistic ideologies, or nomothetic and idiographic approaches, as ideal for training scientist-professionals in Boulder model programs. Despite this vision, prospective students preferring nomothetic approaches were increasingly selected on the basis of a normative ideology, an experimentation factor, objectively perceived reality, and social responsibility ethics. These Alpha students were distinguished from Beta students who shared a humanistic ideology, a social concern factor, subjectively perceived reality, and personal conscience ethics (Dana, 1982a, 1987; Dana & May, 1987).

Shaffer (1953) identified objective or intuitive attitudes of Alpha and Beta students, respectively, that became more polarized over time (Garfield & Kurtz, 1976). Many Beta students and faculty (Lipsey, 1974) were alienated by a psychological science predicated on values and methods implying a subject–object split and professionally socializing "a clinician who does *something* to someone else and observes the outcome in a scientific if not an Olympian manner" (Dana, 1966a, p. 132).

Kimble (1984) subsequently identified relevant values (scientific vs. humanistic), lawfulness of behavior (determinism vs. indeterminism), basic knowledge sources (observation vs. intuition), setting-for-discovery (laboratory vs. field study/case history/comprehensive assessment), generality of laws (nomothetic vs. idiographic), and level of analysis (elementarism vs. holism) that characterized these polarized psychologists. Frank (1984) described their vocational differences, needs, personality traits, cognitive abilities and predisposing childhood experiences as

correlates of scientific and humanistic values. Conway (1988; 1992) systematically documented these individual differences in a survey of clinical
psychologists who were scientists (Alphas), practitioners (Betas), and scientist-practitioners (Alpha-Betas). These differences in epistemic values and
theoretical orientations, cognitive and personality attributes, and critical
developmental incidents in professional development provided a milestone
description of psychologists' scientific and humanistic values (Conway,
1992). The Scientist-Practitioner Inventory (Leong & Zachar, 1991; Zachar
& Leong, 2000) subsequently provided quantified measures of the personality styles responsible for differences among these professional
groups (Zachar & Leong, 1992).

Although Boulder model training was originally designed to accommodate both Alpha and Beta students (e.g., Clark, 1973; Dana, 1978), professional preparation fostered an explicit normative ideology and over
time preferred students who were comfortable with method-centered
psychological science. Although the Vail model was designed at a later
date to implement a practitioner-scholar perspective (see Dana & May,
1987), diluted Boulder model science requirements ultimately prevailed
in these programs and eventually in all professional programs (e.g., for
assessment implications, see Dana, 1992).

Boring's positivist-empiricist science, employed in Boulder model
scientist-professional training, was a precursor of contemporary method-
derived and evidence-based practice. A small number of standard tests
and methods with predominantly low inference interpretation were
mandatory in assessment training. Research was restricted to the psychometric properties of these instruments predicated on the assumed universality of their applications with all persons.

LOW INFERENCE INTERPRETATION: NECESSARY
AND INCOMPLETE

During the 1940s and 1950s, psychodynamically oriented psychologists
(Betas) assumed major responsibility for assessment training but were
gradually replaced by Alpha graduates from Boulder model programs.
Some early student consumers of high inference interpretation assessment training eschewed objective scoring and low inference interpretation
especially for projective methods, whereas others scrupulously developed
low inference objective TAT scores and normative data that gradually
became the *sine qua non* of personality assessment instruments described as

tests. For example, my own undergraduate Rorschach and TAT instruction preceded training in a Boulder model program and development of objective TAT scores in a dissertation (Dana, 1955).

Preoccupation with method-oriented assessment increased over time and precluded development of comprehensive scoring systems or sustained attention to the range and richness of human problems germane to TAT interpretation (Shneidman, 1951, 1999). Only a small number of these early scores were represented in subsequent TAT training (Vane, 1981) that soon became "a doctrinaire integration of inferred psychoanalytic interpretation" (Rossini & Moretti, 1997, p. 395) that deprived the TAT of status as a test (Moretti & Rossini, 2004).

Thus, the potentially rich early interpretation harvest of TAT scores was put on hold. The TAT was used clinically primarily within a variety of restrictive interpretive frames-of-reference by high inference assessors. In a similar vein, this inattention coincided with an increasingly limited focus and process of psychological assessment. Over time, academic assessment training minimized preparation of competent psychological reports (Clemence & Handler, 2001) although there has been renewed attention to the difficulty of report writing per se (Handler, 2005) and particularly for description of assessees who are not middle-class, White Euro-Americans (Dana, 2005).

Within the positivist-empiricist climate in the United States, psychologists quickly embraced the scientific virtue of general laws for group behavior derived from methodological concern with data, or nomothesis. Individual differences were subsequently minimized by prioritization of a statistical-actuarial approach. This dichotomy was expressed by actuarial versus clinical prediction in clinical settings, crystallizing the distinctiveness of low and high inference interpretive approaches. The study of individuals, or idiography, represented historically in measurement by Allport (1962) and practiced by psychoanalysts, gradually became of secondary interest. The dilemma of how to make the particular express the general, elucidated by Gide (1952), is a reminder that falsely dichotomizing nomothesis and idiography by contrasting actuarial and clinical prediction in assessment practice has not served psychological science well over time.

This debate, described historically as a false dichotomy (e.g., Dana, 1966b, 1982a; DuMas, 1955; Holzberg, 1957), has always been amenable to resolution. Nonetheless, empirically informed rapproachment is recent (Westen & Weinberger, 2004) and predicated on acceptance of an enlarged frame-of-reference for understanding the necessity for clinical practice incorporating both low and high inference interpretation. In the immediate present, these scientific issues contribute to an artificial separation of human similarities and differences represented by a search for general laws and individual/cultural differences. These polarized etic or universal and emic or culture-specific perspectives deterred acceptance of an etic–emic paradigm in cross-cultural assessment as well as recognition of the necessity for employing both culture-general and culture-specific instruments and interventions (Dana, 1998, 2005).

SCORING SYSTEMS: ELUSIVE, BELATED, AND MANDATORY

The failure of Murray's comprehensive scoring system to be accepted also signaled a disinclination to combine objective TAT scores into comprehensive interpretive systems in the United States. In the absence of similar historical constraints, a comprehensive scoring system was feasible in Spain (Avila-Espada, 2000). Although the TAT still retains significant popularity, frequency of usage has somewhat diminished over time in psychological constituencies (Piotrowski, 1999), exclusive reliance on psychoanalytic interpretation has been questioned (Moretti & Rossini, 2004), and the instrument has been repeatedly evaluated as poor science (e.g., Lilienfeld, Wood, & Garb, 2000, 2001).

Nonetheless, the recent APA-published retrospective–prospective TAT appreciation (Gieser & Stein, 1999) signaled a renewal of professional recognition and interest. The TAT was not only useful for assessment of multicultural populations (Dana, 1999, 2005), but the TAT-derived TEMAS was designed and validated for this purpose (Costantino & Malgady, 1999). A compilation of objective TAT scores into a reference handbook may rekindle professional interest in the TAT (Jenkins, in press). Earlier organized reviews of TAT scoring variables have also contributed to the likelihood of developing a comprehensive and consensual TAT scoring system (Teglasi, 1993, 2001). These recent TAT contributions serve to legitimize the employment of picture-story narrative instruments with low inference objective scores for comprehensive assessment objectives.

ASSESSMENT PRACTICE: INTERPRETATION AS INTERVENTION

There has been a recent shift in understanding the assessment process predicated on reconciling discrepant views of the nature of assessment science and the relationship of this science to practice. A demonstrable role for therapeutic assessment has occurred as a result of increasing recognition that assessment and intervention are part and parcel of the same healing process. This role also informs the assessment process as a major component in a judgment-based practice of care that can "address the whole life of an individual … aim(s) at the betterment of specific life areas" (Polkinghorne, 2004, p. 1).

Polkinghorne (2004) examined the history of psychotherapy during three time periods or phases in case study format. In Phase 1 (1890–1950), diagnostic tests and psychotherapy were considered as medical practice. In Phase 2 (1950–1990), Boulder model training, "the scientist-practitioner model turned out to be a scientist model that generated findings to be implemented by practitioners" (p. 183). A very small number of these practitioners preferred an instrumental stance in which decisions were based exclusively on research-generated knowledge due to the belief that anecdotal and experiential knowledge was faulty (Cohen, Sargent, & Sechrest, 1986). Confirming what was suggested earlier in this chapter, approximately one third of practitioners preferred their in-situation judgment rather than academic research, whereas others practitioners used this research merely as an information resource.

In Phrase 3 (1990–now), managed care replaced indemnity policies with limited payment for medically necessary services required for a return to functional daily living. Utilization review boards gradually replaced practitioner judgment. Health care management technification questioned the cost-effectiveness of conventional psychotherapies and led to the use of brief, manualized interventions of empirically demonstrated effectiveness employed by subdoctoral therapists. These changes contrasted with Seligman's (1995) report that psychotherapy effectiveness was not predicated on applying particular techniques with specific diagnoses and Wampold's (2001) conclusion that a common core of psychotherapeutic practices abets recovery and growth. Polkinghorne (2004) concluded that it is not technification of practice that dramatically affects psychotherapy but judgment-based practice.

PICTURE-STORY INSTRUMENT PERSPECTIVES

This section begins by identifying the range and variety of available picture-story performance instruments. A number of instruments differing from TEMAS in stimuli, construction, and administration are described at the onset to provide an introductory context for a few similar and potentially competitive instruments. Subsequent sections present an abbreviated history of adapted multicultural/cross-cultural picture-story instruments and critical reviews of these instruments, leading to a discussion of a number of previously developed desiderata or criteria for this purpose. These desiderata are then applied to TEMAS and similar instruments.

Dissimilar Instruments

Seven of these instruments are nonverbal, require card selection, present partial stories for completion, depict nonhuman figures, or have histories of use exclusively with child/adolescent White populations. These instruments include: (a) the Missouri Children's Picture Series (Sines, Pauker, & Sines, 1963), a unique, 238-card, nonverbal sorting task requesting children to make "fun" and "nonfun" choices related to personality scores by behavioral and other test data; (b) The School Apperception Story Procedure (Jones, 2001) that requires selection of three cards from 15 cards for "good school," "bad school," "happy school," "sad school," "liked school," and "disliked school" stories; (c) The Make-A-Picture-Story Test (Shneidman, 1951) that requires selection from a large number of characters for placement on cards before storytelling and a modified administration requiring selection of both cards and characters by assesses; (d) The Once-Upon-A-Time Test (Fagulha, 1993) which presents partial-story cartoon pictures developed from psychoanalytic functions of play to be completed by children's stories; (e) The Blacky Pictures (Blum, 1950) and (f) the Children's Apperception Test (Bellak & Bellak, 1949), which employ animal pictures designed to represent psychoanalytic concepts; and (g) The Fairy Tale Test that uses cartoon fairy tale figures (Coulacoglou & Kine, 1995).

Two of these tests with applications primarily in Europe, the Once-Upon-A-Time Test and the Fairy Tale Test, were reviewed elsewhere for comparison with TEMAS (Dana, 2006). These instruments were excluded from further consideration and are not reviewed in greater detail here because of limited comparability with TEMAS due to their stimuli, nature of task, directions, paucity of normative and validation data, and minimal use with multicultural populations.

Similar Instruments

Other picture-story performance instruments employ pictorial stimulus cards, use standard storytelling directions, analyze stories with reliable coding procedures, and provide scores for interpretation employing normative data and validation information. The following instruments meet these criteria: Apperceptive Personality Test (APT; Holstrom, Karp, & Silber, 1990); Children's Apperceptive Story-Telling Test (CAST; Schneider, 1989); Michigan Picture Test (MPT; Hutt, 1980); Roberts Apperception Test for Children (RATC; McArthur & Roberts, 1982); and the Symonds Picture Story Test (SPST; Symonds, 1949). The MPT and SPST were constructed primarily for employment with White child/adolescent populations, make no provisions for multicultural assessment, and are no longer published or readily available (Kroon, Goudena, & Rispens, 1998).

ADAPTING PICTURE-STORY INSTRUMENTS FOR MULTICULTURAL POPULATIONS

Culture-Specific Instrument Adaptations

A large number of picture-story instruments have used redrawn Murray TAT cards (M-TAT; 1943) with altered features and/or skin color, clothing, backgrounds, and situations, designed new cards, or employed combinations of both procedures. These adaptations were designed historically for multicultural populations in the United States, particularly African Americans and Native Americans as well as for indigenous populations worldwide. Many adapted card sets were developed, and these early studies had considerable face validity and popular appeal. A number of reviews describe these culture-specific sets of TAT cards adapted for children and adults in the United States and throughout the world (e.g., Bellak & Abrams, 1997; Dana, 1993, 1999, 2005; Jacquemin, 1982; Retief, 1987; Ritzler, 2004; Yeh & Yeh, 2002). Bellak and Abrams describe a variety of culture-specific TAT cards worldwide and in a context of culture, gender, and power bias. The reviews by Jacquemin, Retief, and Yeh and Yeh, in particular, introduce a wider range of M-TAT variants employed in Africa and Asia.

This history of adapted card set examples is predicated on early recognition and delineation of the range and importance of research reviews of picture stimuli (see, Dana, 1982a; Murstein, 1961). Sherwood's (1957) independent outline of psychological dimensions and characteristics important in designing adapted cards for applications with South African cultural/racial groups contributed to this awareness. Thirteen design characteristics (i.e., image sharpness–vagueness, incompleteness, compression, range of presented objects, emotional tone, representation of basic family relationships as well as other important relationships, familiarity of relationships, symbolism, visual impact contrasts, appropriateness of human figures, physical environment, and interpersonal situations) were used to design 12 pilot cards. The effectiveness of these cards with high and low acculturated Swazi was evaluated by length of responses and number of introduced figures/objects/events, as well as response relevance to specific areas, plot varieties, and imaginative quality. This evaluation resulted in redrawing these modified pictures for application in Sherwood's (1961) unpublished dissertation. Sherwood recommended employment of a theoretical frame of reference to define relevant personality areas for subsequent picture design for empirical studies in the United States (Dana, 1968).

Several selected contemporary examples of adapted card sets used in the United States for African Americans and Native Americans with relevance for TEMAS are described next. For African Americans, the Thompson Modification (T-TAT; 1949) altered the M-TAT cards to represent African Americans by changing only the faces. Other authors questioned Thompson's assumptions of African American population homogeneity, identification difficulty with White figures in M-TAT cards, and the adequacy of comparisons between M-TAT and T-TAT cards (Korchin, Mitchell, & Meltzoff, 1950). Research suggested storytelling was facilitated with redrawn cards that were more like "people in general," although culture-relevant background stimuli was also necessary (Bailey & Green, 1977).

A second measure, with 20 charcoal drawings, the Themes Concerning Blacks Test (TCB; Williams, 1972) depicted aspects of urban and rural African American lifestyles in backgrounds. These scenes yielded common themes; academic motivation, aggression, athletic drive, achievement, autonomy, Black pride, identification, self-confidence, and socialization (affiliation and interpersonal relations) in children. Continuing research comparing the TCB with M-TAT indicated greater TCB story length, identification, achievement, and positive feeling tone, and no significant differences were found between African American samples in the United States, African Dutch, and African Surinamers (Hoy-Watkins & Jenkins-Monroe, in press).

Hoy (1997) subsequently developed the Contemporized-Themes Concerning Blacks Text (C-TCB) to include contemporary African American psychosocial experiences in addition to the original Afrocentric theoretical perspective (Williams & Johnson, 1981). The C-TCB is compared favorably with TEMAS later in this chapter.

Despite this proliferation of M-TAT adaptations for many Native American tribes historically accompanied by a review of these studies (Lindzey, 1961), the only available contemporary set of redrawn pictures is for the Lakota Sioux tribe and other Plains Indians (Dana, 1982b). A review of personality assessment for native populations (Allen, 1998) included these Lakota card reproductions and referred to earlier interpretive guidelines (Dana, 1993) and Monopoli's (1984) summary of TAT expectations for traditional Native Americans. Allen also reiterated the earlier contents of these guidelines "that picture story interpretation can only be performed by assessors familiar with the Indian person's cultural setting, and the accompanying tribal history, philosophy, healing practices, language conventions, and cultural expectations regarding service delivery style" (p. 33). The increasing numbers of these card sets now used for assessment training, research, and practice applications in native communities by culturally competent doctoral-level psychologists should reduce assessment bias in these settings.

Lindzey (1952) described limitations and advantages contained in interpretive assumptions of early cross-cultural studies using picture-story measures. These assumptions include equal card significance, identifications with heroes, other characters, or with introduced characters, separation of real-life past or present personal experiences from fantasy, and difficulty recognizing direct and symbolic referents to conscious behavior contextualized by cultural determinants and group memberships. A half-century later "these assumptions (continue to) articulate what assessees can do with a storytelling task, but interpretation must (still) be augmented by including stimulus values of cards, selection of cards, directions for the storytelling task, and recommended interpretation prerequisites and guidelines for processing story contents" (Dana, 2005, p. 177). Hofer and Chasiotis (2004) illustrated this continuing dilemma with examples emphasizing the need for careful design and culturally informed, consensual procedures at every phase in the comparative TAT research process.

Adaptation: A Controversy

Instrument and interpretation adaptations, or corrections for culture, for psychological tests/methods have been described and examined for many years to reduce bias (e.g., Cuellar, 2000; Dana, 1993; Geisinger, 1994). In addition to stimulus characteristics of the cards, these adaptations include administration directions and social etiquette, translations, moderator variables, special norms (e.g., acculturation status), response sets/styles, and interpretation procedures (Dana, 1995, 2000a, 2000b, 2000c, 2003, 2005).

Historically, however, a primary obstacle to instrument adaptation was the assumption that standard instruments developed in the United States or with Euro-American origins were universal in nature and required only adequate translations for applications in other countries. Translations of psychological tests are indeed necessary for linguistic equivalence (Van de Vijver & Hambleton, 1996), but translation has been used synonymously with adaptation (Butcher, 1996) and always requires subsequent reestablishement of reliability and validity, and cross-cultural practice applications necessitate demonstrations of measurement qualities and adequacy (e.g., Arnold & Matus, 2000; Geisinger, 1994).

However, there are methodological difficulties in establishing equivalence in objective testing (Van de Vijver & Leung, 1997), and there are few documentations of construct validity or demonstrations of metric validity in samples, instruments, and administration, although methodologies are available. Recently, methodological issues in projective assessment have been examined (e.g., Allen & Dana, 2004; Allen & Walsh, 2000; Okazaki & Sue, 1995; Roysircar-Sodowsky & Kuo, 2001; Van de Vijver, 2000), but research applications of recommended methodologies remain limited.

INSTRUMENT ADAPTATIONS FOR MULTICULTURAL AND CROSS-CULTURAL ASSESSMENT

Picture-story instrument adaptations are relevant and necessary for competency in multicultural and cross-cultural assessment, although to date not all of these adaptations have been incorporated in assessment training and practice. These adaptations include the nature of stimulus characteristics, administration directions and social etiquette, moderator variables, special norms (e.g., acculturation status and culture-specific), and culture-specific interpretation guidelines.

First, the history of multicultural assessment instruments described the importance of stimulus cues in developing specific sets of adapted picture-story cards for multicultural and cross-cultural applications as well as for emic populations. However, this information has only been infrequently applied in the design of new instruments.

Second, although the cultural responsiveness hypothesis has been carefully explored (e.g., Sue & Zane, 1987), many assessors are still unfamiliar with the overarching importance of professional etiquette during service delivery that is culturally credible, acceptable, and conducive to developing the trust necessary for responsible attention and participation in the assessment process. Assessment instruction and supervision has not routinely included training in behaviors associated with multiculturally competent professional social etiquette.

Third, routine usage of moderator variables for acculturation/racial identity status, advocated by Dana (2005), Ritzler (2004), and others for multicultural instrument applications within specific countries, has not occurred even in the United States. Van de Vijver and Phalet (2004) have examined several ways of dealing with acculturation during assessment: (a) cut-off scores on acculturation instruments; (b) differential norms for standard tests based on length of stay in host country, exemplified by Mercer (1979); (c) using acculturation scores as covariates or moderators recommended by Cuellar (2000); (d) standardization or centering to eliminate group differences due to response styles using deviation scores from the individual or group mean. Acculturation status measures are now available for many different cultures as well as for ethnic minority groups in the United States (Dana, 1993, 1998, 2000a, 2005).

Fourth, the available apperception instruments rarely provide adequate cultural norms (Bellak & Abrams, 1997), although additional examples of available norms for common themes have been identified (Ritzler, 2004). Acculturation/racial identity status norms are not available (Dana, 2000b), although such norms for standard instruments would facilitate culturally competent interpretations of standard instruments by reducing bias without recourse to use of separate moderators providing only indirect and approximate corrections for test scores.

Fifth, instrument-specific guidelines (e.g., for Rorschach, TAT, MMPI/MMPI–2; Dana, 2005) for interpretation are now available. These guidelines have received only limited exposition and professional attention to date and are not used routinely by assessment practitioners.

Sixth, culture-specific interpretation guidelines for assessment instruments have not been developed for multicultural competence training, although general guidelines for cross-cultural assessment exist that have been applied to data samples from specific cultures (Dana, 2005a; Hays, 2001). Instead, acquisition of the cultural knowledge necessary for multicultural assessment competency has been inconsistently realized in counseling psychology programs for many years although adequate cultural information resources are now available (e.g., Dana, 1993, 1998, 2005). These issues remain salient for multicultural competency with adapted assessment instruments.

SELECTING INSTRUMENTS FOR MULTICULTURAL AND CROSS-CULTURAL POPULATIONS

Dana's desiderata/criteria (1993, 1999, in press) for cross-cultural/multicultural assessment instrument applications were described in chapter 2, Table 2–3. This chapter continues and elaborates the earlier discussion with the question, "Why employ TEMAS in preference to other picture-story narrative instruments for multicultural populations?" There is some necessary overlap between instrument adaptations and these desiderata because empirically documented instrument adaptations are necessary but do not suffice for ethical and responsible practice.

First, these desiderata begin with the overarching importance of participation by informed members of the cultural community for which assessment is planned. Consent, representation, and responsible aegis by these communities are mandatory in all phases of instrument development. This consideration, incorporated in multicultural research competency (Sue & Sue, 2003), has particular relevance for research and practice in cultural communities (Manson, 1997), and was endorsed as a research prerequisite by four major groups in the United States (CNPAAEMI, 2000).

Second, theoretical models precede the development of assessment instruments and interventions/treatment. These models assume that general laws governing human behavior are ultimately feasible because human beings are remarkably similar. Thus, standard assessment instruments are assumed to have universal applicability. Nonetheless, a theoretical model that can be empirically scrutinized and evaluated for cultural relevance is ultimately mandatory. Models for examining the rationales of standard assessment instruments and for the development of new instruments as well as for interventions and treatments are sorely needed. For new assessment instruments, a theoretical model leads to the selection, development, and evaluation of scoring variables for cross-cultural equivalence. Although an examination of some components for such a model is currently in process by the Hogg Foundation, there is only limited consensus on the applicability of specific psychological interventions at present.

Third, as indicated in the preceding section of this chapter, culturally/racially recognizable figures in a range of appropriate backgrounds are necessary for assessee identification and have been associated with productivity. Figures and backgrounds also contribute to the design of cards for particular scoring variables, or "card pull," as evidenced by Murray needs (Dana, 1968).

Fourth, administration social etiquette conforming to assessee expectations is mandatory. This behavior may occur simply and routinely as a consequence of assessor–assessee cultural/racial match. In the absence of explicit matching, however, cultural competence training for assessors may be needed. Whenever translated directions are read by an assessee or presented orally by the assessor, the client's language proficiency should be evaluated. Cultural match may also be needed to ensure sufficient cultural knowledge for proper professional social etiquette during test administration or for competent interpretation of test findings.

Fifth, scoring variables for personality/psychopathology should exhibit demonstrated cultural equivalence. This occurs initially in conceptualizing variables of known and empirically documented cultural relevance and subsequently in the availability of normative data from cultural groups for which the scoring variables were designed.

Sixth, this normative data should be representative of the ethnic minority population and stratified by relevant demographic variables (age, gender, socioeconomic status, education, occupation, urban–rural residence, etc). Normative data should include acculturation status for multicultural populations in the United States.

Seventh, in addition to normative data, interpretation of the meaning of scoring variables should be informed by in-depth knowledge of the culture. For example, prior to employing normative data for interpretation, assessee typicality should be explored. Typicality is ascertained by goodness-of-fit with modal cultural group identity in terms of gender, social class, age, education, and health status and the extent that normative data conforms to population demographics.

TEMAS AND OTHER PICTURE-STORY INSTRUMENTS

These desiderata/criteria are reexamined as preparation for Table 3–1 comparisons of TEMAS with other picture-story instruments (APT, CAST, C-TCB, RATC) and the relative multicultural and cross-cultural usefulness of these instruments.

APT

The 8-card pen-and-ink APT drawing set has been used with relatively large numbers of male and female college students from one private

TABLE 3–1.   Comparison of Picture-Story Instruments for Multicultural
Children/Adolescents

Instrument	Aegis	Theory	Stimuli	Etiquette	Scores	Norms	Interpretation
APT	No	No	Yes:	No	No	Yes	No
RATC	No	No	Yes	No	No	No	No
CAST	No	No	Yes	No	No	Yes	No
C-TCB	Yes	Yes	Yes	Yes	?	No	Yes
TEMAS	Yes	?	Yes	Yes	?	Yes	Yes

university and with smaller samples of adolescents, geriatric groups, and racial/ethnic groups described as Whites, Blacks, Orientals, and Hispanics. These cards are primarily adaptations of TAT cards, by one artist, with recognizable persons in familiar everyday settings. Two cards contain modified African American figures and an ambiguous figure perceived as Caucasian or Hispanic (Holstrom, Silber, & Karp, 1990). A scoring questionnaire of over 400 variables is completed by the assessee independently of the narrative stories and restricted to two story characters, a central figure and the next most important figure. Combinations of type of character, feelings, and actions are compared with nine semantic-differential ratings. Scoring for a small number of these variables, either 21 or 22, is by hand, computer, or publisher scoring service (Silber, Karp, & Holstrom, 1990). There is satisfactory test–retest reliability for college students and limited concurrent validity information is available. However, the scoring variables appear too limited for comprehensive assessment, concurrent validity comparisons have been made primarily with the TAT, normative data is meager, and differences of Blacks and Hispanics from Caucasians are minimal. There are no formal reviews by other authors.

CAST

The CAST was designed with 17 cards in color of moderate ambiguity for children 6 to 13. An Adlerian rationale provides cards for family, peer, and school settings. The cards contain White, African-American, Hispanic, and Asian children. Ratings of ethnic representativeness of stimuli were recognizable by these groups. Scores for thematic and problem-solving scales and thematic indicators are used. Reliability and validity data are available. Adaptive, nonadaptive, immature, and uninvested factor scores are obtained. Standardization is representative of 1980 census for age, gender, race, parent education, geographic location, and community size. Administration, scoring, and interpretation take nearly two hours. Moderate relationships with RATC provide concurrent validity.

C-TCB

The C-TCB is predicated on an Afrocentric theoretical orientation of traditional culture-specific values, beliefs, and practices learned in family/ extended family, church, and society. There are 27 chromatic cards that depict African American daily life experiences and yield themes concerning academic and social motivation, autonomy, Black pride, extended family/unity, institutionalized racism, media portrayal, political leadership, single parenting, teenage pregnancy, and drug abuse/unsafe vs. safe sex. These cards were developed on 18- to 32-year old students. A scoring system for ten personality traits and nine affective functioning characteristics based on these thematic card contents was adapted from TEMAS, and limited research evidence is available.

RATC

The RATC contains 27 cards, pretested for clinically useful responses, containing line drawings for children 6 to 15. Faces are somewhat ambiguous; warmth and support are indicated by posture. Children and parents are depicted in family and school situations. Sixteen male or female and both gender cards are individually administered. There are scores for 13 scales, 8 adaptive and 5 clinical are described as profile scales, and three critical indicators (ego functioning, aggression, level of projection). Normative data from 200 teacher-nominated, well-adjusted California children does not include ethnicity and socioeconomic status information. Comparisons with the TAT and CAT provide clinically useful data, although no studies more recent than 1980 are reported in the 1995 manual update. Waller (2001) suggested, "Although the RATC has been marketed for more than 15 years, it still has no established validity for its intended purposes" (p. 1032). More recently, Bell and Nagle (1999) concluded that 6 adaptive and 3 clinical scales support earlier research concerning deficiencies in the norms that argue strongly against RATC use for clinical diagnosis before restandardization is completed.

Supplemental RATC pictures paralleling the original stimuli are available for Black and Hispanic children and adolescents. Unpublished dissertation studies with these pictures indicate conflicting cultural sensitivity findings. These dissertations suggest important subscale differences across cultural groups, in collectivist societies for Asian Americans (Yeh & Yeh, 2002) as well as Egyptian and Canadian Children (Barbopoulos, Fishman, Clark, & El-Katib, 2002). Restandardization as the Roberts - 2 (Roberts & Gruber, 2005) have not altered Waller's 2001 conclusions.

TEMAS

TEMAS was developed from a dynamic-cognitive model combining aspects of cognitive, ego, and interpersonal psychology, with social-cognitive learning theory for 5- to-13-year-old children and adolescents. TEMAS has 12 gender-neutral cards and 11 gender-specific, and one card with child and adolescent, male and female versions. There were 23 long-form and 9 short-form cards. These cards were designed with reference to research findings indicating that ethnicity, gender, age, and stimuli in color led to increased verbalization. Unambiguous faces and scenes were used for White, Hispanic/Black, Hispanic, and Asian children and adolescents from 5 through adolescence. Individual and group administration conflict-laden scenes were employed to observe social problem-solving skills. Norms for Whites, Blacks, Puerto Ricans, and Other Hispanics were relatively small, with geographic restrictions, and were influenced by cultural variables affecting scorable indices (Costantino, Malgady, & Rogler, 1988).

MULTICULTURAL/CROSS-CULTURAL COMPETENCY OF PICTURE-STORY INSTRUMENTS

Table 3–1 contains multicultural competency comparisons. An evaluation of the multicultural/cross-cultural competency of these instruments follows from least to most similar in their relative standings with TEMAS on these desiderata.

The APT has only minimal applicability for child and adolescent multicultural groups as suggested by partial and limited relevance of two desiderata. Only two cards contained African American and possibly Hispanic figures, and small, unrepresentative samples of Black, Oriental, and Hispanic students were used as normative data. These racial/cultural group designations are overly inclusive, homogenizing, and serve primarily as ethnic glosses (Trimble, 2000) rather than providing reliable information on ethnicity/racial identity. Moreover, the relatively small numbers of adolescents used, the presence of racial/ethnic figures in only two stimulus cards, and minimal score differences between these groups and Whites suggests only marginal and limited multicultural applicability.

The RATC had faces and figures on cards redrawn for African American and Hispanic assessees. This degree of stimulus alteration may be insufficient without attention to other desiderata, particularly up-to-date representative norms instead of the meager California data from three school districts without information concerning the ethnicity of selected children. If these supplementary pictures receive continued use with ethnic populations, the development of an empirical literature documenting such usage is mandatory.

The CAST uses stimulus figures representing three ethnic/racial child/adolescent groups in addition to Whites, and these groups are included in standardization data based on the 1980 census. Although this test is competent psychometrically, the adequacy of 1980 census figures for use 25 years later is problematic due to changes in the demographic composition of the entire population. In addition, the very small ethnic/racial samples employed in normative data for these instruments obscures within-group heterogeneity and fails to incorporate acculturation status.

The C-TCB has adopted TEMAS scores and designed stimuli explicitly for African Americans. The C-TCB is a bona fide emic instrument rather than an instrument useful for multicultural or cross-cultural populations. By dovetailing Afrocentric theory with the thematic contents elicited by the picture stimuli, the C-TCB has a unique distinctiveness and appeal for picture-story assessment of African Americans not only in the United States but elsewhere in the world. The instrument was developed for assessors with adequate knowledge of African American history, problems, and culture. White assessors using this instrument require training and experience with African American populations in order to provide competent C-TCB interpretation. The C-TCB meets five of seven desiderata for picture-story instrument applications to ethnic minority populations. Issues concerning the adequacy of scoring variables for African Americans are shared with TEMAS and discussed later. It is unfortunate that norms for scoring variables are unavailable at present. However, updating of the 1972 TCB was accomplished in a 1997 dissertation, and the C-TCB description is available in an unpublished source (Hoy-Watkins & Jenkins-Monroe, in press); normative data should be forthcoming.

Comparisons of TEMAS multicultural/cross-cultural usefulness with somewhat different versions of Dana's desiderata/criteria (i.e., 1993,

1999, in press), as well as with competing instruments, has been consistent and positive. TEMAS still has no rivals among performance measures per se, and this subset of picture-story instruments for children and adolescents provides no exceptions. The additions of culture-specific sets of TEMAS picture stimuli and the empirical basis for applications with multicultural populations in the United States and cross-culturally in other countries has been continued and elaborated.

As Table 3–1 indicates, TEMAS meets five of seven desiderata including stimuli, assessment etiquette, norms, and cultural interpretation knowledge. With regard to theory and scores, a strong argument can be made for imposed etic status at present. The fact that the C-TCB rationale and scoring variables mirror TEMAS is reassuring, although the cultural adequacy of theory applied in TEMAS scoring variables has not been sufficiently examined or received substantive empirical support for equivalence to date. On the basis of a review of rationales and derived scoring across picture-story instruments in this chapter, TEMAS has the most comprehensive system of personality/psychopathology variables. As with objective tests, however, the question may be raised concerning what is omitted in these variables that could be identified by parallel emic measures constructed in different countries.

With regard to normative data within the United States, the existing standardization sample is somewhat dated, primarily urban, limited to Puerto Rican and Caribbean Hispanics, and admittedly geographically narrow. Subsequent data supports applications in other parts of the United States and with Mexican Americans. However, the heterogeneity of the Hispanic and African American populations in the United States in addition to the acculturation and racial identity status of these populations have not been reflected in the samples collected for normative purposes or validation studies. Since acculturation and racial identity status are of overarching importance in the acceptability and outcomes of different kinds of interventions for multicultural clients, fine tuning of research to include these omissions appears necessary in the immediate future.

REFERENCES

Allen, J. (1998). Personality assessment with American Indians and Alaska Natives: Instrument considerations and service delivery style. *Journal of Personality Assessment, 70,* 17–42.

Allen, J., & Dana, R. H. (2004). Methodological issues in cross-cultural and multicultural Rorschach research. *Journal of Personality Assessment, 7,* 272–280.

Allen, J., & Walsh, J. A. (2000). A construct-based approach to equivalence: methodologies for cross-cultural/multicultural personality assessment research. In R. H. Dana (Ed.), *Handbook of cross-cultural and multicultural personality research* (pp. 63–85). Mahwah, NJ: Lawrence Erlbaum Associates, Inc.

Allport, G. W. (1962). The general and the unique in psychological science. *Journal of Personality, 30,* 405–423.

Arnold, B. R. & Matus, Y. E. (2000). Test translation and cultural equivalence methodologies for use with diverse populations. In I. Cuellar & F. A. Paniagua (Eds.), *Handbook of multicultural mental health: Assessment and treatment of diverse populations* (pp. 121–136). San Diego, CA: Academic.

Avila-Espada, A. (2000). Objective scoring for the TAT. In R. H. Dana (Ed.), *Handbook of cross-cultural and multicultural personality assessment* (pp. 465–480). Mahwah, NJ: Lawrence Erlbaum Associates.

Barbopoulos, A., Fisharah, F., Clark, J. M., & El-Khatib, A. (2002). Comparison of Egyptian and Canadian children on a Picture Apperception Test. *Cultural Diversity and Ethnic Minority Psychology, 8,* 395–403.

Bailey, B. E., & Green, J. (1977). Black Thematic Apperception Test stimulus material. *Journal of Personality Assessment, 41,* 25–30.

Bell, N. L., & Nagle, R. J. (1999). Interpretive issues with the Roberts Apperception Test for children: Limitations of the standardization group. Psychology in the Schools, 36, 277–283.

Bellak, L., & Abrams, D. M. (1997). *The Thematic Apperception Test, the Children's Apperception Test, and the Senior Apperception Technique in clinical use* (6th ed.). Boston: Allyn & Bacon.

Bellak, L, & Bellak, S. S. (1949). *The Children's Apperception Test.* New York: CPS.

Blum, G. S. 1950). *The Blacky Pictures: Manual of instructions.* New York: Psychological Corporation.

Boring, E. G. (1929). *A history of experimental psychology.* New York: Century.

Butcher, J. N. (1996). Translation and adaptation of the MMPI-2 for international use. In J. N. Butcher (Ed.), *International adaptations of the MMPI-2* (pp. 26–43). Minneapolis, MN: University of Minnesota Press.

Clark, R. (1973). The socialization of clinical psychologists. *Professional Psychology, 3,* 329–340.

Clemence, A. J., & Handler, L. (2001). Psychological assessment on internship: A survey of training directors and their expectations for students. *Journal of Personality Assessment, 76,* 18–47.

Cohen, L. H., Sargent, M. M., & Sechrest, L. B. (1986). Use of psychotherapy research by professional psychologists. *American Psychologist, 41,* 198–206.

Conway, J. B. (1988). Differences among clinical psychologists: Scientists, practitioners, and scientist-practitioners. *Professional Psychology: Research and Practice, 19,* 642–655.

Conway, J. B. (1992). Presidential Address: A world of differences among psychologists. *Canadian Psychology, 33,* 1–24.

Costantino, G., & Malgady, R. (1999). The Tell-Me-A-Story Test: A multicultural offspring of the Thematic Apperception Test. In L. Gieser & J. Stein (Eds.), *Evocative images: The Thematic Apperception Test and the art of projection* (pp. 191–206). Washington, DC: American Psychological Association.

Costantino, G., Malgady, R., & Rogler, L. (1988). *TEMAS (Tell-Me-A -Story) manual.* Los Angeles: Western Psychological Services.

Coulacoglou, C., & Kine, P. (1995). The Fairy Tale Test: A novel approach in projective assessment. *British Journal of Projective Psychology, 40(2),* 10–31.

Council of National Psychological Associations for the Advancement of Ethnic Minority Interests (CNPAAEMI) (2000). *Guidelines for research in ethnic minority communities.* Washington, DC: American Psychological Association.

Cuellar, I. (2000). Acculturation as a moderator of personality and psychological assessment. In R. H. Dana (Ed.), *Handbook of cross-cultural and multicultural personality assessment* (pp. 113–129). Mahwah, NJ: Lawrence Erlbaum Associates, Inc

Dana, R. H. (1955). Clinical diagnosis and objective TAT scoring. *Journal of Abnormal and Social Psychology, 50,* 19–24.

Dana, R. H. (1966a). The clinical psychologist: A generalist with specialist training. *Psychological Reports, 19,* 127–138.

Dana, R. H. (1966b). *Foundations of clinical psychology: Problems of personality and adjustment.* Princeton, NJ: D. Van Nostrand.

Dana, R. H. (1968). Thematic techniques and clinical practice. *Journal of Projective Techniques and Personality Assessment, 32,* 202–214.

Dana, R. H. (1978). Comparisons of competence training in two successful clinical programs. *Psychological Reports, 42,* 919–926.

Dana, R. H. (1982a). *A human science model for personality assessment with projective techniques.* Springfield, IL: Thomas.

Dana, R. H. (1982b). *Picture-story cards for Sioux/Plains Indians.* Fayetteville: University of Arkansas.

Dana, R. H. (1987). Training for professional psychology: Science, practice, and identity. *Professional Psychology: Research and Practice, 18,* 9–16.

Dana, R. H. (1992). A commentary on assessment training in Boulder and Vail model programs. *Journal of Training and Practice in Professional Psychology, 6(2),* 19–26.

Dana, R. H. (1993). *Multicultural assessment perspectives for professional psychology.* Boston: Allyn & Bacon.

Dana, R. H. (1995). Culturally competent MMPI assessment of Hispanic populations. *Hispanic Journal of Behavioral Sciences, 17,* 305–319.

Dana, R. H. (1998). *Understanding cultural identity in intervention and assessment.* Thousand Oaks, CA: Sage.

Dana, R. H. (1999). Cross-cultural-multicultural use of the Thematic Apperception Test. In L. Gieser & M. J. Stein (Eds), *Evocative images: The Thematic Apperception Test and the art of projection* (pp. 177–190). Washington, DC: American Psychological Association.

Dana, R. H. (2000a) (Ed.). *Handbook of cross-cultural and multicultural personality assessment*. Mahwah, NJ: Lawrence Erlbaum Associates.

Dana, R. H. (2000b). Culture and methodology in personality assessment. In I. Cuellar & F. Paniagua (Eds.), *Handbook of multicultural mental health: Assessment and treatment of diverse groups* (pp. 97–120). San Diego, CA: Academic Press.

Dana, R. H. (2000c). Multicultural assessment of children and adolescent personality and psychopathology. In A. L. Comunian & U. Gielen (Eds.), *International perspectives on human development* (pp. 233–258). Lengerich, Germany: Pabst Science Publishers.

Dana, R. H. (2003). Assessment training, practice, and research in the new millennium: Challenges and opportunities for professional psychology. *Ethical Human Sciences and Services, 5*(2), 127–140.

Dana, R. H. (2005). *Multicultural assessment principles, applications, and examples*. Mahwah, NJ: Lawrence Erlbaum Associates

Dana, R. H. (2006). TEMAS among the Europeans: Different, complementary, and provocative. *South African Rorschach Journal, 3*(1), 11–22.

Dana, R. H. (in press). Using performance measures of personality with multicultural child and adolescent school populations. In H. Teglasi & R. Flanagan (Eds.), *Psychology in the Schools Special Topics Issue*.

Dana, R. H., & May, W. T. (1987). Overview. In R. H. Dana & W. T. May (Eds.), *Internship training in professional psychology* (pp. 3–74). Washington, DC: Hemisphere.

DuMas, F. (1955). Science and the single case. *Psychological Reports, 1*, 65–75.

Fagulha, R. (1993). *"Era uma vez ..." Prova projective para criancas. Manual* (2nd ed). (Once upon a time ... a projective test for children). Lisbon: CEGOC-TEA.

Frank, G. (1984). The Boulder model: History, rationale, and critique. *Professional Psychology: Research and Practice, 15*, 417–435.

Garfield, S., & Kurtz, R. (1976). Clinical psychologists in the 1970s. *American sychologist, 31*, 1–9.

Geisinger, K. F. (1994). Cross-cultural normative assessment: Translation and adaptation issues influencing the normative interpretation of assessment instruments. *Psychological Assessment, 6*, 304–312.

Gide, A. (1952). *The counterfeiters*. New York: Knopf.

Gieser, L. & Stein, M. I. (1999). *Evocative images: The Thematic Apperception Test and the art of projection*. Washington, DC: American Psychological Association.

Handler, L. (2005). Why is it so difficult to write a psychological report? *SPA Exchange, 17*(2), 1–3, 4–5.

Hays, P. (2001). *Addressing cultural complexities in practice: A framework for clinicians and counselors*. Washington, DC: American Psychological Association.

Hofer, J., & Chasiotis, A. (2004). Methodological considerations of applying a TAT-type picture-story test in cross-cultural research: A comparison of German and Zambian adolescents. *Journal of Cross-Cultural Psychology, 35*, 224–241.

Holstrom, R. W., Silber, D. E., & Karp, S. A. (1990). Development of the Apperceptive Personality Test. *Journal of Personality Assessment, 54*, 252–264.

Holzberg, J. D. (1957). The clinical and scientific methods: Synthesis or antithesis? *Journal of Projective Techniques, 21,* 227–242.

Hoy, M. (1997). Contemporizing the Themes Concerning Blacks Test (C-TCB). *Dissertation Abstracts International, 58(5-B),* 2679.

Hoy-Watkins, M., & Jenkins-Monroe, V. (in press). Personality and affective functioning of the C-TCB. In S. Jenkins (Ed.), *A handbook of clinical scoring systems for Thematic Apperceptive Techniques.* Mahwah, NJ: Lawrence Erlbaum Associates.

Hutt, M. L. (1980). *The Michigan Picture Test: Revised manual.* New York: Grune & Stratton.

Jacquemin, J. (1982). Les variants du "Thematic Apperception Test" pour l'etude des groupes culturels (Variants of the Thematic Apperception Test for the study of cultural groups). *Revue belge de Psychologie et de Pedagogie, 44 (No. 180),* 135 –144.

Jenkins, S. (in press). *A handbook of clinical scoring systems for Thematic Apperceptive Techniques.* Mahwah, NJ: Lawrence Erlbaum Associates.

Jones, R. A. (2001). The School Apperception Story Procedure. *British Journal of Guidance & Counseling, 29,* 47–64.

Kimble, G. A. (1984). Psychology's two cultures. *American Psychologist, 39,* 833–839.

Koch, S. (1969). Psychology cannot be a coherent science. *Psychology Today, 3,* 14, 64–68.

Koch, S. (1981). The nature and limits of psychological knowledge: Lessons of a century qua "science." *American Psychologist, 36,* 257–269.

Korchin, S. J., Mitchell, H. E., & Meltzoff, J. (1950). A critical examination of the Thompson Thematic Apperception Test. *Journal of Projective Techniques, 14,* 445–452.

Kroon, N., Goudena, P. P., & Rispens, J. (1998). Thematic Apperception Tests for child and adolescent assessment: A practitioner's consumer guide. *Journal of Psycheducational Assessment, 16,* 99–117.

Leong, F. T. L., & Zachar, P. (1991). Development and validation of the Scientist-Practitioner Inventory for psychology. *Journal of Counseling Psychology, 38,* 331–341.

Lilienfeld, S. O., Wood, J. M., & Garb, H. N. (2000). The scientific status of projective techniques. *Psychological Science in the Public Interest, 1(2),* 27–66.

Lilienfeld, S. O., Wood, J. M., & Garb, H. N. (2001). What's wrong with this picture? *Scientific American, May,* 81–87.

Lindzey, G. (1952). Thematic Apperception Test: Interpretive assumptions and related empirical evidence. *Psychological Bulletin, 49,* 1–25.

Lindzey, G. (1961). *Projective techniques and cross-cultural research.* New York: Appleton-Century-Crofts.

Lipsey, M. (1974). Research and relevance: A survey of graduate students and faculty in psychology. *American Psychologist, 29,* 541–555.

Manson, S. M. (1997). One small step for science, one giant step for prevention. *American Journal of Community Psychology, 25,* 215–219.

McArthur, D. S., & Roberts, G. E. (1982). *Roberts Apperception Test for Children: Manual*. Los Angeles: Western Psychological Services.

Mercer, J. R. (1979). *Technical manual. System of multicultural pluralistic assessment*. New York: Psychological Corporation.

Monopoli, J. (1984). *A culture-specific interpretation of Thematic Apperception Test protocols for American Indians*. Unpublished master's thesis, University of Arkansas, Fayetteville.

Moretti, R. J., & Rossini, E. D. (2004). The Thematic Apperception Test (TAT). In M. J. Hilsenbroth & D. L. Segal (Eds.), *Comprehensive handbook of psychological assessment. Vol. 2: Personality assessment* (pp. 356–371). New York: Wiley.

Murray, H. A. (1943). *Thematic Apperception Test Manual*. Cambridge, MA: Harvard University Press.

Murray, H. A. (1959). Preparation for a scaffold of a comprehensive system. In S. Koch (Ed.), *Psychology: A study of a science* (Vol. 3; pp. 7–54). New York: McGraw-Hill.

Murstein, B. I. (1961). The role of the stimulus in the manifestation of fantasy. In J. Kagan & G. S. Lesser (Eds.), *Contemporay issues in thematic apperceptive methods* (pp. 229–287). Springfield, IL: Thomas.

Nesbitt, M. (1959). *Friendship, love, and values*. Princeton, NJ: Educational Testing Service.

Okazaki, S., & Sue, S. (1995). Methodological issues in assessment research with ethnic minorities. *Psychological Assessment, 7*, 272–280.

Piotrowski, C. (1999). Assessment practices in the era of managed care: Current status and future directions. *Journal of Clinical Psychology, 55*, 787–796.

Polkinghorne, D. E. (2004). *Practice and the human sciences: The case for judgment-based practice of care*. Albany, NY: State University of New York Press.

Retief, A. I. (1987). Thematic appercetion testing across cultures: Tests of selection versus tests of inclusion. *South African Journal of Psychology, 17(2)*, 47–55.

Ritzler, B. (2004). Cultural applications of the Rorschach, Apperception Tests, and Figure Drawings. In M. J. Hilsenroth & D. L. Segal (Eds.), *Comprehensive handbook of psychological assessment. Vol. 2: Personality assessment* (pp. 573–585). New York: Wiley.

Roberts, G. E. & Gruber, C. (2005). *Roberts - 2 Manual*. Los Angeles, CA: Western Psychological Services.

Rossini, E. D., & Moretti, R. J. (1997). Thematic Apperception Test (TAT) interpretation: Practice recommendations from a survey of clinical psychology doctoral programs accredited by the American Psychological Association. *Professional Psychology: Research and Practice, 28*, 393–398.

Roysircar-Sodowsky, G., & Kuo, P. Y. (2001). Determining cultural validity of personality assessment: Some guidelines. In D. B. Pope-Davis, & H. L. K. Coleman (Eds.), *The intersection of race, class, and gender in multicultural counseling* (pp. 213–239). Thousand Oaks, CA: Sage.

Sampson, E. E. (1985). The decentralization of identity: Toward a revised concept of the personal and social order. *American Psychologist, 40,* 1202–1211.

Schneider, M. F. (1989). *Children's Apperception Test manual.* Austin, TX: PRO-ED.

Seligman, M. E. P. (1995). The effectiveness of psychotherapy: The Consumer Reports study. *American Psychologist, 50,* 965–974.

Shaffer, L. (1953). Of whose reality I cannot doubt. *American Psychologist, 8,* 608–623.

Shakow, D. (1976). What is clinical psychology? *American Psychologist, 31,* 553–560.

Sherwood, E. T. (1957). On the designing of TAT pictures, with special interest to a set for African people assimilating Western culture. *Journal of Social Psychology, 45,* 161–190.

Sherwood, E. T. (1961). *Swazi personality and the assimilation of Western culture.* Unpublished Ph.D. thesis, University of Chicago.

Shneidman, E. S. (1951). *The Make-A-Picture Story Test.* New York: Psychological Corporation.

Shneidman, E. S. (1999). The Thematic Apperception Test: A paradise of psycho-dynamics. In M. L. Gieser & M. J. Stein (Eds.), *Evocative images: The Thematic Apperception Test and the art of projection* (pp. 87–97). Washington, DC: American Psychological Association.

Silber, D. E., Karp, S. A., & Holmstrom, R. W. (1990). Recommendations for the clinical use of the Apperceptive Personality Test. *Journal of Personality Assessment, 55,* 790–799.

Sines, J. O., Pauker, J. D., & Sines, L. K. (1963). *The Missouri Children's Picture Series Manual.* Iowa City: Psychological Assessment and Services, Inc.

Sue, S., & Sue, L. (2003). Ethnic science is good science. In G. Bernal, J. E. Trimble, A. K. Burlew, & F. T. L. Leong (Eds.), *Handbook of racial and ethnic minority psychology* (pp. 198–207). Thousand Oaks, CA: Sage.

Sue, S., & Zane, N. (1987). The role of culture and cultural techniques in psychotherapy. *American Psychologist, 42,* 37–45.

Symonds, P. M. (1949). *Adolescent fantasy: An investigation of the picture-story method of personality study.* New York: Columbia University Press.

Teglasi, H. (1993). *Clinical use of storytelling: Emphasizing the TAT with children and adolescents.* Needham Heights, MA: Allyn & Bacon.

Teglasi, H. (2001). *Essentials of TAT and other storytelling techniques assessment.* New York: Wiley.

Thompson, C. E. (1949). The Thompson modification of the Thematic Apperception Test. *Rorschach Research Exchange and Journal of Projective Techniques, 13,* 469–478.

Tomkins, S. (1963). The ideology of research strategy. In S. Messick & J. Ross (Eds.), *Measurement of personality and cognition* (pp. 285–295). New York: Wiley.

Trimble, J. E. (2000). Social psychological perspectives on changing self-identification among American Indians and Alaska Natives. In R. H. Dana (Ed.), *Handbook of cross-cultural and multicultural personality assessment* (pp. 197–222). Mahwah, NJ: Lawrence Erlbaum Associates, Inc.

Van de Vijver, F. (2000). The nature of bias. In R. H. Dana (Ed.), *Handbook of cross-cultural and multicultural personality assessment* (pp. 87–106). Mahwah, NJ: Lawrence Erlbaum Associates.

Van de Vijver, F., & Hambleton, R. K. (1996). Translating tests: Some practical guidelines. *European Psychologist, 1,* 89–99.

Van de Vijver, F., & Leung, K. (1997). *Methods and analysis for cross-cultural research.* Newbury Park, CA: Sage.

Van de Vijver, F., & Phalet, K. (2004). Assessment in multicultural groups: The role of acculturation. *Applied Psychology: An International Review, 53(2),* 215–236.

Vane, J. (1981). The Thematic Apperception Test: A review. *Clinical Psychology Review, 1,* 319–336.

Waller, N. G. (2001). Review of Roberts Apperception Test for Children. *The fourteenth mental measurements yearbook* (pp. 1032–1033). Lincoln, NE: Buros Institute of Mental Measurements.

Wampold, B. E. (2001). *The great psychotherapy debate: Models, measures, findings.* Mahwah, NJ: Lawrence Erlbaum Associates.

Westen, D., & Weinberger, J. (2004). When clinical description becomes statistical prediction. *American Psychologist, 59,* 595–613.

Williams, R. L. (1972). *Themes Concerning Blacks Test.,* St. Louis, MO: Washington University.

Williams, R. L., & Johnson, R. C. ((1981). Progress in developing Afrocentric measuring instruments. *Journal of Non-White Concerns, 1,* 3–18.

Yeh, M., & Yeh, J. W. (2002). The clinical assessment of Asian American children. In K. Kurasaki, S. Okazaki, & S. Sue (Eds.), *Asian American mental health: assessment theories and methods* (pp. 233–249). New York, NY· Kluwer Academic/Plenum Publishers.

Zachar, P., & Leong, F. T. L. (1992). A problem in personality: Scientist and practitioner differences in psychology. *Journal of Personality, 60,* 665–677.

Zachar, P. & Leong, F. T. L. (2000). A 10-year longitudinal study of scientist and practitioner interests in psychology: Assessing the Boulder model. *Professional Psychology: Research and Practice, 31,* 575–580.

4

TEMAS: Description and Development

BACKGROUND

TEMAS has the same meaning in several languages: in English, TEMAS is an acronym for *tell me a story*; in Spanish, it means *themes*, in Italian, TEMA means *theme*. This felicitous cross-linguistic combination of names represents the most appropriate title for a narrative test (Costantino, 1987; Costantino, Malgady, & Rogler, 1988; Ritzler, 1993). Rooted originally in the memory of the first author since his elementary school years in Italy—where il *tema* was class work or a homework assignment to develop a narrative composition based on an assigned title such as, "If I had a million lire," or "Grandmother's birthday,"—it became the test's title following his toddler's bed-time request, "Papa, tell me a story." The TEMAS test is a multicultural narrative instrument designed for use with minority and non-minority children and adolescents aged 5 to 18 years old.

The TEMAS test represents a number of departures and improvements relative to previous narrative/thematic apperception tests. First, the test was specifically developed for use with children and adolescents (Ritzler, 1993). Second, the test comprises two parallel sets of stimulus cards, one set for minorities and the other for nonminorities, thus making it multicultural in nature. Third, the test abandons the construct of pictorial ambiguity common to the TAT and Rorschach to pull for specific conflicts, and utilizes structured stimuli with pictorial problem solving (Costantino, Flanagan, & Malgady, 2001; Flanagan, Losapio, Greenfeld, Costantino, & Hernandez, 2004; Flanagan & Di-Giuseppe, 1999). Fourth, the test has normative data for Black, Puerto Rican, Other Hispanic, and White children thus increasing multicultural validity and diminishing test bias against minorities (Dana, 1993, 1998; Ritzler, 1996). Fifth, the stimulus cards are in color, which attracts and maintains children's interest (Costantino, 1978; Costantino, Malgady, & Rogler, 1988) and facilitates narratives of emotional states (Costantino, Flanagan, & Malgady, 1995; Lubin, 1955; Murstein, 1963; Exner, 1993; Thompson & Bachrach, 1951).

Narrative Techniques

Thematic apperception techniques, also known as narrative techniques, and other projective tests, such as the Rorschach, are based on psychoanalytic theory positing that an individual projects onto ambiguous stimuli unconscious drives and presses (Murray, 1951). (Even the Rorschach Comprehensive System assumes that there is an element of projection in the Rorschach responses; Exner, 1993).

The cognitive nature of TAT and CAT stories was recognized in the early 1950s. In fact, Bellak (1954) criticized the limitations and failures of projective tests in general and the TAT in particular because they were based on the psychoanalytic model of projective hypothesis in addressing unconscious conflicts by bypassing the ego defenses; hence, he proposed that TAT stories could be best understood in terms of ego functioning. In addition, Holt (1960a, 1960b), for example, argued that TAT stories are not fantasies or products of primary processes, but rather are cognitions or products of conscious cognitive processes. Kagan (1960), although he labeled TAT productions "fantasies," emphasized the importance of analyzing the ego defenses of the stories in addition to their symbolic content. More recently, Teglasi (2001) wrote that the TAT stimuli, notwithstanding their ambiguity, are to large degree structured to assess both the process and content, thus allowing the evaluation of both the structure and the content of the story.

Notwithstanding these theoretical reconsiderations (Dana, 2000; Teglasi, 2001), in clinical practice, the TAT stories continue to be analyzed primarily only with respect to their content within a psychodynamic framework, in the absence of an objective scoring system (Costantino & Malgady, 1996; Costantino, Malgady, & Rogler, 1988; Dana, 2000). On the other hand, the Rorschach Comprehensive System overcame some of these limitations with its objective scoring system and development of norms (Exner, 1993)

The emphasis on cognitive processes in projective/narrative testing was the natural progression of the theoretical development of cognitive psychology in the 1970s. In the past two decades, there has been a movement among cognitive-behavioral psychologists to integrate the basic assumptions of ego psychology and cognitive psychology in the application of projective analyses (Anderson, 1981; Forgus & Shulman, 1979; Singer & Pope, 1978; Sobel, 1981; Teglasi, 2001). Sobel (1981) proposed the development of a "projective-cognitive" instrument to assess an individual's problem-solving strategies, coping skills, and self-instructional styles. Bruner (1986) posited that there are two modes of thoughts: the paradigmatic mode, which deals with general causes in the attempt to discover empirical truths; and the narrative mode, which deals with life experiences. The narrative mode of thought, as presented by Bruner (1986), is an important element of special interest for our theoretical formulation of narrative assessment both in the way in which individuals understand their life events and in the way psychologists endeavor to understand the lives of examinees through narrative. Teglasi (2001), in her reformulation of the theoretical framework of the TAT, wrote that the projective hypothesis and cognitive schema theory are essentially similar because both assume the importance of the role of previously learned mental sets in responding to "projective" stimuli and both indicate that these responses fall outside the realm of consciousness. Because these modes of thoughts are organized into narratives, storytelling becomes a valid medium in personality assessment while using the TAT.

In the tradition of psychologists who have proposed a narrative conceptualization of human thinking, Howard (1991), among others cited later in this chapter, suggested that storytelling is fundamental to the development of self-identity, which he calls "life story construction." Psychopathology occurs when life stories go awry. Hence, the effectiveness of a culturally sensitive storytelling technique may correspond to Howard's view of psychotherapy as an "exercise in story repair." (Costantino, Malgady, & Rogler, 1994). Hence, TEMAS narrative test may correspond to a valid multicultural assessment in understanding why life stories go wrong, thus linking culturally appropriate assessment to treatment.

RATIONALE FOR TEMAS DEVELOPMENT

The principal rationale for the development of TEMAS was to address the emic and etic validity in constructing psychometrically sound multicultural narrative tests developed specifically for use with children and adolescents (Dana, 1993).

The TEMAS test is based largely on social, cognitive, and narrative theoretical models, which posit that personality development occurs within a sociocultural system where individuals internalize the cultural values and beliefs of family and society (Bandura, 1977, 1986, 1989, 1991; McAdams, 1994; Piaget & Inhelder, 1971; Sullivan, 1953). Personality functions are learned initially through modeling (Bandura, 1977) and are then developed through verbal and imaginal processes (Paivio, 1971; Piaget & Inhelder, 1971; Singer & Pope, 1978). When narrative test pictorial stimuli are similar to the situations in which the personality functions were originally learned, these functions are attributed to the characters and situations in the cards and narrated as personal life events and life stories (Auld, 1952, 1954; Bandura, 1991; Bruner, 1986; Mancuso & Sarbin, 1983; Sarbin, 1986; Teglasi, 2001).

Traditionally, projective/narrative tests have fared well in clinical settings, but have presented a host of problems with respect to psychometric rigor (Dana, 1993; Murstein, 1963, 1972). However, since the 1980s, there has been interest in clinically useful narrative techniques satisfying psychometric standards (Avila-Espada, 1986; Costantino & Malgady, 2000; Dana, 1986, 2000; Sobel, 1981). There is a need to develop psychological tests for reliable and valid diagnosis and personality assessment of culturally and linguistically diverse children (Costantino, 1992; Costantino & Malgady, 1996; Dana, 1996; Padilla, 1979) as well as nonminority children, and to create culture-specific norms for projective tests (Dana, 1986, 1993, 2000; Exner & Weiner, 1982, 1995).

Based on these considerations, the TEMAS (Tell-Me-A-Story) narrative test was developed with culturally relevant stimuli. There are parallel minority and nonminority versions of TEMAS stimuli (Costantino, 1978, 1987) embodying the following features: structured stimuli and diminished ambiguity to pull for specific personality functions; chromatically attractive, ethnically relevant, and contemporary stimuli to elicit diagnostically meaningful stories; representation of both negative and positive intrapersonal functions in the form of conflicts or dilemmas that require a solution; and objective scoring of both thematic structure and content. The rationale for these and other departures from traditional projective techniques (e.g., reduced ambiguity, color) is based on empirical research conducted with the TAT (Costantino & Malgady, 1999; Murstein, 1972; Teglasi, 2001).

The presentation of culturally relevant and familiar projective test stimuli was originally explored in Thompson's (1949) Black TAT, based on the assumption that similarity between stimulus and examinee facilitates identification with the characters in the pictures and therefore promotes greater verbal fluency and self-disclosure. Projective/narrative stimuli traditionally have been ambiguous, in order to bypass ego defenses and allow latent psychological conflict to be more freely expressed (Teglasi, 2001); however, TEMAS was conceived following more recent thinking that diminished ambiguity and increased structure facilitates verbal fluency and enables a more focused understanding of the examinee's personality functioning (Epstein, 1966; 1994; Sobel, 1981). That is, when pictorial stimuli are structured to "pull" specific personality functions, unlike ambiguous stimuli, a more reliable and valid clinical interpretation of thematic content may be achieved (Costantino, 1978; Costantino, Malgady, & Rogler, 1988).

Both clinicians and researchers alike acknowledge that color has an impact on the perception of thematic and projective stimuli (Costantino, Flanagan, & Malgady, 1995; Exner, 1993; Johnson & Dana, 1965; Murstein, 1963) and that integration of color and form is considered a sign of emotional maturity and cognitive organization (Costantino, Flanagan, & Malgady, 1995; Exner, 1993; Siipola, 1950). During the 1950s, several studies documented that chromatic TAT stimuli enhance verbal fluency and more accurately discriminate between clinical and control examinees than achromatic stimuli (e.g., Brackbill, 1951; Thompson, & Bachrach, 1951). Murstein (1963) suggested that color facilitates such differentiation of psychiatric and normal examinees because achromicity reinforces sadness as an affective response to TAT stimuli. In addition, colored pictorial stimuli motivate and maintain longer attention span in children (Ritzler, 1993, 1996). Thus, based on this evidence and reasoning, the TEMAS stimuli were developed in color.

The pictorial representation of psychological conflicts and problem solving in TEMAS pictures is a reformulation of the methodology of Kohlberg (1976), who developed stories portraying moral dilemmas to assess the moral development of children. Similarly, the TEMAS pictures depict a split scene showing psychological dilemmas that require problem solving; the examinee must resolve the antithetical situations portrayed, and the examining clinician evaluates the adaptiveness of the resolution of conflict. The conflicts depicted in TEMAS stimuli were designed to evoke disclosure of specific personality functions that are prominent in personality theory and also are key diagnostic indicators of psychopathology: integrity of interpersonal relations, control of aggressive impulses, control of anxious and depressive feelings, achievement motivation, ability to delay gratification, self-concept of competence, self/sexual identity, moral judgment, and reality testing (e.g., Bandura, 1991; Bellak, Hurvich, & Gediman, 1973; McClelland, Atkinson, Clark, & Lowell, 1953; 1976; Mischel, 1974; Mischel & Mischel, 1983).

Purpose and Uses of the TEMAS

The TEMAS is a cognitive instrument that yields valuable multicultural psychological data, enabling clinicians to: (a) gain better understanding of both strengths and deficits in cognitive, affective, and intrapersonal and interpersonal functioning of the individual; (b) give problem-specific information in order to develop a more accurate treatment plan; and (c) assess therapeutic progress and outcome (Dana, 1996).

The TEMAS stimuli were created by Phil Jacobs, an amateur who developed into a professional artist, he worked closely with the test author (Costantino, 1978; 1987). The pictorial stimuli embody a wide variety of problematic life events and personal experiences in urban environments, such as familial scenes within the home, solitary dreamlike and fantasy states, street scenes involving peers and adults, sports activities, and events occurring in school settings. The antithetical nature of the situations portrayed in the pictures provokes positive and/or negative feelings to be imbedded in the stories and requires adaptive or maladaptive resolutions. These situations pull for themes expressive of varying degrees of psychopathology, ranging from severe pathology (e.g., morbidity, suicidal ideation, depression, impulsivity, isolation, delusion) to highly adaptive functioning.

GENERAL DESCRIPTION

The Stimulus Cards

The TEMAS test is comprised of two parallel versions of pictures: the nonminority version consisting of 23 pictures featuring predominantly non-minority characters in an urban environment and the minority versions also consisting of 23 pictures featuring predominantly minority characters in an urban setting. The two parallel sets of pictures present identical themes.

Both the minority and nonminority versions have a Short Form comprised of 9 cards of the 23-card Long Form. In the 9 Short Form Cards, 4 are administered to both sexes and 5 are sex-specific. In the 23 Long Form cards, 12 are both sexes, 11 are sex-specific, and 1 is age-specific. Additionally, there are 4 cards with multicultural characters, which can be used interchangeably for both the minority and nonminority versions (Cards 15, 16, 20, and 21). Cards are numbered on the back in the upper right-hand corner. For sex-specific cards, the card number is followed by a "B" or a "G" to indicate whether it should be used with boys and with girls. Cards are also identified as belonging to the minority version with an "M" denoting minority after the number and gender identification, such as 1G-M. Card 22B-G, is specific for ages (5 to 13) as well as for sex; hence when testing adolescent (aged 14 to 18) minority boys/girls, an examiner should select the card labeled "22B-G-M (Adolescent)," and for nonminority adolescent girls, the card labeled "22B-G (Adolescent)." Furthermore, Card 15, which is a multicultural card used interchangeably for minority and nonminority children, shows two settings. The card included in the minority set depicts a coach giving an award to a group of baseball players, whereas the card included in the nonminority set depicts a coach presenting an award to a group of soccer players. The two versions of Card 15 can be used interchangeably, depending on whether the examinee is more familiar with soccer or with baseball.

The 23-picture version, published by Western Psychological Services (WPS), constitutes the third revision of the original TEMAS cards. The first series was developed in 1978 and consisted of 53 cards. The second, revised series was developed in 1980 and consisted of 47 cards. This third series was developed in 1983.

The following descriptions of the 23 TEMAS pictures are organized by Short Form or Long Form inclusion:

Short Form (Cards 1B, 1G, 7, 10B, 10G, 14B, 14G, 15, 17B, 17G, 20, 21, 22B, 22G)

Card 1B.   A mother is giving a command to her son. A father is in the background. Friends are urging the boy to play basketball with them. (Card. 1 is designed to pull for the personality functions of Interpersonal Relations and Delay of Gratification.)

Card 1G.   A mother is giving a command to her daughter. A father is in the background. Friends are urging the girl to jump rope with them. (Designed to pull for Interpersonal Relations and for Delay of Gratification.)

Card 7.   An angry mother is watching her son and daughter argue over a broken lamp. (Designed to pull for Interpersonal Relations, Aggression, and Moral Judgment.)

Card 10B.   A boy is standing in front of a piggy bank holding money, while imagining himself looking at a bicycle in a shop window and buying an ice cream cone. (Designed to pull for Delay of Gratification.)

Card 10G.   A girl is standing in front of a piggy bank holding money, while imagining herself looking at a bicycle in a shop window and buying an ice cream cone. (Designed to pull for Delay of Gratification.)

Card 14B.   A boy is studying in his room. A group of boys and girls is listening to music in the living room. (Designed to pull for Interpersonal Relations, Achievement Motivation, and Delay of Gratification.)

Card 14G.   A girl is studying in her room. A group of boys and girls is listening to music in the living room. (Designed to pull for Interpersonal Relations, Achievement Motivation, and Delay of Gratification.)

Card 15 (Minority Version).   A policeman is giving an award to a group of PAL baseball players. A policeman is arresting a group of three boys and one girl who have broken a window and stolen merchandise. (Designed to pull for Interpersonal Relations, Aggression, Achievement Motivation, and Moral Judgment.)

Card 15 (Nonminority Version).   A coach is giving an award to a group of soccer players. A policeman is arresting a group of three boys and one girl who have broken a window and stolen merchandise. (Designed to pull for Interpersonal Relations, Aggression, Achievement Motivation, and Moral Judgment.)

Card 17B.   A boy is studying and daydreaming about receiving an "A" from his teacher and receiving an "F" from his teacher. (Designed to pull for Anxiety/Depression, Achievement Motivation, and Self-Concept.)

Card 17G.   A girl is studying and daydreaming about receiving an "A" from her teacher and receiving and "F" from her teacher. (Designed to pull for Anxiety/Depression, Achievement Motivation, and Self-Concept.)

Card 20.   A youngster is in bed dreaming a scene showing a horse on a hill, a river, and a path leading to a castle. (Designed to pull for Anxiety/Depression.)

Card 21.   A youngster is in bed dreaming of a monster eating something and of a monster making threats. (Designed to pull for Aggression, Anxiety/Depression, and Reality Testing.)

Card 22B.   A Latency age boy is standing in front of a bathroom mirror, imagining his face reflected in the mirror with attributes of both sexes. (Designed to pull for Anxiety/Depression, Sexual Identity, and Reality Testing.)

Card 22G.   A latency age girl is standing in front of a bathroom mirror, imagining her face reflected in the mirror with attributes of both sexes. (Designed to pull for Anxiety/Depression, Sexual Identity, and Reality Testing.)

Card 22B (Adolescent).   An adolescent boy is standing in front of a bathroom mirror, imagining his face reflected in the mirror with attributes of both sexes (Designed to pull for Anxiety/Depression, Sexual Identity, and Reality Testing.)

Card 22G (Adolescent).   An Adolescent girl is standing in front of a bathroom mirror, imagining her face reflected in the mirror with attributes of both sexes. (designed to pull for Anxiety/Depression, Sexual Identity and Reality Testing.

Long Form (Cards. 2, 3, 4, 5, 6, 8, 9B, 9G, 11, 12B, 12G, 13B, 13G, 16, 18B, 18G, 19B, 19G, 23B, 23G, plus the nine cards of the short form)

Card 2.   A father is watching television and drinking. A son and a daughter are standing beside him. A mother is seen carrying a baby and vacuuming. Another daughter and son are seen at the mother's side. (Designed to pull for Interpersonal Relations and for Moral Judgment.)

Card 3.   A father is telling his son to do his homework. A mother is holding a plate and getting a glass. A daughter is doing her homework at the kitchen table. Another daughter and son are watching television. (Designed to pull for Interpersonal Relations, Achievement Motivation, and Delay of Gratification.)

Card 4.   An angry father is threatening the mother. Two sons and two daughters are standing with the mother. A young woman lies in bed with her face covered. (Designed to pull for Interpersonal Relations, Aggression, Anxiety/Depression, and Moral Judgment.)

Card 5.   A youngster is sleeping in bed dreaming of a picnic with a woman. A figure enters through the bedroom window at night. (Designed to pull for Interpersonal Relations and for Aggression.)

Card 6.   A boy and a girl dress up in grown-up clothes in the attic, while they look nostalgically at a crib and some baby toys. (Designed to pull for Interpersonal Relations and for Sexual Identity.)

Card 8.   A male teacher is reading to a class of attentive students. A female teacher or principal is showing a broken window to a mother and father with their son and daughter. (Designed to pull for Interpersonal Relations, Aggression, Achievement Motivation, and Moral Judgment.)

Card 9B.   A boy with outstretched arms is standing at the junction of two roads in a forest. Friends call to him to join them for a walk on the right-hand road. (Designed to pull for Interpersonal Relations and for Anxiety/Depression.)

Card 9G.   A girl with outstretched arms is standing at the junction of two roads in a forest. Friends call to her to join them for a walk on the right-hand road. (Designed to pull for Interpersonal Relations and for Anxiety/Depression.)

Card 11.   A woman is carrying bags of groceries with a boy and girl helping her. A woman is trying to protect herself from two boys and a girl who are stealing groceries from her bags. (Designed to pull for Interpersonal Relations, Aggression, and Moral Judgment.)

Card 12B.   A group of four boys is cooperating in the repair of a bicycle. A group of four boys is fighting. (Designed to pull for Interpersonal Relations, Aggression, and Moral Judgment.)

Card 12G.   A group of four girls is cooperating in the repair of a bicycle. A group of four girls is fighting. (Designed to pull for Interpersonal Relations, Aggression, and Moral Judgement.)

Card 13B.   A boy is standing in front of a bathroom mirror, imagining the reflection of his parents in the mirror. (Designed to pull for Interpersonal Relations, Self-Concept, and Sexual Identity.)

Card 13G.   A girl is standing in front of a bathroom mirror, imagining the reflection of her parents in the mirror. (Designed to pull for Interpersonal Relations, Self-Concept, and Sexual Identity.)

Card 16.   A boy is climbing up a rope in a gym, where a girl is jumping over a wooden horse, and a group of two boys and two girls on the right-hand side of the picture is expressing encouragement and admiration. A group of two boys and two girls on the left hand side of the picture is expressing fear. (Designed to pull for Interpersonal Relations, Achievement Motivation, and Self-Concept.)

Card 18B. A boy is studying and daydreaming about becoming an actor, a doctor, and a drunk. (Designed to pull for Achievement Motivation and for Self-Concept.)

Card 18G. A girl is studying and daydreaming about becoming an actress, a doctor, and a bag lady. (Designed to pull for Achievement Motivation and for Self-Concept.)

Card 19B. A boy in a window is imagining himself being saved from a burning building by a fireman and by Superman. (Designed to pull for Anxiety/Depression and for Reality Testing.)

Card 19G. A girl in a window is imagining herself being saved from a burning building by a fireman and by Wonder Woman. (Designed to pull for Anxiety/Depression and for Reality Testing.)

Card 23B. A boy is rejected by his parents, and imagines himself running away from home with a suitcase, and standing on a bridge looking at the sea below. (Designed to pull for Interpersonal Relations and for Anxiety/Depression.)

Card 23G. A girl is rejected by her parents, and imagines herself running away from home with luggage, and standing on a bridge looking at the sea below. (Designed to pull for Interpersonal Relations and for Anxiety/Depression.)

TEMAS Measures

Cognitive Functions. Complete definitions of cognitive functions are reported later in this chapter. There are 18 Cognitive Functions, which can be scored for each TEMAS story:

> Reaction Time (RT)
> Total Time (TT)
> Fluency (FL)
> Total Omissions (OM)
> Main Character Omissions (MCO)

Secondary Character Omissions (SCO)
Event Omissions (EO)
Setting Omissions (SO)
Total Transformations (TRANS)
Main Character Transformations (MCT)
Secondary Character Transformations (SCT)
Event Transformations (ET)
Setting Transformations (ST)
Inquiries (INQ)
Relationships (REL)
Imagination (IMAG)
Sequencing (SEQ)
Conflict (CON)

Personality Functions.   There are 9 Personality Functions assessed by the TEMAS, within the social cognitive-narrative theoretical framework. Each stimulus card pulls for at least one of the following Personality Functions. Complete definitions of the personality functions are reported later in this chapter.

Interpersonal Relations (IR)
Aggression (AGG)
Anxiety/Depression (A/D)
Achievement Motivation (AM)
Delay of Gratification (DG)
Self-Concept (SC)
Sexual Identity (SEX)
Moral Judgment (MJ)
Reality Testing (REAL)

Affective Functions.   The TEMAS scoring system evaluates 7 Affective Functions. Although in psychiatric mental status evaluations these are known as mood states, we have labeled them affective functions because they reflect emotional states:

Happy (HAP)
Sad (SAD)
Angry (ANG)
Fearful (FEAR)

Neutral (NEUT)
Ambivalent (AMB)
Inappropriate Affect (IA)

Examinee Population

The TEMAS is designed to be used with children and adolescents aged 5 to 18. The test can be interpreted normatively for children aged 5 to 13 and used clinically with children and adolescents aged 5 to 18.

THEORETICAL FRAMEWORK

Background

Apperception has been defined in psychodynamic terms as the synthesis of a percept with past experience and learning as well as with the present motivational state of an individual (Kagan, 1960). The thematic apperception technique analyzes examinees' stories told in response to a series of pictures developed to "pull" for the underlying psychological drives and emotional states of the respondent. Thematic apperception tests, such as Murray's TAT (1943), and Bellak & Bellak's CAT (1949) and Bellak's SAT (1986), are considered to be projective instruments because the respondent projects into the story his or her own needs and drives in response to the eliciting stimuli. Projective/narrative tests differ from other projective techniques, such as the Rorschach (Exner, 1978), Goodenough-Harris Drawing Test (Harris, 1963), and Sentence Completion (Rotter, Rafferty, & Lotsof, 1954) in the nature of both the stimuli and the elicited response (Kagan & Lesser, 1961). However, there are some similarities between the TAT and Rorschach stimuli because both provoke responses, that are guided by the constraints of the stimuli (Holt, 1961; Teglasi, 2001).

Narrative and projective tests can be conceived in two ways when used as instruments to assess personality functioning: as perceptual-cognitive tasks and/or as stimuli to fantasy or covert behavior (Exner & Weiner, 1982). The perceptual-cognitive task encompasses the examinee's focus of attention and selective attention, mode and accuracy of perception, and style of thinking, whereas the stimulus to fantasy embodies the examinee's personal beliefs and myths (Forgus & Shulman, 1979) and psychocultural and emotional functioning (Costantino, 1978; Costantino, Malgady, & Rolger, 1988;

Padilla, 1979; Rogler, Malgady, Costantino, & Blumenthal, 1987). Unlike paper-and-pencil tests, which primarily assess verbal processes, narrative and projective tests tap both visual-imaginal and verbal processes.

The TEMAS technique was conceived as a method to assess a person's Cognitive, Affective, and Personality Functions through the scoring and interpretation of examinees' responses to familiar and culturally relevant pictorial stimuli. This conception of the TEMAS as a narrative test integrates the social cognitive–narrative models.

Culturally Relevant and Familiar Stimuli

The TEMAS stimuli are structured, unambiguous, and familiar. However, the pictures do not elicit highly similar stories from different examinees. All TEMAS pictures depict a split scene showing antithetical or conflicting intra and interpersonal situations presenting a relevant psychological dilemma/problem that requires a solution. The resolutions of the antithetical situations depicted in the split TEMAS pictures reflect the degree of a examinee's adaptive and maladaptive personality functioning and also the stage of personality development. In this respect, the TEMAS bipolar stimuli engage the child in problem-solving strategies requiring a choice, thus placing this narrative instrument within the social cognitive and narrative theoretical frameworks (Costantino, Flanagan, & Malgady, 2001; Dana, 2000).

Social Cognitive–Narrative Framework

The theoretical framework of the TEMAS is based on a social cognitive–narrative framework derived from the following theoretical models: interpersonal psychology (Sullivan, 1953), ego psychology (Bellak, Hurvich, & Gediman, 1973), social cognitive approach (Bandura, 1977, 1986, 1989, 1991; McAdams, 1994; Piaget & Inhelder, 1969, 1971), cognitive psychology (Piaget & Inhelder, 1969, 1971; Singer & Pope, 1984; Sobel, 1981), and narrative psychology (Bruner, 1986; Howard, 1991; Kirkman, 2002; Polkinghorne, 1995, 2004; Sarbin, 1986). This section discusses these theories and their relationship to the social-cognitive and narrative models used in as the theoretical framework of the TEMAS test.

According to traditional psychodynamic theory (Freud, 1923, 1961; Murray, 1938), the personality is organized at different levels of consciousness—unconscious, preconscious, and conscious. Although the existence of multiple levels of consciousness is not denied within the TEMAS social cognitive-narrative framework, the TEMAS scoring system focuses primarily on overt behavior as exhibited into the stories that correspond to functions at a conscious ego level and, secondarily, on low inferences that correspond to functions at ego level as encoded in the individual schema. This assessment increases the probability that inferences made about personality functioning are accurate. In fact, it has been shown that the fewer the inferential steps, the more accurate is the resulting prediction that the narrative or projective response will correspond to a specific personality function (Costantino, Malgady, & Rogler, 1988; Exner & Weiner, 1982; Murstein, 1963).

The TEMAS Personality Functions are seen as reformulation of ego functions or as personality metaphors derived from the integration of schemas-encoded knowledge of past experiences with present perception of pictorial stimuli and verbalized and revealed by examinees in their TEMAS stories. Furthermore, these personality constructs or metaphors are defined in terms of the problem-solving functioning of adaptive vs. maladaptive behavior (Costantino, 1978; Costantino, Malgady, & Rolger, 1988).

Ego Psychology. During the 1950s, "id psychology" as posited by Freud (1923, 1961) was reformulated into "ego psychology," originally advanced by Hartman (1951), and into interpersonal psychology, originally formulated by the neo-Freudians such as Sullivan (1953). Ego Psychologists focused on the influence of the ego structure on overt behavior, whereas the neo-Freudians focused on interpersonal psychopathology of the ego or self. Consequently, there has been a tendency to regard the responses to the TAT cards as being cognitive productions controlled by the ego instead of as revelations of unconscious needs (Bellak, 1954; Holt, 1961; Teglasi, 2001).

Bellak, Hurvich, and Gediman (1973) defined ego functions as theoretical constructs based on observations of behavior and on patients' verbalizations of their experiences. Furthermore, Bellak and his associates defined ego constructs in terms of twelve functions that reflect both adaptive and maladaptive behaviors. These ego functions include: reality testing; judgment; sense of reality of the world and of the self; regulations and control of drives, affects, and impulses; object relations; thought processes; adaptive regression at the service of the ego; defensive functioning; stimulus barrier; autonomous functioning; synthetic-integrative functioning; and mastery-competence. The nine TEMAS Personality Functions are based on the TEMAS social cognitive and narrative framework. In addition, the TEMAS Personality Functions are based on further research on aggression (Bandura & Walters, 1959,

1967), achievement motivation (Atkinson, 1958, 1981; McClelland et al., 1953/1976), delay of gratification (Mischel, 1974; Mischel & Mischel, 1983), self-concept of competence (Bandura, 1992; Bandura & Walters, 1967), coping with anxiety/depression (Merluzzi, Rudy, & Krejci, 1986), sexual identity (Kohlberg & Ullian, 1974) and moral judgment (Kohlberg, 1976).

Interpersonal/Social-Cognitive Psychology.   There is an increasing consensus among researchers that children develop their personality structures by internalizing the sociocultural values of their families and communities. Accordingly, there is continuous reciprocal feedback between the intrapsychic structure of the personality and the sociocultural environment in which the individual lives.

Sullivan (1947) postulated that the self is a protective mechanism developed from the interaction between the infant and his or her parents. The child is very sensitive to parental approval and censure. As a result of positive and negative parent–child interactions, the child learns that certain behaviors are rewarded—those aspects of the self are perceived as the "good-me." Other behaviors are punished and, therefore, are conceptualized as the "bad-me." In short, Sullivan posited that the self-system of the self-image "may be said to be made up of reflected appraisals" (p. 10) and that "it is built largely of personal symbolic elements learned in contact with significant people" (p.21).

Thus, Sullivan viewed personality as an abstract construct generated from observed social interactions. Moreover, Sullivan identified several subconstructs within the personality. One of these is dynamism, defined as a recurring behavior pattern or ego functioning. Therefore, achievement motivation and other ego functions, such as delay of gratification, control of aggression, self-concept, sexual identity, and moral judgment, seem to be learned from interaction with significant others, especially the mother. Both clinical observation and research indicate that the relationship with parents is of cardinal importance for the development of personality (or ego) functions in children (e.g, Bandura, 1986, 1989; Bandura & Walters, 1967; Kohlberg, 1976; McClelland & Friedman, 1952; Mischel, 1961; Piaget & Inhelder, 1971).

Learning through modeling.   According to Bandura and Walters (1967) and Bandura (1986, 1989), social leaning and, hence, personality development occur largely through children's observations of salient "models" in their environment, such as parents, teachers, and peers. Social learning theory assumes that children acquire symbolic representations of the behaviors exhibited by models, and as the observed behaviors are internalized, they are encoded in schemas, thus becoming part of the personality of the observer. Therefore, adult and peer models within a psychocultural milieu have been identified as exerting the most important influence on personality development. There is an indication that psychically abusive and rejecting parents foster aggressive and acting-out behavior in their children (Bandura & Walters, 1959). There is also evidence that adaptive personality functions, such as achievement, work behaviors, and sexual identity, are learned through observation (e.g., Bandura & Walters, 1967; Kohlberg & Ullian, 1974)

Learning through modeling is governed by four interrelated subprocesses: attention, retention, motoric reproduction, and reinforcement. In fact, vicarious experience alone is ineffectual unless the child attends to, accurately perceives, and is able to reproduce the salient features of the modeled behavior. Furthermore, reinforcement of the modeled behavior is important for the learning of such behaviors.

Human learning through modeling has three basic effects: (a) an imitative effect, which consists of mimicking the behavior of the model in an identical form; (b) a disinhibitory effect, which triggers responses already available in the repertoire of the observer; and (c) an eliciting effect, which triggers unassociated ideas in the observer, thus facilitating new behavior. Consequently, "modeling influences operate principally through their informative function and observers acquire mainly symbolic representations of modeled events rather than specific stimulus–response associations" (Bandura, 1977, p. 16). Various processes of Bandura's (1977) social learning theory are reflected in the interpersonal-social cognitive framework of the TEMAS. For example, the lifelike color and appearance of the cards attract and maintain the child's attention, and the familiarity of characters, events, and settings has a disinhibitory effect, which elicits responses already available in the child's repertoire.

Cognitive Psychology. Singer (1973) emphasized that Piaget (1951) provided the important cognitive connection between modeling and symbolic behavior by proposing that symbolic representation fosters the development of cognitive skills. Piaget (1951) posited that symbolic representation in young children is the result of two modes of experience: accommodation and assimilation. During the process of accommodation, which occurs during the early period of sensorimotor development, the child can imitate only responses that he or she has previously performed spontaneously. At the final stage of sensorimotor development, which occurs at approximately the age of two, children begin the process of assimilation, during which they are able to experience representative imitation. Schemas are arranged internally to create new and complex behaviors without requiring motoric representations. This covert imitation occurs through imaginal representation of modeled behavior.

Piaget and Inhelder (1969, 1971) postulated that the development of imagery follows a two-stage process. The emergence of imagery at the beginning of the symbolic process, which occurs around the age of two, constitutes the first stage, whereas the development of anticipatory imagery, which is the necessary condition for symbolic thinking, is part of the second stage. Anticipatory imagery is internalized imagery derived from imitative acts. The relationship between images and words is a complementary process of concreteness-and-abstractness, whereby images indicate concrete objects, and words signify concepts. Consequently, the role of modeling and symbolic representation in early and middle childhood, and even in adolescence (Singer, 1973), seems to be an important factor in the development of symbolic functioning.

Moreover, Piaget's theoretical formulation of the cognitive development of the child and the research of Paivio on imagery indicate that cognitive development depends on two separate but interacting encoding systems: the imaginal and the verbal. Paivio (1971) posited that the imaginal system processes abstract linguistic symbols. Therefore, images are related to concrete representations and words are related to abstract thinking. Piaget and Inhelder (1971) argued that images stem not only from perception, but also from the internal focusing on operative schemas. This aspect of the memory image as a symbol or schema, and not as a mere extension of perception, is an important aspect of the schema, that integrates the individual perception of present events with memory of personal past events. According to Piaget and Inhelder (1971), an image is a symbol that uses operational representations in the reconstruction of events and the recall of objects, dreams, play, and artistic activities, and, we add, in narrative assessment. Thus, the memory image elicited by a pictorial representation of the TEMAS becomes a symbol that integrates the present perception, the emotional state, and the elicited past learning of the examinee.

Narrative Psychology

Narrative psychology has not yet fully emerged as a separate field (Sarbin, 1986), but is gaining popularity as narrative theory (Kirkman, 2002) in the form of both narrative assessment (e.g. Costantino, 1978; Costantino, Flanagan, & Malgady, 2001; Costantino, Malgady, & Rogler, 1988; Teglasi, 2001) and narrative treatment (e.g., Bracero, in press; Costantino, Malgady, &

Rogler, 1994; Freedman & Combs, 1996; Howard, 1991). Nonetheless, in this chapter, we present sufficient theoretical evidence to discuss the value of the TEMAS test as a narrative assessment tool.

Bruner (1986) posited that there are two modes of thought in obtaining knowledge, the paradigmatic mode, which deals with general causes and effects in the discovery of empirical truth, and the narrative mode, which deals with the way individuals understand the vicissitudes of their own lives. Traditionally, psychology has been using the mechanistic laboratory and experimental methods in obtaining knowledge about individuals. More recently, however, Sarbin (1986), and Mancuso and Sarbin (1983) proposed the narrative mode as a root metaphor in psychology, which allows psychologists to understand individuals through their narratives or life histories. Narrative theory suggests that there is an interrelationship between cultural narrative and personal narrative because culture influences the individual and in turn the individual narratives reflect the culture in which they are told (Kirkman, 2002). In addition, there is a mutual relationship between individual and cultural narrative and the sociocognitive psychology of human development posited by Bandura (1991), Piaget and Inhandler (1971), and Singer and Pope (1978) because those social learning theorists must explain the development of the self in the different stages of the life span through the narrative identity of the individual. In addition, there is a mutual relationship between individual and cultural narrative, and the socio-cognitive psychology of human development. In fact, cognitive and social learning theorists such as Bandura (1991), Piaget & Inhandler (1971), and Singer & Pope (1978) posit that the self develops through the narrative identity of the individual across different stages of the life span. Narrative identity is developed within the matrix of social and cultural milieu (Bruner, 1990) and through telling about our selves so that we develop a sense of the self (Mancuso & Sarbin, 1983). Earlier we stated that in the cognitive development of the child, the relationship between images and words is a complementary process of concreteness-and-abstractness, whereby images indicate concrete objects and words signify concepts. As narrative theory posits that the self-identity develops through life-story construction, by linking social cognitive psychology and narrative psychology, we can confidently assume that narrative assessment is the most important and valid technique in understanding personality functioning. In addition, the linguist Charlotte Linde (as reported in Kirkman, 2002) stated that individuals need a coherent life story in order to be able to adaptively function in their environment. However, quite often life stories go wrong, and it is the responsibility of psychologists and other mental health professionals to understand these "broken" life stories and engage in "story repair" (Howard, 1991).

Cognitive, Affective, and Personality Functions:
Narrative Psychopathology

The TEMAS Narrative Test assesses both the visual-imaginal and the verbal processes of the individual. Therefore, in addition to assessing the contents of thematic responses, which symbolize the various personality functions, it is important to assess the structure of the stories, which comprise such cognitive functions as reaction time in responding to the pictorial stimuli, total time in telling the story, and fluency or number of words per story. There are 18 cognitive functions assessed by TEMAS, listed earlier in this chapter.

Analysis of thematic content of the stories seems to be a poor predictor of personality functioning and psychopathology. Conversely, it has been pointed out that perceptual-cognitive styles tend to be more accurate predictors of maladaptive behavior and psychopathology (Kagan, 1960; Teglasi, 2001).

Extending the interpersonal theory of Sullivan (1953), it can be assumed that the self-system, which is the core of the Personality Functions and which is developed through observational learning within a cultural milieu, tends to motivate and direct perceptions toward seeking information that is congruent with the individual's self-concept. The self-system tends to defend against information that is threatening to the self-concept by using selective inattention. Although selective inattention is a cognitive style, it precipitates maladaptive behavior and psychopathology when used in excess. As a perceptual defense, selective inattention narrows perception of the psychocultural milieu and sometimes engenders a misunderstanding in obtaining new knowledge.

As we explained earlier, Piaget (1951) and Piaget and Inhelder, (1971) provided the cognitive connection between modeling and symbolic behavior by positing that symbolic representation fosters the development of cognitive skills. Within this social cognitive theory, modeled events are internalized as memory images or personal schemas, which can be defined as a symbolic repository of all life events (affects and actions) experienced by the individual through the various developmental stages and the numerous life vicissitudes. By integrating this schema theory with the narrative theory, we can state that, as the individual uses language to reconstruct those events, narratives or personal stories are metaphorical representations of the self (Mancuso & Sarbin, 1983). Thus, the memory image elicited by the TEMAS pictorial stimuli becomes a symbol reconstruction which integrates the present perception of the event, the emotional state, and the elicited past learning experience of the examinee. Within this reformulated theoretical framework, schemas are not defined as mental structures embodying internal representations, that are unconscious (Teglasi, 2001), but as conscious mental structures that embody symbolic representations of past learning with an on-going feedback system interacting with present perceptions and experiences within a cultural social-cognitive milieu. Schemas can become mental structures outside the conscious awareness in individuals who lose contact with the reality of the outside world, thus cutting off the feedback system from the outside and relying only on the internal self-system.

Furthermore, psychopathology has been reported to be associated with perceptual omissions and/or transformations of significant stimuli within an individual's environment (Costantino, Colon-Malgady, Malgady & Perez, 1991). These omissions are revealed by Omissions of Main Characters and of Secondary Characters, Events, and Settings, and by Personality Functions Not Pulled in a child's TEMAS stories. These types of omissions are also known in the cognition literature as attentional deficits. With respect to learning disabilities and hyperactivity, omissions are labeled as deficits in Selective Attention, which has been defined as a developmental lag in the ability of learning-disabled and hyperactive children to select, and use adaptively, attentional and encoding skills (e.g. Copeland and Wisniewski, 1981; Costantino, Colon-Malgady, Malgady, & Perez, 1991; Costantino, Malgady, Colon-Malgady, & Bailey, 1992; Costantino, Malgady, Rogler, & Tsui, 1988).

With respect to psychopathology, this attention deficit is known in the literature as Selective Inattention (Sullivan, 1953), which may be defined as a disturbance of awareness in which the individual fails to perceive significant details of daily life. This deficit is pathological because the individual tends to overlook his or her own obvious behaviors, as well as the behaviors of others and interactions between the self and others (Sullivan, 1953, 1956). Therefore, the chronic use of Selective Inattention interferes with adaptive interpersonal relations and reality testing, and impedes adaptive personality development. Within the social cognitive/narrative theoretical framework, the terms "adaptive Selective Attention" and "maladaptive Selective Attention" are used to explain both Omissions in Cognitive Functions and Personality Functions Not Pulled. Maladaptive Selective Attention is defined as a perceptual deficit, in which the individual does not attend to relevant stimuli because they are anxiety provoking or because it is socially desirable to repress stimuli depicting undesirable themes such as aggression and stealing.

In addition, individuals presenting maladaptive behavior and/or emotional distress tend to distort pictorial stimuli (e.g, Exner, 1993; Exner & Weiner, 1982; Costantino, Malgady, Colon-Malgady & Bailey, 1992; Costantino, Malgady, Rogler, & Tsui, 1988; Teglasi, 2001). These distortions, which in the Rorschach Comprehensive System (Exner, 1993) are reflected in poor form quality, in the TEMAS test are labeled as transformations. As seen in the following example, there are also four types of omissions and transformations in TEMAS. The following TEMAS stories illustrate both omission and transformations. In response to Card 7 (A mother observing son and daughter arguing in accepting responsibility for a broken lamp), a 7-year-old clinic girl says:

> The mother is pregnant and they are fighting over the mother for the baby. Once the mother says, "I'm pregnant." they get into a fight and they say: "She said to me first" ... "No, she said to me first." ...

In this story, we readily note that the examinee changes the conflict depicted in the card: Boy and Girl arguing over a broken lamp, while the mother is waiting to know: "Who broke the lamp." Hence, we have an omission of setting, the broken lamp, transformations of depicted theme: attributing responsibility of wrongdoing to the other, transformation of the depicted mother from arbiter to finding out the truth to an expecting mother. The seven-year-old female examinee told this story by changing the reality of the pictorial stimuli because she had her story to tell based on her need of wanting a baby brother because she was the only child of two middle-aged parents. This child was referred to a mental health clinic because she continued to "play with an imaginary baby brother; she accused her parents of not loving her because they would not have another child." From this example, it can be observed that omissions and transformations occur not only as cognitive deficits in the structure of the story but also in the content of the story.

Operational Definitions of the Cognitive Functions

A cognitive function is defined as a perceptual pattern according to which the individual organizes information about the self, the environment, and the relationship between the two. Eighteen Cognitive Functions can be assessed using the scoring criteria outlined in chapter 5.

1. Reaction Time (RT) is the latency or time elapsed between the presentation of the TEMAS picture and the moment the respondent begins to verbalize the story.
2. Total Time (TT) refers to the response time plus the time of the tructured Inquiries (See chapter 3). Total Time is the time elapsed between the start of a story and its conclusion, including responses to all relevant enquiries.

3. Fluency (FL) refers to verbal productivity, which is determined by the total word count of each TEMAS story.
4. Total Omissions (OM) refer to a count of the characters, events, and settings that are depicted in the pictures but are not mentioned in an individual's thematic response.
5. Main Character Omissions (MCO) refer to omissions from a thematic response of the principal character or characters present in the picture.
6. Secondary Character Omissions (SCO) refer to omissions from a thematic response of figures other than the main character that are depicted.
7. Event Omissions (EO) refer to the failure of a respondent to identify what is happening in a picture.
8. Setting Omissions (SO) refer to the failure of a respondent to identify the location where the characters are acting and events of the story are occurring.
9. Total Transformations (TRANS) refer to the total number of a respondent's perceptual distortions of the characters, events, and settings depicted in the pictures.
10. Main Character Transformations (MCT) refer to the principal figures that are present in thematic responses but are incorrectly identified by the respondent.
11. Secondary Character Transformations (SCT) refer to characters other than the main character that are mentioned in a thematic response but are incorrectly identified by the respondent.
12. Event Transformations (ET) refer to occurrences depicted in a picture that are incorrectly identified by a respondent.
13. Setting Transformations (ST) refer to the incorrect identification by a respondent of the location where characters are acting and events are occurring.
14. Conflict (CON) refers to the recognition of interpersonal and intrapersonal polarities of Personality Functions depicted in a card. For example, the choice of buying an ice cream cone now (immediate gratification) is contrasted with the choice of saving money to buy a bicycle in the future (delayed gratification).
15. Sequencing (SEQ) refers to relating the order of events to the past (what happened before), to the present (what is happening now), and to the future (what will happen).
16. Imagination (IMAG) refers to the projection of information into the content of the story, as opposed to responding with themes that are stimulus-bound and relate only descriptive details of characters, events, and settings.

17. Relationships (REL) refer to the identification of the characters and how they are related to each other.
18. Inquiries (INQ) refer to questions asked by the examiner both to clarify responses given spontaneously by the examinee during the telling of the story and to elicit omitted information about characters, events, settings, and affective functions during the Structured Inquiries.

The Personality Functions

The dynamic social-cognitive theoretical framework of the TEMAS is based on the concept that personality development occurs within a sociocultural system. In this system, individuals internalize the cultural values of family and society; personality functions are learned initially through modeling and are then integrated and represented symbolically through imaginal and verbal processes. These functions and their underlying motives, which are learned within a sociocultural context, are readily transferred to the testing situation, then projected into thematic stories when the projective stimuli are similar to the circumstances in which those functions were originally learned. To optimize its utility as a projective/narrative test, the TEMAS was developed with structured, familiar, and culturally relevant stimuli.

Operational Definitions of the Personality Functions

Within the stated dynamic social-cognitive theoretical framework, the following nine Personality functions are assessed by the TEMAS.

1. Interpersonal Relations (IR) refer to the degree and quality of relatedness to parental and authority figures, siblings, and peers, as revealed in the child's TEMAS stories. Adaptive and maladaptive interpersonal relationships are defined by the storyteller's ability to synthesize the polarities of dependence–individuation, respect–disrespect, and nurturance–rejection. An adaptive interpersonal relationship refers to the individual's ability to relate to others in an age-appropriate (mature) manner free from conflicts and aggressive needs.
2. Aggression (AGG) refers to the direct verbal and physical expression of the intent to kill, harm, or injure oneself or others, or to destroy property. An Aggression fantasy/ideation reflects loss of impulse control, or acquired and maintained maladaptive social behavior.

3. Anxiety/Depression (A/D) refers to irrational fears or worries about situations that are perceived as dangerous and/or threatening at the present time or in the future. Other manifestations of this function include: worries about school; pervasive feelings of unhappiness; psychosomatic symptoms (e.g., headaches, stomachaches, palpitations, dizziness, helplessness, or loneliness); crying; and being shy and withdrawn.

At this point, it is important to clarify the rationale for labeling Anxiety/Depression as a Personality Function and for having integrated the two into a single function. First, although anxiety and depression are generally defined as emotional reactions and/or conditions characterized by feelings of tension and helplessness (e.g., Beck, 1972; Speilberger, 1971), anxiety and depression are also associated with coping styles and/or defense mechanisms (e.g., Forgus & Shulman, 1979; Sobel, 1981). Within the dynamic social-cognitive theoretical framework of TEMAS, anxiety and depression are defined as coping styles and defense mechanisms: therefore, they are labeled as a Personality Function. Second, anxiety and depression symptoms tend to be exhibited in a combined form by children. Within the TEMAS theoretical framework, anxiety and depression are viewed as symptoms, which tend to be exhibited by children in an integrated manner; thus, they are scored under the same function. Nonetheless, clinicians can differentiate between the presence of anxiety vs. depression in a TEMAS protocol by "correlating" the low score in Anxiety/Depression with the high scores in the Affective Functions of Fearful and Sad. For example, if an examinee has a T-score (< 50) in Anxiety/Depression and a High T-score (> 50) in Fearful with a Low T-score (< 50) in Sad, it can be stated that the examinee may present an anxiety reaction "disorder." Conversely, if an examinee has a T-score (< 50) in Anxiety/Depression and a High T-Score (> 50) in Sad with a low a Low T-score (< 50) in Fearful, it can be stated that the examinee presents a depression reaction "disorder." It is important to note that Anxiety/Depression as well as aggression scores in TEMAS protocols are inversely related. For example, a low score in anxiety/depression denotes high anxiety/depression, whereas a high score denotes low anxiety/depression.

4. Achievement Motivation (AM) refers to the desire to attain a goal or to succeed in an endeavor that is measured by some standard of excellence. Achievement Motivation could refer to personal accomplishment or to competition with others in areas such as sports and games, school and learning, or vocation and avocation.

5. Delay of Gratification (DG) refers to the ability to forgo an immediate reward or gratification in order to await or work to achieve a greater future reward or gratification.

6. Self-Concept (SC) refers to the realistic self-perception of intellectual, social, physical, and vocation abilities, and also to an individual's ability to master his or her environment.

7. Sexual Identity (SEX) refers to the positive perception of the self in various social roles, and to age-appropriate psychosocial maturity. More specifically, Sexual Identity refers to an individual's realistic perception of roles appropriate to his or her gender—sex roles can be perceived as gender-appropriate, inappropriate, or androgynous. Inappropriate sex role behavior may be indicated by the presence of anxiety about behavior.

8. Moral Judgment (MJ) refers to the developmental stage at which the superego or social conscience is operational. More specifically, Moral Judgment refers to the ability to discriminate between right and wrong and to act accordingly, to accept responsibility for wrongdoing, and to experience appropriate guilt for wrongdoing.

9. Reality Testing (REAL) refers to the ability to distinguish between fantasy and reality. Furthermore, it refers to an individual's ability to recognize problematic situations and to anticipate the personal and social consequences of his or her behavior.

Adaptive Versus Maladaptive Cognitive, Affective, and Personality Functions

Within the social cognitive-narrative framework of the TEMAS, psychopathology is conceptualized as a maladaptive interaction between the perceptions and personal schema, causing an individual to make perceptual mistakes about himself or herself and the psychocultural environment.

The relationship between cognition, affect, and psychopathology has been explored both theoretically and empirically by Beck (1971), a cognitive theorist, who posited that:

> The relationship of cognition to affect in normal individuals is similar to that observed in psychopathological states. Among normals, the sequence perception-cognition-emotion is indicated largely by the demand character of the stimulus situation. In psychopathological conditions, the reaction to the stimulus is determined to a much greater extent by internal processes. The affective response is likely to be excessive or inappropriate

because of the idiosyncratic conceptualization of the event. The input from the external situation is molded to conform to the typical schemas activated in these conditions. As a result, interpretations of experience embody arbitrary judgments. Overgeneralizations relevant to danger, loss, unjustified attack, and self-enhancement are typical of anxiety neuroses, depression, paranoid states, and hypomanic states, respectively. (p. 495)

Beck (1971) clearly indicated that cognitions precipitate affective states; in fact, anxiety is triggered when an individual is unable to cope with threat or stress that has caused him or her harm, and that threat or stress persists.

Recent cognitive and social cognitive/interpersonal theorists have posited theoretical models that reformulate the ego psychology and cognitive, interpersonal, social cognitive, and narrative models described in this chapter. Following Tegliasi (2001) model of understanding personality through narrative analyses, we also posit, as explained earlier, that schema are conscious mental structures embodying symbolic representations of past learning with an on-going feedback system interacting with present perceptions and experiences within a cultural social cognitive milieu. Schemas can become mental structures outside the conscious awareness in individuals who lose contact with the reality of the outside world, thus cutting off the feedback system from the outside and relying only on the internal self-system. Within this theoretical model, schemas represent explanatory models of perception, memory image, affect, event, and feedback (e.g., Bandura, 1991; Beck & Clark, 1997; Horowitz, 1991; Piaget & Inhelder, 1971; Singer, 1973), thus integrating the various personality theoretical frameworks in understanding personality functioning. The schema theory, therefore, gives a valid explanation of both adaptive and maladaptive personality functions. In this chapter, we have argued that schemas are conscious mental structures embodying symbolic representations of past learning with an on-going feedback system interacting with present perceptions and experiences within a cultural social-cognitive milieu. On the other hand, schemas can become mental structures outside the conscious awareness in individuals who have contact with the reality of the outside world, thus cutting off the feedback system from the outside, and relying only on the internal self-system, which may contains misconceptions. A similar explanation is advanced by Teglasi (2001), which is based on the models of Beck & Clark (1997) and Horowitz (1991), who posit that the schema construct explains both normal and abnormal personality processes because schema-driven information processing affords past knowledge to influence present perception in adaptive or maladaptive ways.

According to the TEMAS definition of psychopathology, the nine Personality Functions depicted in the stimulus cards are assessed along an adaptive–maladaptive continuum according to psychosocial criteria. As indicated earlier, social cognitive psychologists such as Bruner, Bandura, and Sullivan have argued that the most important aspect in adaptive personality functioning is in the interaction of the self-system with the social system, which dictates the values of various covert and overt behaviors by determining which functions are useful and adaptive and which functions are detrimental and maladaptive. In summary, with the TEMAS theoretical model, the memory image of the examinee elicited by the TEMAS pictorial stimuli becomes a symbol reconstruction that integrates the present perception, the emotional state, and the elicited past learning. Adaptive or maladaptive responses are representations of the personal schemas or self-system of the examinee, its influence on the present perception of the pictorial stimuli, the effect of the cultural sensitivity of the stimuli, and the degree of the interactive feedback among the three processes.

REFERENCES

Anderson, M. P. (1981). Assessment of imaginal processes: Approaches and issues. In T. Merluzzi, C. Glass, & M. Genest (Eds.), *Cognitive Assessment* (pp. 149–187). New York, NY: Guilford.

Atkinson, J. W. (Ed.). (1958). *Motives in fantasy, action, and society*. Princeton, NJ: Van Nostrand.

Atkinson, J. W. (1981). Studying personality in the context of an advanced motivational psychology. *American Psychologist, 36,* 117–128.

Auld, F., (1954). Contribution of behavior therory to projective testing. *Journal of Projective Techniques, 18,* 129–142.

Auld, F., Jr. (1952). Influence of social class on personality test responses. *Psychological Bulletin, 49,* 318–332.

Avila-Espada, A. (1986). *Manual Operativo para el Examen de Apercepcion Tematica.* Operating Manual of the Tematic Apperception Test (TAT). Madrid: Ediciones Piramide, S.A.

Bandura, A. (1977). *Social learning theory.* Englewood Cliffs, NJ: Prentice-Hall.

Bandura, A. (1986). *Social foundations of thought and action: A social cognitive theory.* Englewood Cliffs, NJ: Prentice Hall.

Bandura, A. (1989), Social cognitive theory. *Annals of child development, 6,* 1–60.

Bandura, A. (1991), Social cognitive theory of self-regulation. *Organizational Behavior and Human Decision Processes, 50,* 248–287.

Bandura, A. (1992). Self-efficacy: Thought control of action. In R. Schwarzer (Ed.), *Self-efficacy: Thought control of action* (pp. 3–88). Washington, DC: Hemisphere.

Bandura, A., & Walters, R. H. (1959). *Adolescent aggression.* New York: Ronald.

Bandura, A., & Walters, R. H. (1967). *Social learning and personality development.* New York: Holt, Rinehart & Winston.

Beck, A. T. (1971). Cognition, affect, and psychopathology. *Archives of General Psychiatry, 24,* 495–500.

Beck, A. T. (1972). *Depression: Cases and treatment.* Philadelphia: Universtity of Pensylvania Press.

Beck, A. T., & Clark, D. A. (1997). An information processing model of anxiety: Automatic and strategic processes. *Behavior Research and Therapy, 35,* 49–58.

Bellak, L. (1954) A study of limitations and "failures:" Toward an ego psychology of projective techniques. *Journal of Prospective Techniques, 10,* 279–283.

Bellak, L. (1986). *The TAT, CAT and SAT in clinical use.* (4th ed.) New York: Grune & Stratton.

Bellak, L., & Bellak, S. S. (1949). *Children's Apperception Test.* Larchmant, NY: C.P.S.

Bellak, L., Hurvich, M., & Gediman, H. K. (1973). *Ego functions in schizophrenics, neurotics, and normals, 15,* 412–418.

Bracero, W. (in press). *Between the worlds: The assessment and treatment of the culturally diverse.* Northvale, Jason Aronson.

Brackbill, G. A. (1951). Some effects of color on thematic fantasy. *Journal of Consulting and normals, 15,* 412–418.

Bruner, J. (1986). *Actual minds, possible worlds.* Cambridge, MA: Harvard University Press.

Bruner, J. (1990). *Acts of meaning,* Cambridge, MA: Harvard University Press.

Copeland, A.P., & Wisniewski, N. M. (1981). Learning disability and hyperactivity: Deficit in selective attention. *Journal of Experimental Child Psychology, 32,* 88–101.

Costantino, G. (1978, November). *TEMAS, a new thematic apperception test to Measure ego functions and development in urban Black and Hispanic children.* Paper presented at the Second Annual Conference on Fantasy and the Imaging Process, Chicago, IL.

Costantino, G. (1987). *TEMAS (Tell-Me-A-Story) test pictures.* Los Angeles, CA: Western Psychological Services.

Costantino, G. (1992). Overcoming bias in educational assessment of Hispanic students. (In K. Geisinger (Ed.), *The psychological testing of Hispanics.* (pp. 89–97). Washington, DC, American Psychological Association.

Costantino, G., Colon-Malgady, G., Malgady, R. G., & Pérez, A. (1991). Assessment of attention deficit disorder using a thematic apperception technique. *Journal of Personality Assessment, 57,* 87–95.

Costantino, G., Flanagan, R., & Malgady, R. (1995). The history of the Rorschach: Overcoming bias in multicultural projective assessment. *Rorschachiana: Yearbook of the International Rorschach Society, 20,* 148–171.

Costantino, G., Flanagan, R., & Malgady, R. (2001). Narrative assessments: TAT, CAT, and TEMAS. In L. A. Suzuki, P. J. Meller, & J. G. Ponterotto (Eds.) *Handbook of Multicultural Assessment* (2nd ed., pp. 217–237). San Francisco: Jossey-Bass.

Costantino, G., & Malgady, R. G. (1996). Development of TEMAS, A Multicultural Thematic Apperception Test: Psychometric Properties and Clinical Utility. In G. R. Sodowsky & J. Impara (Eds.), *Multicultural Assessment in Counseling and Clinical Psychology.* (pp. 85–136). Lincoln, NE: University of Nebraska.

Costantino, G., & Malgady, R. G. (1999). The Tell-Me-A-Story Test: A multicultural offspring of the Thematic Apperception Test. In L. Geiser & M. I. Stein (Eds.), *Evocative images: The Thematic Apperception Test and the art of projection* (pp. 191–206). Washington, DC: American Psychological Association.

Costantino, G., Malgady, R. G., (2000). Multicultural and cross-cultural utility of the TEMAS (Tell-Me-A-Story) Test. In R. H. Dana (Ed.), *Handbook of cross-cultural/multicultural personality assessment.* (pp. 481–514). Mahwah, NJ: Lawrence Erlbaum Associates.

Costantino, G., Malgady, R. G., Colon-Malgady, G., Bailey, J. (1992). Clinical utility of TEMAS with non-minority children. *Journal of Personality Assessment, 59*(3), 433–438.

Costantino, G., Malgady, R. G., Rogler, L. H., (1988). *TEMAS (Tell-Me-A-Story) test manual.* Los Angeles: Western Psychological Services.

Costantino, G., Malgady, R. G., Rogler, L. H., & Tsui, E. (1988). Discriminant analysis of clinical outpatients and public school children by TEMAS: A thematic apperception test for Hispanics and Blacks. *Journal of Personality Assessment, 52,* 670–678.

Costantino, G., Malgady, R. G., & Rogler, L. H. (1994). Storytelling-Through Pictures: Culturally sensitive psychotherapy for Hispanic children and adolescents. *Journal of Clinical Child Psychology, 23,* 13–20.

Dana, R. H. (1986). Personality assessment and Native Americans. *Journal of Personality Assessment, 50,* 480–500.

Dana, R. H. (1993). *Multicultural assessment perspectives for professional psychology.* Boston: Allyn & Bacon.

Dana, R. H. (1996). Culturally competent assessment practice in the United States. *Journal of Personality Assessment, 66,* 472–487.

Dana, R. H. (1998). *Understanding cultural identity in intervention and assessment.*

Dana, R. H. (2000). Multicultural assessment of child and adolescent personality and psychopathology. In A. L. Comunian & U. Gielen (Eds.), *International perspectives on human development* (pp. 233–258). Lengerich, Germany: Pabst Science Publishers.

Epstein, S. (1966). Some considerations on the nature of ambiguity and the use of stimulus dimensions in projective techniques. *Journal of Consulting Psychology, 30,* 183–192.

Epstein, S. (1994). Integration of cognitive and psychodynamic unconscious. *American Psychologist, 49,* 709–724.

Exner, J. E. (1978). *The Rorschach: A comprehensive system: Vol. 2. Recent research and advanced interpretation.* New York: John Wiley & Sons.

Exner, J. (1993). *The Rorschach: A comprehensive system.* (Vol. 1, 3rd ed.) New York: John Wiley & Sons.

Exner J. E., & Weiner, I. B. (1982). *The Rorschach: A comprehensive system: Assessment of Children and Adolescents.* Wiley-Interscience Series on Personality Processes, (Vol. 3). New York, NY: John Wiley and Sons.

Exner, J. E., & Weiner, I. B. (1995). *The Rorschach: A comprehensive system: Assessment of children and adolescents* (2nd ed,) Vol. 3, pp. New York: Wiley.

Flanagan, R., & DiGiuseppe, R. (1999). A critical review of the TEMAS: A step within the Development of Thematic Apperception Instruments. *Psychology in the schools, 36*(1), 1–10.

Flanagan, R., Losapio, G., Greenfeld, R., Costantino, G., Hernandez, A. (2004, July). *Using narratives to assess children's social problem skills.* 112th APA Convention, Honolulu, Hawaii.

Freedman, J., & Combs, G. (1996). *Narrative therapy: The social construction of preferred realities.* New York: W. W. Norton.

Freud, S. (1961). The ego and the id. In J. Strachey (Ed. and Trans.), *The standard edition of the complete psychological works of Sigmund Freud* (Vol. 19, pp. 3–66). London: Hogarth press. (Original work published 1923)

Forgus, R., & Shulman, B. (1979). *Personality: A cognitive view.* Englewood Cliffs, NJ: Prentice-Hall.

Harris, D.B. (1963). *Children's drawings as measures of intellectual maturity.* New York: Hartcourt, Brace & World.

Hartmann, H. (1951). Ego psychology and the problem of adaptation. In D. Rapaport (Ed.), *Organization and pathology of thought* (pp. New York): Columbia University Press.

Holt, R. R. (1960a). Cognitive controls and primary processes. *Journal of Psychological Researches, 4,*105–112.

Holt, R. R. (1960b). Recent developments in psychoanalytic ego psychology and their implications for diagnostic testing. *Journal of Prospective Techniques, 24,* 251–266.

Holt, R. R. (1961). The nature of TAT stories as cognitive products: a psychoanalytic approach. In J. Kagan & G. Lesser (Eds.), *Contemporary issues in thematic apperceptive methods* (pp. 3–40). Springfield, IL: Charles C. Thomas.

Horowitz, M.J. (1991). States, schemas, and control: General theories for psychotherapy integration. *Journal of Psychotherapy Integration, 1,* 85–102

Howard, G. (1991). Culture tales: A narrative approach to thinking, cross-cultural psychology and psychotherapy. *American Psychologist, 46,* 187–197

Johnson, A. W., Jr. & Dana, R. H. (1965). Color on the TAT. *Journal of Projective Techniques and Personality Assessment, 29,* 178–182.

Kagan, J. (1960). Thematic apperceptive techniques with children. In A. Rabin & M. Haworth (Eds.), *Projective techniques with children* (pp. 105–129). New York: Grune & Stratton.

Kagan, J., & Lesser, G. (1961). *Contemporary issues in thematic apperceptive methods.* Springfield, IL: C. C. Thomas.

Kirkman. M. (2002). What's the plot? Applying narrative theory to research psychology. *Australian Psychologist, 37*, 30–38.

Kohlberg, L. (1976). Moral stages and moralization. The cognitive-developmental approach. In T. Lichona (Ed.), *Moral development and behavior: Theory, research, and social issues.* (pp. 31–53). New York: Holt, Rinehart & Winston.

Kohlberg, L. & Ullian, D. Z. (1974). Stages in the development of psychosexual concepts and attitudes. In R. C. Friedman, R. M. Richart, & R. I. Van de Wiele (Eds.), *Sex differences in behavior* (pp. 209–222). New York: Wiley.

Lubin, N. M. (1955). The effect of color in the TAT on production of mentally retarded subjects. *American Journal of Mental Deficiency, 60*, 336–370.

Mancuso, J. C., & Sarbin, T. R. (1983). The self-narrative in the enactment of roles. In T. R. Sarbin & K. E. Scheibe (Eds.). *Studies in social identity* (pp. 233–253). New York: Praeger.

McAdams, D. P. (1994). *The person: An introduction to personality psychology* (2nd ed.). Fort Worth: Harcourt Brace.

McClelland, D. C., Atkinson, J. W., Clark, R. W., & Lowell, E. L. (1976). *The achievement motive.* New York: Irvington. (Original work published 1953)

McClelland, D. C., & Friedman, G.A. (1952). A cross-cultural study of the relationship between child-training practices and achievement motivation appearing in folktales. In G. E. Swanson, T.H. Newcomb, & E. L. Hartley (Eds.), *Readings in social psychology* (pp. 243–249). New York: Holt.

Merluzzi, T. V., Rudy, T. E., & Krejci, M. J. (1986). Social skill and anxiety: Information processing perspectives. In R. E. Ingram (Ed.), *Information processing approaches to clinical psychology* (pp. 109–129). Orlando, FL: Academic Press.

Mischel, W. (1961). Father absence and delay of gratification: cross-cultural comparison. *Journal of Abnormal and Social Psychology, 62*, 116–124.

Mischel, W. (1974). Processes in delay gratification. In L. Berkowitz (Ed.), *Advances in experimental social psychology* (Vol. 7, pp. 249–292). New York, NY: Academic Press.

Mischel, H. N., & Mischel, W. (1983). The development of children's knowledge of self-control-strategies. *Child Development, 54*, 603–619.

Murray, H. A. (1938). *Explorations in personality.* New York: Oxford Press.

Murray, H. A. (1943). *Thematic Apperception Test Manual.* Cambridge: Harvard University Press.

Murray, H. A. (1951). Uses of the Thematic Aperception Test. *American Journal of Psychiatry, 107*, 577–581.

Murstein, B. I. (1963). *Theory and research in projective techniques.* New York: John Wiley & Sons.

Murstein, B. I. (1972). Normative written TAT responses for a college sample. *Journal of Personality Assessment, 36*, 109–147.

Padilla, A. M. (1979). Critical factors in the testing of Hispanic Americans: A review and some suggestions for the future. In R. Tyler & S. White (Eds.), *Testing, teaching and learning: Report of a conference on testing* (pp. 219–233). Washington, DC: National Institute of Education.

Paivio, A. (1971). *Imagery and verbal processes.* New York: Holt, Rinehart & Winston.

Piaget, J. (1951). *Play, dreams and imitation in childhood.* New York: W.W. Norton.

Piaget, J., & Inhelder, B. (1969). *The psychology of the child.* New York: Basic Books.

Piaget, J., & Inhelder, B. (1971). *Mental imagery in the child.* New York: Basic Books.

Polkinghorne, D. E. (1995). Narrative configuration in qualitative analysis. In J. A., Hatch & R. Wisnieski (Eds.). *Life history and narrative* (pp. 5–22). London: Falmer.

Polkinghorne, D. E. (2004). *Practice and the human sciences: The case for judgment-based practice of care.* Albany, NY: State University of New York Press.

Ritzler, B. (1993). TEMAS (Tell-Me-A-Story). *Journal of Psychoeducational Assessment, 11,* 381–389.

Ritzler, B.A. (1996). Projective methods for multicultural personality assessment: Rorschach, TEMAS, and Early Memory Procedures. In L. A. Suzuki, P. J. Meller, & J. G. Ponterotto (Eds.) *Handbook of Multicultural Assessment: Clinical, psychological and educational applications.* (pp.115–136). San Francisco: Jossey-Bass Publishers.

Rogler, L. H., Malgady, R. G., Costantino, G., & Blumenthal, R. (1987). What does cultural sensitivity mean? The case of Hispanics. *American Psychologist, 42,* pp. 565–560.

Rotter, J. B., Rafferty, J. E., & Lotsof, A. B. (1954). The validity of the Rotter Incomplete Sentence Blank: High School Form. *Journal of Consulting Psychology, 18,* 105–111.

Sarbin, T. R., (1986). *Narrative psychology: The storied nature of human conduct.* New York: Praeger.

Siipola, E. M., (1950). Influence of color reactions to inkblots. *Journal of Personality, 18,* 358.

Singer, J. L. (1973). *The child's world of make believe: Experimental studies of imaginative play.* New York: Academic Press.

Singer, J. L., & Pope, K. (Eds.). (1978). *The power of human imagination: New methods in psychotherapy.* New York: Plenum Press.

Sobel, H. J. (1981). Projective methods of cognitive analysis. In T. Merluzzi, C. Glass, & M. Genest (Eds.), *Cognitive assessment* (pp. 127–148). New York: Guilford.

Spielberger, C. D. (1971). Anxiety as an emotional state. In C.D. Spielberger (Ed.), *Anxiety: Current trends in theory and research.* (Vol. 1, pp. 23–49). Palo Alto, CA: Consulting Psychologist Press.

Sullivan, H. S. (1947). *Conception of modern psychiatry.* Washington, DC: The William Alanson White Psychiatric Foundation.

Sullivan, H. S. (1953). *The interpersonal theory of psychiatry.* New York: W.W. Norton.

Sullivan, H. S. (1956). *Clinical studies in psychiatry.* New York: W.W. Norton.

Teglasi., H. (2001). *Essential of TAT and other storytelling techniques assessment.* New York: John Wiley & Sons.

Thompson, C. E. (1949). The Thompson modification of the thematic apperception test. *Journal of Projective Techniques, 15,* 469–478.

Thompson, C. E., & Bachrach, J. (1951). The use of color in the Thematic Apperception Test. *Journal of Projective Techniques,* 15, 173–184.

II

ESSENTIALS OF TEMAS ASSESSMENT

Since the advent of Alfred Binet's work in the intelligence testing movement in France during the early 20th century, apart from Sir Frances Galton's more biological approach to the task, controversy has surrounded the very definition and nature of the concept of intelligence itself. Racial differences in IQ testing are well documented. Whether or not standardized IQ tests indeed measure such a putative construct has been hotly debated. Those arguing vehemently that intelligence differs across races, perhaps none more strongly than Arthur Jensen's 1969 paper that drew on well-documented empirical data, have been branded "racists."

In all fairness, however, even Jensen was careful to note, drawing on the asymptotic properties of the proverbial normal curve, that African Americans are included at the highest levels of the White bell curve, and moreover, that Whites are included at the lowest levels of the African American distribution. In other words, both racial IQ distributions overlap, but the White curve is displaced about one full standard deviation (an extraordinary effect size for a population) to the right. Since then, there have been numerous attempts to develop so-called culture-free and culture-fair IQ tests—none of which have sustained either rigorous psychometric scrutiny or widespread usage within clinical practice. The debate remains unresolved and resurfaces prominently, seemingly every decade, when a sufficiently imminent scholar (e.g., R. J. Hernstein) tempts fate to broach the subject. Perhaps as an offspring of the intelligence testing controversy, racial and ethnic bias in personality assessment has slowly and somewhat surreptitiously crept into the psychological testing arena. The history of this movement is described in the first section of this book.

The TEMAS test was conceived nearly three decades ago, based on the notion that standard projective/narrative instruments, such as the TAT and even the seemingly amorphous Rorschach test, are not devoid of cultural content. Consequently, the TEMAS test was constructed with specific attention to cultural substance in its depiction of multiracial characters, inner city urban settings, and portrayal of ethnic themes. Unlike much of the research that has transpired with traditional projective/narrative tests, which have enjoyed widespread clinical popularity (i.e., according to a recent APA survey, the Rorschach is still the most popular test used by practicing clinicians), they have been largely exempt from considerations of reliability and validity, unlike virtually all other psychometric instruments. The TEMAS test is an exception.

Chapter 5 covers two important areas of the TEMAS test, Administration and Scoring. The administration uniqueness rests on traditional narrative test instructions requiring a complete story with temporal sequences of now, before and after, as well as structured inquiries at the end of the spontaneous story about missing sequences and other indices from the story. The structured inquiries component provides opportunity for storytellers who need prompting to complete a story without being penalized. In addition to insuring a complete story for scoring purposes, this component was introduced for the first time in a narrative test as part of the administration instructions. The TEMAS problem-solving objective scoring system is also introduced in narrative assessment for the first time, thus giving legimate validity to this narrative test.

Chapter 6 begins with an overview of the epidemiological character of culturally diverse children's mental health status in the United States, portraying this population as high-risk for DSM psychiatric disorders, school dropout, and associated behavioral and forensic problems. The need for culturally appropriate personality assessment leading to accurate diagnosis and treatment planning is paramount. Based on a litany of studies in the U.S. and Puerto Rico, considerable evidence is amassed documenting the internal consistency, interrater, and test–retest reliability of the TEMAS test. Content validity has been established by a panel of psychologists with expertise in conducting assessments of ethnic minority clients. Whereas individual indices of personality functioning exhibit modest correlations with criterion-related indicators such as school performance and self-report scales of anxiety and other symptomatology, TEMAS profiles are highly predictive of external criteria in multiple regression analyses.

Chapter 7 focuses on the validation of the TEMAS test in different cultural settings, including the United States, Puerto Rico, Argentina, Peru, Italy, and Taiwan. Extensive data are presented, documenting evidence of reliability and validity cross-culturally. However, some evidence through qualitative semistructured interviewing suggests that the innercity "New York" nature of the TEMAS pictures needs to be modified for more appropriate administration in less urban settings, and to accommodate details even as recondite as the architecture of the scenes depicted. An Asian version has been developed and the collection of pilot data is presently in progress.

5

Administration and Scoring

This chapter describes the details of the administration and scoring of the TEMAS test. These two procedures are reported together because a standardized administration generates more reliable scoring, thus yielding potentially more valid results.

BACKGROUND

The TEMAS (Tell-Me-A-Story) is a theoretically developed narrative test (Costantino, 1978, 1987; Costantino, Malgady & Rogler, 1988; Costantino & Malgady, 1996), using a psychometrically derived problem-solving scoring system. Although the TEMAS test was created to revive the TAT technique (Costantino & Malgady, 1999; Dana, 1993, 1996), the TEMAS test presents several features that are at variance with the traditional TAT techniques (Murray, 1943; Thompson, 1949).

There are five basic variant features. *First*, the TEMAS is the only test to be developed for both minority and nonminority children and adolescents (Ritzler, 1996); *second*, the picture cards are all chromatic and depict minority and nonminority characters in urban settings that are culturally relevant to the normative groups; *third*, the cards have diminished ambiguity, but the scenes present antithetical events or psychological problems that require a solution; *fourth*, the TEMAS stories are scored in an objective manner; and, *fifth*, the TEMAS is the first and only narrative test to be standardized for Puerto Rican, Other Hispanic, Black, and White children age 5 to 13 (Costantino, Malgady, & Rogler, 1988), thus being the sole narrative test to present multicultural norms (Dana, 1996).

Originally, the TAT (Morgan and Murray, 1935) was conceived as a technique to pull for stories not to be objectively scored, but to be analyzed in order to help the clinician in obtaining information about the patient's underlying dynamics (Winter, 1999). However, following Murray's scoring system of need-press-and-thema, a proliferation of additional scoring systems were developed, such as Tomkins' (1947), which scored for relationships, levels, conditions, and qualifiers, Bellak's (1954) which scored for 10 categories, Dana's (1955) intuitive scoring system, and Eron's (1965) attempt to develop a normative scoring system. Conversely, McClelland, Atkinson, Clark, and Lowell, (1953/1976) and Winter (1973) developed an objective scoring system for specific personality constructs, such as achievement motivation and power motivation. However, the two latter systems are too lengthy and cumbersome, and have limited clinical utility. In addition, relatively recent scoring systems, the Object Relations and Social Cognition Scoring Systems (Westen, Lohr, Silk, Kerber, & Goodrich, 1985) have shown moderate clinical utility, but limited clinical acceptability (Ornduff, Freedenfeld, Kelsey, & Critelli, 1994; Ornduff & Kelsey, 1996). The most systematic attempt to develop an objective scoring system was made by Murstein (1972). After a year-long endeavor, Murstein candidly admitted that except for Card 1, which depicts a White boy pondering over a violin, and a few other cards with medium ambiguity, he could not develop an objective scoring system because of the high ambiguity of most of the TAT stimuli. The failure to reach a clinical consensus on how to objectively evaluate TAT stories is best summarized by Karon (1981), who stated that all the numerous TAT scoring systems lack acceptable psychometric properties and/or require too much time and effort to analyze a protocol.

With respect to multiculturalism, the TAT has been criticized has having poor multicultural and cross-cultural validity, hence little clinical utility in most urban clinical settings. Dana (2000) emphasized that the continued use of the TAT, especially with culturally diverse groups, rests on the development of a consensual formal scoring system. Most recently, Ronan and Gibbs (1999) attempted to overcome the various barriers in developing an objective system by introducing a problem-solving system for the TAT, which they claim "… is the first time that an easily administered and theoretically sound personal problem-solving system has been developed …" for this technique. Although the authors indicate that "idea of using projective tests to measure …" (p. 15) personal problem solving was advanced by Sobel (1981), they fail to report that the TEMAS test may very well be the first narrative instrument using an objective problem-solving scoring system. These authors also fail to indicate that the representation of problem-solving and psychological conflicts in TEMAS cards were presented as early as 1977 (Costantino, 1978). A more systematic approach in the assessment of schemas and problem-solving strategies based on existing projective techniques is presented by Teglasi (1998, 2001), who cites quite extensively the TEMAS problem-solving technique and argues that a problem-solving scoring system may represent a valid method for projective/narrative techniques.

The problem-solving scoring system, which is intrinsically related to the representation of the psychological conflicts depicted in the TEMAS pictures, was originally developed by the primary author to present a pictorial alternative to the TAT stimulus ambiguity, which is the first culprit implicated in the failure to develop an objective TAT scoring system, and thus afford the development of a valid and objective scoring system for a narrative test.

TEMAS ADMINISTRATION

The TEMAS administration is a reformulation of both the traditional TAT administration (Murray, 1943) and the Rorschach Comprehensive System administration (Exner, 1993; Exner & Weiner, 1995).

The TEMAS was designed for use with minority and nonminority children and adolescents aged 5 to 18. It has two parallel versions: minority for Blacks and Hispanics/Latinos, and nonminority for Whites; a third Asian American version is in the process of being validated (Yang, Kuo, & Costantino, 2004). Each version is comprised of a short form of 9 cards, which can be completed within 45–50 minutes, and a long form of 23 cards, which can be completed within 100–120 minutes. The short form is usually administered in clinical as well as in school settings, which can be augmented by two or three additional cards pulling for the specific symptoms presented by a given examinee (e.g, aggression, anxiety, sexual identification conflicts). In order to reduce the examiner's bias, the test should be administered in the child's dominant language by an examiner fully familiar with the child's cultural background and proficient in the standardized administration of the test (Dana, 1998). The test is administered individually; hence, individual administration is important because the normative data were obtained by this method. Recent studies have explored group administration in a classroom setting, with students writing instead of telling a story (Cardalda et. al, 2004; Flanagan, Losapio, Greenfield, Costantino & Hernandez, 2004). Group administration seems a viable alternative for research and educational activities.

Unlike the TAT and Rorschach, the TEMAS cards are administered in a random order, except for card IB-G, which is administered first because of its nonthreatening and familiar content. The random administration is used to neutralize the antagonistic processes of acquaintance and fatigue, thus affording each card its valid pull. The test is administered face to face, and the examiner should make sure that the child is as comfortable as possible and is experiencing a minimum of test anxiety. The TEMAS administration subscribes to the collaborative efforts between the examiner and the examinee, thus changing the vertical relationship between the examiner and the "subject" to a horizontal collaborative relationship (Costantino & Malgady, 2000).

It is important to establish a working relationship with the examinee. The examiner may utilize the following script, which has been found to be an effective one. After introducing himself or herself by using his or her professional title, the examiner says to the youngster: "What is your nickname or how your friends call you? Can I call you the same way your friend calls you?" Subsequently, the examiner introduces the TEMAS cards with the following instructions: "I have several interesting pictures that I am going to show you. Look at the persons and places in the pictures and tell me a complete story about each picture, one that has a beginning and an end. The story should answer three questions: What is happening in the picture now? What has happened before? And what will happen in the future?" Subsequently, the examiner hands the card to the student, and records the story verbatim (standard abbreviation are acceptable). Reaction Time (RT), Spontaneous Time (ST), and Total Time (TT) are recorded on the left column of a pad page. Because there is no normative data for Spontaneous Time, the ratio between spontaneous time and Total Time will give an index of cognitive ability (see scoring section in this chapter for more information). It is encouraged that the examiner write the story in the middle part of a pad page. It is important to draw a free-hand column on the left side of the page to record the RT, ST, and TT, and to draw a column on the right side to note clinically useful test behavior. The maximum time allowed for a story is about typically three to five minutes; in clinical cases more time may be allowed. Examinees are given the opportunity to tell a complete story in a spontaneous manner without structured inquiries. A story is complete if it embodies: (1a–1b) the identities of and relationships among the characters, (2a–2b) identification of the setting, (3a–3b) what the characters are doing and saying: (4a–4b) what the characters did before, (5a–5b) what the characters will be doing in the future, and (6a–6b) what the main character is thinking and feeling upon resolution of the story's conflict/problem. Structured inquiries were developed to afford a complete scorable narrative and to give the opportunity to youngsters who do not speak spontaneously to give a complete story with prompting.

The structure inquiries are conducted only for those indices that are not present in the story. Because the scoring relies on the complete sets of indices embodied in the narratives, it is important that the examiner make sure that the inquiries are conducted thoroughly so that single indices are not missed. Missed indices may deem a story nonscorable. In order to promote a standardized and complete administration, the TEMAS kits have a laminated administration form that can be easily used and read. (see Figure. 5.1). Complete scoring instructions can be found in the TEMAS manual published by Western Psychological Services (Costantino, Malgady, & Rogler, 1988).

TEMAS PROBLEM-SOLVING SCORING SYSTEM

The TEMAS scoring system was based on an objective, problem-solving (Costantino, 1987; Flanagan, 1999) and/or "scoring by consensus" strategy (Dana, 1998). This problem-solving strategy is reflected in the pictures, which were designed to depict antithetical themes and psychological problems (Costantino, 1978, 1987). The representation of psychological problems in TEMAS card stimuli was based on the methodology of Kohlberg (1976), who developed stories portraying moral dilemmas to assess the moral development of children. Similarly, the TEMAS pictures were designed to portray a split scene showing psychological dilemmas or conflicts; the examinee must resolve the problem situation portrayed in a narrative format. The clinician scores selected personality functions according to the adaptiveness of the resolution of the narratives in addition to scoring for other several functions as described later.

The problems depicted in TEMAS were designed to evoke disclosure of specific personality functions that are prominent in personality theory and also are key diagnostic indicators, including: integrity of interpersonal relations (Sullivan, 1953), control of aggressive impulses (Bandura. 1977), control of anxious and depressed feelings (Bandura, 1971; Kovacs, 1992; Spielberger, 1971), achievement motivation (McClelland et al., 1953, 1976) delay, gratification (Mischel, 1974), self-concept of competence (Erickson, 1968), moral judgment (Kohlberg, 1976), self/sexual identity (Kohlberg & Ullian, 1974) and reality testing (Bellak, Hurvich, & Gediman, 1973).

The TEMAS card stimuli were drawn by an artist, Phil Jacobs, who worked closely with the test author (Costantino, 1978, 1987) to pictorially represent a large set of antithetical psychosocial interpersonal situations. The stimuli embody a large variety of problematic life situations and

TEMAS

Administration Instructions

General Instructions

The TEMAS was designed for use with children and adolescents aged 5 to 18. Either the entire protocol of 23 cards or a short version of 9 cards may be administered to a given child.

The TEMAS should be administered individually to each examinee in that child's dominant language by an examiner proficient in the administration of the test. The clinician should choose the set of cards (minority or nonminority) which best corresponds to the racial and cultural identification of the child. Note that the minority version of the cards is distinguished by an "M" added to each card number printed on the upper right-hand corner on the back of each card. Thus, Card No. 10G-M is designed for use with minority girls, while Card No. 10G should be used for nonminority girls.

Initial Instructions

The examiner should read the same instructions and inquiries to all children. After having initiated a working relationship with the child, the examiner should say:

"I'd like you to tell me a story. I have a lot of interesting pictures that I'm going to show you. Please look carefully at the people and the places in the pictures and then tell me a complete story about each picture—a story that has a beginning and an end."

Specific Instructions

Two types of instructions may be used by the examiner: Instructions of Temporal Sequencing and Structured Inquiries.

Instructions of Temporal Sequencing

The examiner will show the first picture to the child and say: "Please tell me a complete story about this picture and all the other pictures I will show you. The story should answer three questions:

1. What is happening in the picture now?
2. What happened before?
3. What will happen in the future?"

These three questions, known as the Instructions of Temporal Sequencing, define how the child should structure the temporal sequence of the events in telling a story. The examiner may repeat these instructions for each picture presented, if necessary. Repetition of the instructions is recommended when an examiner is testing young children and children with short attention spans.

Structured Inquiries

When the child has completed each story, the examiner may need to clarify unclear or omitted narrative elements. The Structured Inquiries are conducted to elicit omitted identifications of relationships between characters, of settings and events, and of characters' thoughts and affective processes. Furthermore, an inquiry should be conducted if the child has omitted a past sequence ("What has happened before?"), a present sequence ("What is happening now?"), or a future sequence ("What will happen or what will the character do next?").

After a child has completed his or her story, the examiner may conduct Structured Inquiries, drawing from the six following queries, as needed, to elicit omitted details.

Inquiry 1. a) Who are these people? Do they know each other? *b)* Who is this person?

Inquiry 2. a) Where are these people? *b)* Where is this person?

Inquiry 3. a) What are these people doing and saying? *b)* What is this person doing and saying?

Inquiry 4. a) What were these people doing before? *b)* What was this person doing before?

Inquiry 5. a) What will these people do next? *b)* What will this person do next?

Inquiry 6. a) What is this person (main character) thinking? *b)* What is this person (main character) feeling?

Inquiry 1. Inquiry 1a is carried out to identify the characters and their relationships when multiple characters are depicted in the pictures; 1a is also conducted to identify the only character in the picture who imagines himself or herself in the situation of facing bipolar choices such as in Card Nos. 10B, 10G, 13B, 13G, 18B, 18G, 19B, 19G, 22B, and 22G. Inquiry 1b is conducted to identify the sole human character in the picture when multiple human characteristics are not depicted in the bipolar choices such as in Card Nos. 20 and 21.

Inquiry 2. Inquiry 2a is conducted to identify a setting populated with more than one character, and to identify a setting in which a single character is imagining himself or herself involved in other activities. Inquiry 2b is conducted to identify the setting of the sole character of a picture.

Inquiry 3. Inquiries 3a and 3b are conducted to elicit the present action or behavior and verbalizations of the depicted character(s).

Inquiry 4. Inquiries 4a and 4b are conducted to elicit an explanation of the prior actions of the character(s) depicted.

Inquiry 5. Inquiries 5a and 5b are conducted to inquire what the character(s) will do to resolve the conflict or polarities depicted.

OVER

FIGURE 5–1. Administration Laminated Card

Inquiry 6. Inquiry 6a is conducted to elicit the ideation of the main character. Inquiry 6b is conducted to elicit the affect/mood state of the main character upon the resolution of the conflict. *Note:* It is of paramount importance that the examiner inquire about the affect/mood state of the main character upon the resolution of the conflict even if such states are mentioned before the conflict was resolved or before the story ended.

The language of the inquiries may be simplified if necessary.

Use of Inquiries

The child should be given the opportunity to tell a complete story in a spontaneous manner following the Instructions of Temporal Sequencing. A story is complete if it relates: (a) the identities and relationships of the characters, the settings, and the events being depicted; (b) what the character(s) did before; (c) what the character(s) will be doing; and (d) what the character is thinking and feeling about the resolution of the dialectic situation. If a child tells a complete story, no inquiry is necessary unless any of the temporal sequences or Structured Inquiries need to be clarified. If a child gives only a general description of the picture in response to a query regarding "What is happening," then the entire sequence of six Structured Inquiries should be conducted. Furthermore, Structured Inquiries should be conducted for any of the items (1a through 6b) that are missing from the content of the story.

Note that each story is scored for the inclusion of the following information: (a) the identification of the characters (Inquiry 1a, 1b); (b) the identification of the setting (Inquiry 2a, 2b); (c) the action or behavior and verbalizations of the characters (Inquiry 3a, 3b); (d) the temporal sequence of what has led to the present occurrence (Inquiry 4a, 4b); (e) the temporal sequence of what the characters will be doing to resolve the depicted conflict (Inquiry 5a, 5b); (f) the ideation process of the main character (Inquiry 6a); and (g) the affect/mood state of the main character at the end of the story or at the resolution of the conflict (Inquiry 6b). Therefore, if the examiner does not make a necessary inquiry, a child may be unduly penalized for an omission.

The examiner should motivate the child to complete ideas and/or sentences and to clarify behaviors and explain motives. It is important to note that the clarifying questions are asked during the telling of the story and are recorded parenthetically with a question mark, "(?)"; the Structured Inquiries are conducted after the child has told the story and are also recorded parenthetically, indicated only by the number of the inquiry used, such as "(1a)" or "(6b)," as appropriate. Clarifying questions are not analyzed in the scoring system but may provide useful clinical information.

Recording Time

The use of a stopwatch is necessary for recording administration time accurately. For accurate scoring, a child's response time must be recorded in two ways: *Reaction Time* (RT) and *Total Time* (TT). As soon as the examiner hands the picture to the child, the examiner should start the stopwatch and then stop it

the moment the child begins to respond; this latency period is the Reaction Time (RT), which is recorded at the beginning of the story. When the child first responds to a given picture, following the latency period, the examiner should restart the stopwatch and allow it to run until the end of the spontaneous storytelling—that is, when the child indicates (overtly or covertly) that the thematic story is complete. The time elapsed from the moment that the child begins to speak, following the Instructions of Temporal Sequencing, to the moment that the child concludes the complete story, is the Total Time (TT). However, if the child has omitted answers to any of the six Structured Inquiries, the examiner should allow the stopwatch to run while making the appropriate inquiries, and write the answers. At the end of the answer to the last inquiry, the examiner should stop the watch and note the Total Time with the transcript of the child's story, on the left-hand column of the tablet of paper being used.

The *minimum* Total Time for a story is 2 minutes: the examiner should motivate the child to speak for at least 2 minutes. If the child is unable to conceptualize a story, the examiner may prompt him or her with phrases such as, "Tell me what's happening in this picture," or, "Tell me what you see." However, if the child speaks very little during the allotted 2 minutes, or if he or she rejects the picture being presented, the actual time of verbalization should be recorded on the right-hand column of the paper being used. A *maximum* time limit of 5 minutes is allowed to complete each story. Most stories are completed in 3 to 4 minutes. After 4 minutes, if the inquiries have been answered and the child appears to be rambling or to be overly verbose, the examiner should prompt him or her to terminate the story by saying, "Fine, now how does the story end?"

Recording the Stories

During the TEMAS administration, the examinee's stories should be recorded verbatim by the examiner on a ruled letter- or legal-sized pad. It is useful to draw a vertical line about two inches from the right margin of the pad, dividing the page into two columns: the left (larger) column for writing down the story, and the right (smaller) column for noting unusual observed behavior such as:

1. Unusual comments by the child
2. Unusual facial expressions and/or body gestures
3. Long pauses (exceeding 30 seconds)
4. Other important events

In order to save time, the examiner should record only the number(s) of the Structured Inquiries used (e.g., 1a, 1b), not the inquiries themselves. Occurrences of clarifying questions should be noted by a parenthetical question mark. This notation, "(?)," indicates that the child has not told the story in specific terms.

[Note: The instructions provided here are a subset of those presented in the TEMAS Manual. The examiner should familiarize himself or herself with the administration and scoring instructions as presented in the Manual.]

FIGURE 5–1.   Administration Laminated Card (*continued*)

experiences, such as familiar scenes within the home or on the street, solitary dreamlike and fantasy states, involving peers and adults, sport activities, and situations occurring in school settings. The problem-solving nature of the situations depicted in the pictures enables positive and negative feelings to be expressed in the stories and manifested as adaptive and maladaptive resolutions of the underlying psychological problems and/or strengths. These situations pull themes expressive of varying degrees of psychopathology ranging from adaptive to maladaptive.

The TEMAS scoring system is comprised of nine personality functions, 18 cognitive functions, and seven affective functions. The cognitive functions are scored in seconds and minutes for Reaction Time, Spontaneous Time, and Total Time, and 1 when the specific function is missing from the story, or "blank" when it is recognized in the story for Conflict (Problem Solution), Sequencing, Imagination, Relationships, Inquiries, Omissions and Transformations. The Affective Functions are scored as 1 when they are present in the stories and "blank" when they are not mentioned. The nine personality functions are scored on a Lykert scale from 1 to 4 and N, where one is the most maladaptive resolution to the conflict, 4 is the most adaptive problem solution, and N is when the personality function is not pulled (not present) in the stories.

Most TEMAS pictures were designed to pull for a minimum of two to a maximum of four personality functions; however, cards. 10B(Boy) & 10 G (Girl) and card 20 pull for only one personality function. Specific picture functions for each card are denoted by a triangle in the scoring boxes of the Personality Functions, as shown in the Record Booklet (see Figure 5.2, on pages 181–184). The pull(s) for each card were originally generated clinically; however, subsequently the functions were empirically assessed. In an early study, Costantino, Malgady, and Rogler, (1988), measured the degree of interrater reliability in a sample of school ($N = 8$) and clinical psychologists ($N = 6$), assessing the nine personality functions pulled by each TEMAS card. Six of the psychologists were PhDs and eight had their MA; their age ranged from 24 to 54 ($M = 36.67$, $SD = 7.53$). The participant psychologists had a mean of 7.79 years ($SD = 5.36$) of professional experience in psychological testing, mental health evaluation, and treatment of culturally and linguistically diverse children, adolescents, and adults; they had a mean of 8.64 years of experience ($SD = 53$) in personality assessment, including projective techniques. With respect to race and ethnicity, seven were White, one was Black, and six were Latino. Their theoretical and clinical orientations were eclectic, cognitive/behavioral, psychoanalytic, and ego psychology based. The participating psychologists

TABLE 5–1. Percentage of Agreement Among 14 Clinicians
Regarding Personality Pulled by TEMAS Pictures

Card	IR	AGG	A/D	AM	DG	SC	SEX	MJ	REAL
1B & 1G*	100	–	–	–	86	–	–	–	–
2	93	–	–	–	–	–	–	71	–
3	93	–	–	86	93	–	–	–	–
4	100	79	71	–	–	–	–	71	–
5	93	79	–	–	–	–	–	–	–
6	79	–	–	–	–	–	86	–	–
7*	79	79	–	–	–	–	–	79	–
8	79	79	–	86	–	–	–	86	–
9B & 9G	86	–	79	–	–	–	–	–	–
10B & 10G*	–	–	–	–	93	–	–	–	–
11	86	100	–	–	–	–	–	100	–
12B & 12G	93	100	–	–	–	–	–	79	–
13B & 13G	86	–	–	–	–	71	86	–	–
14B & 14G*	93	–	–	100	93	–	–	–	–
15*	86	86	–	71	–	–	–	93	–
16	93	–	–	79	–	100	–	–	–
17B & 17G*	–	–	71	100	–	86	–	–	–
18B & 18G	–	–	–	93	–	86	–	–	–
19B & 19G	–	–	71	–	–	–	–	–	100
20*	–	–	71	–	–	–	–	–	–
21*	–	93	86	–	–	–	–	–	71
22B & 22G*	–	–	79	–	–	–	86	–	71
23B & 23G	100	–	100	–	–	–	–	–	–

Note. Asterisks denote cards in the short version.

were given in random order, the 23 TEMAS pictures and individually
instructed to check at least two and not more than four of the nine functions pulled by each card, in accordance with their theoretical orientation
and the TEMAS definition of the nine personality functions. They
recorded their choices on a grid similar to page two of the scoring record
booklet, with the personality functions written horizontally on the top
and the card number written vertically on the left hand-side of the grid.
The percentage of agreement among the 14 clinicians ranged from 100%
on Cards 1B & 1G for Interpersonal Relations to 71% on Card 15 for

Achievement Motivation. Table 5–1 shows the complete percentage of agreement for all the pictures, thus confirming the pulls scored for each personality function. The triangles represent the agreed-on functions for the specific 23 picture cards.

Problems Depicted in TEMAS Cards

The TEMAS scoring system is a theoretical and psychometric derivation of the pictures. Here, below, are brief descriptions of the cards.

Short Form

- Cards 1 Boy & Girl (B & G). Children in front of the house scene: *Obeying the mother vs. playing with friends.*
- Card 7. Family scene: son-daughter-and-mother: *Admitting "who broke the lamp" vs. accusing each other of wrongdoing in the mother's presence.*
- Cards 10B & 10G Child in front of a piggybank thinking: *Saving money in the piggy-bank to buy a bike at later time vs. taking money from the piggy bank to buy ice-cream now.*
- Card 14B & 14G. Home scene: Child: *Studying/doing the homework to get good grades vs. playing/dancing with siblings and/or friends.*
- Card 15. Play field/street scene: *Baseball or soccer team receiving trophies vs. group of children stealing goods from a vandalized electronic store.*
- Card 17B & 17G. Home scene: *Child deciding to study hard to get an A vs. deciding not to study, thus receiving an F.*
- Card 20. Home scene: *Child in bed dreaming about the horse confronted by a road ravine vs. to safely/unsafely reach the castle.*
- Card 21. Home scene: *Child in bed dreaming about two monsters, a fire-breathing monster/dragon vs. a hamburger-eating monster/dragon.*
- Card 22B & 22G. Home scene: *Child in bathroom looking to a male/female face images reflected in the mirror: Identifying with the sexually or body-appropriate image of male vs. female face images.*

Long Form

- Card 2. Family scene: mother, father, and five children: *sharing household chores vs. ignoring family responsibilities and instead watching television.*
- Card 3. Family scene: mother, father, and four children: *obeying parental commands to do the homework vs. watching television.*
- Card 4. Family scene: *showing marital responsibility and acceptance of wrongdoing by the father vs. showing aggression toward wife and children.*

- Card 5. Home scene: *child in bed dreaming about an intruder entering through the window into the bedroom vs. having a picnic with the loved one.*
- Card 6. Boy and Girl in the attic; *feeling proud to wear their parents' clothes and imaging following the parents' achievement vs. longing for their childhood and being fearful of growing-up.*
- Card 8. School scene: students in classroom: *showing interest in the lesson taught by the teacher vs. two students with their parents being reprimanded by the school principal for having broken windows.*
- Cards 9B & 9G. Forest scene: youth at the crossroad: *thinking about taking the road taken by his or her friends to get out of the forest vs. taking a less traveled road to reach the other side.*
- Card 11. Street scene: youth: *showing prosocial and helping behavior by helping an elderly lady in carrying her groceries vs. stealing groceries from an elderly lady.*
- Card 12B & 12G. Street scene: youth: *showing prosocial and helping behavior by working cooperatively in assembling/repairing a bike vs. fighting aggressively and/or inciting fighting.*
- Card 13B & 13G. Home scene: youth in the bathroom looking at the parents' images reflected in the mirror: *identifying with same-sex parent or with parents and deciding to achieve as well as the parents have vs. identifying with the opposite-sex parent and/or rejecting the achievement accomplished by parent(s).*
- Card 16. School gym scene: group of children: *mastering rope climbing and mastering a pummel horse vs. fearing to try those two sport activities.*
- Card 18B & 18G. Home scene: *A boy (B) and a girl (G) studying and day-dreaming about becoming a doctor and/or a TV actor vs. becoming a homeless person.*
- Card 19B & 19G. Home scene, Youth at the window of an apartment building on fire thinking about: *being saved by fireman vs. flying down to safety like Superman or Superwoman.*
- Card 23B & 23G. Home scene: Youth having conflict with parents and fantasizing about: *running away to jump off a bridge vs. running away to a relative/friend to make it on his or her own.*

Scoring Procedures

The TEMAS stories are scored for indices representative of cognitive, affective, and personality functions in the TEMAS Record Booklet. After all the cards have been scored, the card scores should be totaled down the columns of each Scoring Sheet to compute the raw scores for the Cognitive and Affective Functions. For the Personality Functions, these sums should be divided by the number of cards scored to produce a mean score. The Record Booklet is comprised of the face page for demographic data, the "Observed Test Behavior," and other comments regarding clinically relevant information (See Figure 5–2). Page 2 of the Record booklet displays the Quantitative (*T*-Score) Scales; page 3 shows the Percentile Scales; page 4 exhibits the examinee's profile based on the *T*-scores of the transformed quantitative scales raw scores (See Figure 5.2).

Cognitive Functions

Cognitive Functions of the Quantitative Scales, recorded on page 2 of the Record Booklet, are: *Reaction Time, Total Time, Spontaneous Time, Fluency, Total Omissions,* and *Reaction Time. Reaction Time* (RT), which is the latency time between the end of the general instructions and the beginning of the storytelling, is recorded in seconds and entered as two digits (e.g., 5" = 05) in the column labeled "Reaction Time." *Total Time (TT),* which is the time span of the storytelling including the structured inquires, is entered in minutes and seconds (e.g., 3.30 = 3.50) in the upper box of Total Time. *Spontaneous Time* (ST), which represents the narrative time span before the structured inquiries, is entered in the lower half of the Total Time box. The Spontaneous Time is not part of the standardization because it was not obtained during the original TEMAS normative data collection. However, it is an important indicator of cognitive functioning. As there are no *T*-scores conversion for ST, the examiner should sum the ST, sum the TT, and take the difference between the two sums; the smaller the difference between the two sums, the higher is the cognitive functioning of the examinee.

Fluency is a total number of the words used in a story. To score Fluency, sum the number of words of each of the examinee's narratives and enter this score in the appropriate box in the column labeled "Fluency" intersecting with the card number. All contracted words, such as "I'll" or "can't" are counted as two words in English. This rule also applies for other languages that use contracted words, and for Latin languages, such as Spanish and Italian, which use verbs without nouns or adverb, such as "soy" and "sono", which mean "I'm" in English.

Total Omissions are the sum of the omissions of main character, secondary character, setting, and event, which are part of the percentile scales on page 3 of the Record Booklet.

Omissions and Transformations

Omissions are defined as of picture stimuli not present in the story, whereas transformations refer to perceptual distortion of the stimuli. There are four types of *Omissions* and *Transformations*: *Main Character, Secondary Character, Event,* and *Setting. Omissions* are scored as the number omissions in the appropriate box on page 3 of the booklet, but added to the column of Total Omission on page 2 (*T*-score scales). The transformations are scored in the appropriate box on page 3 of the Record Booklet, but added to the column of Total Transformation on page 3 (90th percentile cutoff scores). The specific types of Omissions are entered both in the *T*-Score Scales and the Percentile Score Scales, whereas the specific types of Transformations are entered on page 3 of the Percentile Score Scales (See Figure 5.2). The distinction between the two types of scales reflects differences in the psychometric properties of the two scales rather than any differences in their relative clinical value.

All TEMAS pictures are designed to pull for at least two Personality Functions except for Cards 10B, 10G, and 20, which pull for one personality function. In the Record Booklet, specific predicted pulls for each card are denoted by a triangle in the scoring boxes of the Personality Functions. This part of the scoring system is based on the analysis of 14 clinicians who analyzed all 23 TEMAS pictures and evidenced acceptable interrater agreement ranging from .71 to. 99 as to the specific card pulls, see Table 5–1.

Criteria for Scoring Personality Functions
The nine Personality Functions as defined in chapter 2 of the Manual (published by Western Psychological Services-WPS) are: *Interpersonal Relations, Aggression, Anxiety/Depression, Achievement Motivation, Self-Concept, Delay of Gratification, Sexual Identity, Moral Judgment,* and *Reality Testing.* They are scored on a scale from 1 (highly maladaptive) to 4 (highly adaptive) when these functions are present in the stories; when those personality functions that have been designed to be pulled by the card are not present in the narratives, they are scored as N (the function not pulled) in the marked triangle.

   1: A scoring of 1 for any Personality Function indicates the presence of a highly maladaptive action or resolution for a particular TEMAS card. For example, inclusions of murder, rape, assault, or physical fighting with the intent to harm in TEMAS stories are always scored 1 for *Interpersonal Relations (IR), Aggression (AGG),* and *Moral Judgment (MJ).* Suicide or feeling hopelessly anxious or depressed is scored 1 for *Anxiety/Depression (A/D).* The anticipation of complete failure and a concomitant refusal to attempt to a given task results in a score of 1 for *Self Concept of Competence (SC).* Failure to study because school is not important at all gets a score 1 in *Achievement Motivation.* (AM). Spending one's meager savings on edible goods now instead of saving to buy a larger reward because no one knows what will happen tomorrow is scored 1 for *Delay Gratification* (DG). A character that strongly identifies with the opposite sex and/or who rejects his or her gender earns a 1 in Sexual Identity (SEX). Severely impaired reality testing (REAL) is scored only for the most bizarre and impossible resolutions (e.g., inanimate objects come to life, or a child causes events to occur by a strange power of the mind). In summary, scores of 1 in IR with parental figures and AGG reflects a total disregard for parental command, total lack of respect for parental authority, and harmful threats against parents; 1 in IR and AGG with peers reflects a total disregard for socialized interaction with intent to cause serious harm; 1 in MJ reflects a total lack of regard for the consequences of antisocial behaviors.

2: A scoring of 2 for any Personality Function reflects a maladaptive response or resolution.   The following responses call for a 2: *Interpersonal Relations (IR)*: children fail to obey their parents; *Moral Judgment (MJ)*: children fail to admit wrongdoing, without feeling guilty, and get away with it; *Aggression (AGG)* (Control of) conflicts are resolved by fighting; *Delay Gratification (DG)*: money is spent to achieve immediate gratification (buying an ice cream) rather than saved to buy a bike at a later date; *Achievement Motivation (AM)*: homework is avoided in favor of play; *Anxiety/Depression (A/D)*: a child is extremely frightened by a nightmare about a monster; a child runs away from home and never returns or is thinking about jumping off a bridge; *Self-concept of Competence (SC)*: a youngster is not confident that he or she will get a passing grade even if he or she studies; *Reality Testing* (REAL): the monster in a dream is perceived as a real threat; *Sexual Identity* (SEX): a youngster is confused about his or her gender identity and unable to resolve the confusion in a gender-appropriate manner.

3: A scoring of 3 represents an average adaptive resolution.   Responses are scored as 3 include the following examples: a child compromises between obeying a parental command and playing with his or her friends following compliance (IR and DG); two siblings accept responsibility for wrongdoing instead of fighting (IR; AGG; REAL); money is saved for a time and then is spent to buy a larger reward (DG); homework is completed for fear of punishment or failing in school (AM); a threatening monster in a nightmare is not perceived as a real threat and is neutralized by a benign monster (AGG; A/D; REAL); a youngster who is confused about his or her sexual identity has a clear perception about the feminine and masculine role consequences and resolves the confusion in a sexually adaptive manner (SEX; A/D; REAL).

4: A score of 4 represents a highly adaptive response or resolution. The child must perceive the intended conflict and solve the problem in a mature, socially adaptive manner. A score of 4 includes the following responses: a child rejects the notion of cheating as being antithetical to learning, thinks only of wrongdoing (if depicted in the picture) but rejects it because is socially unacceptable (MJ); conflicts are discussed and compromises reached (IR, AGG, REAL); money is earned by working and saved for the future (DG); homework is completed because good grades are instrumental for excelling in school and obtaining a higher degree (SC; DG; AM); a child decides to reconcile with his or her parents rather than run away (IR; AIO); dreams are never real (REAL); a youngster resolves his/her sexual identity conflict in a highly adaptive and gender-appropriate manner (SEX).

N: An N is entered in the appropriate triangle on page 2 of the Record Booklet whenever an examinee fails to verbalize a theme that is pulled by the specific card but is not explicitly present in the narrative. Conversely, if a specific personality function, which was designed to be pulled by a particular card, is not present in the corresponding story, it is scored in the appropriate box outside the triangle.

For example, with Cards 1B and 1G, (which depict a boy and a girl conflicted between obeying a parental command and/or playing basketball/ jump rope with his or her friends), if the storyteller does not tell a story resolving the TEMAS psychological conflict or problem of the mother sending the child on an errand and the character wishing to play with friends, but, instead, the narrative exhibits a personal conflict between the main and the peers whereby the main character cries to his mother that "the tall Black bully" has beaten him badly and stolen his ball, the scores for this story of the three personality functions pulled by the card are: a 2 in *Interpersonal Relations* (IR) with the mother figure, a 1 in IR with his peers, and N for Delay of Gratification because playing with his friends is not mentioned; but a 1 in *Aggression* is scored in the appropriate box, even though the function is not pulled by Card 1. These types of stories depart from the "popular stories" and reflect the personal motivation of the storyteller. In addition, several other indices, such as solution of the TEMAS conflict, omissions, and transformations are scored accordingly as discussed herein. It is important to note that an N-score for the Personality Function(s) that the card pulls for is almost always associated with Omissions of Events. Furthermore, with Card 15, if the four children stealing electronic goods and the policeman are not mentioned in the story, an N is entered in the *Aggression* and *Moral Judgment* triangles, and 5 is entered in the box of

Omissions of Secondary Character on page 3 of the Record Booklet. With Cards 12B and 12G, if the four youngsters on the left side of the picture are not mentioned, a score of N is entered in the triangle in the Aggression in the appropriate triangle on page 2 of the Record Booklet; in addition, a score of 1 is entered in the box of Omissions of Events and a score of 5 is entered in the Omissions of Secondary Characters box on page 3 of the Record Booklet. An early study Reported that most children in a nonclinical population tended to achieve scores of 2, 3, and 4 in the personality functions, and occasionally N, whereas clinical examinees tended to achieve scores of 1, 2, and more frequently N. This study also showed that clinical children reported more transformations than school children (Costantino, Colon-Malgady, Malgady, & Perez, 1991). The N-scores, Omissions, and Transformations scales were not part of the original Manual submitted to Western Psychological Services; however, these subscales were added to the galleys after several months following this study. This critical study compared clinical (ADHD) and school students on the TEMAS newly developed Omission scale and N values. Results revealed that the ADHD children were significantly more likely than normal children to omit information in the card stimuli about characters, events, settings, and psychological conflicts. Results also indicated that clinical children tended to exhibit more transformations than the school children. Following these significant findings; the psychometric properties of N score, Omissions Scales, and even the Transformations Scale were added to the Manual. The N score and the Omissions Scale are based on the theoretical construct of Selective Inattention, which emphasizes that the continuous use of this mechanism leads to poor perception of reality and psychopathology (Sullivan, 1953). Detailed scoring instruction and examples can be found in the TEMAS manual published by Western Psychological Services (Costantino, Malgady, & Rogler, 1988).

Psychometric Properties of Cognitive, Affective, and Personality Functions

The TEMAS multicultural test represents the first systematic endeavor to develop valid multicultural test scores for a narrative instrument, so that clinicians can avoid using scores that are invalid and thus making clinical judgments that are incorrect and dangerous for the examinees. To this end, TEMAS was standardized on a sample of 642 children (281 males and 361 females) from public schools in the New York City area. These children ranged in age from 5 to 13 years, with a mean age of 8.9 years ($SD = 1.9$). The total sample represented four ethnic/racial groups: Puerto Ricans, Other Hispanics, Blacks, and Whites. With respect to socioeconomic

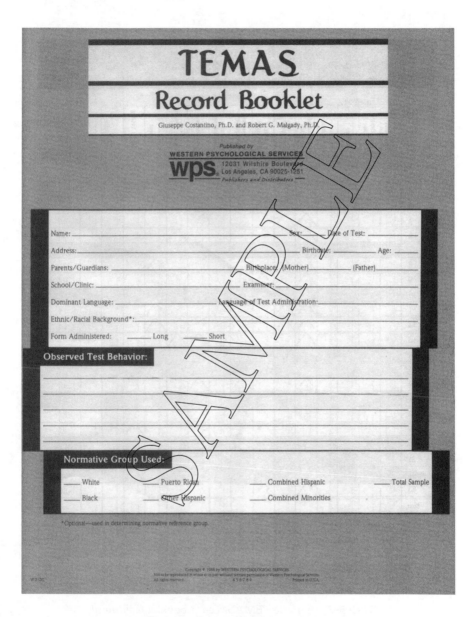

FIGURE 5–2. Sample TEMAS record booklet.

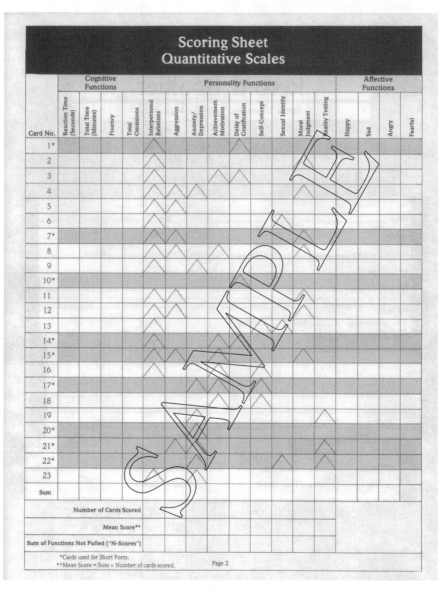

FIGURE 5–2.   Sample TEMAS record booklet (*continued*).

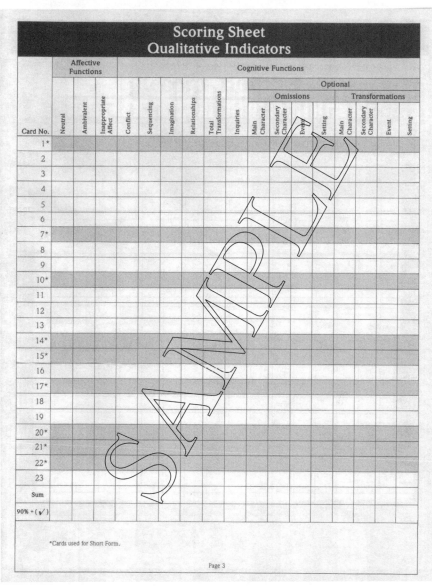

Scoring Sheet
Qualitative Indicators

Card No.	Affective Functions			Cognitive Functions						Optional							
										Omissions				Transformations			
	Neutral	Ambivalent	Inappropriate Affect	Conflict	Sequencing	Imagination	Relationships	Total Transformations	Inquiries	Main Character	Secondary Character	Event	Setting	Main Character	Secondary Character	Event	Setting
1*																	
2																	
3																	
4																	
5																	
6																	
7*																	
8																	
9																	
10*																	
11																	
12																	
13																	
14*																	
15*																	
16																	
17*																	
18																	
19																	
20*																	
21*																	
22*																	
23																	
Sum																	
90% + (✔)																	

*Cards used for Short Form.

Page 3

FIGURE 5–2. Sample TEMAS record booklet (*continued*).

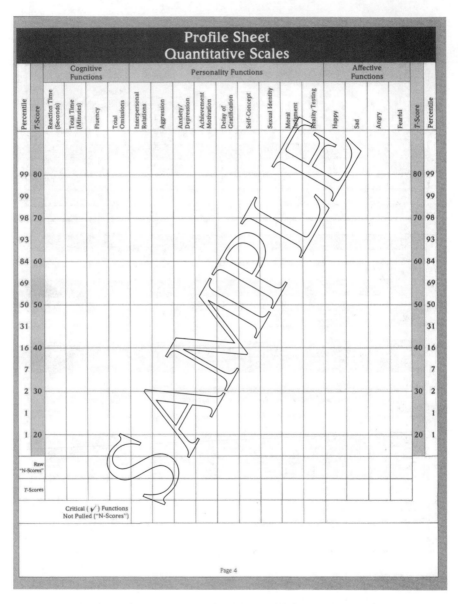

FIGURE 5–2.   Sample TEMAS record booklet (*continued*).

status (SES), the normative sample showed that these children were from predominately lower and middle-income families. Although the TEMAS was standardized in the New York City area, several studies showed that culturally and linguistically diverse groups in other states, such as California, and other countries, such as Puerto Rico, Argentina, Peru, Salvador, and Italy, can appropriately relate to the TEMAS picture cards and produce narratives that can be validly scored (Bernal, 1991; Cardalda, 1995; Cardalda, Santiago-Negron, Jimenez-Suarez, Leon-Velasquez, Martinez, et al., 2005; Cornabuci, 2000; Costantino, Malgady, Casullo & Castillo, 1991; Costantino, Dupertuis, Castillo, Malgady & Faiola, 1997; Costantino, Flanagan & Malgady, 2001; Dupertuis, Silvia-Arancibia, Pais, Fernandez, & Rodino, 2004; Krinsky, 1997; Sardi, 2000; Sulfaro, 2000; Summo, 2000; Walton, Nuttall, & Vazquez-Nuttall, 1997).

QUANTITATIVE SCALES AND QUALITATIVE INDICATORS

The nature of the distribution of some TEMAS cognitive and affective functions made it impractical to convert them to standard scores, because scores other than zero were rare in the standardization sample. These functions were designated "Qualitative Indicators" and scored as cut-off percentile scores. Because of these psychometric properties, these indicators are labeled in this book as Clinical Indicators. However, those TEMAS functions that had relatively normal distributions were designated "Quantitative Scales" and scored as Percentile Score Scales—normalized T-Scores ($m = 50$, $SD = 10$) for profiling.

DERIVATION OF STANDARD SCORES AND QUALITATIVE INDICATORS

To enable users to directly compare scores within a single protocol, and to facilitate comparisons with the performance of the standardization sample, raw scores of Quantitative Scales were converted to normalized T-scores. To minimize irregularities in the raw score distribution, an analytic smoothing technique was also used (Cureton & Tukey, 1951). Because it was inappropriate to transform raw scores of the Qualitative Indicators to standard scores, critical levels based on raw score distributions were developed; based on expert clinical evaluation, the Qualitative Indicators should be named Clinical Indicators.

TABLE 5–2.   Correlations of TEMAS Indexes With age

Cognitive Functions	Hispanic	Black
Reaction Time	.00	.22
Total Time	.11	.01
Fluency	.18	.20
Total Omissions	−.23	−.11
Total Transformation	−.17	−.52*
Inquiries	−.13	−.25
Main Character Omissions	−.17	−.19
Main Character Transformations	−.14	−.35*
Secondary Character Omissions	−.01	−.24
Secondary Character Transformations	−.12	−.40*
Event Omissions	−.13	−.11
Event Transformations	−.05	–
Setting Omissions	−.31*	.00
Setting Transformations	−.19	−.37*
Conflict	−.21	−.18
Sequencing	−.11	−.38*
Imagination	−.14	−.31*
Relationships	−.20	−.39*
Personality Functions		
Interpersonal Relations	−.21	.17
Aggression	−.26*	.02
Anxiety/Depression	−.18	.34*
Achievement Motivation	.02	.23
Delay of Gratification	.07	.20
Self–Concept	−.05	.10
Sexual Identity	−.34*	.29
Moral Judgment	.05	.12
Reality Testing	−.10	.18
Affective Function		
Happy	.16	−.12
Sad	−.28*	.08
Angry	.08	.13
Fearful	.12	.04
Neutral	.00	−.29
Ambivalent	.00	.12
Inappropriate Affect	−.09	−.05

Note. [a]n = 115 (73 Hispanics, 42 Blacks). [b]Father SES, n = 54 Hispanics, 27 Blacks. [c]Mother SES, n = 69 Hispanics, 39 Blacks. *p < .05

STRATIFICATION OF THE STANDARDIZATION SAMPLE

In the standardization sample, significant correlations of low magnitude were found between age and many of the TEMAS functions. Correlations ranged from .01 to −.52 (see Table 5–2). Although these correlations are small, it is believed that they reflect real developmental trends in the children's cognitive, affective, and personality trends; while still retaining adequate sample sizes, age was divided into three age-range groups: 5- to 7-year-olds, 8- to 10-year-olds, and 11- to 13-year-olds.

For each of the 17 Quantitative Scales, three-way analyses of variance (ANOVAs) were conducted by age, ethnic/racial background, and gender of the standardization sample. The three-way interaction terms were not significant for any of the quantitative functions. The two-way interactions between gender and age were also nonsignificant for these scales. However, the two-way interaction of sex and ethnic/racial backgrounds was significant for one of the 17 Quantitative Scales (Sexual Identity). However, given the number of hypotheses tested, this result may be attributable to chance.

There were no significant main effects of gender for any of these functions. This result is consistent with the results of other studies that have investigated the effects of gender on TEMAS functions.

Short Form

Means and standard deviations for the short form were obtained by extracting the scores of the 9 cards from the 23-card protocols of the standardization sample. The correlations between the 23-card long form of TEMAS and the 9-card short form for each function were conducted separately for the total sample and for each ethnic/racial group (see Table 5–3). The correlation between the long form and the short form was uniformly high across samples. The median correlation between forms was .81 for the Total sample, .82 for Whites, .80 for Blacks, .80 for Puerto Ricans, and .81 for Other Hispanics.

RELIABILITY

Internal Consistency

Internal consistency refers to the degree to which individual TEMAS cards are interrelated in measuring specific functions.

TABLE 5–3.   Correlation Between TEMAS Long and Short Forms

Function	White Sample N—r	Puerto Rican Sample N—r	Other Hispanic Sample N—r	Black Sample N—r
Quantitative Scale				
Reaction Time	87—95	117—95	84—94	114—99
Total Time	124—97	122—98	84—97	113—97
Fluency	123—98	125—97	86—97	206—74
Total Omissions	172—72	164—70	93—81	206—91
Interpersonal Relations	143—95	164—87	45—99	206—95
Aggression	136—92	164—96	38—99	206—89
Anxiety/Depression	171—90	151—84	100—83	203—88
Achievement Motivation	172—79	163—79	100—81	203—96
Delay of Gratification	163—89	161—87	84—82	193—82
Self-Concept	166—82	155—70	98—77	127—90
Sexual Identity	145—69	76—86	86—80	197—73
Moral Judgment	158—81	163—78	90—64	206—83
Reality Testing	171—75	125—84	100—66	206—71
Happy	172—87	163—81	94—96	206—72
Sad	172—82	163—79	94—94	206—77
Angry	172—77	163—84	94—87	206—80
Fearful	171—88	163—83	94—88	206—91
Qualitative Indicator	171—86	163—86	94—86	206—94
Neutral	171—72	163—61	94—79	206—74
Ambivalent	171—77	163—39	94—86	206—91
Inappropriate Affect	172—77	163—80	100—82	206—57
Conflict	172—87	163—57	100—79	206—65
Sequencing	172—82	163—97	96—84	206—59
Imagination	172—82	163—76	94—75	206—71
Relationships	172—62	164—80	96—72	206—72
Total Transformations	172—76	162—04	98—66	206—95
Inquiries	172—64	164—82	95—79	206—80
Main Character Omissions	172—78	164—75	98—78	206—64
Secondary Character	172—69	164—65	100—60	206—63
Omissions	172—68	164—66	100—87	206—55
Setting Omissions	172—47	164—57		206—34
Event Omissions	172—60	164—68	96—63	206—61
Main Character	172—66	164—94	100—65	206—70
Transformations	172—83	164—73	100—76	
Secondary Character			100—72	
Transformations				
Setting Transformations				
Event Transformations				

Long Form. Internal consistency reliabilities of the TEMAS functions were derived using a sample of 73 Hispanic and 42 Black children (see Table 5–4). The internal consistency reliability coefficients for the Hispanic sample ranged from .41 for *Ambivalent*, an affective function, to .98 for *Fluency*, a cognitive function, and had a median value of .73. For the Black sample, coefficients ranged from .31 for *Setting Transformations* to .97 for *Fluency*, with a median of .62.

Reaction Time, Fluency, and *Total Time* demonstrated high levels of internal consistency in both Hispanic and Black samples. However, in general, *Omissions* and *Transformations* of perceptual details *(Main Character, Secondary Character, Event, and Setting)* had lower magnitudes of internal consistency than other TEMAS functions in both samples. This may be attributable to the fact that these two functions, being clinical scales, tend to occur less frequently in nonclinical children (Costantino, Colon-Malgady, Malgady, & Perez, 1991). The internal consistency reliabilities for *Omissions* and *Transformations* were uniformly lower for Blacks than for Hispanics.

Conflict, Imagination, and *Relationships* demonstrated moderate-to-high internal consistency reliability in both ethnic/racial groups. The alpha coefficient for *Sequencing,* a cognitive function, was moderately high in the Hispanic sample but low in the Black sample. With respect to affective functions, reliability estimates in the Hispanic sample were highest for *Happy, Sad, Angry, and Fearful,* whereas in the Black sample, the highest reliability was evident for *Sad, Angry, Neutral, and Ambivalent.*

With respect to personality functions, pictures pulling for *Interpersonal Relations, Aggression, and Moral Judgment* showed the highest levels of internal consistency in the Hispanic sample, whereas *Anxiety/Depression, Achievement Motivation, Delay of Gratification, Self-concept, Sexual Identity, and Reality Testing* had a low-to-moderate reliability. For Blacks, alphas were again uniformly lower than for Hispanics, with the highest reliabilities associated with Aggression and Moral Judgment. Low reliabilities for the personality functions may be due partially to the fact that personality function scores are based on relatively few TEMAS cards (see Table 5–4).

The coefficient alphas for the standardization sample, differentiated by ethnic/racial group membership for the long form, were, for the most part, in the moderate range, with a median alpha of .83 for the Quantitative Scales for the Total Sample. On these functions, the median reliability ranged from .80 for Black children to .69 for Other Hispanic children. On the Short Form, alphas were generally lower, with a median reliability of .68 for the Total sample on the Quantitative scales. Reliability coefficients for

ethnic/racial groups on these functions ranged from a median coefficient of
.65 for the White sample to .54 for the Black sample. Reliability coefficients
on the Qualitative Indicators were lower due, in large part, to the nonmetric
nature of the scoring system used with these scales.

TEST–RETEST RELIABILITY (SHORT FORM)

Test–retest stability reliability of the TEMAS functions was computed
for the Short Form by correlating the results of two administrations, separated by an 18-week interval. The sample used in this study consisted of
51 subjects chosen at random from the 210 Puerto Rican students screened
for behavior problems. Results indicated that TEMAS functions exhibited
low-to-moderate stability over an 18-week period (see Table 5–4). The
eight TEMAS functions with significant test–retest correlations were *fluency, event transformations, conflict, relationships, happy, ambivalent, anxi-
ety/depression, and sexual identity*. Two explanations for the generally low
level of test–retest reliability have been proposed. First, test–retest correlations may be lower-bounds estimates of reliability, in this case because
different raters were employed at pre and posttesting. Therefore, they
include error variance due to interrater reliability. Second, the indices of
this test have limited range and hence, the correlation may be reduced.

INTERRATER RELIABILITY

Interrater reliability was estimated in a relatively recent study of the
nonminority version of the TEMAS short form (Costantino, Malgady,
Casullo & Castillo, 1991). Two experienced clinical psychologists (one
with extensive training in scoring TEMAS and the other a newly trained
scorer) independently rated 20 protocols. The results of this study indicated a high interrater agreement in scoring protocols for Personality
Functions, ranging from 75% to 95%. The mean level of interrater agreement was 81%, and in no cases were the two independent ratings different
by more than one rating scale-point. However, the interrater agreement
for Personality Functions in the standardization study ranged from 31%
to 100% (Costantino, Malgady, & Rogler, 1988). The explanation for this
discrepancy is that during the first study, conducted in 1983, the TEMAS
scoring system was still undergoing changes, whereas in the second
study, conducted in 1987, the scoring system and the instructions were

TABLE 5–4. Internal Consistency (Alpha) Reliability and Test-Retest (R)
Reliability Over 18-Week Interval

	Hispanic	Black	N	r
Cognitive Function				
Reaction time	.95	.92	50	.17
Total time	.98	.97	50	.06
Fluency	.98	.97	50	.45
Total omissions	.80	.75	50	.13
Total transformations	.64	.45	51	.05
Inquiries	.82	.59	51	.27
Main character omissions	.76	.59	51	.04
Main character transformations	.52	–	51	−.05
Secondary character omissions	.65	.56	51	−.06
Secondary character transformations	.77	.36	51	−.07
Event omissions	.74	.72	51	.27
Event transformations	.48	–	51	.46
Setting omissions	.75	.60	51	.15
Setting transformation	.55	.31	51	−.08
Conflict	.69	.83	51	.53
Sequencing	.82	.46	51	−.01
Imagination	.98	.75	51	.11
Relationship	.75	.68	51	.39
Personality Function[2]				
Interpersonal relations (16)	.92	.62	50	.24
Aggression (8)	.84	.78	50	.16
Anxiety/depression	.50	.49	50	.45
Achievement motivation	.65	.52	48	.11
Delay of gratification (4)	.45	.45	50	.17
Self–concept (4)	.59	.45	45	−.07
Sexual identity (3)	.58	.63	33	.38
Moral judgment	.72	.70	49	.07
Reality testing	.56	.44	49	.21
Affective Function				
Happy	.86	.67	51	.35
Sad	.89	.79	51	.15
Angry	.76	.77	51	−.04
Fearful	.82	.50	51	.25
Neutral	.50	.84	51	−.03
Ambivalent	.41	.77	51	.45
Inappropriate affect	–	–	–	

Note. [2]The number of pictures pulling each function is indicated in parentheses.

TABLE 5–5.   InterRater Reliability of TEMAS Scales
Reported by Cardalda (1995)

Scales	Reliability
Adaptive Personality Functioning	
Interpersonal relations	.76
Control of aggression	.80
Achievement motivation	.74
Delay of gratification	.84
Self-concept of competence	.78
Cognitive Functioning	
Omissions	.87
Transformations	.73
Recognition of conflict	.83
Narrative imagination	.87

completely formulated. A more recent study (Cardalda, 1995) reports the interrater reliability of the personality and cognitive functions. Two trained clinicians independently scored a random sample of 15 of the 74 protocols. Interrater reliability based on correlations between the two clinicians' assessments is shown in Table 5–5. The adaptive functioning scales showed high interrater agreement, ranging from .74 to .84. Similarly, the cognitive scores were also rated consistently, with interrater correlations ranging from .73 to .87.

CONTENT VALIDITY

TEMAS pictures were designed to pull for specific personality functions based on the nature of the psychological conflict represented in each picture. As previously described in the Scoring section, all TEMAS pictures are scored for at least two and not more than four personality functions. A study was conducted to assess the concordance among a sample of practicing school ($n = 8$) and clinical ($n = 6$) psychologists regarding the pulls of each TEMAS picture for specific personality functions. The psychologists were presented the TEMAS pictures in random order and were asked individually to indicate which, if any, of the nine functions each picture pulled. The percentage of agreement among the 14 clinicians revealed surprisingly high agreement (71%–100%) across the pictures, thus confirming the pulls scored for specific personality functions.

RELATIONSHIP TO OTHER MEASURES

A sample of 210 Puerto Rican children screened for behavior problems were administered a number of measures along with the TEMAS, and their adaptive behavior in experimental role-playing situations was observed and rated by psychological examiners. The measures administered included: the Sentence Completion Test of Ego Development (SCT; Loevinger & Wessler, 1970) or its Spanish version (Brenes-Jette, 1987); the Trait Anxiety Scale of the State–Trait Anxiety Inventory for Children (STAIC; Speilberger, Edwards, Lushene, Montouri, & Platzek, 1973) or its Spanish version, *Inventario de Ansiedad Rasgo-Estado Para Ninos* (Villamil, 1973); the Teacher Behavior Rating Scale (TBR: Costantino, 1980), and the parallel Mother Behavior Rating Scale (MBR: Costantino, 1980) in both English and Spanish. Finally, the children participated in four experimental role-playing situations, designed to elicit adaptive behavior.

Results of the regression analyses indicated that TEMAS profiles significantly predicted ego development (SCT), $R = .49$, $p < .05$; disruptive behavior (DIS), $R = .51$, $p < .05$; and aggressive behavior (AGG), $R = .32$, $p < .05$. However, the multiple correlations for predicting trait anxiety were not significant. TEMAS functions accounted for between 10% (for DG and AGG) and 26% (for DIS) of the variability in scores on the criterion measures. Predictive validity was established using hierarchical multiple regression analysis to assess the utility of TEMAS profiles for predicting posttherapy scores ($N = 123$) on the criterion measures, independent of pretherapy scores. In the first step of the hierarchy, the pretherapy score on a given criterion measure was entered into the regression equation, followed in the second step by a complete TEMAS psychotherapy profile. Results of these analyses showed that pretherapy TEMAS profiles significantly predicted all therapeutic outcomes, ranging from 6% to 22% variance increments, except for observation of *Self-concept of Competence*. Outcome measures were the Sentence Completion Test of Ego Development (14%); Trait Anxiety Inventory for Children (22%); Conner's Behavior Rating Scale (6%); and observational tasks measuring delay gratification (20%); disruptive behavior (17%); and aggression (14%).

DISCUSSION

Developing a consensual formal scoring for the TAT has challenged psychologists for more than a half a century. Historically, endeavors to develop or adapt a personal problem-solving scoring system does not seem to be a valid approach because of the high ambiguity of several TAT cards, which were not designed to depict psychological problems in a dialectic format. There are two possible approaches to develop an "objective scoring system" for the TAT. The first would be to expand the initial work of Murstein (1972) by focusing the scoring on those cards that have medium ambiguity and using the remaining cards as clinical tools; the second, as suggested by Dana (1999), would be to redraw several TAT cards to reflect the emic validity of the various cultural groups, collect a large library of protocols on different groups, and subsequently develop a consensual formal scoring system. A problem-solving scoring system could best be developed by using redesigned contemporary TAT cards with low ambiguity depicting multicultural characters engaged in antithetical situations. In light of the strong criticism of "projective techniques" as invalid and potentially harmful in providing inaccurate diagnostic profiles of clients (Garb, Wood, Lilienfeld, & Nezworski, 2002), we have endeavored to develop a valid scoring system for a narrative technique, which was derived from the traditional thinking about projective tests. Paradigmatic shifts in science, including social science, are common knowledge among historians (Kuhn, 1962). The TEMAS paradigm shifts new psychometric thoughts about projective/narrative testing toward a reconciliation with evidence-based psychometric methodology. It also redirects clinical practice into seminal modes of multicultural assessment that have promise to positively impact on the mental health and educational needs of the growing culturally and linguistically diverse populations.

The TEMAS scoring system presents a systematic, and to a given extent, a psychometrically reliable and valid system to score the complexity of personal narratives. Its clinical utility is based on the design of structured pictures that depict characters that promote identification between the storyteller and the stimuli, and on the development of a scoring system that closely captures the most salient aspects of the projected narratives, thus showing both emic and etic validity (APA, 2003; Cardalda et al., 1998; Cornabuci, 2000; Dana, 1996; Sardi, 2000; Sulfaro, 2000; Summo, 2000; Walton, Nuttall, and Vazquez-Nuttall, 1997).

REFERENCES

American Psychological Association (2003). Guidelines on Multicultural Education, Training, Research, Practice, and Organizational Change for Psychologists. *American Psychologist, 58,* 377–402. Washington, D.C.: Author.

Bandura, A. (1971). Analysis of modeling processes. In A. Bandura (Ed.), *Psychological modeling: Conflicting theories* (pp. 1–62). New York: Aldine-Atherton.

Bandura, A. (1977). *Social learning theory.* Englewood Cliffs, NJ: Prentice-Hall.

Bellak, L. (1954). *The T.A.T. and C.A.T. in clinical use.* New York, NY: Grune & Stratton.

Bellak, L., Hurvich, M., & Gediman, H. K. (1973). *Ego functions in schizophrenics, neurotics, and normals.* New York: John Wiley & Sons.

Bernal, I. (1991). *The relationship between levels of acculturation, The Robert's Apperception Test for Children, and the TEMAS (Tell-Me-A-Story test).* Unpublished dissertation, Los Angeles, CA: California School of Professional Psychology.

Brenes-Jette, C. (1987). *Mother's contribution to an early intervention program for Hispanic children.* Unpublished dissertation, New York University, New York City.

Cardalda, E. (1995). *Socio-cognitive correlates to school achievement using the TEMAS (Tell-Me-A-Story) culturally sensitive test with 6th, 7th, and 8th grades Puerto Rican students.* Unpublished dissertation, New School for Social Research, New York, NY.

Cardalda, E., Santiago-Negron, S., Jimenez-Suarez, V., Leon-Velasquez, M., Martinez, J., Figueroa, M., et al. (2005, July). New directions with the TEMAS test: Interpreting cognitive scales of the TEMAS relative to language problems in high risk Puerto Rican children. In. G. Costantino (Chair), *Multicultural/cross-cultural validation of TEMAS: A projective/narrative test.* Symposium, 9th European Congress of Psychology, Granada, Spain.

Cornabuci, C. (2000). *Relationship between Aggression and Interpersonal Relations in 7 and 8 years old Italian children.* Unpublished dissertation, Universita di Roma "La Sapienza," Rome, Italy

Costantino, G. (1978, November). *TEMAS, a new thematic apperception test to measure ego functions and development in urban Black and Hispanic children.* Paper presented at the Second Annual Conference on Fantasy and the Imaging Process. Chicago, IL.

Costantino, G. (1980). *The use of folktales as a new therapy modality to effect change in Hispanic children and their families.* (National Institute of Mental Health Grant 1-RO1-MH33711). Rockville, MD: NIMH.

Costantino, G. (1987). *TEMAS (Tell-Me-A-Story) Picture Cards.* Los Angeles: Western Psychological Services.

Costantino, G., Colon-Malgady, G., Malgady, R. G., & Pérez, A. (1991). Assessment of attention deficit disorder using a thematic apperception technique. *Journal of Personality Assessment, 57,* 87–95.

Costantino, G., & Malgady, R. G. (1996). Development of TEMAS, a multicultural thematic apperception test: psychometric properties and clinical utility. In G. R. Sodowsky & J.Impara (Eds) *Multicultural Assessment in Counseling and Clinical Psychology.* (pp. 85–136). Lincoln, NE: University of Nebraska.

Costantino, G., & Malgady, R. G. (1999). The Tell-Me-A-Story Test: A multicultural offspring of the Thematic Apperception Test. In L. Geiser & M. I. Stein (Eds.),

Evocative images: The Thematic Apperception Test and the art of projection (pp. 191–206). Washington, DC: American Psychological Association.

Costantino, G., & Malgady, R. G. (2000). Multicultural and cross-cultural utility of the TEMAS (Tell-Me-A-Story) Test. In R.H. Dana (Ed.), *Handbook of cross-cultural/ multicultural personality assessment.* (pp. 481–514). Mahwah, NJ: Lawrence Erlbaum Associates.

Costantino, G., Malgady, R. G., Casullo, M. M., & Castillo, A. (1991). Cross-cultural standardization of TEMAS in three Hispanic subcultures. *Hispanic Journal of Behavioral Sciences, 13,* 48–62.

Costantino, G., Malgady, R. G., Colon-Malgady, G., & Bailey, J. (1992). Clinical utility of the TEMAS with non-minority children. *Journal of Personality Assessment, 59, 433–438.*

Costantino, G., Dupertuis, D. G., Castillo, A., Malgady, R. G. & Faiola, T. (1997, July). Cross-cultural standardization of TEMAS with Argentinean and Peruvian Children. Poster paper presented at the International Congress of Psychology (ICP) Cross-Cultural Conference, Padua, Italy.

Costantino, G., Flanagan, R. M., & Malgady, R. G. (2001). Narrative assessment: TAT, CAT and TEMAS. In L. A. Suzuki, J. G. Ponterotto, and P. J. Meller (Eds.) *Handbook of multicultural assessment (2nd ed.* pp. 217–237). San Francisco, CA: Jossey-Bass.

Costantino, G., Malgady, R. G., & Rogler, L. H. (1988). *TEMAS (Tell-Me-A-Story) test manual.* Los Angeles: Western Psychological Services.

Costantino, G., & Malgady, R. G. (1996). Development of TEMAS, a multicultural Thematic Apperception Test: Psychometric properties and clinical utility. In G. R. Sodowsky & J. Impara (Eds.), *Multicultural Assessment in Counseling and Clinical Psychology.* (pp. 85–136). Lincoln, NE: University of Nebraska.

Cureton, E. E., & Tukey, J. W. (1951). Smoothing frequency distribution, equating tests, and preparing norms. *American Psychologist, 6,* 404–410.

Dana, R. H. (1955) Clinical diagnosis and objective TAT scoring. *Journal of Abnormal and Social Psychology, 50,* 19–24.

Dana, R. H. (1993). *Multicultural assessment perceptive for professional psychology.* Boston, MA: Allyn & Bacon.

Dana, R. H. (1996). Culturally competent assessment practice in the United States. *Journal of Personality Assessment, 66,* 472–487.

Dana, R. H. (1998). *Understanding cultural identity in intervention and assessment.* Thousand Oaks, CA: Sage.

Dana, R. H., (1999). Cross-cultural and multicultural use of the Thematic Apperception Test. In M. L. Gieser & M. I. Stein (Eds.), *Evocative images: The Thematic Apperception Test and the Art of Projection.* (pp. 177–190). Washington, DC: American Psychological Association.

Dana, R. H. (2000). Multicultural assessment of child and adolescent personality and psychopathology. In A. L. Comunian & U. Gielen (Eds.), *International perspectives on human development* (pp. 233–258). Lengerich, Germany: Pabst Science Publishers.

Dupertuis , D. G., Silva Arancibia, V., Pais, E., Fernandez, C., & Rodino, V. (2004). Similarities and differences in TEMAS test functions in Argentinean and European-American children. *Universidad de Buenos Aires—Argentina.*

Erikson, E.H. (1968). *Identity: Youth and crisis.* New York: Norton.

Eron, L. D. (1965). A normative study of the Thematic Apperception Test. In B. I. Murstein (Ed.), *Handbook of projective techniques* (pp. 469–507). New York, NY: Basic.

Exner, J. E., & Weiner, I. B. (1995). *The Rorschach: A comprehensive system: Vol. 3. Assessment of children and adolescents (2nd ed.).* New York: Wiley.

Exner, J. E., Jr. (1993). *The Rorschach: A comprehensive system: Vol. 1. Basic foundations.* (3rd Edition). New York, NY: Wiley.

Flanagan, R. (1999). Objective and projective personality assessment: The TEMAS and the Behavior Assessment System for Children, self-report of personality. *Psychological Reports, 48,* 865–867.

Flanagan, R., Losapio, G., Greenfeld, R., Costantino, G., & Hernandez, A. (2004, July). *Using Narratives to Assess Children's Social Problem Solving Skills.* Poster presented at the 112th Annual Convention of the American Psychological Association, Honolulu, Hawaii.

Garb, H. N., Wood, J. M., Lilienfeld, S. O., & Nezworski, T. M. (2002). Effective uses of projective techniques in clinical practice: Let the data help with selection and interpretation. *Professional Psychology: Research and Practice, 33,* 454–463.

Jensen, A. (1969). How much can we boost IQ and scholastic achievement? *Harvard Educational Review, 39,* 1–23.

Karon, B. P. (1981). The Thematic Apperception Test (TAT). In A. I. Rabin (Ed.), *Assessment with projective techniques* (pp. 150–162). New York, NY: Springer.

Krinsky, R. E. (1997). Children of alcoholics/substance abusing parents: Delay gratification, achievement *motivation, and aggression.* Unpublished doctoral dissertation. Adelphi University, Garden City, NY.

Kohlberg, L., (1976). Moral stages and moralization. In T. Lichona (Ed.), *Moral development and behavior: Theory, research, and social issues* (pp. 170–199). New York: Holt, Rinehart & Winston.

Kohlberg, L. & Ullian, D. Z. (1974). Stages in the development of psycho sexual concept and attitudes. In R. C. Friedman, R. M. Richart, & R. I. Van de Wiele (Eds.) *Sex differences in behavior* (pp. 209–222). New York: Wiley.

Kovacs, M., (1992). *The children's depression inventory.* North Tonawanda, NY: Multi-Health System.

Kuhn, T. S. (1962). *The structure of Scientific Revolutions.* Chicago, IL: University of Chicago Press.

Loevinger, J., & Wessler, R. (1970). *Measuring ego development 1. Construction and use of a sentence completion test.* San Francisco: Jossey-Bass.

McClelland, D. C., Atkinson, J.W., Clark, R. W., & Lowell, E. L. (1976). *The achievement motive.* New York: Irvington. (Original work published 1953)

Mischel, W. (1974). Processes in delay gratification. In L. Berkowitz (Ed.), *Advances in experimental social psychology* (Vol. 7, pp. 210–225). New York: Academic Press.

Morgan, C. D., & Murray, H. A. (1935). A method for investigating phantasies: The Thematic Apperception Test. *Archives of Neurological Psychiatry, 34,* 289–306.

Murray, H. A. (1943). *Thematic Apperception Test Manual.* Cambridge: Harvard University Press.

Murstein, B. L. (1972). Normative written responses for a college sample. *Journal of Personality Assessment, 41,* 194–247.

Ornduff, S. R., Freedenfeld, R. N., Kelsey, R. M., & Critelli, J. W. (1994). Object relations of sexually abused female subjects: A TAT analysis. *Journal of Personality Assessment, 63,* 223–238.

Ornduff, S. R. & Kelsey, R. M. (1996). Object relations of sexually abused and physically abused female children: A TAT analysis. *Journal of Personality Assessment, 66,* 91–105.

Ritzler, B. A. (1996). Projective methods for multicultural personality assessment: Rorschach, TEMAS, and Early Memory Procedures. In L. A. Suzuki, P. J. Meller, & J. G. Ponterotto (Eds.), pp. 115–136. *Handbook of Multicultural Assessment: Clinical, psychological and educational applications.* (pp. 115–136). San Francisco: Jossey-Bass

Ronan, G. F. & Gibbs, M. S. (1999) *The personal problem-solving system for scoring thematic apperception Test responses,* Mount Pleasant, MI: Central Michigan University.

Sardi, G. M. (2000) *Relationship between aggression and cognitive functions in conflict resolution in 7 and 8 years old Italian children.* Unpublished Dissertation, Universita di Roma "La Sapienza," Rome, Italy.

Sardi, G. M., Summo, B., Carnabuchi, C., & Sulfaro, C. (2001, July). Relationship between aggression, cognition and moral judgement in conflict resolution among Italian children. Paper presented by E. Costantino in G. Costantino (Chair), *Multicultural/cross-cultural validation of TEMAS: A new projective test.* Symposium conducted at the VII European Congress of Psychology, London, England.

Sobel, H. J. (1981). Projective methods of cognitive analysis. In T. Merluzzi, C. Glass, & M. Genest (Eds.), *Cognitive assessment* (pp. 127–148). New York: Guilford.

Spielberger, C. D. (1971). Anxiety as an emotional state. In C.D. Spielberger (Ed.), *Anxiety: current trends in theory and research.* Palo Alto, CA: Consulting sychologist Press.

Spielberger, C. D., Edwards, C. D., Lushene, R. E., Montouri, J., & Plaztek, D., (1973). *Preliminary test manual for the State–Trait Anxiety Inventory for Children.* Palo Alto, CA: Consulting Psychologist Press.

Sulfaro, C. (2000). *Relationship between aggression and moral judgment,* Unpublished dissertation, Universita di Roma "La Sapienza," Rome, Ital.y

Sullivan, H. S. (1953). *The interpersonal theory of psychiatry.* New York: W. W. Norton.

Summo, B. (2000). *Relationship between aggression and emotional functions in conflict resolution of 7 and 8 years old children.* Unpublished dissertation, Universita di Roma "La Sapienza," Rome, Italy.

Teglasi, H. (1998). Assessment of schema and problem-solving strategies with projective techniques. In A. S. Bellak and A. M. Hersen (Eds.), *Comprehensive clinical psychology* (pp. 439–499). New York: Pergamon Press.

Teglasi, H. (2001). Essentials of TAT and other storytelling techniques assessment. New York: John Wiley & Sons.

Thompson, C. E. (1949). The Thompson modification of the thematic apperception test. *Journal of Projective Techniques, 15,* 469–478.

Tomkins, S. S. (1947). *The Thematic Apperception Test: The theory and technique of interpretation.* New York, NY: Grune & Straton.

Villamil, B. (1973). *Desarollo del Inventario de Ansiedad Estado Y Rasgo para ninos.* (Development of the State–Trait Anxiety Inventory for Children). Unpublished master's thesis, University of Puerto Rico, San Juan.

Walton, J. R., Nuttall, R.L., & Vazquez-Nuttall, E. (1997). The impact of war on the mental health of children: A Salvadoran study. *Child Abuse & Neglect, 21,* 737–749.

Walton, J. R., Nuttall, R. L., & Vazquez-Nuttall, E. (1997, August). Effects of war on children's motivation reflected in TEMAS Stories. In G. Costantino (Chair), *Multicultural/cross-cultural motivation as assessed by TAT and TEMAS.* Symposium presented at the 106th annual APA Convention, San Francisco, CA.

Westen, D., Lohr, N., Silk, K., Kerber, K., & Goodrich, R. (1985). *Object relations and social cognition TAT scoring manual.* Ann Arbor: University of Michigan.

Winter, D. G. (1999). Linking personality and "scientific" psychology: The development of empirically derived Thematic Apperception Test measures. In L. Gieser & M. I. Stein (Eds.), *Evocative images: The Thematic Apperception Test and the art of projection* (pp. 107–124). Washington, DC: American Psychological Association.

Winter, D. G. (1973). *The power motive.* New York, NY: Free Press.

Yang, C-M., Kuo, L-H., & Costantino, G., (2004, July). Validity of Asian TEMAS in Taiwanese Children: Preliminary data. In G. Costantino (Chair), *Multicultural/cross-cultural validation of TEMAS: A projective/narrative test.* Symposium conducted at 8th European Congress of Psychology, Vienna, Austria.

6

Psychometric Properties

INTRODUCTION

For several years, standardized psychological assessment techniques have been criticized by some researchers as culturally biased toward ethnic minority children and adolescents (e.g., Dana, 1998, Costantino & Malgady, 1996; 2003; Malgady, Rogler, & Costantino, 1987; Olmedo, 1981; Rogler, Malgady, & Rodriguez, 1989). If these allegations are true, a significant problem confronting the delivery of effective mental health services to ethnic minority youth is the need for culturally sensitive assessment techniques with acceptable psychometric properties (American Psychological Association, 2003; 1993; US Department of Health and Human Services (US HHS), Mental Health: Culture, Race and Ethnicity, A Supplement to Mental Health: a Report of the Surgeon General, 2001). The need for culturally sensitive assessment models that are both reliable and valid is essential not only for screening and diagnostic purposes, but also because such assessments subsequently inform effective psychotherapeutic and pharmacological interventions (Rogler, Malgady & Rodriguez, 1989). Thus, research on the development of culturally sensitive measurement techniques is a critical need in the delivery of mental health services to minority populations.

Consistent with this need, the TEMAS ("Tell-Me-A-Story") test was developed as a culturally sensitive technique for personality assessment and diagnosis of Hispanic, Black, and White children and adolescents (Costantino, 1978). Extensive research documenting the reliability and validity of the TEMAS test has been conducted over the past decade (Costantino & Malgady, 1996), including research exploring the utility of TEMAS in discriminating common DSM-IV disorders of childhood and adolescence.

Since its publication in 1988, the use of the TEMAS test in clinical settings has grown rapidly, especially in large urban cities with large minority populations. The TEMAS test has been adopted by several major school systems, it has been included in university curricula for professional psychology training, and it has been widely used by school, community, and clinical psychologist practitioners.

BACKGROUND AND SIGNIFICANCE
OF THE PROBLEM

Recent statistics indicate that there are approximately 75 million school-age children under the age of 18 in the United States (The New York City Public School System alone has more than one million pupils). According to a recent study, "School Mental Health Services in the United States, 2002–2003" (SAMHSA, 2004), school-age children throughout the nation present severe mental health problems. More specifically, the study shows that 80% of the girls and 73% of the boys present social, interpersonal and family problems; 63% of the boys and 27% of the girls show aggression, disruptive behavior and bullying; 42% of the boys and 20% of the girls exhibit behavior problems related to neurological disorders; 24% of the boys and 36% of the girls present adjustment disorders; 18% of the boys and 41% of the girls show anxiety, stress and school phobia; and 13% of the boys and 29% of the girls exhibit depression disorders. In addition, the World Health Organization Global Burden of Disease Study indicates that by 2020, children mental health disorders will increase by more than 50%, thus becoming one of the five most common causes of disability and mortality among children (WHO, 2001). The Surgeon General emphasized that a large percentage of children with mental illness are not receiving any services. The situation is even worse for African-American, Latino, and other youngsters from ethnically and culturally diverse communities. Tragically, these children often bear the burden of unmet mental health needs. (US Department of Health and Human Services (US HHS), Mental Health: Culture, Race and Ethnicity, A Supplement to Mental Health: a Report of the Surgeon General, 2001). These significant percentages of mental health problems indicate that the schools play a very critical role in mental health interventions; hence school-based mental health programs become the necessary agent to provide psychological assessment and treatment on-site to the high numbers of affected pupils in the nation. The public schools in big cities such as New York, Chicago, Atlanta, Miami, Boston, Los Angeles and others have high percentages of racial/ethnic minorities such as Latinos and African-Americans.

THE MULTICULTURAL POPULATION IN
THE UNITED STATES

In 2003, there were 73 million children ages 0-17 in the United States, or 25% of the population, down from a peak of 36% at the end of the baby boom in 1964. Children are projected to comprise 24% of the total population in

2020. The racial and ethnic diversity of America's children continues to increase over time. In 2003, 60% of U.S. children were White non-Hispanic, 19% were Latino, 16% were Black-alone, and 4% were Asian-alone. The proportion of Hispanic/Latino children has increased faster than that of any other racial and ethnic group, growing from 9% of the child population in 1980 to 19% in 2003. (America's Children, 2005)

In 2004, more than one-fourth of the population 3 years and older (74.9 million people) were enrolled in schools in the United States: 33 million in elementary school, 17 million in high School, and 17 million in college. (US Census Press Releases, 2005).

The multicultural distribution of school age children in large metropolitan cites for school year 2004 are:

In Los Angeles, California, according the Board of Education in California, the total school age enrollment was 1.7 Million: 7.7% Asian, 61.7% Hispanic/Latino, 10.4 % African American, 0.3% American Indian or Alaska Native, 16.5 % White (not Hispanic), and 0.9%. Multiracial or no response.

In Chicago, Illinois, according to the Illinois Board of Education, there were 426,812 enrollees. Students' racial distribution was as follows: 49.8% African-American, 38.0% Latino, 8.8% White, 3.2% Asian/Pacific Islander, and 0.2% Native American.

In Miami, Florida, there were a total of 371,773 students enrolled: with 10% White non-Hispanic student enrolled; 29% black non-Hispanic enrolled; 59% Hispanic/Latino; 1.0% Asian/Pacific Islanders; 0.1% American Indian enrollees; and 0.1% Multiracial enrollees.

In New York City, New York, the New York City Department of Education had a total of 1,055,986 students enrolled: American Indian 0.46%; Asian 13%; Hispanic/Latino 39%; Black 33%; and White 15%.

In Atlanta, Georgia, there were a total of 50,770 enrollees: .003% American Indian, 0.6% Asian, 86% Black, 4.0% Hispanic /Latino, 1.0% Multiracial and 8.0% White.

Boston Massachusetts, According to the Massachusetts Board of Education, had a total of 57,742 students enrolled: 0.4% Native American, 9% Asian, 46% African American, 14% White and 31% Hispanic/Latino.

In Newark, New Jersey, the Newark Public Schools 2004-2005 Annual Report showed a total student enrollment of 41,899: with 59% Blacks; 32% Hispanic/Latino; 7.9% White; 0.8% Asian and 0.1% Native American.

In Washington, DC, for the 2003 school year, according to the District of Columbia Public School, there was a total of 65,009 enrollees. 12% of the student population were identified as minorities: 84.4% African Americans; 9.4% Hispanic/Latinos; 4.6% Whites: 9.6% Asian American; and 0.5% were classified as Others.

A controversial issue in the delivery of effective mental health services for culturally diverse children and adolescents is the questionable cultural sensitivity of standard psychological assessment and diagnostic procedures with documented reliability and validity for ethnic minorities. The propriety of assessing ethnic minorities with instruments conceived, standardized, and validated from a White middle-class perspective has been questioned for many years (Dana, 1998, 1996; Olmedo, 1981; Malgady, Rogler, & Costantino, 1987). Nonetheless, despite years of rhetoric in the clinical literature, litigation in the public domain, special considerations in government funding policies, and ethnic minority caveats in the testing procedures and policies established for professional practice (APA, 1999, 2003; Bernal & Castro, 1994), little knowledge has emerged regarding how current assessment procedures can be sensitized or modified (with the exception of non-English-language translations) to reliably and validly accommodate children's cultural diversity. The achievement of this goal is a prerequisite to adequate assessment and, ultimately, the delivery of effective health services to minority populations.

Development of TEMAs

The "Tell-Me-A-Story" (TEMAS) test was developed as a storytelling technique, pictorially representing multiracial and multiethnic characters interacting in familiar family and urban settings, and also in fantasy situations (Costantino, 1987; Costantino, Malgady, & Rogler, 1988). The test consists of two versions: a minority (multiracial/ethnic characters) version for Hispanics and Blacks, and a parallel nonminority (White characters) version for Whites. Each version consists of a 9-picture short form and a 23-picture long form; some pictures are gender specific. According to the TEMAS administration procedure, after establishing rapport, the examinee is asked to tell a story about the pictures, relating "who/what/where" information and how each story ends. Structure probes are used by the clinician to elaborate this information if necessary. Many pictures involve bipolar dilemmas, such as choosing to comply with a parental demand or noncompliant playing with friends. The pictures, which are chromatic, were designed and have been empirically confirmed to provoke or "pull" distinct themes (e.g., aggressive conduct, depressive feelings). The thematic content of the stories, including the resolution of the dilemma posed, are rated by a clinician on a 4-point scale of symptom severity, ranging from severe pathology (e.g., themes of murder, suicide, physical abuse) to adaptive adjustment. Symptomatology detected in story themes is scored in a number of domains:

affect, attention deficit, anxiety, depression, interpersonal functioning, sexual/moral identity, self-concept, reality testing, and aggression.

The test has been standardized on four major groups of children and adolescents, ranging from 5 to 18 years old: Puerto Ricans; Other Hispanics, including Dominicans, Central/South Americans, and Mexican Americans; Blacks; and non-Hispanic Whites. Extensive evidence of interrater, internal consistency, and test–retest reliability and criterion-related validity, collected in the developmental research on the TEMAS test, are reported in the test's *Technical Manual* (Costantino, Malgady, & Rogler, 1988). Early research showed that bilingual Hispanics were more likely to speak Spanish and to tell longer stories when administered the TEMAS test as compared with the traditional TAT (Costantino, Malgady, & Vasquez, 1981). More recent studies showed that TEMAS profiles accurately discriminate between children with attention-deficit disorders and normal children (Costantino, Colon-Malgady, Malgady, & Perez, 1991) and between conduct disordered children and public school children (Costantino, Malgady, Rogler, & Tsui, 1988).

Another study demonstrated the diagnostic sensitivity and specificity of the TEMAS test (scored for DSM-IV criteria) to discriminate among multinational Hispanic children with conduct, anxiety, and adjustment disorders. Another recent study used selected TEMAS pictures as a modality for conducting "storytelling" therapy with diverse groups of Hispanic adolescents (Costantino, Malgady, & Rogler, 1994).

SOME RECENT PSYCHOMETRIC STUDIES OF TEMAS

TEMAS and RATC, a study by Bernal (1991), was conducted to determine the relationship between level of acculturation, the TEMAS test (Costantino, 1987), and nonminority instrument, the *Robert's Apperception Test for Children* (RATC; Roberts McArthur, 1982), which at that time had only a version for white children. Bernal's study was based on a relatively small sample of 40 Mexican American ($n = 32$) and a comparison group of European-American ($n = 8$) children. The children ranged in age from 10 to 12 years old, were about evenly split by gender and birthplace (i.e., U.S. vs. Mexico), and were recruited from regular and gifted classrooms (Grades six through eight in a Los Angeles school district). Children's parents were administered the Vineland Adaptive Behavior Scales (Sparrow, Balla & Cicchotti, 1984), and the SOMPA Acculturation Scale (Mercer & Lewis, 1977), while teachers were administered the adaptive behavior scale classroom version of the Vineland Scales. The order of the RATC and TEMAS (9-card short form) was counterbalanced; furthermore, all tests were administered in the participant's preferred language, English or Spanish.

A number of findings of Bernal's comparative study of the two instruments are compelling. Highly adaptive behavior scores on the RATC were associated with speaking English at home, household income, parental income, and Anglo-ethnicity; however, there were no age or gender differences in RATC assessments of adaptive behavior. In contrast, no demographic factors were correlated with the TEMAS indices of adaptive personality functioning.

With respect to acculturation, Bernal showed that RATC adaptive scores were significantly correlated with levels of (U.S.) acculturation, but surprisingly, clinical status scores on the RATC were negatively correlated, indicated greater clinical impairment with increasing acculturation. Although Bernal was unable to interpret the latter finding, this is consistent with an earlier meta-analysis of the literature on acculturation and mental health (Cortez, Rogler, & Malgady, 1994). Unlike the RATC, the TEMAS scores were uncorrelated with level of acculturation, which is consistent with the theoretical rationale underlying the development of TEMAS; namely, that it provides a clinical bridge between languages and cultures in assessing personality functions of culturally diverse children.

Bernal also tested correlations between the RATC and various TEMAS scales, finding that the two instruments similarly assessed self concept/need for support, but only the TEMAS validly assessed clinical status in both White and Mexican-American students (Bernal, 1991).

Temas Achievement Motivation and School Achievement

In another study, Cardalda (1995) explored the relationship of TEMAS assessment to school achievement and performance measures in reading and mathematics of Puerto Rican children in Grades six to eight, ranging in age from 11 to 15 years old. Specifically, Cardalda correlated the TEMAS personality functions of *Interpersonal Relations, Aggression, Achievement Motivation, Delay of Gratification*, and *Self-Concept* with reading and mathematics scores; the TEMAS cognitive variables of *Fluency, Omissions, Conflict, Imagination*, and *Transformations* with reading and math scores; and she examined the relationship between TEMAS adaptive personality function scores and cognitive scores, as a function of grade level.

In this study, 74 Puerto Rican children (44 males, 30 females) were recruited from a public school in a low SES district in New York City.

TABLE 6–1. Interrater Reliability of TEMAS Scales
Reported by Cardalda (1995)

Scale	Reliability
Adaptive Personality Functioning	
Interpersonal relations	.76
Control of aggression	.80
Achievement motivation	.74
Delay of gratification	.84
Self-concept of competence	.78
Cognitive Functioning	
Omissions	.87
Transformations	.73
Recognition of conflict	.83
Narrative imagination	.87

[1]Reported by Cardalda (1995)

Students were administered the 9-card minority version of the TEMAS in their preferred language, and protocols were scored according to the standardized procedures in the Manual (Costantino, Malgady, & Rogler).

Reliability of the TEMAS scales was exceptionally high in the Cardalda study. Two trained clinicians independently scored a random sample of 15 of the 74 protocols. Interrater reliability based on correlations between the two clinicians' assessments are shown in Table 6–1. As is evident in the table, the adaptive functioning scales showed high interrater agreement, ranging from .74 to .84. Similarly, the cognitive scores were also rated consistently, with interrater correlations ranging from .73 to .87.

Reading and mathematics achievement and performance measures were obtained from their school records. Table 6–2 shows the correlations of TEMAS scales with the New York City school achievement and performance measures, controlling for grade level.

As Table 6–2 shows, the correlations of TEMAS personality functioning and cognitive indices with school achievement and performance indicators were largely nonsignificant and relatively weak in magnitude. The notable exception to this pattern was a significant, low to moderate correlation of *Achievement Motivation* with reading and mathematics achievement, and a moderate correlation of *Delay of Gratification* with mathematics achievement. When cast into multiple regression equations, TEMAS profiles were significant predictors of both reading and mathematics achievement; with

TABLE 6–2. Partial Correlations of TEMAS Scales With Reading and
Mathematics Achievement and School Performance (N = 74)

Temas Scale	Reading	Math	Performance
Interpersonal relations	.11	.10	.17
Control of aggression	.13	.00	.19
Achievement motivation	.24*	.28*	.16
Delay of gratification	.19	.29*	.16
Self-concept of competence	.04	.06	.11
Verbal fluency	.11	.20	.16
Omissions	.01	−.07	.06
Recognition of conflict	.09	.00	−.02
Narrative imagination	−.04	−.06	−.13
Transformations	−.11	−.20	−.13

Note. * p < .05

respect to reading achievement, $R = .60$, $p < .01$, and with respect to mathematics achievement, $R = .64$, $p < .05$.

Cardalda further explored the relationship between TEMAS assessment as a predictor of school achievement and performance within grade levels. These results are shown in Table 6–3.

The pattern of within-grade-level correlations of TEMAS scores with achievement and performance is more interesting than the total sample analysis. Despite the smaller within-group sample size, more correlations were statistically significant within groups, and the magnitude of the correlations was uniformly higher.

For sixth graders, Cardalda identified moderate correlations between *Interpersonal Relations* and reading and mathematics achievement; between *Control of Aggression* and mathematics achievement; between *Achievement Motivation* and mathematics achievement; and between *Delay of Gratification* and reading and mathematics achievement.

For seventh graders, moderate correlations were found for *Control of Aggression* with reading achievement, *Achievement Motivation* with mathematics achievement and school performance, and *Delay of Gratification* with reading achievement and school performance.

Finally, Cardalda introduced an interesting new index for scoring TEMAS protocols, the "Dysfluency" score. The dysfluency index consists of a count of a number of dysfluent utterances, such as "um," "eh," and so forth. The range of dysfluency scores for the combined sample ranged

TABLE 6–3. Correlations of TEMAS Scales With Reading and Mathematics Achievement and School Performance With Grade Levels

TEMAS Scale	Reading	Math	Performance
Grade 6 (N = 25)			
Interpersonal relations	.48*	.45*	.23
Control of aggression	.28	.40*	−.25
Achievement motivation	.53**	.43*	−.02
Delay of gratification	.33	.52**	−.08
Self-concept of competence	.17	.16	.27
Verbal fluency	.16	.13	.20
Omissions	.11	.16	.28
Recognition of conflict	.21	.30	.33
Narrative imagination	−.23	−.26	−.13
Transformations	−.05	−.11	−.20
Grade 7 (N = 27)			
Interpersonal relations	−.04	.14	.08
Control of aggression	−.29	−.25	.34
Achievement motivation	.15	.25	.46*
Delay of gratification	.09	.32	.39*
Self-concept of competence	−.02	.10	.12
Verbal fluency	.19	.36	−.01
Omissions	.03	−.16	.21
Recognition of conflict	−.20	−.38	−.05
Narrative imagination	.23	.25	−.30
Transformations	.07	−.25	.13
Grade 8 (N = 22)			
Interpersonal relations	.04	.07	.17
Control of aggression	.34	−.19	.24
Achievement motivation	.19	.47*	.51*
Delay of gratification	.30	.24	.32
Self-concept of competence	.17	.09	.08
Verbal fluency	−.17	.12	.35
Omissions	.04	−.01	.32
Recognition of conflict	.02	.07	.15
Narrative imagination	.11	−.24	.02
Transformations	.06	.06	−.04

Note. * p < .05, ** p < .01

from 1 to 80 (M = 12.44, SD = 15.59). The correlation between Dysfluency and Fluency scores was moderate (r = .39, p < .001), indicating that there was a tendency for the more verbal respondents to also present more meaningless speech utterances. Dysfluency was not related to grade level or bilingual language switching. Unfortunately, this index was not correlated with school achievement and performance indicators.

Cardalda's (1995) work represents perhaps the most comprehensive body of psychometric research conducted on the TEMAS test, independent of the TEMAS authors. Her work augments the reliability and validity studies reported in the TEMAS Manual (Costantino, Malgady, & Rogler, 1988), and in their subsequent work. Based on her findings, Cardalda offered some insightful directions for further research on the TEMAS test.

In the Cardalda (1995) study it was also found that sixth graders showed high achievement motivation in TEMAS and comparable high school achievement; however, these achievements tended to decline in grades seventh and eighth. This result seems to be important because it may contribute to the high school dropout rates of Latino students at the Middle School level. To further assess the steady step-wise decline of achievement motivation from grades sixth through eighth, Cardalda suggested that it would have been useful to examine the archival data from student records. This would have entailed a longitudinal analysis of the participants' school functioning from the lower grade to the higher grade to uncover variables associated with this decrease. An additional direction would be to conduct a content analysis of the TEMAS protocols to explore social representations of achievement motivation. A probability sample of the protocols for the three Middle School grades should be analyzed by three psychologists to assess the relationships between achievement motivation and psychosocial factors such as positive school experiences, role models, future expectations, the strength of identification with the main character in the story, and primacy and length of the achievement theme. In summary, further research in TEMAS Achievement motivation among Latino students as related to general school achievement is a very important topic and needs to be closely followed up.

Mujica (1997) conducted a study to explore school psychologists' familiarity, training, and experience with the TEMAS test, and their evaluation of TEMAS's utility in comparison to the TAT. Surveys were mailed to 120 school psychologists in New York City public schools, serving in six different school districts in low SES areas, enrolling mostly Latino and African American student populations. The mailing was a survey composed of questions pertaining to school psychologists' demographic background, their theoretical orientation, and familiarity, training, and experience with the TEMAS and TAT. This was accompanied by a questionnaire with a 29-item rating scale, which compared the TEMAS and TAT.

Three fourths of the surveys ($N = 90$) were returned, representing a reasonably good response rate of 75%. The majority of psychologists were female (65%); half identified themselves as White, 25% as Hispanic/Latino, 8% as African American, and one as Asian American. Three fourths were State certified, one fourth had doctoral degrees, and most were "eclectic" in their theoretical orientation. The vast majority had at least five years of experience in their field. All had previous experience evaluating and working with Hispanic/Latino and African American children.

Of the 90 school psychologists surveyed, 26 had previous experience using both the TEMAS and the TAT. The 29 criteria comparing the utility of the TEMAS and TAT are presented in Table 6–4, which shows the item, mean and SD of rating, and significance of paired t-tests comparing mean TEMAS and TAT ratings.

The results indicated that among school psychologists with experience using both the TEMAS and TAT to evaluate minority children, on the average the TEMAS test was rated more clinically relevant and more interesting. The TEMAS test was rated significantly higher on 10 of the 13 items assessing clinical utility. Similarly, the TEMAS test maintained a child examinee's interest on all four items composing this criterion. Mujica also reported that the TEMAS test received good ratings with regard to multicultural relevance. Although TEMAS was not rated as more sensitive than the TAT in terms of stimulus cards or thematic content, TEMAS rated more culturally relevant and less biased toward minorities compared to the TAT. Mujica found this, understandably, a perplexing result. Her conclusion was that although the psychologists had extensive practical experiences and were familiar with both tests, they may have had unclear or variable conceptualizations of what constitutes multicultural sensitivity. Furthermore, she distinguishes between cultural sensitivity (awareness) and cultural competence (skills), suggesteding that cultural sensitivity and competency skills need to be systematically introduced into graduate training programs in school psychology.

Directions for future research, as suggested by Mujica (1997), include evaluation of the effectiveness of multicultural training programs, setting clearly delineated specific standards, and involving multiple curriculum components such as didactic and supervisory, expert consultation, support groups, cultural immersion, and training in racial identity formation. Mujica also recommends replicating the study with samples from different

TABLE 6–4.   Mean Comparisons Evaluating the TEMAS
Test vs. The TAT ($N = 27$)

Attribute	TEMAS		TAT		T
	M	SD	M	SD	
A. Ease of Administration/Scoring/Interpretation					
Ease of administration	3.50	1.00	3.70	0.81	1.05
Ease of interpreting data	3.50	1.10	3.30	1.00	0.48
Ease of integrating test clinical data in report	4.00	0.84	3.30	1.00	2.58*
Ease of integrating test data in the battery	3.00	1.03	3.00	1.03	0.00
Facility of training required to master test	3.50	1.20	3.40	1.00	0.30
Ease of scoring	3.10	1.30	3.00	1.20	0.18
Substance of psychometric properties	3.50	0.99	2.20	1.00	4.71*
B. Cultural Sensitivity					
Cultural sensitivity of test stimuli	1.60	0.79	1.60	0.79	0.00
Cultural sensitivity of thematic content	1.90	0.84	1.90	0.84	0.00
Multicultural relevance	4.50	0.64	1.60	0.79	13.28*
Utility of multicultural norms	4.00	1.00	2.20	1.10	5.69*
Lack of bias toward minority students	3.50	1.30	2.00	1.10	3.29*
C. Eliciting/Maintaining Interest					
Stimulating/maintaining interest in the task	3.90	0.74	2.50	0.81	7.86*
Utility in eliciting rich protocols	3.60	0.89	2.90	0.87	2.71*
Attractiveness of stimuli	4.50	0.57	1.80	0.88	12.10*
Utility of test eliciting imaginative stories	3.60	0.94	2.50	1.00	4.24*
D. Clinical Utility					
Utility of objective scoring versus subjective interpretation	3.80	0.76	2.60	1.00	5.05*
Comprehensiveness of assessment	3.70	1.00	2.50	0.94	4.17*
Temporal efficiency in obtaining clinical data	3.40	1.00	2.70	1.20	0.18
Utility of ambiguous versus unambiguous stimuli	3.50	1.20	2.70	1.40	1.53
Relevance of test to theoretical orientation	4.00	0.80	3.00	1.20	0.02*
Validity assessing personality functioning	3.60	0.80	3.00	0.97	2.98*
Validity predicting clinical profiles	3.60	1.00	3.00	1.10	2.18*
Utility of test in school setting	4.10	0.80	3.10	1.10	4.15*
Utility in assessing strengths of examiners	3.80	0.80	2.50	1.00	5.49*
Utility in assessing weaknesses of examiners	3.70	0.82	2.80	1.00	4.31*
Substance of theoretical/ research info in manual	3.80	0.90	2.40	1.20	4.50*
Utility of color	4.20	0.84	1.60	1.00	8.22*
Utility of familiarity of stimuli	2.40	1.20	2.40	1.20	0.00

Notes.   * p < .05, 1 = poor; 2 = fair; 3 = good; 4 = very good; 5 = excellent

populations, in rural and suburban areas, in the private sector, and in other areas of the country.

TEMAS and RCS

Another comparative study of projective techniques was conducted by Elliott (1998), who examined the differential validity of the TEMAS test with the Rorschach Comprehensive System (RCS). The RCS was developed by Exner (1993) in an effort to produce a psychometrically sound basis for scoring the Rorschach, along with standardized administration, scoring, and interpretation procedures. The RCS elicits a behavioral demonstration of the examinee's personality functioning, and is based on a structural score-based content analysis that enables an interpretation of the examined ideographic character (Ritzler, 1996). According to Butcher and Rouse (1996), the RCS is one of the more extensively researched and most utilized clinical tools in the field today.

Accordingly, Elliott studied 84 11 to 15-year-old Hispanic ($n = 30$), African American ($n = 29$), and Caucasian ($n = 25$) junior high school students, about evenly distributed by gender, in New York City. Students were administered both the minority and nonminority versions of the 9-card short form of TEMAS and the RCS. Tests were administered in counterbalanced order, in three sessions separated by a 3-week interval. TEMAS pretests were scored for the following standardized indices: R, Lambda, Isolate/R, S, Es, X% (see RCS scoring definitions).

A random sample of 12 of RCS protocols and 16 TEMAS protocols were scored by two independent raters. Raters were intercorrelated to determine interrater reliability, as shown in Table 6–5.

Thus, as Table 6–5 shows, both the TEMAS and the RCS achieved high levels of interrater reliability.

CRITERION VALIDITY

The first phase of this study explored the criterion validity of the minority and nonminority versions of the TEMAS as predictors of the same selected RCS outcome criterion. This was completed in two steps. First, using Pearson correlational coefficients, the relationships between the scores on the minority version of the TEMAS as predictors of select RCS outcomes were calculated. The relationships between the scores on the nonminority version of the TEMAS as separate predictors of the same selected RCS outcomes were also calculated. As the direction of each

TABLE 6–5.   Interrater Reliabilty of TEMAS and RCS Tests

Score Index:	TEMAS	RCS	
Fluency	1.00	R	1.00
Anxiety/Depression	0.85	Isolate/R	0.98
Aggression	0.87	Lambda	0.97
Interpersonal Relations	0.89	S	0.96
Reality Testing	0.93	Es	0.99
		X%	0.88

correlation had been hypothesized, the Pearson correlational coefficients were tested for statistical significance with one-tailed significance tests at probability level < .05. The results of these tests were used to accept or reject the null hypotheses.

TOTAL SAMPLE ANALYSIS—IGNORING ETHNICITY

Of the 12 analyses conducted (six variables for both the minority and non-minority versions of the TEMAS), four were statistically significant. Both versions of the TEMAS variable AGG showed no relationship to the RCS criterion measure "S". In addition, although the nonminority TEMAS variable Interpersonal Relations (IR) was significantly correlated with the RCS criterion variable Isolate/R ($r = .197, p < .05$) the direction of the correlation coefficient was in the predicted direction but was not statistically significant ($r = -.050, p = .330$). There was also no relationship found between the TEMAS variable Fluency and the RCS criterion measure Lambda. The strongest correlation was found between the TEMAS variable Anxiety/Depression (A/D) and the RCS criterion variable "Es." The minority version of the TEMAS variable A/D and the RCS criterion variable "Es" shared 13% of their variance ($r = -.354, p < .01$); and the nonminority version of the TEMAS A/D variable shared 12% of its variance with the RCS criterion variable "Es" ($r = -.350, p < .01$). Finally, the minority version of the TEMAS variable REAL was significantly correlated in the predicted direction with the RCS criterion variable X% ($r = -198, p < .05$). The Pearson correlational coefficient for the nonminority version was also in the hypothesized direction, but was not statistically significant with the corresponding RCS variable X% ($r = -.030, p = .8$). This is not surprising given that the initial analyses of this project demonstrated a lack of correspondence between the minority and nonminority versions of the TEMAS on this variable. See

TABLE 6–6.   Pearson Correlation Matrix for Minority and Nonminority TEMAS
Variables and RCS Criterion Ignoring Ethnicity (*N* = 79)

Rorschach	Fluency	IR	AGG	AD	REAL
		Minority TEMAS			
Rank R	.118	—	—	—	—
Lambda	.070	—	—	—	—
Isolate/R	—	−.050	—	—	—
Space	—	—	.035	—	—
X%	—	—	—	—	—.198*
		Non-Minority TEMAS			
Rorschach	Fluency	IR	AGG	AD	REAL
Rank R	.147	—	—	—	—
Lambda	−.050	—	—	—	—
Isolate/R	—	.197*a	—	—	—
Space	—	—	.095	—	—
Es	—	—	—	−.340**	—
X%	—	—	—	—	−.030

Note. *p < .05, **p < .01, 1-tailed significance level.
aAlthough this correlation is statistically significant, it is in the direction opposite
to that hypothesized.

Table 6–6 for the Pearson correlations for the minority and non-minority
variables ignoring ethnicity.

SEPARATE ETHNIC GROUP ANALYSES

The second step in assessing the criterion validity of the minority and
nonminority versions of the TEMAS was to look separately at the three
ethnic groups. Again using Pearson correlational coefficients, the relationships between the scores on the minority version of the TEMAS as predictors
of select RCS outcomes were calculated, this time for each ethnic group. The
relationships between the scores on the nonminority version of the TEMAS
as separate predictors of the same selected RCS outcomes were also calculated for each ethnic group. As the direction of each correlation had been
hypothesized, the Pearson correlational coefficients were tested for statistical
significance with one-tailed significance tests at probability level *p* < .05. The
results of these tests were used to accept or reject the null hypotheses.

For the African American sample (n = 29), out of the 12 analyses conducted (6 variables for both the minority and nonminority versions of the TEMAS), two were statistically significant and an additional two showed trends toward statistical significance. The minority version of the TEMAS variables A/D (r = −.481, p < .01) and REAL (r = −.383, p < .05) were statistically significant predictors of the RCS criterion variables "Es" and X% and shared 23% and 15% of their variance respectively. In addition, the minority and nonminority versions of the TEMAS variable Fluency demonstrated Pearson correlational coefficients that were in the hypothesized direction and approached statistical significance (minority, r = −.272, p = .08; nonminority, r = −.306, p = .053) in their prediction of the RCS criterion variable Lambda. As predicted, the nonminority version of the TEMAS variable IR was approaching statistical significance in predicting the RCS criterion variable Isolate/R, and it was in the predicted direction of that hypothesized (r = .276, p = .07). Also statistically insignificant, but noteworthy, was that both the minority and nonminority versions of the TEMAS variable Fluency were moving in the direction opposite to that hypothesized to predict the RCS criterion variable Ranked R, and the non-minority version was at a level approaching statistical significance (minority, r = −.181, p = .173; non-minority, r = −.264, p = .084). Refer to Table 6–7 for the Pearson correlation matrix for the minority and nonminority TEMAS variables and RCS criterion for the African American sample.

For the Hispanic sample (n = 26), none of the 12 analyses conducted (6 variables for both the minority and nonminority versions of the TEMAS) were statistically significantly, although three approached significance. The correlational coefficients for both the minority and nonminority versions of the TEMAS variable Fluency were in the predicted direction and approached statistical significance in their prediction of the RCS criterion variable Lambda (minority, r = −.293, p = .07; nonminority, r = −.326, p = .052). Both the minority and nonminority versions of the TEMAS variable Fluency were in the hypothesized direction in their prediction of the RCS criterion variable Ranked R, while the nonminority version approached significance (r = .292, p = .07). Refer to Table 6–8 for the Pearson correlation matrix for the minority and nonminority TEMAS variables and RCS criterion for the Hispanic sample.

For the Caucasian sample (n = 24), three of the 12 analyses conducted (6 variables for both the minority and nonminority versions of the TEMAS), were statistically significant and an additional two approached significance. Both the minority and nonminority versions of the TEMAS variable Fluency were in the hypothesized direction and significant predictors

TABLE 6–7. Pearson Correlation Matrix for Minority and Nonminority TEMAS Variables and RCS Criterion for African Americans ($N = 29$)

| Rorschach | Minority TEMAS | | | | |
	Fluency	IR	AGG	AD	REAL
Rank R	−.181	—	—	—	—
Lambda	−.272	—	—	—	—
Isolate/R	—	−.203	—	—	—
Space	—	—	−.177	—	—
Es	—	—	—	−.481**	—
X%	—	—	—	—	−.383*

| Rorschach | Non-Minority TEMAS | | | | |
	Fluency	IR	AGG	AD	REAL
Rank R	−.264	—	—	—	—
Lambda	−.306	—	—	—	—
Isolate/R	—	.276	—	—	—
Space	—	—	−.130	—	—
Es	—	—	—	−.236	—
X%	—	—	—	—	−.224

Note. $*p < .05$, $**p < .01$, 1–tailed significance level.

of the RCS criterion variable Lambda and shared 19% and 45% of their variance, respectively (minority, $r = −.431$, $p < .05$; nonminority $r = −.674$, $p < .01$). The nonminority version of the TEMAS variable A/D was also statistically significant ($r = −.513$, $p < .01$) as a predictor of the RCS criterion variable "es" and shared 26% of the variance. The minority version approached significance in the predicted direction ($r = −.281$, $p = .09$). The nonminority version of the TEMAS variable Fluency also approached significance in the hypothesized direction as a predictor of the RCS criterion variable Ranked R ($r = .290$, $p = .085$). Refer to Table 6–9 for the Pearson correlation matrix for the minority and nonminority TEMAS variables and RCS criterion for the Caucasian sample.

DIFFERENTIAL VALIDITY

The second phase of this research project was an analysis of the differential validity of the minority and nonminority versions of the TEMAS as predictors of the same RCS outcome variables. This was examined first in

TABLE 6–8. Pearson Correlation Matrix for Minority and Nonminority TEMAS
            Variables and RCS Criterion for Hispanics ($N = 26$)

| | | Minority TEMAS | | | |
Rorschach	Fluency	IR	AGG	AD	REAL
Rank R	.259	—	—	—	—
Lambda	−.293	—	—	—	—
Isolate/R	—	.223	—	—	—
Space	—	—	.224	—	—
Es	—	—	—	−.239	—
X%	—	—	—	—	−.227
		Nonminority TEMAS			
Rorschach	Fluency	IR	AGG	AD	REAL
Rank R	.292	—	—	—	—
Lambda	−.326	—	—	—	—
Isolate/R	—	.045	—	—	—
Space	—	—	.063	—	—
Es	—	—	—	−.090	—
X%	—	—	—	—	.183

Note. $*p < .05$, $**p < .01$, 1-tailed significance level.

the total population, ignoring ethnicity, and then within each ethnic
group. The Pearson correlational coefficients for the relationship between
the minority and nonminority versions of the TEMAS variables to the
same RCS outcome criteria were previously calculated for the total population (see Table 6–6) and for each ethnic group separately (see Table 6–7,
Table 6–8, Table 6–9). These validity coefficients were then evaluated using
a test of the significance of the difference between the two dependent
correlations. As the hypotheses were directional in nature, the tests for
significance were one-tailed at the .05 probability level.

DIFFERENTIAL VALIDITY: TOTAL SAMPLE
ANALYSIS—IGNORING ETHNICITY

For the total sample, the null hypotheses that the minority and nonminority TEMAS variables are not statistically different from each other as
predictors of the RCS criteria was not refuted. For five of the six variables,

TABLE 6–9. Pearson Correlation Matrix for Minority and Nonminority TEMAS Variables and RCS Criterion for Caucasians ($N = 24$)

Rorschach	Fluency	IR	AGG	AD	REAL
		Minority TEMAS			
Rank R	.101	—	—	—	—
Lambda	−.431*	—	—	—	—
Isolate/R	—	−.079	—	—	—
Space	—	—	−.174	—	—
Es	—	—	—	−.281	—
X%	—	—	—	—	.0.58

Rorschach	Fluency	IR	AGG	AD	REAL
		Nonminority TEMAS			
Rank R	.290	—	—	—	—
Lambda	−.674**	—	—	—	—
Isolate/R	—	.159	—	—	—
Space	—	—	.143	—	—
Es	—	—	—	−.513**	—
X%	—	—	—	—	−.004

Note. $*p < .05$, $**p < .01$, 1-tailed significance level.

there was no statistical difference between the minority and nonminority TEMAS versions as predictors of RCS criterion variables. In the remaining analyses, the TEMAS variable IR was hypothesized to negatively correlate the RCS criterion variable Isolate/R. A statistical difference was found between the minority and nonminority versions of the TEMAS variable IR as predictors of the RCS criterion variable Isolate/R ($t = -1.798$, $df = 76$, $p = .038$). On closer examination, it is important to note that although the correlation between the minority version of the TEMAS variable IR and the RCS criterion variable Isolate/R was in the hypothesized direction ($r = -.050$, $p = .330$, one-tailed significance test) it was not statistically significant. In addition, the correlation between the nonminority version of the TEMAS variable IR and the RCS criterion variable Isolate/R represents a confirmation of the hypotheses. Taken as a whole, these results represent a partial confirmation of the hypotheses that the minority and nonminority versions of the TEMAS are differentially valid.

DIFFERENTIAL VALIDITY: SEPARATE ETHNIC
GROUP ANALYSES

Differential validity was also examined within each ethnic group separately. Here, the differential hypotheses were that for the minority groups
(Blacks and Hispanics) the minority version of the TEMAS variables
would be better predictors (as compared to the nonminority version) of
the RCS criteria. The nonminority versions of the TEMAS variables were
hypothesized to be better predictors of the RCS criteria for the Caucasian
ethnic group. Within each ethnic group, the validity coefficients were
compared in order to test for evidence of differential criterion validity
between the two versions of the TEMAS. Again, as the directionality of
the correlations had been hypothesized, all validity coefficients were
tested for statistical significance with one-tailed significance tests at the
probability level .05. The results were used to accept or reject the null
hypotheses that for each ethnic group separately, the minority and nonminority versions of the TEMAS would perform equally in predicting the
RCS criterion outcome variables.

For the African American sample ($n = 29$), inconsistent with expectations,
the null hypothesis that the minority and nonminority TEMAS variables are
not statistically different from each other as predictors of the RCS criteria was
not refuted. For five of the six variables, there was no statistical difference
between the minority and nonminority TEMAS versions as predictors of the
RCS criterion variables. In the remaining analyses, the TEMAS variable IR
was hypothesized to negatively correlate with the RCS criterion variable
Isolate/R. As seen in the total population analysis, a statistical difference was
found between the minority and nonminority versions of the TEMAS variable IR as predictors of the RCS criterion variable Isolate/R ($t = -1.949$,
$df = 26$, $p = .031$). The correlation between the minority version of the TEMAS
variable IR and the RCS criterion variable Isolate/R was in the hypothesized
direction ($r = -.203$, $p = .146$, one-tailed significance test), but was not statistically significant, and the correlation between the nonminority version of
the TEMAS variable IR and the RCS criterion variable Isolate/R was neither
statistically significant nor in the hypothesized direction ($r = .276$, $p = .07$,
one-tailed significance test). These results suggest that for African Americans
the minority version of the TEMAS variable IR is a better predictor of the RCS
criterion variable Isolate/R than the nonminority version. The rest of these
results represent a disconfirmation of the hypotheses that the minority and
nonminority versions of the TEMAS are differentially valid for the African
American sample.

For the Hispanic sample ($n = 26$), similar results were found. For five of the six variables examined, there were no statistical differences between the minority and nonminority TEMAS versions as predictors of RCS criterion variables. In the remaining analyses, the TEMAS variable REAL was hypothesized to negatively correlate with the RCS criterion variable X%. A statistical difference was found between the minority and nonminority versions of the TEMAS variable REAL as a predictor of the RCS criterion variable X% ($t = -1.952$, $df = 23$, $p = .031$). The correlation between the minority version of the TEMAS variable REAL and the RCS criterion variable X% was in the hypothesized direction ($r = -.227$, $p = .135$, one-tailed significance test), but was not statistically significant. The correlation between the nonminority version of the TEMAS variable REAL and the RCS criterion variable X% was neither statistically significant nor in the hypothesized direction ($r = .183$, $p = .186$, one-tailed significance test). These results suggest that for Hispanics the minority version of the TEMAS variable REAL is a better predictor of the RCS criterion variable X% than the nonminority version. The rest of the results represent a disconfirmation of the hypotheses that the minority and nonminority versions of the TEMAS are differentially valid for the Hispanic sample.

For the Caucasian sample ($n = 24$), similar results were found. For five of the six variables examined there was no statistical difference between the minority and nonminority TEMAS versions as predictors of the RCS criterion variables. In the remaining analyses, the TEMAS variable Fluency was hypothesized to negatively correlate with the RCS criterion variable Lambda. A statistical difference was found between the minority and nonminority versions of the TEMAS variable Fluency as a predictor of the RCS criterion Lambda ($t = 1.829$, $df = 21$, $p = .041$). The correlation between the minority version of the TEMAS Fluency variable and the RCS criterion variable Lambda was significant and in the hypothesized direction ($r = -.431$, $p = .018$, one-tailed significance test). In addition, the correlation between the nonminority version of the TEMAS variable REAL and the RCS criterion variable Lambda was also statistically significant and in the hypothesized direction ($r = -.674$, $p < .001$, one-tailed significance test). In congruence with the predicted hypotheses, the nonminority version of the TEMAS variable Fluency was a better predictor of the RCS criterion variable Lambda than the minority version. This result provides strong evidence for the differential validity of the minority and nonminority versions of the TEMAS variable Fluency as a predictor of the RCS criterion variable Lambda for Caucasians. Although this is a solid indication for differential validity, this is the only result consistent with the predicted hypotheses. The rest of the results represent a discon-firmation of the hypotheses that the minority and nonminority versions of the TEMAS are differentially valid for the Caucasian sample.

CROSS-CULTURAL CRITERION DIFFERENTIAL VALIDITY

The third area examined by this research project was the cross-cultural differential criterion validity of the minority and nonminority versions of the TEMAS. The research question is whether there are any statistically significant differences that exist between the minority and nonminority versions of the TEMAS across the three ethnic groups. Six estimated correlations were calculated and compared (the separate relationships between the minority and nonminority versions of the TEMAS and the RCS criterion variables for African Americans, Hispanics, and Caucasians) for each TEMAS predictor and associated RCS criterion variable (Ranked R and Fluency, Lambda and Fluency, es and A/D, Isolate/R and IR, X% and REAL, S and AGG) by the Linear structural relations (LISREL) pro-gram. These correlations were then tested statistically to evaluate the null hypotheses that there were no differences between the TEMAS versions or the ethnic groups in terms of differential validity. The previously com-puted Pearson correlational coefficients for the minority and nonminority versions of the TEMAS and their relationship to the RCS criterion vari-ables were used. Two constraints were imposed on the statistical analysis: first, that the correlations between the minority and nonminority versions of the TEMAS will be equal within each ethnic groups, and second, that these correlations will be equal across sample groups. Using these con-straints, the LISREL program estimates what the correlations would be under those conditions and then uses a two-tailed test of significance at the probability level of .05 to evaluate the results. An insignificant result indicates that the actual correlations are not different enough from the imposed estimates to conclude that the constraints are inappropriate and therefore we are unable to reject the null hypotheses. Results for all three ethnic groups were unable to refute the null hypotheses. See Table 6–10 for the chi-square results for cross-cultural differential validity.

Based on these findings, Elliott (1998), highlighted the assets and deficits of both projective techniques, suggesting that more clinical insight is gained integrating both elements of a psychological assessment profile. She concurs with Meyer (1996), who also grappled with cross-method

TABLE 6–10.   Chi-Square Results for Cross-Cultural
Differential Validity (N = 79)

Rorschach Index	Chi-Sq.	p	Goodness of Fit
R	6.82	.235	.952
Lambda	5.53	.354	.892
Isolate/R	5.88	.318	.963
S	3.83	.574	.961
Es	4.52	.477	.960
X%	7.91	.161	.966

Note. $df = 5$, two-tailed significance level.

disagreement, while maintaining faith in what each individual technique has to offer uniquely to the assessment protocol.

CONCLUSIONS

The use of the TEMAS test has been rapidly growing in clinical practice, particularly in large urban cities where the mental health service system is populated by a high proportion of culturally diverse clients. The test is most widely used with referrals from public school teachers to school psychologists for behavioral assessment, and from school psychologists to community mental health centers for psychiatric diagnosis and treatment. The TEMAS test has been adopted by the Boards of Education in New York City, Miami, and Los Angeles as part of their standard psychological assessment batteries. The test has been integrated into the graduate curriculum for training professional psychologists not only across the U.S., but also in Argentina, Italy, and Puerto Rico. Because the TEMAS has been acknowledged as an increasingly used measure of personality and symptomatology, it was included by Meyer and Handler in their 1994 review of those personality tests that were able to predict valid outcomes in health care (Meyer, personal communication, 2006). More recently, Abraham (2003) writes that Richard Dana has been an instrumental and successful pioneer in advocating the use of multiculturalism and human diversity into personality testing. In addition, Costantino and his colleagues have been instrumental in introducing TEMAS as the first multicultural test for best practices in multicultural assessment. She concluded: "the contributions of Dana, Costantino, Malgady & Rogler are noteworthy for consciousness raising and influencing changes in our practices to better meet the assessment needs of a pluralistic society (p. 10)."

As mental health services such as assessment and diagnosis become modified to better serve multicultural populations, such as culturally diverse youth, there is a subsequent need to summatively evaluate the effectiveness of these special services. Specifically, there is a need to determine whether mental health practitioners who take culture into consideration in the provision of services report that more accurate assessments and diagnoses are achieved using the TEMAS test. In addition, a more fundamental issue in research on cultural sensitivity is to determine what particular elements of culture are consequential to the delivery of mental health services.

REFERENCES

Abraham, P. (2003). The teacher's block Multicultural/Diversity Assessment: An evolving process. *Society For Personality Assessment Exchange, 15,*10–11, 22.

America's Children: Key National Indicators of Well-Being, 2005 (n.d) Retrieved on February 8, 2006, from http://www.childstats.gov/americaschildren/i ndex.asp.

American Psychological Association (1993). Guidelines for providers of psychological services to ethnic, linguistic, and culturally diverse populations. Washington, D.C.: *American Psychologist, 48,* 45–48.

American Psychological Association (2003). Guidelines on multicultural education, training, research, practice, and organizational change for psychologists. *American Psychologist, 58,* 377–402. Washington, D.C.: Author.

American Psychological Association, American Educational Research Association, National Council on Measurement in Education (1999). *Standards for Educational and Psychological tests.* Washington, D.C.: American Psychological Association.

Bernal, M. E., & Castro, F. (1994). Are clinical psychologists prepared for service and research with ethnic minorities. Report of a decade of Progress. *American Psychologist, 49,* 797–805.

Bernal, I. (1991). The Relationship between level of Acculturation, the Robert's Apperception Test for Children, and the TEMAS: Tell-Me-A-Story. Unpublished doctoral dissertation, California School of Professional Psychology, Los Angeles, CA.

Butcher, J. N, & Rouse, S. V., (1966). Personality: Individual differences and clinical assessment. *Annual Review of Psychology, 47,* 87–111.

California Department of Education, Educational Demographics Unit: California Public Schools – County Report County Level Enrollment Reports. Created on 3/31/2006. Retrieved on April 14, 2006, from http://data1.cde.ca.gov/dataquest/

CoEnr.asp?cChoice=CoEnrEth&cYear=2004-05&TheCounty=19%2CLOS% 5EANGELES&cLevel=County&cTopic=Enrollment&myTimeFrame=S&sub-mit1=Submit.

Chicago Illinois Board of Education. Retrieved on April 14, 2006, from http://www.cps.k12.il.us/AtAGlance.html.

Cardalda, E. (1995). Socio-Cognitive Correlates to School Achievement using the TEMAS (Tell-Me-A-Story) Culturally Sensitive Test with 6th, 7th, and 8th grades at risk Puerto Rican Students. Unpublished doctoral dissertation, New School for Social Research University, New York, NY.

Cortez, D. E., Rogler, L. H., & Malgady, R. G.(1994). Biculturality among Puerto Rican Adults in the United States. *American Journal of Community Psychology*, 22, 707–21.

Costantino, G. (1978). *Preliminary report on the TEMAS ("Tell-Me-A-Story") test for ethnic minority children*. Paper presented at the Second American Conference on Fantasy and the Imaging Process, Chicago, IL.

Costantino, G. (1987). *TEMAS (Tell-Me-A-Story) Multicultural Test Cards*. Los Angeles, CA: Western Psychological Services.

Costantino, G., Colon-Malgady, G., Malgady, R. G., & Perez, A. (1991). Assessment of attention-deficit disorder using a thematic apperception technique. *Journal of Personality Assessment, 57*, 87–95.

Costantino, G., & Malgady, R. G. (1996). Psychometric research on the TEMAS test: A thematic apperception test for minority and non-minority children and adolescents. In *Buros-Nebraska Symposium on Measurement and Testing Series: Multicultural Assessment*. Lincoln, NE: Buros Institute of Mental Measurements.

Costantino, G., Malgady, R.G., & Rogler, L. H. (1988). *Technical manual: The TEMAS Thematic Apperception Test*. Los Angeles: Western Psychological Services.

Costantino, G., Malgady, R. G. & Rogler, L. H. (1994). Storytelling through pictures: Culturally sensitive psychotherapy for Hispanic children and adolescents. *Journal of Clinical Child Psychology, 23*, 13–20.

Costantino, G., Malgady, R. G., Rogler, L. H., & Tsui, E. (1988). *Discriminant analysis of clinical outpatients and public school children by TEMAS: A thematic apperception test for Hispanics and Blacks. Journal of Personality Assessment, 52*, 670–678.

Costantino, G., Malgady, R. G., & Vasquez, C. (1981). Comparing Murray's TAT to a new thematic apperception test for urban ethnic minority children. *Hispanic Journal of Behavioral Sciences, 3*, 291–300.

Dana, R. H. (1998). Cultural identity assessment of culturally diverse groups: *Journal of Personality Assessment, 70*, 1–16.

Dana, R. H. (1996). Culturally competent assessment practice in the United States. *Journal of Personality Assessment, 66*, 472–487.

Dana, R. H. (1995). Cultural competence in school psychology. *The School Psychologist, 49*(4), 87, 90.

Elliot, T. L., (1998). Differential Validity of the TEMAS (Tell-Me-A-Story) With Rorschach as Criterion: A Comparison of Projective Methods. Unpublished doctoral dissertation, Long Island University, Brooklyn, NY.

Exner, J. E., Jr. (1993). *The Rorschach: A comprehensive system: Vol. 1. Basic foundations*. (3rd Edition). New York, NY: Wiley.

Florida Department of Education Profiles of Florida School Districts, Student and Staff Data, 2003-2004 Dade County. Created in April, 2005.Retrieved on April 14, 2006 from http://www.firn.edu/doe/eias/eiaspubs/pdf/ssdata04.pdf. Main page http://www.firn.edu/doe/eias/eiaspubs/profiles.htm.

Georgia Department of Education (2005-2006 school year). *Enrollment by Gender, Race/Ethnicity and Grade*. Retrieved on April 14, 2006 from http://app.doe.k12.ga.us/ows-bin/owa/fte_pack_ethnicsex.display_proc.

Malgady, R. G. (1994). Hispanic diversity and the need for culturally sensitive mental health services. In R. G. Malgady & O. Rodriguez (Eds.), *Theoretical and Conceptual Issues in Hispanic Mental Health*. Melbourne, FL: Krieger Publishing Company.

Malgady, R. G., Rogler, L. H., & Costantino, G. (1987). Ethnocultural and linguistic bias in mental health evaluation of Hispanics. *American Psychologist, 43*, 228–234.

Massachusetts Department of Education, Retrieved on April 14, 2006, from http://profiles.doe.mass.edu/state.asp.

Mercer, J. R., & Luis, J. F. (1978). *System of multicultural pluralistic assessment (SOMPA)*. New York, NY: The Psychological Corporation.

Meyer, G. J. (1996). The Rorschach and MMPI: Toward a more scientifically differentiated understanding of cross-method assessment. *Journal of Personality Assessment 67*, 558–578

Mujica, C. (1997). *Multicultural assessment: School psychologists' experience with the TEMAS test*. Unpublished doctoral dissertation, Yeshiva University, NY.

Newark Public Schools (2004-2005). Annual Report. Student Statistics, pg.13. Retrieved on February 8, 2006, from http://www.nps.k12.nj.us/annualreport 2004b.pdf.

New York City Department of Education Statistical Summaries. Retrieved on February 8, 2006, from http://www.nycenet.edu/offices/stats/default.htm.

Olmedo, E. L (1981). Testing linguistic minorities. *American Psychologist, 36*, 1078–1085.

Roberts, G. E., & McArthur, D. S. (1982). *Roberts Apperception Test for Children*. Los Angeles, CA: Western Psychological Services.

Rogler, L. H., Malgady, R. G., & Rodriguez, O. (1989). *Hispanics and mental health: A framework for research*. Malabar, FL: Kreiger.

Ritzler, B. A. (1996). Projective methods for multicultural personality assessment: Rorschach, TEMAS, and the Early Memories Procedures. In L. A. Suzuki, P. J. Meller, and J. G. Ponterotto (Eds.) *Handbook of multicultural assessment* (pp. 115–135). San Francisco, CA: Jossey-Bass, Inc.

Roberts, G. E. & McArthur, D. S. (1982). *Roberts Apperception Test for Children*. Los Angeles, CA: Western Psychological Services.

Sparrow, S. S., Balla, D. A., & Cicchetti, D. V., (1984). *Vineland Adaptive Behavior Scale: Interview Edition Expanded Form Manual.* Circle Pines, MN: American Guidance Service.

Substance Abuse and Mental Health Services Administration (SAMHSA) (2004). School Mental Health services in the United States, 2002-2003. Retrieved on April 14, 2006, from http://www.mentalhealth.samhsa.gov/publications/allpubs/sma05-4068/.

U.S. Census Press Releases (2005). U.S. Census Bureau News, U.S. Department of Commerce. Facts for Features Back to School. Released June 1, 2005, from http://www.census.gov/Press-Release/www/releases/archives/education/005157.html

U.S. Department of Health and Human Services. (2001). U.S. Surgeon General 2001 Report on Mental Health: Culture, Race and Ethnicity. *A Supplement to Mental Health: A Report of the Surgeon General.* Retrieved on April 14, 2006, from http://www.mentalhealth.org/cre/toc.asp; http://www.surgeon-general.gov/library/mentalhealth/cre/release.asp www.surgeongeneral.gov/library/mentalhealth/cre/release.asp.

Washington District of Columbia Public Schools (2003 school year), *Just the Facts.* Retrieved on April 14, 2006, from http://www.k12.dc.us/DCPS/offices/facts1.html.

World Health Organization Global Burden of disease Study (2001). Retrieved on April 14, 2006, from http://www.hsph.harvard.edu/organizations/bdu/GBDseries_files/gbdsum6.pdf.

7

Cross-Cultural Findings

BACKGROUND

From the inception of cross-cultural studies using projective/narrative tests during the 1940s, it was noted that the traditional TAT (Murray, 1943) pictures had questionable relevance to individuals of different cultures; hence, culturally sensitive TAT stimuli were developed to study various racial groups such as Mexican Indians, Ojibwa Indians, Southwest Africans, and South Pacific Micronesians (Henry, 1947). However, this early research to provide culture-specific and competent interpretative TAT personality profiles has not been regularly pursued by behavioral, social, and/or anthropological scientists (Dana, 1986). In the 1980s, Monopoli (1984) argued that culturally specific thematic pictures were necessary for personality assessment of unaccultured Hopi and Zuni Indians, but the TAT showed some utility with acculturated individuals.

Notwithstanding the paucity of systematic cross-cultural assessment research, the work of Dana (2000, 2005) has evaluated best practices in personality assessment in Europe, Central, and South America. In the United States, a flawed health care policy subordinated mental health care within an entrepreneurial rubric with assessment time restrictions of less than two hours in managed care settings (Camara, Nathan, & Puente, 2000). Comprehensive assessment with standard projective/narrative methods has been derided as pseudoscience (Lilienfeld, Lynn, & Lohr, 2003; Wood, Nezworski, Lilienfeld, & Garb, 2003). Instead, brief, domain-specific measures of behaviors/symptoms address referral questions and provide clinical diagnoses. These instruments have largely replaced comprehensive assessment emphasizing "psychodynamics, defenses, character structure, and object relations" (Piotrowski, 1999, p. 793). Such simplification of human nature has been described as a scientific byproduct of the behaviorism flourishing in the United States throughout much of the 20th century (Leary & Tangney, 2003).

Within psychology, the crucial contributions of feeling and thought were minimized historically in favor of a narrow, empirical, laboratory-based human science, a legacy of Boring's (1929) careful selection among European antecedents. As a consequence, there was benign neglect of the self and identity, as well as the critical role of comprehensive assessment in understanding the complexity of the human self. Nonetheless, in this new millennium, the self emerges as an organizing construct (Leary & Tangney, 2003), with necessity for understanding cultural models of the self (Cross & Gore, 2003), particularly as a primary cross-cultural and multicultural assessment objective (e.g., Dana, 1998, 2000, 2005). These new directions are fueled by the necessity for a positive psychology (Snyder & Lopez, 2003) in which a recovery-oriented service system (Anthony, 2000) emphasizes symptom relief, personal safety, client assessment, skills development, equal opportunity, basic survival support, empowerment, and healthy lifestyle promotion. These new directions can exert a major impact in a renewal of comprehensive assessment for children and adolescents. Projective methods in the United States, now referred to as performance measures of personality (Teglasi, 1998), can provide an impetus for nondiagnostically related interventions within a new holistic developmental science emphasizing prevention (Cairns, 2000; Magnussen, 2000).

In Europe, the mental health status of children and adolescents remains a serious societal responsibility (e.g., see Fagulha & Dana, 1997). Comprehensive assessment is considered a vital and necessarily time-consuming professional preoccupation, and these performance measures are esteemed and employed within various interpretive frames of reference including psychodynamic and empirically derived resources. There is evidence that the idiographic and nomothetic extremes of the TAT interpretation dilemma in the United States are also present in Europe. The false dichotomy of idiography–nomothesis still persuades assessors of the uncompromising virtues of either clinical skill or empirical data for interpretation. However, European assessment instruments are more evenly balanced in their employment of high and low inference interpretation. These parallel traditions have prevailed because high inference assessment is fueled by acceptance of a psychoanalytic vision of science, whereas low inference assessment prioritizes parsimony and explicit empirical dimensions as the essence of science.

The usage of specific performance measures in Spain, Portugal, and Latin American countries, for example, is similar to U.S. survey results, but the rank orders of major assessment instruments, including performance measures, varies dramatically between countries (Muniz, Prieto, Almeida, & Bartram, 1999), rather than between practice areas of psychology (Piotrowski, 1999). The Muniz et al. survey did not include the amount of time available for test administration, analysis, and report writing, probably because time considerations are not of overarching importance. Our experience in several of these countries suggests that time restrictions for assessment batteries are generally not imposed and that several reports may be prepared for different client audiences.

In addition, the work of Dana (2000, 2003) emphasized that, both nationally and internationally, there has been a need to develop narrative tests for reliable and valid diagnosis and personality assessment of culturally and linguistically diverse children and adolescents. To this end, the TEMAS (Tell Me-A-Story) test (Costantino, 1987) was developed with multicultural relevant stimuli. As explained in chapter 4, there are two published versions of TEMAS, minority and nonminority, and the third version, the Asian-American version, is in the process of validation and standardization.

This chapter presents the following, several cross-cultural studies. **Caribbean and Latin America studies:** *Cross-cultural validation of TEMAS in three different Hispanic cultures* (Costantino, Malgady, Casullo, & Castillo, 1991); *Cross-cultural standardization of TEMAS with Argentinean and Peruvian children* (Costantino, Dupertuis, Castillo, Malgady & Faiola, 1997; 2004); *Differences and Similarities between Argentine and European-American children on TEMAS* (Dupertuis, Silva-Arancibia, Pais, Fernandez, & Rodino, 2004); *Cross-cultural comparison with the TEMAS test using group versus individual methodology* (Cardalda, 2005; Cardalda, Costantino, Jiménez-Suárez, León-Velásquez, Martínez, & Perez, 2005); *Comparing the TEMAS projective/narrative test with the BASC self report measure in Hispanic students* (Cardalda, Costantino, Jiménez-Suárez, León-Velásquez, Martínez, & Perez, Ortiz-Vargas, 2005). **Italian studies:** *Relationship between aggression and cognitive functions in conflict resolution in 7 and 8 years old Italian children* (Sardi, 2000); *Relationship between aggression and cognitive functions in conflict resolution in 7 and 8 years old Italian children* (Sardi, 2000); *Relationship between aggression and emotional functions in conflict resolution in 7 and 8 years old Italian children* (Summo, 2000); *Relationship between aggression and moral judgment in conflict resolution in 7 and 8 years old Italian children* (Sulfaro, 2000); *Relationship between aggression and interpersonal relations in conflict resolution in 7 and 8 years old Italian children* (Cornabuci, 2000). A more recent qualitative study was conducted in Italy comparing the TEMAS protocols of seven Latino children living in Milan

(Fantini, 2005); this study is not reported here, but a case study from this study is reported in chapter 11. **Taiwanese study:** *Validity of Asian TEMAS in Taiwanese children: Preliminary data* (Yang, Kuo, & Costantino, 2003).

CROSS-CULTURAL VALIDITY: LATIN-AMERICAN AND CARIBBEAN STUDIES: CROSS-CULTURAL VALIDATION OF TEMAS IN THREE DIFFERENT HISPANIC CULTURES

The cross-cultural validity of TEMAS began to be investigated in New York City, San Juan, Puerto Rico, and Buenos Aires, Argentina, (Costantino, Malgady, Casullo, & Castillo, 1991), as well as in Lima, Peru (Costantino, Dupertuis, Castillo, Malgady, & Faiola, 1977; 2004). This research compared the normative profiles, the reliability, and the criterion-related validity of TEMAS with school and clinical children from the four different Hispanic cultures.

METHOD

Participants

The native Puerto Rican children were public and private school students ($n = 280$) and psychiatric outpatients ($n = 50$) from San Juan, Puerto Rico. The school sample consisted of 140 public and 140 private school students, nearly equally distributed with respect to gender in kindergarten through sixth grade. The public versus private school distinction, introduced to ensure variability due to socioeconomic status (SES), was restricted in previous studies. The psychiatric sample consisted of outpatients from the University of Puerto Rico Medical Center diagnosed according to DSM-III as experiencing conduct, anxiety, or adjustment disorders.

The public, private, and clinical groups were comparable in gender and age distribution ($M = 8.63$ years old, $SD = 2.12$). However, there were rather dramatic differences between groups with respect to household composition and SES. The father was present in 90% of the households of private school families, compared to only 59% in the public school and 40% in the clinical families. Moreover, 7% of the private school families were receiving some form of public assistance (e.g., food stamps, subsidized housing) relative to 65% of the public school and 60% of the clinical families. Parental occupations were much higher on the Hollingshead SES scale in the private school group (fathers $M = 4.83$, $SD = 1.60$; mothers $M = 5.29$, $SD = 1.27$) compared to public school and clinical groups (fathers $M = 2.84$, $SD = 1.73$; mothers $M = 3.50$, $SD = 2.10$). Parents of the private school children also were better educated, with a mean of 15.5 years of education, compared to parents of the public school ($M = 9.8$ years) and clinical children ($M = 10.75$ years).

The New York Puerto Rican examinees consisted of 167 first to sixth graders in public schools and 67 outpatients from a community mental health center, both groups nearly equally distributed with respect to gender. The public school students' mean age was 9.26 ($SD = 2.35$), whereas the outpatient children were slightly older ($M = 10.15$, $SD = 2.78$). All New York examinees were from low to lower-middle SES families (Hollingshead SES; $M = 4.65$, $SD = 1.28$). The clinical and public school samples also were comparable in terms of household composition: The father was present in 31 % of the households.

About half of the clinical children were diagnosed as having adjustment disorders. The next most common diagnosis was conduct disorder (22%), followed by developmental disorder (14%). The remaining cases were diagnosed as anxiety disorders.

The South American examinees—59 public school children from Grades two to seven in Buenos Aires, Argentina—were also nearly equally divided by gender, with a mean age of 9.67 ($SD = 2.62$). These children were largely from middle-class families with fathers primarily employed in managerial or professional occupations and mothers who were housewives or employed in skilled occupations.

Procedures

The full set of 23 TEMAS pictures (minority version) was administered on an individual basis to the native Puerto Rican children in Spanish and to the New York Puerto Rican children in their preferred language (usually English) by Puerto Rican examiners, who were graduate psychology students trained to administer the test. The Argentinean children were also tested individually in Spanish by two clinical psychologists using the nonminority short form of 9 TEMAS pictures. The short form was administered because of time constraints on the two examiners.

The full set of 23 pictures was administered either in two one-hour sessions, or in a single session with a break after one hour. The short form was administered in a single 45-minute session. All TEMAS tests were scored by bilingual graduate psychology interns who were blinded to examinees' demographic backgrounds.

In order to assess concurrent validity in the native Puerto Rican groups, the children were also administered the trait scale of Spielberger's State–Trait Anxiety Inventory (Inventario de Ansiedad Estado Y Rasgo para Ninos), the Piers-Harris Self-Concept Scale (Spanish translation), and the NIMH Center for Epidemiological Studies–Depression Scale (CES-D; Spanish translation). Validity estimation for New York Puerto Ricans has been reported elsewhere (see Costantino, Malgady, & Rogler, 1988). Officials in the public schools in Argentina permitted only the Piers-Harris scale to be administered.

TEMAS Administration and Scoring

The TEMAS pictures were administered according to the standardized instructions (see chapter 5 for complete details). The TEMAS narratives were scored according to standardized instructions (see chapter 5 for complete details) on indices of cognitive, affective, and personality functioning.

RESULTS

Means and standard deviations on the main TEMAS scoring indices (cognitive, affective, and personality functions) for the six Hispanic groups are shown in Table 7–1, where scores are averaged across pictures. A one-way analysis of variance (ANOVA) was conducted to determine whether the group means differed; however, because there were 22 TEMAS variables and relatively small sample sizes in three groups (ns = 50–67), a multivariate analysis was precluded. Therefore, a Bonferroni procedure was used to control the family-wise Type I error rate; setting the significance level at .001 for each of the ANOVAs, an overall error rate was established at .022. When groups differed significantly on a given TEMAS index, post hoc contrasts were conducted by the Scheffe test (p = .001). The results of the ANOVAs and series of Scheffe tests are reported in Table 7–2.

Table 7–2 shows that the six groups differed significantly on all major cognitive indices except transformations, all affective functions except fearfulness, and on all personality functions. However, because the Scheffe test is more conservative (particularly with six groups) than the omnibus F test, in three instances of significant omnibus F tests (sad affect, congruence of affect with theme, and reality testing) no Scheffe contrasts

TABLE 7-1 TEMAS Means and Standard Deviations in Six Hispanic Groups

Index	PR Public (n = 140)		PR Private (n = 140)		PR Clinic (n = 50)		NY Public (n = 167)		NY Clinic (n = 67)		ARG Public (n = 59)	
	M	SD	M	SD	M	SD	M	SD	M	SD	M	SD
Inquiries	.36	.59	.20	.53	.58	.76	.02	.08	.06	.15	.06	.14
Fluency	85.97	27.75	101.64	36.02	68.35	20.72	111.48	40.59	107.22	33.48	181.00	8.43
Time	3.63	1.09	3.41	1.05	1.14	.33	3.78	1.04	3.16	1.32	3.52	1.53
Omissions	1.62	.77	1.60	.59	2.97	.96	.82	.50	1.61	.76	.74	.71
Transformations	.17	.18	.11	.01	.21	.73	.12	.11	.18	.19	.17	.19
Conflict	.21	.19	.12	.14	.19	.19	.09	.10	.07	.06	.17	.16
Happy	.40	.20	.43	.22	.40	.21	.47	.21	.33	.22	.32	.18
Sad	.28	.19	.28	.15	.39	.18	.38	.22	.29	.20	.32	.20
Angry	.09	.10	.08	.09	.11	.13	.17	.13	.11	.12	.10	.11
Fearful	.08	.10	.10	.11	.07	.07	.07	.10	.09	.09	.10	.09
Neutral	.13	.25	.10	.19	.17	.26	.05	.08	.06	.16	.01	.13
Ambivalent	.01	.04	.01	.03	.02	.05	.01	.02	.01	.04	.08	.10
Congruence	.06	.09	.03	.06	.07	.11	.02	.03	.05	.12	.03	.10
Person Relations	2.52	.22	2.67	.29	2.45	.20	2.87	.21	2.49	.33	2.77	.43
Aggression	2.06	.22	2.31	.39	2.14	.25	2.78	.20	2.44	.38	2.66	.42
Anxiety/Depression	2.27	.29	2.48	.37	2.16	.22	2.90	.18	2.33	.35	2.58	.37
Achievement Motivation	2.80	.29	2.92	.30	2.80	.28	3.03	.25	2.79	.35	3.17	.49
Delay Gratification	2.66	.40	2.76	.44	2.55	.37	2.79	.23	2.62	.52	3.14	.61
Self-Concept	2.70	.47	2.89	.50	2.63	.46	3.00	.46	2.73	.33	3.19	.68
Sexual Identity	2.80	.42	2.83	.55	2.64	.48	3.40	.51	2.50	.52	2.76	.88
Moral Judgment	2.32	.31	2.56	.39	2.29	.30	2.91	.36	2.52	.34	2.74	.68
Reality Testing	2.45	.54	2.77	.50	2.47	.37	2.73	.65	2.62	.62	2.77	.71

TABLE 7–2.   ANOVA and Scheffe Results Comparing Groups on TEMAS

Indices		
Index	F (5, 617) Significant* Scheffe Contrasts	
Inquiries	20.65* 3–2, 4, 5, 6; 4–1	
Fluency	115.25* 6–1, 2, 3, 4, 5; 3–2, 4, 5; 4–1	
Time	70.23* 3–1, 2, 4, 5, 6	
Omissions	117.74* 3–1, 2, 4, 5, 6; 4–1, 2, 5; 6–1, 2, 5	
Transformations	1.96	none warranted
Conflict	12.09* 1–4, 5; 3–5	
Happy	8.87* 4–5, 6	
Sad	5.62* none significant	
Angry	6.48* 4–1, 2	
Fearful	1 .86	none warranted
Neutral	8.15*	3–6
Ambivalent	33.20*	6–1, 2, 3, 4, 5
Congruence	5.19*	none significant
Person Relations	32.96*	3–2, 4, 6; 4–1, 2, 5; 6–1, 5
Aggression	71.70*	1–2, 4, 5, 6; 4–2, 3, 5; 5–3; 6–2, 3
Anxiety/Depression	68.93*	4–1, 2, 3, 5, 6; 6–1, 3, 5; 2–3
Achievement Motivation	20.15*	6–1, 2, 3, 5; 4–1,3, 5
Delay Gratification	21.24*	6–1, 2, 3, 4, 5
Self-Concept	15.79*	6–1, 3, 5; 4–3
Sexual Identity	29.30*	4–1, 2, 3, 5, 6
Moral Judgment	31.44*	4–1, 2, 3, 5; 6–1, 3
Reality Testing	5.32*	none significant

Note. Group 1 = PR Public, 2 = PR Private, 3 = PR Clinical, 4 = NY Public, 5 = NY Clinical, 6 = ARG Public. *$p < .001$ (family-wise significance level, $p = .022$).

were significant. In addition, not all the significant Scheffe outcomes presented in Table 7–2 are meaningful comparisons (e.g., Argentina public school vs. Puerto Rican clinical difference in neutral affect). Therefore, only meaningful comparisons on the remaining TEMAS indices are discussed further: intracultural comparisons between school and clinic samples, and intercultural comparisons of school or clinic samples.

Intracultural Comparisons

Native Puerto Rican children. Comparisons among Puerto Rican samples (see Tables 7–1 and 7–2) indicated that the clinical children required more inquiries or prompts to complete a story and told shorter stories (less fluency) than the private school children; they also spoke for less time and more often omitted details (characters, setting, event) than the children in either the public or private school samples. Affectively, there were no significant differences between these three groups. With regard to personality functioning, private school children had themes expressing more adaptive person relations and greater control of anxiety and depressive feelings than the clinical children, and better control of aggressive impulses than public school children.

New York Puerto Rican Children. The Puerto Rican children in New York public schools differed cognitively from their clinical counterparts only in a tendency to commit fewer omissions, and affectively, only in expressing happier themes. The public school children also related themes expressing more adaptive person relations, control of aggression, coping with anxiety/depression, achievement motivation, sexual identity, and moral judgment.

INTERCULTURAL COMPARISONS

Public School Groups

Among public school children, native Puerto Ricans required more inquiries, were less fluent, and demonstrated less recognition of conflict than New York Puerto Ricans; they made more omissions than both New York and Argentinean children. Argentinean children were more verbally fluent than New York children. Affectively, New York children expressed happier themes than Argentineans, but paradoxically, angrier themes than native Puerto Ricans. Conversely, Argentinean children's stories were more ambivalent than the other two subcultures.

In terms of personality functioning, the New York Puerto Rican and Argentinean children expressed themes with more adaptive person relations, control of aggression, achievement motivation, and moral judgment than native Puerto Rican children. New York children's stories also revealed more adaptive coping with anxious/depressive feelings and sexual identity than did Argentinean or Puerto Rican children's stories. On the other hand, Argentinean children expressed the most ability to delay gratification, and also expressed more positive self-concepts than Puerto Rican children.

Clinical Groups

The comparisons between the native and New York Puerto Rican clinical groups revealed consistently higher cognitive functioning in the latter sample. New York Puerto Ricans required fewer prompts to complete stories, their stories were lengthier, they spent more time telling stories, they omitted fewer details, and they more often recognized the conflict depicted in the TEMAS pictures.

There were no differences between these two groups in scoring affective functioning. Personality profiles were also similar, with one exception. New York children expressed better control of aggressive impulses than native Puerto Rican children.

RELIABILITY AND VALIDITY

Native Puerto Rican Children

Internal consistency (alpha) reliability estimates of the TEMAS indices are reported in Table 7–3 for the native Puerto Rican school and clinical groups. As Table 7–3 shows, the more objectively scored cognitive indices (i.e., number of inquiries, fluency, time, number of omissions, and recognition of conflict) generally exhibited acceptable internal consistency estimates within the three groups. However, in stories told in response to numerous TEMAS pictures, no transformations were recorded, thus leading to many pictures with zero variance and lower estimates of internal consistency in the private school and clinical groups. With respect to the affective state attributed to the main character upon story resolution, internal consistency reliabilities of happy, sad, neutral, and congruence indices were moderate to high. Ambivalence had very low reliability in the private school group, again because of many pictures with no variance.

Scoring of fearful and angry affect evidenced marginal reliabilities. The ratings of personality functions exhibited generally lower internal consistencies compared to the more objective indices. Self-/sexual identity, moral judgment, and reality testing showed low reliability estimates, but

TABLE 7–3.   Internal Consistency of TEMAS With Native Puerto Rican Groups

Index	Public	Private	Clinical
Inquiries	.89	.95	.95
Fluency	.93	.91	.90
Tame	.96	.95	.95
Omissions	.87	.76	.80
Transformations	.80	.51	.50
Conflict	.86	.82	.87
Happy	.88	.83	.83
Sad	.81	.71	.73
Angry	.65	.68	.77
Fearful	.79	.76	.58
Neutral	.96	.93	.96
Ambivalent	.70	.25	.83
Congruence	.78	.73	.70
Person Relations	.87	.78	.75
Aggression	.78	.69	.77
Anxiety/Depression	.75	.54	.48
Achievement Motivation	.79	.38	.53
Delay Gratification	.65	.49	.62
Self-Concept	.82	.81	.92
Sexual Identity	.61	.45	.49
Moral Judgment	.31	.25	.46
Reality Testing	.58	.36	.95

this can be attributed to the relatively few pictures that pull these functions (i.e., these are analogous to 3- to 6-item tests). More acceptable reliability estimates were obtained across the three groups on person relations, control of aggression, and self-concept.

Concurrent validity was evaluated separately for school and clinical groups by regressing the criterion-related measures (trait anxiety, depression, self-concept) on the profile of nine personality functions. In the combined public and private school group, the three multiple correlations were significant. In the analysis of trait anxiety, $R = .31$, $p < .005$, and ability to delay gratification was the only significant predictor. In the analysis of depression, $R = .29$, $p < .01$, and delay of gratification again was the sole predictor. In the analysis of self-concept, $R = .26$, $p < .05$, and achievement motivation and moral judgment were significant predictors. Multiple correlations were not significant in the clinical group, due in part to the small sample size. The magnitude of concurrent validity coefficients was somewhat lower in the native Puerto Rican group compared to validity reported on New York Puerto Ricans (see Malgady, Costantino, & Rogler, 1984).

A two-group discriminant analysis was conducted using TEMAS personality profiles to predict clinical vs school group status. The two groups differed significantly in TEMAS profiles, F $(9, 321) = 3.52$, $p <. 001$, with about 9% of the variance explained. The strongest discriminators were person relations and anxiety ($p < .001$). Classification analysis revealed that 69% of the children were correctly reclassified into their designated groups. Thus, the results of this analysis lend some support to the validity of TEMAS personality profiles as a gross discriminator of clinically impaired vs nonimpaired status.

New York Puerto Rican Children

The psychometric properties of TEMAS, such as internal consistency, test–retest and interrater reliability, concurrent validity, and clinical utility in predicting psychotherapy outcomes were reported in earlier studies with New York Puerto Rican children (Costantino, Malgady, & Rogler, 1988; Malgady, Costantino, & Rogler, 1984). The validity of TEMAS personality profiles in discriminating between DSM-III diagnostic groups is also reported elsewhere (Costantino, Malgady, Rogler, & Tsui, 1988). Generally, the outcomes of these earlier New York studies have produced more favorable reliability and validity estimates (e.g., 89% accuracy in discriminant classification analysis) than in the San Juan, Puerto Rico research.

Argentinean Children

The interrater reliability of scoring TEMAS personality functions was established with two Argentinean clinical psychologists (one with extensive training in scoring TEMAS and the other a newly trained scorer). The two raters, who independently scored a sample of 20 protocols, reached a high level of agreement (75%–95%) across the nine pictures. Median interrater agreement was 81% and in no case were the two independent ratings discrepant by more than one rating scale point. This level of agreement is somewhat higher than that reported in an earlier study (27%–100% across 23 pictures, median = 59%; see Malgady, Costantino, & Rogler, 1984). This discrepancy may reflect the refinement of the TEMAS scoring system, instructions, and training examples with the test's manual publication in 1988.

The nine personality function indices of the TEMAS short form were correlated with the total and subscale scores on the Piers-Harris scale. The only correlations that were significant involved the Happiness subscale of self-concept with person relations ($r = .30$, $p <. 05$) and delay of gratification ($r = .34$, $p < .05$). Thus, there is modest evidence of the concurrent validity of TEMAS within the Argentinean culture.

DISCUSSION

The need to create cross-cultural norms for projective/narrative tests (Dana, 1986; Exner & Weiner, 1982) was addressed by the standardization of TEMAS on Hispanic, Black, and White children in the United States (Costantino, Malgady, & Rogler, 1988), and by our present efforts to collect comparative data on native Puerto Rican and Argentinean children. This research is similar to Avila-Espada's (1986) efforts to develop a comprehensive scoring system for the TAT to assess, among other variables, interpersonal functioning, aggression, depression, and achievement motivation in adult Spaniards. The minority and nonminority versions of the TEMAS narrative test were originally developed as a clinical tool, presenting ethnically/ racially familiar characters in urban and fantasy settings, in order to facilitate minority and nonminority children's identification with the stimuli and thereby enhance verbal fluency and self-disclosure. Earlier studies with New York City examinees indicated that Hispanic and Black children, and to a lesser extent, White children, were indeed more verbally fluent in telling stories about TEMAS pictures in comparison to TAT pictures (Costantino, Malgady, & Vazquez, 1981; Costantino & Malgady, 1983). Other studies established the reliability of TEMAS, some rudimentary evidence of concurrent validity, and clinical utility in detecting psychotherapeutic outcomes (Costantino et al., 1988; Malgady et al., 1984). The results of the present study lend support to the use of TEMAS with examinees in Puerto Rico and Argentina. However, reliability and validity estimates for the native Puerto Rican children were less favorable than for mainland groups studied. Further analyses of the TEMAS pictures with native Puerto Rican children to examine the characteristics of individual pictures were conducted. Preliminary scrutiny suggested that some of the pictures did not pull the designated personality functions as consistently in Puerto Rico. This seems to be associated with pictures depicting urban settings common in New York City, which contrast sharply with the ambiance of rural Puerto Rico and metropolitan

San Juan. To this end, several pictures such as 1B-G, which depicts New York City urban brownstone architecture, have been redesigned to reflect European Spanish architecture for the international version of TEMAS.

The Argentinean children, who were administered the nonminority short form, showed significantly higher means on six of the nine personality functions (i.e., more adaptive profiles) than native Puerto Ricans, but largely on a par with the New York group. This difference in normative profile may be attributable to several factors, such as the different number of TEMAS pictures, differential training of examiners, and psychosocial or sociopolitical conditions.

Further analyses in the Argentinean research program also are in progress to assess the characteristics of the individual pictures. Preliminary evidence suggests that the characters, setting, and events of some pictures are not appropriate in Argentinean culture. For example, Card 1B-G was redrawn showing children playing soccer instead of basketball; in another, card 15, a policeman rewarding a baseball team was redrawn to depict a coach rewarding a baseball team; and parallel Card 15 was redrawn to depict a coach rewarding a winning soccer team. Similarly, a picture showing report card grades of A and F was changed to the Argentinean and European school grading systems of 10 and 1, respectively. It was interesting to note that the majority of these children scored lowest in moral judgment in telling stories about a policeman (as a rewarding authority), who was perceived as a punitive agent. This appeared to be associated with historical events, as Argentina was emerging from a military regime in which police were associated with punitive actions and not positive reinforcement. These preliminary results demonstrate that the standardization of a thematic apperception test in cross-cultural research must take into serious account variations in the stimuli necessitated by many aspects of cultural diversity. The Argentina study by Dupertuis, Silva–Arancibia, Pais, Fernandez and Rudino (2004) reported later in this chapter details the process of redesigning several TEMAS cards, thus making them more culturally relevant.

SECOND ARGENTINEAN STUDY: CROSS-CULTURAL COMPARISON OF ARGENTINEAN AND PERUVIAN CHILDREN

In another Latin-American cross-cultural research, Costantino, Dupertuis, Castillo, Malgady and Faiola (1997; 2004) conducted a second study in Argentina and a first study in Peru.

METHOD

In this study, examinees were 46 nonclinical Argentinean (25 males and 21 females) elementary school children from Buenos Aires and 44 Peruvian (25 males and 19 females) elementary school children from Lima. The groups were relatively homogeneous in age; the Argentinean students had a mean age of 9.33 years and the Peruvians had a mean age of 9.50 years. The Peruvian and Argentinean samples were comprised of children whose parents generally had high school, normal school, or university educations. The 23-card version of TEMAS was administered in Spanish to the Argentinean and Peruvian children. The Argentinean children were administered the non-minority form because all children were of European descent. The Peruvian children were administered the minority version of TEMAS because all examinees were of native South American descent. The TEMAS protocols for both groups were scored according to the standardization procedures.

RESULTS

The means and standard deviations of the main TEMAS scoring indices for the Argentinean and Peruvian samples are presented in Table 7–4. The reported scores represent averages across pictures. The mean scores of the two groups were compared by independent t-tests for each TEMAS index. The between-groups variances were compared using the Levene Test, which indicated that in no case were they significantly different. Because of the large number of univariate comparisons being made, the Bonferroni test was applied with a level of .001, giving a family-wise significance level of .027. An ANOVA was also performed to test for the effects of country and sex of examinees. No significant interactions were found and there were no main effects for sex of participants.

Significant differences between the two groups were found in the area of cognitive functioning. The results indicate that the Argentinean children had significantly higher verbal fluency scores than the Peruvian children, with an effect size of .6 SD units. The most notable differences between the two groups were in the area of omissions. The Peruvian children had significantly more Omissions than the Argentineans, with an effect size of 4.8 SD units. Of the different types of omissions (i.e., inattention to essential aspects of the stimulus pictures, which include omissions of event, omissions of primary character, omissions of secondary character, and omissions of settings), omissions of Event contributed the greatest amount of variance. Omissions of Setting and Omissions of Secondary Character were also

TABLE 7–4. Means and Standard Deviation of Argentinean and Peruvian Children

	Argentina (n = 46)		Peru (n = 44)		
TEMAS Index	M	SD	M	SD	T
Inquiries	.02	.09	.009	.04	1.04
Fluency	87.77	25.49	61.87	43.18	3.48*
Time	2.45	.91	3.08	1.09	−2.62
Omissions	.16	.12	.74	.42	−8.88*
Omission/Event	.08	.09	.37	.23	−7.88*
Omission/Setting	.03	.05	.18	.16	−5.85*
Omission/Secondary Character	.05	.06	.14	.12	−4.44*
Omission/Main Character	.004	.01	.02	.04	−3.08
Transformations	.26	.22	.14	.24	2.57
Transformation/ Secondary Character	.09	.09	.02	.05	4.33*
Conflict	.26	.24	.13	.19	2.95
Happy	.38	.20	.22	.13	4.51*
Sad	.23	.14	.24	.16	−.42
Angry	.20	.11	.13	.12	2.56
Fearful	.18	.14	.17	.12	.24
Neutral	.08	.15	.08	.13	.04
Ambivalent	.12	.12	.04	.01	3.63*
Congruence	.02	.06	.01	.04	1.53
Person Relations	2.64	.16	2.57	.24	1.58
Aggression	2.52	.23	2.53	.36	−.19
Anxiety/Depression	2.48	.23	2.52	.37	−.70
Achievement Motivation	2.74	.22	2.71	.56	.58
Delay Gratification	2.68	.32	2.64	.30	.66
Self-Concept	2.83	.20	2.72	.29	2.21
Sexual Identity	2.78	.33	2.83	.26	−.78
Moral Judgment	2.47	.30	2.48	.33	−.15
Reality Testing	2.61	.26	2.60	.36	.13

Note. *p < .001, (Family-wise significance level, p = .027)

significant. Coupled with the significant difference between the two groups on omissions, there was also a significant difference on the conflict score. The latter indicates that the Peruvian children produced stories that did not acknowledge or resolve the pulled-for interpersonal conflict embodied in the story to a greater extent than the Argentinean children. Although there was no significant difference between the two groups in the total number of transformations for each picture, the Argentinean children scored significantly higher on transformations of secondary character than the Peruvian children.

The two groups also differed in terms of affective functions. The Argentineans expressed significantly more happy affect in their themes than did the Peruvians, with an effect size of 1.23 *SD* units. The two groups did not differ significantly in the expression of other affects. However, in terms of percentage of total affective responses given, the Peruvian children expressed sad affect in 31.41% of their affect responses as compared to 23.14% for the Argentinean children. The Argentinean and Peruvian children did not show significant differences on any of the nine personality functions, pulled for on the stimulus cards. The major difference between the two groups was seen in the high number of "*N*" responses scored by the Peruvians. "*N*" scores are closely related to omissions scores; whenever an "*N*" is scored for a personality function, an omission of event is also scored. The high "*N*" of the Peruvian students accentuated the fact that they frequently responded with stories that did not incorporate the pulled-for personality functions.

DISCUSSION

This study presents some interesting results with respect to the cross-cultural and multicultural validity of TEMAS as applied to the two diverse Hispanic Latino cultures tested. Cultural similarities and differences of the two groups are highlighted, as well as the effects of sociopolitical variables on cognitive styles and cognitive functioning. A previous study, which compared cognitive, affective, and personality functions of children from Argentina and Puerto Rico with New York children of Puerto Rican descent, indicated that there were significant differences in areas of cognitive, affective, and personality functioning as measured by TEMAS indices (Costantino, Malgady, Casullo, & Castillo, 1991). That such differences were demonstrated, along with the support for the concurrent validity provided by other assessment instruments, confirmed the utility of TEMAS for personality assessment with the Argentinean and Puerto Rican children as well as the New York children of Puerto Rican descent that represent one of the major cultural groups for whom TEMAS was originally standardized. The Argentinean and Peruvian children under present investigation did not manifest differences in personality functions, perhaps indicative of the relative degree of cultural similarity between the two groups.

At the same time, the significant cognitive differences between the Argentinean and Peruvian responses must be acknowledged. To some extent, the differences may be explained as a consequence of sociopolitical and psychosocial variables in the two countries at the time the data for this study was collected. The year 1989, when this study was conducted, was a time of considerable social turmoil and demographic change in Peru. As a result of insurgent activity by the *Sentero Luminoso*, a considerable portion of the rural population of the country relocated. Of the Peruvian children tested, a number had fathers who were in the military, some of whom were deceased. The omissions scale of TEMAS serves as a clinical indicator of repression or selective inattention (Costantino, Malgady, & Rogler, 1988; Costantino, Malgady, Colon-Malgady & Bailey, 1992). The relatively higher score on omissions by the Peruvian children may be reflective of psychological distress caused by stimuli presenting potentially violent situations and a relative cognitive inability to make sense of them. Because all potentially mediating variables were not controlled for in the collection of the data for the present study, the sources of variability can only be speculated at present. Further investigation, with greater control of variables, is indicated for a future study.

An important difference between Peru and Argentina relates to the ethnic composition of the populations. The population of Lima is largely mestizo and indigenous, whereas Buenos Aires is predominantly European with a large influx of immigrants from Italy and other European countries, especially within the last century. The more open expression of happy affect by the Argentinean participants and the relatively higher percentage of expression of sadness by the Peruvians may reflect ethnocultural differences in expression of affectivity. Indigenous populations in South America tend to internalize emotions to a large degree. The combined effect of traditional culture, sociopolitical marginalization, and exploitation contribute to a sense of helplessness and passivity. The difference in happy response of Argentinean and Peruvian children may be associated with ethnocultural and psychosocial factors in expression of happy emotions.

This study is a preliminary investigation for a more thorough cross-cultural TEMAS standardization. Although the relative similarity of scores of the Argentinean and Peruvian groups on personality functions indicates that TEMAS is appropriate for both groups, differences in cognitive scores, such as omissions and conflict, must be investigated with greater control of mediating variables.

THIRD ARGENTINEAN STUDY: DIFFERENCES AND SIMILARITIES BETWEEN ARGENTINE AND EUROPEAN-AMERICAN CHILDREN ON THE TEMAS

The TEMAS research program in Argentina has spanned about 20 years. In the last 15 years, Professor Daniel G. Dupertuis and his research team have been investigating the validity of this narrative technique. This third study (Dupertuis, Silva-Arancibia, Pais, Fernandez, & Rodino, 2004) assesses differences and similarities between Argentinean in Argentina and European-American (white) children narrative sample of the TEMAS. Only partial results of the study in progress are reported here. At the beginning of the 21st century, one of the problems confronting psychology is the scarcity of psychological tests for children. Mental health and clinical services studies have stressed the urgency of developing culture-sensitive instruments for psychological assessment and psychodiagnosis of cultural, racial, and linguistic variables in children. Research studies done until the present show that the TEMAS is a valid instrument for the analysis of children's cognitive, affective, and personality functions.

The first purpose of the present study was to compare the characteristics of the different groups of Argentinean children, middle-class and impoverished urban schoolchildren as well as children in institutional care, with those of North American school or clinical children. The second purpose was to develop the Argentinean standardization of the TEMAS long form.

METHOD

The sample comprises 240 urban middle-class children from both state (public) and private schools in Buenos Aires and Greater Buenos Aires, aged between 6.0 and 9.11. It includes four subsamples of 60 participants (30 females, 30 males) for each of the age groups: 6.0–6.11; 7.0–7.11; 8.0–8.11; and 9.0–9.11. The children's socioeconomic status (SES) was established according to parents' (or parent's, in case of single-parent families) occupational and educational level, according to Hollingshead Scale, (1957). The difference between state (public) and private schools was introduced to ensure variability due to SES.

Data collection instruments include: (a) semistructured interviews for teachers, (b) interview to record the children's demographic data, (c) the TEMAS test (complete series of 23 stimulus cards). In order to study concurrent validity, two other measures were administered: (d) the CES-D-R questionnaire (Radloff's 1977 Center for Epidemiologic Studies Depression Scale, Revised by the Johns Hopkins University Prevention Research Center), and (e) the STAIC questionnaire, Forms C-1 and C-2 (Spielberger, Edwards, Lushone, Montuori & Platzek's 1973 State–Trait Anxiety Inventory for Children, STAIC).

The average estimated time of administration for the TEMAS was 2 hours, for the CES-D-R and the STAIC, about 20 minutes each, so two sessions were established for each child.

Codification of Obtained Results

- Qualitative analysis and construction of the TEMAS norm for Argentinean urban middle-class children between the ages of 6.0 and 9.11.
- Comparative analysis: Argentinean data by comparison with American white sample TEMAS norms.
- Comparative analysis: data collected with TEMAS by comparison with data collected with the CES-D-R and the STAIC.
- Qualitative analysis of psychosocial and affective function indicators.

Participants

Criteria for Inclusion in the Sample: (a) children without learning disabilities (Indicators: children who have not repeated school grades; teacher's statement indicating the child has no special learning disabilities); (b) children without disruptive behavior problems (Indicator: teacher's assessment during a semistructured interview before the administration of the tests).

The total sample of this research study was obtained with children from state and private schools in the city of Buenos Aires (Federal District) and its surrounding area. The sample comprised $N = 240$ middle class children, between the ages of 6 and 9.11 years. Except for free access to state hospitals, middle-class families that send their children to private schools do not receive any kind of welfare support.

In the group attending private schools, parents' occupation was on a higher level, and many of them were professionals. Parents' educational level was also higher in this group, with an average of 17 years of education, although many have 19 and 20. Not only fathers were employed: in many cases, mothers were employed and professional as often as fathers, and had similar educational levels.

Procedures

All the children in the study were given the long form of the test (23 stimulus cards) in Spanish. The test was administered by qualified psychologists or by graduate students who had completed 4+ years of professional training and had been especially trained in the administration of TEMAS. All the children were examined individually.

The necessary time for the administration of the long form of the test was of approximately two hours in all cases. Because of this, the youngest children (ages 6–7) were given the test in three separate sessions. All the TEMAS protocols were scored by research team members who were well acquainted with the scoring procedures and with the children's cultural background. Each test was subsequently revised by an instructor to ensure that no scoring errors were made.

The test was administered in accordance with the standard TEMAS Manual instructions. Similarly, the stories were scored according to the instructions in the original TEMAS Manual (Costantino et al., 1988).

RESULTS

Intercultural Comparisons

We noticed several of similarities with the TEMAS responses of North American children. Perceived similarities are on two different levels: (a) The profile of responses from Argentinean children offers the same normal parameters as the European American children's standardized profiles of White children in the TEMAS normative sample., and (b) The stories produced by Argentinean children are, while obviously not identical, very similar to the stories produced by North American White children. (2) We have also noticed differences with the TEMAS responses of North American White children. Maybe the most important of them is that in Argentinean children we have not found totally maladaptive responses or stories related with death or killing. Where similar stories do appear, they are structured around loss instead.

Cognitive Functions

The Cognitive Functions showed Argentinean children to be more punctually exact and concrete in organizing their stories. Argentinean children produced stories referring to more concrete situations than North American White children. Argentinean children reported the conflict in fewer words. Their stories were shorter and simpler than North American White children's stories; however, this did not mean that any important elements were omitted. Results showed that the scores of Argentinean children in verbal fluency were within the low to average categories, (T-scores ranging between 40–50). This was in proportion with Argentinean children's lower T scores in total omissions, which implied that they had an adaptive capacity of selective attention.

Personality Functions

Argentinean children's scores for these functions were within the high-average range, except for the *Anxiety-Depression* and the *Self-Concept* functions. This indicates the scores are above the mean, nearer to $T = 60$ than $T = 50$.

Interpersonal Relations is the function where Argentinean children's results were most indicative of adaptive stories, with higher mean scores, in contrast to those of North American children.

Concerning the function of *Interpersonal Relations* with peers or with authority figures, the stories produced by Argentinean children present a good pull for this function. Remarkably, relations with authority figures (teacher, school principal, sports coach) pulled for a more adaptive response than relations with parents. Relationships were well understood by Argentinean children, and this is what the test proposes, that is, assessing children's ability to perceive relationships.

Card 1

The first thing we should note is that in the Argentinean version of the test, this card has been modified and differs from the North American version. In the North American card, there are children playing basketball, a sport with deep roots in the US. Although basketball is common in Argentina, it has not taken as extensively as in the United States; in that sense, volleyball, soccer, and tennis are more popular in Argentina. Therefore, it was decided that the Argentinean card should depict a sport of more cultural relevance, such as soccer, and this effected a visible change in the children's verbalizations because they identified immediately and could see themselves as participants in the situation.

The original Brownstone architectural style was also substituted with a local architectural style. However, we do not regard this change as significant, because Argentinean children, regardless of the predominance of French architecture in Argentina, are used to an array of different architectural styles. In contrast with other Spanish-speaking countries, Argentinean urban architecture is ornate and not uniform. The French style is clearly predominant, but so is English architecture, particularly in the southern part of Buenos Aires. However, the variation in the card has introduced a modest decrease in setting transformations. For instance, before the card was changed, children tended to speak about a school and games in the schoolyard, whereas now they tend to tell stories about a games in the street.

Reaction time for this card was average to high, and so is the total time, which means that Argentine children tell their stories within the same reaction time and total time as North American children, but they use fewer words.

The similarity of reaction times for both shorter and longer stories indicates an absence of impulsiveness, and this implies an adaptive response in the structure of the cognitive functions in order to comply with the proposed task. Regarding the total time, the mean scores (which are within average range, i.e., adaptive) show how time is employed for the correct incorporation of cognitive functions such as *Sequencing* and *Imagination*, including the majority of stimuli present in the card, and for the correct perception of conflict, among others.

We therefore analyzed the particular features in Argentinean children's responses to TEMAS, and subsequently compared them to North American children's responses. *Interpersonal Relations*, the conflict in Card. 1, is generally omitted; this omission, however, happens only in this card.

Considering that children must give adaptive responses in their individuation process according to their upbringing, we could say that Argentinean children, when faced with the stimuli, projected stories that reflect adaptive relationships. It was observed that in Card 1, for instance, the central conflict was distorted (they tended to overlook the interrupted game); this, however, did not imply that at ego level the function of *Interpersonal Relations* was not pulled, even if another function (for instance, *Delay of Gratification*) was scored as omitted.

The reason for this is that in other cards where *Delay of Gratification* is pulled, the function was well identified by the children, and in the Argentinean sample it tended to be close to the norm. Therefore, in the sample of Argentinean children, the presence of a greater number of "N" responses in Card 1, for example, was compensated for in other cards

Card 7

The responses of the majority of Argentinean children for Card 7 regarding both *Interpersonal Relations* and management of aggressive impulses (*Aggression*) presented a highly adaptive score. Faced with this TEMAS card, Argentinean children produced cliché stories. There are children playing in the living room, a lamp is broken, and there follow mutual accusations between the children. This kind of response did not occur with other cards.

The particular characteristic observed in Argentinean children with regard to this card was the frequent manifestation of irresponsibility in not acknowledging a bad action as their own. The responsibility was attributed to the other child, but the conflict was not resolved and then the two children quarrel and they are punished.

This means that the point at issue was generally not resolved during the process of the story, and when this happened, punishment fell on both characters without reaching a solution of whose responsibility it was exactly. It would seem that to a great extent, and already at this early age, the foundations of Argentinean culture are already laid in this aspect that has been so hurtful to the country: No characters do ever take the blame for their acts, and as a result, all the other characters (the whole country) have to suffer the consequences.

It is worth noting that in the age group observed in this study, Argentinean children are developmentally prepared, not only to discern right from wrong, but to take the inherent responsibility for wrongdoing. Why, then, does the story remain unresolved? Why is there always the same structure in the children's stories? If they are developmentally ready to understand the situation, why does no one take responsibility for the bad action?

For example, in one case, the situation is presented as unfair, and both are made responsible: "The brother and sister were playing and they broke the lamp, and then, when their Mom arrived they were fighting and blaming each other. They blamed each other and their Mom punished them both, and they fought."

In other protocols, we see a different aspect of *Moral Judgment*. The children do not take responsibility for their actions: They will not acknowledge breaking the lamp, and consequently, there is no atonement or reparation. We find this particular feature repeatedly, and therefore the *Moral Judgment* function, although it is still within the normal range, was one of the lowest of the mean scores.

Card 15

The first issue we should make clear is that in the Argentinean version, this card has been modified because North American baseball is nonexistent in Argentina, the same way that it does not exist in Europe. The figure of the policeman as a sports coach or person who otherwise collaborates with a group of children, contrarily to what happens in the US (where there are police programs promoting sports among children) is not possible as a perception for Argentinean children. For sociopolitical reasons, both recent and remote, police forces are perceived as punitive authorities, and as a result they are generally regarded in fear, not trust. As they do naturally with many other socially determined notions, children internalize this particular perception as they grow up.

This negative vision of the forces that are meant to be custodians of the law, with the inference of evil that any person in uniform has for Argentinean children, comes, on the one hand, from the role that the police played during the military rule, as well as from the decadence into which law enforcement sunk during those years. We should take into account here the fact that, in contrast to what happens in the North American context, the Argentinean police are not prepared to play a preventive role.

Card 15 is organized on the bases of a bipolarity, which for Argentinean children, at least, makes it difficult to produce stories integrating all the characters in a single narration. Therefore, they tend to produce two parallel stories with the two groups they see in the card, both groups become connected at the end of the story, although in most cases they remain separated.

Therefore, we must remark about the extent of the influence of what is culturally relevant in the production of stories around this stimulus card. The children associate the situation of winning the trophy with football. In this way, in the stories there is always a winning team and a losing team. The latter is the one that, out of envy and anger at having lost the match, go on a rampage of theft and violent behavior, property damage, and so forth. This situation is relatively frequent in Argentine football championships. Argentinean *"Barras bravas"* act in much the same way as English "Hooligans." There is an unburdening of Aggressive Impulses in the form of violent acts; the aggression comes from frustration.

In all the stories on Card 15, Argentinean children reflected the idea of discipline as a punitive act for bad actions. However, we have mentioned in a previous card that, in the narratives, nobody takes responsibility for wrongdoing. Therefore, we can see that this is not because the problem is ignored, as we said before. The children do see the problem and its consequences quite well, but they also act according to their culture. They perceive and point out a "logical" punishment as long as the event falls in a broader social context, where the reparation is necessary, but they do not see it when the events develop in a family environment.

This indicates that the function of *Moral Judgment* was present, as this function acknowledges the differences between good and bad behavior, as well as the necessity of taking responsibility for bad behavior. (For instance, the "bad children" have to "pay" with jail, fines, correctional institutions, etc.) In this sense, we can see very clearly that punishment for bad actions is dealt by the police, and not by the parents who, on the contrary, try not to engage themselves in the situation.

Card 17

This card has been modified in the Argentinean version, as the grades "A" and "F" shown in the original version do not apply to Argentina, where school grades are not identified with letters, but with numbers. Hence, the report card grades "A" and "F" were changed in the Argentinean system of "10" and "1" respectively. The children produced good stories, integrating both assessment situations and the teacher as well, with an active role in the child's situation. (There is something that may be worth noting: The fact that there are practically no male teachers in Argentina does not disturb the integration of the character).

Card 20

Argentinean children established a clear difference between oneiric content and reality, with a good integration of the different elements present in this picture, and a clear perception that it is more convenient to deal with reality.

Card 21

In this card, too, there was good ability to distinguish between dreams and reality as well as a clear understanding of the latter, so most of the stories were scored as 4. There appears a greater variation between scores of 3 and 4 in the *AnxietyDepression* function. In the *Aggression* function, there are very few children with a score of 2, because the description of the dragon generally refers to the environment of the dragon's own life, and not to the relationship between the dragon and the storyteller.

DISCUSSION

Although this study-in-progress is reported here through qualitative analysis, it highlights the lengthy process of adapting a narrative test to a culturally and linguistically distinct group of youngsters. The first part of this research has focused on the face and content validity of several TEMAS cards, which dictated the redrawing of pictures to make them more culturally relevant. The second part of the research described cognitive and personality variables of Argentinean youngsters in comparison with their European American counterparts. Notwithstanding their Spanish language, the Argentinean children in Buenos Aires are racially White, so they were administered the nonminority version of TEMAS. Hence, their scores were compared with the TEMAS White normative data. The third part of this research program is to create Argentinean TEMAS norms.

SECOND PUERTO RICAN STUDY: CROSS-CULTURAL COMPARISONS WITH THE TEMAS: TEST USING GROUP VERSUS INDIVIDUAL METHODOLOGY

The TEMAS narrative test research program at Carlos Albizu University began in the mid 1990s under the coordination of Elsa Cardalda, PhD, Director of the Clinical Psychology Program. Several hundred clinical and school psychologists at the CAU have been trained in the TEMAS narrative techniques over the years, and effective the Fall semester of 2006, the TEMAS test will become a required course in the doctoral program at this university, which promotes cultural competence training. In the present study, Dr. Cardalda and her team assess the validity of group as opposed to individual administration of the TEMAS test. (Cardalda, E., B., Costantino, G., León-Velázquez, M., Jiménez-Suárez, V., Martinez, J. V., & Perez, M., 2005)

BACKGROUND

The current status of assessment for minority children reveals a need for culturally sensitive approaches capable of identifying relative strengths and weaknesses to evaluate both clinical needs and the effectiveness of programs designed to develop their psychological skills (Cardalda, 1995; Costantino, Flanagan & Malgady, 2000). Recent advances in test development have resulted in the availability of standardized, objectively scorable projective/ narrative measures for Hispanic/Latino children, such as the TEMAS (acronym for Tell-Me-A-Story; also meaning themes in Spanish) multicultural projective/narrative test (Costantino, 1987; Costantino, Malgady, & Rogler, 1988). At the present time, the TEMAS is unique because it is the only projective/narrative test standardized for Hispanic children.

Although the TEMAS was originally constructed to be administered individually, as most projective/narrative tests, we recently have been evaluating whether it is possible to administer the TEMAS in a group format vs. the traditional individual format. A pilot project compared the clinical utility of the TEMAS group method as administered to high risk Hispanic students from community schools in Puerto Rico and in New York. The pilot aimed to examine the differences between the TEMAS individual and group methods in Puerto Rico, as well as the differences between the application of the group TEMAS in Puerto Rico and New York. In order to examine the implementation of the TEMAS group methodology, the first area of inquiry was the variable of Verbal Fluency, as this is the cornerstone of self-disclosure in projective testing. As measured in the TEMAS, Verbal Fluency is a cognitive function defined as the total word count used in the story, (i.e., length of stories, oral or written). Verbal Fluency, whether oral or written, was a main concern, given that although group methodologies might seem more cost-effective, these should not inhibit the richness of the material required for the analysis of personality issues. Related to this concern was the question of how high risk (poor) children, who often present learning problems, might respond to writing the stories (instead of giving them orally to an examiner).

The TEMAS test has been standardized with Hispanic/Latino children in New York City (Costantino, Malgady, & Rogler, 1988). Research on the TEMAS to date has included establishing the psychometric properties of the test, such as preliminary studies of its reliability and validity (Costantino, Malgady, Colon-Malgady, & Bailey, 1992; Costantino, Malgady, Rogler, & Tsui, 1988) and clinical utility (Cardalda, Costantino, Sayers, Machado, &

Guzman, 2002). Several studies have shown the multicultural and cross-cultural Research on the TEMAS instrument indicates that Hispanic/Latino children and adolescents tell substantially longer stories with the TEMAS pictures than with pictures lacking culturally sensitive elements, such as TAT cards (Costantino, Flanagan, & Malgady, 200 The research work reported in this chapter is part of a larger NIH study (Cardalda, 2002–2005) that aims to determine the applicability of the TEMAS as a narrative group method to assess how low SES Hispanic children cope with their social environment. The study's second aim was to assess if culturally sensitive narrative techniques could be used for developing valid measures of coping strategies associated with dysfunctional symptomatology in Hispanic children at high risk for mental illness. Thus, we are evaluating the hypothesis that different types of coping strategies of social problem solving (as measured from the TEMAS stories) are related to personality adjustment (as measured by the BASC: Behavior Assessment System for Children) and school success (as measured by school grades). This study was conducted with fifth and sixth graders (boys and girls) of public schools in San Juan, Puerto Rico and fifth graders of public schools in New York City.

Research Questions

Several research questions were posed. The first question pertained to whether children would write shorter stories as a function of the group format when compared to the individual method. (All Verbal Fluency scores are expressed in T-values). Second, with respect to the group format, the question was about the relative length of stories when comparing Hispanics/Latinos living in Puerto Rico or in New York. Third, the significance of length of stories was explored in association with the identification of affects in the TEMAS stories. In order to explore the contribution of Verbal Fluency as a cognitive resource, the Verbal Fluency scale was correlated with school grades for children in Puerto Rico (school grades were not collected in New York). An issue was how bilingualism might play a role. Hence, language of written sample (Spanish vs. English stories) was analyzed in the New York group. Gender and grade were analyzed in terms of their relationship to Verbal Fluency. Finally, early fieldwork data highlighted the importance of distinguishing verbal and speech/language delays; therefore, a qualitative analysis was developed to address this concern.

Puerto Rico Sample

In Puerto Rico we used a list of all active public schools from the local Department of Education to target several schools in the metropolitan San Juan area that served poor communities. Four elementary schools were selected. After obtaining the appropriate permission from the Central Board of the Department of Education, we invited the schools to participate in the study.

The cases with individual TEMAS administrations had been collected in a previous study and were selected from an existing data bank with comparable SES, age, and gender characteristics. This sample consisted of 31 children from one school (23 boys [72%] and 8 girls [25%], ages 9 to 15 ($M = 11.52$, $SD = 1.08$. Then, we recruited 162 children (70 boys [43%] and 92 girls [57%], ages 6 to 16 ($M = 10.78$, $SD = 1.08$) from four schools in Puerto Rico using the TEMAS group methodology. Therefore, altogether, the total number of cases in Puerto Rico consisted of 193 children ages 6 to 16, with 82 participants in Grade 5 (42%) and 111 participants in Grade 6 (58%).

New York Sample

The recruitment procedure in New York was more limited to those public schools where the Lutheran Medical Center Sunset Park Mental Health Center directs a school-based mental health program. Participants included 108 fifth-grade children (47 boys [44%] and 61 girls [56%], ages 9 to 12 years ($M = 10.31$, $SD = 54$), from two public schools of a low SES community in Brooklyn, NY. In New York we reached an 82% response rate (see table 7–5).

Instruments

The TEMAS instrument has a well-researched and standardized scoring system that includes norms for Puerto Rican children (ages 5–13), both in Puerto Rico and New York. The TEMAS cards are administered according to standardized instructions and structured inquiries.

Procedure

Children were invited to participate through their teachers. Informed consent was obtained in writing from the children's parents, and assent from

TABLE 7–5. Puerto Rico and New York Sample Characteristics

Site		Gender		Grade	
Puerto Rico	*n*	F	M	5th	6th
Individual	31	8	23	15	16
Group	162	92	70	67	95
New York	*n*	F	M	5th	6th
Group	108	61	47	108	N/A
TOTAL	301	161	140	190	111

the children. Confidentiality was assured by identifying the participants with only a code number. The permission that was obtained from the Department of Education did not allow us to gather personal demographic information. Only the Project Director had access to the master list linking the names of the students to code numbers. Thus, all scoring was done completely blind.

The group format required that the child write a story about a picture projected on a screen instead of it being recorded by an examiner. A prestructured writing sheet was assigned to each card projected. This form was designed based on TEMAS standard questions and inquiries. TEMAS stimuli were presented in a digital form—floppy (CD) with saved images of TEMAS cards, using a laptop and a projector, that were taken to the school. The stories collected were scored in accordance with standard instructions.

The TEMAS was administered in the community schools during regular hours in classrooms or the library. In Puerto Rico the test was administered in Spanish and the children wrote the story in Spanish, whereas in New York City, the Hispanic/Latino children wrote the stories in English or Spanish according to their preference. Graduate clinical psychology students supervised by the project director conducted the testing. At least two research assistants were assigned to each group administration. Interrater reliability on verbal fluency was obtained as follows: after one group of practicum students had scored the Verbal Fluency scale, the research assistants double-checked these scores by counting all the words in the narratives again. If there was a disparity in counting or understanding some words, then the independent coders convened for a consensus meeting.

This type of research did not seem to pose risks to participants and no adverse reactions among the children were noted. Nevertheless, following the protocol established for the Internal Review Board of the University, should any need be evident, an immediate referral would have been made to the University Community Clinic or to the school-based mental health Program in New York.

We learned that it was not convenient to administer the TEMAS cards stimuli in a numerical order, in order not to get a serial effect for fatigue and acquaintance in the production of stories. Thus, we randomized the order of the cards and created four sets of scrambled stimuli that were presented in identical order to the boys and girls. The TEMAS group instructions were modified to require children to write in capital letters because when the instructions were given to write in small letters, some stories were very difficult to read and one case was left as illegible after several attempts to rewrite it.

In the group administration, more than one examiner were used to give the children adequate supervision if they asked questions about the format.

RESULTS

Effects of Individual Vs. Group Methodology in Puerto Rico

A one-way analysis of variance was conducted to test for differences on Verbal Fluency between the individual and group methods in Puerto Rico. Results ($n = 193$) showed no significant differences between the methods, $F(1,191) = .002$, $p = .97$. Verbal Fluency in the individual method had a mean score of 40.45 ($SD = 13.01$) and in the group method, the mean score was 40.55 ($SD = 11.18$). To further examine how the school that was tested using the TEMAS individual method performed in Verbal Fluency when compared to the four schools that used the group method in Puerto Rico, we decided to assess differences with ANOVAS. Results indicated a significant effect of method ($p < .01$) in only one of the schools. Only in one school out of four, the group method showed lower Verbal Fluency ($M = 32.35$; $SD = 8.40$) than the individual method ($M = 40.45$; $SD = 13.01$).

CROSS-CULTURAL COMPARISONS BETWEEN PUERTO RICO AND NEW YORK

Differences between testing sites (Puerto Rico vs. New York) in Verbal Fluency were assessed conducting a one-way analysis of variance (ANOVA). Results showed significant differences between sites $F(1,268) = 55.44$, $p < .000$. Children in New York ($M = 31.31$, $SD = 7.89$) showed much lower Verbal Fluency than the Puerto Rico sample ($M = 40.55$, $SD = 11.18$).

In Puerto Rico, all participants presented their stories in Spanish, but in New York 87 children (80.6%) chose to respond in English whereas 21 children (19.4%) responded in Spanish. In New York, the children who responded in Spanish had significantly higher Verbal Fluency in the TEMAS stories than the children who responded in English, $F(1, 106) = 5.82$, $p < .018$. These children developed longer stories in Spanish ($M = 34.95$, $SD = 6.76$) than in English ($M = 30.43$, $SD = 7.93$).

Gender Differences

In the Puerto Rico group sample, girls wrote longer stories than boys, $F(1,160) = 17.74$, $p < .000$). However, this sex difference in Verbal Fluency result was not evident with the Puerto Rico individual sample, $F(1, 29) = 1.84$, $p = .19$ or the New York group sample $F(1,106) = 1.25$, $p = .27$. However, in the latter results, although not significant, there was a tendency for girls to produce longer stories than boys (see Table 7‑6).

School Grades

School grades were also significantly different between girls and boys in the group sample in Puerto Rico. In the TEMAS group method in Puerto Rico, girls obtained significantly higher school grades ($M = 2.85$, $SD = .80$) than boys ($M = 2.41$, $SD = .85$); $F(1,158) = 11.05$, $p < .001$. School grades were reported by the teachers (in a 4-point scale using A, B, C, and D).

Grade

In Puerto Rico, children from fifth and sixth grade were not significantly different in Verbal Fluency in the individual method or the group method (see Table 7–7: The New York sample did not have sixth graders).

TABLE 7–6. Verbal Fluency and Gender

| Sample | Total | | Gender | | | | | |
| | | | Female | | Male | | | |
	Mean	SD	Mean	SD	Mean	SD	F	p
Puerto Rico Individual ($n = 31$)	40.45	13.01	45.75	12.54	38.61	12.92	1.84	.19
Puerto Rico Group ($n = 162$)	40.55	11.18	43.62	10.91	36.51	10.26	17.74	.000*
New York Group ($n = 108$)	31.31	7.89	32.05	8.00	30.34	7.73	1.25	.27

Note. $*p < .05$; $* p < .01$

TABLE 7-7. Verbal Fluency and Grade

| Sample | Verbal Fluency | | | | | |
| | 5th grade | | 6th grade | | | |
	Mean	SD	Mean	SD	F	p
Puerto Rico Individual ($n = 31$)	36.53	10.90	44.13	14.06	2.80	.105
Puerto Rico Group ($n = 162$)	39.64	10.35	41.19	11.73	.75	.39

Correlations of Verbal Fluency and TEMAS Affective Scales, and Verbal Fluency and School Grades

Bivariate correlations were used to test the hypothesis regarding the association between Verbal Fluency and the affective scales (Happy, Sad, Angry, Fearful, Neutral, Ambivalent, Inappropriate). In the TEMAS group sample in Puerto Rico, a modest significant correlation was found between Verbal Fluency and Happy ($r = .20$, $p < .01$). In the New York group sample, no significant correlations were found with the affective scales.

The other set of correlations pertained to the association between Verbal Fluency and school grades in the TEMAS group sample in Puerto Rico (grades were not collected in New York). In the Puerto Rico sample, Verbal Fluency was significantly correlated with school grades ($r = .26, p < .001$).

QUALITATIVE RESULTS

Another area of significant findings was with the speech and language screening form developed to further examine the written samples with the TEMAS group test. The problem was that Verbal Fluency as a cognitive variable could reveal a delay, which needed to be distinguished from language deficits. Thirty cases (12 boys & 18 girls) were selected from the total sample of 162. This small sample was composed of high-risk girls and boys attending fifth ($n = 13$) and sixth ($n = 17$) grade classes in Puerto Rico. The TEMAS protocols of these students were given to three speech and language pathologists (10 cases each) so they could deliver a clinical impression of verbal delays and specific problems exhibited in the use of language. Then, these findings were compared with those results exhibited in the TEMAS protocols. Speech and language pathology experts found significant difficulties in written language in the following components: content (semantics) and form (grammar, syntax, morphology, and phonology). Errors most commonly observed were: limited complexity of sentence structure, poor vocabulary, underdeveloped morpho-syntactic skills, difficulty in applying capitalization and punctuation rules, inadequate use of conjunctions and prepositions, and poor narrative discourse skills. Problems in topic continuation and reasoning skills were also identified. Children were assessed to be at least two years behind in language skills, and had significant difficulties identifying conflicts in the TEMAS stories.

Limitations of the Study

Only public schools were used in the study. However, children from private schools as well and SES contributions to mental health need to be considered. The contribution of SES and gender need to be controlled for, from results based on ethnicity. Therefore, future studies should consider evaluating this SES aspect. In addition, we need to explore what can happen if we administer this design in other sites in order to adequately assess the risks and protective factors in poor Hispanic/Latino school children. We need to compare our group sample collected in New York to other high-risk sites in the United States, and perform a more systematic comparison between group and individual methods.

DISCUSSION

Results indicate that cognitive resources as well as delays need to be considered for a more balanced view of relative strengths and weaknesses. In some cases, Verbal Fluency tended to be a cognitive resource for girls. Verbal Fluency was significantly different by gender in Puerto Rico, and this tendency was observed in New York as well. This result confirms earlier research presenting girls with higher narrative ability, which may be a key factor, that may help them present their plight and seek out support. Whether girls use this relative resource to their advantage in delivering their coping strategies is something that needs to be further examined. Also in favor of girls is that they achieved the highest school grades in Puerto Rico. Higher cognitive and academic scores for girls may suggest a protective factor that they can develop.

The study indicated that the TEMAS test is a useful technique to gather information about cognitive resources, which are germane to problem-solving ability. Overall the TEMAS group method was superior to individual method in most cases, and this is a valuable finding as it provides a technique to reach out to more children that present psychological problems, as well as being cost effective as a secondary preventive measure.

The fact that only in one school Verbal Fluency in the group method was significantly lower than the individual method indicates that the group method might have some utility. It should be noted that in the school that showed lower Verbal Fluency with the group method, the school administration informed us that children had witnessed several violent episodes the preceding year, which required police intervention. The principal reported that the atmosphere in the school was tense, which may have impacted verbal productivity. Therefore, we need to study further what environmental factors contribute to an adequate choice of method.

In order to explore the validity of the group method more extensively, we intend, indeed, to analyze the complete TEMAS scales of the samples in Puerto Rico and New York to determine what other cognitive resources, such as omissions and conflict, are exhibited—or not, in the narratives. These cognitive variables could give us an indication of how complete the stories are and the importance of narrative skills in personality functioning. Given the advantage of girls in Verbal Fluency and school grades, evidently we need to look more closely to the contribution of narrative techniques like the TEMAS in order to determine if in fact gender plays a role in narrative ability. In the long term, the study attempts to improve the area of culturally sensitive assessment of risk factors for mental disorder in Hispanic/Latino children in order to design more appropriate and effective clinical interventions.

THIRD PUERTO RICAN STUDY CROSS CULTURAL CONCURRENT VALIDITY OF THE TEMAS AND THE BASC IN THE ASSESSMENT OF LATINO SCHOOL CHILDREN

BACKGROUND

The Behavior Assessment System for Children (BASC) is comprised of objective subscales for preschoolers, children, and adolescents aged 4.0 to 18.9 years. The instrument is a self-report personality inventory (Reynolds, C. & Kamphaus, K., 1992), available in Spanish that measures numerous aspects of behavior and personality dimensions (including positive/adaptive and negative/clinical). The Self-Report Scale includes four composites: Clinical Maladjustment, School Maladjustment, Personal Maladjustment and Emotional Symptoms Index. The TEMAS test has been standardized with Hispanic/Latino children in New York City, with Hispanic children in Puerto Rico, and with Argentinean children in Buenos Aires (Costantino, Malgady, Casullo, & Castillo, 1991). Research on the TEMAS to date has included establishing the psychometric properties of the test (Costantino, Malgady, & Rogler, 1988) as well as preliminary studies of its validity (Costantino, Malgady, Colon-Malgady, & Bailey, 1992; Costantino, Malgady, Rogler, & Tsui, 1988) and clinical utility (Cardalda, Costantino, Sayers, Machado & Guzman, 2002). The psychometric properties of the BASC measure are good, and in the opinion of reviewers (Flanagan, 1995; Sandoval & Echandia, 1994), the BASC represents one of the most widely used behavioral self-report measures of mental disorders symptomatology in the field. The internal consistency coefficients for the scales are high with an average of .80. Both the TEMAS and the BASC raw scores were translated to T scores according to standardized norms. School grades were rated on a scale of 1-5. Preliminary research with TEMAS and BASC suggest that TEMAS measures coping skill with emotionally laden situations, while the BASC measures the emotion or skill in an independent situational context. Other research indicate an inverse relationship between TEMAS Personality Functions and BASC Scales that measure clinical and school problems, while a positive relationship was found with the Personal Adjustment Composite and its components. These results were expected since low T scores on the TEMAS correspond to poor ability to cope with the conflict/problem solving, thus indicating that TEMAS measures what it was purported to measure (Flanagan et al., 1999).

METHOD

Sample and Procedures

The same samples as in the second Puerto Rican Study were used in the present study, 193 in San Juan Puerto Rico and 108 in New York City. (see Table 7–5 for sample characteristics). In Puerto Rico 193 children were administered the TEMAS and the BASC self report. In New York the 108 participants were administered the TEMAS and the BASC. (Cardalda, E. B., Costantino, G., León-Velázquez, M., Jiménez-suárez, V., Martinez, J. V., & Ortiz-Vargas, N., 2005).

RESULTS

ANOVA analyses revealed several significant differences in the following the TEMAS scales in Puerto Rico and New York: Delay of gratification, Sexual Identity and Reality Testing Verbal Fluency and Total Omissions (see Table 7–8). Several significant differences were also found on the following BASC scales between Puerto Rico and New York: School maladjustment, Attitude to Teachers, Personal adjustment, Relations with Parents, Interpersonal Relations, and Emotional Symptoms Index (see Table 7–9).

In Puerto Rico the following significant Pearson correlations were found between the TEMAS and BASC scales: Interpersonal relations in the TEMAS were significantly correlated with the BASC -Clinical Maladjustment, –Locus of Control, -Anxiety, and -Depression, -Sense of Inadequacy, -Emotional Symptom Index. In addition, the TEMAS -Total Omissions were significantly correlated with the BASC-Locus of Control, -Depression, and -Relations with Parents. Similarly the, TEMAS-Verbal Fluency was significantly correlated with the BASC-Social Stress, and -Personal Adjustment. TEMAS aggression was correlated with the BASC-Personal Adjustment,

TABLE 7–8.   Puerto Rico and New York: Mean and SD for TEMAS scales

	Mean (SD) Puerto Rico	Mean (SD) New York	F
Interpersonal Relations	42.98 (11.07)	41.21 (9.49)	1.58 (.210)
Aggression	39.06 (9.16)	38.81 (10.25)	.04 (.848)
Depression/Anxiety	37.61 (9.74)	35.41 (11.86)	2.22 (.138)
Achievement motivation	39.79 (14.62)	41.76 (12.92)	1.09 (.297)
Delay of gratification	35.25 (12.80)	43.43 (11.49)	24.24 (.000)***
Self-concept	38.65 (11.34)	40.98 (10.61)	2.43 (.121)
Sexual Identity	29.40 (20.35)	43.71 (9.29)	43.31 (.000)***
Moral Judgment	39.57 (15.14)	38.59 (10.98)	.294 (.588)
Reality Testing	41.11 (11.01)	39.68 (11.02)	.91 (.341)
Verbal Fluency	41.88 (11.01)	31.16 (7.82)	67.21 (.000)***
Total Omissions	47.05 (10.39)	44.02 (8.35)	5.50 (.020)***

Note. *p <. 05; **p <. 01; ***p <. 001

TABLE 7–9.   Puerto Rico and New York: Mean and
SD for BASC self report scales

	Mean (SD) Puerto Rico	Mean (SD) New York	F
BAC composites/scales:			
School maladjustment	52.54 (9.75)	49.35 (8.83)	6.27 (.013)*
Attitude to School	50.29 (8.58)	48.80 (8.71)	1.60 (.208)
Attitude to Teachers	54.87 (8.70)	49.88 (10.11)	15.14 (.000)***
Clinical maladjustment	51.79 (8.70)	49.97 (8.71)	2.29 (.132)
Atypicality	51.48 (9.17)	49.44 (9.81)	2.47 (.118)
Locus of Control	52.40 (7.87)	50.60 (8.66)	2.54 (.112)
Social Stress	50.85 (9.70)	49.28 (8.50)	1.60 (.208)
Anxiety	51.53 (8.25)	50.34 (8.12)	1.03 (.312)
Depression	52.79 (10.10)	51.72 (10.28)	.32 (.575)
Sense of Inadequacy	53.19 (10.11)	52.70 (10.69)	.12 (.727)
Personal adjustment	45.63 (9.96)	50.40 (10.37)	11.76 (.001)**
Relations With Parents	45.18 (12.34)	49.47 (10.17)	7.68 (.006)**
Interpersonal Relations	44.58 (11.16)	49.22 (11.52)	8.97 (.003)**
Self Esteem	47.93 (7.13)	50.10 (10.36)	3.25 (.073)
Self Reliance	48.83 (9.83)	49.21 (10.14)	.08 (.779)
Emotional symptoms Index	53.10 (9.13)	50.34 (9.66)	4.57 (.034)**

Note. *p <. 05; **p <. 01; ***p <. 001

TABLE 7–10.   Puerto Rico: Significant correlations
between TEMAS & BASC scales

Scales	Correlation (p)
TEMAS-Interpersonal relations and BASC–Clinical maladjustment	−.20 (.040)
TEMAS-Interpersonal relations and BASC–locus of control	−.25 (.009)
TEMAS-Interpersonal relations and BASC–anxiety	−.21 (.033)
TEMAS-Interpersonal relations and BASC–depression	−.25 (.010)
TEMAS-Interpersonal relations and BASC–sense of inadequacy	−.26 (.007)
TEMAS-Interpersonal relations and BASC–emotional symptom index	−.21 (.033)
TEMAS-Total omissions and BASC–locus of control	.22 (.021)
TEMAS-Total omissions and BASC–depression	.24 (.014)
TEMAS-Total omissions and BASC–relations with parents	−.20 (.041)
TEMAS-Verbal fluency and BASC–social stress	−.19 (.050)
TEMAS-Aggression and BASC–personal adjustment	.22 (.019)**
TEMAS-Aggression and BASC–relations with parents	.20 (.039)**
TEMAS-Aggression and BASC–interpersonal relations	.25 (.009)*
TEMAS-Aggression and BASC–emotional symptom index	−.19 (.046)**
TEMAS-Achievement motivation and BASC–sense of inadequacy	−.23 (.016)**
TEMAS-Moral judgment and BASC–school maladjustment	.21 (.025)**

Note. *$p < .05$; **$p < .01$; ***$p < .001$

Relations with Parents, Interpersonal Relations, and -Emotional Symptom Index. TEMAS-Achievement Motivation was correlated with the BASC-Sense of Inadequacy and TEMAS-Moral Judgment was correlated with the BASC-School Maladjustment. (see Table 7–10).

In New York, five significant correlations were found between the TEMAS and BASC scales as follows: TEMAS Verbal Fluency and BASC School Malajustment; TEMAS Verbal Fluency and BASC Attitude to School; TEMAS Total Omissions and BASC Locus of Control; TEMAS Delay of Gratification and BASC Depression; and TEMAS Sexual Identity and BASC self esteem. (see Table 7-10).

School Grades

In Puerto Rico, with respect to school grades, several statistically significant Pearson correlations (although relatively low) were found between the TEMAS scales of verbal Fluency, Omissions, Achievement Motivation, Moral Judgment and school grades. (see Table 7–12).

TABLE 7–11. New York: Significant Correlations
Between TEMAS and BASC Scales

Scales	Correlation (p)
TEMAS-Verbal fluency and BASC-school maladjustment	−.22 (.021)*
TEMAS-Verbal fluency and BASC-attitude to school	−.27 (.005)*
TEMAS-Total omissions and BASC-locus of control	.19 (.047)*
TEMAS-Delay of gratification and BASC-depression	−.32 (.048)*
TEMAS-Sexual identity and BASC-self-esteem	.30 (.002)**

*Note. *p < .05; **p < .01; ***p < .001*

TABLE 7–12. Puerto Rico: Significant Correlations
Between TEMAS Scales and School Grades

Scales	Correlation (p)
TEMAS-Verbal fluency	.26 (.006)**
TEMAS-Aggression	.19 (.048)*
TEMAS-Achievement motivation	.24 (.010)*
TEMAS-Moral judgment	.21 (.031)*

*Note. *p < .05; **p < .01; ***p < .001*

Statistically significant correlations were also found between BASC scales: School maladjustment, Attitude to school, Attitude to teachers, Clinical maladjustment, Atypicality, Locus of control, Social stress, Depression, Sense of Inadequacy, Personal Adjustment, Relations with Parents, Interpersonal Relations, Self Reliance and Emotional Symptoms Index and school grades (see Table 7–13).

In New York no analyses were conducted between the two tests and school grades, because school grades were not obtained for the students in Brooklyn, N.Y.

DISCUSSION

Both in PR and NY, the TEMAS scales showed maladaptive results in Aggression, Depression and Moral Judgment. In PR relative weaknesses were noted in Achievement Motivation, Delay of Gratification, Self-concept and Sexual Identity. In NY relative weaknesses were noted in reality testing and verbal fluency. BASC showed average results. Significant differences

TABLE 7–13.   Puerto Rico: Significant correlations
Between BASC Scales and School Grades

Scales	Correlation (p)
BASC-School maladjustment	−.35 (.000)***
BASC-Attitude to school	−.31 (.001)***
BASC-Attitude to teachers	−.26 (.006)**
BASC-Clinical maladjustment	−.26 (.007)**
BASC-Atypicality	−.19 (.046)*
BASC-Locus of control	−.26 (.007)**
BASC-Social stress	−.25 (.008)**
BASC-Depression	−.33 (.000)***
BASC-Sense of inadequacy	−.45 (.000)***
BASC-Personal adjustment	.37 (.000)***
BASC-Relations with parents	.28 (.003)**
BASC-Interpersonal relations	.35 (.000)***
BASC-Self reliance	.29 (.003)**
BASC-Emotional symptom index	−.36 (.000)***

Note. *$p < .05$; **$p < .01$; ***$p < .001$

were found between PR and NY in the TEMAS and the BASC. From these differential results, it was noted that the cognitive variables were lower in NY and personality variables lower in PR. BASC composite scales were lower in PR in Personal Adjustment, and in NY in School maladjustment, Clinical maladjustment and Emotional symptoms index. Significant correlations between several TEMAS scales and school grades indicate the utility of this measure in assessing cognitive and intellectual abilities. Also, the scales of personal adjustment and clinical symptoms showed correlations with school graders. Two limitation of this study are the inability to obtain school grades in New York City and to use also 3rd and 4th graders as in Puerto Rico. However, there are several barriers within the school system, which at times does not allow matching the comparison samples. Notwithstanding these limitations the TEMAS shows good concurrent validity with the BASC, a valid objective, paper-and pencil test.

This study replicates the results of Flanagan, 1999 conducted with Latino and European American children in New York City; where significant correlations were found between the BASC and the TEMAS. The results of the present study show the concurrent validity of TEMAS test in assessing personality functioning in Latino children. Earlier cross-cultural studies as reported in the next section (Sardi, 2000; Summo, 2000 Cornabuci, 2000; and Sulfaro, 2000) show a robust relationship between the TEMAS Aggression Scale and the Child Behavior Check List Aggression; thus confirming the clinical validity of TEMAS in assessing children personality functioning. The present findings contribute to an expanding area of research on the validity of the TEMAS instrument in assessing in cross-cultural settings. The correlations between the TEMAS Verbal Fluency cognitive function and school grades indicate the predictive validity of the TEMAS test and its utility in multicultural school settings.

ITALIAN STUDIES

The TEMAS research program began its European exposure at the University of Rome "La Sapienza" in 1997, when four master-level psychology students at this university completed their theses using this culturally competent test. As Italian society becomes culturally and linguistically diverse, the need for the TEMAS technique is growing. More recently, several theses are being conducted at the Catholic University of Milan. The case study of "Maria," presented in chapter 12, is taken from one of the master theses at this university (Fantini, 2005).

GENERAL STUDY

The general study, *Relationship between the aggression scales in TEMAS (Tell-Me-A-Story) and the Child Behaviour Checklist Child (CBCL)* was conducted to assess the construct of aggression as revealed in the children TEMAS stories and as shown in CBCL with mothers as informants. The literature shows that studies assessing aggression in children have used primarily behavioural observation, psychiatric evaluations, and or paper and pencil tests with parents, teachers or significant others as the respondents. Seldom, children have been assessed in an objective manner with a projective/narrative test in order to uncover the underlying dynamics of aggression, and thus making a valid comparison between the *genotypic* motivation as revealed by children in TEMAS stories and *phenotypic* behavior as reported by parents. In summary, based on the social learning context of aggression (Bandura, 1977), this study used TEMAS (Tell-Me-A-Story), a multicultural projective/narrative test to assess the

TABLE 7–14.   Contingency Table

| SES | Gender | | Total |
---	Males	Females	Total
A	15	25	40
B	13	18	31
Total	28	43	71

genotypic motivation and the (CBCL) to assess the phenotypic behavior in 7 and 8 year old Italian children in Rome.

The four related studies as presented later—*Relationship between aggression and cognitive functions in conflict resolution in 7 and 8 year old Italian children* (Sardi, 2000), *Relationship between aggression and emotional functions in conflict resolution in 7 and 8 year old Italian children* (Summo, 2000), *Relationship between aggression and moral judgment conflict resolution in 7 and 8 year old Italian children* (Sulfaro, 2000), *Relationship between aggression and interpersonal relations in conflict resolution in 7 and 8 year old Italian children* (Cornabuci, 2000)—are based on the general study, use the same sample of participants, but assess different cognitive and personality functions as related to aggression.

Method

Consent forms were sent to 252 parents in School District 130 in Rome, 92 consented to participate, 11 were excluded because they were single parents, and 71 mother-child dyads were included in the general study. The children were administered the short form of TEMAS (9 cards) while their mothers completed the CBCL. Demographic data were collected with emphasis on the socio-economic status (SES) and occupation; the latter two variables were obtained according to Hollingshead Two Factor Index of Social Position. Table 7-14 shows the sample distribution with respect to gender and SES, where A represents middle-low SES and B represented middle-high SES.

To examine the construct validity of aggression in the two tests, *Adaptive Aggression* in TEMAS was correlated with *Behavioral Aggression* in CBL, when SES and gender were taken into account. A multimethod approach, thus served to explore how aggression is mediated through cognitive functioning and vice versa when SES and gender are considered.

RESULTS

Pearson correlation between adaptive aggression (TEMAS) and Behavioral Aggression (CBCL) was statistically significant at $r = -.41, p < .0001$. When gender is factored in, the correlations are higher for boys than girls, r boys $= -.54, p = .002$ and r girls $= -.29, p = .029$, respectively. With regard to SES, the correlation is higher for the higher SES group than the lower group, r higher SES $= -.51, p = .002, r$ lower SES $= -.21, p = .089$, respectively.

With regard to the CBCL (Behavioral Aggression), gender did not contribute to a statistical difference, SES did. The lower SES participants had higher level of aggression, according to their mothers (see table 7-15). When examined together (gender and SES), there was no interaction among the two. To further investigate the significant results of the ANOVA with respect SES using the CBCL data, the sample was divided in two groups of males and females, and analyses were conducted to assess the level of aggression based on gender differences. Results indicated that boys in the medium-low socioeconomic status (SES) significantly showed more behavioral aggression than boys belonging to medium-high socioeconomic status (SES), as rated by the mothers (see Table 7-16); whereas results indicated that girls in the medium-low SES showed only trends toward significance in behavioral aggression in comparison with girls in the medium-high socioeconomic status (SES) (see Table 7-17).

With regard to the TEMAS (Adaptive Aggression), gender did not contribute to any statistical difference and there is a trend based on SES (e.g., the lower SES group used aggression in less adaptive manner). When these factors are examined together with the TEMAS, there was no interaction between gender and SES. Furthermore, differently from the CBCL, no statistical differences are found between boys and girls based on SES.

DISCUSSION

The results of the general study confirm the hypothesis on the construct validity of aggression. The negative correlation of -0.41 ($p < .0001$) shows the concurrent validity of the TEMAS narrative test and CBCL objective paper-and-pencil test in the assessment of the same construct of aggression. The data are particularly encouraging, taking into consideration that the two tests are very different both in structure and theoretical framework.

TABLE 7–15   Univariate Analysis

Dependent Variable: Aggressive Behavior (CBCL)
Factor: Socioeconomic Status

Group	N	Mean	SD	F Crit.	F Prob.
SES A	40	4.72	3.32	12.84	0.0006
SES B	31	7.84	4.00	/////////////////	/////////////////
Total	71	6.08	3.93	/////////////////	/////////////////

Hence, these results encourage research to continue using complementary measures to study a multidimensional construct such as aggression. Results showing that participating males scored higher than females in both TEMAS and CBCL seem to be confirmed by daily events where boys tend to be more aggressive than girls. These results also indicated that the two tests possess good discriminant validity in assessing the aggression construct. The CBCL findings showing that poor-working class mothers significantly rated their children as being aggressive, while middle-upper class mothers failed to perceive aggression in their children, reflect social class differences among mothers. Lower class mothers seem to be less influenced by social desirability and more candid than their middle-upper class mothers in talking about aggression in their children. These results were also in part confirmed when mothers rated their participating children according to gender. Boys of poor-working class families significantly showed more behavioral aggression than middle-upper class boys, whereas girls in the poor-working families showed only trends toward significance of being more aggressive than their middle class counterpart. The differential class attitude explanation is valid only for low-working class mothers in attributing aggression in their sons; however, these mothers tended to be more protective of their girls. In this respect low-working class mothers were similar to middle-upper class mothers in recognizing aggression in their participating daughters. The results in adaptive aggression as measured by TEMAS did not show any statistical gender differences; however, poor-working class boys, although non significant, tended to deal with aggression in a more maladaptive manner than their middle-upper class counterparts. In addition there were no interaction effects between gender and SES. These non-significant results can be interpreted that TEMAS seems to be a less biased test than the CBCL in assessing children aggression. Furthermore, this interpretation begs the question, if poor and middle class children do not show difference in narrative aggression, why poor children are differentially perceived as more aggressive than middle

TABLE 7–16. Univariate Analysis—Males

Dependent Variable: Aggressive Behavior (CBCL)
Factor: Socioeconomic Status

Males	N	Mean	SD	F Crit.	F Prob.
SES A	15	5.07	3.06	10.63	0.0031
SES B	13	9.23	3.70	/////////////////	/////////////////
Total	28	7.00	3.93	/////////////////	/////////////////

TABLE 7–17. Univariate Analysis—Females

Dependent Variable: Aggressive Behavior (CBCL)
Factor: Socioeconomic Status

Females	N	Mean	SD	F Crit.	F Prob.
SES A	25	4.52	3.51	4.04	0.0051
SES B	18	6.83	4.00	/////////////////	/////////////////
Total	43	5.49	3.86	/////////////////	/////////////////

class children even by their respective mothers? Although we have attempted to explain this differences earlier, this question, which implies both test bias and social bias, needs to be further investigated.

The first Study, conducted by Sardi, in 2000 explored cognitive functions and aggressive functions of personality in the participating students. Four hypotheses were proposed. The first assessed the relationship between an impulsive cognitive style, determined with the Reaction Time on TEMAS and hyperactivity as measured by the CBCL. The second hypothesis focused on the relationship between an impulsive cognitive style in TEMAS and adaptive aggression also in TEMAS, and the relationship between adaptive aggression in TEMAS and hyperactivity in CBCL. The third explored the relationship between the Omissions in TEMAS and hyperactivity in CBCL. The fourth measured the relationship between the Transformations in TEMAS and hyperactivity in CBCL.

RESULTS

Results indicated that with respect to the first hypothesis, there was no correlation between the TEMAS reaction time and CBCL hyperactivity.

The second hypothesis was statistically supported. There was a statistically significant correlation between an impulsive cognitive style and adaptive aggression (Pearson $r = -.19$, $p = 0.038$) and between adaptive aggression and hyperactivity (Pearson $r = -.25$, $p = 0.019$).

The third and fourth hypotheses were not supported statistically, but showed a trend in the hypothesized direction.

DISCUSSION

The second study explored the relationship between aggression and emotional functions in conflict resolution of 7-and 8-year-old children (Summo, 2000). Using the cognitive theory of engagement and disengagement by Lazarus & Folkman (1984) dealing with appraisal or attribution and coping styles, the author tested the following hypotheses:

1. The attribution of the emotional state Happiness to the main character would be correlated with the (TEMAS) personality function of Adaptive Moral Judgment.
2. The attribution of the emotional state Happiness to the main character would be correlated with the (TEMAS) cognitive variables Omission and Transformations.

RESULTS

Results of the first hypothesis indicated that, for children who reported that the main character experienced Happiness at least once, this variable was significantly correlated with the TEMAS Personality Function of Adaptive Moral Judgment as follows: $r = .31$ (66 Ss), $p = 0.006$. When the participants were subdivided in terms of low and high SES, the same was true only the higher SES participants: $r = .41$ (S = 37), $p = 0.006$.

The second hypothesis was not supported, but tended toward significance: r (transformations) $= .20$ (Ss $= 66$), $p = 0.056$, and r (omissions) $= 0.1880$ (Ss $= 66$), $p = 0.065$. However, when the participants were subdivided along the SES category, a statistically significant correlation emerged for the lower SES group: r (transformations) $= .32$ (Ss $= 29$), $p = 0.045$ and r (omissions) $= .35$ (Ss $= 29$), $p = 0.033$.

Furthermore, when participants were subdivided based on frequency of scores in Happiness (e.g., at least 4, 1–3, and 0), it became apparent how Adaptive Aggression was highly correlated with Adaptive Moral Judgment. Indeed, analysis of variance including gender and SES as independent variables and frequency of attribution of Happiness (at least 4 times) as the dependent variable, it was found that SES was statistically significant ($p = 0.015$) and not its interaction with gender ($p = 0.853$).

With respect to Personality Functions, whereas there is a trend for gender to be correlated with Adaptive Aggression for girls ($r = 0.2362$, $p = 0.071$) but not for boys, there was a statistically significant correlation between Adaptive Interpersonal Relations and the frequency of scores in Happiness for both boys ($r = 0.4037, p = 0.020$) and girls ($r = 0.3795, p = 0.008$), with girls higher than boys.

Lastly, based on SES, appraisal of Happiness was statistically significantly correlated with Adaptive Aggression and with Adaptive Interpersonal Relations for the higher SES and not for the lower SES:

r (Aggr—Happ) $= .46$ ($Ss = 37$), $p = 0.002$
r (Inter—Happ) $= .54$ ($Ss = 37$), $p < .001$

The third study assessed aggression and moral judgment in conflict resolution among 7-and 8-years-old Italian children (Cornabuci, 2000). Based on cognitive theory of engagement and disengagement (Lazarus & Folkman, 1984), the authors hypothesized that the development of moral judgment is influenced by SES and differential educational standards based on gender stereotypes, and that Aggression and Moral Judgment would be correlated.

RESULTS

Results indicated that Moral Judgment and Adaptive Aggression measured by the TEMAS were significantly correlated with behavioral aggression measured by the CBCL: $r = .74$ (71-Ss), $p < 0.001$.

Furthermore, Moral Judgment measured with the TEMAS was also significantly correlated with Behavioral Aggression measured with the CBCL, albeit relatively low: $r = -.29, p = 0.007$.

Confirming one of the hypotheses, an analysis of variance showed that when SES was used as the independent variable, there was a trend for the higher SES than the lower SES group to have higher Adaptive Moral Judgment.

When these groups were subdivided according to gender, no differences were evident in terms of Adaptive Moral Judgment. Nonetheless, when girls were subdivided based on SES, the higher SES had a significantly higher level of Adaptive Moral Judgment than the lower SES girls. Gender and SES did not interact when a MANOVA was used.

The fourth study assessed the relationship between interpersonal relations and aggression in children between 7 and 8 years old (Sulfaro, 2000). In the following analyses, based on cognitive theory of engagement and disengagement (Lazarus & Folkman, 1984), the authors hypothesized that the relationship between adaptive interpersonal relations and adaptive aggression was influenced by (a) SES and (b) differential educational standards based on gender stereotypes. In order to quantitatively support these hypotheses, variables from the TEMAS and the CBCL were used as follows: Happiness (TEMAS), Total Time (TEMAS), Verbal Fluency (TEMAS), Aggressive Behavior (CBCL), and Social Competence Scale (CBCL). The following statistically significant Pearson correlations were found between Adaptive Interpersonal Relations and

Adaptive Aggression	$r = .87, p < .00100 \ (N = 71)$
Happiness	$r = .39, p = 0.001 \ (N = 66)$
Total Time	$r = -.29, p = 0.01 \ (N = 71)$
Verbal Fluency	$r = -.30, p = 0.01 \ (N = 71)$
Aggressive Behavior	$r = -.33, p = 0.002 \ (N = 71)$

but not with the Social Competence Scale for the CBCL, nor the subcomponent scales for the social competence scale. An analysis of variance did not support the hypotheses that neither SES or gender were factors in the development and level of Adaptive Interpersonal Relations.

DISCUSSION

The Italian General study and the four Italian studies revealed several significant results thus confirming that the TEMAS narrative test can be as valid as the CBCL paper-and-pencil objective test. The significant correlations between the several TEMAS cognitive, affective and personality functions and the corresponding CBCL functions indicate that personality functioning can be validly assessed at both covert or genotype level and overt phenotype level of functioning.

ASIAN STUDY: VALIDITY OF ASIAN TEMAS IN TAIWANESE CHILDREN: PRELIMINARY DATA

The development of the Asian American version of TEMAS was a logical outgrowth of the continuous efforts to create a culturally appropriate narrative test with Asian American children and adolescents, thus further validating the construct of cultural congruence, that states that similarity between the examinee and the characters in the narrative pictures increases the identification between the storyteller and stimuli and thus generates more valid narratives. Because the TEMAS emphasizes the influence of the cultural context of the test stimuli, there was a need to develop an Asian American version of TEMAS pictures with characters and context to better fit Asian culture (Costantino, 2000; Costantino, Flanigan, & Tsui, 2001). The present study assessed the validity of the Asian American TEMAS with Taiwanese children in Taiwan (Yang, Kuo, & Costantino, 2003).

METHOD

Participants were 48 children (23 boys and 25 girls) from public elementary schools in Taipei. They were administered the short versions of the Asian and nonminority TEMAS cards in a counterbalanced order by trained psychology students. Several paper–pencil tests were also administered to serve as validation criterion, such as the ESCLAI, the CDI, and the CAI.

RESULTS

Repeated-measures ANOVAs comparing the scores obtained from the two versions showed no significant mean differences for all scores. Pearson correlations showed negative correlation between Total Omissions and performance on Verbal Fluency tests, and positive correlation between total transformations and omissions scores. Some personality functions of both versions showed significant correlations with some subscales of the ESCLAI, especially those measured negative aspects of daily life adjustment. Also, many of the personality functions correlated with the scores on the CDI and the CAI. The Asian American TEMAS showed better correlations with the ESCLAI on the Interpersonal Relations and Aggression scores. Significant correlations were obtained between some affective functions of both versions of TEMAS with the CDI, the CAI, and the ESCLAI. Correlations were shown on negative emotion not on positive one. Also, nonminority version of TEMAS appeared to obtain better correlations than Asian TEMAS on affective functions.

DISCUSSION

Overall, the personality and affective functions of the Asian TEMAS can validly reflect the level of negative affect and the difficulty of daily life adjustment in Taiwanese children. No correlations were found between the TEMAS cognitive functions and the performance tests of attention to details and verbal fluency. When comparing the correlations between TEMAS scores and scores on tests for daily life adjustment; it appeared that Asian TEMAS was superior to the non-minority TEMAS on Interpersonal Relationship and Aggression functions. It is possible that Taiwanese children project more information related to interpersonal conflicts when the cultural context of the cards is closer to their own culture. Hence, the development of an Asian version of TEMAS is warranted.

CONCLUSION

The development of projective instruments with both emic and etic validity and the collection of multicultural and cross-cultural norms is an arduous process that has spanned more than half a century (APA, 2003; Costantino, 1987; Costantino, Malgady, & Rogler, 1988: Dana, 1986, 1993; Exner & Weiner, 1995; Henry, 1947; Murray, 1943; Padilla & Medina, 1996; Thompson, 1949; Vane, 1981; Williams, 1983). The standardization of TEMAS on Hispanic, Black, and White children in the United States, and our gathering of comparative normative data on native Puerto Rican, Argentinean, Peruvian, Italian, and Taiwanese children, is a systematic attempt to create a narrative test that has multicultural and cross-cultural validity (APA, 1990, 2003; Dana, 1993, 1998; Flanagan & DiGiuseppe, 1999; Malgady, Rogler, & Costantino, 1987, 1988; Ritzler, 1993, 1997). Similarly, the TEMAS test has been recognized as a culturally competent test for culturally diverse youngsters (APA, 2003; Abraham, 2003). In addition the cross-cultural research with postwar adjustment of Salvadoran children showed that selected TEMAS cards and selected WISC-III subsets with other observed cognitive functions were the two most valid measures in assessing the psychosocial functioning and resiliency of 54 Salvadoran children exposed to the war (Walton, Nuttall, & Vazquez-Nuttall, 1997, 1998). In a way, the TEMAS research is similar to the early attempts to use the TAT in cross-cultural studies (Henry, 1947) and to Avila-Espada's (1986) development of the TAT comprehensive scoring system and norms for European Hispanics. In another way, our research has followed Anastasi's (1988) suggestion and has followed the TAT as a valuable model to develop a more valid and more culturally sensitive narrative instrument (Dana, 1993, 1998; Elliot, 1998; Flanagan & DiGiuseppe, 1999). The minority version of the TEMAS apperception test was originally developed as a clinical tool, presenting ethnically/racially familiar characters in urban and fantasy settings, in order to facilitate minority children's identification with the stimuli and thereby enhance verbal fluency and self-disclosure. Earlier studies with New York City examinees indicated that Hispanic/Latino and African American children were indeed more verbally fluent in telling stories about TEMAS pictures in comparison to TAT pictures (Costantino & Malgady, 1983; Costantino, Malgady, & Vasquez, 1981). Other studies established the reliability of TEMAS and gave some evidence of concurrent validity and clinical utility in predicting psychotherapeutic outcomes (Costantino, Malgady, & Rogler, 1988; Malgady et al., 1984). Additional studies have shown the predictive validity of the TEMAS achievement motivation with multicultural youths (Cardalda, 1995, 1998; Torres, 1995), and in Salvadoran youngsters (Walton, Nuttall, & Vazquez-Nuttall, 1997, 1998). Furthermore, Bernal (1991) has shown that the TEMAS test was superior to the Robert's Apperception Test in assessing the clinical profiles of Mexican and Mexican American youngsters. The results of the two cross-cultural studies lend support to the use of TEMAS with children and adolescents in Puerto Rico, Argentina, Peru, Italy, and Taiwan. However, further analyses of the early Puerto Rican and Argentinean study suggested that the characters, setting, and themes of some pictures were not appropriate in Argentinean and Puerto Rican cultures; hence several cards were redesigned to depict more culturally relevant settings and events for those countries. For example, the Puerto Rican and Argentinean children, when responding to Card 1 that shows a typical New York City urban setting with brownstones, often remarked, "Why all these houses have outside stairs" because houses and buildings in these two Latin countries have stairs inside the main entrances. New pictures, which are used in cross-cultural research, have been redesigned depicting European architecture styles, which are prevalent in the Hispanic Caribbean countries, South America, Europe, and Asia.

In addition the first Argentinean study, Costantino, Malgady, Casullo and Castillo, (1991) found that the majority of children scored very low in moral judgment as revealed in their stories about a policeman (depicted as rewarding authority in card 15) who was perceived as a punitive authority. This misperception seemed to be associated with historical and sociopolitical events, as Argentina was emerging from a military regime in which the police were perceived as punitive agents in 1984-1985 when the study was completed. These redesigned TEMAS cards: 1B-G; 15, 17 B-G were used in subsequent studies in Argentina and Peru and results also lend support to the use of TEMAS with children and adolescents in these two countries.

The most recent cross-cultural research in Puerto Rico (Cardalda et al., 2005; Cardalda, Costantino, Sayers, Machado, & Guzman, 2002) and Argentina (Dupertuis & Ropaldo, 2001; Dupertuis et al., 2004) confirms that the original and revised TEMAS pictures show adequate cross-cultural validity and clinical utility. Furthermore, the studies conducted at the University of Rome (Cornabuci, 2000; Sardi, 2000; Sulfaro, 2000; Summo, 2000) indicate a significant correlation between the TEMAS and the CBCL, a paper-and-pencil test, thus showing adequate concurrent validity of the TEMAS and also indicating that TEMAS is a valid instrument to assess Italian school-age children.

A new set of TEMAS pictures has been created for Asian American children and adolescents in the United States. Preliminary results of a pilot study indicate that Asian American examinees exhibit higher verbal fluency and more adaptive themes when responding to the Asian American version than to the nonminority version of TEMAS (Costantino, Flaningan, & Tsui, 2001; Yang, Kuo, & Costantino, 2003).

REFERENCES

Achenbach, T. M., & Edelbrook, C. S. (1991). *Manual for the child behavior checklist and revised child behavior profile.* Burlington, VT: University of Vermont.

American Psychological Association. (2003). *Guidelines on multicultural education, training, research, practice, and organizational change for psychologists.* Washington, DC: Author.

American Psychological Association. (1990). *Guidelines for providers of psychological services to ethnic, linguistic and culturally diverse populations.* Washington, DC: Author.

Anastasi, A. (1988). *Psychological testing* (6th ed.). New York: Macmillan.

Anthony, W. A. (2000). Recovery from mental illness: The guiding vision of the mental health systems in the 1990s. *Psychiatric Rehabilitation Journal, 16(4)*, 11–23.

Ávila-Espada, A. (1986). *Manual operativo para el Test de Apercepción temática*. [Working manual for the Thematic Apperception Test]. Madrid, Spain: Ediciones Pirámide, S.A.

Bandura, A. (1977). *Social learning theory*. Englewood Cliffs, NJ.: Prentice-Hall.

Bernal, I. (1991). *The relationship between level of acculturation, The Robert's Apperception Test for Children, and the TEMAS (Tell-Me-A-Story Test)*. Unpublished dissertation, California School of Professional Psychology, Los Angeles, CA.

Boring, E. G. (1929). *A history of experimental psychology*. New York: Appleton-Century.

Brackbill, G.A. (1951). Some effects of color on thematic fantasy. *Journal of Counseling Psychology, 15*, 412–418.

Cairns, R. B. (2000). Developmental science: Three audacious implications. In L. R. Bergman, R. B. Cairns, L. G. Nelson, & L. Nystedt (Eds.), *Developmental science and the holistic approach* (pp. 49–62). Mahwah, NJ: Lawrence Erlbaum Associates.

Camara, W. J., Nathan, J. S., & Puente, A. E. (2000). Psychological test usage: Implications for professional psychology. *Professional Psychology: Research and Practice, 31*, 141–154.

Cardalda, E. B. (1995). *Socio-cognitive correlates to school achievement using the TEMAS (Tell-Me-A-Story) culturally sensitive test with sixth, seventh and eighth grade*. Unpublished doctoral dissertation, The New School for Social Research, New York.

Cardalda, E. B. (2002–2005). *Evaluation of the effectiveness of narrative techniques in the assessment of mental disorders symptomatology and coping skills of Hispanic children at high risk of mental disorders*, National Center on Minority Health and Health Disparities (Grant Number- 1 R24 MD00152–01).

Cardalda, E., B., Costantino, G., León-Velázquez, M., Jiménez-Suárez, V., Martínez, J. V., & Ortiz-Vargas, N. (2005). Comparing the TEMAS projective/narrative test with the BASC self report measure in Hispanic students. Carlos Albizu University, San Juan Puerto Rico.

Cardalda, E. B., Costantino, G., Jimenez-Suarez, V., Leon-Velazquez, M. Martinez, J. V., & Perez, M. (2005, August). *Cross cultural comparisons with the TEMAS test using group versus individual methodology*. Poster presented at 114th annual convention of the American Psychological Association, Washington, DC.

Cardalda, E. B., Costantino, G., Sayers, S., Machado, W., & Guzmán, L. (2002). Use of TEMAS with patients referred for sexual abuse: Case studies of Puerto Rican children. *Revista Puertorriqueña de Psicología; Asociación de Psicología de Puerto Rico, (13)*, 167–183.

Cardalda, E. B., Quintero, N., Costantino, G., & Malgady, R. (2000, August). *The development of achievement motivation among Hispanic students*. Poster presented at the 107th annual convention of the American Psychological Association, Boston, MA.

Cardalda, E. B., Santiago-Negrón, S., & Costantino, G. (1999, July). *Cross-cultural achievement motivation in Hispanic, African American, and Anglo Children, as measured by TEMAS*. Paper presented at the 6th European Congress of Psychology, Rome, Italy.

Cornabuci, C. (2000). *Relationship between aggression and interpersonal relations in 7 and 8 years old Italian children*. Unpublished dissertation, Universita di Roma "La Sapienza," Rome, Italy.

Costantino, G. (1978, November). *Preliminary report on TEMAS: A new thematic apperception test to assess ego functions in ethnic minority children*. Paper presented at the Second American Conference on Fantasy and the Imaging Process, Chicago, IL.

Costantino, G. (1987). *TEMAS (Tell-Me-A-Story) test cards*. Los Angeles: Western Psychological Services.

Costantino, G. (2000). Development of the Asian-American version of TEMAS. Brooklyn NY: American Multicultural Institute.

Costantino, G., Dupertuis, D.G., Castillo, A., & Faiola, T. (2004, August). *A comparison of TEMAS scores of Peruvian and Argentinean children*. Paper presented at the 113th annual convention of the American Psychological Association, Honolulu, Hawaii.

Costantino, G., Flanagan, R., & Malgady, R. G. (2001). Narrative assessment: TAT, CAT and TEMAS. In L. Suzuki, J. Ponterotto, & P. Meller (Eds.), *Handbook of multicultural assessment* (2nd ed.,). San Francisco: Jossey-Bass.

Costantino, G., Flanagan, & Tsui, E. (2001). Clinical utility of the Asian-American version of TEMAS. Brooklyn, NY: Sunset Park Mental Health Center.

Costantino, G., & Malgady, R. (2000). Multicultural and cross-cultural utility of TEMAS (Tell-Me-A-Story) Test. In R.H. Dana (Ed.), *Handbook of cross-cultural/multicultural personality assessment*. Hillsdale, NJ: Lawrence Erlbaum Associates.

Costantino, G., Dupertuis, D. G., Castillo, Malgady, R.G., & Faiola, T, (1997, July). Cross-cultural standardization of TEMAS with Argentinean and Peruvian children. ICP Cross-Cultural Conference, Padua, Italy.

Costantino, G., Malgady R., Colon-Malgady, G., & Bailey, J. (1992). Clinical utility of the TEMAS with nonminority children. *Journal of Personality Assessment, 59*(3), 433–438.

Costantino, G., Malgady, R., Casullo, M., & Castillo, A. (1991). Cross-cultural standardization of TEMAS in three Hispanic subcultures. *Hispanic Journal of Behavioral Sciences, 13*, 48–62.

Costantino, G., Malgady, R. G., & Rogler, L. H (1988). *Technical manual: The TEMAS, thematic apperception test*. Los Angeles: Western Psychological Services.

Costantino, G., Malgady, R. G., Rogler, L. H., & Tsui, E. (1988). Discriminant analysis of clinical outpatients and public schools children by TEMAS: A thematic apperception test for Hispanics and Blacks. *Journal of Personality Assessment, 52*, 670–678.

Costantino, G., & Malgady, R. G. (1983). Verbal fluency of Hispanic, Black and White children on a new thematic apperception test for urban minority children. *Hispanic Journal of Behavioral Sciences, 5*, 199–206.

Costantino, G., Malgady, R. G., & Vazquez, C. (1981). Comparing Murray's TAT to a new thematic apperception test for urban ethnic minority children. *Hispanic Journal of Behavioral Sciences, 3*, 291–300.

Cross, S. E., & Gore, J. S. (2003). Cultural models of the self. In M. R. Leary & J. P. Tangney (Eds.), *Handbook of self and identity* (pp. 536–564). New York: Guilford.

Dana, R. H. (1986). Personality assessment and Native Americans. *Journal of Personality Assessment, 50*, 480–500.

Dana, R. H. (1993). *Multicultural assessment perspectives for professional psychology.* Boston: Allyn & Bacon.

Dana, R. H. (1996). Culturally competent assessment practice in the United States. *Journal of Personality Assessment, 66*, 472–487.

Dana, R. H. (1998). *Understanding cultural identity in intervention and assessment.* Thousand Oaks, CA: Sage.

Dana, R. H. (2000). Multicultural assessment of child and adolescent personality and psychopathology. In A. L. Comunian & U. Gielen (Eds.), *International perspectives on human development* (pp. 233–258). Lengerich, Germany: Pabst Science Publishers.

Dana, R. H. (2003). Assessment training, practice, and research in the new millennium: Challenges and opportunities for professional psychology. *Ethical Human Sciences and Services, 5(2)*, 127–140.

Dana, R. H. (2005). *Multicultural assessment principles, applications, and examples.* Mahwah, NJ: Lawrence Erlbaum Associates.

Dupertuis, D. G., & Ropaldo, M. (2001, August). *Differences and similarities between Argentinean and North American children.* Poster presented at the 111th APA Convention, San Francisco, CA.

Dupertuis , D. G., Silva Arancibia, V., Pais, E., Fernandez, C., & Rodino, V. (2004). Similarities and differences in TEMAS test functions in Argentinean and European-American children. *Universidad de Buenos Aires – Argentina.*

Elliot, T. L. (1998). *Differential validation of the TEMAS (Tell-Me-A-Story) with Rorschach as criterion: A comparison of projective methods.* Unpublished doctoral dissertation. Long Island University, N.Y

Exner, J. E. & Weiner, I. B. (1982). *The Rorschach: A comprehensive system: vol. 3. Assessment of children and adolescents.* New York: John Wiley & Sons.

Exner, J. E. & Weiner, I. B. (1995). The Rorschach: A comprehensive system: vol. 3. Assessment of children and adolescents (2nd Ed.) New York: John Wiley & Sons.

Fagulha, T., & Dana, R. H. (1997). Professional psychology in Portugal. *Psychological Reports, 82*, 1211–1222.

Fantini, F. (2005). Risvolti teorici e applicativi in contesto multiculturale [New Theoretical and Applied Developments in Multicultural Context]. Unpublished dissertation, Facoltà Psicologia, Università Cattolica del Sacro Cuore di Milano, Milan, Italy.

Fiorentino, L., & Howe, N. (2004). Language competence, narrative ability, and school readiness in low-income preschool children. *Canadian Journal of Behavioural Science, 36*, 280–294.

Flanagan, R. (1995). A review of the Behavior Assessment System for Children (BASC): Assessment consistent with the requirements of the individuals with disabilities education act (IDEA). *Journal of School Psychology, 33,* 177–186.

Flanagan, R. (1999) Objective and projective personality assessment. The TEMAS and the Behavior Assessment System for Children, self report of personality. *Psychological Reports, 48,* 865–867.

Flanagan, R., & DiGiuseppe, R. (1999). A critical review of the TEMAS: A step within the development of thematic apperception instruments. *Psychology in the Schools. 36(1),* 1–10.

Flanagan, R., Losapio, G., Costantino, G., Greenfeld, R., & Hernandez, A. (2004, July). *The use of narratives to assess children's social problem solving skills.* Paper presented at the 113th American Psychological Association, Honolulu, Hawaii.

Henry, W. E. (1947). The thematic apperception technique in the study of culture-personality relations. *Genetic Psychology Monographs, 35,* 501–35.

Hollingshead, A.B., (1957). Two factor index of social position. In A. B. Hollingshead and F. C. Redlich (Eds.) (1958) *Social Class and Mental Illness.* (pp. 398–407). New York; John Wiley & Sons.

Hyde, J. S. (1990). Meta-analysis and the psychology of gender differences. *Journal of Women in Culture and Society, 16,* 55–73.

Lazarus, R. S., & Folkman, S. (1984). *Stress, appraisal and coping process.* New York: McGraw-Hill.

Leary, M. R., & Tangney, J. P. (2003). *Handbook of self and identity.* New York: Guilford.

Lilienfeld, S. O., Lynn, S. & Lohr, J. M. (2003). *Science and pseudoscience in psychology.* New York: Guilford.

Lindzey, G., & Heinemann, S. H. (1955). Thematic Apperception Test: Individual and group administration. *Journal of Personality, 24,* 34–55.

Malgady, R. G. (1996). The question of cultural bias in assessment and diagnosis of ethnic minority clients: Let's reject the null hypothesis. *Professional Psychology: Research and Practice, 27,* 1–5.

Malgady, R. G. Costantino, G., & Rogler, L. H. (1984). Development of a thematic apperception test (TEMAS) for urban Hispanic children. *Journal of Consulting and Clinical Psychology, 52,* 986–996.

Malgady, R. G., Rogler, L. H. & Costantino, G. (1987). Ethnocultural and linguistic bias in mental health evaluation of Hispanics. *American Psychologist, 42,* 228–234.

Malgady, R. G., Rogler, L. H., & Costantino, G. (1988). Reply to the empirical basis for ethnocultural and linguistic bias in mental health evaluations of Hispanics. *American Psychologist, 43,* 1097

Magnussen, D. (2000). The individual as the organizing principle in psychological inquiry: A holistic approach. In *Developmental science and the holistic approach* L. R. Bergman, L.-G. Nilsson & L. Nystedt (Eds), (pp. 33–47). Mahwah, NJ: Lawrence Erlbaum Associates.

Mc Arthur, D. S., & Roberts, G. E. (1982). *Technical manual: The Roberts Apperception Test for Children.* Los Angeles: Western Psychological Services.

Monopoli, J. (1984). *A culture-specific interpretation of thematic test protocols for American Indians.* Unpublished master's thesis, University of Arkansas, Fayetteville.

Muniz, J., Prieto, G., Almeida, L., & Bertram, D. (1999). Test use in Spain, Portugal, and Latin American countries. *European Journal of Psychological Assessment, 15,* 151–157.

Murray, H.A. (1943). *Thematic Apperception Test Manual.* Cambridge, MA: Harvard University Press.

Padilla, A. M., & Medina, A. (1996). Using test in culturally appropriate ways. In L. A. Suzuki, P. J. Meller, & J. G. Ponterotto (Eds.), *Handbook of multicultural assessment: Clinical, psychological, and educational applications* (pp. 3–28). San Francisco: Jossey-Bass.

Piotrowski, C. (1999). Assessment practices in the era of managed care: Current status and future directions. *Psychological Assessment, 7,* 787–796.

Radloff, L. S. (1977). The CES-D Scale: A self-report depression scale for research in the general population. *Journal of Applied Psychological Measures, 1*(3) 385–401.

Reynolds, C. R., & Kamphaus, R. W. (1992). *Technical Manual: Behavior Assessment System for children.* Circle Pines, MN: American Guidance Services.

Ritzler, B. (1993). A new slant on an old theme. *Journal of Psychoeducational Assessment, 11,* 381–389.

Ritzler, B. (1997), Projective methods for multicultural personality assessment: Rorschach, TEMAS, and the Early Memories Procedures. In L.A. Suzuki, P. J. Meller, & J. G. Ponterotto (Eds.), *Handbook of multicultural assessment: Clinical, psychological, and educational applications* (pp. 115–135). San Francisco: Jossey-Bass.

Sardi, G. M. (2000) *Relationship between aggression and cognitive functions in conflict resolution in 7 and 8 years old Italian children.* Unpublished dissertation, Universita di Roma "La Sapienza," Rome, Italy.

Snyder, C. R., & Lopez, S. J. (2003). *Positive psychological assessment: Handbook of models and measures.* Washington, DC: American Psychological Association.

Spielberger, C. D., Edwards, C. D., Lushene, R. E., Montuori, J., Platzek, D. (1973). State-Trait Anxiety Inventory for Children (STAIC). Palo Alto, CA: Consulting sychologists Press. CA: Mind Garden.

Sulfaro, C. (2000). *Relationship between aggression and moral judgment.* Unpublished dissertation, Universita di Roma "La Sapienza", Rome, Italy

Summo, B. (2000). *Relationship between aggression and emotional functions in conflict resolution of 7 and 8 years old children.* Unpublished dissertation, Universita di Roma "La Sapienza," Rome, Italy.

Teglasi, H. (1998). Assessment of schema and problem-solving strategies with projective techniques. In A. S. Bellack and A. M. Hersen (Eds.), *Comprehensive clinical psychology* (pp. 439–499). New York: Pergamon.

Thompson, C. E. (1949). The Thompson modification of the Thematic Apperception Test. *Journal of Projective Techniques, 15,* 469–478.

Vane, J. R. (1981). The Thematic Apperception Test: A review. *Clinical Psychology Review*, 1, 319–336.

Walton, J. R., Nuttall, R. L., & Vazquez-Nuttall, E. (1997). The impact of war on the mental health of children: A Salvadoran study. *Child Abuse & Neglect, 21*, 737–749.

Walton, J. R., Nuttall, R. L., & Vazquez-Nuttall, E. (1998, August) Effects of war on children's motivation reflected in TEMAS stories. In G. Costantino (Chair), *Multiculturalism/cross-cultural motivation as assessed by TAT and TEMAS.* Symposium presented at the 106th annual APA convention, San Francisco, CA.

Williams, R. L. (1983). *Themes for Blacks.* St. Louis, MO: Williams & Associates.

Wood, J. M., Nezworski, M. T., Lilienfeld, S. O., & Garb, H. N. (2003). *What's wrong with the Rorschach? Science confronts the controversial inkblot test.* San Francisco, CA: Jossey-Bass.

Yang, C-M, Kuo, H., Costantino, G. (2003, July). *Validity of Asian TEMAS in Taiwanese children: Preliminary results.* Paper presented at the VII European Congress of Psychology, Vienna, Austria.

CLINICAL UTILITY OF
TEMAS: CASE STUDIES

The following five brief chapters exemplify the clinical utility of TEMAS by illustrating several clinical cases (i.e., European American, Hispanic/Latino, Asian American, Diverse Cross-Cultural, and African American and Latino Forensic) representing culturally and linguistically diverse children and adolescents.

The clinical interpretation of projective/narrative stories, as well as responses to other projective techniques, have generally been associated with psychodynamic theory. This practice may not be acceptable to clinicians who do not share this theoretical orientation (e.g., Flanagan, 2002) or may be deemed invalid because of failure to rely on a sound psychometric scoring system (e.g., Dana, 1993, 1998, 2000, 2001a, 2001b).

Clinicians in general and psychologists in particular should be informed about the validity of test results so that they will not use invalid test scores and thus generate erroneous clinical judgment and develop individual treatment plans that may be contraindicated and potentially dangerous for clients. The use of valid psychological test scores is important for making clinical and forensic practices more effective and less prone to malpractice (Garb, Wood, Lilienfeld, & Nezworski, 2002), and more cost effective because it focuses and shortens the therapeutic process.

The psychometric properties of the TEMAS test have been empirically validated by several studies. The validity and reliability of the minority version was investigated by administering TEMAS to 73 public school and 210 clinic Puerto Rican children of low socioeconomic status in Grades K–6 (Malgady, Costantino, & Rogler, 1984). TEMAS scoring for personality, cognitive, and affective functions indicated internal consistency and interrater reliability, and TEMAS indices significantly discriminated between public school and clinical samples.

Another study investigated TEMAS clinical utility in discriminating between public school and clinical Hispanic and Black children (Costantino,

Malgady, Rogler, & Tsui, 1988). The examinees were 100 outpatients at psychiatric centers and 373 public school students from low SES, inner city families. These participants were tested individually by examiners of the same race/ethnicity. The TEMAS profiles significantly discriminated between the two groups ($p < .001$) and explained 21% of the variance independently of race/ethnicity, age, and SES. Classification accuracy, based on the discriminant function, was 89%. The TEMAS profiles interacted with ethnicity, and better discrimination was evident for Hispanics than African Americans.

Attention deficit hyperactivity disorder (ADHD) is regarded as being relatively common among school-age children, although the literature reveals a number of confounding factors with standard assessment for this disorder. Attention deficit was examined by using TEMAS to measure attention to pictorial stimuli depicting characters, events, settings, and covert psychological conflicts (Costantino, Colon-Malgady, Malgady, & Perez, 1991). This study was conducted with 152 normal and 95 clinical Hispanic, Black, and White school-age children. The ADHD children were significantly more likely than normal children to omit information contained in the stimuli about characters, events, settings, and psychological conflicts. Differences between these groups were large and persistent in the presence of structured inquiries made by the test examiners. These results suggested the potential utility of structured narrative techniques for assessment of ADHD and eventually to facilitate DSM-IV diagnosis, although users are also invited to give closer scrutiny to carefully controlled validity studies.

Cross-cultural standardization of TEMAS in three diverse Hispanic cultures compared the normative profiles, the reliability, and the criterion-related validity of TEMAS with school and clinical children from three different Hispanic cultures: Puerto Ricans in New York City; natives of San Juan, Puerto Rico; and South Americans in Buenos Aires, Argentina (Costantino, Malgady, Casullo, & Castillo, 1991). In this study, children in New York and Puerto Rico were administered 23 minority TEMAS cards, the Spielberger Trait-Anxiety Scale for Children, and the Piers-Harris Children's Self-Concept Scale. The Argentinean children were administered the nonminority short form consisting of nine TEMAS cards and the Piers-Harris Scale. The results of the study supported the use of TEMAS with examinees in the three cultures; it also suggested that the original TEMAS Card 15 was biased toward Argentinean children.

Bias was suggested because the original Card 15 depicted "a policeman awarding a group of P. A. L. baseball players and a policeman arresting a group of three boys and one girl who have broken a window and stolen merchandise." These Argentinean children scored lower than the other two Hispanic groups in Moral Judgment because the team of children playing baseball was also perceived as responsible for thievery. Analysis of these results indicated that the Argentinean children tended to perceive the baseball players as young thieves because the presence of the policeman as a P. A. L. coach suggested a punitive agent due to experience of these children during the military regime. The presence of a policeman among a group of young baseball players motivated these children to reason that because a policeman was present, the children must also have stolen the award. Card 15 also may be perceived as culturally inappropriate because soccer and not baseball is the national sport in Argentina. This card in the nonminority version was subsequently modified to show a coach giving awards to a group of soccer players.

The validity of the nonminority version for discriminating between public school ($n = 49$) and outpatient ($n = 36$) samples of White examinees from inner city, low to lower middle SES, largely female-headed households, has also been examined (Costantino, Malgady, Colon-Malgady, & Bailey, 1992). TEMAS profiles significantly discriminated between the normal functioning and clinical groups ($p < .001$), with 86% classification accuracy.

The appropriateness of projective/narrative instruments utilized with ethnic/racial minority populations is scarce, and traditionally such research has overlooked acculturation issues. Bernal (1991) investigated cultural competence and emic validity by describing the relationship between acculturation level in the Robert's Apperception Test for Children (RATC) and TEMAS, two popular narrative tests. The participants were 40 Mexican American and European-American children, 24 females and 16 males, in Grades 4 through 7 who were between the ages of 10 and 12. This study utilized a nonexperimental cross-sectional design to test seven research hypotheses. The Vineland Adaptive Behavior Scales Survey Form Classroom Edition was utilized to define examinee wellness-adjustment, and the System of Multicultural Pluralistic Assessment (SOMPA) Urban Acculturation Scale was utilized to define acculturation level. Results showed that TEMAS was more culturally sensitive in assessing Mexican Americans than the RATC, although both the RAT-C and the TEMAS seemed to be valid instruments for assessing personality functioning among European-American children.

Other recent studies, as reported in chapter 7, show the clinical utility of the three versions of TEMAS cross-culturally in Argentina, Italy, Puerto Rico, and Taiwan.

The TEMAS test has been developed to resolve the TAT paradox. Murray (1943) emphasized that the thematic apperception characters needed to be ambiguous and dissimilar from the storyteller in such a way that the defensive system could be easily deceived so that the individual could reveal the "unconscious conflicts." But at the same time, the clinical validity of a TAT story is based on the identification of the storyteller with the characters in the pictures. In the tradition of Thompson (1949), the TEMAS has proven that the congruence between storyteller and picture characters fosters identification between the storyteller and the test characters; and thus increases the validity and clinical utility of TEMAS with culturally diverse individuals.

The following culturally diverse cases exemplify the clinical validity of the test. Chapter 8 shows the clinical utility of the non-minority version in assessing a 12-year-old European American adolescent, whose psychiatric evaluation misguided the treatment plan; the results of the TEMAS test pointed out a more appropriate diagnosis of major depression and revealed several strengths, thus redirecting the treatment plan to a positive treatment outcome. Chapter 9 reports the case of a 9-year-old Latino youngster who was given a diagnosis of ADHD (Attention Deficit Hyperactivity Disorder), based on the presenting problems, that dictated an erroneous treatment. Conversely, the TEMAS minority version results gave a more appropriate diagnosis of generalized anxiety disorders, which changed the treatment plan and resulted in a positive treatment outcome. Chapter 10 reports the case of a 14-year-old Chinese American adolescent, whose results of the Asian American version gave a more accurate personality profile than the results of the nonminority (American) version of the test. This chapter also reports the clinical utility and concurrent validity of TEMAS in assessing a nine-year-old Chinese American boy referred to a mental health clinic because of poor school achievement, short attention span, and constant playing with electronic games. Chapter 11 illustrates the utility and the cross-cultural validity of both the minority and nonminority version of TEMAS in describing the clinical profiles of three Latina youngsters in Argentina, Italy, and Puerto Rico. Chapter 12 shows the cultural competence and clinical utility of the minority version in accurately assessing the cognitive, affective, and personality function of a Latino adolescent and Black youngster forensic cases. It is important to note that all cases reported in Chapters 8, 9, 10, 11, and 12 record the TEMAS inquiries in different formats. All of the various formats are acceptable because they satisfy the TEMAS standard structured inquiries administration.

REFERENCES

Bernal, I. (1991). *The relationship between level of acculturation, the Robert's Apperception Test for Children, and the TEMAS (Tell-Me-A-Story)*. Unpublished doctoral dissertation, California School of Professional Psychology, Los Angeles.

Costantino, G., Colon-Malgady, G., Malgady, R. G., & Perez, A. (1991). Assessment of attention deficit disorder using a thematic apperception test. *Journal of Personality Assessment, 57,* 87–95.

Costantino, G., Malgady, R. G., Casullo, M. M., & Castillo, A. (1991). Cross-cultural standardization of TEMAS in three Hispanic subcultures. *Hispanic Journal of Behavioral Sciences, 13,* 48–62.

Costantino, G. , Malgady, R. G., Colon-Malgady, G., & Bailey, J. (1992). Clinical utility of the TEMAS with non-minority children. *Journal of Personality Assessment, 59,* 433–438.

Costantino, G., Malgady, R. G., Rogler, L. H., & Tsui, E. (1988). Discriminant analysis of clinical outpatients and public school children by TEMAS: A thematic apperception test for Hispanics and Blacks. *Journal of Personality Assessment, 52,* 670–678.

Dana, R. H. (1993). *Multicultural assessment perspectives for professional psychology.* Boston: Allyn & Bacon.

Dana, R. H. (1998). *Understanding cultural identity in intervention and assessment.* Thousand Oaks, CA: Sage.

Dana, R. H. (2000). Multicultural assessment of child and adolescent personality and psychopathology. In A. L. Comunian & U. Gielen (Eds.), *International perspectives on human development* (pp. 233–258). Lengerich, Germany: Pabst Science Publishers.

Dana, R. H. (2001a). Clinical diagnosis of multicultural populations in the United States. In L. Suzuki, J. Ponterotto, & P. Meller (Eds.). *The handbook of multicultural assessment* (2nd ed., pp. 101–131). San Francisco, CA: Jossey-Bass.

Dana, R. H. (2001b). Psychological assessment in diagnosis and treatment of ethnic group members. In J. A. Aponte & J. Wohl (Eds.). *Psychological interventions and cultural diversity.* (2nd ed., pp. 59–74). Boston, MA: Allyn & Bacon.

Flanagan, R. (2002). A review of Essentials of Narrative Assessment with the TAT and other story-telling instruments. *The School Psychologist, 56,* 116-120

Garb, H. N., Wood, J.M., Lilienfeld, S.O., & Nezworski, M.T. (2002) Effective uses of projective techniques in clinical practice: Let the data help with selection and interpretation. *Professional Psychology: Research and Practice, 33(5),* 454–463.

Malgady, R. G., Costantino, G., & Rogler, L. H. (1984). Development of a thematic apperception test (TEMAS) for urban Hispanic children. *Journal of Consulting and Clinical Psychology, 52,* 986–996.

Murray, H. A. (1943). *Thematic Apperception Test Manual.* Cambridge, MA: Harvard University Press.

Thompson, C. E. (1949). The Thompson modification of the Thematic Apperception Test. *Journal of Projective Techniques, 15,* 469–478.

European American Case Study

BACKGROUND

This first clinical case, Kathy, illustrates the utility of TEMAS with respect to differential diagnosis and provides additional clinical information on the youngster's covert behaviors. This female examinee received individual psychotherapy for approximately six months, and the clinician requested psychological testing because the youngster was making very slow therapeutic progress.

CLINICAL UTILITY: EUROPEAN AMERICAN CASE STUDY

Psychological Test Report

Name:	Kathy
Age:	12 years
Date of Evaluation:	October 2004

Examiner:	K. C., M.A.
Language(s) of Examinee:	English
Language of Tests:	English
Collateral Interviews:	Parents. School Principal. Teacher's Report.

Tests Administered:

Wechsler Intelligence Scale for Children-Fourth Edition (WISC-IV)

Rorschach Comprehensive System
Bender–Gestalt Visual Motor Test

House-Tree-Person Projective Drawings
TEMAS (Tell-Me-A-Story) Multicultural Test

Reason for Referral

Kathy was a 12-year-old European American female at the time of testing. She was referred by her therapist for a complete psychological evaluation to assess her cognitive, emotional, and intellectual functioning to assist in treatment planning.

Brief Psychosocial and School History

Kathy was born in New York to Southern European parents. Her father emigrated in 1968 and her mother joined him following their marriage in 1981. According to the parents, the student was born full term following normal pregnancy and delivery. The child achieved all developmental milestones within normal limits. No history of major hospitalizations was reported. She lived with her parents and her two older brothers. Her parents reported that she related well with her brothers despite the age difference. The student was attending a private school since kindergarten, and she was in 8th grade at the time of the evaluation. She was one of four girls in a classroom of 25 students.

There were no previous formal psychological evaluations. According to the mother, the student exhibited academic difficulties since the 5th grade, when one of her older brothers stopped helping her with her homework. However, her school grades were reported to be above average, except for mathematics and science, and she passed all of her city-wide standardized tests the previous year. She received private tutoring in mathematics and her mother was in the process of finding her a science tutor.

According to her parents and therapist, Kathy was an extremely shy adolescent who avoided eye contact and had poor interpersonal skills. The parents expressed great concern about her maladaptive social and emotional functioning and related that the student had been shy and withdrawn since childhood, especially toward people outside her family. Nonetheless, the student occasionally did her homework with a female friend and socialized with a second female student. Kathy enjoyed solitary activities such as reading and writing; her favorite books exhibit themes of death and violence. Both of her grandmothers died one month apart in 2002. Kathy was very close with her paternal grandmother.

In order to assess her academic and her psychosocial school functioning, her school principal was interviewed and her three teachers completed the Child Behavior Checklist (CBCL), following parental consent. The principal reported that the student's grades were in the B+ and A levels of academic achievement; however, he expressed several concerns about Kathy's overt school behavior and socio-emotional functioning. In particular, the principal reported that the student "appears to have difficulty relating to her classmates and to most teachers despite numerous efforts on their behalf to engage her in activities." Furthermore, he described the student "as a very shy, withdrawn, ashamed about her boy image, harboring a lot of anger and emotionally distressed child who seems to repress her feelings ... who shows emotional meltdowns which often result in her fleeing situations and running abruptly out of the classroom." He also indicated she was unwilling to share her experiences and to interact with others because, when she was forced to respond, she often replied, "What's the use? No one cares." In addition, the principal reported he had noticed that she "sometimes squats in a ball-like position as if to protect herself or presses her body up against the wall when reprimanded as if in an effort to disappear." He verbalized great interest in helping the student because she had great academic potential and he was willing to continue providing additional information.

The overall results of the CBCL completed by her three teachers indicated that the student exhibited clinically significant Internalizing Problems, especially in regard to withdrawn behavior, high levels of anxiety and depression that fell in the borderline clinical range, social problems, and aggressive behavior.

Behavioral Observations

Kathy was an attractive, slender, and tall Caucasian female. She tended to avoid eye contact and spoke very softly; at times, her words were inaudible, and she was urged to repeat them. Her mother escorted her to the evaluation. She appeared very well groomed and wore her corrective glasses during the testing. During the first testing session, the student was guarded, reluctantly answered questions, and when asked to draw figures, she turned her body away from the examiner, hid her drawings from sight, and then handed them in. When asked to tell a story about the drawings, she spoke in a very low tone. When asked to repeat her answers, she would quickly verbalize in a somewhat low voice or state that she had forgotten what she had said. However, in the subsequent sessions, the student began to establish a rapport with the examiner. Her interest in the testing was minimal, as she kept asking when the sessions would end. Nonetheless, she seemed interested in knowing if her answers were correct. Her overall attention span was somewhat adequate; but her testing had to be reduced to 90 minutes because of her poor stress tolerance. She coped with difficult items by frequently expressing and by criticizing tasks as being "stupid," "ugly," and "boring," or by saying, "I don't know." Following encouragement, the student was able to complete the tasks at hand to the best of her ability.

During the TEMAS narrative test, the student was *extremely* verbal and in fact stated that "I could go on and on and on if I wanted to" about any particular story. She approached the task of storytelling with what appeared to be enthusiasm in comparison to her previous sessions. However, both her enthusiasm and interest in storytelling waned rapidly after one third of the test was complete. Interestingly, this did not seem to affect the length of her stories, which were all very lengthy. The storytelling task motivated the student to become more verbal outside the testing situation when she told the examiner in minute details and with pressured speech of a fiction book she was reading on the journeys of a princess who encounters great hardship and dragon-slayers in a forest.

Intellectual Functioning

The Wechsler Intelligence Scale for Children—Fourth Edition was administered over three testing sessions because she became easily fatigued and showed limited interest. The student's overall functioning was in the Average range of intelligence. The majority of her index scores (i.e., Verbal Comprehension, Working Memory, and Processing Speed) were all within normal limits with the exception of her score for the Perceptual Reasoning Index (PRI), which fell in the Low Average range. The student's PRI score indicated that her nonverbal and/or verbal concrete and abstract information skills were less developed than her peers.

Intersubtest scores revealed that the majority of her performance subtests fell within normal limits with a few exceptions. Specifically, scores in verbal reasoning and concept formation tasks were identified as a weakness and fell in the Borderline/Marginal range of functioning. Conversely, her scores on a task measuring understanding of social conventions placed her in the High Average range. Because of the high scatter between the intersubtest scores, it possible that her index score for Verbal Comprehension may not be an adequate indicator of her overall ability to comprehend orally presented material.

Lack of homogeneity of subtest scores was also found in Processing Speed Index, suggesting that her scores on related subtests may not be an adequate indicator of her overall ability to rapidly process visual material. In particular, the student's performance on a task involving cognitive flexibility, visual memory, visual–motor coordination, processing speed, and visual discrimination and concentration fell within the High Average range. Her performance on a different processing speed task that relies on more graphomotor skill and endurance was found to be within normal limits. This is supported by her performance on a supplemental test of processing speed of visual stimuli that fell in the Mildly Impaired range. Overall, these findings indicated that the student seemed to have the ability to learn through perceptual organization and planning, but these results may have been associated with her lack of interest and poor motivation to achieve.

In the supplemental subtest administered, her performance on tasks that measured fund of knowledge and computational skills fell within the Average range; and her performance on tasks that measured her verbal deductive ability fell in the Low Average range. In addition, her ability to visually recognize essential details of objects also placed her in the Low Average range. This finding was also confirmed by her Low Average performance on a core subtest that measures perceptual organization and involves more concrete visual–motor coordination.

The Bender–Gestalt Visual Motor Test

On the Bender–Gestalt, the student obtained an error score of 6, according to the Koppitz scoring system, which corresponds to a chronological age 7–0 to 7–5 age-equivalent visual motor coordination maturation thus indicating a lag in visual motor development. However, some of her errors seemed to be associated with carelessness and haste in completing the task. Nonetheless, utilization of space indicated fairly good planning and organizational skills; her short-term visual memory in design recall fell within the average range. In fact, she recalled 6 of 9 designs.

House-Tree-Person

The drawings of the House-Tree-Person test, while somewhat inadequately drawn for her age, also showed the human figure drawn as angry, fearful/confused, and devoid of details; the tree was drawn simplistically and far away from both the person and the house. However, the house was drawn in relatively more detail. Her responses to questions about each drawing were spare and ineloquent. It is important to note that these drawings were completed during her first testing session when she appeared to be the most guarded and least motivated of all testing sessions.

Test Results: Personality Functioning

Rorschach Comprehensive System (CS)

The results of the Rorschach CS (Interpretation Assistance Program Interpretative Report) indicated that Kathy clinically "may be susceptible to episodes of affective disturbance which are likely to involve features of depression." In the area of coping with stress, results indicated that she seemed to lack a consistent coping style as she alternates between expressive and ideational ways in dealing with situations. Her vacillating style tended to reduce her usual level of effectiveness in making decisions. However, she seemed to have "the potential to cope with the demands being imposed on her by internal and external life events." In the area of cognitive functioning, the student "exhibits serious difficulty in thinking logically and coherently and is less capable than her peers to understand relationship between events." In the area of interpersonal functioning, she exhibited oppositional behavior, which seemed to be associated with underlying feelings of anger and resentment toward people and the world in general. She appeared to show low self-esteem and poor self-confidence. Although she showed much interest in other people, she had limited abilities establishing and maintaining adaptive interpersonal relationships. She also had limited abilities to identify with real people in her life; instead, she seemed to identify with imaginary figures and people who were not regular parts of her life. In the area of reality testing, she had abilities to perceive events in a conventional manner and to interpret actions and intentions of others in an accurate manner. However, she used unconventional ways to perceive people and events; consequently, at times, she acted in idiosyncratic ways without caring about the consequences of her behavior.

TEMAS Multicultural Test (Nonminority Version)

On the TEMAS test, when compared with a 12-year-old Caucasian girl, the student scored within the high average to low average range in the Cognitive functions, overall. More specifically, she scored within the low average range in Reaction Time, indicating that she responded quite rapidly in integrating visual stimuli into lengthy and meaningful stories ($T = 42$). In addition, she scored within the extremely high average in

Total Time ($T = 71$), and within the extremely high average in Fluency ($T = 70$), thus showing excellent verbal ability. It is important to note that her verbal ability in the WISC-IV test was generally below average; however, in the TEMAS, the student was verbally extremely productive and spent a great deal of time in elaborating themes, and narrated excellent stories correct in both grammar and syntax. On the other hand, she scored above the 90 percentile cutoff point in resolving the Conflict depicted in the cards, thus showing poor problem-solving skills; it needs to be clarified that she was able to recognize the conflict, but she did not have adaptive cognitive and psychosocial skills to resolve them. In the Personality Functions, she scored within the deficient to the low average range overall. More specifically, the student scored within the deficient average in Interpersonal Relations ($T = 28$), which corresponds to the 1st percentile; within the moderately deficient range in Aggression ($T = 28$), which also corresponds to a 1st percentile; deficient in Coping with Anxiety and Depression ($T = 20$), which also corresponds to a 1st percentile and suggests a symptomatology of major depression. She also scored within the borderline range in Sexual Identity ($T = 37$), which corresponds to a 2nd percentile, Moral Judgment ($T = 30$), and Reality Testing ($T = 32$), which corresponds to a 2nd percentile. However, Kathy scored within the low average category in Self-Concept of Competence ($T = 49$), which fell within the 49th percentile, within the low average category in Delay Gratification ($T = 40$), which fell within the 16th percentile, and within the averange range in Achievement Motivation ($T = 46$), which fell within the 46th percentile. The student scored within average range in "Happy" ($T = 50$), within very high average range in "Sad" ($T = 64$), which corresponds to a 88th percentile, within high average in "Angry" ($T = 60$), which corresponds to a 84th percentile, and within the extremely high average in "Fearful" ($T = 70$) that corresponds to a 98th percentile. These scores indicate Kathy was prone to experience difficulties with the environment and in interpersonal relations. In addition, she showed maladaptive coping skills in dealing with anxiety and depression-provoking situations, as well as a much higher likelihood of interacting less maturely and more aggressively than might be expected for a youngster of this age.

Perseverative themes across Kathy's stories included those of extremely high levels of interpersonal difficulties, aggression, anxiety, and depression. Her stories depicted main characters that felt fearful, had difficulty relating to others, or were very competitive and aggressed upon as a result of jealousy, competitiveness, or punishment. Kathy's extremely competitive and fearful worldview was particularly evident in her response to Card 10 that depicts only one character in front of a piggy bank thinking about buying ice cream or saving money to buy a bike. In response to this picture, Kathy told two stories. In the first one, she wanted both the ice cream and the bike, bought the ice cream, and in the afternoon, she sold lemonade, made some money, and went to buy the bike at the urging of "a mystery man" "who came from nowhere" and she bought the bike. Subsequently, she entered a bike race and, as she was leading the group of bikers to victory, the mystery man enters the story as a bike racer competing with her; but he took a short cut through the woods in order to be first at the finish line . . . However, he was seen cheating and the girl won the race. Kathy's competitiveness appeared to reflect her strong motivation to achieve; however, her maladaptive psychosocial skills and poor reality testing made her fall short of achieving her goals in real life and at the same time caused further conflict in her interpersonal relations.

The student's poor body image and maladaptive perception of her sexual identity was evidenced by her deficient score in self-sexual identity. In the story in response to Card 22, the student described the main character, a girl looking at the mirror and seeing a composite face of a boy and a girl, as someone who became permanently disfigured following a vicious assault by her peers. She described this main character as becoming "the ugliest person in the world" who was destined to never leave her home due to her irreparable disfigurement and societal rejection. In addition, Kathy's difficulties relating to others and the environment appeared to be further complicated by her unconventional way of viewing the world and her selfish manner of relating to others. Specifically, her score in Reality Testing fell in the borderline range, indicating a very maladaptive ability to distinguish fantasy from reality; and her deficient score in Moral Judgment also indicated a difficulty with understanding right from wrong and acting appropriately. In summary, it appears that the student had difficulty anticipating the consequences of her behavior due to her maladaptive perceptions and worldviews.

In contrast, Kathy scored within the average range for self-concept. That is, she appeared to realistically perceive her competence in psychosocial, academic, and/or intellectual domains of functioning. In addition, her ability to delay gratification in order to meet a future goal was found to be in the low average range, and her desire to achieve in school and in competitive sports was within the average range. These scores indicated relative strengths in the area of self-concept of competence, and very relative strengths in her ability to delay gratification and her desire to achieve. These relative strengths partly redeem her serious weaknesses in the other personality functions.

In the Affective Functions, Kathy scored within the average range in attributing "happy feeling" ($T = 50$), within the very high average range in attributing "angry" feelings ($T = 60$), and within the very high range in "Sad" feelings ($T = 64$), and extremely high average "Fearful' feelings ($T = 70$). These emotional indicators, taken together with the low and extremely low score in personality functions, especially in the area of interpersonal relations, aggression, and anxiety/depression, suggest a diagnostic impression of *Depressive Disorder Not Otherwise Specified (Nos)* on Axis I and possibly, *Borderline Personality* on Axis II.

Summary
Kathy was an attractive 12-year-old Caucasian adolescent who was referred by her therapist for assessment of her personality and intellectual functioning in order to make recommendations for treatment and possible educational placement (e.g., private or public high school). The student attended the 8th grade in a regular classroom at a private middle school. Her intellectual functioning fell within the low average range of intelligence overall. However, there were indications that she had the potential to function within the upper end of the average range in verbal ability, verbal comprehension and processing speed, as is indicated by the above-average range cognitive scores in the TEMAS test. Furthermore, her school achievement was within the above-average range; her school grades were in the B+ to A range as reported by her school principal and mother.

The results of the Rorschach CS and TEMAS indicated that the student presented features of clinical depression. However, the TEMAS results in Personality Functions suggested a more complete diagnosis of *Depressive Disorder (NOS)* on Axis I and possibly, *Borderline Personality* on Axis II. In addition, she exhibited poor interpersonal skills, limited abilities in coping skills and problem-solving skills. Also, she showed very poor reality testing, although she had the potential to perceive her world in a realistic manner. She also showed inadequate sexual identity, very poor control of aggressive ideation, and very poor ability to distinguish right from wrong. Whereas results in the Rorschach CS indicated that she exhibited serious difficulties in thinking logically and coherently, the TEMAS results indicated that she showed high cognitive abilities in storytelling verbal fluency, story content, and story temporal sequencing. In addition, the TEMAS results identified relative strengths in the area of self-concept of competence, and to a lesser degree in delay gratification and school achievement. The TEMAS results also showed an extremely high score in Fearful, high scores in Sad and Angry, and an average score in Happy; thus showing a positive relationship between the personality functions scores in Aggression, and Anxiety/Depression.

Recommendations

1. Continue in individual psychotherapy to help her develop a meaningful therapeutic alliance, and decrease her feelings of depression and anxiety while enhancing her self-esteem and positive sexual identity. Related issues for therapy also should include exploring her emotional withdrawing and assisting her in thinking through, and fostering skills in problem solving of social interactions and communication. The use of narrative treatment which will utilize her story telling ability and will strongly contribute to her therapeutic progress.
2. Psychiatric evaluation to confirm the diagnostic impression of Depressive Disorder (Nos) and Borderline Personality, and to determine the need for psychotropic medication.
3. Possible family therapy or collateral sessions to assist her parents in gaining a better understanding of their daughter's psychological and psychiatric difficulties and provide them techniques to deal with her and modify her behavior.
4. Possible group psychotherapy with a focus on social skills training concomitant with individual therapy or within six months of individual therapy.
5. Continue remedial tutoring in science and math.
6. Psychological evaluation in one year to assess her progress and inform treatment and planning.
7. Her story telling ability should also be utilized through the technique of Language Experience Chart Method in order to foster more effective communication skills.

Discussion

The utility of psychological tests in general and narrative tests in particular are important for youngsters in order to clarify diagnostic impressions that are usually based on problems presented by parents, significant others, and/or teachers. Children and adolescents are poor informants and often report absence of emotional and/or behavioral problems during clinical evaluations, but they reveal underlying emotional problems in narrative techniques. In addition, narrative techniques usually help the therapist in refocusing the treatment process and identify additional problem areas to be directly addressed in the Individual Treatment

Plan, thus affording the achievement of therapeutic goals and objectives in a relatively short-term intervention (Costantino, Malgady, & Cardalda, 2005; Dana, 2000a, 2000b, 2001).

In this case, the WISC-IV results indicated that the student's IQ fell within the normal range, but noted deficits in tasks of verbal reasoning and concept formation. These results seem accurate in assessing the student's present cognitive and intellectual functioning, which appear to be inhibited by her emotional and behavior problems, thus pointing to a potentially higher intellectual functioning.

The validity of a psychological test rests on the accuracy of the results of the instruments in generating a clinical profile of the examinee and providing sufficient data on the underlying emotional problems in order to give an appropriate diagnostic label of the examinee. However, the predictive validity of tests ultimately rests on the positive relationship between test results obtained from the youngster and the presenting problems provided by her significant others. Both the Rorschach CS and the TEMAS test results pointed out the presence of depression symptoms, maladaptive interpersonal relations, poor sexual identity, limited coping skills in problem-solving situations, maladapative control of aggressive ideation, avoidant behavior, and a need to relate to imaginary individuals. In addition, the TEMAS test revealed a more definite diagnostic impression of Depressive Disorder (NOS) Disorder associated with Depressive Disorder NOS. In addition, the test results showed superior cognitive strengths in perceptual organization, verbal fluency, and temporal sequencing organization.

The student's intake diagnosis, based on the problems presented by her parents, was Selective Mutism. The diagnosis was changed after four therapy sessions by the student's psychotherapist to Social Phobia. After four months of individual therapy, a psychological evaluation was requested by her therapist because the student had made only limited therapeutic progress.

Following the psychological evaluation and specific recommendations, the student underwent a psychiatric evaluation, which confirmed a diagnosis of *Depressive Disorder NOS* with prescription of Risperdal .25 mg once a day at night (for disruptive and impulsive behavior) and Zoloft 25 mg AM for anxiety and depression. In addition, the psychotherapist refocused the treatment, emphasizing a working therapeutic alliance, storytelling as narrative treatment, and cognitive approach in psychosocial problem solving.

The 90-day Treatment Plan Review, completed as of June 2005, revealed that this adolescent had made progress in academic achievement, and personal and psychosocial skills; she graduated from the 8th grade with an 85 plus average and participated with strong interest in all graduation class trips and parties. In addition, she showed an improved body image with a different hair color, she used nail polish, and lipstick, and she wore an attractive minidress.

In summary, the utility of the psychological tests, especially the narrative test, is evident in the therapeutic progress made by the student following the recommendations based on the results of those tests. This case strongly illustrates the effectiveness of TEMAS narrative test as a cost-effective evaluation in the successful treatment of a female adolescent.

TEMAS STORIES

Card 1G

RT   (Reaction Time)   9 sec.
SP   (Spontaneous Time)   4 min.18 sec.
TT   (Total Time)   10 min. 43 sec.
Fluency 260

There was October and it was nice and sunny and they [Question (Q): the girls] thought it would be bad weather but it wasn't. All the kids thought they could go outside and play. And they had a jump rope competition and while there they had got into a fight because two won but 1 was supposed to win. And then one of the mothers came so that they [Q: one of the girls] can send a letter to the mailbox and while one girl was sending the letter she had to cross the street and a car was coming really fast and the girl she was fighting with of the two girls was angry with her and wanted her to get killed by the car and then she realized that's her friend. She ran so that she could go get her to go save her. Then she pushed her and told her to come back and then they had a jump rope competition and they were always friends.

1a: Who are these people? Do they know   They are friends.
each other?

2a: Where are these people?   In a neighborhood.
                                                                     Playing in the middle of
                                                                     the street where no cars
                                                                     come unless it's crazy.

3a: What are these people doing and saying?	You can't beat me. I'm better than you. See who will win the jump rope competition.
4a: What were these people doing before?	They were inside their houses, playing until time to go out.
5a: What will these people do next?	They will try not to get into a fight with each other because they don't want anything to happen.
6a: What is this person [main character] thinking?	[Kathy chose the girl in yellow pointing at the girl who crossed the street and was going to get killed.] I'll win because I'm good.
6b: What is this person [main character] feeling?	She was first happy because she won. Then she was scared because of the car coming and when her friend warned her.

Card 15

RT   8 sec.
SP   9 min.18 sec.
TT   10 min.24 sec.
Fluency 333

What are these people? It was Monday morning in the school and the gym teacher was getting the little kids ready for the soccer tournament. And the soccer tournament was supposed to be on Tuesday and those kids were the best little soccer players around, and then they got ready and played the game and won.

  And while they were playing one of the kids kicked a soccer ball by mistake and it went across the street and broke one of the windows. And then the other team, these kids while no one was looking they went across the street and they took some TVs that were showing in the window across the street that the kids like and they tried to run as fast as they can and one of the kids from the other team saw them and told their coach and the coach told one of the police officers about what happened and the Police Officer started screaming at the kids [Q: which kids?] the ones who stole the TVs. And the kids tried to run away from the Police Officer and the Police Officer caught them and arrested them and the other team won automatically because the other team stealed and they got a nice trophy.

Where are these people?	In a soccer field playing near the school.
3a: What are these people doing and saying?	Telling each other, no give me the ball, making plans.
4a: What were these people doing before?	Practicing but not in the same area or place.
5a: What will these people do next?	The team that won will try to find another team to play and get better and try to win the world tournament. Other kids that stole have to face the consequences [Q: consequences?]Getting screamed at and grounded by parents; being in jail for 1 day to see how it feels if the police are crazy.
6a: What is this person [main character] thinking?	[Chose the team that stole] How are we going to get out of this mess? Should have never done this.
6b: What is this person [main character] feeling?	[The team that stole] Sad and scared now. [The team that won] feel kind of bad. [Q: Bad?] Sorry for them, for the other team but happy they won.

Card 20

RT   1 sec.
SP   8 min.
TT   10 min. 39 sec.
Fluency 330

What is that? It's a person dreaming. I didn't notice that. There is this person, this girl sleeping and she was in her room and she was dreaming about a huge place, a castle, a castle with a gate, and she was dreaming then ... Let me start again.

She was dreaming that she was on top of a horse riding on a horse trying to jump down the cliff with the horse and she was trying to reach the castle with her horse and while they were going they got attacked by another person riding a horse and who was going to the castle also. She didn't know nothing about the castle, it had secret money, and the boy with the horse was trying to stop her from going because he knew there was money and he wanted to get it, he didn't want her to get it. But the girl didn't know anything about the castle. She just thought it was beautiful and she was like leave me alone and was running away from the boy and the boy had rocks and he threw a couple at the girl and she fell from the horse. And then the boy said to her, I'm not going to let you get to the castle because it's my money and I'm going to let you die here and the girl was like what are you talking about? Some people [Q: people?] people on other horses started bombing the castle and then she couldn't take it anymore seeing this [Q: this?] the battle and as she was walking back to her horse she tripped on a rock and fell into the water and she woke up.

1a: Who are these people? Do they know each other?	No.
2a: Where are these people?	Somewhere far away in the country.
4a: What were these people doing before?	Riding horses to get where they wanted.
6a: What is this person [main character] thinking?	Why am I having a dream like this? When she woke up. In the dream, she thought

... Where am I? Where should I go?

6b: What is this person [main character] feeling?

Scared because someone might come to kill her and throw rocks at her.

Card 17G

RT   2 sec.
SP   6 min. 03 sec.
TT   7 min. 18 sec.
Fluency 273

There is this girl named Emily. She is in her room studying for a math test and while she was studying half of the test was too hard and half was too easy. And then she couldn't study and was tired, she was studying for 3 hours straight and while she was studying, half she got, half she didn't.

While she was studying she was thinking how about if the teacher might put on the test stuff she didn't know and she would get an F and the teacher would start beating her up because she's strict. And then she was thinking the teacher might be nice for once and put the things she knows and she might get an A+. And then she stopped thinking, looked at the book, studied a couple more hours and then she fell asleep and when she woke up while going to school she was late because she slept really late and she was going to school and thought "What am I going to do? I'm really late. My teacher is really strict." She went at 9am and school starts at 8am. She's like Oh, What should I do? She started panicking. She went with her eyes closed, she didn't see the teacher there when she opened them. She asked "where is the teacher?" And she got lucky. The other kids said, "She's not in today and we're waiting for the substitute teacher." She went home after the day was over. She went back the next day and passed the test.

4a: What were these people doing before?

She was studying for a really big test.

6b: What is this person (main character) feeling?

Panicky, then she gets happy when she passes.

Card 7

RT   5 sec.
SP   4 min.
TT   6 min. 10 sec.
Fluency 242

I don't like these stories. I don't know how they draw. I don't have to give titles, do I? [The examiner answered, "only if you want to."] Should I start on it? [Yes.]

It was Monday morning and the two kids' mom left so she could go shopping. While she was out the two kids were running, playing tag with each other at the same time while playing tag their hand [Q: their?] the girl reached out her hand so she could touch her brother to tag him and while she was doing that by mistake she hit the lamp and it fell down. And the mother was almost there to come back she was at the door. The girl was hiding. She first told her brother to tell her "you did it because I don't want to get in trouble" and he said, "No, I'm going to tell on you." She panicked and didn't know what to do and she was going to go hide and her mother came in and said what did you two break? And together they said "she did it, he did it," and then they both got grounded. The End.

2a: Where are these people?	In the house.
4a: What were these people doing before?	Watching TV.
5a: What will these people do next?	They will never talk to each other because they are mad at each other. You never know someone might be a crazy person.
6a: What is this person (main character) thinking?	[She chose the girl as the main character.] Thinking what am I going to do now? My brother won't take the blame now that I broke it.
6b: What is this person (main character) feeling?	Panicking. She doesn't know what to do. Feels angry and sad.

Card 22G

RT   1 second
SP   3 min. 50 sec.
TT   5 min. 46 sec.]
Fluency 195

What about her? She's in the bathroom looking in the mirror. She's ugly. There's a girl coming back from school. Bullies were picking [Q: picking?] on her, attacking her, and she...they put some stuff on her face and they cut her hair and then she started crying. And then she started running to her house and then she went to the bathroom and she looked in the mirror and she saw her face was covered with disgusting stuff and her hair was cut and then she saw gum in her hair and then she had to cut her hair off ... bald. And then she never went back to school, and other schools didn't accept her, and she didn't get a job. And she turned out to be the ugliest person in the world. And she never regrew the hair when she cut her hair off.

5a: What will these people do next?	She can't be seen. She'll never go outside. She was closed in the house all her life.
6a: What is this person (main character) thinking?	She can't get wigs because then she has to go outside.
6b: What is this person (main character) feeling?	She feels sad there is no one to talk to. She could go outside but doesn't because she is bald, people make fun of her.

Card 21

RT   1 sec.
SP   5 min. 09 sec.
TT   7 min. 15 sec.
Fluency 271

What is that? A mutated alligator. There was this ugly boy dreaming. He's ugly can't you see. He had two dreams and he was dreaming he was a servant to the mutant alligator. He always had to give him hamburgers and he was a servant. [Q: Why are they both together?] Because he was trying to find this stone that was made from a volcano that is worth a lot of money and then he found it and saw the volcano wouldn't erupt. Then when he grabbed the stone the mutated alligator grabbed it also and the boy said "let go, it's mine," and the alligator said, "No, I want it. It's mine. Let go if you don't want to die." The boy said, "I'll do anything for you but you have to give me the stone" and the alligator said, "I really like hamburgers and if you are . . . can you be my servant for one year and give me hamburgers then I'll let you go." They agreed. And then one year later while the alligator was letting him go. The alligator grabbed him and was ready to eat him and at that moment the kid woke up. He was all scared and looking for alligators. Then he said he's safe because he didn't find anything.

2a: Where are these people?	In his dream, he was somewhere in the country near a volcano.
3a: What was this person doing before?	Watching a horror alligator movie.
5a: What will this person do next?	Tell his friends about his scary dream so that they never watch the scary movie on mutated alligators.
6a: What is this person (main character) thinking?	If no alligators are around, I'm safe . . . . Never go near water. No one knows if one will come to attack him.
6b: What is this person (main character) feeling?	Scared.

Card 14G

RT   1 sec.
SP   2 min. 20 sec.
TT   5 min. 06 sec.
Fluency 188

This is a stupid one. There is a class in school and everyone does their homework. Except for one kid because she forgot. The teacher really hated that kid and some kids didn't do it [Q: the homework] either. She said go play and do what you want and she whispered make the other kid jealous and then the other girl got jealous and she read a little of what she is supposed to do and she slammed the book and said "I had enough" and then she walked out of the room. And she went and told the principal what happened and then the teacher got expelled and got fired. The End.

1a: Who are these people? Do they know each other?	Classmates.
2a: Where are these people?	In School.
3a: What are these people doing and saying?	Kids are saying "What do you want to do?" They left and went to play.
4a: What were these people doing before?	They were in their houses sleeping.
5a: What will these people do next?	Her friends will try to get revenge with the teacher. They will do something to get the teacher mad.
6a: What is this person (main character) thinking?	She's like, some other people didn't do it. Why am I in trouble? Why do I have to do it?
6b: What is this person (main character) feeling?	She's jealous, sad and angry.

Card 10G

RT   1 sec.
SP   7 min. 30 sec.
TT   8 min. 52 sec.
Fluency 326

There is this girl and she had a lemonade stand and was raising money. In the morning, she saw a bike that she wanted and a new ice cream that came out and she had to choose between the two. (I'll make it a happy ending.) And then in the afternoon she made the lemonade she got money and then she was walking between the two stores and then she had to choose because she really loved ice cream and wanted to try the ice cream and she wanted the bike because all her friends have bikes and make fun of her because she doesn't have one and when she was walking this person [Q: person? A: Don't know.] out of nowhere came and told her she should buy the bike. And she bought the bike and listened to the person and bought the bike. And then she learned how to ride the bike and then she saw a poster for a bike competition. And she saw whoever wins first place gets $500 and then she saw the person who walked past her at the competition and he was one of the persons on the bike and he's like I told you to buy the bike and we'll have fun racing each other. And now they are racing and she's like "I really want to win", and it was between her and the mystery guy and everyone falls behind really behind and when no one was looking, the mystery person took a shortcut and went through the woods and won and then they [Q: they?]…the people in charge saw him in the cameras and so they gave the prize to the 2nd person in place and that was the girl. And then she got the money and went to buy some ice cream.

2a: Where is this person?	In her house.
4a: What was this person doing before?	Thinking about new ice cream and the bicycle.
6b: What is this person [main character] feeling?	She feels like angry at the race because the mystery man, he cheated and then she got happy.

For complete scoring of Kathy's Nine TEMAS cards see record booklet, Figure 8-1.

TEMAS

Record Booklet

Giuseppe Costantino, Ph.D. and Robert G. Malgady, Ph.D.

Published by
WESTERN PSYCHOLOGICAL SERVICES
WPS 12031 Wilshire Boulevard
Los Angeles, CA 90025-1251
— Publishers and Distributors —

Name: _____KATHY_____ Sex: _F_ Date of Test: _10/27/04_

Address: _____ Birthdate: _____ Age: ____

Parents/Guardians: _____ Birthplace: (Mother)_____ (Father)_____

School/Clinic: _____ Examiner: ___I.K._____

Dominant Language: _ENGLISH_____ Language of Test Administration: _ENGLISH_

Ethnic/Racial Background*: _____

Form Administered: _____ Long ✓ Short

Observed Test Behavior:

_____
_____
_____
_____
_____

Normative Group Used:

✓ White _____ Puerto Rican _____ Combined Hispanic _____ Total Sample
_____ Black _____ Other Hispanic _____ Combined Minorities

*Optional—used in determining normative reference group.

FIGURE 8–1.   Scored record booklet.

Scoring Sheet
Quantitative Scales

Card No.	Cognitive Functions				Personality Functions									Affective Functions			
	Reaction Time (Seconds)	Total Time (Minutes)	Fluency	Total Omissions	Interpersonal Relations	Aggression	Anxiety/Depression	Achievement Motivation	Delay of Gratification	Self-Concept	Sexual Identity	Moral Judgment	Reality Testing	Happy	Sad	Angry	Fearful
1*	9	4 18/10.43	260	1	2,3	2	2	4	3					(1)			(1)
2																	
3																	
4																	
5																	
6																	
7*	5	4 10/6	242		2	2	2					2			(1)	(1)	(1)
8																	
9																	
10*	1	7 39/8.52	326	2	2			3	3	3		2	2	(1)		(1)	
11																	
12																	
13																	
14*	1	2 20/59.6	188	2	2	2	2	2	2				2		(1)	(1)	
15*	8	9 2#/10	333	2.6	N		3					2		(1)	(1)		(1)
16																	
17*	2	6 03/.18	273	3	2	2	3		3					(1)			(1)
18																	
19																	
20*	1	8 39/18.8	330	1	2	1	2					2					(1)
21*	1	5 65/5	271			2	2						3				(1)
22*	L1	3 46/5.30	195	2	2	2	2					1	2		(1)		
23																	
Sum	29	50 28/72.13 2418		8	17.9	13	14	15	8	6	1	8	9	4	4	3	6
Number of Cards Scored					8	8	7	5	3	2	1	4	4				
Mean Score**			2.24	1.63	2.0	3	2.66	3	1		2	2.25					
Sum of Functions Not Pulled ("N-Scores")																	

*Cards used for Short Form.
**Mean Score = Sum ÷ Number of cards scored

Page 2

FIGURE 8–1. Scored record booklet. (*continued*)

Scoring Sheet
Qualitative Indicators

Card No.	Affective Functions			Cognitive Functions						Optional — Omissions				Optional — Transformations			
	Neutral	Ambivalent	Inappropriate Affect	Conflict	Sequencing	Imagination	Relationships	Total Transformations	Inquiries	Main Character	Secondary Character	Event	Setting	Main Character	Secondary Character	Event	Setting
1*																	
2																	
3																	
4																	
5																	
6																	
7*				(1)													
8																	
9																	
10*								2								1	1
11																	
12																	
13																	
14*				(1)				2								1	1
15*																	
16																	
17*																	
18																	
19																	
20*				(1)				1					1				
21*								1							1		
22*				(1)				2		1						1	
23																	
Sum				4				8		2		1	1			3	1
0% ÷ (✓)				✓				✓		✓		✓	✓			✓	

FIGURE 8–1. Scored record booklet. (*continued*)

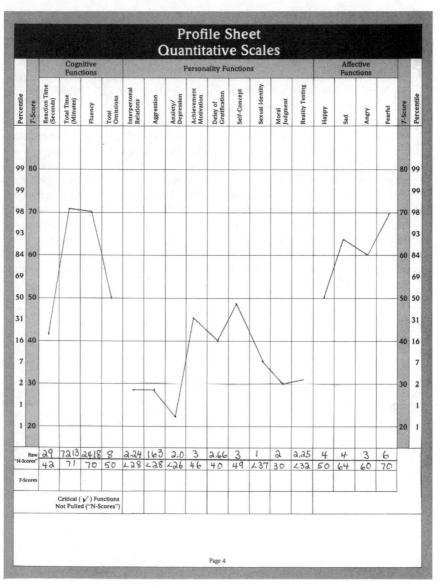

FIGURE 8–1. Scored record booklet. (*continued*)

REFERENCES

Costantino, G., Malgady, R. G., & Cardalda, E.(2005). TEMAS narrative treatment: And evidence-based culturally competent therapy modality. In E. D. Hibbs and P. S. Jensen (Eds). *Psychosocial treatments for child and adolescent disorders. Empirically based strategies for clinical practice.* (2nd ed., pp. 717–765) Washington, D.C.: American Psychological Association.

Dana, R. H. (2001a). Clinical diagnosis of multicultural populations in the United States. In L. Suzuki, J. Ponterotto, & P. Meller (Eds.). *The handbook of multicultural assessment* (2nd ed., pp. 101–131). San Francisco, CA: Jossey-Bass.

Dana, R. H. (2001b). Psychological assessment in diagnosis and treatment of ethnic group members. In J. A. Aponte & J. Wohl (Eds.). *Psychological interventions and cultural diversity.* (2nd ed., pp. 59–74). Boston, MA: Allyn & Bacon.

Dana, R. H. (2000a). Multicultural assessment of child and adolescent personality and psychopathology. In A. L. Comunian & U. Gielen (Eds.), *International perspectives on human development* (pp. 233–258). Lengerich, Germany: Pabst Science Publishers.

Dana, R. H. (Ed). (2000b). *Handbook of cross-cultural and multicultural personality assessment.* Mahwah, NJ: Lawrence Erlbaum Associates.

9

Hispanic/Latino Case Study

BACKGROUND

Originally, the TEMAS minority cards and the TEMAS test (Costantino, 1978; 1987) were developed to overcome bias and create a culturally competent narrative instrument for the assessment of Hispanic/Latino children. In fact, the title embodies a Spanish word, TEMAS, which means themes and an English acronym that stands for "Tell-Me-A-Story." The early studies (Costantino & Malgady, 1983; Costantino, Malgady & Vazquez, 1981; Malgady, Costantino & Rogler, 1984) and subsequent studies (e.g., Bernal, 1991; Cardalda, 1995; Costantino, 1992; Costantino & Malgady, 2000; Millan, 1990; Torres, 1995) confirm the validity of this instrument in assessing Latino youngsters. However, from its inception, it was realized that the TEMAS test was also a valid and necessary instrument for non-minority children and adolescents; thus the parallel non-minority TEMAS test was developed (Costantino, 1987). Here, we report the clinical utility of the non-minority version of the TEMAS test (Costantino, 1978, 1987) with a complete case study of a Latino child.

CLINICAL UTILITY: HISPANIC/LATINO CASE STUDY

This clinical case, Jose, illustrates the utility of TEMAS with respect to differential diagnosis of a Latino youngster, and contains additional clinical information regarding the child's overt behaviors. This Latino male examinee was receiving individual psychotherapy for approximately three months when the therapist's supervisor suggested a complete psychological evaluation because the youngster was not making therapeutic progress.

PSYCHOLOGICAL TEST REPORT

Name: Jose
Age: 9 years, 5 months
Sex: Male
Date of Evaluation: November 1998
Examiner: S.C. Psy.D.
Ethnic/Racial Background: Hispanic/Latino
Language(s) of Examinee: English/Spanish
Language of Tests: English

Tests Administered

Wechsler Intelligence Scale for Children – Third Edition (WISC-III)
Bender–Motor Gestalt Test
TEMAS (Tell-Me-A-Story) Multicultural Test (minority version)
Child Behavior Checklist (CBCL)
Conner's Scale
Clinical Interview
Parent Interview

Reason for Referral

Jose was a 9 year, 5-month-old Puerto Rican male of average height and
weight for his age at the time of the psychological evaluation. His appearance was neat and he was casually dressed. The student was referred to a
mental health center by his father and stepmother because of his poor
school achievement, situational aggressive behavior, and hyperactive
behavior. A complete psychological evaluation was requested by the clinician's supervisor because the student was making very limited progress
in psychotherapy.

Psychosocial History

A psychosocial evaluation was conducted with Jose's father, who appeared
to be a reliable informant. It was reported that the child was born without
complication following a full pregnancy and normal delivery. Developmental milestones were achieved within normal age limits. The child experienced
age-appropriate childhood illnesses, and no serious injuries or hospitalizations were reported in his early infancy. However, he developed asthma

when he was five years old, which has been treated with Proventyl and Albuterol. At about this time, the pediatrician also discovered he was near-sighted and to correct his nearsightedness, the child was prescribed and wore glasses. Jose lived at home with his father, stepmother, and his 2-month-old stepbrother at the time of the testing.

Jose was raised by both biological parents until the age of six months, when his father left the household following a legal separation and went to live with a second wife. During this time, the child remained with his mother, while his father came to visit. His mother experienced great diffi-culty in taking care of Jose by herself and managing her own life events. By age 3, therefore, the child went to live with his father and his second wife. In the new setting, the student experienced strong separation anxiety from his natural mother; this emotional state prevented him from developing a trust-ing relationship with his stepmother, according to his father. Jose apparently rejected her, disobeyed her, exhibited frequent tantrums when he could not have his own way, and, at times, he tended to withdraw. These behaviors recurred less frequently as Jose started to see his biological mother on a more regular and consistent basis. His teachers reported poor school achievement disruptive behavior. He exhibited hyperactivity and short attention span, and showed poor relations with his male peers, who usually teased him. At times, he exhibited aggressive behavior against those students who made fun of him.

Parent Interview

His parents described him as a highly anxious, fearful, and moody child, and added that he was extremely demanding of their attention and often acted like a very young child. Jose frequently experienced anxiety while learning a new task or when placed in a novel situation, they informed. He constantly feared that he might do something wrong or that his schoolwork would not be perfect. Overall, this anxiety manifested in somatic complaints (i.e., headaches, stomachaches), as well as an inability to cope and concen-trate, and had difficulty sleeping. In addition, he sleepwalked and had nightmares.

To further determine how his parents perceived his socioemotional functioning, they were administered the CBCL, independently. Although their scores differed slightly with respect to his behavior, overall results revealed that the student was exhibiting "at risk" maladaptive behaviors and met the criteria for Generalized Anxiety Disorder.

To rule out Attention Deficit Disorder, his parents also completed the Attention Deficit Disorder Evaluation Scale. Results of this instrument indicate that the student also met the criteria for Attention-Deficit/Hyperactivity Disorder, Predominantly Hyperactive-Impulsive Type. More specifically, they reported he was frequently restless, impulsive, and acted without thinking about the consequence of his behavior. They added that he could not follow parental commands. The parents also indicated that he became very upset and ran around the house and climbed on chairs.

Following the TEMAS sexual identity scale results, it was necessary to conduct a brief second parental interview by telephone with both the biological mother and the stepmother. The biological mother said that Jose was toilet trained by the age of 2 and that his pediatrician indicated normal psychosexual development. However, the stepmother clarified that she had noticed Jose sitting on the toilet seat when he had to urinate, instead of standing. The stepmother added that she first observed this behavior since he started kindergarten, and that she did not report it because she did not think it was abnormal. When she was told that this behavior is more appropriate for girls than boys, she added that Jose preferred to be with girls rather than with boys; in fact, she added that in the lunchroom in school, he liked to sit with the girls at lunchtime, instead of with the boys.

Behavioral Observations

His father escorted Jose to the psychological evaluation. The student was cooperative and was easily engaged and motivated to perform to the best of his ability during the administration of verbal tests. When questions were asked, he maintained good eye contact, listened attentively, and responded appropriately in well-organized and coherent sentences. His speech was clear, his thought process organized, and his long-term and short-term memory seemed adequate. His affect was moderate; his mood fluctuated from neutral to anxious. His attention span was also adequate and psychomotor activity was within normal limits. He remained seated without much unnecessary movement.

However, during the administration of performance tests, the student's ability to concentrate, to attend to details, and to persevere were noted to be markedly impaired. More specifically, on nonverbal tasks, he worked impulsively, neglected accuracy for speed, made careless rotation errors, and neglected to pay attention to the demands of the task, thus exhibiting deficits in visual perceptual and visual motor coordination skills. Furthermore, his anxiety level heightened as tasks became more complex.

When coping with difficult items, he usually remarked, "These are too hard," and when encouraged to complete them to the best of his ability, he usually asked, "Is that right?" or "Can I use the other side of the paper?" in the case of the figure drawing test or drawing the Bender– Gestalt test designs. Although he lived in a bilingual, Spanish–English home, he was English dominant, hence all psychological tests were administered in English.

Intellectual Functioning

WISC-III Results

According to the New York City Public Schools Chancellor, the results of this Intelligence Test should be used with caution because of possible test bias when assessing culturally and linguistically diverse children.

Verbal IQ Index = 102   Performance IQ Index = 79   Full Scale IQ = 90

Verbal Subtests: Scaled Scores		Performance Subtests: Scaled Scores	
Information	10	Picture completion	10
Similarities	12	Coding:	7
Arithmetic	11	Picture Arrangement	3
Vocabulary	10	Block design	6
Comprehension	11	Object Assembly	7
(Digit span)	(12)	(Mazes)	(5)
		(Symbol search)	(7)

The results of the WISC-III indicated that the student obtained a Verbal IQ Score of 102 (average range) and a Performance IQ score of 79 (borderline range), with a Full Scale IQ Score of 90 (average range). This placed him at the 25th percentile when compared to same-aged peers. Further analysis of the student's subtest scores revealed wide intra and intertest scatter as scores ranged between borderline and above-average range. A comparison between his Verbal IQ score, and his Performance IQ score, furthermore, indicated that a significant discrepancy favored his verbal skills.

Overall analysis of Jose's verbal skills showed that his verbal comprehension abilities fell within the average range. This suggests that the student showed average ability to organize and synthesize his thoughts, to readily process auditory information, and to use his previously acquired knowledge and general information to solve problems. The student's highest scores were on subtests that measured his short-term memory and ability to think and reason abstractly and logically. His scores within these domains fell within the above-average range. On subtests that measured his long-term memory, word knowledge, numerical skills, and ability to use common sense in social situations, the student demonstrated average abilities. Overall, scores on these subtests suggest that he was alert to his environment, recognized the demands of social situations, and was knowledgeable about societal rules and regulations.

Jose's nonverbal reasoning abilities and Performance IQ score fell within the borderline range, thus suggesting that his visual–motor organizational skills, ability to see spatial relationships and to mentally manipulate visual images were significantly below those of peers. However, a relative strength was noted in the area of paying attention to missing details in common objects, thus showing adequate skills in visual object memory. In general, it appeared that anxiety tended to reduce his abilities to function effectively in the performance subtests.

Visual Motor Functioning

The Bender–Gestalt Test was administered. According to the Koppitz scoring system, Jose achieved a negative score of 3, placing his visual motor and graphomotor coordination maturation at the age 9.3 years, thus showing age-appropriate visual motor coordination. Qualitatively, his drawings showed waved lines instead of straight lines and he exhibited somewhat poor utilization of space.

Social Emotional Functioning

TEMAS Results
To obtain a better understanding of the student's personality functioning, how he viewed the world and related to others, the TEMAS test was administered along with a clinical interview. In the area of cognitive functioning, when compared with the 8 to 10-year-old Puerto Rican child of the normative sample, the student scored within average category in Reaction Time ($T = 51$) thus showing some ability in cognitive organization; within the lower end of the average range in Storytelling Time ($T = 47$) because his stories were moderately short; and within the lower end of the average range in verbal fluency ($T = 47$), thus showing moderately adequate verbal ability. His ability to resolve conflicts fell above the 90th percentile cutoff point thus showing deficits in problem solving; more specifically, he showed adequate skills in recognizing conflicts, but poor skills in resolving them. In addition, his slightly above-average score in Selective Attention

(T = 52) indicated that, at times, he did not pay attention to events. In the area of Personality Functions, his scores fell within the deficient to low average overall. However, he scored within almost the average to the average range in achievement and self-concept. More specifically, he scored within the upper end of the average range in Achievement Motivation (T = 48), whereby showing some school achievement motivation and desire to be successful in other activities, such as sports. The student also scored within the upper end of the average range in Self-Concept of Competence (T = 48); and he scored within the very low average range in Delay Gratification (T = 39). In his stories, Jose described characters who struggled between appeasing their immediate pleasure, such as buying an ice cream, versus saving their money to buy a larger reward such as a bicycle; or studying versus playing. However, the immediate gratification prevailed most of the time. On the other hand, he tended to identify with characters who tried to do well in school and who felt confident about themselves in an average way.

The student also revealed that he was a very anxious, sensitive, and angry youngster who showed very poor interpersonal skills, an extremely dysfunctional gender identity, and very poor aggressive impulse control. In addition, he showed borderline ability to distinguish right from wrong and reality from fantasy. More specifically, the following six personality functions were found to be significantly maladaptive. They are: (a) his Interpersonal Relations (T = 36), which was within the very low range; (b) his Control of Aggression (T = <32), which fell within the borderline range; (c) Anxiety/Depression (T = <31), which fell within the borderline range, and where he showed significant maladaptive selective attention; (d) Sexual Identity (T = <27), which fell within the deficient range and was his lowest score; (e) Moral Judgment (T = <29), which fell within the upper end of the deficient range; and (f) Reality Testing (T = <29), which also was within the upper end of the deficient range.

His interpersonal skills were noted to be maladaptive due to his inability to negotiate effectively with peers, cope with frustration, and resolve problems in a socially acceptable manner. Through his responses, Jose indicated that when faced with a problem, he often became confused, easily upset, or tended to react impulsively. When confronted by peers, he defended against his anxieties by asking for parental help, or by becoming aggressive or withdrawn. Being scolded or criticized by his parents also elicited tears, stubbornness, or a tantrum. Poor reality testing and a low frustration tolerance distorted his understanding of situations, ability to anticipate consequences, and decision-making abilities. His most dysfunctional score was in his gender identity, whereby he completely identified as being a girl in his narrative. Overall, this sexual identity problem may shed light on why he chose to sit with the girls at lunchtime and to sit on the toilet while urinating.

Jose's narration of his life story onto TEMAS story characters indicated the severity of his maladaptive psychosocial skills. For example, when shown a card depicting the child's ability to delay gratification and to carry out a parental command, he transformed the theme and events of the picture. (See story Card1B). Although the card depicts a boy playing basketball with his friends and a mother asking the boy to mail a letter for her, the student saw the young boy being victimized by a bully in the group. Furthermore, he used the mother in the card to resolve the problem for him. More specifically, the mother was sending a note to the bully's parents, asking them to tell their son to return the ball to her child. Feelings of anger were expressed at the end of his story because the student felt so incompetent. This story is also consistent with true-life events. During the interview, Jose related that he was sometimes victimized by a bully in school who demanded his lunch money. He shamefully confessed that when those events occurred, he usually became so scared and angry that he just ran away.

Jose's strong need to be accepted as "one of the guys" may also be contributing to his lack of moral judgment and aggressive behaviors. These feelings were reflected in his story when shown a card intended to elicit feelings about interpersonal relationships, antisocial behavior, aggression, and moral judgment; his story was about a boy his age who robbed a store with peers and got caught in the process by a police officer. Among the objects stolen was a knife. Although Jose recognized that the boys were "doing something bad," and may be severely punished, (i.e., go to jail), the main character showed no remorse. In fact, he was very angry about getting caught and thought to himself, "I'm going to stab the police officer."

Finally, in a card designed to evoke conflicting feelings about one's sexual identity, Jose became so overwhelmed by the stimuli that he transformed the card and in doing so denied his male identity. More specifically, when shown a picture of a boy who is looking into a mirror that reflects back a composite of a male–female image, Jose stated, "When she looked in the mirror, she was thinking if she was a lady. She wishes she was." Considering how threatened and anxious he became when surrounded by male peers, it's no surprise that he was having difficulty with his male identity. His sexual confusion also appeared to be a manifestation of his fantasies. By imaging himself as female, he was able to relax. He did not have to assert himself, be tough around bullies, or assume the male Hispanic macho role he was expected to play. Overall, his anxiety about being male was being exhibited at home as well. Jose continued to sit on the toilet when urinating rather than standing.

In the areas of Affective Functioning, the student scored within the very high average in "Angry" ($T = 60$), within the above average range in "Fearful" ($T = 54$), and within the high average range in "Happy" ($T = 56$) and within the upper end of the average range in "Sad" ($T = 57$). The two above-average affective functions (Angry and Sad) correlate with his depression and aggression, whereas his low score in "Sad" shows a dysfunctional defense, such as repression; and the above-average score in "Happy" shows some ability in perceiving positive aspects of life events.

Summary

Jose was a 9-year, 5-month-old-Latino youngster. He was referred to the mental health clinic because of poor achievement and behavior problems in school and disruptive and hyperactive behavior at home. He was attending the 3rd grade in a public school at the time of referral. Results of the WISC-III indicated that his Verbal Scale IQ fell within the upper middle of the average category; his Performance Scale IQ fell within the upper end of the borderline range, with his Full Scale IQ falling with the lower end of the average category. However, if his bilingual background, low SES, and emotional problems are taken into account, his IQ functioning could fall within the middle of the average category. His strengths were in the areas of verbal tasks, requiring verbal fluency, comprehension, and abstract reasoning, whereas his weaknesses were in the areas of performance operations, requiring visual and psychomotor functioning. Results of the parental version of CBCL indicated that the child exhibited high anxiety, and the parental version of the Conner's Scale indicated that the student also exhibited hyperactive behavior. TEMAS results indicated that the student showed somewhat adaptive cognitive functions in the areas of responding to pictorial stimuli, storytelling time, verbal fluency and selective attention; however, he showed somewhat dysfunctional skills in problem solving. Results of the personality functions indicated he showed weaknesses in interpersonal relations, aggression, anxiety/depression, sexual identity, moral judgment, reality testing; and he showed relative strengths in achievement motivation, self-concept of competence, and to a lesser extent, delay gratification. In the affective functions, he scored within the upper end of the average range in "Sad" within the high average range in "Angry," and within the average range in "Happy" and "Fealful." Emotional indicators presented a diagnostic impression of *Depressive Disorder Not Otherwise Specified (NOS)*.

Recommendations

1. Jose should continue receiving individual psychotherapy to foster more adaptive impulse control, augment his limited interpersonal skills, and resolve his sexual identity conflict.
2. A behavior modification program should be implemented at school and at home to help Jose focus on goals he needs to achieve, and to positively reinforce them when they are attained. These goals should include: (a) improving his interpersonal relationships with peers, (b) increasing his ability to cope with the frustration when denied his own way, (c) learning to assert himself in appropriate ways, and (d) using the toilet in an age-appropriate manner.
3. Jose should be also referred to group psychotherapy in order to foster more adaptive psychosocial skills. In school, the guidance counselor should encourage him to participate in team sports and/or group activities to help him in developing a stronger self-concept and a more adaptive competitive achievement motivation.

Discussion

The utility of psychological tests in general and narrative tests in particular are important for youngsters in order to clarify diagnostic impressions that are usually based on problems presented by parents, significant others, teachers, and/or police/judicial authorities. Children and adolescents are poor informants and often report absence of emotional and/or behavioral problems during clinical evaluations, but they reveal underlying emotional problems in narrative test stories. In addition, narrative techniques, such as the TEMAS test, usually help the therapist in refocusing the treatment process and identifying additional problem areas to be directly addressed in the Individual Treatment Plan, thus affording the achievement of therapeutic goals and objectives in a relatively short-term intervention, (Cardalda, Costantino, Jimenez-Suarez, León-Velázquez, Martínez, et al., 2005; Dana, 2000).

In this case, the WISC-III results indicated that the student's IQ fell within the normal range in the Verbal subtests, whereas his Performance IQ fell within the borderline range, thus indicating serious deficits in his visual motor and psychomotor functioning. However, as his score in the Bender–Gestalt test fell within the appropriate age of psychomotor development, we can assume that his below-average functioning in nonverbal tasks may be associated with emotional factors such as depression. This clinical interpretation is also confirmed by the findings that minority children usually score lower in verbal IQ than performance IQ (e.g., Costantino, 1992; Costantino & Malgady, 1996).

The validity of psychological tests rest on the accuracy of the results of the instruments in generating a clinical profile of the examinee and in providing sufficient data of the underlying emotional problems in order to give an appropriate diagnosis. However, the predictive validity of tests ultimately rests on the positive relationship between test results obtained from the youngster and the presenting problems provided by the significant others. Diagnostically, the TEMAS test results pointed out the presence of strong depression symptoms manifested by elevated scores in angry and sad feelings, very low scores in control of aggressive behavior, and very low scores in coping with depression-provoking life events or intrapsychic events, such as strong sexual identity conflicts. In addition, the TEMAS Quantitative Scales showed that the student had poor psychosocial skills in dealing with his male peers, poor aggressive impulse control, limited ability to distinguish right from wrong and reality from fantasy, and above all highly maladaptive sexual identity. All these variables were strongly associated with the reported presenting problems. On the other hand, he showed some strength in his ability to achieve in school and to a lesser degree, in self-concept and in delaying gratification.

The student's admitting diagnosis was ADHD, which was based on the problems presented by his parents on the Conner's Scale, parent's version. However, following the results of the CBCL and the TEMAS, the working diagnosis was changed to *Depressive Disorder* (NOS), consequently the treatment plan, problems, goals, and objectives were also revised. A subsequent psychiatric evaluation ruled out ADHD diagnosis in favor of Depressive Disorder Not Otherwise Specified, with possible prescription of psychotropic medication if his acting-out behavior in school and at home did not stop. The TEMAS diagnostic profile was confirmed by the CBCL and the presenting problems. In addition, the TEMAS findings revealed maladaptive psychosocial and interpersonal skills and, above all, highly maladaptive sexual identity. These dysfunctions were confirmed by his parents during the second interview, who revealed that he sat on the toilet seat to urinate as if he were a girl, and that he felt more comfortable to have girls as friends instead of boys.

Therapy Progress

By the end of the psychological testing, Jose had been in treatment for three months, he remained in therapy for an additional three months. The 90-day treatment plan review indicated that the student had made marked progress in therapy over the previous three months. Whereas he initially presented himself as a tearful and anxious boy who was afraid of going to school, he showed more adaptive school and home adjustment. He was able to cope, concentrate in school, complete assignments in a timely manner, and began to exhibit less aggression. Overall, good progress was made with assistance of his parents, who had implemented a behavior modification program designed by the clinician, rearranged their schedule at home to spend more time with the student, and rewarded and praised him for his adaptive behavior. At the end of the 6 months of treatment, the clinician had a case conference with his parents to share the student's progress. However, the clinician also pointed out that Jose continued to require individual psychotherapy and group therapy to foster more adaptive psychosocial skills, to be more assertive and appropriate with peers, and to address his sexual identity conflict. The parents apparently were satisfied with his adaptive school adjustment and declined further treatment. The father indicated that under guidance, Jose would learn to be more assertive with his peers; "I will teach him boxing," he remarked; in addition, he added that he felt confident that Jose would resolve his sexual identity problems, if he really had those problems, because he would outgrow them.

In summary, the utility of the psychological tests, especially the TEMAS narrative test, is evident in the therapeutic progress made by the student following the recommendations based on the results of those tests. This case strongly illustrates the effectiveness of the TEMAS narrative test as a cost-effective procedure in the successful assessment and treatment of a Latino youngster.

TEMAS STORIES

Card 1

RT   2 sec.
ST   1 min. 30 sec.
TT   2 min..45 sec.
Fluency 91

They were playing basketball and the boy took the ball. He's pointing and telling his parents. The parents are pointing to the boy to talk to his parents. She's giving him a note. His parents gave back the ball.

1. Friends.
2. In the park.
3. Mother is giving him a note to give to his parents telling the boy to give back the ball.
4. Boys were playing basketball.
5. The bully's parents gave back the ball.
6. Angry and sad.

Card 7

RT	8 sec.
ST	46 sec.
TT	3 min. 19 sec.
Fluency	72

They were fighting over the lamp because one of them broke it. They are saying you broke it—you broke it. The mother is mad.

1. A family.
2. Inside the house.
3. Blaming each other.
4. Children were playing together mother was washing dishes.
5. Mother will tell them to clean up the mess. She has a clue—she sees the wire, they will clean it up.
6. Boy is thinking she did it; boy is angry.

Card 10

RT	7 sec.
ST	1 min..03 sec.
TT	2 min..18 sec.
Fluency	56

The mother gave him allowance and he was thinking of saving it until he could either buy a bike or ice cream and he decides to pick the ice cream.

1. In a house.
2. Thinking which one should I buy?
3. Doing the work for his allowance.
4. Buy ice cream.
5. Thinking he's confused – which one should I buy?
6. Feeling happy and sad.

Card 14

RT   10 sec.
ST   41 sec.
TT   2 min. 19 sec.
Fluency   57

This person right here, he was watching them dancing and playing music. He decided to write a book about them.

1. Friends and family.
2. In the house.
3. He was doing his homework.
4. He will go play with them.
5. Boy is thinking about what they are doing.
6. Boy is feeling happy. He finished his homework and went to play.

Card 15

RT   4 sec.
ST   2 min. 20 sec.
TT   220 min. sec.
Fluency   181

Part I. On this part they broke the window and stole the VCR and TV. One of them stole a book. The cop is saying who did this? He is pointing to them. The next thing that's gonna happen is that he's going to find out who did it and talk to their parents.

1. All are friends doing something bad.
2. In the street.
3. Saying "oh no!" because the cop is gonna find out.
4. Thinking about (planning it).

5. Going to get in trouble, some will go to jail; others will get punished for a long time.
6a. Thinking – I'm going to stab the police officer.
6b. Feeling – mad.

Part II. In the other part, they were playing baseball and they won a trophy. The coach is taking a picture and after that they are gonna celebrate and the coach will buy 6 sodas. Before they won it, they were playing hard.

1. Family.
2. In the park.
3. Playing baseball, taking pictures and saying, "we won!"
4. They were playing the game.
5. Go home and tell their parents.
6a. Thinking – we won the championship.
6b. Feeling—very happy.

Card 17

RT   5 sec.
ST   36 sec.
TT   1 min. 23 sec.
Fluency 48

He's thinking about if he didn't study he would get an F." But, if he studied as hard as he could he would get an "A."

1. He's a 9 year old kid.
2. In school.
3. Studying.
4. He was thinking about if he studied or not.
5. Studies.
6b. Feeling—happy.

Card 20

RT   6 sec.
ST   36 sec.
TT   56 sec.
Fluency 43

The kid is dreaming of a castle and a horse and background mountains. That's it!

1. A boy named Daniel, age 4.
2. In the house his room.
3. Dreaming.
4. Watching TV about a castle.
5. Wakes up.
6a. Thinking—that was a nice dream.
6b. Feeling—happy, sad because he wanted to be real.

Card 21

RT   5 sec.
ST   57 sec.
TT   1 min. 47 sec.
Fluency   54

Same boy, this time he was watching a bad movie and he dreamed of a terrible dragon. One of them had to slay the other. He wanted to eat him.

1. Some boy.
2. In his room.
3. Saying nothing.
4. Sleeping.
5. Wakes up and call his mom into the room.
6a. Thinking—I won't watch a bad movie again.
6b. Feeling—Scared.

Card 22 B-M

RT   5 sec.
ST   34 sec.
TT   57 sec.
Fluency   85

Her name is Cynthia and when she looked in the mirror. She was a lady. She wishes she was. That's it!

1. A girl.
2. In the bathroom.
3. Looking in the mirror.
4. Using in the bathroom.
5. Go play with her toys.
6a. Thinking—I wish I was a lady.
6b. Feeling—happy no sad wishes she were a lady.

Testing limits: (What's the best part about being a lady?)
Answer: The good part about being a lady is she can stay up late. She won't be bossed around like when she has to go to bed.

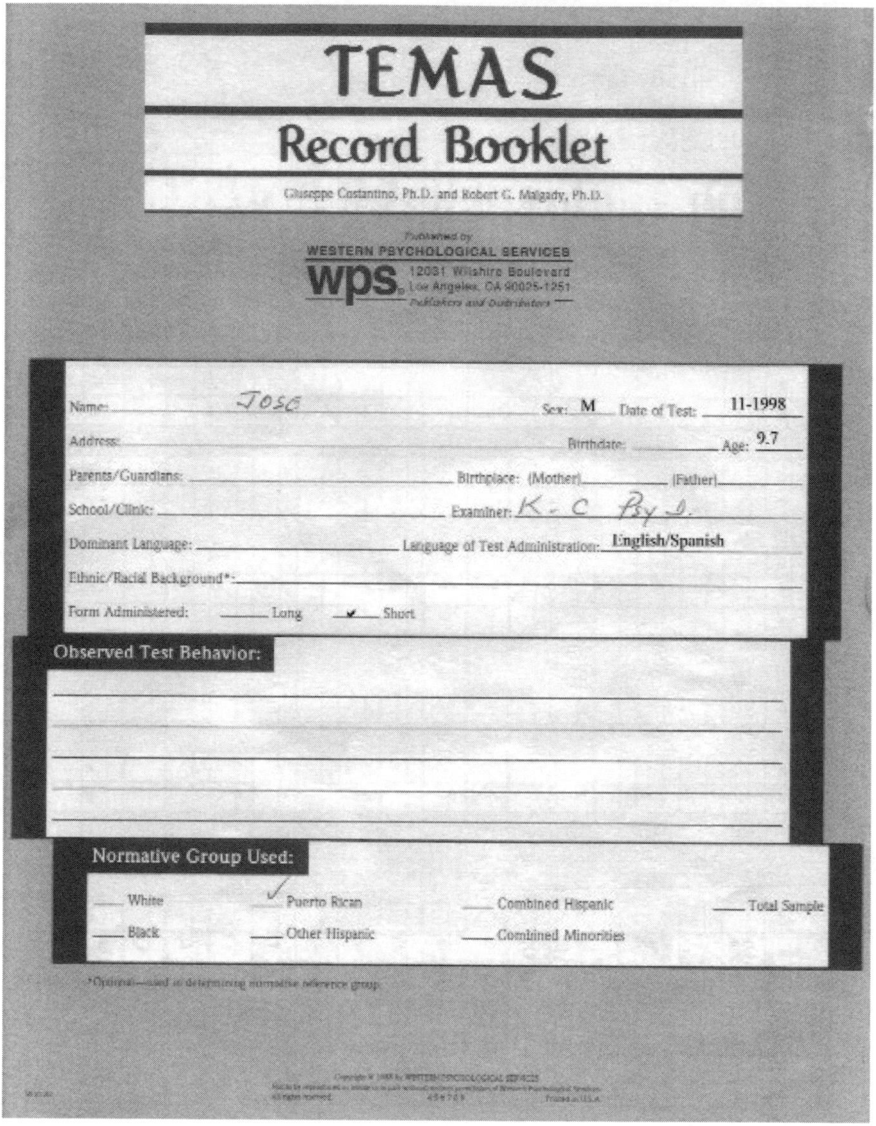
TEMAS

Record Booklet

Giuseppe Costantino, Ph.D. and Robert G. Malgady, Ph.D.

Published by
WESTERN PSYCHOLOGICAL SERVICES
wps 12031 Wilshire Boulevard
Los Angeles, CA 90025-1251
Publishers and Distributors

Name: JOSE Sex: M Date of Test: 11-1998

Address: Birthdate: Age: 9.7

Parents/Guardians: Birthplace: (Mother) (Father)

School/Clinic: Examiner: K - C Psy. D.

Dominant Language: Language of Test Administration: English/Spanish

Ethnic/Racial Background*:

Form Administered: ___ Long ✓ Short

Observed Test Behavior:

Normative Group Used:

___ White ✓ Puerto Rican ___ Combined Hispanic ___ Total Sample

___ Black ___ Other Hispanic ___ Combined Minorities

*Optional—used in determining normative reference group.

FIGURE 9–1. Scored record booklet.

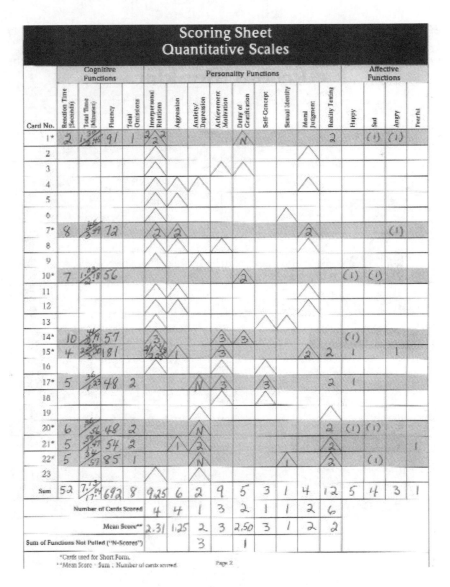

FIGURE 9–1. Scored record booklet. (*continued*)

Scoring Sheet
Qualitative Indicators

Card No.	Affective Functions			Cognitive Functions						Optional							
										Omissions				Transformations			
	Neutral	Ambivalent	Inappropriate Affect	Conflict	Sequencing	Imagination	Relationships	Total Transformations	Inquiries	Main Character	Secondary Character	Event	Setting	Main Character	Secondary Character	Event	Setting
1*				1				2					1			1	1
2																	
3																	
4																	
5																	
6																	
7*				(1)													
8																	
9																	
10*																	
11																	
12																	
13																	
14*								1								1	
15*				(1)				2								1	1
16																	
17*				(1)							2						
18																	
19																	
20*				(1)									2				
21*								1				1	1			1	
22*				1				2		1				1		1	
23																	
Sum				6				8		3	2	3		1	1	5	1
% + (✓)				✓				✓						✓		✓	

FIGURE 9–1.   Scored record booklet. (*continued*)

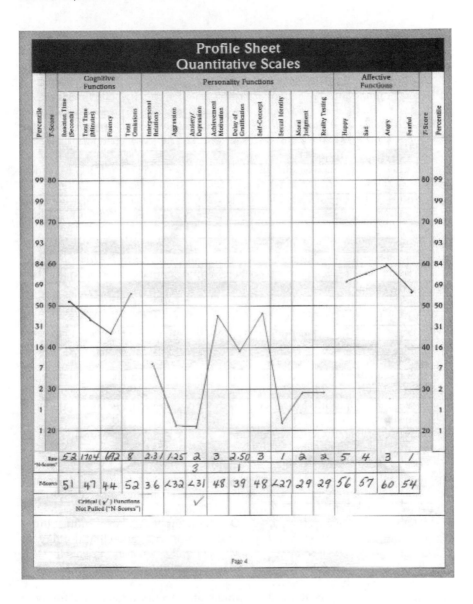

FIGURE 9–1. Scored record booklet. (*continued*)

REFERENCES

Bernal, I. (1991). *The relationship between level of acculturation, The Robert's Apperception Test for Children, and the TEMAS (Tell-Me-A-Story Test)*. Unpublished dissertation, California School of Professional Psychology, Los Angeles, CA.

Cardalda, E. B. (1995). *Socio-cognitive correlates to school achievement using the TEMAS (Tell-Me-A-Story) culturally sensitive test with sixth, seventh and eighth grade*. Unpublished doctoral dissertation, The New School for Social Research, New York, NY

Cardalda, E., Costantino, G., Jiménez-Suarez, V., León-Velázquez, M., Martínez, J. V., & Perez, M. (2005, June). *Second Puerto Rican study: Cross-Cultural comparisons with the TEMAS test using group versus individual methodology*. Project Export Minority Health Disparity Conference. San Juan, PR: Carlos Albizu University.

Costantino, G. (1978, November). *Tell-Me-A-Story test (TEMAS), a New Thematic Apperception Test to Measure Ego Functions and Development in Urban Black and Hispanic Children*. Paper presented at the Second Annual Conference on Fantasy and the Imaging Process. Chicago, IL.

Costantino, G. (1987). *TEMAS (Tell-Me-A-Story) Test cards*. Los Angeles, CA: Western Psychological Services.

Costantino, G., (1992). Overcoming bias in the educational assessment of Hispanic students. In: K. F. Geisinger (Ed.) *Psychological testing of Hispanics*. (pp. 89–97) Washington, DC: American Psychological Association.

Costantino, G. (1993). School dysfunctions in Hispanic children. In E. H. Wender (Ed.), *School dysfunctions in children and youth (pp. 106–212)*. Report of the 24th Ross Roundtable on Critical Approaches to Common Pediatric Problems, Columbus, OH.

Costantino, G., Malgady, R. G., & Vazquez, C. (1981). Comparing Murray's TAT to a new thematic apperception test for urban ethnic. *Hispanic Journal of Behavioral Science, 3*, 291–300.

Costantino, G., Malgady, R. G. (1983). Verbal Fluency of Hispanic, Black and White Children on TAT and TEMAS, A New Thematic Apperception Test. *Hispanic Journal of Behavioral Sciences, 5*, 199–206.

Costantino, G., & Malgady, R. G. (1996). Development of TEMAS, A multicultural Thematic Apperception Test: Psychometric properties and clinical utility. In G. R. Sodowsky & J. Impara (Eds) *Multicultural assessment in counseling and clinical psychology* (pp. 85–136). Lincoln, NE: Buros Institute of. Mental Measurements University of Nebraska.

Costantino, G., & Malgady, R. G. (2000). Multicultural and Cross-cultural utility of the TEMAS (Tell-Me-A-Story) test. In R.H. Dana (Ed.) *Handbook of Cross-cultural/Multicultural Personality Assessment*. (pp. 481–513). Mahwah, NJ: Lawrence Erlbaum Associates, Inc.

Dana, R. H. (2000). Multicultural assessment of child and adolescent personality and psychopathology. In A. L. Comunian & U. Gielen (Eds.), *International perspectives on human development* (pp. 233–258). Lengerich, Germany: Pabst Science Publishers.

Malgady, R. G., Costantino, G., & Rogler, L. H. (1984). Development of a thematic apperception test (TEMAS) for urban Hispanic children. *Journal of Consulting and Clinical Psychology, 52,* 986–996.

Millan-Arzuaga, F.(1990). Mother-child differences in values and acculturation: Their effect on Atonement motivation and self-concept in Hispanic children. Unpublished doctoral dissertation, Columbia University, New York, NY.

Torres, G. (1995). The relationship of bilingualism and school achievement to self-concept and trait anxiety in 4th, 5th, 6th grade Puerto Rican Children. Unpublished doctoral dissertation. Centro Caribeno de Estudios Postgraduados, Caribbean Center for Post Graduate Studies, San Juan, Puerto Rico.

10

Asian American Case Studies

BACKGROUND

Following the Hispanics/Latinos, Asian Americans are the second fastest growing ethnic minority group in the United States (U.S. Bureau of the Census, 2000). When combined with Pacific Islanders, the expanded Asian American population represents the fastest growing ethnic group (Maki & Kitano, 2002). The Asian Americans tend to settle in the coastal areas of the nation, such as California, New York, Hawaii, Texas, and New Jersey (U.S. Bureau of Census, 2000). Chinese students are perceived as a model minority group, with high academic achievement. However, stress associated with acculturation process and intergenerational conflicts are usually obfuscated by their school success (Liu & Lin, 1998). The literature indicates that Asian American children and adolescents experience several filial and psychosocial conflicts and need mental health services no less than other ethnic/racial groups (Lung & Sue, 1997), and tend to exhibit anxiety, depression, psychosomatic complaints, ADHD, lack of interest in school, antisocial behaviors (Liu & Li, 1998), and self-identity problems (Matoba Alder, 2001). Kim & Chun (1993) compared the psychiatric diagnoses among Asian American and European-American adolescents; the authors found that Asian American youngsters in general had higher rates of academic and personal problem, and Asian American females experienced more mood disorders. Consequently, major depression and suicide are reported to be more prevalent among this group. Yu, Chang, Liu, and Fernandez (1989) reported higher suicide rates for adolescents and young adults in the Chinese community (16.8%) than in the European-American community (11.9%). More recently, Reese-Albright and Chung (2002) indicated that depression in Asian American youngsters tends to be associated with significant morbidity and mortality. Chiu and Ring (1998) suggested that Asian adolescents experience intragroup stressors as well as social realities. Prillerman (1988) defined intragroup stressors as pressures from within one's own racial group as well as challenges to group commitment and racial identity. Chiu and Ring (1998) also suggested that Asian youths' mental health could be affected by the realities of racism, bias, stereotypes, and prejudice.

Although recent studies indicated that Asian children and adolescents need mental health services, it has been documented in various studies that Chinese communities underutilize mental health services (Kim & Omizo, 2003; Leong & Lau, 2001; Sue & Morishima, 1982; Sue & Zane, 1987; Zhang & Dixon, 2003). Researchers have identified several barriers that affect the utilization of mental health services in the Asian American groups. These barriers exist within and without the Asian American culture, such as stigma against mental health services (Lung & Sue, 1997), expressing psychological problems in the form of psychosomatic symptoms (Owan, 1985), biased assessment of mental health symptoms (Leong & Lau, 2001), and biased mental health treatment modalities and lack of culturally competent assessment instruments (Leong & Lau, 2001; Snowden, 2003; Woo, 1998).

Woo (1998) cautioned the assessment of Asian children by using standardized tests because of their cultural bias and linguistic distortions. He defined cultural bias as (a) concepts and objects unknown in the students' culture, (b) concepts and objects with different degrees of familiarity or importance, (c) facts not taught in the child's home country, (d) different customs, (e) different ethics, (f) unfamiliar or culturally inappropriate forms of assessment, and (g) different pedagogical practices. To be specific, the socialization process in the Asian culture varies significantly from the Western American culture and places the focus on impulse control, respect for authority figures, emotional restraint, and academic success (Ho, 1986; Lung & Sue, 1997). Existing psychological and personality tests that have been standardized on the European-American population are not clinically or ethnically appropriate for the Asian American groups (Leong & Lau, 2001).

To this end, the Asian American version of TEMAS was developed to overcome bias in assessing Asian American youngsters (Costantino, 1998; Tsenge & Hsu, 1972). The TEMAS characters were designed to depict the physical features of the Asian individuals in order to enhance the similarity between the picture stimuli and the characteristics of the examinees, and to depict settings and themes culturally relevant to the Asian American youngsters (Costantino, 1998). Earlier studies showed the emic and etic validity and clinical utility of the TEMAS minority and nonminority versions (Costantino, Malgady, & Vazquez, 1981; Costantino &

Malgady, 1983; Costantino, Malgady, & Rogler, 1988; Costantino, Malgady, Rogler, & Tsui, 1988; Costantino, Malgady, Colon-Malgady, & Bailey, 1992; Costantino & Malgady, 1996; Malgady, Rogler, & Costantino, 1987). In the first Asian study, Liu and Lin ((2001) utilized the nonminority version of TEMAS with White characters (Costantino, 1987) in two samples of Taiwanese school children and clinical children in first, third and fifth grades in Taiwan. Results indicated that these students in general failed to identify with white TEMAS characters in several cards. However, when these students were able to identify to white characters in a few other cards, significant differences were found between school and clinical children on several personality scales, such as Anxiety/Depression, Delay Gratification, Self-Concept, and Reality Testing. In a second study, comparing the non-minority and AsianAmerican versions of TEMAS with Taiwanese children, Yang, Cou, and Costantino (2003) found that the Asian American version was superior to the nonminority TEMAS in predicting daily life adjustment and negative mood, especially in affective functions and in the following personality scales: Interpersonal Relationship, Aggression, Moral Judgment, and Achievement Motivation.

CASE STUDIES: CHINESE AMERICAN CASE STUDIES

Two cases were used to explore Chinese American children's stories to the Asian American version of TEMAS in terms of the response time, verbal fluency, cultural themes, and clinical utility. The first case, Amy, was evaluated by a licensed Chinese American, PhD psychologist, through clinical analysis because the student was 14 years old and the TEMAS norms end at the age of 13.

CASE STUDY 1: AMY

Presenting Problems

Amy was a 14.2-year-old Chinese American girl of average weight and height at the time of the evaluation. She attended eighth grade and was an average student. Her parents sought psychotherapy for Amy because she had been stealing. She normally stole a few dollars from her mother to buy candies and small items.

Brief Family and Developmental History

The student was born in the United States, following a normal pregnancy and delivery. She had a normal developmental history. She began attending kindergarten at the age of five, and continued attending public schools. She had an older brother who was in college. Her parents emigrated from China in the mid-1980s and met and married in New York City. They worked long hours, and the student was by herself or with relatives after school hours. The parents spoke Cantonese at home, whereas the children spoke primarily English. Apparently there was very little family inter-action, except for holidays and other celebrations.

Evaluation and Treatment

The student was seen for weekly individual therapy and monthly family therapy in private practice. At intake, the parents complained that the girl stole money from them on a regular basis. However, it was discovered that Amy's parents were very tight with money and never gave her an allowance. The student was administered the nonverbal Intelligence Test, 2nd ed., where she obtained an average IQ score. In addition, she was administered the short forms (9 cards) of the non-minority version of TEMAS at the beginning of treatment and the Asian American version at the end of therapy to assess her therapeutic progress and the clinical utility of the latter version of TEMAS. The goals of therapy were to eliminate her stealing, reduce her impulsive behavior, and increase her ability to delay gratification; the objectives were to help Amy realize her need for parental attention, and learn how to interact and negotiate with her parents to have quality time with them. Parental skill training was also implemented to help Amy's parents understand her developmental needs for attention and independence. Amy's parents adopted an allowance system to rein-force Amy's study and work habits and delay of gratification, as well as the understanding of saving. Amy's stealing behavior ceased after fifteen sessions of individual therapy and family therapy.

TEMAS STORIES: NON MINORITY
(WHITE AMERICAN) VERSION

Card 1   RT: 44 sec.   TT: 4 min. 28 sec.

They are playing. The mother is telling the girl to bring the note to some-body. May be the mother wants them to play somewhere else.

The girl is feeling scared. The mother doesn't want them to play. They will go where the mother wants them to be.

Card 2   **RT: 34 sec.   TT: 3 min. 01 sec.**

While these two kids are playing, they drop the lamp. The mother wants to know who did it. They both want to blame each other. Mother is going to punish them.

Feeling?   The girl is angry. The mother is upset.

Card 10   **RT: 30 sec.   TT: 1 min. 51 sec.**

The girl is looking at how much money she has. She is thinking to buy a bicycle. Maybe she is going to buy ice cream. I think the girl is happy because she saved enough money to buy what she wants, the ice cream.

Card 14   **RT: 13 sec.   TT: 2 min. 12 sec.**

The girl is doing her homework. Her sisters and brothers are playing music to disturb her. The girl is trying to ignore them because she is trying to concentrate to study for a test. Maybe she feels angry with her friends. This is it.

Future?   She is going to tell her mother if she can study her work in her room.

Card 15   **RT: 31 sec.   TT: 1 min. 54 sec.**

These kids broke in the store to steal TV and stuff. The police caught them. The kids look scared.

Future?   They know better not to steal.

Card 17   **RT: 35 sec.   TT: 2 min. 02 sec.**

The girl is trying to study hard for the test. She is thinking about the teacher might ask her if she studied or not. And she took the test. The teacher might recommend her in the class and tell the class that she did good on the test.

Future?   She might bring books home to study.

Feeling?   She is happy.

Card 20   **RT: 30 sec.**   **TT: 2 min. 31 sec.**

The girl is dreaming. Maybe she is dreaming she will live in a castle. In her dream, there are a yellow horse, a castle, mountain, and water. She might want to live in the castle because it is a peaceful place.

Card 21   **RT: 14 sec.**   **TT: 1 min. 31 sec.**

The girl is dreaming about 2 things. One dream is about a dragon running a place. And the other dream is that someone is feeding the dragon a hamburger. The dragon in the first dream is mean and angry. And the dragon in the second dream is hungry.

Future?   She wants to dream about the nice dragon.

Feeling?   Worry.

Card 22   **RT: 15 sec.**   **TT: 2 min. 20 sec.**

There is a girl in the bathroom looking at the mirror. May be she is feeling a little sick. Half part of it is a different color. The girl is looking at the mirror because she wants to look at how she will look when she is better.

Feeling?   Worry.

TEMAS STORIES: ASIAN AMERICAN VERSION

Card 1   **RT: 26 sec.**   **TT: 2 min. 17 sec.**

These girls are playing. One of the mothers asked her to give the letter to someone. The girl did not want to send the letter. She point to another girls to want her to go.

Feeling?   Happy playing.

Card 10   **RT: 11 sec.**   **TT: 2 min. 05 sec.**

The girl saves her money in the piggy bank. One day she took out the money to count how much all together. She was thinking if she could go to buy ice cream or spend on a bike. I think she might want to spend the money on the bike because she can play with it. She was feeling concerned. She was not sure how to spend the money, and then she saved the money and bought the bike.

Feeling?   Happy.

Card 14   RT: 26 sec.   TT: 2 min. 23 sec.

One day after school, there was a girl who was doing her homework. Her sister invited her friends to come over. The girl does not want her sister's friends come over because she wants to study. She looks like she is feeling disappointed. I think she might want to go up to her room to study.

Card 15   RT: 15 sec.   TT: 1 min. 45 sec.

There were 4 kids who broke the window of a store and took the TV and a VCR. The police caught them told them to return the stuff. The kids were feeling scared. I think by the time the years pass, they learn not to steal. They are happy. On the other side the kids were playing and won the game. They were given Awards and are very happy.

Card 17   RT: 19 sec.   TT: 1 min. 45 sec.

This girl, she was studying and thinking if she fails and what would happen to her. On the other side, if she studies hard she might have A+. I think she might want to study so she will not get embarrassed. She feels proud of herself.

Card 20   RT: 14 sec.   TT: 1 min. 28 sec.

One day during the night, the kid was dreaming about living in the castle. He was imagining the beautiful place. There is the horse that will take him to wherever he wants. He feels happy to live in this place.

Card 21   RT: 7 sec.   TT: 2 min. 17 sec.

There is another kid dreaming of a dragon burning the entire place surrounding him. He was thinking what would happen if the dragon came to town. On the other dream, he is dreaming the dragon is kind and nice to him. The dragon looks more friendly than the other part of the dream. He might want to have the nice dragon as a friend.

Feeling?   Happy. He thinks the dragon might be a friend.

Card 22   RT: 5 sec.   TT: 1 min. 46 sec.

This picture is about a girl going to the bathroom to look at her reflection. One side looks different from the other. On the left side she thinks herself being a boy. On the right side, she is thinking how she might look as a girl. She thinks she looks better as a girl. She feels happy that she is a girl.

Discussion

A comparison of the cognitive indices of the stories to the two versions of TEMAS showed that in the area of Cognitive Functioning, the student achieved significant shorter response time in the Asian American Version (RT = 2 min. 3' sec.) than in the Nonminority Version (RT: 3 min. 32 sec.), thus exhibiting more adaptive cognitive/organizational skills when responding to cards depicting Asian characters than when responding to cards depicting white characters. In addition to fluency, her stories in response to the Asian American Version of TEMAS were more organized and grammatically structured than the stories given to the non minority version of TEMAS. Furthermore, she resolved the depicted conflicts in a more adaptive manner in the Asian American version.

In the areas of personality functioning, analysis of the stories indicated that in the Asian American version, Amy showed more ability to delay immediate gratification and engage in delay gratification and higher self-concept of competence in school achievement; and she was more assertive with her parents; in addition she showed more ability to explore and resolve the conflict of sexual identity on Card 22 in the Asian version, whereas, she could not even perceive the sexual identity conflict in the Nonminority version. In terms of the chief complaint of stealing, she clearly showed more ability in discussing the conflict of satisfying immediate needs and resolving it by delaying the gratification on the Asian American version.

Notwithstanding that the TEMAS Nonminority version was administered during the initial interview, and the Asian American version was given at the termination of the treatment, the Asian American stories show more adaptive functioning in the area of cognition and personality functioning, which goes beyond the confounding variable of the student's therapeutic gains, thus showing the sensitivity and competence of the TEMAS Asian American version in pulling the strengths of this Chinese American adolescent.

CASE STUDY 2: JAY

The second Asian American case, Jay, was administered a complete test battery.

In addition to the other tests, the student was administered the Asian American version of TEMAS. The pictures of this version show adequate face validity; however, this version is undergoing validation at this time and norms are not available. The TEMAS scores of this student were compared with the norms of the combined minority of the TEMAS Multicultural Test. The student was evaluated by a Chinese American psychologist in training.

Psychological Evaluation Report

Client's Name: Jay
Age: 10 years old
Test Dates: 12/17 & 12/29/04
Examiner: S. H, MA
Tests and Procedures Used for Assessment
Wechsler Intelligence Scale for Children—Fourth Edition (WISC-IV)
Woodcock-Johnson Test of Achievement-Third Edition
Tell-Me-A-Story (TEMAS)-Asian Version (Combined minority norm used for scoring)
The Bender–Gestalt Test
Clinical Interview with Child and Parent
Record Review

Reason for Referral

Jay was referred by his therapist for psychological testing in order to identify his strengths and weaknesses in cognitive and intellectual functioning, academic achievement, personality, and social/emotional functioning.

Background Information

Jay was an American-born 10-year-old boy of Chinese descent who attended fourth grade in a private school. He was held back in third grade because of poor academic performance, especially in reading and writing. He was referred for treatment the first time in 2001 at the age of 7, when he was diagnosed as having ADHD Combined Type (314.01). His symptoms included having difficulty sitting still and paying attention while doing schoolwork or homework. No aggressive behavior was reported. The student remained in treatment for about six months in 2001. He received individual therapy and Ritalin for his ADHD condition. At that time, he showed some improvement and his parents, claiming that they were too busy with their business, terminated the treatment. The student was brought back to the clinic in the spring of 2004, when his behavior and academic problems became worse. He began to receive individual therapy and he was prescribed Ritalin, 10mg twice a day. According to his parents, the student responded positively to medication.

Jay was born as a full-term healthy baby. He began to speak simple words around the age of one year and no speech delay was reported. According to the parent's report, the child achieved all his developmental milestones within a normal age range. His father came from China to the U.S. in the late 1980s and his mother in the early 1990s. Both parents speak limited English, but at home they speak Cantonese. They are self-employed. Since birth, Jay has been living in an intact family with his parents and his sister, who is 2 years older.

During the clinical interview, the student revealed that he had been having problems in reading, writing, and spelling. In addition to his learning problems in school, however, he did not seem to understand his presenting behavior problem. For example, he did not appear to know why he came to the clinic for treatment. Regarding inattentiveness, he said that he always thought about games in class. He proudly showed the examiner his brand-new Game Boy that he was given by his uncle as a Christmas gift. Socially, he appeared to be quite isolated as he reported that he had only a few friends in school.

A clinical interview with Jay's mother indicated the student's problems began in the first grade, when his teachers started to complain that the child could not sit still in the classroom. Following the teacher's recommendation, the child was brought to the clinic, where he underwent psychiatric evaluation and assignment for individual psychotherapy; however, his parents did not follow up and the case was terminated. The youngster was brought back to the clinic after he was left back in the third grade and his behavior deteriorated. According to the school report, Jay showed very poor school achievement in most subjects except math. He spent most of his time playing video games at home. According to his mother, he was able to sit still only when he was playing games. Moreover, he did not listen to his parents.

Mental Status Evaluation and Behavioral Observations

Jay was a 10-year-old boy of average height and somewhat chubby for his age. He was casually dressed, but well groomed. Although he seemed to be somewhat guarded, he readily followed the examiner to the testing room. Soon after the session began, he started asking questions and voluntarily made positive self-references, such that as he was able to write in script. His psychomotor movements were within normal range during the two testing sessions. He was able to remain seated until the evaluation was completed. Good eye contact was maintained after he became more familiar with the examiner. He tended to talk fast in conversation even when there was no need to be rushed. He displayed full range of affects, which were appropriate to the content and situation. Thought content included preoccupation with video games, conflicting relationships with peers in school, and some concerns about his own poor academic performance.

Jay was cooperative most of the time during the testing sessions. He was able to keep focused when the testing tasks were challenging and interesting to him. However, he easily became distracted when he did not like the tasks and his attention span dropped markedly. During the transition between two subtests of the WISC-IV, he saw a game in the testing room and asked if he could play with it. Another time while in the middle of a subtest, he saw another toy and wanted to play with it right away. After playing for a brief period of time, he was willing to go back to working on the testing tasks.

Jay was verbal and replied quickly when he knew the answers. When he was required to find similarities between two seemingly different objects, his responses were to the point and brief. When he was not sure about the answers, he tended to elaborate more. On a subtest of the IQ test that measured numerical skills, he often blurted out answers right after the examiner finished the questions, occasionally even before the questions were completed. When asked if he did a lot of math exercises, he said that he played a Math Journey Game on a CD in the second and third grades. He seemed to be aware of his personal strength in math.

Jay showed a disorganized and random approach in solving problems. When he was required to scan a random and structured arrangement of pictures and mark target pictures within a time limit, he used the same method approaching the tasks no matter whether the pictures were arranged randomly or with a structure. It seemed that the structure of the tasks did not help him better manage the tasks. Instead of noticing and taking advantage of the structure or cues, he started crossing out the pictures randomly until he reached the time limit.

Assessment Results and Interpretations:
Intellectual Functioning

On the WISC-IV, Jay achieved a Full Scale IQ score of 106, indicating that his overall cognitive abilities fell in the upper end of the average range and were ranked at the 66th percentile. There were indications of some fluctuation in his cognitive abilities across the four areas. His Verbal Comprehension Index Score, an indicator of his acquired verbal-related knowledge and verbal reasoning skills, was 104 (61st percentile) and fell in the average range. His Perceptual Reasoning Index Score was 104 (61st percentile), suggesting that his visual-perceptual organization skills fell in the average range. On the Working Memory Index, he obtained a standard score of 97 (42nd percentile), which suggested that his abilities to retain and process information in memory were also in the average range. Lastly, his Processing Speed Index Score was 121 (92nd percentile), which showed that his ability to process information rapidly was in the superior range.

Discrepancy comparisons of his index scores showed that there was a significant difference between his Processing Speed Index Score and all the other three Index Scores. This consistent discrepancy indicated that his ability to process information rapidly was significantly better developed than his acquired verbal-related knowledge and verbal reasoning skills, his visual-perceptual organization skills, and his abilities to hold and process information in memory.

On the 10 core subtests of the WISC-IV, the student's skills ranged from average to superior. More dramatic inconsistencies were detected on his performance on some supplemental subtests. In the Verbal Comprehension area, his skills on verbal reasoning, concept formation, and word knowledge were in the average range. His verbal comprehension, expression, and ability to demonstrate practical information were within the high average range. His performance on the two supplemental subtests in this area suggested that his ability to acquire, retain, and retrieve general factual knowledge was in the high average range and that his analytic and general reasoning ability fell in the average range. Overall, Jay showed average or higher verbal skills when compared with children his age.

His skills in the Perceptual Organization area consistently ranged from average to high average. Specifically, his ability to analyze and synthesize abstract stimuli and visual recognition of essential details of objects fell in the high average range. His categorical reasoning ability and his ability to manipulate abstractions and logical relationships were in the average range.

In the Working Memory area, Jay showed more fluctuations in his skills, which ranged from average to superior. His performance on the two core subtests indicated that his short-term auditory memory and attention fell in the average range. On the supplemental subtest, which measures mental manipulation, concentration, and numerical reasoning skills, he performed in the superior range. His numerical reasoning skills seemed to be his strength.

In the Processing Speed area, Jay demonstrated the most inconsistent performance. His performance on the two core subtests suggested that his visual perception and visual-motor coordination in a specified time limit were in the superior range. In the contrast, his performance on the supplemental subtest, which tests processing speed, visual selective attention, vigilance, and visual neglect indicated that his ability was in the borderline range. His poor performance on this subtest may be related to his disorganized approach to the task as described earlier.

In summary, Jay's overall cognitive functioning fell within the average range. Among the four index areas, there was a significant difference between his Processing Speed Index Score and all the other three Index Scores, suggesting that his ability to process information rapidly was significantly better developed than his verbal skills, his visual-perceptual organization skills, and his ability to retain and process information in memory. Comparisons of abilities in each of the four index areas indicated fairly consistent abilities on all the 10 core subtests, ranging from average to superior range with one exception indicative of his poor (borderline range) skills on visual selective attention, vigilance, and visual neglect.

Academic Achievement

Six subtests on the Woodcock Johnson Achievement Test-III were administered to evaluate the student's academic skills in vocabulary, spelling, reading comprehension, and mathematics. His performance on Letter-Word Identification was equivalent to a Grade Equivalent of 3.0. Similarly, his Grade Equivalent was 3.1 on Spelling. Taken together, these results suggested that his vocabulary in English was limited and that he had difficulty spelling some simple words. On Passage Comprehension, he obtained a Grade Equivalent of 2.7, far below his repeated third grade level. His performance on Oral Comprehension corresponded to a Grade Equivalent of 3.5. On the two math subtests Calculation and Applied Problems, Jay achieved eighth-grade level skills in fluency and solving word problems.

In summary, Jay's vocabulary, spelling skills, and reading comprehension were far below his grade level. In contrast, his math skills, including calculation and solving word problems, were above grade level and more advanced than most of his peers. Math skills were certainly his strengths. Clearly, there was a significant discrepancy between his overall intellectual abilities and his actual academic performance, especially his skills in vocabulary, spelling, and reading comprehension. This implies that even though he had potential to do as well in school as most of his peers, his bilingual home environment, limited attention span, oppositional behavior, and his obsession with play behavior interfered with his school achievement.

Visual-Motor Coordination

On the Bender–Gestalt Test, an individually administered test that measures a child's visual-motor coordination, the student made two errors, according to the Koppitz scoring system, thus achieving an age equivalent of 9 years to 9 years 11 months in psychomotor maturation development. This score indicated approximately age-appropriate visual-motor coordination skills.

Personality and Emotional Functioning

The student was administered the Asian American version of TEMAS, the short form, to evaluate his personality and his cognitive and emotional functioning. Since this version was in the process of validation, the student's raw scores were compared with the norms of combined Hispanics because he lived in a bilingual home. His parents spoke Cantonese at home. In the Cognitive functions, he scored within the average to the low average overall. More specifically, he scored within the average range in Reaction Time ($T = 51$), thus indicating skills in cognitive organization and in transforming visual stimuli into meaningful narrative. In addition, he scored within the above average range ($T = 55$) in Total Time, thus indicating that he told stories within a moderately elevated time frame; however, he told complete stories following structured inquiries as he showed a large discrepancy between spontaneous and total storytelling time. The student achieved a score within the very average range ($T = 34$) in verbal Fluency, thus indicating poor verbal skills. He scored within the above average range in Total Omission ($T = 54$), thus indicating somewhat poor selective attention (Please note: low scores in Total Omission are most adaptive). Furthermore, he scored above the 90th percentile cut-off point in his conflict and problem solving function, thus indicating poor social problem-solving skills. In the Personality Functions, he scored within the low average to borderline ranges overall. More specifically, he scored in the low average range in Interpersonal Relations ($T = 40$), within the very low average range in control of Aggression ($T = 35$), within the borderline range in coping with anxiety/depression ($T = 32$), within the very low average range in Achievement Motivation ($T = 39$), within the borderline range in Delay Gratification ($T = 31$), within the borderline range in Self-Concept of Competence ($T = 31$), and within the low average range in the following functions, Sexual Identity ($T = 40$), Moral Judgment ($T = 40$).

Content analysis of the stories revealed that Jay would like to interact with his peers on play activities, but both his parental overprotection and his fear of being rejected reinforced his avoidant behavior in psychosocial activities. In addition to being fearful, at times he manifested anger in the form of oppositional behavior toward his parents, especially the father. His repeated failure in school fostered a negative self-concept of competence; hence, he regressed to solitary video games, which gave him a false sense of mastery. Consequently, he was constantly driven by this pleasure-seeking behavior, thus further inhibiting the development of his delay gratification skills. He showed moderate weaknesses in his desire to do well in school, in his ability to distinguish right from wrong and reality from fantasy, and, to a lesser extent, in his gender identity. Cognitive and emotional indicators presented the profile of a youngster with deficits in verbal fluency, associated with his bilingual background, poor skills in resolving psychosocial problems, and poor ability to cope with anxiety-provoking situations. His poor selective attention skills also pointed to a diagnostic impression of ADHD.

Summary

On the WISC-IV, Jay achieved a Full Scale score of 106, indicating that his overall cognitive abilities were in the average range and ranked at the 66th percentile. Although his four index scores ranged from average to superior, discrepancy comparisons of his index scores showed that there was a significant difference between his Processing Speed Index Score and the other three Index Scores, suggesting that his ability to process information quickly was better developed than his verbal knowledge, visual-perceptual organization, and ability to hold and recall information. His performance on a supplemental subtest indicates that his ability in processing speed, visual selective attention, vigilance, and visual neglect was in the borderline range. His performance on the subtests on the Woodcock-Johnson Achievement Test-III showed below-grade-level skills in vocabulary, spelling, and reading comprehension but strong and above-grade-level math skills in both computation and solving word problems. Results of the TEMAS Narrative Assessment indicated that the student showed limited verbal ability and psychosocial problem-solving skills. In addition, he showed weaknesses in the areas of controlling aggressive drives, coping with anxiety-provoking situations, ability to delay gratification, and in self-concept of competence; and he showed moderate weaknesses in the area of relating with peers, gender identity, and ability to distinguish right from wrong and reality from fantasy. In addition, he showed relative strengths in selective attention. In the affective functions, he showed a full gamut of feelings, with high scores in "Happy," "Angry," and "Fearful." Emotional indicators presented a diagnostic impression of Generalized Anxiety Disorder with predominant symptoms of restlessness and poor concentration.

Recommendations

1. The student and his parents should be informed of the testing results, especially his strengths and weaknesses in his cognitive functioning, so that they could have a better understanding on how to make best use of his strengths.
2. The youngster would benefit from group therapy where he can learn social skills and how to interact with peers appropriately.
3. He would benefit from participating in some sport teams in order to practice competitive sports on a regular basis. Meanwhile, the time he spends in playing video games should be limited.
4. It would be beneficial to Jay if a big brother role model would be found within his male relatives, with whom he can share some sport and social activities.
5. Individual Psychotherapy should focus on helping the student develop more adaptive delay mechanism, self-esteem, aggressive impulse control, and coping with anxiety-provoking situations.
6. Parents and teachers should communicate on a regular basis in regard to his behaviors and academic progress. Consistent approaches for behavior management should be used both in school and at home.
7. Based on the present level of reading achievement, he would benefit from individual or small-group instruction from a qualified tutor or a reading specialist.

Discussion

As we discussed in the previous case studies, the TEMAS validity rests on the tripartite positive relationship among the TEMAS test data, the WISC-IV data, and the presenting problem of the youngster.

There was a positive relationship between the WISC-IV and TEMAS data showing deficits in verbal skills, but also showing adaptive skills in cognitive organizations. In addition there were positive relationships between TEMAS results showing deficits in selective attention, ability to delay gratification, control of aggression, and poor self-concept of competence in school, and the student's presenting problems of short attention span, continuous playing with electronic games, oppositional behavior, and poor self-concept regarding school achievement. Furthermore, the TEMAS results indicated relative strengths in the areas of interpersonal relationships, achievement motivation, gender identity, moral Judgment, and reality testing, which were utilized in treatment in order to develop a more positive self-concept and develop a more positive attitude toward school.

There is also concordance between the psychiatric evaluation, which gave the student a diagnosis of ADHD, and the TEMAS relatively high score in selective attention, which pointed out attentional deficits. However, the TEMAS data indicated the presence of anxiety disorder, which may also contribute to his poor attention Span and hyperactivity.

In summary, the positive relationship between the TEMAS test results and the child's presenting problems strongly suggest a diagnosis of *Generalized Anxiety Disorder* with predominant symptoms of restlessness and poor concentration.

Conclusion

The student has received very discontinuous treatment because of his mother's ambivalence toward psychotropic medications. The youngster had remained in treatment for only approximately six months each time the case was reopened. During his last reopening, he underwent psychological evaluation and continued to receive individual psychotherapy and psychotropic medication. In addition, his parents became more attentive toward the youngster and reinforced his positive behavior at home. The student showed more adaptive behavior both in school and at home. He graduated from a private elementary school and was promoted to attend sixth grade in Middle School within the public school system. His parents terminated treatment after he graduated from fifth grade.

JAY: ASIAN-AMERICAN TEMAS STORIES

The stories given by Jay to the nine cards, the short form of the Asian American version of TEMAS, are presented below. The TEMAS Record Booklet with the scores is shown at the end of the narratives (see Fig. 10–1).

Card 1B

RT   2"
ST   1.02
TT   1.19
Fluency   70

A boy is playing with his friend. But then his mother told him to deliver a letter to someone or somewhere. But he wants to play with his friends. But then the mom said, "go now." Then he refused to delivery the letter.

1a.   His friends.
2b.   At the sidewalk.
3c.   Come on and play basketball.
4d.   Playing.
5a.   Ask the kid to play.
6.   He wants to play basketball but not deliver letter. Feeling angry.

Card 22B

RT   2 sec.
ST   105 sec.
TT   185 sec.
Fluency   48

The boy is in the bathroom thinking about a girl in mirror. He's thinking what this girl is wearing. And he's thinking this girl is wearing half shirt and half bathing suit.

4a.   Using the bathroom.
5a.   Wash his hands.
6a.   He's thinking about a girl and he likes her.
6b.   Happy.

Card 7

RT	5 sec.
ST	58 sec.
TT	119 sec.
Fluency	58

One day a boy and his sister were fighting over a lamp. Then they broke it. Then the mother came, they argued about who broke the lamp.

2a. At their home.
4a. Fighting over the lamp.
5a. Nothing but argue about who broke the lamp.
6a. Both of them think they didn't do nothing. They blame on each other.
6b. Mad. [Which one?] Both.

Card 17B

RT	5 sec.
ST	80 sec.
TT	215 sec.
Fluency	92

One day a boy is studying. Studying and then he was thinking about if he is gong to get an F for the grade, or he was thinking he might get an A+ for grade.

1a. One is student one is teacher.
2a. In school.
3a. Teacher is asking why he got the poor grade. Other one said good job. And he is saying you've got good grade.
4a. He was studying.
5a. Do his homework.
6. He might get a poor grade, he'll be crying. If he got a good grade, he'll be happy.

Card 14B

RT	4 sec.
ST	71 sec.

TT   171 sec.
Fluency   70

One day a boy is studying. His brother invited his friends over and to dance and the boy was thinking if he could do his homework at night and they party first and then do his homework.

2a.   At someone's house.
3a.   Five of them dancing, one of them is thinking.
4a.   Sitting on floor.
5a.   Dance.
5b.   He's putting on his song.
6a.   He wants to dance but he has to do his homework.

Card 21M

RT   7 sec.
ST   101 sec.
TT   172 sec.
Fluency   54

A boy is having a nightmare. He saw a monster that could burn him. But after a while, he became a servant because he didn't want to get burnt. Then everyday he gets burgers to feed the monster.

2b.   In bed.
4b.   Covered his eyes.
5b.   Go to sleep.
6.   Scared. That he might get killed or burnt.

Card 15

RT   15 sec.
ST   75 sec.
TT   245 sec.
Fluency   94

One day four kids robbing a store, a police is there. Five kids won a baseball game and the police was proud of them. The other side, the police was telling the kids not to steal stuff.

2a. Five of them are at sidewalk. Six of them are in the baseball game.
4a. Baseball people were playing; other four people were stealing.
5a. Go away there people who steal. The people who won will take pictures.
6b. Baseball people are happy. Stealing people are sad. They are proud they won the baseball game. People who steal are not proud.

Card 10B

RT   3 sec.
ST   61 sec.
TT   214 sec.
Fluency: 89

One day a boy was putting money in his piggy bank and thought if he want to use his money to buy ice cream or a bike and his piggy bank is at his room.

2b. At home, bed room.
3b. He's putting money in piggy bank and he's saying he wants to use money to buy ice cream or a bike.
4b. Putting money is his piggy bank.
5b. He might take out the money and use it for ice cream.
6a. Thinking what he's going to get.
6b. And happy.

Card 20

RT   6 sec.
ST   58 sec.
TT   123 sec.
Fluency: 51

One day a person is sleeping in his bedroom and covering his eyes to go to sleep. And he had a good dream about a golden horse and a kingdom.

4b. Tried to go to sleep.
5b. Covers his eyes and then go to sleep.
6a. About a golden horse and a kingdom.
6b. Happy.

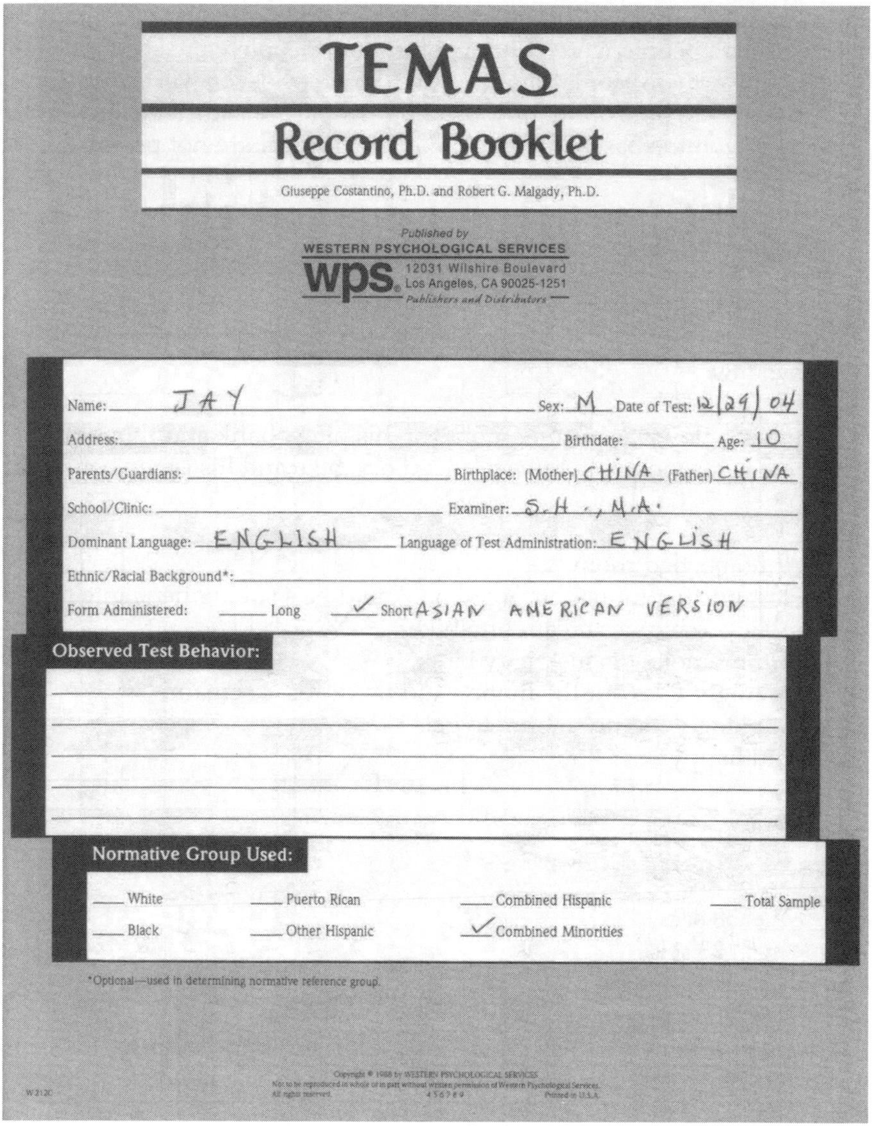

TEMAS

Record Booklet

Giuseppe Costantino, Ph.D. and Robert G. Malgady, Ph.D.

Published by
WESTERN PSYCHOLOGICAL SERVICES
12031 Wilshire Boulevard
WPS Los Angeles, CA 90025-1251
— *Publishers and Distributors* —

Name: _JAY_ Sex: _M_ Date of Test: _12|29|04_

Address: ___ Birthdate: ___ Age: _10_

Parents/Guardians: ___ Birthplace: (Mother) _CHINA_ (Father) _CHINA_

School/Clinic: ___ Examiner: _S.H., M.A._

Dominant Language: _ENGLISH_ Language of Test Administration: _ENGLISH_

Ethnic/Racial Background*: ___

Form Administered: ___ Long ✓ Short _ASIAN AMERICAN VERSION_

Observed Test Behavior:

___

___

___

___

___

Normative Group Used:

___ White ___ Puerto Rican ___ Combined Hispanic ___ Total Sample

___ Black ___ Other Hispanic ✓ Combined Minorities

*Optional—used in determining normative reference group.

FIGURE 10–1. Scored record booklet.

Scoring Sheet
Quantitative Scales

Card No.	Reaction Time (Seconds)	Total Time (Minutes)	Fluency	Total Omissions	Interpersonal Relations	Aggression	Anxiety/ Depression	Achievement Motivation	Delay of Gratification	Self-Concept	Sexual Identity	Moral Judgment	Reality Testing	Happy	Sad	Angry	Fearful
1*	2	103/119	70	1	3 2/2,5				2							1	
2																	
3																	
4																	
5																	
6																	
7*	5	58/119	58	1	3/2 2/2	2						2				1	
8																	
9																	
10*	3	61/214	89					2						1			
11																	
12																	
13																	
14*	4	71/171	70		3			2	2								
15*	15	75/245	94		3 2,5/3	2		3				2		1	1		
16																	
17*	5	80/215	92				2	2		2				1	1		
18																	
19																	
20*	6	58/123	51	2			N							1			
21*	7	101/172	54			2	2 N						3				1
22*	2	105/185	51	1			N					2	2	1			
23																	
Sum	49	7/15.63	629	5	12	6	4	7	6	2	2	4	5	5	2	2	1
Number of Cards Scored					5	3	2	3	3	1	1	2	2				
Mean Score**	2,4				2	2	2	2,3	2	2	2	2	2.5				
Sum of Functions Not Pulled ("N-Scores")						2											

*Cards used for Short Form.
**Mean Score = Sum ÷ Number of cards scored.

Page 2

FIGURE 10–1. Scored record booklet. (*continued*)

	Scoring Sheet — Qualitative Indicators																
	Affective Functions			Cognitive Functions													
											Optional						
											Omissions				Transformations		
Card No.	Neutral	Ambivalent	Inappropriate Affect	Conflict	Sequencing	Imagination	Relationships	Total Transformations	Inquiries	Main Character	Secondary Character	Event	Setting	Main Character	Secondary Character	Event	Setting
1*											1						
2																	
3																	
4																	
5																	
6																	
7*				(1)								1					
8																	
9																	
10*																	
11																	
12																	
13																	
14*																	
15*				(1)				2							1	1	
16																	
17*				(1)													
18																	
19																	
20*												1	1				
21*																	
22*B				(1)				2				1			1	1	
23																	
Sum				4				4		1	3	1			2	2	
90%+ (✓)				✔				✔							✔	✔	

*Cards used for Short Form.

Page 3

FIGURE 10–1.　Scored record booklet. (*continued*)

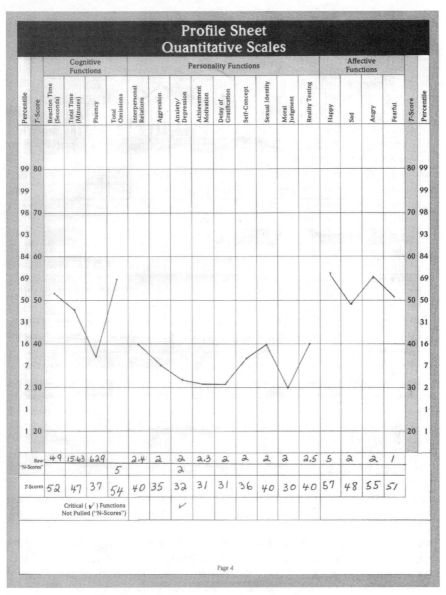

FIGURE 10–1. Scored record booklet. (*Continued*)

REFERENCES

Chiu, Y., & Ring, J. M. (1998). Chinese and Vietnamese immigrant adolescents under pressure: Identifying stressors and interventions. *Professional Psychology: Research and Practice, 29 (5),* 444–449.

Costantino, G. (1987). *TEMAS (Tell-Me-A-Story) test cards.* Los Angeles, CA: Western Psychological Services.

Costantino, G., Malgady, R. G. (1983). Verbal fluency of Hispanic, Black and White Children on TAT and TEMAS, A New Thematic Apperception Test. *Hispanic Journal of Behavioral Sciences, 5,* 199–206.

Costantino, G., & Malgady, R. G. (1996). Development of TEMAS, A multicultural thematic apperception test: Psychometric properties and clinical utility. In G. R. Sodowsky & J. Impara (Eds.),. *Multicultural assessment in counseling and clinical psychology.* (pp. 85–136). Lincoln, NE: Buros Institute of Mental Measurements. University of Nebraska.

Costantino, G., Malgady, R. G., Colon-Malgady, G., & Bailey, J. (1992). Clinical utility of TEMAS with non-minority children. *Journal of Personality Assessment, 59*(3), 433–438.

Costantino, G., Malgady, R. G., & Rogler, L. H. (1988). *TEMAS (Tell-Me-A-Story) Test manual.* Los Angeles: Western Psychological Services.

Costantino, G., Malgady, R. G., & Vazquez, C. (1981). A comparison of the Murray-TAT and a new thematic apperception test for Hispanic children. *Hispanic Journal of Behavioral Sciences, 3,* 291–300.

Costantino, G., Malgady, R. G., Rogler, L. H., & Tsui, E. (1988). Discriminant analysis of clinical outpatients & public school children by TEMAS: A thematic apperception test for Hispanics and blacks. *Journal of Personality Assessment, 52,* 670–678.

Ho, D. Y. (1986). Chinese patterns of socialization. In M. H. Bond (Ed.), *The psychology of the Chinese people* (pp. 1–37). London: Oxford University Press.

Kim, L. S., & Chun, C. A. (1993). Ethnic differences in psychiatric diagnosis among Asian American adolescents. *Journal of Nervous and Mental Disease, 181*(10), 612–617.

Kim, B., & Omizo, M. (2003). Asian cultural values, attitudes toward seeking professional psychological help, and willingness to see a counselor. *The Counseling Psychologist, 31,* 343–361.

Liu, C. T., & Lin, C. (1998). Psychoeducational interventions with southeast Asian students: An ecological approach. *Special Services in Schools, 1,* 129–148.

Leong, F. T., & Lau, A. S., (2001). Barriers to providing effective mental health services to Asian Americans. *Mental Health Service Research, 3,* 201–14.

Lung, A. Y., & Sue, S. (1997). Transcultural child psychiatry: A portrait of Chinese-American children. In G. Johnson-Powell & J. Yamamoto (Eds.), *Transcultural child development* (pp. 208–236). New York, NY: John Wiley & Sons.

Malgady, R. G., Rogler, L. H., & Costantino, G. (1987). Ethnocultural and linguistic bias in mental health evaluation of Hispanics. *American Psychologist, 42,* 228–234.

Maki, M. & Kitano, H. I. (2002). Conseling Asian Americans. In P. Pedersen, J. Draguns, W. Lonner, & J. Trimble (Eds). pp. 254–274. Counseling Across Cultures, Fifth Edition, Sage Publications, and New York.

Matoba Alder, S. (2001). Racial and ethnic identity formation of Midwestern Asian-American children. *Contemporary Issues in Early Childhood, 2,* 265–294.

Prillerman, S. L. (1988). Coping with a stressful situation: A prospective study of Black student adjustment to a predominantly White university. Unpublished doctoral dissertation, University of California, Los Angeles.

Reese-Albright, A., & Chung, H. (2002). Case-based reviews: Depression in Asian American children. *Western Journal of Medicine, 176,* 244–248.

Snowden, L. R. (2003). Racial/ethnic bias and health bias in mental health assessment and intervention: Theory and evidence. *American Journal of Public Health, 93,* 239–243.

Sue, S., & Morishima, J. (1982). *The mental health of Asian Americans.* San Francisco: Jossey-Bass.

Sue, S., & Zane, N. (1987). The role of culture and cultural techniques on psychotherapy. *American Psychologist, 42,* 37–45.

Tseng, W., & Hsu, J. (1972). The Chinese attitude toward parental authority as expressed in Chinese children' stories. *Archives of General Psychiatry 26*(1), pp. 28–34.

Woo, J. Y. T. (1988). *Handbook on the assessment of east Asian Students.* New York: Hunter College of CUNY, Department of Special Education, Training Program for Teachers of Handicapped Children of Asian Origin. Reston, VA: The Council for Exceptional Children.

Yang, C-M., Kuo, L-H., & Costantino, G. (2003, July). *Validity of Asian TEMAS in Taiwanese children: Preliminary Data.* 8th Europen Congress of Psychology, Vienna, Austria,

Yu, E., Chang, C. F., Liu, W., & Fernandez, M. (1989). Suicide among Asian American youth. In M. Feinleib (Ed.), *Report of the secretary's task force on youth suicide* (pp. 157–176). Washington, DC: U.S. Department of Health and Human Services.

Zhang, N., & Dixon, D., (2003). Acculturation and attitudes of Asian international students toward seeking psychological help. *Journal of Multicultural Counseling and Development, 31,* 205–222.

11

Diverse Cross-Cultural Studies

This chapter reports three cross-cultural case studies. The first school case is a Central American girl, who immigrated to Milan, Italy at the age of seven with her parents. The second school case is an Argentinean girl who was born and lived in Buenos Aires, Argentina. The third is a clinical case of a girl born and raised in Puerto Rico.

ITALIAN CASE STUDY: MARIA

The first case, Maria was administered the minority version of TEMAS by a graduate psychology student in Milan, Italy as part of her thesis (Fantini, 2005). The child was not undergoing psychotherapy, but she presented academic and adjustment problems in school. The TEMAS stories were tape-recorded and then transcribed.

Brief Psychological Report

Name:	Maria
Age:	10
Grade:	4th
Language Dominance:	Spanish/Italian
Test Language:	Italian
Test Administered:	TEMAS (Minority Version; Short Form)

Reason for Referral

The student was not formally referred for psychological assessment. However, her parents indicated that she was presenting academic and psychosocial problems in school and consented for her to be tested as part of a thesis to generate personality profiles of culturally and linguistically diverse children living in Italy.

Brief Family History

Maria was born in Ecuador following normal pregnancy and delivery. It is reported that she achieved her developmental milestones within normal time limits. She attended kindergarten and first grade in Ecuador. The student emigrated to Milan, Italy with her parents at the age of 7. Her mother has a Bachelor of Arts degree and worked as a home health aide to an elderly man; her father has a Bachelor of Arts degree and worked as a taxi driver.

Test Results

The scoring of Maria's TEMAS stories was based on norms of Other Hispanics between the ages of 8 and 10 years old. For each scale, the scores are related to the T-score obtained. The stories were told in Italian.

Quantitative Scales

Cognitive Functions:

Reaction Time:	$T = 47$ (47th percentile) is within the low average range.
Total Time:	$T = 64$ (93rd percentile) is within the high average range, suggesting that Maria required time to tell her stories.
Fluency:	$T = 57$ (69th percentile) is within the average range and along with the Total Time T score suggests that Maria was adequately productive in the task at hand.
Total Omissions:	$T = 41$ (17th percentile) is within the low average range, and it suggests that Maria included in her stories most of the presented stimuli, such as main character, secondary characters, events, and settings, which indicates adaptive Selective Attention.

Qualitative Indicators

Conflict: In this function, which refers to her ability to recognize and resolve the TEMAS conflict depicted in the cards, Maria obtained a significant score of 3 that fell above the cutoff point; thus indicating that she had the ability of recognizing, but not resolving psychosocial and or personal conflicts.

Transformations: In this function, which refers to perceptual distortion of characters, setting and events, Maria obtained a N-score of 7, that is above the cutoff point; thus indicating a strong need to distort her psychosocial environment.

Personality Functions:

Interpersonal Relations: $T = 39$ (14th percentile) is within the border-line range, which suggests a maladaptive ability to relate to others.

Aggression: $T = 35$ (7th percentile) is within the border-line range, indicating that Maria showed maladaptive control over her aggressive impulses.

Anxiety/Depression: $T = < 30$ (1st percentile) is within the deficient range, indicating that Maria exhibited maladaptive coping skills in dealing with anxiety and depression-provoking situations.

Achievement Motivation: $T = 41$ (16th percentile) is within the low average range, indicating that Maria showed poor motivation to excel.

Delay of Gratification: $T = 33$ (7th percentile) is in the borderline range and it indicates that Maria had a poor ability to delay a reward in order to meet a future objective.

Self-Concept: $T = 54$ (69th percentile) is within the average range, which indicates that Maria had realistic perception of her psychosocial, academic, and/or intellectual competence.

Sexual Identity: $T = 32$ (7th percentile) is within the border-line range, demonstrating that Maria had a maladaptive perception of her sexual identity.

Moral Judgment: $T = 32$ (7th percentile) is within the border-line range, indicating that Maria exhibited maladaptive ability to distinguish right from wrong and to behave rightfully.

Reality Testing: $T = 37$ (7th percentile) is within the borderline range, indicating that Maria had maladaptive ability to distinguish between fantasy and reality and to anticipate consequences.

Affective Functions:

Happy: $T = 65$ (93rd percentile) is within the high average range, indicating that Maria exhibited a predominantly cheerful mood.

Sad: $T = 68$ (96th percentile) is within the high average range, demonstrating that Maria exhibited a predominantly sad mood.

Angry: $T = 56$ (60th percentile) is within the high average range, indicating that Maria tended to frequently verbalize angry feelings.

Fearful: $T = 54$ (55th percentile) is within the average to within the average range, demonstrating that Maria tended to internalize fearful mood states. (For complete scoring, see record booklet Figure 11–1.)

Profile Interpretation

TEMAS results indicate that the student showed adaptive cognitive skills in the area of Cognitive Functions, evidenced by the rapid reaction time in cognitive organization in converting visual stimuli into narrative, by above-average fluency, which showed high verbal skills, and by a low score in selective attention, thus showing adaptive perceptual and emotional ego defenses. However, in the areas of personality functioning, she showed below-average skills in psychosocial functioning, somewhat poor control of aggressive ideation and inadequate skills to cope with anxiety and depression-provoking situations. In addition, she exhibited poor ability to delay gratification, to distinguish right from wrong or reality from fantasy, and above all, she showed maladaptive sexual identity. Conversely, she showed adaptive self-concept of competence, thus indicating adequate self-esteem; to a lesser extent, she showed somewhat adequate achievement motivation. In the area of Affective Functions, Maria, showed very high to high scores in "Sad" and "Fearful", which correlated with low scores in coping with anxiety/depression; thus indicating a diagnostic impression of Anxiety Disorder Not Otherwise Specified (mixed anxiety-depressed disorder). She also showed an elevated score in "Happy", which may indicate some ability to cope with adverse life situations. In the areas of Qualitative Indicators, she showed some ability to recognize the psychosocial conflicts, but very poor ability to resolve them. Although she showed adequate selective attention, she tended to distort characters and events; this seemed to be related to her acculturation process and some mistrust towards the environment.

In summary, Maria's personality profile indicates that she was experiencing difficulties interacting with new peers in a foreign country. Her mood, in fact, was quite often sad, fearful, and angry and she has difficulty coping with depressive and anxiety symptoms. To counteract her difficulties, Maria relied on a "Pollyannaish" outlook and tended to modify her perceptions to fit her needs, including inadequate delay of gratification. However, given her poor coping abilities, it is likely that Maria also had frequent experiences of anxiety and depression which manifested in fearfulness, sadness, and anger associated with the acculturation process. As such, in spite of her best efforts, she is unable to adequately manage excessive negative self-perceptions when she compared herself to Italian counterparts. Poignantly, in fact, she stated that she was sad "because she does not like how she look[s] … because she would like to be in another way … of skin a bit lighter color and have another dress."

Overall, Maria was a 10-year-old child who emigrated from South America to Italy at the age of 7 and was having difficulties adjusting to her new environment, in spite of her best efforts. Sadness, anxiety, and anger often ensued and predominated her mood states. Maria often compared herself to others, whom she was likely to see as better, smarter, and better looking than she was. As such, racial and acculturation issues were at the forefront of the difficulties for her, whereas issues of academic achievement may be in the background, possibly causing her to engage in poor delay of gratification in order to compensate for feeling deprived. Consequently, Maria's interactions with others may not be optimal and were impeding the development of appropriate psychosocial skills.

MARIA'S STORIES

LEGEND

I = interviewer; instructions about temporal sequence
M = Maria
(?) = incomprehensible part in the taping
… = long pause in speech
… = interrupted word

Card 1

RT: 5 sec.
TT: 3 min. 25 sec.
FLUENCY: 105

M: There are these two (girls) that are jumping rope and ... and the
     mother tells to mail this letter to the post office but the daughter
     wants to go play jump rope ... mmm

I: *Try to tell more.*

M: They are in the middle of the street near a, near some buildings are
     five children, three are playing jump rope and the other two girls ...

I: *What were they doing before?*

M: Mmm, playing jump rope.

I: *They were playing jump rope?*

M: No, they were playing jump rope and before they were playing
     something else ...

I: *What do you think will happen? What will these people do?*

M: Mmm she will go to the post office to bring this paper and the
     others will go home.

I: *And what do you think she was thinking about?*

M: That she wants to play with the girls.

I: *And what does she feel at the end of the story? How does she feel?*

M: Happy?

I: *Why happy?*

M: Because she played with them.

Card 7

RT: 5 sec.
TT: 3 min. 29 sec.
FLUENCY: 162

M: There are these two children that made the lamp fall and their mother is angry with both of them.. Both of them say that it was his fault or her fault … at the end this girl trips (?) because they …

I: *At the end?*

M: Eh, not really at the end, when they leave.

I: *Explain well to me how these things happen in succession, what happens first?*

M: Ok, first these two children make the lamp fall and the wire gets entangled in her legs, then when they want to going to the kitchen or in the bathroom (?) they trip

I: *Now I understand.*

M: And their mother is mad.

I: *Where do you think these people are?*

M: At home.

I: *And what were these people doing before?*

M: Maybe their mother was cooking and the two children were playing.

I: *They were playing and?*

M: All of a sudden they made the lamp fall

I: *And what do you think they will do then?*

M: They will clean the house.

I: *They will clean the house?*

M: From the glass.

I: *Can you choose one person and tell me what he/she was thinking?*

M: The mother, that her children. That her children are a disaster.

I: *That they are a disaster. why?*

M: Eh, because they make everything fall.

I: *And how does she feel at the end of the story?*

M: A little mad and a bit relaxed.

I: *Why?*

M: A bit mad because they made the lamp fall , a bit relaxed because she is old.

I: *And thus a bit relaxed meaning what? That ...*

M: She wasn't very worried.

Card 10

RT: 3 sec.
TT: 2 min. 15 sec.
FLUENCY: 115

M: This girl wants to put a lot of money in her piggy bank to buy an ice cream or a bicycle and so she puts them in the piggy bank and thinks the bicycle or the ice cream...

I: *Where do you think she is?*

M: At home.

I: *At home?*

M: Yes in her room.

I: *And what was she doing before?*

M: Thinking of what to do.

I: *That is?*

M: To see how she would gather the money.

I: *To do what?*

M: To buy the bicycle and the ice-cream.

I: *What will she do next?*

M: Go to the ice-cream store and buy the ice cream and ride a bicycle to play a bit with the bicycle.

I: *Then she will buy the bicycle?*

M: If she can, if she has money.

I: *What do you think?*

M: I think she, she will buy the ice cream because the bicycle costs too much.

I: *And how do you think she feels at the end of the story?*

M: Happy and sad because she wanted the bicycle too; Happy because she ate the ice-cream.

Card 14

RT: 3 sec.
TT: 5 min. 52 sec.
FLUENCY: 155

M: Ehm ok, there is this girl that was doing her home work and can't concentrate because there is another girl plays music and two dance and others make noise with this thing.

I: *What is it?*

M: I don't know… and it will happen that she will get a note from school because she did not do her homework because she could not concentrate.

I: *Where are these people?*

M: At home.

I: *Whose home?*

M: Hers.

I: *Who are these people, do they know each other?*

M: Yes, they could be her friends, parents.

I: *What do you think?*

M: Friends.

I: *Friends?*

M: Yes.

I: *And what do you think they were doing before?*

M: Ehm, they were playing.

I: *They were playing? All of them?*

M: Not all of them before, they (the boys) weren't there.

I: *Yes?*

M: They were playing jump rope.

I: *And then she will get a note (from school)?*

M: Yes.

I: *What do you think she was thinking?*

M: What to do … ehh what to write.

I: *What to write?*

M: And what are they doing they are playing she too.

I: *What do you think she feels at the end of the story?*

M: Ehm … tired

I: *Tired?*

M: Yes because the others were making such confusion and she could not concentrate.

I: *And what does she feels as tired?*

M: what do you mean?

I: *Well, I would like to know what does she feel?*

M: Tired and …

I: *Do you know what I mean?*

M: Yes ehm she is nervous because she did not finish her homework.

I: *Ok, nervous, then can you explain it to me a bit better? I would like to know her emotions.*

M: Chills.

I: *Chills?*

M: Yes.

I: I didn't understand well what does she feels when she is nervous.

M: …

I: *Can you imagine it?*

M: She feels a bit lonely because she wanted to play with them.

I: *Then how does this make her feel?*

M: Sad.

Card 15

RT: 4 sec.
TT: 4 min. 15 sec.
FLUENCY: 167

M: There are these two children that won the cup (trophy) for a soccer game and these others that that the policeman is yelling at them because they broke the glass to take these things, a television; they are in an open space.

I: *Where?*

M: In a park and they were stealing and broke the glass instead they won a cup (trophy) for a game of soccer (?) that's all

I: *Who do you think these people are? Do they know each other?*

M: No...

I: *Who are they?*

M: Friends.

I: *Are they all friends?*

M: Or parents.

I: *What do you think?*

M: Parents.

I: *Parents? All of them?*

M: Not all ...

I: *And what do you think they were these people doing before?*

M: Eh these were playing soccer and these were taking the things that they have in their hands.

I: *And what do you think these people will do?*

M: These will go home happy or will play.. play another game these will go to the police.

I: And ...

M: And will call their mother.

I: And ...

M: And they will go to.. they will pay for the glass.

I: *Can you chose one of these people and tell me what was he/she thinking?*

M: She (the girl among the robbers) fearful she is afraid.

I: *Why?*

M: Because the policeman stopped them and because she is not calm because she thought her Parents would beat (punish) her.

I: *And then how do you think she feels at the end of the story?*

M: Mmm sad because, sad because she broke the glass and for taking those things.

Card 17

RT: 4 sec.
TT: 1 min. 56 sec.
FLUENCY: 92

M: This girl was doing, was redoing her homework no was studying because she got an F on her homework and would like to get an A+ on her homework; so she is studying and when she got the F the teacher yelled at her and when she gets an A she will be happy for having gotten that result.

I: *Then, sorry, this is what will happen?*

M: Yes.

I: *And where are these people?*

M: Oh here they are in class and here she is home studying.

I: *What is she thinking?*

M: Sadness for having gotten an F and for not having studied a lot and ...

I: And *how do you think she will feel at the end of the story?*

M: Happy because she will get an A.

Card 20

RT: 4 sec.
TT: 4 min. 33 sec.
FLUENCY: 165

M: There is this boy that was dreaming of being in a castle with a water-fall in the mountains and an angry horse.

I: *Why is it angry?*

M: No well not angry it was falling from these rocks here … and this horse was galloping and … can I change it?

I: *Yes*

M: There is this horse that wants to go in this castle and and …

I: *Why does it want to go in the castle?*

M: … I don't know.

I: *What do you think?*

M: Because it wants to go wants to find a man that hurt him or his family …

I: *Therefore?*

M: Therefore ehm it is angry with everybody because it wants to go inside and wants to find that man.

I: *Which?*

M: This one (the person in bed).

I: *Ah a man?*

M: A woman, I don't know.

I: *How would you prefer it is your story.*

M: …

I: *And tell me where is this person?*

M: Ehm in the coun..in the country.

I: *This person (points to the person in bed)*

M: Ah at home in bed.

I: *And what was he doing before?*

M: Sleeping.

I: *And what do you think he will do in the future?*

M: He will get up because he will have a bad dream.

I: And...

M: And will go to wash his face.

I: *And how does the story end?*

M: Eh that he will wake up and will see that it is all over.

I: *And how does he feel at the end of the story? What he feel?*

M: Relief because ...

I: *Because?*

M: Because ... well it was all a dream...

Card 21

RT: 2 sec.
TT: 2 min. 45 sec.
FLUENCY: 137

M: There is that man again that was sleeping and before dreams that that there is a monster with fire and then he dreams that there is another monster that eats and that he gives him food to eat . . . what happens is that this man, this monster wanted to eat him because it was hungry and then he ehm made sandwich and gave to eat so it wouldn't eat him and though he had bit of fear but then had mmm was relaxed because it didn't eat him.

I: *What do you think this person was doing before?*

M: Sleeping.

I: *And what will he do in the future?*

M: He will wake up and will go to have breakfast.

I: *And how will he feel at the end of the story?*

M: Excited.

I: *Excited?*

M: Yes because he always dreams of things that at the end don't kill him.

I: *But then what does he feel in being excited?*

M: … Still fear.

I: *Why is he still afraid?*

M: Because if he was afraid that he was killed and relaxed.

I: *Why?*

M: Because at the end it didn't kill him.

Card 22

RT: 6 sec.
TT: 4 min. 16 sec.
FLUENCY: 170

M: There is this girl … ehm there is this girl that looks at herself in the mirror; she is in the bathroom and is looking at herself in the mirror and is this way (boy side) but she would like would like to be like this (girl side) and is sad because this way she doesn't like how she is.

I: *How is that?*

M: Because she does not like how she look.

I: *Why?*

M: Because she would like to be in another way.

I: *How do you mean?*

M: Of skin a bit lighter color and have another dress…

I: *And instead how is she?*

M: A bit darker skin and with different dress from that one that she would like …

I: *Can you tell me more?*

M: First she was washing her hands and then she decided to take a stool to look in the mirror how she was ehm … (sighs).

I: *Where is this person?*

M: In the bathroom.

I: *And before she was washing her hand and what will she do in the future?*

M: She will go eat.

I: *Why?*

M: Because it was dinner time.

I: *And what was she thinking?*

M: That would really like to be like that girl and she would like to be taller.

I: *And what do you think she will feel at the end of the story? How does she feel?*

M: … Mmm bits not well sad because she wants to be like that girl there.

I: Ok.

ARGENTINIAN CASE STUDY: ABIGAIL

Abigail's TEMAS stories were collected in Buenos Aires, Argentina (Dupertuis et al., 2004). The student was eight years old at the time of testing. She was not receiving psychotherapy at the time. The *T* scores of Abigail's TEMAS protocol are based on norms of Other Hispanics between the age of 8 and 10 years old. For each scale, the interpretation will therefore be related to the T-score and Percentile scores obtained. (For complete scoring, see record booklet, Figure 11–2.)

Analysis of Results: Quantitative Scales

Cognitive Functions
    Reaction Time: $T = 66$ (95th percentile) is above a high average range, which indicates that Abigail responded very slowly. This may denote anxiety, inhibition, or ideational rehearsal of projective stimuli (e.g., interfering factors). In analyzing her RT card by card, it appears that the longest RT occurred on Card 1 and Card 20, not on all the cards, suggesting that interfering factors such as anxiety associated with maternal conflict and falling fom a horse, may have delayed her ability to make up a story on these two cards.

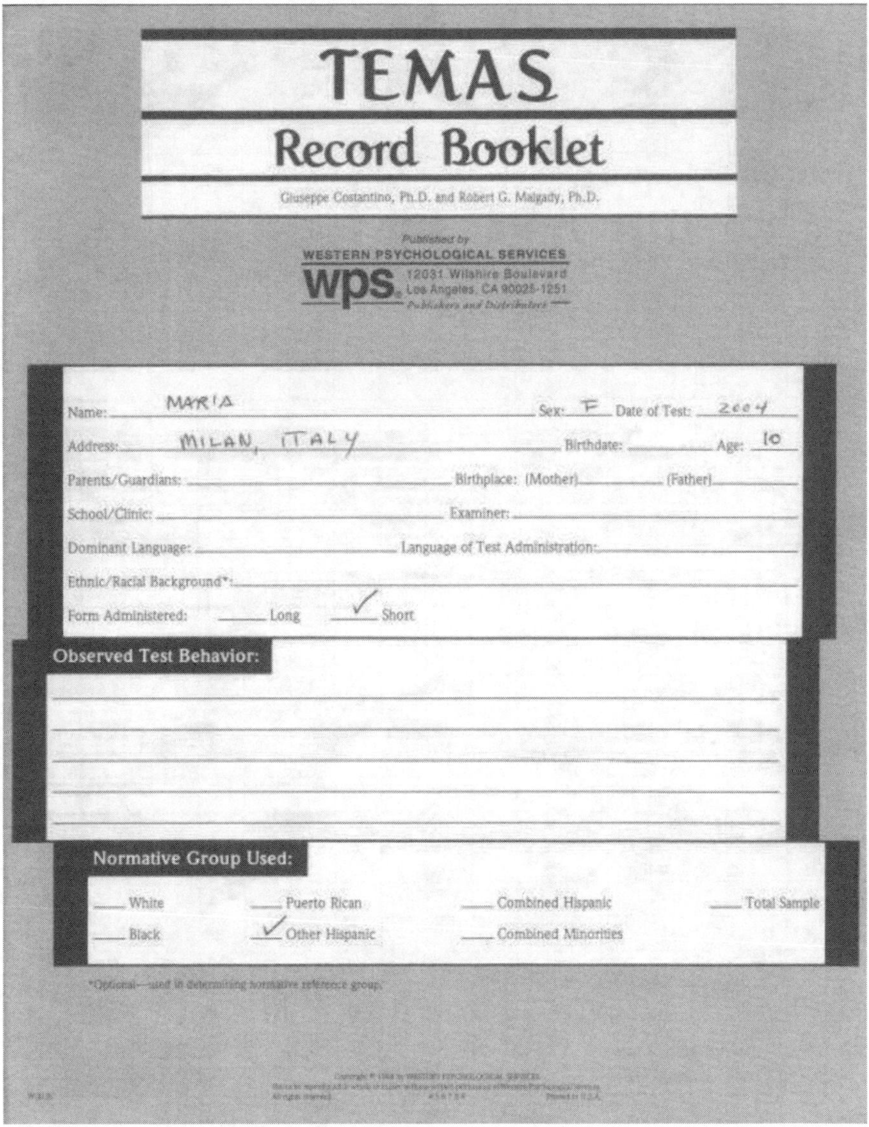

FIGURE 11–1. Scored record booklet.

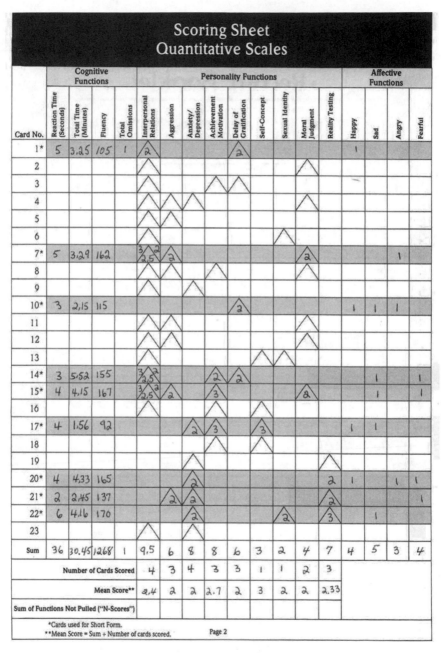

FIGURE 11–1.   Scored record booklet. (*Continued*)

Scoring Sheet
Qualitative Indicators

Card No.	Affective Functions			Cognitive Functions						Optional — Omissions				Optional — Transformations			
	Neutral	Ambivalent	Inappropriate Affect	Conflict	Sequencing	Imagination	Relationships	Total Transformations	Inquiries	Main Character	Secondary Character	Event	Setting	Main Character	Secondary Character	Event	Setting
1*											1						
2																	
3																	
4																	
5																	
6																	
7*				(1)													
8																	
9																	
10*																	
11																	
12																	
13																	
14*				(1)				1								1	
15*								1								1	
16																	
17*																	
18																	
19																	
20*				(1)				3						1	1	1	
21*								1						1			
22*								1						1			
23																	
Sum				3				7	1					3	2	2	
90% + (✓)				✓				✓						✓	✓	✓	

*Cards used for Short Form.

FIGURE 11–1. Scored record booklet. (*Continued*)

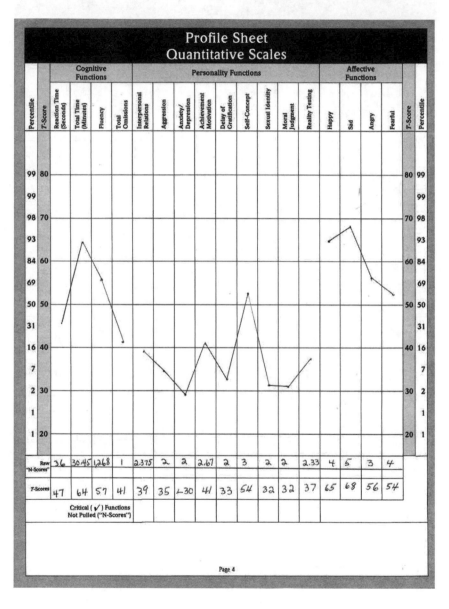

FIGURE 11–1.   Scored record booklet. (*Continued*)

Total Time: $T = 52$ (55th percentile) is within the average range, suggesting that Abigail utilized an average amount of time to tell her stories once she began.

Fluency: $T = 48$ (48th percentile) is within the slightly average range and along with the Total Time T-score suggests that Abigail was adequately productive in the task at hand, though somewhat economical.

Total Omissions: $T = 52$ (65th percentile) is within the above average range and it suggests that Abigail generally did not include in her stories most of the presented stimuli, such as main character, secondary characters, events, and settings.

Selective Attention: Abigail obtained a $T = 52$ (55th percentile) in total omissions, which fell within the above average range, indicating that she often failed to perceive all elements in the pictures. This T- score coupled with the N-scores of 1 in the aggression scale and N-score of 3 in the anxiety/depression scale, which are above the cutoff point for these personality functions, indicated that the student exhibited a maladaptive defense mechanism in perceiving the environment as whole and in perceiving aggressive and anxiety/depression provoking situations.

Total Transformations: These refer to perceptual distortions of characters, events, and settings. In this protocol, Abigail showed a significant number of transformations for main characters, reaching a critical cut-off score indicating that she most frequently changed the main characters (e.g., in Cards 20 and 21). Abigail transformed the gender of the main characters in these two cards, suggesting the role of defense mechanism akin to denial. The interaction of these significant transformations with significant omissions and N-values of Personality Functions not Pulled of Aggression and Anxiety/Depression, and poor ability to resolve conflicts points out a pathological personality functioning, which needed to be addressed by a therapeutic intervention.

Personality functions

Interpersonal Relations: $T = 36$ (7th percentile) is within the very low average range, which suggests a maladaptive ability to relate to others.

Aggression: $T = 35$ (7th percentile) is within the very low average range, which indicates that Abigail showed maladaptive control over her aggressive impulses. Given an "N-score" of 1 above the critical cutoff score (e.g., Personality Functions Not Pulled as part of the content of some TEMAS stories), the very low average T-score may also be interpreted as indicating that Abigail did not pay attention to aggressive stimuli out of fear of retaliation or of the disapproval of authority figures. She thus failed to show adaptive control of her aggressive impulses.

Anxiety/Depression: $T = < 30$ (1st percentile) is within the deficient range, which indicates that Abigail exhibited extremely maladaptive coping skills in dealing with anxiety and depression-provoking situations. Given an "N-score" of 3 above the critical cutoff score for anxiety/depression, the extremely low T-score may be interpreted as indicating that Abigail exhibited a maladaptive selective attention or strong repression, thus manifesting a very maladaptive defense system in dealing with anxiety/depression provoking situations. Also, see Total Omissions and Total Transformations in the previous section.

Achievement Motivation: $T = 35$ (7th percentile) is within the very low average range, indicating that Abigail showed very poor motivation to excel.

Delay of Gratification: $T = 40$ (40th percentile) is within the low average range and it indicates that Abigail showed poor delay mechanisms. This finding confirmed Abigail's poor ability to delay gratification in real life.

Self-Concept: $T = 54$ (69th percentile) is within the above average range, which indicated that Abigail had realistic perception of her psychosocial, academic, and/or intellectual competence.

Sexual Identity: $T = 51$ (52nd percentile) is within the above average range, suggesting that Abigail had an adequate perception of her sexual identity.

Moral Judgment: $T = 32$ (4th percentile) is within the very low range, indicating that Abigail exhibited maladaptive ability to distinguish right from wrong and to behave rightfully.

Reality Testing: $T = 31$ (3rd percentile) is within the borderline range, indicating that Abigail had very maladaptive ability to distinguish between fantasy and reality and to anticipate consequences, indicating psychological and cognitive immaturity.

Affective Functions

Happy: $T = 58$ (80th percentile) is within the high average range, suggesting that Abigail often exhibited a cheerful mood.

Sad: $T = >72$ (98th percentile) is within the extremely high averge range, suggesting that Abigail showed a high sad mood.

Angry: $T = 50$ (50th percentile) is within the average range, suggesting that Abigail showed average recurrence of angry mood states.

Fearful: $T = 35$ (7th percentile) is within the very low range, suggesting that Abigail did not exhibit fearful mood. Also, see Total Omissions and Total Transformations in a prior section.

Personality Functions Not Pulled: Abigail obtained the majority of "N-scores" in Anxiety/Depression on Cards 20, 21, and 22. This suggests that fearfulness may have been suppressed and/or denied by her in order to cope with threatening situations. This defense mechanism suggests inadequate emotional development and coping abilities, as well as the effects of an anxious and/or dependent attachment style, whereby she relied on adults.

Conflict: In this function, which refers to her ability to recognize and resolve the TEMAS conflict depicted in the cards, Abigail obtained a significant score of 3 that fell above the cutoff point; thus indicating that she had the ability of recognizing, but not resolving psychosocial and or personal conflicts.

Summary

Abigail was an 8-year-old Argentinean girl at the time of the testing. She was attending 2nd grade and doing average work in school. She was not receiving mental health treatment at that time. In the Cognitive Functioning area she showed strength in verbal ability and in telling stories within an average time frame; however she showed weaknesses, in responding to the presented stimuli within the average time frame, in selective attention whereby she tended to omit characters and settings, and in misperceiving the environment. In addition, although she showed ability in understanding the main conflict or problem depicted in the pictures, she had difficulty in resolving them.

In the area of personality functions, she showed strengths in self-concept of competence and sexual identity; but showed weakness in relating to others, in control of aggression, achievement motivation, moral judgment, and reality testing.

In the area of Affective Functions, she showed elevated score in "Sad" and "Happy," average score in "Angry", and a very low score in "Fearful."

Analysis of the results indicated that Abigail often failed to self-regulate her emotions, and thus she manifested behaviors that others may have perceived as aggressive and/or impulsive. It is likely that she lacked adequate social skills to cope when interacting with peers and adults and most likely attributed to others her own interpersonal difficulties. Abigail, therefore, was a child who had much difficulty accepting responsibility, understanding right from wrong, and appeared immature, lacking insight, and who may alternate between a depressed and a dependent attachment coping style.

Her interpersonal difficulties, furthermore, tended to negatively impact her daily functioning, especially in school settings. Although she wished to be liked by others, it is possible that she was quite often rejected. This seemed to be a strong disappointment for her, negatively impacting her self-esteem. Although repression and overcompensation may help her to function somewhat adaptively, however, even when she was able to experience intermittent "happy" feelings, she felt very sad and depressed, and this state required an inordinate amount of assurance and comfort by significant others, such as parents and teachers. Abigail showed difficulty in self-regulating and relating to her peers, whom she may attempt to ingratiate in order to obtain acceptance. In addition, these emotional problems may make it difficult to sustain her academic potential and she tended to have difficulty concentrating in class and paying attention, choosing to focus on other distractions that were less threatening to her.

Overall, Abigail was an immature 8-year-old who showed difficulty relating to her peers, dependence on adults, helplessness, and difficulty regulating her emotions. Sadness was a predominant emotional experience that frequently overwhelmed her. She attempted to cope with these stressful events by using repression, attribution, withdrawal, and overcompensating for her deficits with "play" rather than work and/or obeying the rules. Consequently, intermittent acting out was likely to occur at home and/or classroom as well as difficulty with concentrating and demonstrating her academic potential.

ABIGAIL'S STORIES

(*Please note that only the nine cards of the short form marked with an asterisk were scored and analyzed. The additional cards are reported for the reader's information*).

Card 1*

RT:	*42 sec.*
TT:	*28 sec.*
Structured Inquiries:	*1 min. 05 sec.*

The girls are playing, they are jumping rope, and her Mom told Claudia to go home, but she wanted to go on playing, and her Mom is very angry.

1) They are friends.
2) On the street.
4) They were jumping rope.
5) After that, they will ask another friend because Claudia had to go home; the girls didn't want her to, but she had to go.
6a) That they could play with Claudia some other day.
6b) Bad. (?) Sad.

Card 2

RT:	*5 sec.*
TT:	*40 sec.*
Structured Inquiries:	*1 min. 10 sec.*

Then the Mom had a baby and she had a whole lot of children, and the Dad was always watching the TV. The family was always bothering the Dad and the Mom who cleaned the house. The Mom was angry because the Dad didn't clean the house; he just watched TV and drank beer.

4) Before that, they … the children were playing.
5) After that they are going to sleep. The parents are going to prepare the beds for sleeping.
6a) They were thinking that they wanted to play next morning, but I don't know if the Mom will let them.
6b) Good. (?) So-so; the girl and the boy were happy.

Card 3

RT:	*3 sec.*
TT:	*1 min. 20 sec.*
Structured Inquiries:	*40 sec.*

Then the Mom and the Dad scolded them because of the homework and then the two children felt sad; the others were watching the TV. Then the Dad was going out to work. The girl wanted to do the homework, but she was a little afraid because she didn't know if she was going to be able to write well. There were ten pages [to write] for homework.

4) Before they were doing. … They were getting out of bed.
5) After they finished their homework, they were allowed to go out to play.

6a) They were thinking they wanted to go outside and play.
6b) The ones doing the homework were sad, because they had to do the homework.

Card 4

RT: 1 min.
TT: 50 sec.
Structured Inquiries: 50 sec.

Then, just when the Dad wanted to sleep, the grandmother wanted to play with the children, and the Mom too wanted to sleep, and she started to cry because the Dad scolded the children, and then the grandmother came to look after them.

4) Before they were... the son called them, and the Dad said, Don't bother me.
5) Then in the evening they were going to eat with the grandmother.
6a) The children were thinking their Dad didn't love them, and they felt sad.

Card 5

RT: 1 sec.
TT: 1 min. 05 sec.
Structured Inquiries: 1 min. 12 sec.

Then a boy came along and he is dreaming that a man was coming, and the man wanted to steal, he stole everything from the boy except the house and his clothes, and then he dreamed they were going to a really nice park and it was near the waterfalls, and he was afraid of falling into the water.

4) Before that he was sleeping and dreaming that a boy came in and robbed him.
5) Then he dreamed that he and his sister were in the woods.
6a) He is thinking that he wanted to get into the water, but they couldn't, they were on the shore.
6b) Good. (?). Happy.

Card 6

RT:	*1 sec.*
TT:	*1 min. 29 sec.*
Structured Inquiries:	*15 sec.*

One girl wanted to dress up like a cook. Another boy wanted to be a policeman and they had a gun and toys, and they were on the highest story in the building, and the gun was for the policeman. As their Mom was a cook and their Dad was a policeman, they wore their clothes, and then came their Dad and told them to take off the clothes, and they took them off and felt sad, and then they went downstairs to eat.

6a)   She was thinking that when she grew up she wanted to be a cook, and the boy was thinking that when he grew up he wanted to be a policeman.

Card 7*

RT:	*2 sec.*
TT:	*1 min. 24 sec.*
Structured Inquiries:	*2 min. 04 sec.*

The children were fighting with each other and then the Mom said enough! Don't fight any more, and they both broke the lamp, and now they will have to go buy [another] ... And the girl said but it wasn't me, and the Mom said but nothing! and they are going out to buy [a lamp].

4)   Before that they were fighting.
5)   Afterwards they are going to get a lamp because they broke it.
6a)   They are thinking that the Mom will not scold them, and that one will scold the other and this one will scold someone else, and the mother was thinking that all three (?) were to blame, because she thought that she, too, was to blame, because she didn't want to scold the children.
6b)   A little sad. (?) Because they broke the lamp, because they were both pulling at it.

Card 8

RT:	*2 sec.*
TT:	*1 min. 50 sec.*
Structured Inquiries:	*1 min. 25 sec.*

Then they went to school and they broke all the windows, and one of the girls felt bad and the boy felt good. The teacher [female] wanted to scold him, because she couldn't hit him, and the professor [male], while teaching class, scolded the girl who was looking the other way. The teacher called the Mom and Dad so they could see what their children had done.

4) They were breaking the windows.
5) Then they are going home, and they are not going to eat anything for a whole day, and then no watching TV for another day, because they broke the windows.
6a) They thought that the one to blame was the girl who felt sad, and Camilla was thinking she would not be able to watch the Tom and Jerry cartoons, and she would not be able to eat cookies.
6b) The boy was happy because he thought that the girl did it, because she did more [breaking] than him, and the girl is sad.

Card 9

RT:	*2 sec*
TT:	*2 min. 55 sec*
Structured Inquiries:	*37 sec.*

There were some children who were in the woods and the youngest child went farther away, and then the older child went where the youngest had gone, and the girl in yellow said they should go somewhere else, and then they went away. Then they fell upon the younger child but the girl in yellow didn't find anyone and she was scared, so she went the opposite way so as to find the children's friends, and then she said they should go there (the other way), and they did, and they found the way out.

4) The girl went that way all by herself (the one in yellow).
5) Then she went the opposite way.
6a) They were thinking that they would never find the way out, but they were able to find it.
6b) They felt sad.

Card 10*

RT: 1 sec.
TT: 1 min. 34 sec.
Structured Inquiries: 20 sec.

Then the girl put the coin in the piggy bank and she thought she could get an ice cream, and then she thought she could also get a bicycle, but as she had only one coin, she would not be able to buy it. She went to find out how much was the bicycle, and if it was expensive, she would not buy it, and then she went to buy an ice cream.

4) She put the coin in the piggy bank.
6a) She was thinking she could get a bicycle that cheap.
6b) She was happy.

Card 11

RT: 2 sec
TT: 1:31 sec.
Structured Inquiries: 1 min. 12 sec.

Now there is a little old lady ... the children were stealing from her because they were poor. The children told her they were going to hold the bag for her and then they stole it from her, and the little old lady was striking at them with her cane. The children on this side were carrying the stuff for the old granny and they were not stealing from her, but the others did.

4) Before they were running so that she would not hit them with the cane.
5) Then they were going to take the stuff home so they could eat a little ... and they were thinking that they could get to eat something instead of eating things they picked out of the garbage cans.
6b) Rather ... (?) Happier.

Card 12

RT: 3 sec.
TT: 26 sec.
Structured Inquiries: 1 min. 20 sec.

Some girls were fixing the bicycle, and the others wanted to take the little papers from them, and they started pulling on each other's hair and call them names, and a girl that was not pulling the others' hair was watching the moment when the bicycle would already be fixed, so she could steal it.

4) Before that they were fighting.
5) They were going to try to calm down and not pull each other's hair.
6a) They were thinking … because they wanted to steal they bicycle, and the others did, too, and they came to the same place, that's why they all pulled each others' hair.
6b) A little bad, because she got her hair pulled. (?) One was angry and the other was sad.

Card 14*

RT: 5 sec.
TT: 1 min. 12 sec.
Structured Inquiries: 1 min. 08 sec.

Now the older girl put some music on, no, she was doing her homework. She had to do three pages. And the younger girl put on some music. The older one felt bad because she had to do her homework, and the others were playing and they felt very good.

4) Before that she was looking for the CD.
5) After that she was going to dance [to the music], the one who was doing her homework was about to finish it.
6a) She was thinking she could do the homework.
6b) Bad. (?) Sad.

Card 15*

RT: 2 sec.
TT: 34 sec.
Structured Inquiries: 1 min. 54 sec.

The children won the soccer game. They won a cup and a diploma. And some other children who wanted to cross the street were carrying stuff, one was carrying an alarm clock and another one a radio and some books, because they had stolen them. The policeman told them to go put the things back where they had taken them and their parents were going to be put in jail because the children had stolen stuff.

4) Before that they had broken the shop window.
5) Then they were going to put the stuff back where the policeman told them.
6a) They thought they could get away with stealing, but they couldn't.
6b) One was angry, another was sad … all three were sad and one of them was angry because they could not steal the stuff.

Card 17*

RT: 9 sec.
TT: 1 min. 32 sec.
Structured Inquiries: 45 sec.

Claudia was dreaming that she was going to get a zero [lowest grade] at school and she did not want to do the homework, and then, if she did her homework, she was going to get a ten [highest grade], so then she got down to doing the homework and she had two books on her right and two on her left, that's why she did all the homework, and then she went to school and she got a ten and she was very happy.

4) Before that she was thinking.
6a) She was thinking that the teacher was going to scold her if she didn't do the homework.
6b) Sad. (?) Because she thought she was going to get a bad grade.

Card 20*

RT: 52 sec.
TT: 1 min. 20 sec.
Structured Inquiries: 1 min. 05 sec.

The boy was dreaming that he was a horse and that he could jump up to the sandcastle, and when he jumped he fell into the water and then he went to the sandcastle, and it was all falling apart, and then he could not even open the doors, that's why he decided to get out of there and go home, and he took the unpaved road.

4)   Before that he was jumping, and he fell into the water.
5)   Then he was going to get out of bed.
6a) He was thinking about the dream.
6b) He feels sleepy, good, happy.

Card 21*

RT: *13 sec.*
TT: *27 sec.*
Structured Inquiries: *20 sec.*

The boy went home to sleep and he was dreaming that a monster was hungry and it ate the whole town and it gave off fire all over, and then the boy gave the monster a burger and it was not hungry any more, and it went away.

4)   Before that he was about to go to sleep.
5)   He got up.
6b) He was asleep. (?). Good.
6a) He was thinking about the dream. (?). Happy.

Card 22*

RT: *19 sec.*
TT: *1 min. 17 sec.*
Structured Inquiries: *1 min. 08 sec.*

The girl stood up on a stool and she looked in the mirror and she saw part boy part girl, a woman and a boy, that's why she didn't know what to choose, boy or girl, then she chose girl and she went to take a bath, but the Mom didn't tell her to go take a bath, but she went anyway. And the Mom wanted to turn on the shower but she saw that the girl was taking a bath.

4)   Before that she asked her Mom if she could go take a bath, and the Mom said no.
5)   Then she was going to get her clothes changed.
6a) She was thinking that her Mom was going to scold her and punish her, but she didn't punish her, she only scolded her.
6b) Bad because she got scolded. (?) Sad.

Card 23

RT:	*47 sec.*
TT:	*46 sec.*
Structured Inquiries:	*2 min. 13 sec.*

I don't know anything [about this]. [Who are they?] The Mom, the Dad and the daughter were watching the boats float, and the girl threw a stone at the small boat, and the Dad scolded her and the Mom was looking on with a scared face.

2) They were on a harbor.
4) Before that they were about to go, getting ready to go to the harbor.
5) Then the next morning they were going to go to the cinema to watch a movie.
6a) She was thinking that she was not going to be able to, but she did get to go to the cinema.
6b) The Dad was angry, the Mom was scared and the girl was sad. (For scoring of the nine TEMAS cards, see Figure 11–2.)

PUERTO RICAN CASE STUDY: ANA

Ana was a 10-year-old Puerto Rican girl at the time of the testing. The student was attending 4th grade in Public Schools. She was receiving psychotherapy because she had been sexually abused. Ana was administered the nine cards of TEMAS short form plus three additional cards, usually administered to sexually abused children. She was also administered two additional experimental TEMAS cards. However, only twelve standard cards were scored.

Test Results and Interpretation

The test scores of Ana's protocol are based on norms for Puerto Ricans between the age of 8 and 10 years old. For each scale, the interpretation will therefore be related to the T-scores and percentile scores obtained. (See record booklet, Figure 11–3).

Analysis of Results: Quantitative Scales

Cognitive Functions
Reaction Time: $T = 61$ (85th percentile) is within the extremely high average range, which indicates that the Ana responded slowly to the stimuli.

This may denote anxiety, inhibition or ideational rehearsal of projective stimuli (e.g., interfering factors).

Total Time: $T = 61$ (85th percentile) is within the superior range, suggesting that Ana utilized an extremely high amount of time to tell her stories once she began.

Fluency: $T = 47$ (40th percentile) is within the average range and along with the Total Time T-score suggests that Ana needed a high number of inquiries in order to tell complete stories.

Total Omissions: $T = 34$ (7th percentile) is within the low range and it suggests that Ana generally included in her stories most of the presented stimuli, such as main character, secondary characters, events, and settings, which generally indicates adaptive Selective Attention.

Total Transformations (5): A prorated score of 3.75 is above the 90th percentice, of critical cut-off point hence a significant cognitive deficit. This refers to Ana's perceptual distortions of characters (main and secondary) and events. Ana showed a significant amount of transformations for main characters and events, reaching a critical cut-off score indicating that she most frequently changed the main characters suggesting the role of poor defense mechanism. Furthermore, the interaction between these transformations and "N" value of the Personality Function Not Pulled (see Personality Functions not pulled, in the next section) showed a maladaptive defense mechanism and a very poor reality testing.

Personality Functions

Interpersonal Relations: $T = 37$ (10th percentile) is within the very low range, which suggests a maladaptive ability to relate to others.

Aggression: $T = 32$ (5th percentile) is within the borderline range, which indicated that Ana showed maladaptive control over her aggressive impulses. Furthermore, Ana consistently avoided addressing aggressive stimuli in the pictures, indicating that she did not pay attention to aggressive stimuli out of fear of retaliation or of the disapproval of authority figures.

Anxiety/Depression: $T = 31$ (5th percentile) is within the borderline low range, which indicated that Ana exhibited highly maladaptive coping skills in dealing with anxiety and depression-provoking situations.

Achievement Motivation: $T = 26$ (1st percentile) is within the borderline range, indicating that Ana showed poor motivation to excel.

Delay of Gratification: $T = 35$ (7th percentile) is within the low average range, indicating that Ana had fair ability to delay a reward in order to meet a future objective.

Self-Concept: T = 48 (45th percentile) is within the average range, which suggested that Ana had adequate perceptions of her psychosocial, academic, and/or intellectual competence.

Sexual Identity: T = 38 (10th percentile) is within the very low average range, indicating that Ana had a maladaptive perception of her sexual identity.

Moral Judgment: T = 34 (7th percentile) is within the very low range, indicating that Ana had exhibited maladaptive ability to distinguish right from wrong and to behave rightfully.

Reality Testing: T = 34 (7th percentile) is within the very low range, indicating that Ana had maladaptive ability to distinguish between fantasy and reality and to anticipate consequences, indicating psychological immaturity.

Affective Functions

Happy: T = 40 (37th percentile) is within the very low range, suggesting that Ana predominantly exhibited a low recurrence of happy mood states.

Sad: T = >72 (> 98th percentile) is within the extremely high average range, suggesting that Ana predominantly exhibited a sad mood.

Angry: T = 55 (69th percentile) is within the high average range, suggesting that Ana showed recurrence of frequent angry mood states.

Fearful: T = 54 (68th percentile) is within the above average range, suggesting that Ana exhibited frequent fearful mood.

Conflict: Results of Cognitive Functions of the Qualitative Indicators showed that Ana achieved a score above the cutoff critical point in this function, thus indicating that she had the ability to recognize the depicted conflict or problem, but did not have the cognitive skills to resolve them.

Summary

Ana was an 8 year-old Puerto Rican girl at the time of the testing. She was receiving psychotherapy as result of being sexually abused by an adult. Her presenting problems were, inability to verbalize the traumatic events and to verbalize her feelings in general, crying spells and general depressed mood, and problems in relating to both peers and adults.

Results of the cognitive functions revealed that the student showed a very high reaction time to the cards and very high total time in telling stories; this indicated that she was withdrawn and needed much structure in completing her narratives. Nonetheless, once engaged in the task, she was able to be verbally productive and reveal her underlying conflicts. In addition she

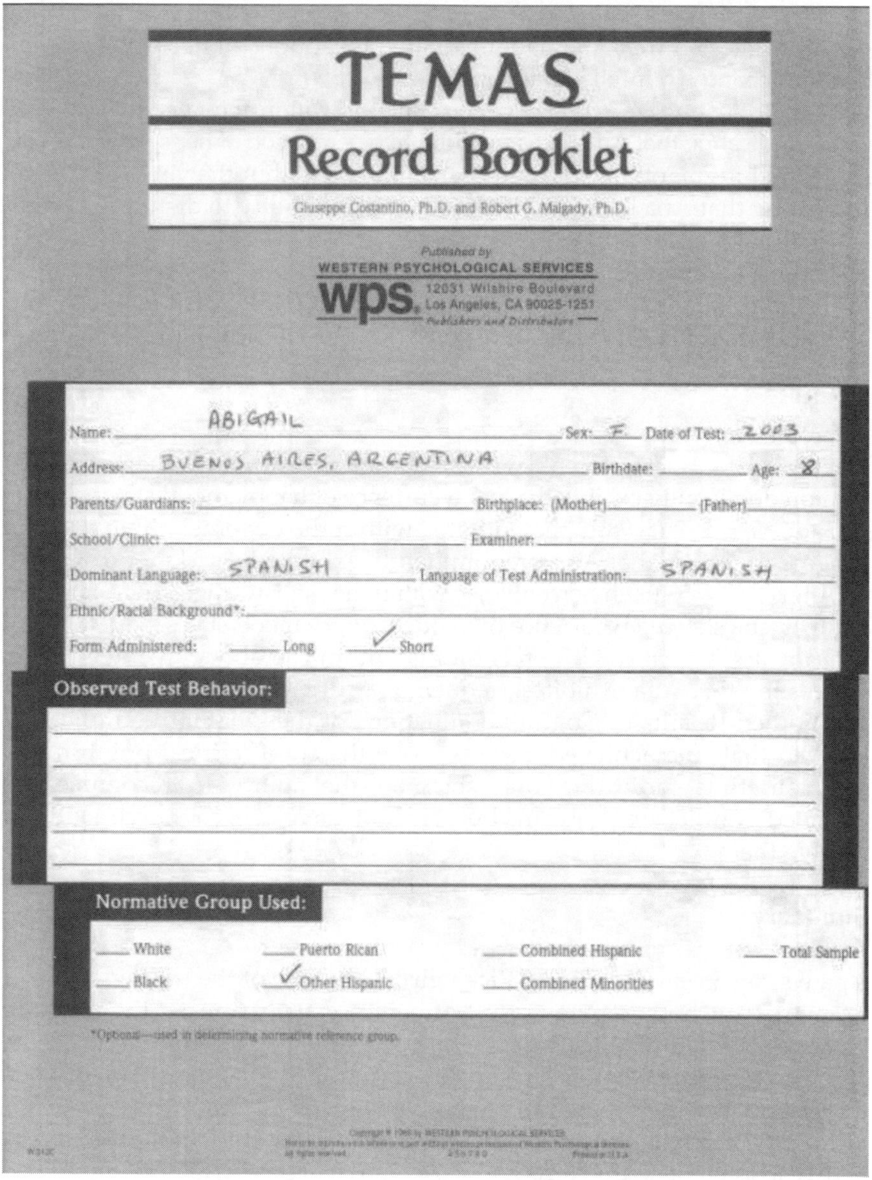
TEMAS
Record Booklet
Giuseppe Costantino, Ph.D. and Robert G. Malgady, Ph.D.

Published by
WESTERN PSYCHOLOGICAL SERVICES
wps 12031 Wilshire Boulevard
Los Angeles, CA 90025-1251
Publishers and Distributors

Name: ABIGAIL Sex: F Date of Test: 2003
Address: BUENOS AIRES, ARGENTINA Birthdate: ______ Age: 8
Parents/Guardians: ______ Birthplace: (Mother) ______ (Father) ______
School/Clinic: ______ Examiner: ______
Dominant Language: SPANISH Language of Test Administration: SPANISH
Ethnic/Racial Background*: ______
Form Administered: ______ Long ✓ Short

Observed Test Behavior:

Normative Group Used:
___ White ___ Puerto Rican ___ Combined Hispanic ___ Total Sample
___ Black ✓ Other Hispanic ___ Combined Minorities

*Optional—used in determining normative reference group.

FIGURE 11–2. Scored record booklet.

Scoring Sheet
Quantitative Scales

Card No.	Reaction Time (Seconds)	Total Time (Minutes)	Fluency	Total Omissions	Interpersonal Relations	Aggression	Anxiety/ Depression	Achievement Motivation	Delay of Gratification	Self-Concept	Sexual Identity	Moral Judgment	Reality Testing	Happy	Sad	Angry	Fearful
1*	42	1.33	75	2	/2				/2						1		
2					/\				/\			/\					
3					/\		/\ /\										
4					/\	/\	/\					/\					
5					/\	/\											
6					/\			/\									
7*	2	3.28	143		/2	/2						/2			1		
8					/\												
9							/\										
10*	1	1.54	94						/3					1			
11					/\							/\					
12					/\			/\									
13					/\			/\ /\									
14*	5	2.20	89	1	3/2.5 /2		/2	/2							1		
15*	2	2.28	133	1	3/2.5 N		3				/2	2		1	1	
16					/\												
17*	9	2.17	120			/2	/2	/3						1	1	
18							/\										
19					/\						/\						
20*	52	2.25	99		N							2	1			
21*	13	.47	71		/2 N						/2	1				
22*	19	2.25	141		2 N			/3	/2			1				
23					/\		/\										
Sum	145	17.26	965	4	9	6	2	7	7	3	3	4	8	4	6	1	0
Number of Cards Scored					4	3	1	3	3	1	1	2	4				
Mean Score**					2.25	2	2	2.33	2.33	3	3	2	2				
Sum of Functions Not Pulled ("N-Scores")						1	3										

*Cards used for Short Form.
**Mean Score = Sum ÷ Number of cards scored.

Page 2

FIGURE 11–2. Scored record booklet. (*Continued*)

Scoring Sheet
Qualitative Indicators

Card No.	Neutral	Ambivalent	Inappropriate Affect	Conflict	Sequencing	Imagination	Relationships	Total Transformations	Inquiries	Omissions Main Character	Omissions Secondary Character	Omissions Event	Omissions Setting	Transformations Main Character	Transformations Secondary Character	Transformations Event	Transformations Setting
1*											I		I				
2																	
3											.						
4																	
5																	
6																	
7*				(1)													
8																	
9																	
10*																	
11																	
12																	
13																	
14*				(1)							I						
15*								I			I					I	
16																	
17*																	
18																	
19																	
20*				(1)				(1)							I		
21*															I		
22*								I									I
23																	
Sum				(3)				3			3		1	2		1	1
90% + (✓)				✓				✓			✓			✓			

*Cards used for Short Form.

Page 3

FIGURE 11–2.   Scored record booklet. (*Continued*)

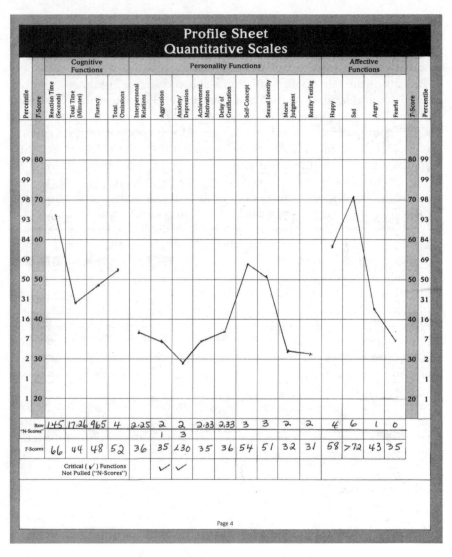

FIGURE 11–2. Scored record booklet.

showed poor skills in resolving personal and psychosocial conflicts, although she had the ability to recognize them. She showed adequate perceptual understanding of the situations, but under stressful situations, she tended to misperceive characters and events.

Results of the Personality Functions showed severe weaknesses in her interpersonal relations, control of aggression and coping with depression and to a lesser degree to anxiety, delay gratification, sexual identity and reality testing. But she showed strength in self-concept of competence, thus exhibiting strong reliance to cope with adverse events and negative feelings. Analysis of the results of the Affective Functions showed an extremely high score in "Sad" with above average scores in "Angry" and "Fearful." These scores correlated with the low score in coping with depression, thus suggesting a diagnosis of major depression.

With respect to her sexual abuse, she was able to talk about her traumatic events. She related two revealing stories about sexual abuse. In the first story told in response to card No. 4, she tells of a father who is asking his children to look to a naked woman in bed, while the mother is very angry "because he should not teach the children this." In the second story told in response to card No. 22, which depicts a girl looking at a face half-boy half-girl reflected, at first she repeatedly says that she does not know what is happening in the picture, however, upon inquiry she relates that "she shouldn't look because there is one part of her and other part of a boy." And she feels very sad. These two stories reveal her depression associated with sexual abuse.

Overall, the TEMAS results showed a profile of a youngsters whose was withdrawn and depressed and strongly avoidant of interpersonal relationships, and who needed much nurturance and "help" in order to overcome her sense of helplessness.

ANA'S STORIES

Name: Ana
Age: 10
Date of Testing: 5/03
Case: Clinic

Ana was administered the nine cards of the TEMAS short form, plus three cards (Nos. 2, 4, and 6) which are usually used with sexually abused children. In addition, she was administered new research cards (Nos. 24 and 25), which were designed for sexually abusing and abused children. Only the nine cards of the short form and the three additional cards were scored and analyzed. The raw scores of the 12 administered cards were prorated before obtaining the *T*-scores and the other Qualitative Indicators Cutoff scores.

Card 14G

Reaction Time (RT) 3 sec.
Spontaneous Time (ST) 1 min. 32 sec.
Total Time 6′
Fluency 88

There are many children dancing and playing and one other girl doing her homework and the girl is sad and they are playing the radio and they are in a house.

1. Children.
2. There are inside the house.
3. There are dancing and saying "Let's go dancing."
4. They are studying and doing the homework.
5. They go dancing.
6a. They are thinking to stop the homework and return to dance.
6b. She feels sad because she'd like to continue dancing with her friends.

Card 20

RT 20 sec.
ST 1 min. 25 sec.
TT 3 sec.
Fluency 86

There is a child sleeping and dreaming of having a castle and that the castle has a river and at the end a lake and a horse on two legs to be mounted and go around and mountains and places plains and others …

1. Is a boy.
2. He's in his house.
3. He's sleeping and dreaming

4. Is getting ready to go to sleep.
5. Sleeping.
6a. That she was in a castle, ah, ah, ah.
7b. Happy because he's sleeping.

Card 6**

RT 12 sec.
ST 1 min. 18 sec.
TT 4 min.
Fluency 107

That there is a girl and a boy that are going to wear clothes of whom they think would like to be when they grow up. [She hesitated]. They're up in the house in the last floor the above.

1. A boy and a girl.
2. They're in their house in the last floor the above.
3. They're wearing clothes of adults they like to be when they are grown-up and they are not talking they're only looking at each other.
4. Looking for clothes.
5. They're wearing clothes.
6a. When they're small.
6b. Sad because they're seeing a cradle. This I think and nothing else.

Card 7

RT 8 sec.
ST 1 min. 25 sec.
TT 4 min.
Fluency 105

There's a mother and her two children and they're in their house and they're fighting because one of them broke the lamp and I don' know. The mother is going to decide who is guilty.

1. Two children and their mother.
2. In the house.

3. They're fighting and saying: "you did it ..." "... no I didn't ..." "... you did it..." "... no I didn't ... "
4. Playing, I think.
5. Picking up the lamp that broke.
6a. The mother is thinking who did it, wishing that this would end because I am like that with my sister. The mother feels sad because she has headaches ... and nothing else.

Card 10G

RT 11 sec.
ST 1 min. 25 sec.
TT 3 min. 41 sec.
Fluency 106

There's a girl with her piggybank to get money and she's thinking of buying a bike. But she's not sufficient money and she's buying an ice cream and nothing else.

1. A girl.
2. She's in her room.
3. She's taking out money from her piggybank and she's saying nothing.
4. Working hard to have all the money.
5. Buying an ice cream because she'd like to buy a bike,
6. but she doesn't have all the money and she goes to buy the ice cream.
7a. That she's hungry and wishes to buy something sweet.
8b. Sad because she really likes the bike.

Card 1G

RT 10 sec.
ST 1 min. 29 sec.
TT 4 min.
Fluency 144

The same girl from the other story and 4 girls and the mother and the father and the girls are playing outside. The girl with the yellow dress, her mother is asking her to bring a letter to someone and the girls who are in the street are playing, and nothing else.

1. The girls and the mother and the father.
2. The girls are playing in the street and the parents in the house.
3. The mother is saying that the girl deliver the letter and the girls are playing jump rope.
4. They're calling the girl who was writing a letter.
5. She'd like to play with the girls, but the mother is calling her to deliver the letter and to deliver the letter now.
6a if her mother could leave her playing with her friends.
6b. She feels sad.

Card 24***

RT 9 sec.
ST 2 min.
TT 5 min. 14 sec.
Fluency 185

There is a group of students in a bus and there's one girl and 2 boys and one of them is pulling up her skirt and the other is trying to give her something strange and other three students are in the back of the bus and nothing else.

1. Are 2 boys. The 2 boys know each other and the girl feels upset.
2. They are in a school bus.
3. They are doing bad things and they are saying nothing. And the girl is pushing them that they should leave her alone and they should stop pulling up her skirt and to the other to stop giving her that strange thing.
4. They were studying in the school.
5. Doing something bad to her. The other boys and the girl are telling the girl to call the bus driver.
6a. She's thinking that they'd leave her alone and she's thinking that maybe they're going to hurt her.
6b. She's a feel very fearful and sad.

Card 17

RT 13 sec.
ST 50 sec.
TT 4 min.
Fluency 86

There's a girl studying with her teacher who gave a test and she got an A and on the other side she got an F and that is.

1. There is a girl and a teacher or her mother.
2. Was in the school studying.
3. She' saying that she got an A and feels very happy and proud of herself.
4. Learning.
5. Take a test.
6a. She's thinking that she got an F and has to retake the test.
6b. She felt sad that she could do better.

Card 4**

RT 9 sec.
ST 50 sec.
TT 4 min.
Fluency 115

This, is that there are a father, a mother and 4 children, 2 daughters and two sons and the father is offering at one of the boys to see a naked woman; and the mother is very angry because he should not teach the children this. And that's it.

1. The father his children, the mother and another woman.
2. They are in the house.
3. Is telling to come in the room.
4. They were going to see their father.
5. Get away from the father because he is offering them to see something bad.
6a. This woman is thinking that he is doing something bad.
7b. She feels bad (?) Sad

Card 21

RT 3 sec.
ST 1 min. 3 sec.
TT 3 min.
Fluency 80

There's a boy who is dreaming that there're monsters in his nightmare or dream and that there's one that is eating and the other very angry; and the boy is very afraid and that's it.

1. A boy.
2. He's in his house and in his room.
3. Is dreaming and is saying nothing.
4. Was going to sleep.
5. Waking up in the morning.
6a. That he doesn't like nightmare.
7b. Feels sad because he had nightmare.

Card 2**

RT 9 sec.
ST 40 sec.
TT 3 min.
Fluency 92

There is the father and the mother and five children and a dog; and the mother is cleaning by herself; and that's it.

1. There's a father and his children.
2. There are in their house in the living room.
3. The children are playing and the other is cleaning the house.
4. They were watching Television.
5. They are going to do naughty things.
6a. The father is thinking what channel he should see and the mother is thinking that the husband is not helping.
7b. And she feels sad.

Card 22

RT 10 sec.
ST 54 sec.
TT 2 min.
Fluency 118

There's a girl in the bathroom on top of a stool. She is looking herself in the mirror. And that's it.

1. A girl.
2. She's in her house and in the bathroom.
3. She's looking herself in the mirror and saying nothing.
4. Don't know.
5. Don't know.
6a. That she shouldn't look because there is one part of her and other part of a boy.
7b. And she's sad.

Card 25***

RT 10 sec.
ST 1 min. 33 sec.
TT 3 min. 27 sec.
Fluency 118

There's a family and a neighbor with his son ready to kill a deer and the father is saying that there's a deer in the garden and the boy of the neighbor also wants to kill the deer with that thing there. That's it.

1. The father and his family.
2. In the back patio cooking something.
3. The mother is cooking something and placing it on the table and she is saying: ah, ah, ah!
4. And they are preparing everything to go outside.
5. To eat.
6a. They're thinking that the deer should come to eat the apple.
6b. And the girl is feeling bad that they shouldn't kill the deer because they haven't done anything bad.

Card 15

RT 14 sec.
ST 45 sec.
TT 5 min.
Fluency 192

There is a baseball team and a group that is stealing and there's the police apprehending them. But the groups are of children. That's it.

1. The team of good children.
2. The others are on the street taking away the stolen things.
3. The police is saying why they stole and why they broke the window,
4. They were playing baseball.
5. They are running away to hide those things in a place where they cannot be found.
6a. The coach of the good team is thinking that he is proud because the team won.
6b. The girl feels sad because they are going to take her in prison.

It is important to note that the examinee of theses stories was administered a total of 15 cards: the short form nine cards, marked with an asterisk, on the record booklet, plus cards 2, 4 and 6, which are also administered to sexually abused children, marked with two asterisks next to cards numbers in this chapter. In addition, this examinee was administrated two additional experimental cards: 24 and 25, marked with three asterisks next to cards numbers in this chapter, which pull for sexual abuse and aggression (for complete scoring see record booklet, Figure, 10–3).

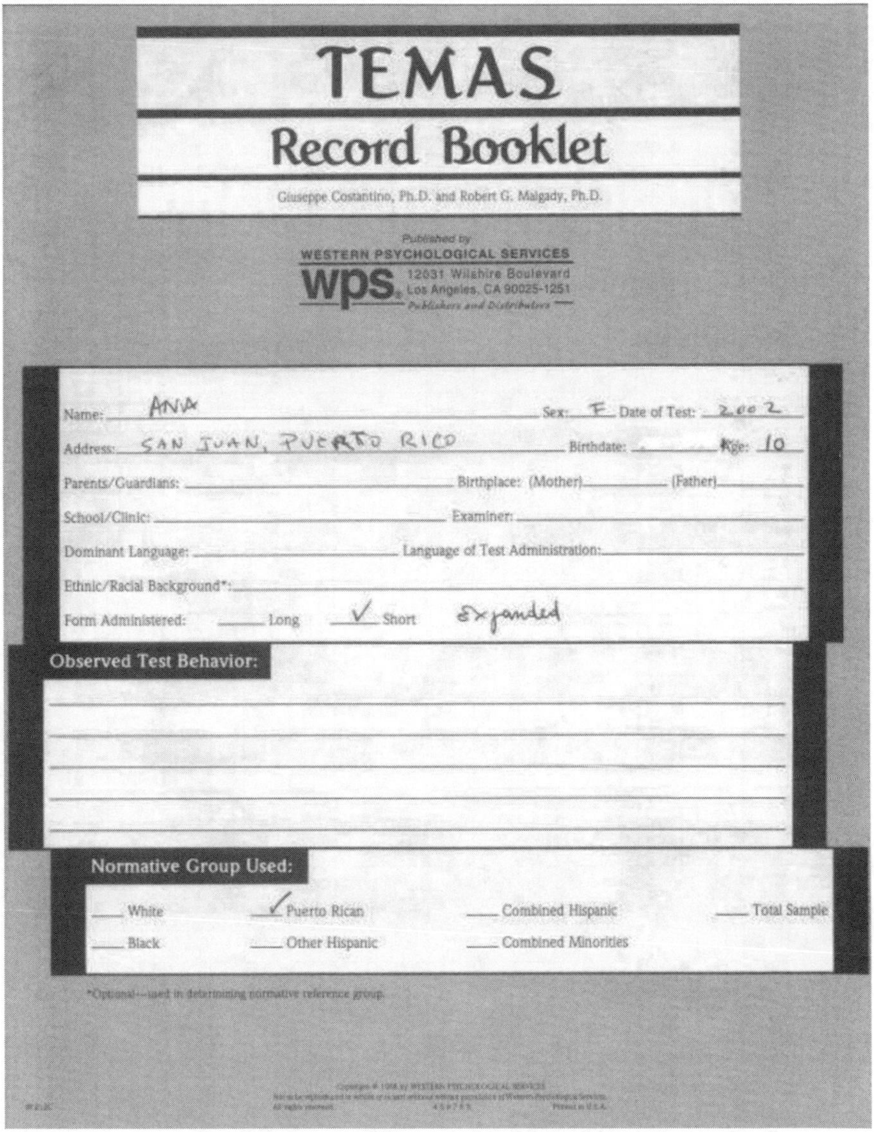
TEMAS

Record Booklet

Giuseppe Costantino, Ph.D. and Robert G. Malgady, Ph.D.

Published by
WESTERN PSYCHOLOGICAL SERVICES
wps 12031 Wilshire Boulevard
Los Angeles, CA 90025-1251
Publishers and Distributors

Name: ANA Sex: F Date of Test: 2002

Address: SAN JUAN, PUERTO RICO Birthdate: ______ Age: 10

Parents/Guardians: ______ Birthplace: (Mother) ______ (Father) ______

School/Clinic: ______ Examiner: ______

Dominant Language: ______ Language of Test Administration: ______

Ethnic/Racial Background*: ______

Form Administered: ___ Long ✓ Short Expanded

Observed Test Behavior:

Normative Group Used:

___ White ✓ Puerto Rican ___ Combined Hispanic ___ Total Sample

___ Black ___ Other Hispanic ___ Combined Minorities

*Optional—used in determining normative reference group.

FIGURE 11–3. Scored record protocol.

Scoring Sheet
Quantitative Scales

	Cognitive Functions				Personality Functions									Affective Functions			
Card No.	Reaction Time (Seconds)	Total Time (Minutes)	Fluency	Total Omissions	Interpersonal Relations	Aggression	Anxiety/Depression	Achievement Motivation	Delay of Gratification	Self-Concept	Sexual Identity	Moral Judgment	Reality Testing	Happy	Sad	Angry	Fearful
1*	10	1.24/4	144		2/2.5 3				2						1		
2	9		92		2/2.5 3								2/2.5 3		1		
3																	
4	9	50/4	115		1/2 3	N	2					3	2		1	1	
5																	
6	12	1.18/4	107		2					N					1		
7*	8	1.23/4	105		3/2 2	2						2			1		
8																	
9																	
10*	11	1.25/3.41	106						2						1		
11																	
12																	
13																	
14*	3	1.33/6	88		3			2	3						1		
15*	14	45/5	112		2/2.5 3	2		3				2			1		
16																	
17*	13	50/4	86			N	2		3				2	1	1		
18																	
19																	
20*	20	1.25/3	85	1		N							2	1			
21*	3	1.30/3	80		N	2							2		1	1	1
22*	10	.54/2	73			2					2		3				
23																	
Sum	123/91	7.53/5.65	1.193/895	1/21	16.5	4	6	7	7	3	2	9.5	11	2/1.5	10/7.5	2/1.5	1/21
Number of Cards Scored					7	2	3	3	3	1	1	4	5				
Mean Score**					2.35	2	2	2.33	2.33	3	2	2.37	2.2	*PRORATED SCORES			
Sum of Functions Not Pulled ("N-Scores")					1.5*	1.5*					>1*						

*Cards used for Short Form.
**Mean Score = Sum ÷ Number of cards scored.   Page 2

FIGURE 11–3.   Scored record protocol. (*Continued*)

Scoring Sheet
Qualitative Indicators

| Card No. | Affective Functions | | | Cognitive Functions | | | | | | Optional | | | | | | | |
| | | | | | | | | | | Omissions | | | | Transformations | | | |
	Neutral	Ambivalent	Inappropriate Affect	Conflict	Sequencing	Imagination	Relationships	Total Transformations	Inquiries	Main Character	Secondary Character	Event	Setting	Main Character	Secondary Character	Event	Setting
1*				(1)				1								1	
2																	
3																	
4						1										1	
5																	
6				(1)													
7*				(1)													
8																	
9																	
10*				(1)													
11																	
12																	
13																	
14*				(1)													
15*				(1)													
16																	
17*				(1)		1									1		
18																	
19																	
20*				(1)		1							1	1			
21*				(1)		1									1		
22*				(1)	1												
23																	
Sum				10/2.5	>1*			5/3.75*						>1⁺ 2/1.5*	>1⁺ 2/1.5*		
90% + (✓)				✓				✓									

PRORATED SCORES

*Cards used for Short Form.

Page 3

FIGURE 11–3.   Scored record protocol. (*Continued*)

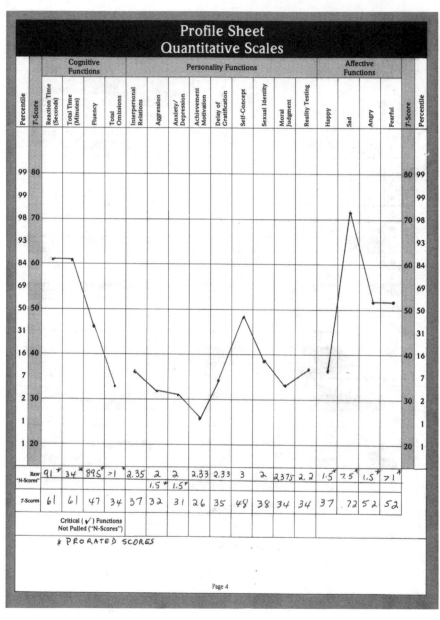

FIGURE 11–3. Scored record protocol. (*Continued*)`

DISCUSSION

The three TEMAS protocols in this chapter reflect diverse Latino cultures with the third case representing a Latino girl transplanted with her family in Italy for about one year. Each narrates a unifying theme of *marianismo*. This confirms how the TEMAS pictures are culturally sensitive in pulling the identical underlying theme in three Latino girls living in three different cultures (Bernal, 1991; Costantino, 1987; Costantino, Malgady & Vasquez, 1981; Dana, 1993). The three protocol presentations herein each can be viewed as examples of young girls struggling with the traditional Latino cultural expectations, or culture tales, of *Marianismo* as defined here.

Marianismo has been defined as the cultural antithesis of *machismo*, and focuses on the cultural ideal of female subjugation to male domination. Marianismo takes its name from a male-centered view of the religious icon of the Virgin Mary as a woman whose fate was both to carry (give birth to and nurture) and to honor and serve the Lord (her son Jesus). The Virgin Mary thus became the cultural ego ideal for all Latina women. Ramos-McKay, Comas-Diaz, and Rivera (1988) argued that the positive interpretation of *marianismo* implies that women are spiritually superior to men and thus serve as their moral guide and anchor, and share with Jesus the capacity to endure the cruelties and injustices of men. This capacity for endurance is not, as is argued elsewhere (Bracero, 1998), so much a female reflection of *macho* attitudes as it is an adaptation of the ancient Roman philosophy of stoicism, which taught that a person revealed their moral superiority by not only enduring but disregarding the suffering and injustices built upon them by the social elite of the Empire.

Bracero (in press) has incorporated his own previous work with that of feminist writers, narrative therapy theorists, and Latina psychotherapists and social commentators (most notably Gil and Vazquez, 1996), in the construction of a list of seven personality characteristics ("The Seven Habits") of women who subscribe to marianista cultural expectations:

The 7 Habits of Marianista Women

1. A pervasive sense of obligation to others, regardless of justification or merit.
2. A pervasive sense of personal guilt, regardless of justification or merit.
3. Suppression of female sexual desire.

4. Suppression of self-assertion and expression of anger, regardless of
    justification.
5. Silencing of the self, which includes self-resignation (*resignarse*), self-
    suppression (*sobreponerse*), self-censorship (*no pensar*), self-sacrifice
    (sacrificarse), and moral and emotional self-discipline (*controlarse*).
6. Unconditional acceptance of dysfunctional relationships with men.
7. Martyrdom as a source of self-esteem and as an ego-ideal

Three Child Narratives of Marianismo

Maria, the 10-year-old emigrant from Ecuador residing for about three
year in Milan, Italy, constructs TEMAS narratives that illustrate an avoid-
ance of expression of angry feelings against her mother 's wishes on Card
1; the attribution of guilt and ensuing criticism and punishment of the girl
for her failure to act appropriately on Cards 2, 14, 15, and 17 , even in situations where her actions were the result of the behaviors of others; and
the pervasive low self-esteem and sadness expressed in almost every
TEMAS narrative. What is reflected in stories is a young girl who has been
made to feel guilty about whatever bad things happen to her, and to feel
ashamed of her femininity. What has been described as a "Pollyannaish"
outlook may be more accurately described as the consequence of her
unfortunate acceptance of the cultural mandates of *marianismo*. However,
Maria also expresses a sense of alienation and shame about her own cultural heritage when she feels sad about her dark skin color because she
does not blend with the white- skinned Italian girls at school and in the
community.

Abigail, the 8-year-old resident of the sprawling metropolis of Buenos
Aires, Argentina, constructs TEMAS narratives that illustrate further the
ready self-attribution of guilt and acceptance of the anger and criticism of
others, as reflected in her stories to Cards 1, 3, 4, 8, 22, and 23. An interesting correlate is the character of the mother in her stories, which also
shows difficulty in expressing her anger appropriately and appears afraid
to exact punishment from those who might deserve it, as seen on Cards
4, 22, 23, and 7 (where the mother specifically attributed blame for others
on herself as well!). A additional example of the *marianista* tendency to
subjugate the self in favor of male privilege are the two stories where the
female is punished, while the male gets a lesser or no punishment for his
behavior, as shown in the story to Card 8, and the complete disavowal of
any sexual wrong-doing on the part of the father on Card 4, with the
children left feeling sad because their father did not love them. Indeed,

the male privilege can be summed up in the last line of her last narrative to Card 23 ("The Dad was angry, the Mom was scared, and the girl was sad."). Indeed, a subtext of many of her narratives reveal an intimate familiarity with a world filled with poverty, violence, and organized street crime, which she appears to have accepted as the norm. The happy dreams of one's childhood are abandoned as fantasy from a harsh reality ('the unpaved road" of Card 20) to which one must return. Again, it is argued that her responses do not reflect "*macho*" or anxiety-free images, but rather another instance of adoption of *marianista* attitudes of silencing the self in order to bind anxiety and aggression and demonstrate the socially desirable behaviors of the ego ideal of *marianismo*.

The case of Ana, the 10-year-old Puerto Rican girl, is perhaps the clearest case of the *marianista* silencing of the self, as her TEMAS tales of implied personal trauma are told in narratives of a sad girl who repeatedly says nothing when molested by her peers on Card 24, witnesses sexual misconduct on Card 4, and the intentions of men to destroy innocent life on Card 25, thus showing the female self-sacrifice. Again and again, the female suffers punishment while others are unpunished, as on Card 15, and even the mother figure cannot pass judgment or punish those who are guilty, and only suffers herself in headaches, as on Card 7. Again, Card 22 is noteworthy for its illustration of a pervasive sense of shame and alienation over sexual identity and feminine self-image, which cannot even be spoken about ("She's looking in the mirror and saying nothing."). This silence is not *macho* posturing, but the consequence of *marianista* self-subjugation to male privilege and abuse, thus showing the true meaning of the *marianismo*, the silence of the self.

In summary, the narratives of these three Latina female cases show a strong cultural trait-*marianismo*, which is seems to be integrated in the Latina personality and reveals itself cross-culturally in the life stories of three Latina girls living in three different cultures in response to culturally sensitive and competent TEMAS pictures.

REFERENCES

Bernal, I. (1991). *The relationship between level of acculturation, The Robert's Apperception Test for Children, and the TEMAS (Tell-Me-A-Story Test)*. Dissertation, California School of Professional Psychology, Los Angeles, CA.

Bracero, W. (1998). Intimidades: Confianza gender, and hierarchy in the construction of Latino-Latina therapeutic relationships Cultural *Diversity & Mental Health*. 4 (4).

Bracero, W. (in press). *Between the worlds: The assessment and treatment of the culturally diverse.* Northvale, NJ: Jason Aronson.

Costantino, G. (1987). *TEMAS (Tell-Me-A-Story) cards.* Los Angeles: Western sychological Services.

Costantino, G., Malgady, R. G., & Vazquez, C. (1981). Comparing Murray's TAT to a new thematic apperception test for urban ethnic minority children. *Hispanic Journal of Behavioral Sciences, 3,* 291–300.

Dana, R. H. (1993). *Multicultural assessment perspectives for professional psychology.* Boston: Allyn & Bacon.

Dupertuis , D. G., Silva Arancibia, V., Pais, E., Fernandez, C., & Rodino, V. (2004). Similarities and differences in TEMAS test functions in Argentinean and European-American children. *Argentina: Universidad de Buenos Aires.*

Fantini, F. (2005). Risvolti teorici e applicativi in contesto multiculturale. Unpublished dissertation, Facoltà Psicologia, Università Cattolica del Sacro Cuore di Milano, Milan, Italy.

Gil, R. M., & Vazquez, C. I. (1996). *The Maria paradox: How Latina can merge old world traditions with new world self-esteem.* New York: Perigee

Ramos-McKay, J. M., Comas-Diaz, L., and Rivera, L. A. (1988). Puerto Ricans. In L. Comas-Diaz & E. E. H. Griffith (Eds.), *Clinical Guidelines in Mental Health* 204–232. New York: Wiley.

12

Forensic Case Study

Given the growing importance of using narrative and projective tests that are culturally competent and ethically valid with forensic patients, this chapter presents the clinical utility of TEMAS with two youngsters. The first study reports the case of a 12-year-old sexually abusing youngster; this protocol is analyzed both psychometrically and clinically because it falls within the normative sample of the TEMAS test. The second case, a 16-year-old sexually abusing adolescent, is only analyzed clinically because it falls outside the TEMAS normative group,

BACKGROUND

TEMAS Utility With Forensic Patients

The forensic patient presents the clinician with a significant variation in the application of psychological measurements, theories, and principles. Our experience in utilizing TEMAS in the area of forensic psychology has stimulated thinking as to ways in which TEMAS can be particularly useful. This chapter is a harbinger of clinically useful information in this area. Given the TEMAS track record in the area of multicultural and culturally competent assessment and the validation of this narrative instrument for use with minority and nonminority children and adolescents, it is expected that the discussion of the utility of TEMAS with the forensic population will be an ongoing and fruitful enterprise.

TEMAS History With Forensic Patients

TEMAS development has co-occurred in an urban clinic, which by coincidence also developed a program for Sexually Abusing Youngsters (SAY). The availability of court-mandated youngsters provided a ready population for utilizing TEMAS for assessment purposes. These evaluations could immediately be translated into treatment plans for sexually abusing youngsters. The adaptation of TEMAS to this population offered a valid alternative of the utility of this test with the forensic population.

Description of The Treatment Program—Sexually Abusing Youngsters (SAY)

The program was developed in 1991 with funding from the Office of Juvenile Justice and Delinquency Prevention, through the New York State Division of Criminal Justice Services. It was designed to provide treatment services to sexual abusing youngsters in the age range of 5 to 12. Now in its 14th year of operation, the SAY Program has provided treatment to about 600 referred youngsters, maintaining an active caseload of about 40 youngsters at any given time. Eighty per cent of the youngsters are court referred and mandated for treatment.

The SAY Program is culturally sensitive and competent, providing a tripartite approach to mental health care: initial assessment, treatment intervention, and posttreatment assessment and recidivist prevention. The initial assessment includes intake assessment, psychosocial assessment, mental status examination, and psychological evaluation including the administration of the TEMAS test. The approach of the SAY program is based on understanding the youngsters as a whole in their affective, cognitive, and personality functions within a psychocultural environment. Young sexual perpetrators are different from adult sexual offenders both in the way the law views them and also in the way the psychological clinician views them. Youngsters demand to be viewed as developing "whole individuals." Although sexual behaviors can be identified and singled out as targets of treatment, it is our understanding that of necessity the youngster must be seen from a "person as a whole" perspective. This is because the clinician is responsible not only for eliminating the delinquent behavior, but at the same time she or he is also charged with the responsibility of fostering the child's adaptive overall development. An instrument such as TEMAS is exemplary in identifying a multiplicity of factors needing to be assessed and addressed in the child.

Research has shown the numerous psychological components contributing to sexually abusing youngsters. (e.g., Sgroi, 1989). These include personality characteristics, as well as affective functions. Among the personality characteristics are gender identity, interpersonal relations, self-concept, aggression, and moral development. Among the affective functions are anger and fear. TEMAS has been shown to be effective in validly identifying these personality and affective characteristics in both minority and nonminority youngsters (Costantino & Malgady, 1996).

In testing youngsters involved in sexually abusing behavior, the options range from the narrowest approach of assessing for the presence or absence of a specific diagnosis of pedophilic behaviors to a larger focus, which includes assessment of a broad band of personality functions, affective functions, and cognitive indicators. Furthermore, the assessment can vary from either a Eurocentric model, in which the issues of language difference and ethnic/racial difference between examiner and examinee are not addressed and majority norms of behavior, values, and test data are applied, or a culture-centric, etic model in which examiner, evaluations, and interpretations are culturally competent.

The tendency to focus specifically on the sexually abusing behaviors is driven by a problem-focused treatment model. This model assumes that behaviors can be identified, isolated, and targeted for treatment with good outcomes. However, this model does not address the child as a whole. Frequently, sexual offense behaviors of children are the first manifest presenting problems of sufficient severity to lead to a referral of the child for treatment. Once the child is referred, however, typically a vast array of psychological, interpersonal, family, and academic problems are revealed. From that point of view, the sex offense leads to the beneficial outcome that a youngster with severe need is able to access treatment. At this point, a complete understanding of significant personality and cognitive factors in the child's life can be fully addressed. Narrative testing fosters this kind of depiction of the child's functioning from a multifaceted perspective.

What is being suggested here is that accurate psychological data elicited on culturally competent normed and validated narrative tasks can directly inform treatment planning in connection with young sexual offenders. Consequently, the individual treatment plan, which describes goals and objectives, can be framed in a measurable way. These goals and objectives would be addressed by multiple modalities, including individual dynamic therapy, cognitive/behavior therapy, group therapy, and psychoeducational interventions. In addition, a parental component informs parents about the specific goals of treatment of the child and engages parents to become therapy assistants in the treatment.

TEMAS Description (Including Psychological Information That Can Be Obtained From TEMAS in Assessing Young Sexual Offenders).

In the treatment of sex offenders, an instrument that provides a broad range of psychological data, as well as a culturally competent, perspective, tends to provide more complete, relevant, and significant psychological information. The information is relevant both for addressing the specific sexual behavior and for several variables needing to be addressed when treating behavioral problems in these youngsters.

Furthermore, for reasons of low socioeconomic status, cultural, and possibly ethnic/racial bias, the overwhelming majority of youthful sexual offenders that go through the family courts are ethnic/racial minorities in our locale. The questionable utilization of Eurocentric testing instruments exclusively in working with minorities has been well documented (Costantino, 1992; Costantino & Malgady, 1996; Dana, 1993, 2000). Consequently, the necessity for the use of multicultural and culturally competent narrative tests such as TEMAS, and to further promote the efficacy of such measures in working with these children, cries out to us if we are to do accurate and useful assessments.

CLINICAL UTILITY: AFRICAN AMERICAN CASE STUDY

This clinical case illustrates the utility of TEMAS with respect to differential diagnosis and offers significant clinical data regarding the youngster's covert behaviors. This male examinee received individual psychotherapy for approximately one month in a Sex Abusing Youngster Program (SAY), when the examinee was administered a complete psychological evaluation, a requirement in this program. This case contains the following format: Psychological Report; Discussion; TEMAS stories, complete set; and Record Booklet, scored.

Psychological Evaluation Report

Name:	Myron
Age:	12 Years Old
Date of Testing:	October 2002
Language:	English
Examiner:	S.B., M.S.

Reason for Referral

The Director of the SAY program referred Myron for psychological testing to determine his current level of intellectual, cognitive, emotional, and personality functioning. The SAY program requires complete psychological evaluations of all youngsters admitted for treatment.

History and Background Information

Myron was a 12-year-old African American male at the time of the testing. He was mandated for treatment by the Family Court after being charged with forcing his 8-year-old sister to touch his penis. Myron was 11 years and 5 months old and his sister was six at the time when the alleged incident occurred. Myron denied these charges, stating, "The charges are outrageous." He claimed his sister lied about him because he relentlessly teased her. He explained that he would often jokingly tell her that "she was adopted," that "she didn't belong to the family," and that he "hoped she died." He strongly believed the teasing motivated his sister to make these accusations. In addition, the student claimed that prior to being charged, she had threatened "to do something like this." He felt his sister has destroyed his life and was conflicted about forgiving her.

Myron's family moved to New York City from an urban area in Mississippi three years before. His childhood was significant for parental separation, migration, and domestic violence. Myron lived with his mother in New York City. His parents divorced almost two years before they came to New York City and his father lived in a different state. His sister was recently sent back to Mississippi to live with their maternal grandmother for six months. His mother worked as a teacher's aide and his estranged father's occupation was unknown. Myron described a pattern of family migration in which his mother migrated first and the rest of the family joined her a year later. During that year, when his father was the primary caregiver, he reported fighting frequently with other kids at school and in his neighborhood. His father often complained to his mother that he "couldn't control him."

Myron reported they argued frequently, and that his father was physically abusive toward his mother. When asked how the divorce affected him, he stated, "It didn't really matter to me." He reported having a close relationship with his mother, although there had been conflicts between the two of them since his sister made the charges against him. The student indicated that the mother did not believe his side of the story; this bothered him. However, he reported a more distant relationship with his father whom he only saw occasionally. In fact, he had not seen his father in eight months.

Myron was currently enrolled in the 7th grade. He reported doing well academically, and noted that his favorite subjects were math, science, and gym. He explained that he had some difficulty adjusting to school in New York City, but believed the teachers were good and helped him significantly. The student also explained he made a strong effort to change his Southern accent because it called too much attention. He reported having some friends at school and was involved in extracurricular activities at the International Youth Leadership Institute, a community and public service organization for African American and Latino students.

The student reported no past psychiatric history, and denied any family history of mental illness. He was receiving individual therapy in the SAY project. He was not prescribed psychotropic medications as part of treatment, had never been seriously ill or hospitalized, and denied any substance use.

Behavioral Observations

The student dressed appropriately for all testing sessions. Rapport was easily established from the first session, and he continued to be cooperative and friendly throughout the testing. He made good eye contact and displayed appropriate verbal skills. He was fully oriented to person, place, and time. His mood ranged from neutral to anxious; his affect was moderate. He denied any current suicidal or homicidal ideation. Myron showed adequate attention span on the WISC-III, Bender–Gestalt, Tower of London, and Sentence Completion tests. His approach to the House-Tree-Person, Rorschach, and Tell-Me-A-Story was adequate. He appeared more anxious with tasks that were less structured or open-ended. For example, on the HTP test, where he was instructed to draw a person, a house and a tree, he repeatedly asked for clarification and specific instructions. When he was not given specific instructions, he left out details in the house and tree drawings, and drew stick figures for his person drawings. He laughed defensively when presented with some test materials that pulled for sexual themes. The data gathered seemed to be an accurate assessment of Myron's current personality and cognitive functioning. Because he was English-speaking, all tests were administered in English.

Tests Administered

> Bender–Gestalt Test
> Clinical Interview
> House-Tree-Person (HTP)
> Review of intake report and progress notes
> Rorschach CS
> Wechsler Intelligence Scale for Children-Third Edition (WISC-III)
> Tell-Me-A-Story (TEMAS) (Minority Version)

Test Results

According to the New York City Public Schools Chancellor, the results of these Intelligence tests should be used with caution because of possible test bias whenever assessing culturally and linguistically diverse children.

WISC-III: Full Scale IQ   = 98

          Verbal IQ   = 99

          Performance IQ   = 98

Information	9	Picture Completion	15
Similarities	10	Coding	6
Arithmetic	12	Picture Arrangement	11
Vocabulary	8	Block Design	8
Comprehension	10	Object Assembly	8

Intellectual Functioning

Myron achieved a Full Scale IQ of 98 (45th percentile), Verbal IQ of 99 (47th percentile), and a Performance IQ of 98(45th percentile) on the WISC-III. Overall, this placed him within the Average range of intellectual functioning for children his age. There was little intratest variability between the first two domains assessed by the WISC-III. However, within the Performance domain, there was significant intratest variability. Myron displayed a relative strength in his ability to follow simple verbal directions and in his awareness of environmental details. This was demonstrated in his performance on a subtest requiring him to identify missing details in a series of pictures. Despite his adequate visual acuity in this task, the student performed relatively poorly on a subtest assessing his capacity to learn and imitate new visual material. These two subtests suggested that although he had adequate long-term visual memory, his visual short-term memory was less efficient. There was little variation on the remaining subtests, as his abilities were average on all of them.

His performance on the Bender–Gestalt test fell within normal range. His drawings were relatively accurate and showed no indication of neurological dysfunction.

Personality Functioning: Rorschach Comprehensive System (CS)

The results of the Rorschach CS indicated that Myron clinically presented "a distinct possibility of schizophrenia and this should be considered among diagnostic alternatives." In addition, the student's "...current personality organization was very similar to those who have frequent and reasonably intense experience of depression." In the area of Cognitive Functioning, he presented serious thinking deficits evidenced by frequent ideational discontinuity, faulty judgment, and errors in decision making. The data also indicated significant deficits in perceptual accuracy, resulting in poor reality testing. Consequently, he exhibited unconventional behaviors. This unconventionality drove the student to distance himself from his immediate environment, perceived as dangerous, stressful, and tricky. Hence, he had developed a hypervigilant style of dealing with the environment. However, when the student was not under stress, he was highly motivated to engage in problem solving and decisionmaking, and the quality of his thought process suggested above-average intelligence and academic achievement. In the area of Interpersonal Relations, he was emotionally distant from people because of mistrust and social isolation, but at the same time, displayed marked interest in people; consequently, he experienced frequent interpersonal difficulties. In the area of Self-Perception, he tended to have a negative self-image. In the areas of Emotional Functioning, he avoided emotional stimuli and showed a very negative and angry attitude toward the environment. Consequently, he was very much socially isolated.

TEMAS Multicultural Test (Minority Version)

When his TEMAS results were compared with those of a 12-year-old black youngster of the narrative sample, the student scored within the high average range in overall Cognitive Functioning. More specifically, he scored within an extremely high average range in Reaction Time, indicating that he responded in a slow manner in integrating visual stimuli into lengthy and meaningful stories ($T = 72$), which corresponds to 98th percentile. As his stories were lengthy and complete, we can categorize his cognitive organizational style as pensive and/or reflective. He scored within the very high average range in Total Time ($T = 66$), which corresponds to 93rd percentile, and very high average in Fluency ($T = 58$), which corresponds to 93rd percentile, thus showing excellent verbal ability. It is important to note that his verbal ability in the WISC-III test was within the average range; however, in the TEMAS, the student was verbally very productive, spent a great deal of time in elaborating themes, and narrated excellent and grammatically correct stories. He also scored within the average range in recognizing and resolving interpersonal and personal conflicts, thus showing adaptive problem-solving skills in all areas except sexual identity function. In the Personality Functions, however, he scored within the borderline range, overall. More specifically, the student scored within the borderline range in Interpersonal Relations ($T = 31$), which corresponds to the 2nd percentile; within the very low average range in Aggression ($T = 39$), corresponding to the 7th percentile; and within the deficient range in Coping with Anxiety and Depression ($T = 27$), which corresponds to the 1st percentile and points toward a symptomatology of major depression. The student also scored within the very low average in Sexual Identity ($T = 39$), which corresponds to the 7th percentile, Self-Concept of Competence ($T = 31$), which corresponds to the 2nd percentile, and Moral Judgment ($T = 38$), which corresponds to the 7th percentile. Conversely, the student scored within the very high average in Achievement Motivation ($T = 63$), corresponding to the 90th percentile, and Reality Testing ($T = 52$) corresponding to the 60th percentile. In the area of Affective Functions, he scored within the very low average in "Happy" ($T = 38$; 7th percentile); within the extremely high average range in "Sad" ($T = 72$; 98th percentile); within the above-average range in "Angry" ($T = 55$; 65th percentile), and within the average range in "Fearful" ($T = 50$; 50th percentile). The very high score in "Sad" affective function confirms a possible diagnosis of major depression.

With respect to total omissions ($T = 43$), corresponding to about the 25th percentile, he showed a nonsignificant selective attention in the areas of coping with anxiety and depression, controlling aggressive ideation, ability to delay gratification, moral judgment, and reality testing, thus indicating a somewhat adaptive defensive mechanism. It needs to be pointed out, however, that Myron showed significant omissions in the area of sexual identity; thus indicating a maladaptive defense mechanism in dealing with this function. This significant score coupled with the low score in sexual identity scale indicates that sexual identity was a problematic function for this youngster. In addition, he tended to use his maladaptive selective attention in the areas of aggression, anxiety/depression, moral judgment, and reality testing, which, although were statistically non-significant, have clinical significance.

In summary, Myron experienced serious difficulties in interpersonal relationship. In addition, he showed seriously maladaptive skills in controlling his aggressive impulses and in coping with anxiety/depression provoking situations. He also showed serious dysfunctions in the areas of self-concept of competence and above all in sexual identity. Conversely, his desire to achieve in school, his ability to forgo immediate gratification, and his ability to distinguish right from wrong constituted his strengths. In the area of Affective Functions, a statistically and clinically significant score in "Sad" correlated positively with his very low scores in Anxiety/Depression and pointed to a diagnostic impression of Major Depression, because his scores in "Fearful" were less clinically significant.

Myron's test profile revealed a deeply depressed and isolated young man. He mostly felt like a failure and struggled to perceive himself as a good and worthy person. He stated, "I failed life," "the future sure seems to suck," and "Life is a pain in the ass" on the Sentence Completion Test. His poor self-image was further illustrated in the story he gave to a TEMAS card depicting a child dreaming about two dragons. Myron saw the boy facing his two sides: "a ferocious and fearless side and a side that eats too much and is cowardly." Myron stated that inside he was feeling "like a whole lot of nothing." Myron's drawings also hinted at the mental confusion that he was experiencing and the isolation he felt.

Throughout his Rorschach responses, his TEMAS stories, and the clinical interview, Myron also revealed an attitude of mistrust toward his social environment. He revealed that he felt insecure and unsupported in his relationships with family members and peers. He also perceived adolescent peer relationships as difficult. He often felt inadequate and left out and perceived hostility and ridicule in his peers' actions, a likely source of his depression. To cope with what he perceived as a hostile environment, Myron attempted to maintain emotional distance in his interpersonal relationships and avoided deep relationships with his peers.

Serious conflict in sexual identity and its psychosocial implication remained the most troublesome areas for Myron. His story to TEMAS Card 22 confirmed this problematic area: "I guess he's thinking about cross-dressing …thinking if he'll look better as girl or boy. Friends call him pussy or ass. Now he is looking at himself and… probably says he does act like a girl. He is thinking maybe he does act feminine…" This unresolved conflict tended to alienate him from both males and female peers and could have motivated him to act out his sexual fantasies with his sister.

The charges that were filed against Myron impacted his family life situations. He felt betrayed by his little sister and rejected by his parents. In addition, his parents' divorce also negatively affected his perception of family life, although he struggled to acknowledge this in the interview. Myron's projection of his family's problems onto the TEMAS cards revealed the anger he felt toward his father and his empathy for his mother. Several of his stories also illustrated his feelings of being left out and unhappy within his family. He also projected these feelings on other family members, especially his mother, whom he depicted as a victim of his father's deception and abuse (see story to Card 4). To cope with his unhappy family life, Myron isolated and immersed himself in several positive activities such as writing poetry, doing homework, and engaging in extracurricular activities.

Despite feeling disconnected from his family, Myron still recognized interdependence among family members. For instance, Myron acknowledged that his behavior carried consequences that impacted his entire family and not just himself. He considered them when making difficult decisions. He also ascribed a very important role to adults and parents in defining appropriate behavior and delivering reward or punishment to children. It was likely that the values that he had learned from his family and other adults in his community played a significant role in guiding Myron's behavior and helping him to cope with his peers.

Diagnostic Impression

AXIS I: R/O 296.22 Major Depression Disorder, Single Episode Moderate Severity R/O 312.81 Conduct Disorder, Childhood-Onset Type
AXIS II: None
AXIS III: None
AXIS IV: Family conflict
AXIS V: 67

Summary and Recommendations

Myron was a 12-year-old youngster at the time of testing. He was referred for psychological evaluation to assess his current level of affective and personality functioning for allegedly sexually abusing his younger sister. Myron was easily engaged in all testing sessions, and displayed adequate attention and cooperation. The results reported should be considered an adequate measure of his current functioning, except for his IQ full scale scores. He seemed to have higher IQ potential.

Test results placed Myron's level of intellectual functioning within the average range for children his age. There were no significant differences between his Verbal and Performance scores. He displayed a relative strength in his long-term visual memory and a relative weakness in his working memory. Some difficulty in executive planning was also noted. In general, Myron was a bright youngster who was motivated to achieve and had the ability to do so.

Personality testing highlighted Myron's struggles with feelings of sadness, isolation, and confusion, especially in the area of sexual identity, which left him feeling depressed and empty inside. Myron defended against these feelings by presenting his strong fearless side to the world and resisting lasting and meaningful relationships with both female and male peers. Myron needed to protect himself and thus kept himself isolated from his family and his peer group.

Myron also expressed feelings of hopelessness throughout this evaluation. It is important to explore these feelings during treatment. He believed factors outside of his control, such as his sister's lying, could impact negatively on his future. It was important for Myron to gain a realistic sense of control in his life. Related to this was his anger toward his sister; Myron maintained his innocence and saw himself as the victim of circumstances. It was recommended that therapy should motivate him to explore these feelings. Given the test data, a parental consultation prior to terminating treatment was recommended. It will be useful for Myron and his mother to prepare for the return of his sister. Myron's therapist should also consider assessing his family's attitude toward sexuality in anticipation of the sister's return to the home, and Myron's own psychosexual development. Notwithstanding his denial of the sexual abuse incident, therapy should also focus on clarifying his gender identification, and thus lead him toward a socially acceptable manner of expressing sexual needs.

Therapy should also help Myron to develop adaptive relationships with adult male authority figures. He had a positive relationship with adult female maternal figures. He tended to perceive male authority figures as threatening, and hence tended to aggress against them. TEMAS narratives (see story to Card 15-M) indicated that he had the potential to externalize this aggressive feeling. Hence, therapy should also focus on having him develop socially acceptable skills to control these aggressive feelings. Therapy should also help Myron to enhance his self-esteem and social skills, and encourage his educational and artistic pursuits. Myron's poor self-image likely caused some distortion in his perception of social interactions with his peers. With a more positive self-concept and improved social skills, Myron tended to have the potential to develop adaptive relationships with his peers. These relationships could also foster age-appropriate psychosexual development.

Discussion

Clinical Utility. The utility of psychological tests in general and narrative tests in particular are important in the area of assessment of child/adolescent psychopathology because they clarify diagnostic impressions that are usually based on problems presented by parents, significant others, and/or teachers. Children and adolescents are poor informants and often report absence of emotional and/or behavioral problems during clinical evaluations, however youngsters do reveal underlying emotional problems in narrative techniques. In addition, narrative techniques usually help the therapist to refocus the treatment process and identify additional problem areas that can be directly addressed in the Individual Treatment Plan, thus affording the achievement of therapeutic goals and objectives in a relatively short-term intervention (Cardalda, Costantino, Jiménez-Suárez, León-Velázquez, Martínez, & Perez, 2005; Dana, 2000).

In addition, the validity of a psychological test rests on the accuracy of the results of the instruments in generating a clinical profile of the examinee and sufficient data on the underlying emotional problems in order to provide an appropriate diagnostic label for the examinee. However, the predictive validity of tests ultimately rests on the following relationships: the positive relationship between the findings of test results obtained from the various tests and the presenting problems, the relationship among the results of the various tests, and between the single or collective test results and the youngster's relationship between the presenting problems provided by the significant others.

Differential Test Utility. In this case, the WISC-III results indicated that Myron's IQ fell within the normal range, with the potential to function at a higher intellectual level. The results of the Cognitive Functions on the TEMAS also revealed the youngster's high average cognitive organizational ability and verbal fluency. The Rorschach CS results indicated that the student showed above average intellectual abilities only in stress-free situations, but he exhibited limited cognitive organization. The WISC-III results showed an average IQ. However, the TEMAS results indicated above-average intellectual abilities even in stressful situations, above-average cognitive skills, and above-average verbal ability; thus giving a more accurate prediction of Myron's cognitive and intellectual abilities.

Both the Rorschach CS and TEMAS test results suggested the presence of depression symptoms, maladaptive interpersonal relations, poor self-esteem, poor control of aggressive ideation, avoidant behavior, and a tendency to act in an unconventional manner. These test findings were confirmed by the presenting problems at admission. However, the Rorschach also pointed to a diagnostic impression of Schizophrenia, which was not supported by his adequate reality testing in TEMAS and in real-life situations. In addition, TEMAS revealed a more appropriate diagnostic impression of Major Depression evidenced by the very low score in depression and very high score on "Sad" feelings. This diagnostic impression of Major Depression was confirmed by the psychiatric evaluation conducted within a month of the psychological evaluation. The psychiatrist recommended antidepressant medication, but the student refused. In addition, TEMAS findings indicated a serious sexual identity conflict, which may have precipitated the alleged sexual offense against his sister. These specific results generated specific treatment planning goals and objectives, which became the focal point of treatment. Furthermore, the TEMAS results indicated strengths in academic achievement motivation and ability to forgo immediate gratification. The student was reported by the parents to do well in school, thus confirming the TEMAS findings (Eliot, 1998).

Therapeutic Progress.   Myron lived with his single-parent mother and 8-year-old sister. His father left the household after the birth of his sister. Following a complaint by his 8-year-old sister of being forced to touch his penis, his mother lodged this complaint with the Family Court and the student was given an 18-month probation and mandated to receive psychotherapy. Myron at first admitted to this offense, following legal advice. However, he complained that it was just an accident. After taking a shower, he came out in his underwear, was teased by his sister, and they began to wrestle. During the friendly struggle, he inadvertently rubbed his penis against his sister's hands. Nevertheless, his mother believed the sister's complaint of an intentional act. The student underwent individual therapy with monthly family therapy sessions. During the initial stage, the treatment dealt with his angry feelings toward his sisters false accusations, feelings of betrayal, and feelings of abandonment by his mother. After six months, he learned to control his anger and even wrote a letter of apology to his sister. The mother began to express some positive feelings toward the son, and they began to work out some of the conflicts in filial therapy sessions. The second phase of treatment focused on his rebellion and his deliberate plans to do poorly in school so that he could be remanded to attend summer school, and thus be given attention by authority figures.

In summary, the utility of the psychological tests administered to Myron rests on a somewhat positive relationship between the results of WISC-III, the Rorschach CS and the TEMAS, which predicted average and above average cognitive abilities. With respect to psychopathology, the Rorschach CS results indicated the presence of a possible schizophrenic process, depression symptoms, maladaptive interpersonal relationship, poor self-esteem, poor control of aggressive ideation, and avoidant behavior. However; only TEMAS attributed a more accurate diagnostic label of Major Depression. This diagnosis was confirmed by a psychiatric evaluation and presenting problems. This case strongly illustrates the effectiveness of narrative tests in providing a valid clinical profile of a forensic case, which was acceptable in the Family Court and which successfully contributed to a positive treatment outcome. (For complete scoring, see Fig. 12–1.)

MYRON'S TEMAS STORIES

Myron's stories in response to the expanded short form of TEMAS are reported, together with the scoring in the Record Booklet. The 9 cards of the short form were increased to 12 to assess this youngster accused of sexual abuse in order to augment the validity of the pulled functions and thus present a more complete clinical forensic case.

TEMAS Stories

Myron: 12 Years Old

Card 1B-M*

RT   5 sec.
ST   1 min.
TT   3 min.18 sec.
Fluency: 130

There is this boy who wants to go play basketball with his friends. His mom is giving him some list and telling him to go do that first. If he's a good boy he'll go do what mom tells him first and play with his friends later.

1. His friends, his mom and father.
2. They live near a school.
3. They're pointing and saying , "aah" (laughs).
4. He was probably inside the house – the friends came…no. He was sitting out on step, then friends wanted to play. Mom said "go do something for me first."
5. Boy will do what Mom says, then play.
6. Probably thinking that "why didn't she ask before."
   Kinda disappointed (?), sad, I guess. But if he hurried and do what mother asks, he'll do what he wants.

Card 13 B-M

RT   7 sec.
ST   1 min. 20 sec.
TT   4 min. 57 sec.
Fluency: 145

This boy is feeling like doing something wrong. He's analyzing what, or who he'll hurt and his parents come to his vision.

1. (a)a boy (?) a teenager. I guess he has troubles. That's why he's thinking of something bad. Probably trying to fit in.
2. In the bathroom.
3. This is the only place to be alone without being bothered. Went to wash his face, and take a good look at himself. Thinking about who he would disappoint and parents faces appear.
4. He was thinking hard about doing something bad. Probably with friends, so he needed to be alone, so said he had to use the bathroom.
5. Depends on how he's feeling. If he feels like he has to, he will. But if he feels he can't live with self, he won't.
6. (a) Same exact thing.
   (b) Confused, sad.

Testing the Limits

Q: What is he struggling with?
A: He's a teenager. Peer pressure. Friends want him to rob liquor store, join a gang, shoot somebody.

Card 14 B-M*

RT	5 sec.
ST	1 min.25 sec.
TT	4 min. 06 sec.
Fluency:	152

What happened before is that everybody came in and started goofing around. That kid wants to do homework. They saw only one kid doing it. They made fun of him. He didn't care because he had to do it. They went and partied. In the future he'll be better off. Gotta be book-smart too. Can't only be street smart.

1. (a) Guess his friends from school. But, why are they all in his house dancing? I would kick them out.
2. (b)He's in the living room—they're in there, but moved away for him to concentrate.
3. They're dancing. The kid with a painting in his hands is trying to get his mack on. (laughs).
4. ———
5. Leave after they finish, or ask to copy from him.
6. (a) What is he thinking...probably thinking, "what a bunch of dumb asses." Probably tempted, but parents taught him better.
   (b) What is he feeling? Left out, sad.

Card 7-M*

RT	5 sec.
ST	30 sec.
TT	3 min. 15 sec.
Fluency:	119

What happen before is brother and sister were playing around. Someone broke the lamp. Mom came down. She doesn't know what to do so she'll punish both.

1. (a)Mother, brother, sister.
2. At home in the living room.
3. Brother and sister blaming each other. Mom looks irritated.
4. Brother and sister playing around...playing tag. Mom was chilling upstairs, she had cleaned the house, now the damn kids.
5. Mom is going to punish them. Who did it will be happy because they got the other one in trouble. The other will be mad.
6. (a) Mother—what the hell to do with damn kids. Don't know who to believe, so probably thinking of punishing both of them.
    (b) Irritated, upset, confused, mad.

Card 20-M*

RT   35 sec.
ST   2 min.50 sec.
TT   5 min. 24 sec.
Fluency: 134

It's a girl and she's dreaming. What happened before...she's probably adopted. Probably thinking she's the horse. Trying to get into the castle. The castle represents home. The horse is trying to find a way home. Bridges represent problems. Water represents things pushing you away. The water pushing you away always ends up where everyone else is (points to lake). That's why the road starts here.

1. don't know—girl
2. At her adopted parents or foster home. If foster home would be other people. Uhm...(pause)...lost my thought there.
3. She's dreaming—she's dreaming of a home or a better place.
4. Just found out she's adopted. Or had argument—and hates foster parents.
5. Probably run away, searching for home.
6. (a) Wants to find better home.
    (b) Depressed, deceived, manipulated, angry, impatient.

Card 17 B-M*

RT   10 sec.
ST   1 min. 02 sec.
TT   4 min. 09 sec.
Fluency: 137

He's thinking if he doesn't study he'll get an F, and he'll be mad. And the guy—teacher—he'll be mad. If he studies, he'll get A and father will be happy, and take him anywhere he goes. However, if he does study too hard his mind will go blank. But that's a different story.

1. (a)Boy and his father.
2. Boy's at home—when daydreaming. I guess he's in class or someone's house . . . No, most likely class.
3. He's thinking. Kinda balancing whether he should study or not.
4. The boy he probably just came home, father told him to go study. He's thinking if he really should do it.
5. Probably end up doing it.
6. (a) If he should study.
   (b) If it's really necessary (?) confused (?), sad, I guess.

Card 4-M**

RT   9 sec.
ST   1 min. 15 sec.
TT   4 min. 50 sec.
Fluency: 138

You got caught! (laughs). What happened before...father was cheating on wife. Sleeping with other woman. What happened is that the wife and kids caught him in the act. Father is pissed. Naturally, family is shocked. Mother is pissed she married him in the first place.

1. Pops and mom and family. Her best friend (person in the bed).
2. at home.
3. Sister is shocked, and covering her mouth. Son is pointing and saying "Ooh, I saw her naked." Mom is thinking, "What a dog."

4. Kids were playing around or just came home with mom. They ran in to see pops caught him.
5. Guess get a divorce. He'll try to come around, but mom will get a new boyfriend.
6. (a) "Ooh I saw a girl".
    (b) Feels lucky (?), happy. He'll probably go tell his friends at school he saw a girl naked.

Card 10B*

RT   3 sec.
ST   1 min. 20 sec.
TT   3 min. 07 sec.
Fluency: 107

This boy worked for money, or just got some. He goes to his piggy bank, and is contemplating if he should get ice cream or save up to get new bike in the future. He'll probably get the ice cream.

1. probably me.
2. in his room.
3. –
4. working I guess – he did something for someone.
5. –
6. (a) Should I buy the ice cream or get bike. If he saves to get the bike, he'll still want the ice cream. And he'll have to ask his mom for money and he doesn't want to do that. I guess that's just like life.
    (b) Feels hungry, confused…sad.

Card 6-M**

RT   44 sec.
ST   1 min. 50 sec.
TT   3 min. 36 sec.
FT   4 min. 13 sec.
Fluency: 103

What happened was that their mom and dad probably separated, or one of them died.

Or…ok, what happened was that while they were playing dress-up—their little brother died or got killed in a drive by—every time they see it (points at toy) they get sad.

1. Brother and sister.
2. In the attic.
3. –
4. Running upstairs (laughs). Feeling bored, so they felt like they wanted to go play dress up.
5. Probably go to sleep feeling depressed.
6. (a) Both are mainly thinking of how things use to be before it happened.
   (b) Feeling depressed. [?—Main character] both, feeling the same thing. The father is angry and wants revenge.

Card 2M**

RT   22 sec.
ST   1 min. 10 sec.
TT   3 min. 42 sec.
Fluency: 118

Don't know what happened before. There are kids all over. Pops being a bum watching TV, while mom is doing everything all at once. I don't know how she does it. Typical family.

(Should've shown this before other one-referring to card 4M). They need to stop having kids.

1. At home in the living room.
2. –
3. (?) They were making a mess. They boy looks like he spilled juice.
4. Mom probably won't talk to husband or father. He's going to wonder why and she's not going to tell him.
5. –
6. (?) a. Mother thinking – her husband is a lazy bum. Kids are pain in the ass. She doesn't get help from any of them.
   b. She's feeling unwanted, no, unappreciated, sad.

Card 15 M*

"That's bullshit. Why it has to be a minority" (points to kid with "knife")

RT   28 sec.
ST   1 min. 41 sec.
TT   4 min. 13 sec.
Fluency: 178

What happened was that this baseball team won. A ball was hit foul and hit a window in the appliance store. These kids were walking by, one took a TV, one a radio. They're so ghetto. One has a knife and thinks he's so brave he's probably going to try and slice the cop. But he'll not get away.

1. Coach and team, and looters and cops. (looters) don't know each other. Saw they were robbing the place and joined in.
2. At the park and across the street at the appliance store.
3. Baseball team playing and won. The looters were walking by.
4. –
5. One with the knife will try and stab cop. Baseball team will try to hide baseball, because they broke it and don't want to say anything.
6. (a) Kid trying to stab cop is thinking "I'm not getting caught I'm going to stab him and run. Thinks he's braver than everyone.
   (b) Feeling he won't get caught (?) cornered, sad.

Card 21M*

RT   35 sec.
ST   1 min. 00 sec.
TT   3 min. 30 sec.
Fluency: 99

Well he's thinking he's a monster. He's dreaming one is ferocious and fearless. The other one eats too much and is a coward. I guess those are the two faces of himself.

1. A boy (?) 13 or 14.
2. He's in his room.
3. The ferocious side's talking shit, but deep inside he's feeling unwanted and eats his problems away. The ferocious side is a front. Inside he's feeling like a whole lot of nothing.
4. Probably got beat up.
5. Change his life around.
6. (a) Thinking if ferocious side is a front.
   (b) Feeling inside, depressed and unwanted.

Card 22 B-M*

"What the hell is this"

RT   6 sec.
ST   1 min.50 sec.
TT   4 min. 07 sec.
Fluency: 132

I guess he's thinking about cross-dressing. He's deciding if he'll look better as a girl or boy. His friends called him 'pussy' or 'ass.' Now he's looking at himself and ... probably saying he acts like a girl. He's thinking that maybe he does act feminine. Maybe he's a half boy half girl, a hermaphrodite.

1. (?) Too short to be that old, so maybe 9 or 10, maybe 7- why 7 pop in my head. Maybe friends didn't call him pussy, might be thinking of sister who makes up half of him.
2. In bathroom.
3. ———
4. Probably someone wanted to fight him and called him pussy.
5. Go to sleep and think things over.
6. (a) Maybe he acts feminine. Probably wears exact size pants.
    (b) Like a girl (?) left one, coward, sad.

LATINO FORENSIC CASE STUDY

In this section, we present the second forensic case. As the Latino youngster was 16 years old at the time of the testing, the TEMAS test was administered according to the standard administration, scored according to the step-down method, and compared to a 13-year-old Hispanic normative case. This case was only analyzed clinically without reporting TEMAS test scores.

Miguel was a 16-year-old male who was referred after being found guilty in a juvenile Family Court of multiple counts of "forcible touching and sexual abuse in the third degree." He denied all allegations. He was

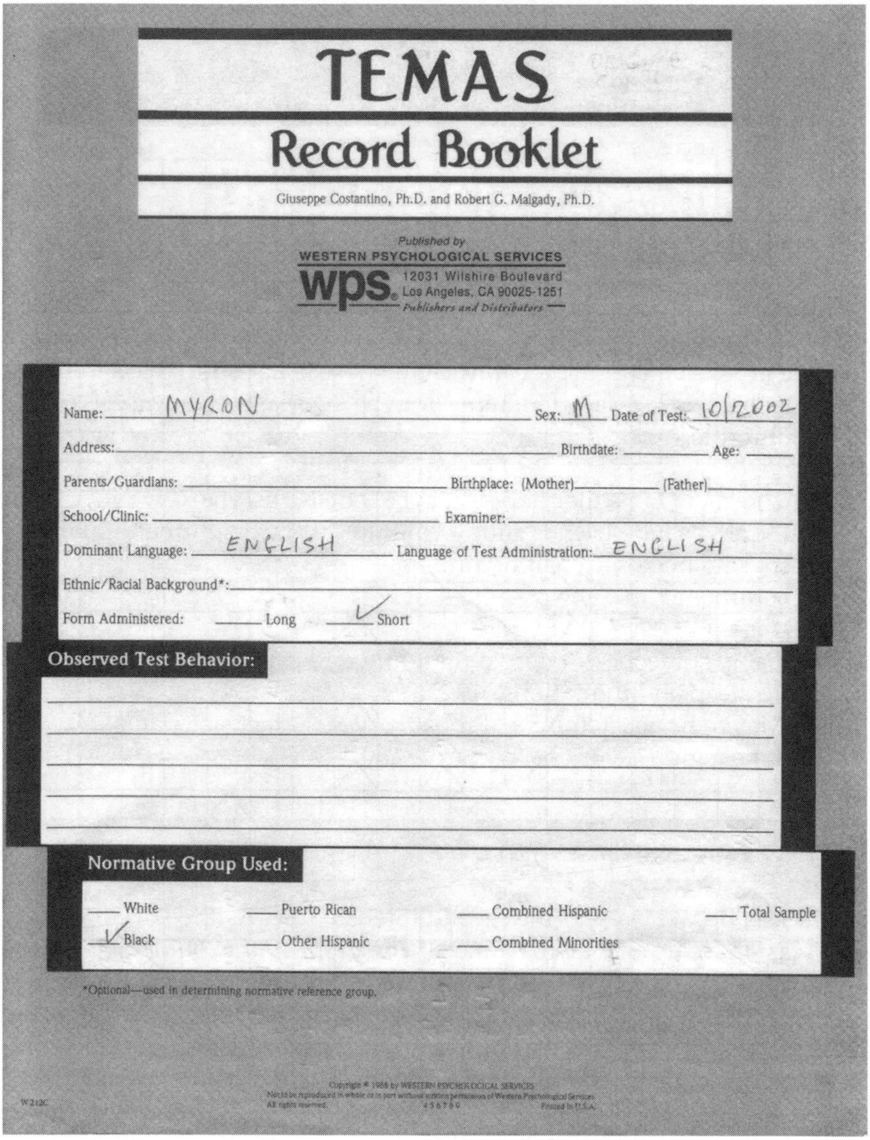

TEMAS
Record Booklet

Giuseppe Costantino, Ph.D. and Robert G. Malgady, Ph.D.

Published by
WESTERN PSYCHOLOGICAL SERVICES
wps. 12031 Wilshire Boulevard
Los Angeles, CA 90025-1251
Publishers and Distributors

Name: MYRON Sex: M Date of Test: 10/2002

Address: Birthdate: Age:

Parents/Guardians: Birthplace: (Mother) (Father)

School/Clinic: Examiner:

Dominant Language: ENGLISH Language of Test Administration: ENGLISH

Ethnic/Racial Background*:

Form Administered: ___ Long ✓ Short

Observed Test Behavior:

Normative Group Used:

___ White ___ Puerto Rican ___ Combined Hispanic ___ Total Sample

✓ Black ___ Other Hispanic ___ Combined Minorities

*Optional—used in determining normative reference group.

FIGURE 12–1. Scored record booklet.

Scoring Sheet
Quantitative Scales

Card No.	Reaction Time (Seconds)	Total Time (Minutes)	Fluency	Total Omissions	Interpersonal Relations	Aggression	Anxiety/ Depression	Achievement Motivation	Delay of Gratification	Self-Concept	Sexual Identity	Moral Judgment	Reality Testing	Happy	Sad	Angry	Fearful
		Cognitive Functions						Personality Functions							Affective Functions		
1*	5	3.18	130		3/3				4						1	1	
2	22	3.42	118	1	1		2					N			1	1	
3																	
4	9	4.50	138	2	1/2 3	N	N					2		1			
5																	
6	44	3.38	103	1	1		1				N				1		
7*	5	3.15	119		2	3						2				1	
8																	
9																	
10*	13	3.07	107						3						1		
11																	
12																	
13	7	4.57	145	1	1/2 3		2			2	N	3			1		
14*	5	4.06	152		2			4	4						1		
15*																	
16																	
17*	10	4.09	137					2	3			2					
18																	
19																	
20*	35	5.24	134			1									1		
21*	35	3.35	99	1		2	1						N		1		
22*	6	3.30	132	1		2						2	3		1		1
23																	
Sum	224/155	59.34/353	1693/171	7/4.8	16	8	10	7	12	5	2	10	3	>1	9/6.7	3/2.2	>1
Number of Cards Scored					9	4	7	2	4	3	1	4	1				
Mean Score**					1.8	2	1.4	3.5	3	1.7	2	2.5	3				
Sum of Functions Not Pulled ("N-Scores")					>1	>1					2/1.5	>1	>1		*PRORATED SCORES		

*Cards used for Short Form.
**Mean Score = Sum ÷ Number of cards scored.   Page 2

FIGURE 12–1.   Scored record booklet. (*Continued*)

Scoring Sheet
Qualitative Indicators

Card No.	Affective Functions			Cognitive Functions													
										Optional							
										Omissions				Transformations			
	Neutral	Ambivalent	Inappropriate Affect	Conflict	Sequencing	Imagination	Relationships	Total Transformations	Inquiries	Main Character	Secondary Character	Event	Setting	Main Character	Secondary Character	Event	Setting
1*																I	I
2																	
3																	
4																	
5																	—
6																	
7*																	
8																	
9																	
10*																	
11																	
12																	
13																	
14*																	
15*																	
16																	
17*										I							
18																	
19																	
20*			(1)														
21*																	
22*			1														
23																	
Sum			$\frac{2}{1.5}^4$							>I $^+$						>I $^+$	>I $^+$
90% + (✓)																	

+ PRORATED SCORES

*Cards used for Short Form.

Page 3

FIGURE 12–1.   Scored record booklet. (*Continued*)

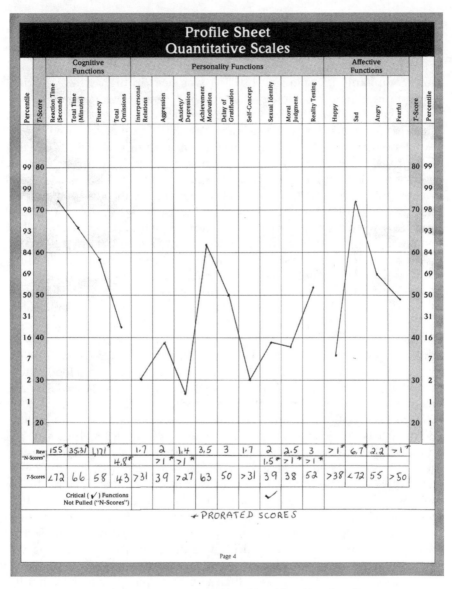

FIGURE 12–1. Scored record booklet. (*Continued*)

initially accused of "sexually harassing a female peer," when he was in ninth grade, at the age of 14. Prior to that incident, he had been suspended numerous times in seventh and eighth grades for fighting with other students, and for throwing stones at cars. Following the sexual harassment complaint, a suspension hearing was held in high school, during which numerous other female students had come forward to complain that he had touched each of them on the buttocks at various different times. Miguel denied each of these accusations. He never admitted to any sexual molestation activity, or to fondling or pinching any girls. When the student was transferred to another high school later in the year, he was again accused by numerous girls of touching them. He also denied these charges, and claimed that the accusers were friends of the girls in the previous school. He indicated that there was a conspiracy by these girls, inasmuch they were entirely from the same immigrant group. He claimed all of his accusers emigrated from a country in Eastern Europe. On beginning 10th grade, he was accused by students of following them around and fondling them in summer school classes during the previous summer. At that point, he was arrested and charged with numerous counts of forcible touching and of sexual abuse in the third degree. He was housed in a secure juvenile facility for a time, but after his release, while awaiting disposition, he was again arrested for the same sexual molestation act. This time he was charged as an adult, and was adjudicated in a local criminal court. He persisted in denying that he had ever committed any sexual abuse. His parents stood steadfastly by his denials, and took the position that he was the unfortunate victim of an ethnically and racially motivated conspiracy.

Upon examination for "risk assessment," he acknowledged that fondling and forcible touching was wrong, but denied ever committing those acts. He admitted, however, that, in the past he had tapped female acquaintances on the buttocks as was he walking down the hallways at school, just like baseball players do to teammates, but he insisted that he had never done this to a stranger. He said that he had tapped a girl on the buttocks, but that this was a girl who was his friend, and that she was not offended. He indicated that he was the type of person who would play the game of tapping someone on the shoulder and then quickly withdrawing his hand, leaving the object of the game confused as to who had tapped him or her. He added that by this time, the girls had lodged the same complaint against him, but he denied that he had ever seen any of them before. When asked if these kinds of offenses were serious, he said: "Yes. It's violating their boundaries."

Review of the TEMAS protocol of this youngster provided four kinds of information: Personality Functions that were significant, Affective

Functions, Cognitive Function, and individual response stories or story segments of clinical significance.

Utility and Applicability of Personality Functions

Review of the personality functions of this youngster showed significant impairment in controlling his Aggression, coping with Anxiety/Depression, Self-concept of Competence, Sexual Identity, and in Interpersonal Relationships. Although he showed a wide inconsistency in relating to others in real life.

Our work with sexually acting out youngsters has shown many instances in which the youngsters exhibited impairment in Sexual Identity. Frequently, this takes the form of a male showing a prevailing feminine identification. Although no relationship of causation can be posited based on this result, the finding does suggest a hypothesis that the youngster's aggressive sexual behavior may serve to help resolve a conflict associated with sexual identity problems. This youngster, in addition, manifested problems in self-concept, in coping with anxiety and depression-provoking situations, controlling aggression, and in relating to others. Again, no casual relationship is implied, but these findings suggest areas of weakness that are variables associated with the psychological and clinical profile of this sexual offender. The TEMAS protocol directs the clinician to areas of psychological weakness that can be targeted in subsequent clinical work.

The literature suggests that *general systems theory* offers a paradigm for explaining how the sexual misconduct can be remedied by addressing the numerous weaknesses identified in the personality functions (e.g., Sgroi, 1989). In taking a systems point of view, the identified maladaptive behavior, in this case the sexual acting out can only exist in a homeostasis with other elements of the psychic system. The psychic system includes both the sexual acting out as well as the configuration of personality factors, including the weaknesses identified by TEMAS. The expectation is that once these areas of weakness are improved, the personality configuration will be rearranged and the sexual abuse will no longer be supported within the new personality structure.

Furthermore, qualitative analysis of stories suggested the presence of other psychological factors, relevant for understanding the sexual offending youngster. For example, in one story (Card 4), the youngster portrayed a father caught with a "smoking gun," so to speak. The father is standing at the door of his bedroom, confronted by his wife and children, as another woman is in his bed trying to hide her face. When asked how the father responded to the confrontation, the patient stated: "...the father is saying with an angry tone of voice: 'There's nobody in the bed!'" This response was striking in that the youngster told a story in which a nonambiguous percept is assertively denied, even though others can validate its existence. In fact, despite what the youngster may say, somebody was in the bed. This story demonstrates distortion of the picture in order to protect his fragile self-image and his "innocence," thus showing some malingering. This finding, as demonstrated in the TEMAS story, lends support to the idea that Miguel lacked credibility.

Failures in credibility are inimical to sexual offenders, both adults as well as youngsters. With youngsters, standard assessment procedures require that the clinician come armed with all corroborating information available. When such information is lacking, and even in some cases when the information is available, denials by the sexually acting out youngster are to be expected. Clinically relevant information of the type described in this case serves as aids to the clinician who is attempting to separate the truth from fiction. Clinicians take pains to avoid the role of finders of fact. The clinician working with the forensic population is well aware that only a court has that role. Yet, it is common that clinicians find themselves in the situation of trying to determine the facts as they attempt to turn a mandated case into a treatment case. Data such as the kind available in TEMAS stories helps in this venture.

Development of the Individual Treatment Plan (ITP)

TEMAS is particularly useful in that it assists the forensic clinician in the development of the specific treatment plan, including treatment goals and objectives for the youngster. In the case of Miguel, the treatment plan addressed the following areas:

1. Interpersonal relations. Inconsistencies were identified, and the youngster was to be taught skills in interpersonal behavior, how to identify his own aggressive feelings, and alternative ways of expressing these feelings.
2. Sexual identity. The issue of sexual identity was to be raised in an effort to help the youngster clarify conflicts, and to address issues of gender interest and sexuality. As a result of this work, it was expected that he would gain an appreciation of socially acceptable behaviors with peers of his own gender and of the opposite gender.

3. Denial, and Self-Concept. By addressing these issues, the youngster's capacity to deal honestly with reality and to develop his coping skills in uncomfortable realistic situations would be improved.
4. Anxiety and Depression. By addressing these two clinical symptoms, it was expected that the youngster would develop skills to adaptively cope with stress.

CONCLUSION

Following the psychological evaluation and the development of the ITP, the youngster was terminated at the SAY program because he had been rearrested following an additional "pinching incident" in school. Miguel was referred to a residential program for sexually abusing youngsters by the juvenile court. The utility of the psychological assessment and clinical analyses were sent to the court, which in turn, forwarded them to the new residential treatment facility.

REFERENCES

Cardalda, E., Costantino, G., Jiménez-Suárez, V., León-Velázquez, M., Martínez, J. V., & Perez. M (2005). *Second Puerto Rican study: Cross-Cultural comparisons with the TEMAS test using group versus individual methodology*. San Juan, P R: Carlos Albizu University.

Costantino, G. (1992). Overcoming bias in the educational assessment of Hispanic students. In K. F. Geisinger (Ed.), *Psychological testing of Hispanics* (pp. 89–98). Washington, DC: American Psychological Assn.

Costantino, G., & Malgady, R. G. (1996). Development of TEMAS, A multicultural thematic apperception test: Psychometric properties and clinical utility. In G. R. Sodowsky & J. Impara (Eds.), *Multicultural assessment in counseling and clinical Psychology*. (pp. 85–136). Lincoln, NE: Buros Institute of Mental Measurements University of Nebraska.

Dana, R. H. (1993). *Multicultural assessment perspectives for professional psychology*. Boston: Allyn & Bacon.

Dana, R. H. (2000). Multicultural assessment of child and adolescent personality and psychopathology. In A. L. Comunian & U. Gielen (Eds), *International perspectives on human development* (pp. 233–258). Lengerich, Germany: Pabst Science Publishers.

Sgroi, S. M., (1989). *Vulnerable populations: Sexual abuse treatment for children, adult survivors, offenders and persons with mental retardation* (Vol. 2). Lexington, MA: Lexington Books/D.C. Health and Company.

Author Index

A

Abe-Kim, J. S., 64, 90
Abraham, P., 223, 224
Abrams, D. M., 109, 113, 121
Abreu, J. M., 68, 90
Achenbach, R. M., 22, 26, 49
Achenbach, T. M., 282
Albano, A. M., 22, 53
Alexander, C. M., 85, 97
Allen, I. I., 36, 59
Allen, J., 33, 34, 37, 49, 52, 60, 88, 90, 111, 112, 120, 121
Allen-Meares, P., 72, 81, 90
Allison, K., 68, 90
Allport, G. W., 105, 121
Almeida, L., 231, 287
Ambrosini, P., 7, 59
Anastasi, A., 281, 283
Ancis, J. R., 81, 90
Anderson, M. P., 130, 156
Anderson, M. Z., 70, 96
Andrews, H., 48, 50
Angold, A., 7, 8, 49, 51
Anthony, W. A., 16, 18, 49, 50, 230, 283
Aragon, M., 36, 37, 38, 42, 52, 53, 63, 93
Archer, R. P., 26, 50
Arellano, L., 36, 37, 42, 53, 63, 93
Arnold, B. R., 45, 48, 51, 112, 121
Arredondo, P., 98
Atkinson, D. R., 68, 90
Atkinson, J. W., 133, 144, 156, 160, 166, 169, 197
Attkisson, C. C., 27, 58
Auld, F., Jr., 132, 156
Austin, R., 62, 97
Ávila-Espada, A., 106, 121, 132, 156, 241, 281, 283

B

Bachrach, J., 130, 133, 162
Bailey, B. E., 110, 121
Bailey, J., 149, 158, 196, 246, 256, 265, 284, 291, 293, 347, 370
Baines, T. C., 70, 96
Baird, M., 24, 53
Balla, D. A., 205, 227
Bandura, A., 131, 132, 133, 142, 143, 144, 145, 147, 155, 156, 157, 169, 195, 271, 283
Barbopoulos, A., 118, 121
Barker, J. C., 78, 81, 91
Barnum, R., 22, 54
Bartolomeo, M., 79, 93
Battle, C. L., 71, 91
Becerra, R. M., 72, 94
Beck, A. T., 26, 50, 153, 154, 155, 157
Beck, J. S., 26, 50
Behn, J. D., 37, 52
Belizaire, L., 9, 57
Bell, N. L., 117, 121
Bellak, L., 108, 109, 113, 121, 130, 133, 141, 142, 143, 157, 166, 169, 195
Bellak, S. S., 108, 121, 141, 157
Bellamy, D. E., 68, 96
Bellow, S., 34, 50
Belter, R. W., 87, 96
Bent-Goodley, T. B., 72, 81, 91
Berglund, P., 18, 60
Berkel, L. A., 70, 96
Bernal, G., 19, 47, 57
Bernal, I., 185, 195, 205, 206, 224, 281, 283, 291, 293, 321, 342, 425, 427
Bernal, M. E., 204, 224

Bernier, J. E., 62, 98
Bernstein, L., 82, 91
Berry, J. W., 33, 50, 63, 91
Bertram, D., 231, 287
Beutler, L. E., 70, 91
Bird, H., 7, 48, 50, 59
Bishop, K. K., 73, 97
Blanch, A., 17, 50
Blum, G. S., 108, 121
Blumenthal, R., 142, 161
Booker, K., 70, 91
Borgman, A. L., 70, 96
Boring, E. G., 102, 121, 230, 283
Boucher, J. D., 33, 50
Bracero, W., 146, 157, 425, 427, 428
Brackbill, G. A., 133, 157, 283
Brandt, M. E., 33, 50
Brasic, J., 7, 59
Brenes-Jette, C., 193, 195
Briggs, D., 70, 96
Brislin, R. W., 33, 50
Brittan-Powell, C. S., 68, 97
Brobst, K., 79, 93
Brook, R. H., 65, 99
Brown, M. T., 70, 91
Brown, S. D., 81, 91
Bruner, J., 131, 132, 142, 147, 157
Brunk, M., 48, 50
Burlew, A. K., 34, 50
Burns, B. J., 8, 47, 49, 54
Butcher, J. N, 112, 121, 213, 224

C

Cairns, R. B., 18, 50, 230, 283
Camacho-Gonsalves, T., 36, 59
Camara, W. J., 26, 48, 50, 87, 91,
    229, 283
Cardalda, E. B., 167, 185, 192,
    194, 195, 206, 207, 210, 225,
    231, 255, 256, 257, 265, 266,
    281, 282, 283, 284, 305, 320,
    321, 330, 342, 441, 459
Cardemil, E. V., 71, 91
Carnabuchi, C., 198

Carter, R. T., 68, 81, 91
Casas, J. M., 85, 97
Case, L., 70, 91
Castillo, A., 185, 190, 196, 231,
    232, 242, 245, 265, 282,
    284, 290, 293
Castillo, R., 76, 81, 91
Castro, F., 204, 224
Casullo, M. M., 185, 190, 196, 231,
    232, 245, 265, 282, 284,
    290, 293
Cataldo, M. F., 8, 53
Cauce, A. M., 18, 51
Cauffman, E., 22, 54
Chang, C. F., 345, 371
Chasiotis, A., 111, 123
Chassman, J., 17, 50
Chau, K. L., 72, 91
Chauhan, R. V., 67, 97
Chen, E. C., 62, 97
Cheung, M-K., 36, 58
Childs, R. A., 87, 91
Chin, J. L., 64, 91, 92, 93
Chiu, Y., 345, 346, 370
Chow, D., 36, 59
Chow, J., 12, 51
Chun, C. A., 345, 370
Chung, H., 345, 371
Chung, R. H. G., 68, 90
Cicchetti, D. V., 205, 227
Clark, D. A., 155, 157
Clark, J. M., 118, 121
Clark, R. W., 133, 144, 160,
    166, 169, 197
Clark, R., 104, 121
Clarke, G. N., 22, 53
Clemence, A. J., 87, 92, 105, 121
Clemente, R., 81, 99
Cochran, B. N., 18, 51
Cohen, D., 17, 56
Cohen, L. H., 107, 121
Coleman, H. L. K., 61, 68, 79, 80, 81,
    84, 92, 97
Collins, R. C., 24, 57

Colon-Malgady, G., 149, 157, 158,
    180, 189, 195,196, 205, 225,
    246, 256, 265, 284, 290, 291,
    293, 347, 370
Comas-Diaz, L., 425, 428
Combs, G., 147, 159
Conner, M. G., 21, 22, 29, 37,
    51, 52
Conners, C. K., 26, 51
Conway, J. B., 104, 121
Copeland, A. P., 149, 157
Copeland, E. J., 67, 69, 92
Cornabuci, C., 185, 194, 195,
    231, 271, 272, 277,
    282, 284
Cortez, D. E., 206, 225
Costantino, G., 106, 118, 122, 129,
    130, 131, 132, 133, 134, 141,
    142, 143, 146, 149, 157, 158,
    159, 161, 165, 166, 167, 168,
    169, 172, 180, 185, 189, 190,
    193, 195, 196, 197, 199, 201,
    204, 205, 207, 210, 225, 226,
    231, 232, 234, 240, 241, 242,
    245, 246, 249, 255, 256, 257,
    265, 266, 279, 280, 281, 282,
    283, 284, 285, 286, 288, 289,
    290, 291, 293, 305, 320, 321,
    330, 331, 342, 343, 346, 347,
    370, 371, 425, 428, 430,
    432, 441, 459
Costello, A., 7, 51
Costello, E. J., 7, 8, 49, 51
Cottrell, D., 9, 53
Coulacoglou, C., 108, 122
Crawford, I., 68, 90
Critelli, J. W., 166, 198
Cross, S. E., 230, 285
Cross, T., 8, 58
Crothers, L., 70, 91
Csikszentmihalyi, M., 18, 58
Cuellar, I., 45, 48, 51, 111, 113, 122
Cummings, N., 8, 51
Cureton, E. E., 185, 196

D

Dana, J., 69, 93
Dana, R. H., 31, 32, 33, 34, 35, 36,
    37, 38, 41, 42, 45, 46, 47, 49, 51,
    52, 53, 54, 60, 63, 66, 67, 69, 70,
    76, 81, 82, 85, 87, 88, 91, 92, 93,
    101, 102, 103, 104, 105, 106,
    108, 109, 110, 111, 112, 113,
    114, 119, 120, 122, 123, 129,
    130, 131, 132, 133, 134, 142,
    158, 159, 165, 166, 167, 169,
    194, 196, 201, 204, 225, 229,
    230, 231, 241, 280, 281, 285,
    289, 293, 305, 320, 330, 342,
    425, 428, 432, 441, 459
Davies, M., 7, 58
Davis, D. C., 48, 57
De La Cancela, V., 64, 93
DeLeon, P. H., 24, 59, 70, 93
Del Valle, A. G., 72, 93
Denmon, J., 73, 94
Der-Karabetian, A., 36, 37, 42, 52, 53,
    54, 63, 93
Detweiler, J. B., 18, 58
Dibble, S. L., 77, 81, 95
Dierker, L. C., 22, 53
Dies, R. R., 26, 56
Dietrich, A. J., 8, 60
DiGiuseppe, R., 129, 159, 266, 280,
    281, 286
Dixon, D., 346, 371
Dixon, L., 18, 53
Dolan, J. P. Jr., 70, 96
Domenech-Rodriguez, M., 18, 51
Donabedian, A., 64, 93
Donenberg, G. R., 19, 60
Draguns, J. G., 83, 96
Drake, R. E., 18, 53
Duchowski, A. J., 6, 7, 53
Dulcan, M. K., 7, 48, 50, 58
DuMas, F., 105, 123
Dupertuis, D. G., 185, 196, 197, 231,
    232, 242, 247, 282, 284, 285,
    388, 428

Duran, A., 62, 98
Durlak, J. A., 24, 25, 53

E

Echandia, A., 265
Echemendia, R., 68, 90
Edelbrock, C., 7, 51
Edelbrook, C. S., 282
Edlefsen, M., 24, 53
Edwards, C. D., 193, 198, 248, 287
Elbert, J. C., 19, 56
Eldridge, W. D., 72, 93
El-Khatib, A., 118, 121
Elliot, T. L., 213, 222, 226, 281, 285, 442
Elster, A. B., 8, 53
Epstein, S., 133, 158
Erikson, E. H., 169, 197
Erkanli, A., 8, 49
Eron, L. D., 166, 197
Etzkom, J., 68, 97
Exner, J. E., 130, 132, 133, 141, 143,
    149, 159, 167, 197, 213, 226, 241,
    280, 285
Eyde, L. D., 26, 56, 87, 91

F

Fabrega, H. Jr., 75, 81, 96
Fagulha, T., 108, 123, 230, 285
Faiola, T., 185, 196, 231, 232, 242, 284
Fantini, F., 232, 271, 285, 373, 428
Farkas, M., 18, 50
Farmer, E. M. Z., 8, 18, 49, 53, 66, 93
Farmer, T. W., 18, 53, 66, 93
Feinberg, L., 62, 98
Fernandez, C., 185, 197, 231, 242, 247,
    282, 285, 388, 428
Fernandez, M., 345, 371
Figueroa, M., 167, 185, 194, 195
Finn, S. E., 26, 56
Finney, F. I., 8, 53
Fiorentino, L., 285
Fischer, P., 7, 59

Fisharah, F., 118, 121
Fisher, D., 17, 50
Fisher, P., 7, 22, 58
Flanagan, R., 129, 130, 133, 142, 146,
    157, 158, 159, 167, 169, 185, 196,
    197, 256, 257, 265, 266, 270, 279,
    280, 281, 282, 284, 286, 289, 293
Fletcher, K. E., 22, 54
Flores, L. Y., 70, 96
Flynn, L., 21, 22, 54
Folkman, S., 276, 277, 278, 286
Fonagy, P., 9, 53
Forgus, R., 130, 141, 153, 159
Forness, S. R., 7, 53
Foster, S. L., 67, 95
Foulks, E., 76, 93
Fox, R. E., 26, 53
Frank, G., 103, 123
Franklin, C., 75, 81, 94
Freedenfeld, R. N., 166, 198
Freedman, J., 147, 159
Freud, S., 142, 143, 159
Frick, P. J., 26, 55, 57
Friedman, G. A., 144, 160
Friedman, R. M., 6, 7, 10, 27, 53, 59
Fuertes, J. N., 62, 79, 93, 97
Fujino, D. C., 36, 58

G

Gadnow, K., 22, 53
Gamst, G., 36, 37, 38, 40, 41, 42, 52, 46,
    52, 53, 54, 56, 63, 93
Ganju, V., 40, 48, 59
Garb, H. N., 87, 95, 106, 124, 194, 197,
    229, 288, 289, 293
Garcia-Vazquez, E., 67, 98
Garfield, S., 103, 123
Garvin, C., 72, 81, 90
Gaw, A., 75, 93
Gediman, H. K., 133, 142, 143, 157,
    169, 195
Geisinger, K. F., 111, 112, 123

Gibbs, M. S., 166, 198
Gide, A., 105, 123
Gieser, L., 106, 123
Gil, R. M., 425, 428
Gilliam, M., 69, 93
Goh, M., 79, 94
Goldman, H. H., 18, 53
Gomez, S. P., 18, 58
Gonwa, T., 37, 52
Goodman, S., 48, 50
Goodrich, R., 166, 199
Gopaul-McNichol, S., 81
Gore, J. S., 230, 285
Gorham, D. R., 40, 48, 57
Goudena, P. P., 109, 124
Gould, M., 7, 59
Green, J. W., 72, 94
Green, J., 110, 121
Greenfeld, R., 129, 159, 167, 197, 286
Greenfield, P. M., 63, 94
Green-Hennessy, S., 17, 54
Greenley, D., 17, 54
Gretchen, D., 62, 67, 97
Grisso, T., 22, 54
Gruber, C., 118, 125
Guarino, A. J., 40, 41, 52, 54, 56
Guzmán, L., 256, 265, 282, 283

H

Haggerty, R. J., 8, 23, 25, 57
Hall, G. C. N., 36, 56, 70, 94
Hambleton, R. K., 112, 127
Han, S. S., 19, 60
Handler, L., 87, 92, 105, 121, 123
Hanson, A., 8, 55
Harris, D. B., 141, 159
Hartmann, H., 143, 159
Hatch, J. P., 68, 87, 98
Hayes, S. A., 61, 95
Hays, P. A., 81, 94, 113, 123
Hedburg, V., 21, 57
Heimberg, R. G., 22, 53
Heinemann, S. H., 286

Hennessy, K. D., 8, 17, 54, 55
Henry, W. E., 229, 280, 281, 286
Hensen, D. J., 12, 55
Hernandez, A., 129, 159, 167, 197, 286
Herrera, J., 75, 94
Hill, C. L., 67, 96
Hills, H. I., 68, 94
Ho, D. Y., 346, 370
Hoagwood, K., 47, 54
Hofer, J., 111, 123
Hogan, M., 21, 22, 54
Hollingshead, A. B., 248, 286
Holmstrom, R. W., 109, 116, 123, 126
Holt, R. R., 130, 141, 143, 159
Holzberg, J. D., 105, 124
Hornik, J., 40, 48, 59
Horowitz, M. J., 155, 159
Howard, G., 131, 142, 147, 159
Howe, N., 285
Hoy, M., 110, 124
Hoy-Watkins, M., 110, 119, 124
Hsu, J., 346, 371
Huff, R. M., 78, 81, 94
Hurvich, M., 133, 142, 143, 157,
    169, 195
Hutt, M. L., 109, 124
Hwang, W-C, 19, 47, 57
Hyde, J. S., 286

I

Iglehart, A., 72, 94
Inhelder, B., 131, 132, 142, 144, 146,
    147, 148, 155, 161
Ivey, A., 67, 96

J

Jackson, L. C., 71, 94
Jacobson, N., 17, 54
Jacquemin, J., 109, 124
Jenkins, S., 106, 124
Jenkins, Y. M., 64, 93
Jenkins-Monroe, V., 110, 119, 124
Jennings, L., 79, 97

Jensen, A., 163, 197
Jensen, P. S., 47, 54
Jerrell, J. M., 36, 54
Jimenez-Suarez, V., 167, 185, 194, 195, 231, 255, 266, 282, 283, 330, 342, 441, 459
Johnson, A. W., Jr., 133, 159
Johnson, J. R., 40, 48, 59
Johnson, R. C., 110, 127
Johnson, S. B., 19, 56
Jolly, J. B., 26, 50
Jones, R. A., 108, 124
Jones, R., 34, 55
Jordan, C., 75, 81, 94

K

Kagan, J., 130, 141, 148, 159, 160
Kahn, J. S., 73, 94
Kalas, R., 7, 51
Kamphaus, R. W., 22, 26, *55*, 58, 265, *287*
Karon, B. P., 166, 197
Karp, S. A., 109, 116, 123, 126
Kataoka, S. H., 8, 9, 55
Kay, G. G., 26, 56
Kazdin, A. E., 19, 55, 60
Keeler, G., 7, 51
Keilin, W. G., 68, 98
Kelsey, J. L., 34, 56
Kelsey, R. M., 166, 198
Kendall, P. C., 19, 22, 53, 55
Kerber, K., 166, 199
Kerl, S. B., 68, 94
Kessler, M., 7, 51
Kessler, R. C., 18, 60
Kiesler, C. A., 12, 55
Kim, B., 346, 370
Kim, L. S., 345, 370
Kimble, G. A., 103, 124
Kirkman. M., 142, 146, 147, 160
Kitano, H. I., 345, 371
Klaric, S., 7, 51
Kleinman, A., 73, 75, 81, 94, 96

Kline, M. V., 78, 81, 94
Kline, P., 108, 122
Knepp, D., 68, 90
Knitzer, J., 6, 7, 24, 53, 55, 57
Koch, S., 102, 124
Kohatsu, E. L., 85, 94
Kohlberg, L., 133, 144, 145, 160, 169, 197
Kohn, L., 19, 47, 57
Korchin, S. J., 110, 124
Kouyoumdjian, H., 12, 55
Kovacs, M., 169, 197
Kramer, T., 36, 37, 38, 52, 53, 54
Kratchowill, T. R., 19, 55
Krejci, M. J., 144, 160
Krinsky, R. E., 185, 197
Kroon, N., 109, 124
Kuhn, T. S., 194, 197
Kuo, H., 232, 279, 282, 288
Kuo, L-H., 167, 199, 347, 371
Kuo, P. Y., 112, 125
Kurtz, R., 103, 123
Kurtz, Z., 9, 53
Kutash, K., 6, 7, 53

L

Lachar, D., 26, 55
LaFromboise, T. D., 19, 33, 47, 55, 57, 67, 95
Lahey, B. B., 26, 57
Larson, D. B., 76, 95
Larson, R. W., 18, 55
Lau, A. S. L., 12, 55
Lau, A. S., 346, 370
Lau, A., 36, 55
Lawson, W., 75, 94
Lay, A., 19, 47, 57
Lazarus, R. S., 276, 277, 278, 286
Leaf, P. J., 23, 24, 55
Leary, M. R., 229, 230, 286
LeBuffe, P. A., 22, 57
Lee, M.-Y., 73, 95
Leff, H. S., 36, 59

Leff, S., 18, 53
Lehman, A. F., 18, 48, 53, 55
Leininger, M., 76, 77, 81, 95
Lent, R. W., 81, 91
Leong, F. T. L., 12, 55, 104, 124, 127, 346, 370
Leon-Velasquez, M., 167, 185, 194, 195, 231, 255, 266, 282, 283, 330, 342, 441, 459
Lesser, G., 141, 160
Leung, K., 112, 127
Levin, B. L., 8, 55
Levy, R. J., 36, 59
Lewis, J. F., 205, 226
Lewis-Fernandez, R., 76, 95
Liao, Q., 27, 56
Liberman, R. P., 64, 95
Like, R. C., 78, 81, 95
Lilienfeld, S. O., 26, 56, 87, 95, 106, 124, 194, 197, 229, 286, 288, 289, 293
Lin, C., 345, 347, 370
Lin, R. F., 75, 95
Lin, S. S., 34, 56
Lindzey, G., 111, 124, 286
Lipsey, M., 103, 124
Lipson, J. G., 77, 81, 95
Liu, C. T., 345, 347, 370
Liu, W. M., 61, 68, 80, 81, 84, 97
Liu, W., 345, 371
Loevinger, J., 193, 197
Lohmann, N., 72, 81, 95
Lohmann, R. A., 72, 81, 95
Lohr, J. M., 26, 56, 229, 286
Lohr, N., 166, 199
Lonigan, C. J., 19, 56
Lonner, W. J., 33, 56, 61, 83, 95, 96
Lopez, S. J., 18, 56, 230, 287
Lopez, S. R., 67, 95
Losapio, G., 129, 159, 167, 197, 286
Lotsof, A. B., 141, 161
Love, K. M., 70, 96
Lovett, M., 34, 50

Lowell, E. L., 133, 144, 160, 166, 169, 197
Lu, F. G., 75, 76, 95
Lubin, N. M., 130, 160
Lucas, C., 7, 22, 58
Lum, D., 72, 95
Lung, A. Y., 345, 346, 370
Lunnen, K. M., 48, 57
Lushene, R. E., 193, 198, 248, 287
Lynn, S., 26, 56, 229, 286
Lyons, J. S., 12, 13, 27, 28, 56

M

Machado, W., 256, 265, 282, 283
Magnussen, D., 18, 56, 230, 286
Maki, M., 345, 371
Maldonado, R., 45, 48, 51
Malgady, R. G., 25, 56, 106, 118, 122, 129, 130, 131, 132, 133, 141, 142, 143, 146, 149, 157, 158, 161, 165, 168, 169, 172, 180, 185, 189, 190, 195, 196, 201, 204, 205, 206, 207,210, 225, 226, 227, 231, 232, 234, 240, 241, 242, 245, 246, 249, 256, 257, 265, 280, 281, 282, 283, 284, 285, 286, 289, 290, 291, 293, 305, 320, 321, 331, 342, 343, 346, 347, 370, 371, 425, 428, 430, 432, 459
Mancuso, J. C., 132, 147, 148, 160
Manson, S. M., 18, 24, 25, 56, 114, 124
Maramba, G. G., 36, 56, 70, 94
Marcell, A. V., 8, 53
Martin, T. W., 36, 56
Martinez, J. V., 231, 255, 266, 282, 283, 330, 342, 441, 459
Martinez, J., 167, 185, 194, 195
Matoba Alder, S., 345, 371
Matus, Y. E., 112, 121
May, W. T., 70, 93, 103, 104, 105, 106, 123
McAdams, D. P., 131, 142, 160

McArthur, D. S., 109, 125, 205, 226, 286
McClelland, D. C., 133, 144, 160, 166, 169, 197
McConaughy, S. H., 26, 49
McCubbin, M., 17, 56
McDavis, R. J., 98
McFarland, M. R., 76, 77, 95
McGlynn, E. A., 64, 95
McKinney, J., 40, 48, 59
McMiller, W. P., 73, 96
McNeill, B. W., 18, 58
McPhatter, A. R., 73, 96
Mecklenberg, E. C., 70, 96
Medina, A., 280, 287
Meleis, A. I., 77, 95
Melendez, G., 48, 57
Meller, P. J., 87, 98
Meltzoff, J., 110, 124
Mendelsohn, J., 9, 57
Mercer, J. R., 113, 125, 205, 226
Merdinger, J. M., 72, 93
Merikangas, K. R., 22, 53
Merluzzi, T. V., 144, 160
Meyer, G. J., 26, 56, 222, 223, 226
Meyers, L., 40, 41, 52, 54, 56
Mezzich, J. E., 75, 81, 95, 96
Millan-Arzuaga, F., 321, 342
Miller, D., 72, 93
Millon, T., 26, 56
Minarik, P. A., 77, 81, 95
Miranda, J., 19, 47, 57
Mischel, H. N., 133, 144, 160
Mischel, W., 133, 144, 160, 169, 197
Mitchell, H. E., 110, 124
Mohatt, G. V., 33, 55
Mollen, D., 67, 96
Monopoli, J., 111, 125, 229, 287
Montouri, J., 193, 198, 248, 287
Moreland, K. L., 26, 56
Moretti, R. J., 88, 97, 102, 105, 106, 125
Morgan, C. D., 165, 198
Morishima, J., 346, 371
Morrow, G., 42, 53, 63, 93
Mrazek, P. J., 8, 23, 25, 57

Mueser, K. T., 18, 53
Mujica, C., 210, 211, 226
Muniz, J., 231, 287
Munley, P. H., 70, 96
Murphy, M. C., 68, 96
Murray, H. A., 101, 109, 125, 130, 141, 142, 160, 165, 167, 198, 229, 280, 287, 292, 293
Murstein, B. I., 109, 125, 130, 132, 133, 143, 160, 166, 194, 198
Mustillo, S., 7, 51

N

Nagle, R. J., 117, 121
Naglieri, J., 22, 57
Nathan, J. S., 26, 48, 50, 87, 91, 229, 283
Neeper, R., 26, 57
Nesbitt, M., 102, 125
Nezworski, M. T., 229, 288
Nezworski, T. M., 194, 197, 289, 293
Nichols, C. M., 79, 93
Nilsson, J. E., 70, 96
Norquist, G. S., 64, 95
Nuttall, R. L., 185, 194, 199, 281, 288

O

Ogles, B. M., 48, 57
Okazaki, S., 112, 125
Olfson, M., 14, 57
Olmedo, E., 201, 204, 226
Omizo, M., 346, 370
Ornduff, S. R., 166, 198
Ortiz-Vargas, N., 231, 266, 282, 283
Oswald, D. P., 18, 59
Overall, J. E., 40, 48, 57
Owan, T. C., 346

P

Pack-Brown, S. P., 71, 75, 81, 96
Padilla, A. M., 132, 142, 161, 280, 287
Pais, E., 185, 197, 231, 242, 247, 282, 285, 388, 428
Paivio, A., 132, 146, 161
Paniagua, F., 76, 96

Paperny, D. M., 21, 57
Paradise, M., 18, 51
Parron, D. L., 75, 81, 96
Pauker, J. D., 108, 126
Pedersen, P. B., 62, 67, 83, 96, 98
Pellegrino, E. D., 17, 57
Pérez, A., 149, 157, 180, 189, 195, 205, 225, 290, 293
Perez, M., 231, 255, 283, 330, 342, 441, 459
Petti, T., 47, 54
Peuslchold, D., 22, 54
Pfeiffer, S., 22, 57
Phalet, K., 34, 45, 60, 113, 127
Phillips, J., 9, 53
Phinney, J. S., 45, 48, 57
Piacentini, J., 7, 58
Piaget, J., 131, 132, 142, 144, 145, 146, 147, 148, 155, 161
Piotrkowski, C. S., 24, 57
Piotrowski, C., 26, 57, 87, 88, 96, 106, 125, 229, 231, 287
Plaztek, D., 193, 198, 248, 287
Polkinghorne, D. E., 107, 125, 142, 161
Ponterotto, J. G., 9, 57, 62, 67, 71, 85, 87, 96, 97, 98
Pope, K., 130, 132, 142, 147, 161
Pope-Davis, D. B., 61, 68, 80, 81, 84, 97
Prieto, G., 231, 287
Prieto, L. R., 18, 58
Prillerman, S. L., 345, 371
Prince, R., 75, 99
Puente, A. E., 26, 48, 50, 87, 91, 229, 283

Q

Quintero, N., 283

R

Radloff, L. S., 248, 287
Rafferty, J. E., 141, 161
Ramos-McKay, J. M., 425, 428
Reese-Albright, A., 345, 371
Retief, A. I., 109, 125

Reynolds, C. R., 22, 26, 58, 265, 287
Reynolds, W. M., 26, 58
Reza, J. V., 67, 98
Richardson, T. Q., 85, 94
Ridley, C. R., 67, 96
Rieger, B. P., 62, 97
Riley, A, W., 8, 53
Ring, J. M., 345, 346, 370
Ringel, J. S., 8, 58
Rispens, J., 109, 124
Ritzler, B. A., 129, 133, 161, 165, 198, 213, 226
Ritzler, B., 109, 113, 125, 129, 133, 161, 280, 287
Rivera, L. A., 425, 428
Roberts, G. E., 109, 118, 125, 205, 226, 286
Roberts, M. C., 49, 58
Roberts, R. E., 27, 58
Robinson, L., 68, 90
Robinson, R., 24, 57
Rodino, V., 185, 197, 231, 242, 247, 282, 285, 388, 428
Rodriguez, O., 201, 227
Rogers, E. S., 18, 50
Rogers, M. R., 9, 58, 69, 97
Rogler, L. H., 25, 58, 73, 76, 97, 118, 122, 129, 130, 131, 133, 141, 142, 143, 146, 149, 158, 161, 165, 169, 172, 180, 190, 196, 201, 204, 205, 206, 207, 210, 225, 226, 227, 234, 240, 241, 246, 249, 256, 265, 280, 281, 284, 286, 289, 293, 321, 343, 347, 370, 371
Ronan, G. F., 166, 198
Ropaldo, M., 282, 285
Rosenblatt, A., 27, 58
Ross, K., 8, 60
Rossini, E. D., 88, 97, 102, 105, 106, 125
Rothman, A., 18, 58
Rotter, J. B., 141, 161
Rounds, K. A., 73, 97
Rouse, S. V., 213, 224
Roysircar, G., 97

Roysircar-Sodowsky, G., 112, 125
Rubel, A. J., 78, 81, 95
Rudy, T. E., 144, 160
Ruiz, P., 75, 81, 97
Russell, G. L., 36, 58
Rutter, M., 9, 59

S

Salovey, P., 18, 58
Sampson, E. E., 102, 126
Sanchez, L. M., 27, 58
Sandoval, J., 265
Santiago-Negrón, S., 167, 185, 194,
    195, 284
Sarbin, T. R., 132, 142, 146, 147, 148,
    160, 161
Sardi, G. M., 185, 194, 198, 231,271,
    272, 275, 282, 287
Sargent, M. M., 107, 121
Saxe, L., 8, 58
Sayers, S., 256, 265, 282, 283
Schlesinger, H. J., 14, 57
Schneider, M. F., 109, 126
Schoenfeld, L. S., 68, 87, 98
Schwab-Stone, M. E., 7, 58,
    48, 50
Seabrook, M. K., 70, 91
Sechrest, L. B., 107, 121
Seligman, M. E. P., 18, 58, 107, 126
Sevig, T., 68, 97
Sgroi, S. M., 430, 459
Shaffer, D., 7, 22, 58, 59
Shaffer, L., 103, 126
Shakow, D., 103, 126
Shea, J. M., 18, 51
Shernoff, E. S., 19, 55
Sherwood, E. T., 109, 110, 126
Shin, S. M., 36, 59
Shneidman, E. S., 105, 108, 126
Shulman, B., 130, 141, 153, 159
Siipola, E. M., 133, 161
Silber, D. E., 109, 116, 123, 126
Silk, K., 166, 199
Silva Arancibia, V., 185, 197, 231, 242,
    247, 282, 285, 388, 428

Silverman, N., 8, 58
Simon, B. L., 72, 97
Sines, J. O., 108, 126
Sines, L. K., 108, 126
Sing, M., 14, 57
Singer, J. L., 130, 132, 142, 145, 146,
    147, 155, 161
Singh, N. N., 18, 59
Skovholt, T. M., 79, 97
Smith, D. J., 9, 59
Smith, E. J., 62, 98
Smith, T. B., 70, 91
Snowden, L. R., 9, 12, 36, 58, 59, 72,
    98, 346, 371
Snyder, C. P., 18, 56
Snyder, C. R., 230, 287
Sobel, H. J., 130, 132, 133, 142, 153,
    161, 166, 198
Sodowsky, 68
Sparrow, S. S., 205, 227
Spielberger, C. D., 153, 161, 169, 193,
    198, 248, 287
Spratkin, J., 22, 53
Sramek, J., 75, 94
Srebnik, D., 18, 51
Stedman, J. M., 68, 87, 98
Stein, M. I., 106, 123
Steiner, R. P., 78, 81, 95
Stephenson, M., 45, 48, 59
Steward, W. T., 18, 58
Streltzer, J., 81, 98
Stroul, B. A., 6, 10, 27, 59
Strozier, A. L., 68, 94
Sturm, R., 8, 58
Sue, D. W., 62, 67, 71, 79, 81, 98
Sue, D., 67, 79, 98
Sue, L., 25, 59, 64, 81, 98, 114, 126
Sue, S., 25, 36, 58, 59, 64, 81, 98, 112,
    114, 125, 126, 345, 346, 370, 371
Suh, E. M., 33, 59
Sulfaro, C., 185, 194, 198, 231, 271,
    272, 278, 282, 287
Sullivan, G., 64, 95
Sullivan, H. S., 131, 142, 143, 144, 148,
    149, 161, 169, 180, 198

Summo, B., 185, 194, 198, 231, 271, 272, 276, 282, 287
Suzuki, L. A., 85, 87, 97, 98
Swyers, J. P., 76, 95
Symonds, P. M., 109, 126

T

Ta, K., 76, 93
Takanishi, R., 24, 59
Takeuchi, D. T., 64, 90
Tangney, J. P., 229, 230, 286
Target, M., 9, 53
Teague, G. B., 40, 48, 59
Teglasi, H., 106, 126, 130, 131, 132, 141, 143, 146, 148, 149, 155, 161, 167, 199, 230, 287
Thompson, C. E., 110, 126, 130, 132, 133, 162, 165, 199, 280, 287, 292, 293
Thyer, B. A., 73, 98
Tomkins, S. S., 102, 126, 166, 199
Toporek, R. L., 61, 67, 68, 80, 81, 84, 97, 98
Torres, G., 321, 342
Torrey, W. C., 18, 53
Triandis, H. C., 33, 59
Trickett. E. J., 24, 25, 59
Trimble, J. E., 33, 55, 83, 96, 118, 126
Tseng, W., 346, 371
Tseng, W-S., 75, 76, 81, 98
Tsui, E., 149, 158, 205, 225, 240, 241, 256, 265, 279, 282, 284, 289, 293, 347, 370
Tucker, W., 17, 50
Tukey, J. W., 185, 196
Turner, S. M., 27, 58

U

Ullian, D. Z., 144, 145, 160, 169, 197
Utsey, S. O., 62, 97

V

Van de Vijver, F. J. R., 34, 45, 60
Van de Vijver, F., 112, 113, 127
VandenBos, G. R., 70, 93

Vane, J. R., 105, 127, 280, 288
Vazquez, C. I., 425, 428
Vazquez, C., 205, 225, 241, 281, 285, 321, 342, 346, 370, 425, 428
Vazquez, L. A., 67, 98
Vazquez-Nuttall, E., 185, 194, 199, 281, 288
Vernon, A., 81, 99
Villamil, B., 193, 199

W

Waller, N. G., 117, 127
Walls, R. G., 18, 58
Walsh, D., 17, 50
Walsh, J. A., 112, 121
Walters, R. H., 143, 144, 145, 157
Walton, J. R., 185, 194, 199, 281, 288
Wampold, B. E., 107, 127
Wang, P. S., 18, 60
Weaver, H. N., 72, 73, 74, 75, 81, 99
Weil, M., 73, 97
Weinberger, J., 105, 127
Weiner, I. B., 132, 141, 143, 149, 159, 167, 197, 241, 280, 285
Weiss, B., 19, 60
Weisz, J. R., 19, 60, 73, 96
Wells, A. M., 24, 25, 53
Wells, K. B., 8, 9, 55, 64, 65, 95, 99
Wendler, A. M., 70, 96
Wessler, R., 193, 197
Westen, D., 105, 127, 166, 199
Westermeyer, J., 76, 93
Whatley, R., 34, 60
Williams, C. B., 75, 81, 96
Williams, J. W., 8, 60
Williams, R. L., 110, 127, 280, 288
Winter, D. G., 166, 199
Wisniewski, N. M., 149, 157
Wittkower, E. D., 75, 99
Woo, J. Y. T., 346, 371
Wood, J. M., 87, 95, 106, 124, 194, 197, 229, 288, 289, 293
Wrenn, R. M., 72, 93

Wright, B. V., 68, 96
Wyatt, P., 12, 51

Y

Yamada, A-M., 9, 12, 59
Yang, C-M., 167, 199, 232, 279, 282,
    288, 347, 371
Yeh, J. W., 109, 118, 127
Yeh, M., 109, 118, 127
Yu, E., 345, 371

Z

Zachar, P., 104, 124, 127
Zamboanga, B. L., 12, 55
Zane, N., 36, 55, 112, 126, 346, 371
Zhang, L., 8, 9, 55
Zhang, N., 346, 371

Subject Index

A

America's Children, 203, 224
American Psychiatric Association, 27, 45, 47, 49
American Psychological Association, 84, 87, 90, 194, 194, 201, 204, 224, 280, 282

B

Bazelon Center for Mental Health Law, 7, 50

C

California Department of Education, 203, 224
California Department of Mental Health, 38, 50
Chicago Illinois Board of Education, 203, 225
Commission on Chronic Illness, 23, 51
Council of National Psychological Association for the Advancement of Ethnic Minority Interests (CNPAAEMI), 25, 51, 63, 81, 92, 114, 122
Council on Social Work Education, 72, 81, 92

F

Florida Department of Education, 203, 226

G

Georgia Department of Education, 203, 226

I

Institute of Medicine, 8, 54

J

Joint Commission on the Mental Health of Children, 6, 55

M

Massachusetts Department of Education, 203, 226

N

New Freedom Commission on Mental Health, 11, 21, 57
New York City Department of Education, 203, 226
Newark Public Schools, 203, 226

O

Office of Technology Assessment, 8, 57

P

Piaget, J., 131, 132, 142, 144, 145, 146, 147, 148, 155, 161

S

Substance Abuse and Mental Health
    Services Administration
    (SAMHSA), 202, 227

U

U.S. Census Bureau, 8, 9, 59, 60
U.S. Census Press Releases, 203, 227

U.S. Department of Health and
    Human Services, 10, 21, 16, 60,
    201, 202, 227
U.S. Public Health Service, 7, 10, 60

W

Washington District of Columbia
    Public Schools, 203, 227
World Health Organization, 7, 12, 60,
    202, 227